The Fifties
CHRONICLE

CONSULTANTS
Beth Bailey, Ph.D.
David Farber, Ph.D.

WRITERS
Beth Bailey, Ph.D.
Todd Burroughs, Ph.D.
Anthony Edmonds, Ph.D.
David Farber, Ph.D.
Christy Nadalin
Robert Rodriguez
Jeffrey Sanders, Ph.D.
Bradley Shreve, M.A.

FOREWORD
Margaret Truman

LEGACY

Publisher & CEO
Louis Weber

Editor-in-Chief
David J. Hogan

Editor
David Aretha

Associate Editor
Jeremy Weber

Art Director
James Slate

Creative Director
Marissa Conner

Acquisitions Editors
Rebecca Burton
Victoria Smith
Michael Staples

**Director of Acquisitions
& Visual Resources**
Doug Brooks

**Associate Director
of Acquisitions**
Susan Barbee

Production Editors
Valerie Iglar-Mobley
Margaret McConnell

Production Director
Steven Grundt

**Electronic Publishing
Specialist**
Ron Gad

**Visual Resources
Specialist**
Matthew Schwarz

Special Photography
Deborah Van Kirk

Legacy Logo Designer
James Schlottman

Assistant to the Publisher
Renee G. Haring

Editorial Assistants
Kathline Jones
Nicholas Myers

Publications Coordinator
Julie Greene

Director, Pre-Press
David Darian

**Assistant Director,
Pre-Press**
Laura Schmidt

Pre-Press Coordinator
Timothy Griffin

**Imaging Development
Manager**
Paul Fromberg

Imaging Assistants
Sherese Hopkins
Jacob Stickann

Director of Purchasing
Rocky Wu

Manufacturing Manager
Kent Keutzer

Legal Adviser
Dorothy Weber

Legacy Publishing is a division of Publications International, Ltd.

Manufactured in China.

8 7 6 5 4 3 2 1

ISBN: 1-4127-1187-8

Library of Congress Cataloging-in-Publication Data

The fifties chronicle / consultants, Beth Bailey, David Farber ;
writers, Beth Bailey ...[et al.] ; foreword, Margaret Truman.
    p. cm.
  ISBN 1-4127-1187-8
  1. United States—Civilization—1945- 2. Nineteen fifties. I. Bailey,
Beth L., 1957-
  E169.12.F497 2006
  973.921—dc22

2005032663

Contributors

Foreword

Margaret Truman Daniel is the only child of former U.S. President Harry S. Truman and his wife, Bess Wallace Truman. Over a 60-year career, she has been a singer, actress, radio and television personality, and author, turning out more than two dozen fiction and nonfiction books, including a best-selling biography of her father and a popular series of murder mysteries set in the nation's capital. Mrs. Truman Daniel currently lives in New York City.

Consultants and Essayists

Beth Bailey, Ph.D., is a professor of history at Temple University. A cultural and social historian of 20th century America, she is the author of *Sex in the Heartland* and *From Front Porch to Back Seat: Courtship in Twentieth-Century America*. With David Farber, she coauthored *The First Strange Place: Race and Sex in World War II Hawaii* and *The Columbia Guide to America in the 1960s*. She is also coauthor of *A People and a Nation,* an American history textbook. She recently received fellowships from the Woodrow Wilson International Center for Scholars and from the National Endowment for the Humanities.

David Farber, Ph.D., is a professor of history at Temple University. A cultural and social historian of 20th century America, he is the author of *The Age of Great Dreams: America in the 1960s, Taken Hostage: The Iran Hostage Crisis and America's First Encounter with Radical Islam,* and *Sloan Rules: Alfred P. Sloan and the Triumph of General Motors*. With his wife, Beth Bailey, he coauthored *The First Strange Place* and *The Columbia Guide to America in the 1960s*. He also was the consultant for and a coauthor of *The Sixties Chronicle*.

Additional Writers

Todd Burroughs, Ph.D., (sidebars and captions author) is an independent researcher/scholar based in Hyattsville, Maryland. A professional journalist since 1985, he has written for such magazines as *The Source* and *The Crisis,* such Web sites as BlackAmericaWeb.com and Africana.com, and such newspapers as *New York Amsterdam News* and *The* (Newark) *Star-Ledger*. He served as an editor, contributing columnist, and national correspondent for the NNPA News Service. He also was a primary author for *Civil Rights Chronicle*.

Anthony Edmonds, Ph.D., (sidebars and captions author) is a George and Frances Ball distinguished professor of history at Ball State University. He is the author or coauthor of seven books, including *Silhouettes on the Shade: Images of the 1950s Reexamined, The War in Vietnam,* and *Eisenhower, Macmillan and Allied Unity, 1957–61*. He also wrote for *The Sixties Chronicle*.

Christy Nadalin (timeline author and fact-checker) is a documentary television producer, freelance writer, and editorial researcher whose clients have included the National Geographic Society, the Discovery Channel, A&E Television Networks, and Time Life Books. She contributed to *The Sixties Chronicle* and *Civil Rights Chronicle*.

Robert Rodriguez (sidebars and captions author) is a freelance writer specializing in history and pop culture. He authored *The 1950s' Most Wanted* and contributed to *The Sixties Chronicle* and *Great Hispanic-Americans*.

Jeffrey Sanders, Ph.D., (sidebars and captions author) is an assistant professor of history at the University of New England. He is the author of *McClellan Park: The Life and Death of an Urban Greenspace*. He also has contributed to *The Sixties Chronicle, The Columbia Guide to America in the 1960s,* and *Environmental Atlas of the United States and Canada*.

Bradley Shreve, M.A., (sidebars author) is a doctoral candidate at the University of New Mexico. He has published several articles and is currently working on his dissertation. He also wrote for *The Sixties Chronicle*.

Factual Verification

Barbara Cross has contributed to a variety of titles as a researcher, fact-checker, and editor on such topics as history and science.

Index by Ina Gravitz.

Acknowledgments can be found on page 479.

Contents

Benefiting from more than four years of recovery and growth following World War II, the United States was in a position unique among the world's nations: considerably stronger and more prosperous after the war than before. Asia and Europe, America's allies included, were exhausted, but in the U.S. an optimism not felt since the 1920s encouraged unprecedented increases in manufacturing, consumer buying, marriage, and births. America was booming.

The USA, China, and the Soviet Union had come together to defeat Germany and Japan, but by 1950 the alliances had soured. Communists had seized control of the Chinese mainland in 1949, and the Soviets exploded their first atomic bomb the same year. On the Korean Peninsula in 1950, a surprise attack from the North against the South kicked off a campaign to create a single, Communist Korea that lasted into 1951 and beyond. When the UN intervened, U.S. forces were thrust into a bloody war for freedom and global influence.

Increased aggressiveness of Communist regimes encouraged a worried, even paranoid, climate in the United States that was seized upon by ambitious "Red-baiters," none more vociferous than the junior senator from Wisconsin, Joseph McCarthy. Brimming with apocryphal claims of Communist subversion, he brought panic to Washington and set in motion forces that threatened many of the freedoms McCarthy and his supporters claimed to cherish.

Alfred Kinsey's new book, *Sexual Behavior in the Human Female*, shocked many in 1953, but its findings were only the tip of the iceberg. In millions of American homes, wives and mothers labored to fulfill their roles to the satisfaction of society and their husbands. Single and "career" women, meanwhile, were told they existed outside the mainstream, and were falling short of America's feminine ideal. The tensions were very real, and they were growing.

As grand and attainable as the American Dream became in the 1950s, it was not possible for all citizens. Although prosperous, the middle class also was distressingly insular. In the popular imagination, the nation was contentedly homogeneous, which meant of Anglo-Saxon origins. Even "outsiders" of Eastern European extraction, particularly Jews, had to "earn" acceptance, while people of color lived in a rigidly segregated America where rule of law was practiced selectively in the North as well as in the South.

The reweaving of America's social fabric was hastened this year, when white racists in Mississippi murdered a black teenager named Emmett Till, and when NAACP activist Rosa Parks refused to give up her seat on a Montgomery, Alabama, bus. National coverage of the Till case (his killers were acquitted) and the Montgomery bus boycott helped spur the civil rights movement, and encouraged African-Americans to set out on the long road to equality in law and in practice.

Youngsters became a potent economic force in the 1950s, as manufacturing and retailing joined with the advertising industry to reach into the purses and pockets of America's teens. Teens were no longer miniature adults, but free-thinking consumers who were ready to be courted as representatives of a separate culture. Teenagers became the driving force behind fashion, music, and other enterprises that had once been shaped solely by grown-ups.

America had an understandable preoccupation throughout the '50s with "super-science." The atomic bomb had been revealed as recently as 1945, and missile technology had arrived. Imagine, then, U.S. consternation when the first artificial satellite, called Sputnik, was launched into Earth orbit in October 1957 by the Soviet Union. Politicians bewailed America's failed educational system, and regular folks waited for the atomic missiles to fall. The arms race had begun.

For millions of Americans who lived in split-level splendor and drove gaudy new cars, the high-pressure avenue to affluence finally became wearisome. Male bread-winners questioned the sometimes soulless grind of white-collar corporate life, where bosses demanded complete devotion to pursuits that frequently struck trainees, junior executives, and assistant vice presidents as meaningless. And then there was the supposed feminization of the American male on the home front. What was a man, anyway?

In the early 1900s, society's malcontents were called "beady-eyed anarchists." But as America prospered (and fretted) in the volatile postwar era, and as some people questioned the meaning of it all, the new malcontents revealed themselves as Beats, and later as Beatniks. These savvy cats saw through the shuck and jive of Washington and Madison Avenue, and stood ready to liberate the rest of us with music, free-form poetry, some anger, and not a little condescension. Hipsters, unite!

Foreword

AT THE DAWN OF THE 1950s, I was a 25-year-old president's daughter with a budding career as a singer and a wide-open future. Like many Americans, I was enjoying the sense of hope and freedom that arose in the wake of World War II and reveling in the country's prosperity.

In late June 1950, North Korea attacked South Korea and our country's good mood evaporated. No one's outlook was darker, at times, than my father's. Though he believed with all his heart in the policy of containing communism, he abhorred the idea of putting American soldiers in harm's way, especially so soon after a world war and with the Armed Forces demobilized and ill-prepared.

It was this, in part, that embroiled the both of us in a public fracas in 1950. It involved the unfavorable and rather pompous review of my Constitution Hall concert by Paul Hume, the music critic for *The Washington Post.*

Dad had more than Korea on his mind when he read that review the morning after the concert. His oldest friend and press secretary, Charlie Ross, had died of a massive heart attack the previous day. So it didn't surprise me much when I discovered that Dad's letter to Hume contained two pages of vitriol and the suggestion that should he and Hume meet, the latter would need "a new nose, a lot of beefsteak for black eyes, and perhaps a supporter below!"

Dad took a lot of flack over that letter. Many parents supported him, but just as many felt his attack on Hume was unconscionable given that their sons were fighting and dying in Korea. And really, the review did me no harm. In fact, it helped sell tickets to the next concert. Nevertheless, I was grateful to Dad for coming to my defense and glad that at least in the Truman household, chivalry was not dead.

While the postwar housing boom and growing economy meant that many Americans were living in brand-new homes in the 1950s, ours was so rotten that we had been kicked out. In 1948 the interior of the White House was found to be in a dangerously deplorable condition, so much so that the chandelier in the State Dining Room downstairs quivered whenever someone walked back and forth in the family quarters above. The last straw was a piano leg that punched through the floor of my upstairs sitting room, prompting engineers to run steel cables from the roof through the second floor to make sure it stayed up.

Before they moved us catty-corner across the street to Blair House, we lived like that for weeks, dodging in and out of the cables. Early on, Dad led a media tour of the family quarters, stopping outside his bathroom to point out a cable that had been run down through the floor next to the commode. *New York Times* photographer George Tames remembered Dad eyeing the cable suspiciously and saying, "This thing scares me. I'm going to be sitting in here someday, pull the plunger, and wind up in the State Dining Room. And don't you know the band will play 'Hail to the Chief' as I come through the ceiling."

The world's troubles intruded upon us violently in November 1952 when two Puerto Rican nationalists, Oscar Collazo and Griselio Torresola, tried to shoot their way into Blair House and kill Dad in an attempt to draw attention to the cause of Puerto Rican independence. Torresola died in the attempt, as did the fine White House policeman who shot him, Private Leslie Coffelt. I was in Oregon on a concert tour at the time, but Dad was upstairs in Blair House taking a nap. He heard the commotion and went to the window to see what was going on. He actually caught a glimpse of Torresola on the front steps before White House policemen shouted at him to duck back inside.

Margaret Truman

By the time Mother and Dad had retired to Independence, Missouri, in 1953 (Mother would have been happy to stay put in D.C., but Dad insisted that ex-presidents did not retire in Washington), I happily had become part and parcel of America's new favorite pastime—television.

I was lucky enough to work with some of the new medium's brightest stars, including Milton Berle, Sid Caesar, Imogene Coca, Fred Allen, and Groucho Marx. But my favorite was Jimmy Durante. Uncle Miltie tried to teach me how to sing a song, while Sid and Imogene were a little too serious about being funny. I have Fred to thank for any knowledge of comic timing, and Groucho tried to sit on my lap in front of 4,000 people. But Jimmy . . . he was a love.

Jimmy was used to working nightclubs, so he rarely got up before noon. Yet when my train arrived in Los Angeles at 9 A.M. one morning, he was there to greet me, looking a little worse for wear. "What are you doing here at this hour?" I asked. "That's what I'm wondering," he said.

On another occasion, a couple of friends took me to dinner between rehearsals and I let them talk me into a glass of wine, which apparently was a good idea. Jimmy pulled them aside after the evening rehearsal and said, "Wherever you took her to dinner, take her there tomorrow before the show. And whatever you gave her, give it to her again."

Despite all the work in television, my steadiest job during the 1950s was in radio, teamed with Mike Wallace—in the days before he became renowned for his journalistic aggression—on a show called *Weekday.* It was created in 1955 by NBC chief Pat Weaver (actress Sigourney Weaver's dad) in an attempt to lure housewives back from the independent stations. Like *Live with Regis and Kelly,* it had a little bit of everything—news, music, chatter, celebrities, cooking hints, cliff-hanger serials, fashion notes, even lectures on human relations. I had the chance to interview Liberace, playwright Thornton Wilder, and John F. Kennedy, who was then a freshman senator and author of the newly published *Profiles in Courage.*

I signed a 10-year contract with NBC in 1955 and wound up talking them out of it the following year so I could get married. I had gone to a party with Alan Campbell, writer Dorothy Parker's ex-ex-husband (she had married him twice), and there met Clifton Daniel, the assistant to the foreign editor of *The New York Times.* For months, we went sneaking around New York, trying not to be seen together because the press—the rest of it besides Clifton, anyway—was dogging me to see whether or not I was getting married. Finally, on a trip to see Clifton's family in North Carolina, we made the mistake of confiding in Jonathan Daniels, editor of Raleigh's *The News & Observer,* who blabbed, forcing Dad to hold a press conference to announce our engagement.

Dad approved of Clifton, and Clifton always said Dad was the perfect father-in-law in that he kept his nose out of Clifton's business. Still, they got off to a rocky start. Dad didn't like people who drank too much, but he had even less tolerance for teetotalers, not to mention newspapermen. At their first meeting, Clifton—who was recovering from an ulcer—first asked for a glass of milk and then revealed he was a newspaper editor. Dad actually leaned forward in his chair and said, "What?!"

Nevertheless, by the time the 1950s closed, I was a 35-year-old with a career, a husband, and two preschoolers. It had been a golden age. Even with the pall of Korea and the Cold War over us, we were young and exuberant, we had money in our pockets, and there seemed to be no limit to our creativity or what we could achieve.

—MARGARET TRUMAN

Introduction

OF COURSE YOU RECALL "Rock Around the Clock" by Bill Haley and His Comets, and even if you don't actually *remember* it, you know the song was a major hit from the early rock 'n' roll era. The 1950s. That prosperous, sunny decade of cars, music, the suburbs, and sitcoms. An uncomplicated time aswirl in poodle skirts and bathed in the reassuring grin of President Eisenhower. "Rock Around the Clock" has become emblematic of the '50s, and why not? The record is cheerful and upbeat. Just like the 1950s.

What has been forgotten is that "Rock Around the Clock" was recorded as the throwaway "B" side to Haley's version of "Thirteen Women (And Only One Man in Town)," an unsettling novelty tune about the sole fellow left alive—with 13 ladies along for company—after everybody else on the planet has been annihilated by atomic bombs.

Cheerful and upbeat indeed.

Haley supplied a sterling vocal performance for "Thirteen Women," but the recording's real significance is its ironically jokey acceptance of the specter of atomic destruction, a prospect that hung over this Cold War decade like a shroud. Americans could laugh off "Thirteen Women" during the light of day, but the laughter stopped when they lay awake in their beds at 3 A.M., their minds assaulted with visions of Communist attack, mushroom clouds and sundered cities, their families and friends—and themselves—killed.

The true nature of the 1950s has been clouded by a half century of innocent but misrepresented nostalgia, and by traditionalists' attempts to return to the purported innocence and moral clarity of the decade. As *The Fifties Chronicle* makes clear, the period is complex and unarguably revolutionary in such fundamental areas as international relations, economic growth, housing patterns, class distinctions, gender roles, and racial politics. The scale of change was monumental, and not all of it was easily discussed in the polite society of the day.

America's wartime experience and the first wave of postwar consumerism encouraged a broadened cultural perspective among Americans—not to the degree that the white majority was truly interested in being anything other than homogeneous, but so that it was at least receptive to some novel ideas about the look and attitude of everyday culture. Fresh sensibilities of creators and audiences affected fine art; comic books, paperbacks, and other "low" art; movies and television; "exotica" music and black-rooted rock 'n' roll; fashion; furniture design and other home decor; architecture; magazine and ad graphics; and the whole spectrum of industrial design, from kitchen appliances to automobiles.

General anxiety about Communist subversion and atomic war brought about some unavoidable self-examination. Many men felt victimized by the "rat race." Many women found housewifery to be an empty occupation. Teenagers and even pre-teens developed new conceptions of self.

The inevitability of change was embraced as often as it was resisted. In the end, change won out. "Traditional" America was long gone—swept away by the Depression and the fires of war. Attempts to revive it during the '50s, as today, were illusory or purposely misleading.

Challenging, audacious, dangerous, revolutionary—all of these words accurately describe the 1950s, when modern America was born.

"My [college] classmates in the forties, after the war, we wanted to get on with our lives. We were men, not kids, and we had the maturity to recognize we had to go get what we wanted, and not just wait for things to happen to us."

—Returned veteran Chesterfield Smith

Prologue
Peace and Possibilities

THE 1950s MAY BE the most misunderstood decade of the American 20th century. The period looms in the nation's popular imagination as an island of stability and calm in the roiling waters of the mid-1900s, which include the Great Depression of the 1930s, the world war of the 1940s, and the turmoil that threatened to tear the nation apart in the 1960s. The 1950s provide the contrast that throws those eras into sharp relief.

For some, the decade has served as a touchstone, a golden age of traditional values and national consensus that was destroyed by the overblown claims of the 1960s. With little irony and not much historical consciousness, these Americans see the '50s as America's Happy Days. To others, the '50s are an era of conformity and repression, blessedly overthrown by the cultural revolution of the 1960s. These Americans get the irony—*Leave It to Beaver* was just a TV show, not a true reflection of the times—but they may have even less historical consciousness, too easily discounting the relief many Americans felt during the 1950s in the aftermath of two decades of suffering and sacrifice. However, both of these assessments remove the 1950s from the struggles of the era. Both treat the '50s as a decade out of time.

In fact, the 1950s were a complex and volatile decade. They were a time of enormous social change on almost all fronts of American life. It was during the 1950s that the United States tried to figure out how to act as the strongest and most powerful nation in the world; Americans struggled, both internally and internationally, with this not-altogether-comfortable new role. It was during the 1950s that Americans tried to figure out how to live in new landscapes—the physical landscape of the suburbs; the cultural landscape of a consumer society; the political landscape of the Cold War world; the intimate

America's victory in World War II meant the homecomings of countless servicemen, who married, started families, and went to school. The construction industry could not initially keep pace with the furious demand for housing, so for many, life in a house trailer was the best option. In this 1947 domestic moment in Iowa, Ginny Smayda irons while husband Charles studies with baby Sue on his knee.

landscape of the family. It was during the 1950s that America defined itself as a middle-class nation; that "ethnic" Americans from Europe became firmly considered "white"; that African-Americans made powerful claims for equality and began to change the nation's laws, if not its practices.

The 1950s have their grand stories. After all, it was a decade of war, both hot and cold; of the "Red Scare" and "witch hunts"; of the moral grandeur of the Montgomery bus boycott and the bravery of the "Little Rock Nine," who faced hostile mobs as they integrated Arkansas's Central High. But much that was significant about the 1950s took place on a smaller scale, as people who had lived through hard times tried to make sense of a new world—a world with new possibilities but also with new and unfamiliar demands. To understand the 1950s, we need to understand what preceded the decade: economic depression and lost hope; world war, suffering, and loss; grand visions and great dreams.

The United States celebrated the end of World War II in a privileged way: Because homeland America had been physically untouched, and because the nation had suffered relatively few casualties, it entered the postwar era intact, economically strong, and with no shortage of men available for work and marriage. This uninhibited scene was snapped in Cleveland on August 14, 1945.

On August 15, 1945, as news of Japan's surrender reached the United States, people poured into the streets of the nation's cities. In Honolulu, where America's war had begun, impromptu parades snarled traffic. In Times Square, a sailor and a nurse were captured by photographer Alfred Eisenstadt in the kiss that has since symbolized the moment of victory. The war was finally over.

And much of the world lay in ruins. Pacific islands had been transformed into scorched and smoldering hells. In formerly proud cities of Europe and Asia, starving people wandered among the rubble, searching for food. One out of every nine people in the Soviet Union had died. The Chinese estimated their war losses at 10 million. Almost 11 million people had been systematically murdered or worked to death in Nazi death camps. Close to one million people died of famine in Japanese-controlled Indochina. Japan lost two and a half million of its citizens, almost 200,000 of them immediate casualties of the U.S. atomic bombs. More than 55 million people, at least half of them civilians, perished in the global conflagration.

In the calculus of human suffering, the United States was relatively blessed. After the shock of the attack on Pearl Harbor, the war was not waged on American soil. The nation lost fewer than 300,000 men out of a total population of about 132 million. Of all the world's nations, only the United States ended the war more prosperous and stronger than when it began.

Nevertheless, WWII had a profound impact on virtually all Americans. For four years, the war had been at the center of national life. Each of those war deaths left families and communities changed forever. The men who returned from combat in WWII often found a hero's welcome, but that did not cancel out the horrors they had experienced. Those of the 16 million men who served in the military but who were spared combat—the majority, as the U.S. Army had by far the largest "teeth-to-tail" ratio of the combatant nations—nonetheless had lives disrupted. Many returned to children who did not know them, to wives who had learned to make do without them, to a world that seemed vastly different from the one they had inhabited "for the duration."

On the home front, more than 15 million civilians moved during the war—half of them to another state—often in pursuit of well-paid work in war-production factories. The influx of war workers to cities and towns strained existing resources. The migrants crowded into ramshackle trailer parks without adequate sanitary facilities, or lived in tents, cellars, or even woodsheds. The situation was explosive, and when racial difference was involved, violence often arose. Forty-seven American cities saw almost 250 racial conflicts during 1943, with 34 people killed in 30 hours of racial warfare in Detroit that summer. Under difficult circumstances, most Americans tried to "do their part" for the war effort, and many American factories ran 24 hours a day, seven days a week, with workers on a six-day-a-week work schedule.

Though it was thousands of miles away, the war was hard to avoid. Even going to the movies—and 90 million movie tickets were sold each week—was no escape. Theaters offered "plasma premieres," with free admission to those who donated a half-pint of blood. Audiences watched newsreels of combat, laughed at cartoons in which Daffy Duck battled Nazis, and rose to sing the national anthem or to recite in unison the Lord's Prayer.

At war's end, the society to which GIs returned seemed precarious. Veterans were old enough to remember the economic depression that had devastated the nation for a full decade. During the 1930s, unemployment had reached 25 percent. Man and

Soldiers inspect the bombed Royal Hospital in Chelsea, London, on January 3, 1945. London and other British cities took tremendous damage and civilian casualties, and 400,000 men were lost in combat. By 1945 the British economy was exhausted. Like much of the rest of the world, Great Britain could only look at the United States with envy.

nature had seemed to conspire against the nation's farmers, as banks foreclosed on mortgages and drought swept black soil into gray dust that blew into the boiling clouds of the "Dust Bowl" in Kansas, New Mexico, Colorado, Oklahoma, and Texas. Tens of millions of the nation's citizens were desperately poor.

Few Americans in the 1930s felt confident about the future—either the nation's future or their own. Economic security seemed a false hope; social unrest and political instability were persistent threats. And while President Franklin Roosevelt's New Deal had ameliorated the suffering, federal programs did not solve the underlying problems. It was spending for war that lifted America out of economic crisis. With the war over, what would prevent those dark days from returning? The young Americans who would make the postwar world faced the future with a heavy burden of history. It would not be easy to move past the shadows of economic depression and war.

The GI Bill helped millions of former servicemen through college and trade school, and also headed off the economic and social disasters that would have been caused by returned soldiers entering the workforce en masse. As it was, the early postwar period saw serious labor strikes. These Detroit workers picketed the Kelsey-Hayes plant in September 1945.

In 1945 the United States faced a critical problem. Within 10 days of victory over Japan, 1.8 million Americans were laid off from their jobs, as war plants closed. Fifteen million servicemen awaited demobilization. How would the shrinking economy absorb the returning veterans? How could the economy not plunge back into depression?

The first year of adjustment to a peacetime economy was difficult. Unemployment rates stayed high, and as wartime price controls ended, inflation skyrocketed. With paychecks diminished by inflation, and facing the threat of unemployment, the nation's industrial workers launched a series of debilitating strikes in core industries: steel, coal, automobile, and electric, as well as railroad and maritime transportation.

Despite the immediate troubles, the economy regained its strength. During WWII, factories had turned out tanks, planes, and ships instead of cars and appliances, and uniforms and parachutes instead of suits and silk stockings. People had made good money but had little on which to spend it. After the war, corporations had to make a gamble: reconversion and expansion, or careful retrenchment. General Motors rejected predictions of renewed depression and expanded its operations by 50 percent—and found millions of customers eager to buy its cars. And because most of the world's factories were in ruins, the United States faced little competition from abroad. Consumer spending at home, and global dominance abroad, set off an economic expansion that would last, with relatively minor recessions, for many years. The nation's GNP grew, from 1945 to 1960, by 250 percent.

Federal policies also fostered economic stability. The GI Bill, enacted before war's end, offered benefits to the nation's 16 million veterans. Meant to show gratitude, it also was a piece of social engineering designed to prevent veterans from swamping the nation's economy. The $4 billion in unemployment benefits dispensed to veterans by 1949 slowed the pace of demands on the job market.

American production of civilian automobiles was halted early in 1942 and did not resume until late in 1945. Although most new postwar cars were retreads of prewar models, pent-up consumer demand meant that every one found a buyer, giving a significant boost to the U.S. economy. These '46 Fords rolled off the Edgewater, New Jersey, line in October 1945.

Moreover, almost half of all returning veterans took advantage of the GI Bill to attend college or vocational school. Once again, GI Bill benefits reduced pressure on the recovering job market, but these educational benefits also produced a much more highly educated and skilled set of American workers. Before the war, fewer than 8 percent of American youth went to college; the GI Bill democratized American higher education and moved a great many Americans into the new and expanding middle class.

Finally, low-interest-rate mortgages for veterans made it possible for many Americans who had never expected to own a house to become homeowners—and at the same time financed an explosion of new housing construction that spurred growth in many sectors of the economy. Thirteen million new homes were built in the United States from 1948 to 1958; of these, 11 million were in the suburbs.

In the wartime military and defense plants, many Americans had come into contact with people from backgrounds different than their own. They had met people of different religions, from different regions, of different class or ethnic backgrounds. Sometimes, especially in the tension of war, these contacts were explosive, but at other times they created new connections, challenged assumptions, or offered new possibilities. In the postwar world, this process of cultural contact continued, though with less pressure and at a different pace. On the factory floor, in college classrooms, in corporate offices, and in new suburbs, people tried to figure out the rules of the new postwar society in the company of others who had come to the same place by different paths.

Lines still were drawn very firmly, however, at race, which would be the focus of many of the nation's most critical struggles during the 1950s. During the war, African-Americans had pressed for a "Double V": victory abroad, over the Axis powers, and victory at home, over racism and discrimination. In 1941, as the nation's factories began turning out weapons of war, A. Philip Randolph, head of the Brotherhood of Sleeping Car Porters union, proposed a march on Washington to demand that black Americans have equal access to jobs in defense industries. President Roosevelt, to head off the march, issued an executive order prohibiting racial discrimination in defense industries and government positions.

Nonetheless, the United States fought the war with a segregated military. Racism ran so deep in much of white American society that the Red Cross maintained separate "white" and "Negro" blood supplies. But as black Americans contributed to the war effort, membership in civil rights organizations, such as the NAACP, soared. And after the war, African-Americans called upon their wartime service to claim the full rights of citizenship.

President Harry Truman pushed forward civil rights legislation, including an antilynching bill, and in 1948 he desegregated the Armed Forces. Violence and discrimination against black Americans continued throughout the postwar era, but many black citizens used their wartime experiences as a foundation to build better lives. Blacks sought education through the GI Bill, participated in civil service employment preferences accorded to veterans, and organized for civil rights. And small victories, such as Jackie Robinson breaking the color line in major-league baseball in 1947, carried great symbolic weight.

In the wake of so many hard years, young couples of all racial and ethnic backgrounds exhibited a great optimism in their personal lives. They married at the highest rate of any industrialized nation except Hungary; 2.2 million couples married in 1946, double the rate of the preceding year. Those couples quickly began to have children. The baby boom officially began at one second past midnight on January 1, 1946, with the birth of Kathleen Casey in Philadelphia. She was joined, before the baby boom ran its course in 1964, by more than 76 million others.

Black GIs had fought and died in segregated units during World War II. Vets not unreasonably demanded their share of the nation's gratitude and opportunities, but racial tensions remained high, and meaningful work scarce. This strained encounter took place in Harlem on August 1, 1947.

The young men and women who became the parents of Baby Boomers were profoundly shaped by their youthful experiences of economic depression and war. Most sought stability—in marriages they vowed to make the best of; in large families (the ideal number of children jumped from two to four); and in clearly defined gender roles. Millions of postwar men and women embraced the traditional roles of breadwinner and homemaker. For them, it was a more desirable situation than during the Depression, when many men couldn't support their families, and during the war, when mothers had to make do without their husbands. Family was at the center of the nation's public life in the postwar era, and it served both as an expression of optimism about the future and a bulwark against fears of a difficult and dangerous postwar world.

For as the nation struggled with massive social change and new ways of life, it also faced the challenges of a new, complex role in the world. World War II had left international relations radically destabilized and in flux. Though the Soviet Union and the United States had been allies during the war, their relationship was always strained. And as each pursued its own interests in the final days of war and the months that followed, those strains shaped a "Cold War" that would bring the world to the brink of nuclear apocalypse and define the relations among most of the world's nations for decades to come.

Schooled in the "lessons" of WWII, America resolved to hold firm against the Soviet Union and what many saw as the relentless expansion of worldwide communism. As nationalist movements pressed for independence in colonies of exhausted European powers, both Washington and Moscow tried to push those countries into their column of Cold War alignment.

The United States was shocked in September 1949, when President Truman announced that the Soviet Union had successfully test-exploded an atomic device a few weeks earlier. America's nuclear monopoly had ended. And China, the world's most populous nation, "fell" that same September to Communist insurgents led by Mao Zedong.

After only a few years of fragile peace, the world was in flux again. The resulting fears, sometimes used cynically for political advantage and sometimes simply reflecting the assumptions of the age, led to domestic panic. Americans worried about spies and Communist subversion, and wondered if their precarious peace and security might be lost or squandered.

On the cusp of the 1950s, Americans were possessed by both fear and hope. These powerful emotions, born of decades of depression and war, would shape the decade to come in complex and unpredictable ways.

U.S.-Soviet tensions were apparent well before the end of the war, and the sham of alliance was abandoned completely in 1945. The Soviets established Communist rule in Eastern Germany and Eastern Europe, unnerving Americans. This 1949 postage stamp celebrates Soviet dictator Joseph Stalin (*left*) and East German puppet leader Wilhelm Pieck (*right*).

As America saw things, it was bad enough that the USSR was exporting communism into half of Europe, and even worse when the first Soviet A-bomb was successfully tested, on August 29, 1949. America's atomic monopoly had ended, and the Cold War suddenly assumed enormous stakes.

"Take the 3,548,000 babies born in 1950. Bundle them into a batch, bounce them all over the bountiful land that is America. What do you get? Boom. The biggest, boomiest boom ever known in history."

—Sylvia F. Porter, syndicated newspaper columnist

1950

Boom Time

I N 1950 SUNDAY EVENINGS were "Hoppy night" for many of the 10 million American families who had spent up to $500 for a television—at a time when minimum wage was 75 cents an hour. Children crowded around television sets to watch Hopalong Cassidy, the black-clad cowboy hero, riding through the American West to vanquish rustlers and bandits. Though *Hopalong Cassidy* ranked No. 9 for the year in the brand new Nielsen television ratings, the show was nothing more than a set of recycled Hollywood films, B westerns made by actor William Boyd from 1935 to 1948. NBC simply cut them to 54 minutes so they would fit, with commercials, into the one-hour time slot.

Soon there would be new Hopalong Cassidy adventures made especially for television. But in the meantime, Hoppy's success on the small screen signaled something else about postwar America. When an official "Hopalong Cassidy jackknife" was marketed through the show in 1950, one million were sold in just 10 days. Consumption was going to be key to economic growth in the 1950s, and children were going to be a major engine driving that growth.

The young adults of 1950 had been children during the Great Depression of the 1930s. Many had been hungry, cold, and ill-clothed. They had seen seemingly secure jobs disappear and family farms lost to the combined forces of nature and an unforgiving national economy. They had come of age during World War II, and most of the men had been in uniform. Though WWII was America's "good war," the men who had hit the beaches at Nor-

At a suburban housing development in Columbus, Ohio, a couple stands amid the windows and appliances that will be part of their new house. Home and family became integral parts of the postwar boom.

mandy or on Iwo Jima had felt its full horror. They returned to a nation flush with victory, but to an uncertain future.

In 1950 many signs were discouraging. The nation was just emerging from the recession of 1948–49. A new draft disrupted the plans of approximately 200,000 young men—in addition to those of the 62,000 reservists called up by the Army. In summer 1950, the Cold War heated up in Korea.

Despite the shadow of the past and the instability of the present, the young adults of 1950 were optimistic. They were changing the face of the nation through countless individual decisions—to marry, to have babies, to move to the suburbs, and to buy the things that represented, to them, the good life: cars, furniture, appliances, and a vast array of material goods.

Poised on the brink of that good life, Americans were creating a boom that would reverberate through the rest of the American century. "Just imagine how much these extra people, these new markets, will absorb—in food, in clothing, in gadgets, in housing, in services," wrote one syndicated columnist at the time. "Our factories must expand just to keep pace."

Young adults in the 1950s launched themselves into marriage and child-raising with an enthusiasm never seen before or since. The marriage boom that had started during World War II only grew with the return of peace, and Americans married at younger and younger ages. The trend toward earlier marriages was not new. The average age at which men married had dropped from 26 in 1890 to about 23 in 1930; for women, the decline had been less extreme—from 22 to 21. But so many young people had deferred marriage during the Great Depression that the new trend was startling. By the end of the 1950s, about half of all brides would be under 19.

By 1950 American network television had been broadcasting in earnest for two years. TV brought families and friends together in a passive way that, many feared, was killing conversation and relationships.

Even more striking was how much society celebrated the trend toward early marriage. Many of the young women who married in 1950 had read an article in the *Ladies' Home Journal* in '49 about marriage and youth. Accompanying the article was a photo of a young man studying at a ramshackle kitchen table, his very young wife hanging over his shoulder. The caption stated that many young men could "do much better work" if they got "the girl out of their dreams and into their kitchen." That same year, a professor of human relations made the case for early marriage in *Woman's Home Com-*

panion: "When two people are ready for sexual intercourse at the fully human level, they are ready for marriage—and they *should* marry. Not to do so is moral cowardice. And society has no right to stand in their way."

As America's marriage rate surpassed that of nearly all western nations, its birthrate rivaled that of India. It was not that American women suddenly began having large families, but that—uniformly, across lines of class, race, and educational level—Americans married young and quickly had children, an average of three per family.

Where were these young families to live? Due to the Great Depression and World War II, very little new housing had been built for almost two decades. In Lawrence, Kansas, a newly hired assistant professor moved his family into a Quonset hut; in Chicago, 250 trolley cars were sold to families desperate for a place to live. Many married couples doubled up with his parents or hers, waiting for the day they could find their own place. An estimated five million new houses or apartments were needed in the years following WWII, and by 1950 housing starts approached two million.

From 1946 to 1950, the federal government financed $20 billion in Veterans Administration or Federal Housing Administration mortgage loans. Veterans could buy a new house in Levittown, New York, or a similar suburb, with a VA 30-year mortgage and no money down for just $56 a month. People who had grown up in cramped tenement apartments in cities or in rural housing (much of which still lacked electricity and indoor plumbing in the 1930s and even 1940s) looked to the suburbs for comfort, privacy, and a good life for their families. But even without the lure of suburban life, the economics of the situation favored a move to the suburbs. An apartment rental—if one could find the apartment—ran close to $100 a month in many major cities.

America's suburban population would double from 1950 to 1970, but already in 1950 36 million Americans lived in the suburbs. The new suburbs did not grow in concentric rings around city centers. Instead, their locations were determined opportunistically, as developers found cheap land and put up inexpensive starter homes, increasingly using the mass-production building techniques pioneered by William Levitt. Many houses, no more than 800 or 900 square feet, were variations on a developer's "box" plan. And unlike the houses of previous decades, these were usually horizontal, one-story affairs, increasingly with an open floor plan and incorporating a plate-glass window to give the illusion of space and connection to the outdoors. In 1950 subur-

Marriage and motherhood were the presumed destinies of America's young women. Indeed, women were marrying at younger ages, and having more children, than women of the previous generation.

Housing starts, which had been moribund during two decades of depression and war, exploded after 1945. By 1950 jobs were plentiful, and ex-servicemen who had educated themselves on the GI Bill were able to marry and save for homes of their own.

ban developments typically were surrounded by woods and fields, which gradually gave way to more suburban developments and the phenomenon of urban sprawl.

A move to the suburbs changed more than one's surroundings. The new suburbanites were in a sense pioneers, creating new communities and new rituals of family life. Men's and women's roles in the family became more clearly differentiated, as women and children lived in communities essentially devoid of men Monday through Friday. Though women continued to work outside the home during the 1950s (usually part-time, and typically only after their children had entered school), the ideal of the breadwinner husband and homemaker wife was strong.

Suburban life also made Americans much more reliant on automobiles, as men commuted to their jobs and women relied on cars to do their shopping. However, thanks to the luxury of refrigerators and "convenience" processed foods, women did not have to make daily runs to the local market for fresh food. Instead, a weekly trip to the giant supermarket would do.

The automobiles that would transform the American landscape were just becoming widely available in 1950. Before that year, new cars were relatively scarce, and certainly expensive. America's stock of automobiles had declined by about four million during World War II, as factories turned out tanks and ships for the duration before retooling after the war. Acquiring

Because no new automobiles were manufactured in the U.S. during the war years, demand for new cars was immense. By 1950 independent manufacturers and Detroit's Big Three offered an abundance of new lines and models, such as this Ford Crestliner.

even a broken-down used car might require the supplemental purchase of "accessories," such as a $150 battery, during the late 1940s. By 1950, however, General Motors was turning out six million automobiles a year, and American families were buying cars with the same enthusiasm they brought to the purchase of their suburban houses.

In 1950 America was on the brink of an explosion of consumer spending, most of it centering on the home and family. In the five years following WWII, total consumer spending rose 60 percent—with spending on home appliances and furnishings jumping an amazing 240 percent. Americans bought millions of refrigerators and a host of small appliances that would, over the course of the decade, come in increasingly improbable shapes and colors.

Author Thomas Hine describes the style of the 1950s—its homes and cars and furniture and appliances—as "populuxe," a synthetic word itself derived from "populism and popularity.... [I]t has luxury, popular luxury, luxury for all ... [as well as] a thoroughly unnecessary 'e,' to give it class." Populuxe, Hine writes, "speaks of optimism and opulence" in an age when the "objects people could buy took on a special exaggerated quality. They celebrated confidence in the future, the excitement of the present, the sheer joy of having so much."

The pent-up demand for consumer goods had exploded during the immediate postwar years, even when

More than 219,000 American men were drafted in 1950, up from about 9,800 in 1949. With a new war in Asia, good-byes were difficult.

the economy was rocky. But in 1950 American businesses were concerned about the future. The young adults of 1950 were the smallest cohort of the 20th century, Depression babies born in years when the American birthrate dropped precipitously. How would such a small demographic fuel the consumer economy? The answer, of course, was through their children.

The move to the suburbs was justified as "good for the children" (though a host of sophisticated urbanites wrote screeds against the practice). It was in 1950 that Saturday morning cartoons appeared on the American television landscape, that Silly Putty came into the hands of America's kids, that the Aladdin corporation put Hopalong Cassidy on its lunch boxes, which sold so fast that stores couldn't keep them in stock. In 1950, even before the baby boom reached its height or the economic boom of the decade became certain, Hopalong Cassidy toys brought in $100 million. It was clear that the decade of consumption and of the family were coming together in the figure of the American child.

1950: The United Nations Secretariat Building on Manhattan's East Side is completed. • British and American anti-Communist guerrillas infiltrate Albania. • The Saudis strike a deal with the Arabian American Oil Company (Aramco) that funnels 50 percent of oil profits to the kingdom's treasury. • Physicist Ralph Lapp argues that dispersion of the population is the most practical method of American civil defense against atomic attack. • Strategic Air Command (SAC) General Curtis LeMay urges implementation of SAC Emergency War Plan 1-49, which calls for the delivery of "the entire stockpile of atomic bombs . . . in a single massive attack" against the USSR. If implemented, the plan would destroy 70 Soviet cities in 30 days with 133 atomic bombs.

1950: Congressman Adam Clayton Powell (D–NY) introduces an amendment calling for denial of federal funds to projects tainted by racial discrimination. • President Harry Truman establishes the Commission on Internal Security and Individual Rights. • The U.S. Gross National Product reaches $284 billion, nearly three times the 1940 figure. • An ill-fated Army "mock" biological attack kills one and sickens 11 in San Francisco.

1950: Albert Einstein develops his General Field Theory in an effort to expand on his theory of relativity. • David Riesman's book *The Lonely Crowd,* which introduces the concept of inner- and other-directed personalities, is released. • The U.S. census employs a computer, the UNIVAC I, for the first time in history. • Xerox introduces the first electronic copier using xerography, which shines infrared light through an original document, creating an exact copy. • The first mass-production postwar compact car—the Nash Rambler—rolls off the assembly line. • Zenith's *Lazy Bones,* the first television remote control, hits the market.

From 1949 to 1961, General Motors staged a series of promotional extravaganzas throughout the United States. Dubbed the "Motorama," the pre-auto show affair showcased GM's future offerings in order to create a buzz and gauge public response. Highlighting the shows were displays of experimental "concept cars," which rarely entered mass production. GM's 1950 exposition in New York (*pictured*) drew some 320,000 attendees over seven days. Visitors were treated to scores of female models (gowned to match the cars), entertainment figures, and a singing group called the Motorythms.

This ad for industry giant TWA shows smiling passengers preparing to embark on what surely will be an adventure. Wartime technological advances had made air travel a viable alternative to sea and rail transport, but with limitations. In this pre-jet age, industry workhorses such as the Lockheed Constellation and Douglas DC-6 were susceptible to engine breakdowns, excessive noise, and rough flying due to altitude restrictions. Moreover, passenger flight was too expensive for most Americans. Nevertheless, airlines could always count on the allure of faraway places to entice the well-heeled to "come fly" with them.

First flight or fiftieth, you'll be glad you chose TWA

The Mexico City street children of Luis Buñuel's *Los Olvidados* (*The Forgotten*) do not steal, cheat, and kill in order to make their lives more comfortable; they do these things merely to live. Comfort is not a possibility in this bleakly unsentimental view of the urban, Third World underclass, and the children—the sons and daughters of rural peasants now adrift in the city—are its most pathetic victims. Buñuel was a leader in the Surrealist movement, and while *Los Olvidados* indulges in some of that (notably in a disquieting dream sequence), the film is very much in the social realist tradition that arose internationally following World War II. Mexican officials hated *Los Olvidados,* and were harshly critical of Buñuel, who would make many more honest, adventurous movies.

Former State Department official Alger Hiss leaves court with his wife, Priscilla, following his conviction on two counts of perjury in January 1950. Prosecutors charged that Hiss had lied when he denied allegations that he had been a Communist Party member. His accuser, Whittaker Chambers, further alleged that Hiss had passed sensitive materials through him to the Soviets. The sensational charges stirred an ideological firestorm. Freshman Congressman Richard Nixon (R–CA), a member of the House Un-American Activities Committee (HUAC), championed Chambers and pushed for a full investigation, resulting in Hiss's indictment. A guilty verdict (coming after two trials) was handed down in 1950. Nixon's role in the case brought him national exposure and springboarded him to a higher office later that year.

Police question employees near the Brinks Building's vault in Boston on January 17, 1950. Earlier that day, a crack team of robbers had relieved the facility of about $2.7 million in cash and securities, setting a record for the largest theft in U.S. history. Masterminded by Tony Pino, the crime had taken years to prepare for. Detailed research and strict discipline paid off when the thieves, sporting Halloween masks, netted their tremendous payday without incident. Authorities were baffled and the public enchanted until 1956, when one team member cracked. The surviving thieves were tried and convicted, although most of the haul was never recovered.

Alger Hiss's unlikely accuser was a former Communist Party member. Whittaker Chambers had been working as an editor at *Time* magazine when his story of an underground Communist network in Washington became public. Initial skepticism evaporated when, in highly dramatic fashion, Chambers led investigators to his Maryland farm, where he revealed four rolls of microfilm secreted in a hollowed-out pumpkin. The microfilm revealed incriminating documents that Hiss had written. After Hiss's conviction, Chambers wrote a book, *Witness* (1952), justifying his actions. As for Hiss, following his release, he spent the remainder of his life seeking a new trial and working to clear his name.

1950

1950: The San Francisco 49ers, Baltimore Colts, and Cleveland Browns all join the NFL when the All-America Football Conference disbands. • Evangelical preacher Billy Graham begins *Hour of Decision,* his weekly radio program. • The Christian nudist camp *Cedar Waters Village* opens in Nottingham, New Hampshire. • The prescription drug Miltown, a so-called "minor tranquilizer," is introduced in the U.S. and will soon become the abused drug of choice among the postwar middle class. • The National Council of Churches is founded, uniting 45 million congregants from 36 Protestant, Anglican, and Orthodox Christian denominations nationwide.

1950: Tulsa, Oklahoma, installs America's first yield sign. • New Yorker George Jorgensen travels to Denmark for a sex-change operation. • Campbell's Soup withdraws its sponsorship of *Edward R. Murrow with the News* amid concerns that the program has developed a pro-Communist slant. • American businessman Walter Paepcke founds the Aspen Institute. The Colorado-based think tank welcomes leaders ranging from the business world to fine arts to gather at this, in Paepcke's vision, "global forum for leveraging the power of leaders to improve the human condition."

January: The USSR and China recognize the Democratic Republic of Vietnam.

January 6: The British government recognizes Red China.

January 10: The Soviet delegate walks off the Security Council in disgust following the UN's support of Nationalist China.

January 12: A speech by Dean Acheson, U.S. secretary of state, inadvertently implies that South Korea is not under the protection of the U.S.

A seasick sea serpent named Cecil and his pal, Beany, were the stars of one of television's earliest kids shows, *Time for Beany.* The creation of former *Looney Tunes* animator Bob Clampett, the show featured Daws Butler as the title voice (later he would supply vocal talent for Huckleberry Hound), with comic legend Stan Freberg as the voice of both Cecil and Beany's nemesis, Dishonest John. Their seafaring adventures aboard the *Leakin' Lena* were later reinvented in the 1960s as a cartoon. The show's popularity spurred sales of the "propeller beanie" cap in the early 1950s.

Although India was granted independence by the Crown in 1947, three years passed before the last British troops left that country. Years of struggle, spearheaded by the nonviolent tactics of Mahatma Gandhi, had won India its autonomy, but the real upheaval was just beginning. Long-simmering ethnic tensions among the populace resulted in the country's partition. Much of the Muslim population relocated to newly formed Pakistan, while the Hindu majority in India struggled to maintain order. On January 26, 1950, the Indian constitution was formally ratified, and Dr. Rajendra Prasad (*pictured*) took office. He became the first president of the world's largest democracy.

Howdy Doody, which aired in the late afternoons on NBC in the first half of the 1950s, remains a treasured childhood memory for many Baby Boomers. Howdy and his companions, who included Phineas T. Bluster, Princess Summerfall Winterspring, and Clarabell the clown inhabited (where else?) Doodyville. Emceeing the proceedings was Buffalo Bob Smith, whose duties included playing host to the in-studio audience of children who comprised the "Peanut Gallery." Howdy-mania led to an array of spin-off products that flooded the market.

University of Chicago professor David Riesman's *The Lonely Crowd: A Study of the Changing American Character* was the rarest of things—a sociological analysis that became a best-seller. Inspired by De Tocqueville's *Democracy in America,* Riesman *(pictured)* explored how a corporate-driven society reflected the national disposition. He described three distinct character types: the tradition-directed, the inner-directed, and the usefully adaptable (if conformist) other-directed—and how each played a greater or lesser role, suited to the demands of the day.

The GI Bill

DISPLAYING HIS TYPICAL farsightedness, President Franklin Roosevelt in 1944 signed into law the Serviceman's Readjustment Act, universally known as the GI Bill. As both a measure of the nation's gratitude and as a pragmatic safeguard against widespread postwar unemployment, the legislation revitalized the middle class, providing a potent means for millions to realize the American Dream.

The GI Bill funded vocational training or college tuition for returning veterans while also making available low-cost loans for home buying or business start-ups. Input from the American Legion was critical in shaping the bill's final form, which extended the benefits to all veterans, including women and minorities.

The education component of the bill initially met with resistance from some school presidents, who feared an influx of servicemen unable to meet their tuition. Once school officials adjusted to the idea that the entire education was on Uncle Sam's dime, universities across the country opened their doors to millions of veterans. Likewise, the critical postwar housing shortage was met with a construction boom, with 11 million of 13 million new homes financed by GI Bill loans.

Such largesse was paid for with the federal income tax generated by the burgeoning class of entrepreneurs and college-educated employees suddenly entering the workforce. The federal government also offered a year's worth

A former GI and his family starting out in a Quonset hut

of unemployment insurance. But with so many takers for the education and job-training allotments, only 20 percent of this unemployment set-aside was ever tapped.

The GI Bill had a profound broadening effect. Because vocational training was paid for, class distinctions were blurred. The middle class expanded to eventually encompass more than white-collar workers and their families. This, plus an expanded economy, suggest that the GI Bill was the right program at the right time.

1950

January 15: The Leadership Conference on Civil Rights is chartered by A. Philip Randolph, Roy Wilkins, and Arnold Aronson.

January 17: Eight men snag more than $2.7 million in the biggest heist ever, at Boston's Brinks Express Co.

January 21: George Orwell, who penned *1984* and *Animal Farm,* dies at age 46.

January 23: Israel's Knesset proclaims Jerusalem the capital of Israel.

January 25: U.S. government official Alger Hiss, an alleged Communist spy who escaped a treason trial due to the expiration of the statute of limitations, is sentenced to five years for perjuring himself while under investigation. • The Equal Rights Amendment passes the Senate, 63 to 19. However, it contains a rider that invalidates its effectiveness.

January 26: Rajendra Prasad is sworn in as president of India, establishing a new republic.

January 27: Klaus Fuchs, a German who had helped the U.S. and Great Britain build atomic bombs, confesses to passing nuclear secrets to the Soviets. The Fuchs case will provide key evidence leading to the convictions of Julius and Ethel Rosenberg.

January 29: Race riots rage in Johannesburg, South Africa.

January 31: In a message to the Atomic Energy Commission, President Truman announces his decision to proceed with the development of the hydrogen bomb, which would be much more powerful than the atomic bomb. • Chinese Nationalists resume bombing of mainland China in hopes of preventing the Communist invasion of the offshore islands.

On Saturday nights from 1950 to 1954, Sid Caesar (*left*) and his teammate actors defied convention on NBC's *Your Show of Shows.* Scripts were written by such comic geniuses as Woody Allen, Mel Brooks, and Neil Simon. Caesar's cast of performers included Carl Reiner and Imogene Coca (*right*). The comedy was equally inventive with dialogue or without. Caesar and his crew could play everyone from Nazis to automated figures on a broken European clock with the same uproarious result.

In February 1950, China's newly ensconced chairman, Mao Zedong (*left*), signed a 30-year mutual defense treaty with Soviet Premier Joseph Stalin (*right,* pictured with Politburo member Nikolai Bulganin). By doing so, they went a long way toward inflaming western fears of a monolithic Communist bloc bent on world domination. The truth was far more complicated. Relations between the two nations had long been mistrustful, and conflicting claims on Mongolia would remain a particular sore spot for years to come. But the treaty represented a marriage of convenience for both parties, with the Soviets desiring stability with their immediate neighbors and China seeking protection against any aggressive action from the United States.

In a follow-up to his startling proclamation of rampant subversion in the State Department, Senator Joseph McCarthy fired off a lengthy telegram to President Harry Truman, taking the latter to task for not addressing the supposed problem. Furious at the senator's reckless impertinence, President Truman responded with this incendiary, tersely worded missive. Whether or not Truman actually sent it, or simply used it as an outlet to vent, is unknown. What is certain is that at a press conference on March 30, the President didn't equivocate, calling the senator "the greatest asset that the Kremlin has."

Draft

McCarthy
file

My dear Senator:

I read your telegram of February eleventh from Reno, Nevada with a great deal of interest and this is the first time in my experience, and I was ten years in the Senate, that I ever heard of a Senator trying to discredit his own Government before the world.   You know that isn't done by honest public officials. Your telegram is not only not true and an insolent approach to a situation that should have been worked out between man and man but it shows conclusively that you are not even fit to have a hand in the operation of the Government of the United States.

I am very sure that the people of Wisconsin are extremely sorry that they are represented by a person who has as little sense of responsibility as you have.

"Joe couldn't find a Communist in Red Square—he didn't know Karl Marx from Groucho—but he was a United States senator."

—George Reedy, former UPI reporter

McCarthy's List

AT A GATHERING of the Republican Women's Club in Wheeling, West Virginia, Wisconsin's junior senator unleashed a bombshell. Standing before the small assemblage on February 9, 1950, Joseph McCarthy waved a piece of paper and declared, "I have here in my hand a list of 205 that were known to the secretary of state as being members of the Communist Party, and who nevertheless are still working and shaping the policy of the State Department."

Though the paper in his hand was a prop and the speech had been cobbled together from remarks made by Congressman Richard Nixon (R–CA) days before, onlookers were intrigued. As McCarthy's speaking tour proceeded, reporters at the next stop demanded to see the list. Senator McCarthy balked; moreover, the exact number and description of the alleged miscreants changed with each telling. But for the accuser, the facts were less important than the effect.

McCarthy had been elected to the U.S. Senate in 1946, campaigning as a war hero. "Tail-gunner Joe" deposed the incumbent even though much of his "war record," like so much of his rhetoric, was fiction. McCarthy served for four years in the Senate, undistinguished but for his continual stepping on the toes of his colleagues. Then, in February 1950, with a retooled message staged for maximum drama, he claimed national attention. It was less the substance of his remarks than the way the administration reacted to them that gave them such potency.

President Truman pushed for a Senate investigation, led by conservative Senator Millard Tydings (D–MD). Despite the committee's finding in 1953 that McCarthy's accusations were groundless, the movement to hunt for Communists had been set into motion. Throughout the early 1950s, Senator McCarthy found himself at the center of a national crusade.

February 7: Britain and the U.S. recognize Bao Dai's government of South Vietnam. • Viet Minh fighters attack French positions near China's border with North Vietnam.

February 9: In a speech in Wheeling, West Virginia, U.S. Senator Joseph McCarthy (R–WI) asserts that Communists have infiltrated the State Department.

February 14: In a newspaper interview, President Truman claims that the Soviets have broken every postwar promise they have made to the U.S.

February 15: Red China signs a 30-year Treaty of Friendship with the USSR.

February 22: Albert Einstein, whose 1939 letter to President Franklin Roosevelt helped spur the development of the atomic bomb, warns that nuclear war could end in mutual annihilation.

February 25: In perhaps the most notorious assassination plot of the Cold War, U.S. Navy Captain Eugene Simon Karpe, suspected spy, is killed in a suspicious fall from the Orient Express. • The star-studded *Your Show of Shows* debuts on NBC.

February 27: Chiang Kai-shek is elected president of Nationalist China.

March 2: Dow's Earl Warrick, while developing a rubberlike substance, inadvertently invents Silly Putty.

March 5: A devastating winter walk-out by 340,000 miners throughout the U.S. coal belt is settled with a wage increase.

March 8: Soviet Marshal Kliment Voroshilov announces that the USSR has an atomic bomb.

March 14: The FBI introduces its "10 Most Wanted List."

March 16: Secretary of State Dean Acheson promotes his seven-point U.S.-Soviet cooperation plan.

Flair was an oversized monthly devoted to literature, travel, the visual arts, dining, fashion, and the rest of what editor Fleur Cowles called "the fullness of American life." *Flair* immediately attracted attention with bound-in booklets and art cards; complex, die-cut covers; an audacious variety of paper stock; and unusual printing techniques. Cowles's inaugural editorial, for instance, was written in her own hand and printed with simulated gold leaf on a discrete navy blue page. Contributors to the first issue included Jean Cocteau, W. H. Auden, and Tennessee Williams. Although underwritten by the Cowles publishing empire that included newspapers and *Look* magazine, *Flair* was prohibitively expensive to produce, and was discontinued after a dozen issues.

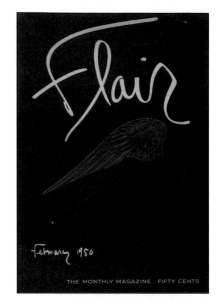

THE MONTHLY MAGAZINE   FIFTY CENTS

On March 15, 1950, picketers express their disapproval with the U.S. government's "superbomb" program, in which scientists worked to develop a weapon 500 times more powerful than those dropped on Hiroshima and Nagasaki. The picketers' views echoed those of physicist J. Robert Oppenheimer, one of the architects of America's atomic bomb program. He spoke for many within the scientific community who questioned the wisdom of unleashing such awful violence into the world. Others, including physicist Edward Teller, had no such qualms, arguing for peace through deterrence. For the Soviets to come into sole possession of such a weapon, he asserted, would be unacceptable. President Truman concurred, giving the go-ahead.

One of the most notorious names to surface during the Cold War was that of Klaus Fuchs, a German-born physicist. Fuchs had fled his homeland prior to World War II and eventually was assigned to the top-secret Manhattan Project, which developed the world's first atomic bomb. Fuchs, however, became part of a spy ring, funneling details of the Manhattan Project straight to the Soviets. Fuchs was convicted by a British court on March 1, 1950, and sentenced to 14 years in prison. His confession implicated a New Yorker named Julius Rosenberg, setting the stage for the biggest espionage case of the century.

Beginning in 1937, Walt Disney produced five consecutive animated classics: *Snow White and the Seven Dwarfs, Pinocchio, Fantasia, Dumbo,* and *Bambi.* Disney's next six films are long forgotten, but he launched his resurgence with 1950's *Cinderella.* For this film, Disney's crew reassembled the elements that pointed the way to future animated classics: a timeless story, vivid characterizations, artful direction (particularly when setting the mood), a memorable supporting cast of talking animals, and a soundtrack loaded with sing-along songs, including "Bibbidi Bobbidi Boo."

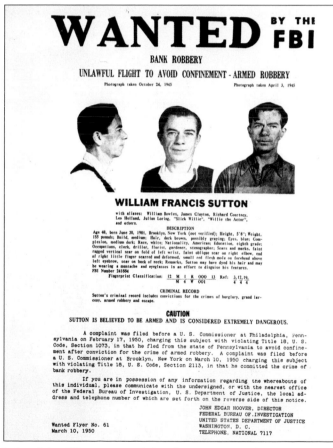

Why did Willie Sutton rob banks? "Because that's where the money is," he said. Known as "The Actor," Sutton became somewhat of a folk hero during the 1930s and '40s for both his skills (he is believed to have scored about $2 million over his career) and for his dramatic flair. He employed disguises, dialects, and physical affectations while plying his trade, and he even escaped from prison several times. On March 9, 1950, Sutton robbed the Manufacturers Bank in New York City of $64,000. He was arrested in 1952 and imprisoned for 17 years.

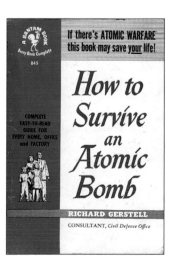

This paperback suggested to Americans that atomic war was survivable if proper precautions were taken. Some of the book's contentions are half-truths: Radiation is dangerous but not necessarily fatal. Others are patently false: Canned foods will not be adversely affected by radioactive fallout. Still others are, at best, wishful thinking: A program of simple home shelters will save families, entire communities, and the nation. Naive and deceptive, and based on poor military intelligence, this book and others like it suggest Washington's uncertainty about the extent of Soviet atomic stockpiles and missile-delivery systems, as well as an understandable desire to avoid a national panic.

1950

March 18: Nationalist Chinese troops capture the Red China city of Sungmen.

March 19: American novelist Edgar Rice Burroughs, the creator of Tarzan, dies at age 74.

March 23: RCA demonstrates the first color television to the FCC.

March 26: Senator Joseph McCarthy denounces former State Department employee Owen Lattimore as a Soviet spy.

March 30: President Truman accuses Joseph McCarthy of sabotaging U.S. foreign policy.

April: Former Nazi scientist Wernher von Braun is appointed director of development operations of Redstone Arsenal's Army Ballistic Missile Agency in Huntsville, Alabama.

April 5: An espionage trial against bishops and priests begins in Prague.

April 7: The State Department issues *National Security Council Document 68.* It urges massive military buildup to counter Soviet expansion in a world increasingly shaped by two contentious superpowers.

April 8: Ten die when a U.S. Navy spy plane is shot down over Latvia.

April 10: The U.S. Supreme Court upholds the contempt of Congress convictions of the "Hollywood Ten" (screenwriters, directors, and producers), most of whom will begin serving one-year prison sentences. The writers had been accused of infusing pro-Communist ideology into their scripts.

April 19: President Truman signs a bill establishing a decade-long Navajo/Hopi economic rehabilitation program.

April 23: Chiang Kai-shek pulls his troops out of Hainan, leaving mainland China to Mao's Communists.

When a kid needed a dribble glass in a hurry, the place to go was the Johnson Smith Company, which advertised its novelty wares in magazines and comic books as well as in mammoth catalogs of the type seen here. If the item was loud, embarrassing, silly, and just plain fun, Johnson Smith had it—and at a bargain price, too. Alfred Johnson Smith founded his mail-order enterprise in Australia in 1905, and brought it to the States in 1914. By the 1950s, schoolteachers across America were confiscating numberless JS gadgets, including joy buzzers, poo-poo cushions, squirt flowers, and chattering teeth.

Months after Red soldiers had driven the Nationalists from the Chinese mainland to the island of Formosa, the American-supported army of Nationalist China leader Chiang Kai-shek *(pictured)* lacked the will to defeat the Communists. Moreover, excesses committed during Chiang's rule left much of the population resentful and receptive to a regime change. Though their fight was all but over by the end of 1949, Chiang vowed to retake his country. While unwilling to further this goal, President Truman did send the Seventh Fleet to the Taiwan Strait in 1950 as a deterrent to further Red Army action.

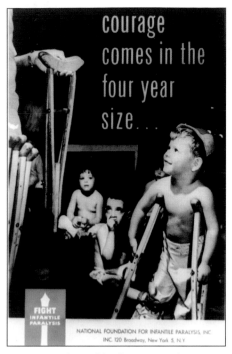

courage comes in the four year size...

FIGHT INFANTILE PARALYSIS

NATIONAL FOUNDATION FOR INFANTILE PARALYSIS, INC.
INC. 120 Broadway, New York 5, N.Y.

Posters such as this drew attention to the fight against infantile paralysis and were a familiar sight in 1950. That year saw 33,300 cases of polio reported, with nine fatalities. Facing an illness that could lead to paralysis or death made polio every parent's worst nightmare. Because doctors lacked insight into the disease's cause, parents placed heavy-handed restrictions upon children, particularly during the summer months, when cases tended to crest. Research funded by the March of Dimes helped give hope to those stricken by the virus.

The Harlem Renaissance was over before World War II, and by 1950 urban blacks were looking forward. But Harlem was far from dead. It was still the greatest black metropolis in the world, still the welcoming stage for a range of artists, such as painter Romare Bearden, writer John Henrik Clarke, and actors Ossie Davis and Ruby Dee. It was still a place to be cool—as cool as, paradoxically, the color "hot pink." As a trend, pink transcended the gender line in the early 1950s, as evidenced by boxer Sugar Ray Robinson's suit and Cadillac on this Harlem street.

Life in a Trailer Park in Florida.

A postcard captures the charm of a trailer park in Florida circa 1950. Originally, house trailers tended to be smaller units used for vacationing. But due to the post-World War II housing shortage, larger versions were marketed as permanent homes. Even after the housing shortage subsided, trailer homes were still sold to thousands of low-income and alternative-living Americans, who considered them more expedient than apartments.

U.S. Admiral Russell Berkey (*left*) meets with Bao Dai (*right*), the nominal head of Vietnam, in April 1950. Ostensibly an independent nation, Vietnam's affairs were still managed by France in the face of Ho Chi Minh's longtime struggle to free the nation from colonial rule. When China and the Soviets granted recognition to Ho's sovereignty in the North, France quickly restored Bao, the former emperor, to power as head of a government recognized by the U.S. and its allies. Bao, however, had little interest in running Vietnam. Meanwhile, nationalist Viet Minh forces began eroding France's resolve to hold on to its former colony.

Harry Truman

FOLLOWING THE IMPOSING Franklin Roosevelt into office in 1945, Harry Truman initially seemed at best a question mark, and at worst a man unfit to fill FDR's shoes. Chosen in a compromise as the least objectionable vice-presidential candidate in 1944, Truman's ascent in the midst of a world war concerned many. But his innate common sense and everyman persona soon won over doubters, including Winston Churchill: "I misjudged [Truman] badly...[M]ore than any other man, [he] saved Western civilization."

Truman had made a name for himself in the Senate as an incorruptible crusader against war profiteering. Though characterized by detractors as an unsophisticated Missouri rube, he demonstrated considerable courage and foresight as President, both in his dealings with the Soviets and with rebuilding Europe. Self-effacing and outspoken, Truman never evaded accountability for setbacks. ("The Buck Stops Here," read the famous sign on his desk.) America rewarded him with an astonishing come-from-behind victory against

Republican challenger Tom Dewey in 1948, sealing his place in political legend. Unfortunately, the election victory proved the high point of his second term. The rise of the "Red Menace" and New Deal fatigue paved the way for GOP victories in coming elections.

While beset by the Korean conflict, Truman doggedly pursued his political agenda, with plans that included universal health care. His desegregation of the armed forces proved a crucial first step toward racial equality, but his stock among the public plummeted when he fired vainglorious General Douglas MacArthur for insubordination during the Korean War. Though insiders deemed the dismissal necessary, the move was cited by the President's enemies as proof of the chief executive's poor judgment. Recognizing an uphill campaign, President Truman announced in early 1952 that he would not seek reelection. Reassessments by both the public and historians alike would rate Harry Truman far higher in later years than when he left office.

Beginning in the early 1950s, the name of Viet Minh leader Ho Chi Minh was increasingly familiar to many Westerners, while the man remained an enigma. He had been educated in both Paris and Moscow, which was, to many, a puzzling contradiction. A nationalist and a Communist, Ho preferred to play his enemies against each other in the name of Vietnamese independence. His successful guerrilla campaign against French colonial occupation (successfully concluded in 1954) would result in a Korea-style partitioning of Vietnam, with Communist forces occupying the North. His desire to unite the country under communism would prompt future American involvement.

With NBC's Milton Berle killing the competition every week, CBS thought that a weekly talent show could work as a successful alternative. So *Toast of the Town,* starring Ed Sullivan (*pictured*) premiered on June 20, 1948. The world of vaudeville—comedy, dance, acrobatics, and all the other bits—entered the living rooms of America, for free, with Sullivan as the ringmaster and taste arbiter. The man nicknamed "Old Stone Face" became one of America's first household television names. His "rilly big shoo" was renamed *The Ed Sullivan Show* in 1955, and became a showcase for new and established talent.

A stretch of America's most fabled highway, Route 66, winds through Seligman, Arizona. Commissioned in 1926, the highway was designed to connect small towns between Chicago and Los Angeles, as officials hoped it would enable farmers to get goods to market more easily. Later, the road facilitated transportation of military goods during World War II. Heavily traveled, Route 66 led to a building boom of ancillary businesses, from gas stations and roadside diners to family-owned motels and Southwest "trading posts" (souvenir shops). Road-trippers loved the charm of what they called the "Mother Road." In later decades, Route 66 became a victim of "progress," i.e., interstate highways.

April 24: The kingdom of Transjordan annexes Arab Palestine, and offers citizenship to its residents. It shortens its name to Jordan.

April 25: African-American Chuck Cooper breaks the NBA color barrier when he signs with the Boston Celtics.

April 27: Great Britain officially recognizes Israel. • The South African system of Apartheid is formalized with the passage of the Group Areas Act.

May: L. Ron Hubbard's *Dianetics,* the foundation of the Church of Scientology, first sees print as a magazine article. It will be published in book form later this year.

May 13: The Diners Club credit card is introduced.

May 14: Turkey ushers in democracy with its first free, multiparty general election.

May 25: The French appeal to the U.S. for assistance following a devastating attack by four Viet Minh battalions. • New York City's Brooklyn Battery Tunnel opens.

May 26: Hearings begin in the congressional investigation of organized crime. They are chaired by Senator Estes Kefauver (D–TN).

June: *Red Channels, A Report of Communist Influence in Radio and Television* is published by American Business Consultants, publishers of *Counterattack, The Newsletter of Facts to Combat Communists.* The paperback names 151 radio and television personalities with alleged ties to communism, including jazz singers Lena Horne and Hazel Scott.

June 5: Two U.S. Supreme Court rulings assert that segregation in state higher-education facilities is unconstitutional. • The U.S. Supreme Court, in its *Henderson v. United States* ruling, reverses a regulation requiring segregated dining cars on interstate trains.

Life imitated art when 18-year-old film actress Elizabeth Taylor, star of soon-to-be-released *Father of the Bride,* married hotel heir Nicky Hilton on May 6, 1950. Although the union lasted less than a year, it helped smooth the way for public acceptance of Taylor's transition from juvenile to adult roles. Until this stage of her career, Liz's renown came more for her beauty than for her acting. That would change with her strong performance opposite Montgomery Clift in George Stevens's *A Place in the Sun* (1951).

Editorial cartoonist Herbert Block, known to his readers as "Herblock," became one of the few people in the country capable of taking on Senator Joseph McCarthy with impunity. Through his daily platform at *The Washington Post,* Block kept up a barrage of outspoken critiques of Red-baiters in general and Senator McCarthy in particular. (Richard Nixon was another favorite target.) In this cartoon, Block underscores the depths to which subversion investigators were willing to plunge in order to support their innuendos. Perhaps Block's most enduring contribution to the discourse was introducing a fitting new term: "McCarthyism."

In May 1950, a former U.S. Department of Justice political analyst named Judith Coplon (*pictured*) got married in New York. The event was unremarkable but for the fact that Coplon's groom was her attorney, and the bride was free on bond after being twice convicted of espionage. When Coplon said "I do," she was looking at a possible 25 years in prison. Throughout 1949–50, America was mesmerized by the pretty ex-government worker—and by revelations during and after her Washington and New York trials of illegal FBI wiretapping and destruction of evidence. On December 5, 1950, Coplon's New York conviction was overturned; six months later, the U.S. Court of Appeals in Washington concurred.

Captain Video and His Video Rangers, on the DuMont Television Network, was one of several low-budget science fiction TV shows of the early 1950s. All of these programs had, essentially, the same Cold War era plot: The hero was a planetary police officer working for an FBI-like organization against evil forces trying to take over Earth. These futuristic versions of FBI "G-Men" were very popular with children who grew up during the Red Scare. Each week, the hero would use a combination of science and fair play, with an occasional ray blast or left hook, to win the day. Seen here are Don Hastings (*left*) and Al Hodge as the captain.

For those who liked their entertainment tuneful, but with a touch of subversion, bandleader Spike Jones filled the bill. Jones was known for his irreverent takes on both the classics and pop standards (for example, his "You Always Hurt the One You Love" was punctuated by cries of pain). In 1948 he made an immortal contribution to the Christmas canon with the irresistible song "All I Want for Christmas Is My Two Front Teeth," which was still high on the charts in 1950.

From 1948 until 1952, the White House was off limits—even to the President. Years of alterations and neglect had taken a heavy toll on the 150-year-old structure. (The final straw came when Margaret Truman's piano leg crashed through a ceiling from the floor above.) In 1948 President Truman authorized a $5.4 million overhaul, in which workers would replace the mansion's decrepit wooden interior with a duplicate, supported by a modern steel skeleton. As the inside was gutted, the Trumans took up residence across the street at Blair House.

A subgenre of crime thrillers that had begun in 1948 with *The Naked City* was elaborated upon in 1950 with John Huston's *The Asphalt Jungle,* which humanized criminals while portraying forces of law in a documentary-style way. Based on a novel by W. R. Burnett, this gritty, realistic depiction of criminals who banded together to pull off the big heist laid the groundwork for scores of films to come. The ensemble cast included (*left to right*) Sam Jaffe, Sterling Hayden, Anthony Caruso, and James Whitmore, all of whom delivered stellar performances. A small but glittering role showcased starlet Marilyn Monroe.

An uncharacteristically cheery Ben Hogan accepts his second U.S. Open Golf Championship trophy on June 11, 1950. The normally stern-faced, taciturn golfer had reason to be jubilant. Just 16 months earlier, he and wife Valerie (*pictured*) were involved in a head-on accident with a Greyhound bus in Texas. Hogan, who suffered fractures to his ankle, collarbone, pelvis, and a rib, was told by doctors that mere walking might be difficult. But with characteristic grit, he worked hard through his recovery to reclaim his place in professional golf. He went on to win 12 more PGA titles, including six majors.

Escapism was very much in vogue during an era in which nuclear annihilation seemed imminent. The 1950 book *The Martian Chronicles* by Ray Bradbury became a classic of the science fiction genre. Though cloaked in fantasy, Bradbury's commentary on the Cold War events of the day is readily discernable. *Chronicles* was presented less as an extended narrative than as a collection of variations on a theme (family, loneliness, nuclear war), each presented through a different voice or perspective. *The Martian Chronicles* became the best selling sci-fi work of the decade.

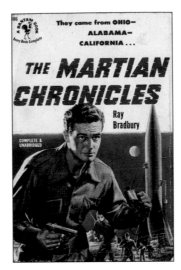

While cartoons seem to go hand-in-hand with television, it wasn't always so. Though some comic shorts (produced by studios for theater viewing) found a home on the tube in the 1940s, not until 1950 was a cartoon specifically conceived for the small screen. *Crusader Rabbit* was the brainchild of Alex Anderson and Jay Ward. Anderson favored characters whose personalities were the opposite of their image. Thus, a brave bunny was paired with a childlike, gentle tiger. In addition to financial backing, Ward (who would go on to produce *Rocky and Bullwinkle*) brought subtly witty dialogue and narration that trumped the shortcomings of the low-budget animation.

Television

THOUGH FEWER THAN A MILLION American households boasted television sets in 1949, a rush on TVs began in the early 1950s. By 1953, the number of TV owners skyrocketed to 20 million.

The American public began to realize that they no longer had to go to the movies or nightclubs to see great entertainment. Individuals and families understood that they could center their evenings and weekends around their big boxes with the little screens. They could view comedy, sports, music, news, and drama every day for the one-time cost of the television set.

This new piece of American furniture made many in the entertainment industry household names. A vaudevillian and radio performer named Milton Berle became "Mr. Television." From 1948 until 1956, he shone weekly on the *Texaco Star Theater,* one of many comedy shows that made a successful transition to TV from its predecessor, radio. Tuesday nights belonged to NBC and Uncle Miltie's broad, physical humor.

The same year that Berle took over the airwaves—often wearing a dress—a Broadway gossip columnist named Ed Sullivan began hosting *Toast of the Town,* a variety show. Sullivan's eccentric diction, posture, and mannerisms—and his extraordinary eye for talent that appealed to Middle America—drew huge ratings.

The new national audience could now see as well as hear live events, such as wrestling (the latest match of Gorgeous

George) or news (Edward R. Murrow's aptly titled *See It Now*). Viewers then would talk about the big show around the water cooler the next day. TV became such a big hit that attendance dwindled at movies and baseball games. In 1954 *Life* magazine lost 21 percent of its circulation in six months due to television.

Products that were advertised on television—such as certain appliances and cigarettes—became national sales sensations, and their television slogans, known as "jingles," became embedded in America's consciousness. By the end of the decade, life prior to television would become a fleeting memory.

June 6: General Douglas MacArthur bans Communists from public service positions in Japanese government.

June 11: Following a near-fatal car crash the year before, golfer Ben Hogan wins the U.S. Open.

June 15: Within hours of his arrest, David Greenglass confesses to spying for the Soviets. He implicates his sister and her husband, Ethel and Julius Rosenberg, as accomplices. *See* March 29, 1951.

June 17: The world's first kidney transplant is performed in Chicago by Dr. Richard Lawler.

June 24: Fifty-eight people die in the worst U.S. airline disaster to date when a Northwest jet crashes into Lake Michigan.

June 25: The Korean War begins as the army of Communist North Korea crosses the 38th parallel and storms toward Seoul, South Korea.

June 27: As North Korean troops reach Seoul, the UN calls on member nations to increase military aid to South Korea.

June 28: South Korean forces blow up the Han River Bridge, cutting off a crucial escape route for the beleaguered population of Seoul. • The Senate extends the Selective Service program and expands President Truman's authority to call up the National Guard and Reserves.

June 29: President Truman approves a naval blockade of the Korean Peninsula.

June 30: President Truman orders U.S. troops into Korea.

July 1: The first U.S. ground troops arrive in South Korea.

July 3: U.S. and North Korean troops skirmish for the first time when the U.S. attacks North Korean airfields near Pyongyang.

Attorney Charles Houston died in 1950, so it was left to his protégé, Thurgood Marshall (*pictured*), to carry on Houston's work of dismantling segregated-education laws case by case. In 1950 Marshall, as NAACP counsel, scored two huge victories in the U.S. Supreme Court. In *Sweatt v. Painter* and *McLaurin v. Oklahoma State Regents,* the court ruled that that the University of Texas Law School and the University of Oklahoma could not ban the enrollments of the African-American plaintiffs. Weeks later, Marshall convened a conference of lawyers with the specific purpose of planning an all-out attack on public-school segregation.

LEARNING IN A TARPAPER SHACK

THE SCHOOL WE WENT TO was overcrowded. Consequently, the county decided to build three tarpaper shacks for us to hold classes in. A tarpaper shack looks like a dilapidated black building, which is similar to a chicken coop on a farm. It's very unsightly. In winter the school was very cold. And a lot of times we had to put on our jackets. Now, the students that sat closest to the wood stove were very warm and the ones who sat farthest away were very cold. And I remember being cold a lot of times and sitting in the classroom with my jacket on. When it rained, we would get water through the ceiling. So there were lots of pails sitting around the classroom. And sometimes we had to raise our umbrellas to keep the water off our heads. It was a very difficult setting for trying to learn.

—AFRICAN-AMERICAN JOAN JOHNS COBBS,
DESCRIBING HER SEGREGATED HIGH SCHOOL IN FARMVILLE, VIRGINIA

Though in existence since 1933, drive-in movie theaters did not become a full-blown phenomenon until the early 1950s. From 1948 to 1958, their numbers rose from fewer than 1,000 to nearly 5,000. The emergent car culture contributed to the theaters' spread, as did the appeal of relative privacy. Indeed, drive-ins gave young lovers, most of whom lived with their parents, a rare chance to be alone. By decade's end, however, the boom had peaked, and drive-ins began to diminish in popularity.

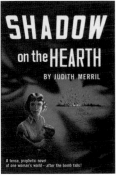

A major writer of speculative fiction during the second half of the 20th century, Judith Merril burned brightly with her first novel, published in 1950 when she was 27. Although very much a product of Cold War preoccupations, *Shadow on the Hearth* is unusual because it focuses on a young suburban mother who protects her home and children following an A-bomb attack that has trapped or killed her husband in Manhattan. It's a deceptively quiet book that gradually reveals the steel beneath the protagonist's soft-spoken exterior. Many post-bomb novels would be written throughout the decade, but few had the sharp yet peculiarly tender focus of Merril's.

Seven of the renowned "Hollywood 10" arrive at a federal court in Washington on June 22, 1950, to face contempt of Congress charges. They are (*from left to right*) Samuel Ornitz, Ring Lardner, Jr., Albert Maltz, Alvah Bessie, Lester Cole, Herbert Biberman, and Edward Dmytryk. These film industry professionals had been called before the House Un-American Activities Committee (HUAC) in 1947. When asked whether they ever had been members of the Communist Party, the men stood on principle and refused to answer, invoking their constitutional rights. All served prison terms and became blacklisted by the industry.

War in Korea

IN THE PREDAWN HOURS of June 25, 1950, the Communist-backed North Korean People's Army (NKPA) began an intense barrage upon targets south of the 38th parallel, the imposed post-World War II boundary separating two political adversaries. Before the South Koreans (America's allies) could collect themselves, more than 90,000 NKPA troops poured in, overrunning the frightened populace while delivering a sucker-punch to diplomats in the West.

Under Japanese rule for much of the 20th century, Korea had barely registered on the scale of Western strategic interest during much of that time. But with the Communist takeover of China in 1949 fresh in everyone's mind, concerns over what Dwight Eisenhower would one day call the "domino effect" led Americans to foresee eventual Red domination of Asia.

Korea had been the subject of much East-West jockeying for position in the aftermath of World War II. Following Japan's postwar pull-out, Korea was divided at the 38th parallel between Soviet occupiers to the north and American forces to the south. Both sides withdrew in 1949, leaving simmering tensions between the two ideologically opposed camps. As potential civil war loomed, fuel was added to the fire from an unexpected source. In a January 1950 speech, U.S. Secretary of State Dean Acheson omitted South Korea from his description of the USA's defense perimeter in Asia. This set the stage for the Soviet-trained North Korean army to invade the south on June 25.

Sensitive to charges that his administration had "lost" China, President Truman consulted with the Joint Chiefs about North Korea's invasion and dispatched General Douglas MacArthur to assess the situation. Their conclusions, bolstered by news that the South Korean army had lost half of its forces and that the capital city, Seoul, had fallen, called for intervention by force. Under the auspices of the United Nations, American forces were ordered into battle on June 30.

U.S. soldiers consoling each other near Haktong-ni

Following that summer's deployment, undertrained UN troops proved no match for the lean, mean NKPA. Humiliating weeks of retreat and staggering casualties demoralized soldiers and the public alike. Not until General MacArthur's stunning sea invasion at Inchon in September did things begin to turn around for the beleaguered troops. Seoul was recaptured, and the NKPA was on the run. But despite warnings from his commanders in Washington not to bait the Chinese army, which was watching on the sidelines, MacArthur overplayed his hand, pushing his men far to the north. The move brought the seemingly limitless Chinese army streaming into Korea, resulting in stunning American losses.

Adding to U.S. woes in late 1950 and early '51 was the cruelest winter in a century, resulting in a ghastly toll on Western forces. These reversals brought widespread erosion of public confidence in the nation's leadership. What President Truman had termed "a police action under the United Nations" was looking, to many, like a no-win war.

According to the original American newswire caption, North Korean men volunteer for duty at a recruiting center in 1950. The partitioning of Korea after Japan's withdrawal in 1945 resulted in two camps, each vying for complete control of the country. Communist dictator Kim Il Sung, bolstered by Soviet support, was able to assemble a robust war machine in North Korea. Syngman Rhee, installed as president of South Korea by Western powers, was denied an extensive military by his sponsors, who feared his eagerness to use it. With tacit approval from Stalin and Mao, Kim invaded the South on June 25, 1950, triggering the Korean War.

The events of June 1950 were unsettling to Americans. For the second time in a decade, an outbreak of hostilities erupted in a far-off Asian land. The 38th parallel in Korea was the dividing line that separated the combatants—the Communist North Koreans and the U.S.-backed South Koreans. Following Japan's withdrawal from Korea after World War II, two of the war's victors, the U.S. and the USSR, allowed Korea to develop into a battleground for a proxy war of ideological influence.

Having presided over the profoundly difficult final stages of World War II, President Harry Truman was not inclined to unnecessary foreign adventuring. Nonetheless, as a student of history, he recognized the peril of inaction. "If [North Korea's aggression] were allowed to go unchallenged," he stated, "it would mean a third world war." While sensitivity to charges that he had "lost" China to communism undoubtedly affected his decision-making, Truman was well aware that nuclear weapons had raised the retaliatory ante. Thus, he chose a course of countering North Korea's invasion with a multilateral response under the auspices of the United Nations. This action had the added benefit of disarming opposition in Congress by circumventing the necessity of a war declaration.

This photo, suppressed for years, depicts some of the victims summarily executed by the South Korean military over a three-day period in July 1950. Fearing possible infiltration by Communist sympathizers, South Korean soldiers rounded up some 1,800 political prisoners. The prisoners were trucked to a location in Taejon, forced to dig trenches, and shot. Several Americans witnessed the slaughter, but details of the massacre didn't begin to filter out until decades later.

1950

July 4: Puerto Rico gains the authorization to write its own constitution when President Truman signs Public Law 600.

July 5: The Law of Return, which opens Israel to worldwide Jewish immigration, is passed by the Israeli Knesset. • In the first U.S.-North Korean clash of the Korean War, Task Force Smith is pushed back by North Korean forces.

July 17: A St. Louis federal court ruling opens city swimming pools to African-Americans.

July 22: Census results reveal that the U.S. population has grown to more than 150 million people.

July 27: President Truman asserts that the U.S. will not drop an atomic bomb on Korea. *See* November 30, 1950.

Late July: U.S. soldiers kill with machine-gun fire an estimated 100 to 300 South Korean civilians in No Gun Ri. Officers believed the group had been infiltrated by North Koreans.

August: Operation Magic Carpet ends. It succeeds in airlifting 45,000 of the 46,000 Jews in Yemen to Israel, to escape religious persecution. • The State Department revokes the passport of singer-actor Paul Robeson for his outspoken criticism of U.S. policy.

August 3: The refugee-choked Waegwan Bridge is destroyed on orders from U.S. Major General Hobart Gay.

August 4: President Truman calls up the National Guard for duty in the Korean War.

August 8: American Florence Chadwick swims the English Channel in record time. • The U.S. Army turns back the North Koreans at the Battle of Naktong Bulge.

August 10: South Korean military police execute up to 300 prisoners of war, including women, near Dokchon.

Director Anthony Mann became one of Hollywood's most reliable purveyors of what became known as "adult westerns." In a departure from old-fashioned good guy/bad guy shoot-'em-ups, Mann presented complex characters, often of ambiguous morality. Eight of his films featured actor Jimmy Stewart, commencing with 1950's *Winchester '73* (*pictured*). The story traces the title weapon through a series of owners after it has been stolen from Stewart. The actor's postwar career saw him tread new ground with increasingly nuanced performances, beginning with an undercurrent of desperation in 1946's *It's a Wonderful Life* and culminating with the intense Hitchcock thriller *Vertigo* in 1958.

Perhaps the biggest destination for Puerto Ricans relocating to the mainland was New York's Spanish Harlem. Though many people regarded the area as a rundown ghetto, newly landed Latinos appreciated the familiarity of language and custom. Some, like the street vendor seen here, went into business for themselves. But typically, for Hispanics in urban centers around the country, service industries such as janitorial work and housekeeping were the only employment available. For most Hispanics, being able to provide opportunities and a better life for their children was a goal worth the hardships.

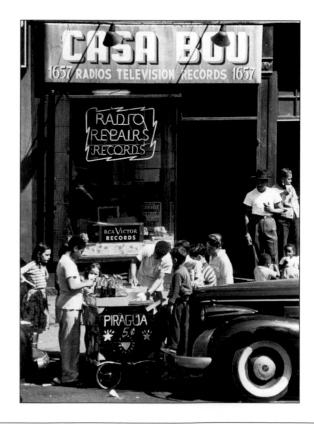

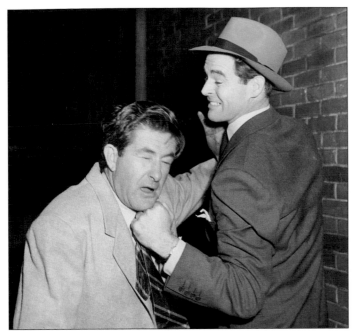

Robert Ryan (*right*) plays a little chin music for Jack Stoney in *I Married a Communist*. While Cold War paranoia in Washington led Senate committees to target Hollywood leftists, some studios produced artful propaganda pieces that fed into the hysteria. In this film, produced by RKO chief Howard Hughes, San Francisco dock workers are "agitated" by a labor leader patterned after real-life organizer Harry Bridges. (To many Red-baiters, *union* was synonymous with *Communist.*) Other entries in the genre included *My Son John, Walk East on Beacon, Pickup on South Street,* and *Big Jim McLain,* starring John Wayne.

A product of the anti-Communist paranoia of the period, *Red Channels* was the brainchild of Theodore Kirkpatrick, a former FBI agent, and Vincent Harnett, a conservative television producer. Published in June 1950, the pamphlet listed the names of 151 people in the entertainment industry who allegedly had been members of subversive organizations before World War II and thus far had not been denied employment because of their pasts. The publisher sent free copies of the pamphlet to all major potential employers in the entertainment industry. Most of those fingered were subsequently blacklisted, including actor Lee J. Cobb, writer Arthur Miller, and composer Aaron Copland.

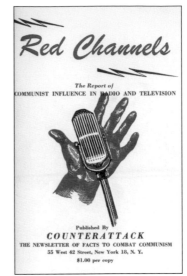

It took a few years for automakers to regroup after World War II, but when they did, innovations followed. The year 1950 saw the introduction of America's first successful compact car, the Nash Rambler. The Rambler's design clearly was inspired by European automobiles (though derided by critics as an "overturned bathtub"). Buyers were treated to a variety of standard features, including a radio and clock, heater, and "luxury" upholstery—all for less than $2,000.

The prototypical singing cowboy, Gene Autry (seen here with his trusted horse, Champion) starred in scores of musical westerns throughout the 1930s and '40s. More success lay ahead. In 1949 he recorded the song "Rudolph the Red-nosed Reindeer," one of the most successful holiday recordings ever. A year later, he produced and starred in *The Gene Autry Show,* a TV western series in which he and sidekick Pat Buttram brought outlaws to justice. Autry eventually would use his millions to buy the Los Angeles Angels, a Major League Baseball expansion team, in 1960.

1950

August 15: An earthquake centered in Assam, India, kills up to 30,000.

August 18–25: The U.S. sustains heavy casualties in the bloody Battle of the Bowling Alley in South Korea.

August 19: Edith Sampson is appointed to the UN's U.S. delegation, becoming the first African-American to hold that seat. • The first TV programming aimed at children, including *Animal Clinic* and *Acrobat Ranch,* airs on Saturday mornings.

August 23: Nearly 80,000 members of the Organized Reserve Corps are called to active duty in Korea.

August 25: President Truman orders a military seizure of U.S. railroads in an effort to prevent a national strike.

August 28: President Truman signs amendments to the Social Security Act, increasing coverage and benefits.

September: The McCarran Internal Security Act, which calls for the registration of all Communists, is passed by Congress over Truman's veto.

September 4: Mort Walker's *Beetle Bailey* comic strip makes its debut in syndication.

September 5: The Army asks for 70,000 draftees by November.

September 9: President Truman announces a four-division increase in U.S. troop presence in Europe.

September 15: In the greatest amphibious attack in history, General MacArthur's X Corps lands on the Korean coast at Inchon and charges inland.

September 19: Communist Party members employed by the West German government are fired from their jobs. • The UN rejects Red China's membership appeal.

Californian Florence Chadwick, 32, attempted to enter the London *Daily Mail*'s competition to swim the English Channel in the summer of 1950, but her application was rejected because she was an unknown. Unfazed, she set out on her own on August 8. Chadwick reached England in 13 hours, 20 minutes, shattering Gertrude Ederle's 24-year-old record by 79 minutes. A year later, she made the more difficult England-to-France channel swim, becoming the first woman to cross in both directions. An incomparable athlete, Chadwick later swam the Dardanelles, the Strait of Gibraltar, the Bosphorus, and the Bristol Channel.

Billy Wilder's *Sunset Boulevard,* starring William Holden and former silent-screen siren Gloria Swanson (*both pictured*), sent shock waves through the Hollywood community. This darkly iconoclastic look at film stardom and the blurring of fantasy with reality touched a nerve among many within the industry. What no one could deny was Wilder's superb direction and brilliant script, supported by pitch-perfect casting (which included silent-era director Erich von Stroheim as a supporting actor). Swanson won kudos for her depiction of Norma Desmond, a deluded and narcissistic fading movie queen. Holden's equally masterful performance, as a washed-up scriptwriter, reaffirmed his stardom and established him as a serious actor.

Levittown

IN THE YEARS immediately following World War II, America faced a housing shortage. One man's solution was to apply the principles of automobile mass production to the problem.

William Levitt, conceptualizer and salesman, came from a family of homebuilders. His experience in construction while serving in the Navy taught him how to build fast and efficiently. Levitt, recognizing a market for low-cost homes on a grand scale, bought acres of farmland in New York (Long Island), Pennsylvania, and New Jersey. What he envisioned were smartly designed communities, planned down to the smallest detail.

At a time when most builders completed four or five houses per year, Levitt planned to construct 10 times that many—in a day! His cost-cutting measures included making nails on site, securing lumber from his own Oregon logging operation, and making each worker responsible for a single task.

Levitt single-family homes ranged from under $8,000 to just over twice that. Typically, they were Cape Cods with unfinished second floors. Common belief notwithstanding, Levittown homes were built to be customized—there were no entire blocks of same-design homes. (Levitt was less a fan of conformity than one might suppose.) Levitt's homes featured 2.3 trees per lot, which when fully grown provided abundant shade. Codes called for no fences, laundry to be hung only on umbrella-designed clothes lines (and

The Levey family, in Levittown, New York

never on a Sunday), and weekly lawn mowings. Perks included a free washing machine and (in some models) an Admiral television.

Critics deplored Levitt's controlled environs and seemingly bloodless social experimentation. His enforced antiminority policy was an embarrassment. Certain amenities, such as a sewer system, went unrealized until the late 1970s. But for the thousands who flocked to the three Levittowns, these issues were not a big concern. They were just happy to have a piece of the American Dream.

WILLIAM LEVITT ON LEVITTOWN

"We are not builders. We are manufacturers."

"Any fool can build homes. What counts is how many you can sell for how little."

"We bought 5,000 acres and we planned every foot of it."

"We can solve a housing problem or we can try to solve a racial problem, but we cannot combine the two."

"No man who owns his own house can be a Communist. He has too much to do."

"I'm not here just to build and sell houses. To be perfectly frank, I'm looking for a little glory, too. . . . I want to build a town to be proud of."

Commissioned to build airstrips as a Navy Seabee during World War II, William J. Levitt had taken on tasks with "impossible" deadlines and accomplished them on time. Applying these skills in civilian life, Levitt perfected an assembly-line style of housing construction that produced many simple houses in a short amount of time. The first Levitt homes, in the late 1940s, went for $7,990. In March 1949, he sold 1,400 homes in one day for the planned Levittown community in New York.

1950

September 22: Colonel David C. Schilling flies 3,300 miles from England to Maine to complete the first nonstop transatlantic jet flight in 10 hours and 1 minute.

September 23: The Mundt Bill, which requires Communist organizations to reveal their officers and financial records, passes over President Truman's veto.

September 25: The Atomic Energy Commission announces that scientists in Chicago have discovered a way to generate electricity using atomic energy alone.

September 26: The U.S. Eighth Army links up with MacArthur's troops on the road to Seoul.

September 27: The U.S. Army and Marines liberate Seoul. • In an effort to assist the French, the Americans establish a Military Assistance Advisory Group in Saigon, Vietnam.

October: England fires up its first nuclear reactor. • UN troops chase the retreating North Koreans over the 38th parallel. • Hank Ketcham introduces the comic strip *Dennis the Menace.*

October 2: Following its sale to United Feature Syndicate earlier in the year, Charles Schulz's comic strip, *Peanuts,* appears in seven newspapers.

October 7: The UN Security Council passes a resolution calling for a united, democratic Korea. • The New York Yankees win Game 4 against the Philadelphia Phillies to sweep the World Series. • Communist China invades Tibet, destroying the Tibetan army. Under Chinese rule, the Tibetan practice of Buddhism will be severely restricted.

October 11: The FCC authorizes CBS's color television technology as the national standard. However, incompatibility with most existing television sets will allow RCA's standard to prevail within three years.

Western star William Boyd, beloved by millions as "Hopalong Cassidy," becomes acquainted with the new forest fire prevention spokescub, Smokey Bear. The badly burned animal had been rescued from a New Mexico wildfire in 1950. Following his recovery, he was sent to the National Zoo in Washington, where he subsequently enjoyed celebrity status. Boyd had been a western film actor facing hard times when he shrewdly bought the television rights to his Hopalong Cassidy movies. He brought "Hoppy" to TV and became an enormous star.

A violent encounter that results in a woman's rape and her husband's death is the subject of Japanese director Akira Kurosawa's 1950 classic film, *Rashomon.* This brilliant, sometimes poetic, examination of the elusiveness of absolute truth is richly deserving of its acclaim. Told in flashback, the event is recalled by four involved parties, with each perspective offering a different interpretation of the crime. Toshiro Mifune (*left*) plays the antagonist while Machiko Kyo (*right*) portrays the victim. Other influential Kurosawa works included *The Seven Samurai* (1954) and *Yojimbo* (1961).

When ever-confident General Douglas MacArthur (*right, forefront, at Inchon*) announced a grandiose, unorthodox plan to achieve victory in Korea, his superiors were aghast. "Operation Chromite" called for a risky amphibious landing (à la Normandy) at the port city of Inchon on September 15, 1950. By striking at this unlikely target, UN forces would blindside the enemy, recoup their losses, drive the Communists from South Korea, and bring the troops home by Christmas. To everyone's further astonishment, much of the gamble worked. Marines are seen here (*left*) at their September 15 landing. Within days, the North Korean army abandoned the city and the Allies regained control of Seoul, South Korea. Tragically, MacArthur's flamboyant bravado would lead to disaster two months later.

Refugees flee a war zone in Korea on September 16, 1950. The outbreak of war multiplied the already considerable stream of Korean refugees heading south across the 38th parallel. Many took temporary sanctuary in and around Pusan, to the southeast. Though largely fleeing the combat and Communist rule, their safety was far from assured. With their swelling numbers clogging the roads, the nomadic civilians came to be regarded as a nuisance by military officials. Once Allied forces realized that enemy troops were blending in among evacuees, the Allied soldiers took innocent lives indiscriminately. In all, an estimated nine million Koreans were displaced by the fighting.

UN troops fight in the streets of Seoul on September 20, 1950. As South Korea's capital, Seoul was a highly symbolic trophy. Coveted by the Communists, the city fell within the first five days of fighting in early summer. In September, its recapture became a top Allied priority. MacArthur's Inchon strategy called for reclaiming Seoul while driving the enemy north. While North Korea offered little resistance during the Allied soldiers' push toward Seoul, forces occupying the capital put up a great fight. The North Koreans barricaded main thoroughfares (stymieing incoming tanks) and peppered UN troops with sniper fire. Intense street fighting required small bands of soldiers to clear houses block by block. Allied forces eventually prevailed, recapturing Seoul by the end of September.

1950

October 14: Chinese Communist troops, posing as Army regulars, infiltrate North Korea.

October 16: The U.S. Supreme Court orders the Florida Supreme Court to reconsider a ruling that permits the Miami Springs Golf Course to limit access to African-American players.

October 19: UN soldiers reach Pyongyang, North Korea.

October 21: Kim Il Sung, North Korean premier, moves the capital to Sinuiju.

October 23: Jazz great Al Jolson dies at age 64.

October 26: Mother Teresa of Calcutta founds the Missionaries of Charity.

October 30: The First Marine Division takes over for South Korea's I Corps in tough fighting at the Chosin Reservoir.

November 1: Pope Pius XII asserts that the bodily assumption of the Virgin Mary into Heaven is established Roman Catholic dogma. • An assassination attempt on President Truman fails when two Puerto Rican nationalists are stopped while attempting to shoot their way into Blair House in Washington, D.C. *See* July 24, 1952.

November 2: Playwright George Bernard Shaw dies at age 94.

November 7: Voters in Massachusetts reelect Democrat John F. Kennedy to his third term in Congress. • Republican Richard Nixon defeats Democrat Helen Gahagan Douglas to win one of California's seats in the U.S. Senate.

November 10: Spain's Generalissimo Francisco Franco ends war in Gibraltar.

November 11: The first meeting of the Mattachine Foundation, an early gay rights organization, takes place.

A romance between a professional gambler and a Salvation Army-type missionary would hardly seem to contain the makings of a hit Broadway show, but 1950's *Guys and Dolls* proved to be a smash, lasting for 1,200 performances. Largely based on Damon Runyon short stories, the musical comedy starred Robert Alda and Isabel Bigley as the romantic leads. But the real draw was the vivid portrayal of Broadway's denizens: the racketeers, do-gooders, showgirls, and small-time operators who populated New York's underbelly. Bringing the characterizations to life was Frank Loesser's superb score, which included the songs "A Bushel and a Peck" and "Luck Be a Lady."

Television's first late-night powerhouse premiered on NBC in May 1950. *Broadway Open House* starred (initially) comedians Morey Amsterdam and Jerry Lester (*right*) as alternating hosts before Lester took over full-time duties. But the show's secret weapon came in the voluptuous form of Virginia Egnor, better known to millions as "Dagmar" (*left*), a prototypical "dumb blonde." The show's success proved to networks the viability of late-night programming, paving the way for Steve Allen and *The Tonight Show* a few years later.

One year after successfully taking control of the mainland, China's army moved on its neighbor, Tibet. On October 7, 1950, some 40,000 soldiers crossed the upper Yangtze River (*left*), brushing aside token resistance. China explained its mission as one of "liberating" Tibet from undue Western influence. Tibet was a fiercely independent Buddhist theocracy, headed by the Dalai Lama, Tenzin Gyatso (*right*), who was just 15 at the time of the invasion. With Tibet's appeals to the West going unanswered, China began a repopulation program that reduced Tibetans to minority status within their own borders.

Mao and Red China

IN OCTOBER 1949, an American-made Sherman tank rolled into Tiananmen Square in Beijing, followed by a limousine. Exiting the limo, its occupant stunned both the crowd and Western observers with the proclamation, "The Chinese people have stood up." His name was Mao Zedong, and his capture of a tank formerly utilized by Nationalist leader Generalissimo Chiang Kai-shek was tangible evidence of the Communists' successful campaign to drive the U.S.-backed Nationalists from the Chinese mainland.

The 55-year-old Mao had led insurgents against corrupt and warring Chinese governments and factions for decades. Largely dismissed as a rural upstart, his revolutionary army coalesced in the countryside, far from the cities. Resuming their part in China's civil war after helping to defeat Japan in World War II, Mao's forces, backed by the Soviet bloc, emerged victorious against Chiang's government. Among Mao's first acts as leader was to institute "land reform." This consisted of seizing privately owned farms from their owners, usually by force. It is estimated that millions lost their lives in the ensuing struggle. Even more would perish later as a result of Mao's disastrous "Great Leap Forward" agricultural reform.

Mao's ambitious goals could be realized more quickly with foreign aid. Because the U.S. had tied itself to the Nationalists, Mao petitioned the Soviets. Western perceptions aside, deep divisions marked relations between the two Communist nations. Mao's decision to enter the Korean War would cost nearly a million Red Army casualties, further taxing China's shaky resources.

Following Stalin's death in 1953, relations improved somewhat between China and the Soviet Union. But the struggle for influence over another Asian region, Manchuria, would remain a sore point. Cold War tensions were further heightened by Mao's adventurism, typified by the seizure of Tibet and attacks on the Nationalist islands of Quemoy and Matsu. Such actions fueled fears that all of Asia would ultimately "turn" Communist.

You Bet Your Life host Groucho Marx contemplates his next one-liner while ogling contestant Sarita Pelkey. The veteran vaudevillian-turned-film star found renewed popularity first on radio, then on television with this comedic quiz program. Though ostensibly centered on guests answering questions for cash and prizes, *You Bet Your Life* was in reality a vehicle for Marx to showcase his uproarious humor during pre-quiz banter. His freewheeling ad-libs made censors nervous but brought laughter to millions throughout the show's run.

In 1950 young readers first became acquainted with the fictional writing of librarian Beverly Cleary. Longing for stories that portrayed real kids with everyday escapades in familiar settings, Cleary created a series of books centered around Henry's neighborhood on Klickitat Street. Along with such friends as Murph, Beezus, and Beezus's little sister, Ramona, Henry and his dog, Ribsy, lived lives not much different from those of Cleary's readers. Splendidly illustrated by Louis Darling, the books were imaginative without being implausible—and funny, to boot.

Peanus

THE MOST BELOVED cartoon strip in history arrived in the fall of 1950, but its origins date further back. Charles "Sparky" Schulz hailed from Saint Paul, Minnesota. From an early age, he aspired to be a cartoonist. He made his professional debut in 1947 with a single-panel strip he called *Li'l Folks*. This early effort was richer in detail than Schulz's more familiar later works, but it revealed unmistakable commonality: precocious dialogue, realistic motivations, and a dog. Grown-ups were absent, though each child character displayed intriguingly adultlike characteristics.

With a deal for syndication struck, the strip was expanded to four panels and, at the publisher's insistence, renamed *Peanuts* (the existence

A 1956 collection of *Peanuts* comic strips

of strips with names similar to *Li'l Folks* mandated it). Despite the creator's austere drawing style, the characters were remarkably sophisticated. They became ingrained in the national consciousness, particularly Charlie Brown, an inveterate pessimist who nonetheless never quit trying. The loudmouthed Lucy served as chief antagonist, while her brother, Linus, often mediated with a liberal dose of theology. (His ever-present "security blanket" soon entered common parlance.) The standout figure was Snoopy, a beagle whose rich fantasy life gave the strip a surreal dimension.

Over time, *Peanuts* became an international phenomenon, spawning thousands of products and (beginning in 1965) television specials. By century's end, more than 1,400 *Peanuts* books had been published. The strip itself appeared in 2,600 newspapers in 75 countries with an estimated readership of 350 million people.

> **"You know, what happens to me personally isn't very important. But that pipsqueak [Nixon] has his eye on the White House, and if he ever gets there, God help us all."**
>
> —HELEN GAHAGAN DOUGLAS, RICHARD NIXON'S OPPONENT FOR A U.S. SENATE SEAT IN 1950

The 1950 U.S. Senate race in California between representatives Richard Nixon (Republican, *left*) and Helen Gahagan Douglas (Democrat, *right*) was one of the dirtiest in campaign history. Nixon, in Congress since 1946, rode his notoriety from the recent Alger Hiss case into national prominence. Douglas, a former stage actress who entered Congress in 1944, was long known as a supporter of progressive causes. Following a brutal primary, she hoped to become California's first elected female senator. But like Jerry Voorhis four years earlier, she didn't anticipate Nixon's treachery. His campaign branded her the "Pink Lady" ("pink right down to her underwear") and a Kremlin stooge. Against this onslaught, Douglas was defeated.

After a summer of stunning defeats, General MacArthur's smashing victory at Inchon decimated the North Korean army and scattered its remains north of the 38th parallel. Reestablishing the status quo had been his mandate, but MacArthur wasn't satisfied to let things lie. Unconcerned by the Chinese troops massing at the border, he drove his forces north to the Yalu River, despite repeated warnings from China that any aggression by the West would be met by force. In late October, battle-hardened Chinese regulars (*pictured*) attacked, sending UN forces reeling. MacArthur's ill-advised offensive had the effect of prolonging the war.

1950

November 14: President Truman nominates Henry Bennett as director of his Point Four Program of foreign aid to developing nations.

November 16: King Farouk ejects British troops from Egypt. • President Truman reassures China that the United States does not intend to invade China during the prosecution of the Korean War.

November 22: A train crash in Richmond Hills, New York, kills 79.

November 24: The UN launches a new wave of assaults against the North Koreans, hoping to speed up progress in the war.

November 25–27: A monster storm blankets the eastern U.S. with wind-driven snow, claiming 383 lives.

November 26: China, now officially involved in the Korean War, puts down an offensive from UN, U.S., and South Korean troops while protecting its border and defending electric power stations along the Yalu River.

November 27: More than 200 U.S. soldiers in Fox Company take heavy casualties in an engagement against Chinese forces east of the Chosin River.

November 30: A UN Security Council resolution calling for Chinese withdrawal from the Korean peninsula is vetoed by the Soviets. • President Truman states that the U.S. would drop an atomic bomb on Korea if necessary.

December: Exceptionally harsh winter weather descends upon Korea.

December 1: President Truman creates the Federal Civil Defense Administration under the Office of Emergency Management.

December 3: Dr. Charles Bailey announces the development of a heart-lung device that has succeeded in restoring life to clinically dead patients.

On October 25, 1950, Sukarno (*standing in car*) was appointed president of the newly minted Republic of Indonesia. For much of the 20th century, the country had chafed under the yoke of foreign control, mostly by the Dutch but also the Japanese, who occupied the nation during World War II. During those years, an underground nationalist movement brewed. Following the war, bloody fighting for sovereignty erupted, ending with a UN-brokered agreement that established Indonesian independence. As president, Sukarno sought to unite the nation's diverse cultures by bringing all factions, including the Communists, into his government, with uneven results.

Puerto Rican gunman Oscar Collazo lies wounded in front of Blair House on November 1, 1950, in the aftermath of a bloody gunfight with President Harry Truman's security guards. Collazo and his accomplice attempted to shoot their way into the First Family's temporary quarters following an unsuccessful coup staged in San Juan days earlier. Collazo and fellow Puerto Rican nationalist Griselio Torresola had arrived in Washington on October 31, naively believing that to kill the President would spark a move toward Puerto Rican independence. With little deliberation, the two launched their attack the next day. The ensuing gunplay claimed Torresola's life; meanwhile, three guards were wounded, one fatally. Collazo's death sentence was later commuted to life imprisonment by Truman.

Arguably, the decade's first cinematic masterpiece arrived in 1950 with director Joseph Mankiewicz's *All About Eve*. This witty, cynical look at Broadway theater's backstage drama boasted a first-rate cast—Anne Baxter (*left*) in the title role opposite Bette Davis (*right*) as Margo Channing—as well as memorable dialogue and superb direction. For his efforts, Mankiewicz won two Academy Awards (best director and screenplay), while the film earned six Oscars out of a record-breaking 14 nominations. Adding to the film's immortality is a young Marilyn Monroe (*background*) in her first all-star film.

Ink-and-wash master Charles Addams sold his first drawing to *The New Yorker* at age 20 in 1932, and remained a mainstay of the magazine until his death in 1988. Along the way he became one of America's favorite cartoonists. Addams published more than 1,300 comical drawings and numerous covers with *The New Yorker,* all with a macabre, sometimes perverse, bent. Gothicism, the supernatural, fiendish children, marital discord that culminated in grotesquely funny murder scenarios—Addams depicted all of these and more. His recurring "family" of characters, seen here on the jacket of a 1950 collection, comprised only a small fraction of Addams's output but is beloved, thanks in part to a television adaptation in the 1960s.

Architect Ludwig Mies van der Rohe was an original with an idiosyncratic style. The German-born designer gained renown for his strikingly modern creations—steel and glass structures that transcended functionality and commented on the surrounding environs. For example, the Farnsworth House (*pictured*) is simultaneously reduced to its basic components with unprecedented transparency while maintaining a "temple-like aloofness" from its organic surroundings. In 1950 Mies van der Rohe built the glass house in Plano, Illinois, for a friend, Dr. Edith Farnsworth. She hated it, claiming it was unlivable.

1950

December 5: Pyongyang falls to the Chinese Communists.

December 9: Harry Gold, a Soviet courier who gained access to the Theoretical Physics Division at the Los Alamos National Labs, is sentenced to 30 years for passing atomic secrets. • General MacArthur asks for the authority to use atomic weapons against North Korea.

December 11: The Nobel Peace Prize is awarded to Ralph Bunche for his mediation of the 1948 Arab-Israeli War. Bunche is the first African-American to win the esteemed prize. • The Supreme Court rules that grand jury witnesses may invoke the Fifth Amendment right against self-incrimination when refusing to answer questions about Communist affiliations.

December 15: President Truman expresses his hope that the U.S. may become an "arsenal of freedom."

December 16: President Truman announces a state of national emergency as Chinese Communists invade deep into South Korea.

December 18: The Conference of NATO Foreign Ministers opens in Brussels. Member nations, including the U.S., Britain, West Germany, France, Belgium, Italy, Luxembourg, and the Netherlands, will approve plans for the defense of Western Europe, and install General Dwight D. Eisenhower as supreme commander of NATO.

December 23: Army General Walton H. Walker dies in a jeep accident in Korea. • Pope Pius XII confirms the discovery of the tomb of St. Peter.

December 25: NBC broadcasts the first Disney television special: *One Hour in Wonderland.*

December 29: Congress passes the *Cellar-Kefauver Act,* which outlaws mergers or acquisitions that would create a monopoly.

... and now the *gift* for thirst

Drink Coca-Cola

In their fight to dominate the soft drink market, Coca-Cola's strategists took no prisoners. World War II saw their advertising linked to patriotism, with images of soldiers enjoying their refreshing product. By the 1950s, Coca-Cola's Christmas-themed ads had become a tradition, enhanced by the iconic work of artist Haddon Sundblom (who crystallized the Santa image we know today in the process). The company's aggressive marketing of Coke overseas was noted in a 1950 *Time* magazine cover story, which suggested that the drink had become a potent American symbol.

In December 1950, Soviet representative Jacob Malik casts the only dissenting vote among the United Nations Security Council in calling for China to withdraw from Korea. Soviet Premier Joseph Stalin's exact role in the events leading up to the Korean hostilities remains unclear. While the North Korean army was armed and trained by the Soviets, China fulfilled a more proactive role aimed at reuniting the country. Most experts doubt that Stalin had territorial designs on the Korean peninsula, but few dispute his tacit acquiescence to the invasion. The United States, however, viewed North Korea's actions as a direct Soviet challenge, and reacted accordingly.

> "I continue to get further away from the usual painter's tools such as easel, palette, brushes, etc. I prefer sticks, trowels, knives, and dripping fluid paint or a heavy impasto with sand, broken glass, or other foreign matter added."
>
> —JACKSON POLLOCK

Pollock's Abstract Expressions

NOTHING CEMENTS THE LEGEND of an artist more effectively than a premature death. So it was with New York painter Jackson Pollock, killed at 44 in a car wreck in 1956 less than a year after actor James Dean. Pollock pulled Abstract Expressionism in a direction termed "action painting." Though his best known works—including "Lavender Mist," "Autumn Rhythm," and "Blue Poles"—appear, to the lay person, as random drippings and splatterings of pigment on canvas, to aficionados they are open windows to the artist's subconscious—a sort of reverse Rorschach Test.

Early on, as a protégé of Regionalist painter Thomas Hart Benton, Pollock moved away from representational work into Modernism. But fueled by explorations into his own troubled psyche (Pollock repeatedly underwent treatment for alcoholism), his work began to assert its own identity. Abandoning the easel, he laid his canvases flat on the floor and stepped "into" them, bonding with creations produced through his unconscious manipulation of the dripped paint. By rejecting the conventions of composition and presenting unfiltered emotion, Jackson forged a uniquely American style of painting, worthy of its European precedents.

Other Abstract Expressionists were likewise based in New York. Dutch-born Willem de Kooning was responsible for 1953's wildly provocative series "Paintings on the Theme of the Woman." Mark Rothko, another mainstay of the scene, evoked a wide range of emotions through his singular use of patterns and color.

Though the work of painters grouped in the "New York School" was stylistically disparate, some common elements included disassociation from natural order, aggressive use of textures, and a rebellion from convention in any form. Weighty subjects were invoked, both personal and topical. The 1950s heyday of such revolutionary art contradicts those who view the decade as monolithically bland and tranquil.

Jackson Pollock's 1950 composition "One" gives an ample illustration of what was termed "action painting." Determined to channel all of his impressions and thoughts into his work, Pollock created a visual experience that suggested energy, rhythm, and mood. He literally stepped onto the canvas to create, allowing his subconscious to flow unfettered: "I'm not aware of what I'm doing," he explained. "It's only after a 'get acquainted' period that I see what I've been about."

1950

New & Notable

Books

Betty Crocker's Picture Cook Book
Dianetics by L. Ron Hubbard
The Drowning Pool by Ross Macdonald
The Labyrinth of Solitude by Octavio Paz
The Liberal Imagination by Lionel Trilling
The Lonely Crowd by David Riesman
     (with Reuel Denney and
     Nathan Glazer)
Look Younger, Live Longer
     by Gayelord Hauser
The Martian Chronicles by Ray Bradbury
The Town and the City by Jack Kerouac

Movies

All About Eve
The Asphalt Jungle
Born Yesterday
Cinderella
The Gunfighter
La Ronde
Rashomon
Sunset Boulevard

Songs

"A Bushel and a Peck" by Perry Como
     and Betty Hutton
"Frosty the Snowman" by Gene Autry
"I'm Moving On" by Hank Snow
"Mona Lisa" by Nat King Cole
"Music! Music! Music!"
     by Teresa Brewer
"Rudolph, the Red-Nosed Reindeer"
     by Gene Autry
"The Tennessee Waltz" by Patti Page

Television

Broadway Open House
The George Burns and Gracie Allen Show
Space Patrol
Truth or Consequences
What's My Line?
You Bet Your Life
Your Hit Parade
Your Show of Shows

Theater

Come Back, Little Sheba
The Country Girl
Guys and Dolls
The Member of the Wedding
Peter Pan

Jon Whitcomb was one of the most admired commercial illustrators of the 1940s and '50s. He was famously adept at painting beautiful women, often in idealized, highly romantic situations, as in this 1950 magazine ad for Oneida's Community brand silverware. Whitcomb also was a master of lighting and composition. Here, the focus is on the upturned, transformed face of the woman; her husband (a secondary player in this tale of tableware) is shadowed and less detailed. Artfully arranged pine boughs provide a suitable backdrop for the product. In addition to ad work, Whitcomb illustrated many covers and interior stories for *Cosmopolitan* and other women's "slicks."

The RAND Corporation

A RAND Corporation scientist

IN SUMMER 1955, a platoon of balloons took off from Western Europe, each carrying a 600-pound gondola containing navigating gear and a camera. Drifting eastward, they entered a programmed descent over Soviet-bloc countries. There, the cameras recorded images before entering a freefall, arrested by parachutes. Most were then collected in midair by airplanes, their reconnaissance mission complete; others landed and were discovered by incensed Communist authorities. Until the advent of the U-2 spy plane one year later, Operation Moby Dick successfully gathered intelligence for the CIA.

The project was the brainchild of the RAND Corporation. Originating under the auspices of Douglas Aircraft following the war, RAND (short for research and development) was an independent "think tank," specializing in security analysis. While almost wholly employed by the U.S. military, its reach also extended to other government agencies as well as the space program.

RAND epitomized the growing trend following World War II to tap the greatest thinkers in the world of science and research and allow them to conceptualize cutting-edge solutions to the Cold War's problems. Among its members were mathematician John Nash (subject of the 2001 film *A Beautiful Mind*) and Daniel Ellsberg, later famed for leaking the Pentagon Papers regarding the Vietnam War.

All wars stir an escalation in brutality. Korea was no different, with fighting between North and South drawing the worst from both sides. While atrocities committed by South Koreans and their UN allies went largely unreported in the West, Communist excesses received widespread coverage in the United States. This photo depicts a group of grieving Hamhung women identifying loved ones. The North Korean army had killed some 300 political prisoners by trapping and sealing them in caves, resulting in suffocation.

Ordered by General MacArthur to pursue the enemy to the Yalu River in the fall of 1950, UN troops soon found themselves outmanned and outgunned by the Chinese army, while suffering further assault from the brutal winter. The resulting fiasco led to the encirclement of U.S. Marines (*pictured*) by the enemy outside the Chosin Reservoir in late November. Facing certain oblivion, the troops tried to punch their way out of the trap by running the gauntlet to Hungnam, nearly 50 miles away. The Marines' bravery became legendary, and was immortalized by Major General O. P. Smith's oft-quoted retort when queried about his men's withdrawal: "We're not retreating. We are just advancing in a different direction."

"If the best minds in the world had set out to find the worst possible location in the world to fight this damnable war, politically and militarily, the unanimous choice would have been Korea."

—SECRETARY OF STATE DEAN ACHESON

1951
The Korean War

O N THE KOREAN PENINSULA on New Year's Day, 1951, 500,000 Red Chinese troops were on the attack, crushing the vastly outnumbered United Nations troops commanded by General Douglas MacArthur. Just five weeks earlier, MacArthur had blustered that the Korean War would be over in a few days and America's fighting men would be home in time for Christmas. Instead, the Americans and their allies were forced into a full-scale retreat.

By January 15, the allied Communist armies of North Korea (Democratic People's Republic of Korea) and China, supported by the Soviet Union, had pushed 50 miles into South Korea (Republic of Korea). Major General Oliver P. Smith, commander of the First Marine Division, conceded nothing: "Retreat, hell. We're just advancing in a different direction." Brave words, but the situation on the ground looked anything but promising.

The war had begun only seven months earlier. On June 25, 1950, North Korean Communist forces led by Kim Il Sung crossed the demarcation line set up in the immediate post-World War II years. That line, the 38th parallel, was meant to temporarily separate the Korean peninsula—which had been for decades a Japanese imperial possession—into two regions until a unifying election could be held. Neither Kim nor his Soviet backers wanted to pursue that electoral option. Kim intended to unify the peninsula through force of arms. Supplied by the Soviet Union with tanks, a formidable number of artillery pieces, and a small air force, his military might far outmatched that of South Korea.

A tired girl carries her brother past an American M-26 tank in June 1951. As the war ebbed and flowed, moving back and forth on the Korean peninsula, hundreds of thousands of refugees were forced to flee their homes.

In a few weeks' time, the North Korean army almost completed its conquest of the South. Only the small region surrounding Pusan at the southern tip of Korea remained out of Communist hands. There, on July 5, Americans began to give support to the nearly vanquished army of the Republic of Korea.

The American forces were officially a component of the United Nations' collective armed response to the North Korean invasion. Because the Soviet Union had been boycotting the UN Security Council over that body's refusal to recognize the new Communist government in China led by Mao Zedong, the United States had been able to gain unanimous acceptance of a security resolution condemning the Communist invasion and calling for an international military response. While the United States carried almost the entire burden in support of South Korea, soldiers from 15 other nations—including the United Kingdom, Canada, France, Greece, Turkey, Australia, Thailand, the Philippines, and Ethiopia—joined the fight.

The American-led counterattack began with a master stroke. On September 15, 1950, General MacArthur launched an amphibious assault against the North Korean army at the port city of Inchon, well behind the Communists' front lines. By late September, American troops took back the South Korean capital city of Seoul, and by late October the North Korean army was in ruins. MacArthur was determined to finish off the North Koreans. Despite warnings from the Chinese government that it would not accept an American invasion of North Korea that threatened its own southern border, MacArthur pushed forward. President Harry Truman authorized MacArthur only to capture the North Korean capital of Pyongyang, but MacArthur, on his own authority, decided to keep moving north all the way to the Yalu River, which marked the Chinese border.

Generals Douglas MacArthur (*center*) and Matthew Ridgway (*right*) tour a Korean battlefield in the winter of 1950–51. In April 1951 President Truman removed MacArthur as supreme commander of the Allied Forces in the Far East for insubordination. Ridgway replaced him.

In the bitterly cold Korean winter, with temperatures plummeting to 35 degrees below zero, the Chinese army descended on MacArthur's forces. MacArthur was shocked. President Truman was shaken to the bone; he wrote privately: "I have worked for peace for five years and six months and it looks like World War III is near."

MacArthur was ready to start that wider war. He demanded that President Truman give him free rein to attack the Chinese Red Army. He wanted Truman to support an invasion of mainland China by the exiled Nationalist forces of Generalissimo Chiang Kai-shek. And he wanted the U.S. Navy to blockade China to prevent the Communist government from gaining outside support that might postpone or prevent the government's destruction at the hands of MacArthur and the Chinese Nationalists. MacArthur wrote to his conservative Republican supporters in Congress, stating, "There is no substitute for victory."

President Truman, demonstrating the grit for which he became famous, fired General MacArthur. As Truman saw it, the general had forgotten that he served the President and that the commander-in-chief had not sought a wider war. Moreover, Truman had explicitly told MacArthur not to advocate publicly for such a war. Truman didn't care that the American public loved General MacArthur, and he did not care that a Gallup Poll revealed that 66 percent of the Americans surveyed supported MacArthur and only 25 percent believed Truman was right to fire the general.

Harry Truman stood up for a vital principle: In the United States, the military took orders from the president. And Truman did not believe that an apocalyptic war with China, a country that likely would have been supported by the Soviet Union, was in the best interests of the United States. In this view, Truman was publicly supported by the cerebral chairman of the Joint Chiefs of Staff, General Omar Bradley, who memorably told the public that a war with Communist China "would involve us in the wrong war, at the wrong place, at the wrong time, and with the wrong enemy."

Despite support from Bradley and other military leaders, Truman's firing of MacArthur and his refusal to support a wider war against communism were savaged by the anti-Communist right wing in the United States. The most fervent of the anti-Communists were sure that Truman was either a dupe of the Soviet menace or an actual member of the Communist Party. Senator William Jenner (R–IN) announced that Truman was surely in league with "a secret inner coterie which is directed by the Soviet Union." Senator Joseph McCarthy (R–WI), who only a year earlier had launched himself into the headlines by declaring that the State Department was overflowing with Communists, gleefully declared that Truman was nothing more than a "son of a bitch."

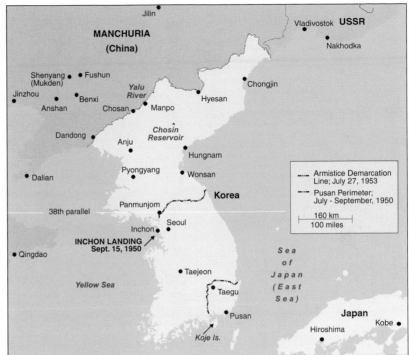

This map illustrates key geographical moments in the Korean War. The North Korean invasion in June 1950 almost pushed South Korean forces into the sea at Pusan, while the Inchon landing in September 1950 pushed back Communist troops. The final demarcation line was only slightly different from the original boundary between the two nations.

McCarthy's demagoguery escalated on June 14, when he rose in the Senate chamber and blamed Secretary of Defense George Marshall for the fall of China to communism in 1949 and for American setbacks in Korea. General Marshall had been one of America's greatest heroes during World War II, and as secretary of state in the immediate post–World War II years had successfully stopped the spread of communism in Europe. Marshall had crafted a massive economic recovery program that brought hope and opportunity to tens of millions of people in France, West Germany, Italy, the Netherlands, and many other nations. Marshall was revered in Europe and was awarded the Nobel Peace Prize in 1953.

Chinese Communist troops march near Kaesong, directly violating an agreement that had created a neutrality zone in Korea. Talks were suspended and then moved in October to Panmunjom, where they continued until a cease-fire was signed in July 1953.

But facts never got in McCarthy's way. Marshall, he orated, was at the heart of "a conspiracy so immense, an infamy so black, as to dwarf any in the history of man." McCarthy predicted that the U.S. would be "contained, frustrated, and finally fall victim to Soviet intrigue from within and Russian military might from without." McCarthy's diatribes were like gasoline poured on the anti-Communist bonfires that were roaring, almost out of control, in the United States.

In Korea, under the new leadership of General Matthew Ridgway, the Chinese-led offensive was stopped in early 1951, and turned. The UN forces pushed the Chinese and North Koreans out of South Korea and held the line at the 38th parallel. The war was not over; men would fight and die for another two years. But the geography of the battlefield shifted very little thereafter.

The two-year stalemate that ensued was frustrating for U.S. soldiers and unsettling for people back home. Americans did not understand the nature of the new wars—wars of decolonization, liberation, and unification—that were breaking out in such faraway places as Indochina, Malaysia, and East and North Africa. On the Korean peninsula, a truce agreement that ended the fighting but did not officially conclude the war was finally signed on July 27, 1953. The Korean peninsula would not be the home of a unified nation; it would remain bitterly divided.

The war had produced some three million Korean casualties—about 10 percent of the total population. Korean War historian Bruce Cummings writes that at war's end, "the Korean peninsula was a smoldering ruin. . . . In the capital at Seoul, hollow buildings stood like skeletons alongside streets paved with weird mixtures of concrete and shrapnel. . . . In the North, modern edifices scarcely stood anymore; Pyongyang and other cities were heaps of bricks and ashes, factories stood empty, massive dams no longer held their water. People emerged from a mole-like existence in caves and tunnels to find a nightmare in the bright of day."

In three years of fighting, more than 33,000 Americans died and more than 100,000 were wounded. Even after the truce agreement was signed, the Korean peninsula remained contested terrain, a continuing flash point in the Cold War that shaped the entire decade of the 1950s and much of the rest of the 20th century.

The Korean War was headline news throughout 1951. But unlike Americans' home front experience during World War II, the distant confrontation did not directly intrude on citizens' everyday lives. In most ways, the nation went about its business even during the hardest days of fighting in 1951. The New York Yankees won the World Series that year, their third of five straight triumphs in the fall classic. Watching the '51 Series on national television, now made possible for the first time by a transcontinental coaxial cable, many baseball fans got their first look at two rookies who would dominate baseball for the rest of the decade: Mickey Mantle and Willie Mays.

At the annual Motorama auto show, General Motors—under the leadership of design chief Harley Earl—introduced a "dream car," the 1951 Buick Le Sabre, which took its inspiration directly from the P-38 Lightning fighter plane. Inspired by the plane's dramatic, twin-boom tail, the Le Sabre had two flaring tailfins. The fins served no practical purpose, but millions of American men looked at the Le Sabre and liked what they saw. Thus, the era of tailfinned, chrome-bedecked, ever-longer autos began.

In 1951 Americans lived amid contradictions. At home, the economy was booming with an overall growth rate in the gross domestic product of 7.7 percent. Jobs were plentiful and consumption soared. Americans owned approximately 12 million television sets, and by the end of the year a majority of them were tuned on Monday nights to CBS's *I Love Lucy,* a ditzy take on married life that starred real-life spouses Lucille Ball and Desi Arnaz.

Even while Americans laughed at the comedienne's antics, men were dying in Korea and Senator Joe McCarthy was insisting that the government was run by Communist traitors. Even more unsettling, the United States and Soviet Union were locked in a frenzied race to build a new generation of "super bombs"—hydrogen bombs—that would be a thousand times more powerful than the atomic detonation that had leveled Hiroshima.

An American soldier fires a recoilless rifle as American troops battle Chinese Communists in June 1951. During the winter and spring of 1950–51, hundreds of thousands of Chinese troops had pushed U.S. forces from northern North Korea back toward South Korea. A virtual stalemate resulted later near the 38th parallel separating the two Koreas.

1951: The Soviets kick off their fifth five-year plan. This failing policy is a Communist construct designed to increase agricultural and industrial output by imposing quotas for a predetermined period of time. • China ejects missionaries and forces Catholics to sever ties with Rome, causing the Vatican to break formal relations with the Asian power. • In a move to strengthen South Africa's system of apartheid, all residents are forced to carry race-specific ID cards. • The American Israel Public Affairs Committee, the flagship U.S. Zionist lobby, is founded.

1951: Actress Dorothy Comingore loses custody of her children to ex-husband and screenwriter Richard Collins, after Collins proved Comingore unfit due to her Communist Party membership. • Actor Zero Mostel is blacklisted for his lack of cooperation with the House Un-American Activities Committee (HUAC). • William F. Buckley, Jr., accepts a Mexico City posting with the CIA. • Marguerite Higgins, a reporter stationed in the Korean War zone, becomes the first woman awarded the Pulitzer Prize for international reporting.

1951: Scientists determine that background radiation levels have increased in the eastern U.S., thousands of miles from areas where nuclear testing has been conducted. According to the Atomic Energy Commission, the elevated radiation exposure is harmless. • Fallout shelters begin to crop up in backyards across the U.S. • *Chicago Tribune* publisher Robert McCormick reveals he has built a bomb shelter. • New York City spends $159,000 on 2.5 million I.D. bracelets, or dog tags, for schoolchildren to facilitate identification following an atomic attack.

American B-29s bomb an enemy supply center in late January 1951. Although eschewing the nuclear option, the United States used airpower very effectively during the war. Close air support helped save the South Korean army when it was almost destroyed at Pusan in 1950. In early 1951, a combination of close air support and strategic bombing helped blunt the massive Communist Chinese advance. After the ground stalemate around the 38th parallel, Communist forces were unable to launch another mass attack because U.S. air power interdicted supply routes and centers during Operation Strangle II in late 1951.

This Communist Chinese political poster illustrates the determination of the People's Republic of China to thwart what its leaders saw as a dangerous American provocation. PRC leader Mao Zedong believed that when United Nations forces crossed the 38th parallel into North Korea, and then continued to advance closer to the Chinese border, they posed a direct threat to China. Given U.S. support for Taiwan and for the French in Indochina, Red China feared that an international capitalist conspiracy was attempting to encircle the fledgling nation. In October 1950, PRC troops crossed the Yalu River and drove UN forces out of North Korea. In January 1951, they captured Seoul, South Korea's capital.

News that U.S. forces had inflicted horrendous civilian casualties in Korea was suppressed in the American press at the time, but the word filtered out elsewhere. Among those appalled by the reports was master painter Pablo Picasso, who in early 1951 created "Massacre in Korea" to register his outrage. Picasso's politics were suspect to many Westerners, for although his anti-fascist stand was well known, he also was perceived as anti-American and a Communist. Perhaps that is why this powerful painting was not as highly regarded as his earlier "Guernica," which depicted Nazi atrocities against Spain.

French philosopher and novelist Albert Camus strikes an especially pensive pose. Born in Algeria and part of the French resistance to Nazi occupation, Camus was best known for his striking novels, *The Stranger* (1942) and *The Plague* (1947), and two major philosophical works, *The Myth of Sisyphus* (1942) and *The Rebel* (1951). This last work praised those who rebelled against injustice without embracing the totalitarianism inherent in Marxism. Committed to battling against human suffering even though the battle could never be completely won, Camus won the Nobel Prize for Literature in 1957. He died in an automobile accident in 1960.

English women maintain stiff upper lips in the face of postwar deprivation. World War II forced Brits to ration a host of necessities, including clothing, fuel, and, most importantly, food items. After the war, an exhausted British economy and a tattered national infrastructure mandated tight resource management, causing many restrictions to remain in place in the late 1940s and even into the '50s. Many complained bitterly and voted the Labour Party out in 1951. By 1954, thanks to a stronger economy, the last restrictions were finally lifted.

1951

1951: Chrysler becomes the first car manufacturer to introduce hydraulic power steering. • Kodak unveils the Brownie 8mm Movie Camera, its first instamatic camera. • Procter & Gamble introduces two new brands of dishwashing detergent: Joy, for hand washing, and Cascade, for the new automatic dishwashers. • Carl Djerassi, a chemist working out of a Mexico City lab, invents a prototype progesterone-based birth control pill. • British firm J. Lyons & Co. manages distribution of its tea cakes using the world's first business computer. • Sugar Pops cereal and Duncan Hines cake mix are the latest additions to America's supermarket shelves.

1951: Vogue Dolls of Bedford, Massachusetts, introduces its popular line of Ginny dolls. • Paint by-number kits are introduced by the Palmer Paint Company, kicking off a fad that will sweep the U.S. • S&H Green Stamps make their debut in a Denver grocery store. • Disc Jockey Alan Freed coins the term "rock 'n' roll" in an effort to make R&B music appeal to a white audience. • The concept of Top 40 radio is developed when Todd Storz and Bill Stewart are hired by Omaha's KOWH to increase the station's ratings. Storz and Stewart are inspired by the repetitive listening habits of patrons playing restaurant jukeboxes. • After nearly 200 films, the final *March of Time* newsreel is produced. The news series has been supplanted by television.

1951: Farnsworth House, Ludwig Mies van der Rohe's masterpiece of international style architecture, is completed near Plano, Illinois. • Chicago's landmark Lake Shore Drive Apartments, or "Glass Houses," another Ludwig Mies van der Rohe creation, is completed. • Elliot Carter's composition *String Quartet No. 1* cements his reputation as one of the leading avant-garde composers of the 20th century.

This scene vividly records the horror visited upon hundreds of commuters near Woodbridge, New Jersey, on February 6, 1951. "The Broker," so named for its abundance of Wall Street workers, was headed home that day on the Pennsylvania Railroad line. Construction of the New Jersey Turnpike forced trains on the line to make a detour across a temporary trestle. Despite prior warnings to slow from 60 to 25 mph when crossing, the Broker's engineer maintained a high speed. The accident killed more than 80 people and injured 500.

A bloody Sugar Ray Robinson (*right*) pummels Jake LaMotta in their world middleweight championship bout on February 14, 1951. This was the sixth and final fight in their epic series of matchups that had begun in 1942. Robinson, the challenger, was in control almost from the beginning, building up a comfortable lead in spite of some telling blows from the champ. But the courageous LaMotta refused to go down despite absorbing an enormous amount of punishment. The referee mercifully stopped the fight in the 13th round. The bout was immortalized in Martin Scorsese's highly acclaimed 1980 film, *Raging Bull*.

In 1951 the Federal Civil Defense Administration made *Duck and Cover,* an informational cartoon in which Bert the turtle hides under his shell to avoid danger. In this sequence, the monkey with the dynamite represents Communists with an atomic bomb. Bert survives because he "ducks and covers" (although the fate of the monkey is unclear!). Directed at young children, the cartoon tried to calm fears by claiming that kids could duck under desks and cover their faces in case of a nuclear attack. The film stated that adults in charge of things would give plenty of warning and basically have the situation under control. Of course, such a response would be fruitless.

Civil Defense

THOUGH HOMELAND SECURITY measures in times of crisis in the United States existed as far back as the Minutemen, most provisions were organized on an *ad hoc* basis. While a jittery American citizenry had been placated by the mobilization of skywatchers during World War II, the Atomic Age required something more substantial. To that end, President Truman ordered the creation of the Federal Civil Defense Administration in 1951. Grossly underfunded by Congress (in what Truman called "a reckless evasion of responsibility"), the department did little more than issue government pamphlets in its first years of existence.

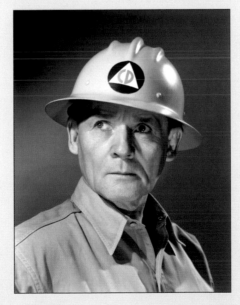

However, the introduction of an animated turtle named Bert soon put a face on their efforts. In an educational short and radio broadcast, Bert showed a generation of schoolchildren that the apocalypse was eminently survivable. All one needed to do upon seeing the flash of a nuclear explosion was to "duck" (to avoid flying debris) and "cover" (to escape radiation burns). Classroom drills became commonplace in schools across the country, with teachers commanding their charges to "drop!" and assume the position. Reassured, many Americans believed that nuclear war would be manageable, if inconvenient.

Preparedness became the watchword. To that end, thousands of sturdy buildings throughout the country were soon sporting black and yellow "Fallout Shelter" signs, beckoning citizens to enter the presumably safe confines should bombs start to fall. Drills and emergency training became commonplace, with mock "raids" staged to test the readiness of civil defense teams and the public alike.

While such efforts did much to satisfy the public's need to "do something," the futility of such planning eventually became apparent. Experts pointed out that the best-stocked shelters could never support great masses of people for any significant length of time. Furthermore, with the warning time of a missile strike reduced from hours to minutes, contingencies for major evacuations became useless.

1951

1951: A point-shaving scandal involving players from several teams—including New York University, University of Kentucky, and City College of New York—casts a long shadow over college basketball. • Althea Gibson becomes the first black tennis player to compete on the grass at Wimbledon. *See* July 6, 1957. • Elroy "Crazy Legs" Hirsch of the Los Angeles Rams amasses 1,495 receiving yards, shattering the NFL record. • Willie Mays captures Rookie of the Year honors after leading the New York Giants to the National League pennant.

Early 1951: Edward Teller redesigns the hydrogen bomb on recommendations made by mathematician Stanislaw Ulam. • More than 200 people are killed and tens of thousands are injured as avalanches sweep the Swiss, Austrian, and Italian Alps.

January: The South Korean port of Inchon is destroyed by evacuating UN forces as the Chinese Army advances to capture the city.

January 1: The Boring & Tilton building on New York City's Ellis Island, long the home of a hospital for contagious disease, closes its doors.

January 4: Communist Chinese and North Korean forces capture Seoul, the capital of South Korea.

January 10: Author Sinclair Lewis, the first American to win a Nobel Prize for Literature, dies at age 65.

January 11: President Harry Truman authorizes the designation of part of the Nevada desert as a nuclear testing site. This area will come to be known as the Nevada Test Site.

January 12: President Truman signs the Federal Civil Defense Act. He also announces the National Industrial Dispersion Policy, which will allocate federal aid for new industrial plants if they are built in atomic-safe, sparsely populated regions.

Columbia University's Jack Molinas was one of 32 players from seven New York colleges arrested for fixing basketball games in the early 1950s. New York District Attorney Frank Hogan even indicted players from City College of New York, which had won both the NCAA Tournament and the National Invitation Tournament in 1950, an unprecedented accomplishment irrevocably tarnished. The scandal also reached the prestigious University of Kentucky program with the arrest of center Bill Spivey in 1952.

A worker for A & D Bomb Shelters, Inc., stands in the backyard of a homeowner in Hermosa Beach, California, in early 1951. The year before, Congress had created the Civil Defense Administration (CDA), largely as a reaction to the Soviets' testing of an atomic bomb in 1949. The CDA disseminated information about constructing fallout shelters and how to stock them, and it created the Emergency Broadcasting System. Although no one knows how many bomb shelters were built in 1951, certainly a trend had begun.

Communist Chinese soldiers capture American troops during the fourth major Chinese offensive of the Korean War in February 1951. Communist troops crossed the 38th parallel on New Year's Eve 1950 and for two months hammered reeling UN forces, causing a large number of casualties. Bitter cold and thousands of fleeing civilian refugees complicated the issue as UN troops retreated. The men in this photograph were among more than 7,000 Americans who became POWs during the course of the war.

Communist Chinese forces participate in a major offensive in early 1951. Since entering the war in late 1950, the Chinese had succeeded in driving UN forces out of North Korea. By January, they took the South's capital, Seoul. Regrouping, the UN command under General Matthew Ridgway struck back in late January. This time, the Communists were caught off-guard, and they retreated north of the boundary that separated north and south. Incensed that his plans for total annihilation of the enemy had been thwarted, China's Chairman Mao ordered reinforcements to mount a massive counterstrike in April. But Ridgway's men were by then battle-seasoned enough to prevail in the fierce fighting, inflicting 160,000 casualties on the withdrawing Chinese.

To facilitate the high-priority retaking of Seoul, General Matthew Ridgway commenced Operation Ripper in March 1951. Designed to simultaneously destroy the enemy's ability to mount offensives while pushing it north, plans called for some of the heaviest artillery bombardments of the war. Machine-gun fire (*pictured*) decimated enemy troops, laying the groundwork for an assault by UN forces. On March 14, the Allies retook Seoul while driving the Communists back across mountain terrain. By April, the enemy had been thoroughly pushed to the north of the 38th parallel.

January 15: In a West German courtroom, Ilse Koch, notorious wife of the Buchenwald death camp commandant, is sentenced to life in prison for her crimes during the Holocaust. • President Truman submits a budget to Congress that includes a deficit of more than $15 billion, with more than $40 billion in defense spending.

January 23: In an effort to provide some oversight of the anti-Communist movement, President Truman establishes the Commission on Internal Security and Individual Rights.

January 25: The U.S. Eighth Army launches Operation Thunderbolt in an effort to push Chinese forces north of the Han River.

January 27: For the first time, an atmospheric test takes place at the Nevada Test Site. The weapon, code-named Able, is detonated 1,060 feet above Frenchman Flat.

February 6: More than 80 people are killed when a commuter train derails in Woodbridge, New Jersey.

February 11: UN forces gain some ground as they push north across the 38th parallel into North Korea.

February 14: The U.S. military orders the B-52 bomber from Boeing. The B-52, a heavy bomber that can fly as many as 8,800 miles without refueling, is the linchpin of the U.S. nuclear strategy. • Israeli Prime Minister David Ben Gurion resigns due to his ongoing inability to reach consensus with the Knesset. • In what is known as the "Valentine's Day Massacre," middleweight boxer Sugar Ray Robinson wins a 5–1 decision over Jake LaMotta.

February 16: New York City bans racial discrimination in public housing.

February 26: With the ratification of the 22nd Amendment, the U.S. presidential term is restricted to eight years.

The Rosenberg Trial

IN THE EARLY YEARS of the Cold War, few Americans would object to executing a man caught spying for the Communists. But when the accused were married and parents of two small children, the case weighed heavily on America's collective conscience.

The story began in 1950, when German-born physicist Klaus Fuchs, living in Britain, was interviewed by British agents. Fuchs admitted to investigators that he had procured top-secret information about the atom bomb from Los Alamos National Laboratory in New Mexico. Fuchs's story led investigators to a former Army sergeant and Los Alamos machinist named David Greenglass, who thereupon incriminated his sister and brother-in-law, New Yorkers named Ethel and Julius Rosenberg.

The Rosenbergs' involvement with the American Communist Party dated back to their youth. Though he typically fulfilled his Party duties by attending meetings, Julius learned in 1944 that Ethel's brother had been assigned to the highly classified Manhattan Project in Los Alamos. He pressured Greenglass to smuggle details of the ongoing atomic mission into a channel that led to the Soviets.

Ethel and Julius Rosenberg, separated following their arrests

The arrest of first Julius, then Ethel, brought fears of widespread Communist infiltration to America's doorstep. Demands that the government "fry the traitors" drowned out the smaller number of those advocating mercy—mostly on behalf of the couple's two young sons, Robert and Michael. The boys brought sympathetic observers to tears when they marched with signs that read "Don't Kill My Mommy and Daddy."

President Eisenhower declined to involve himself in the Rosenbergs' lengthy appeals process. The case went to the U.S. Supreme Court, but only four of the nine justices voted to stay the execution.

While Julius's guilt (motivated by ideological rather than financial grounds) was clearly established, Ethel was never more than a minor player at best. David Greenglass would confirm as much decades later, stating that his testimony against his sister was an effort to draw some leniency for himself and his wife. The Rosenbergs themselves hardly helped their own cause, maintaining a rigid and ideologically dogmatic defense that bordered on arrogance.

On June 19, 1953, Julius and then Ethel were executed in the electric chair at Sing Sing Prison in New York. The first 57-second jolt of electricity failed to kill Ethel. She was restrapped to the chair and electrocuted again.

In 1951 David Greenglass and his wife, Ruth, (*both pictured*) were key figures in the espionage trial of Ethel and Julius Rosenberg, David's sister and brother-in-law. Accused of spying for the USSR themselves, the Greenglasses made a deal with the government to testify against the Rosenbergs. They claimed that Julius and Ethel had recruited David, who worked at Los Alamos during the A-bomb project, to pass on top-secret information about the project. In return for his testimony, David received a 15-year prison sentence (of which he served 10); his wife was never indicted. In interviews with author Sam Roberts and *60 Minutes*, Greenglass claimed he lied about Ethel's role in order to keep his wife out of jail.

IN THE JUDGE'S OPINION . . .

I CONSIDER YOUR CRIME worse than murder. Plain deliberate contemplated murder is dwarfed in magnitude by comparison with the crime you have committed. In committing the act of murder, the criminal kills only his victim. . . . But in your case, I believe your conduct in putting into the hands of the Russians the A-bomb years before our best scientists predicted Russia would perfect the bomb has already caused, in my opinion, the Communist aggression in Korea, with the resultant casualties exceeding 50,000 and who knows but that millions more of innocent people may pay the price of your treason. Indeed, by your betrayal you undoubtedly have altered the course of history to the disadvantage of our country.

—JUDGE IRVING R. KAUFMAN, DURING SENTENCING FOR THE ROSENBERGS

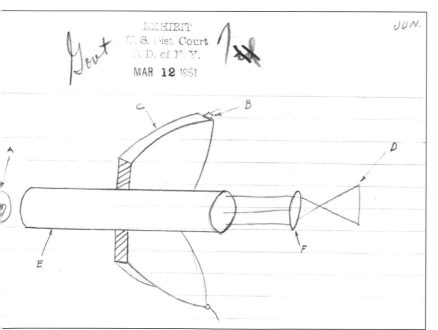

Soviet spy David Greenglass passed sketches and descriptions of lens molds, to be used in the trigger for the A-bomb, to Julius Rosenberg. Greenglass's claim—which he recanted years later—that his sister, Ethel, had typed some of his notes helped send her to the electric chair. Although there is considerable controversy over whether these specific sketches were of any great help to the Soviets, historian Ron Radosh concludes that the information provided by Greenglass via Julius Rosenberg was of "very significant help in accelerating" the Russian nuclear program.

These actors, performing in a weekly *Polish Tea Party* broadcast, contributed to Radio Free Europe (RFE), a potent weapon in America's Cold War propaganda arsenal. Beginning in 1950, RFE promoted democratic values behind enemy lines, with a wide array of programming aimed initially at Iron Curtain countries in Eastern Europe (and later expanding to Asia and the Middle East). Centering on but not limited to news and information, the broadcasts also included musical, religious, comedic, and literary programming. Funding was provided by the U.S. Congress and channeled through the CIA.

1951

March: The Federal Civil Defense Administration requests a $250 million allocation from Congress for a national shelter program. Congress will authorize only $31.75 million, effectively killing the program. • Communist spy Alger Hiss checks into the federal penitentiary at Lewisburg, Pennsylvania, to begin serving a five-year term for perjury.

March 2: The K-1 submarine, the first sub designed to track enemy submarines, is commissioned by the U.S. Navy.

March 7: Operation Ripper, an offensive designed to reorganize the UN line facing the Chinese, is launched under General Matthew Ridgway. • General Ali Razmara, Iranian premier, is assassinated by a fanatic who objects to Iran's trade policies with the West.

March 13: Israel demands $1.5 billion in German war reparations to help pay for the post-Holocaust refugee crisis.

March 14: UN forces retake Seoul from the North Koreans.

March 15: Communist puppet Jacobo Guzman Arbenz begins his tenure as president of Guatemala. • Iranian Premier Mohammed Mossadegh nationalizes Iran's oil industry, prompting U.S. and British intelligence plans for his ouster.

March 19: The European Coal and Steel Community is established, with Holland, Luxembourg, West Germany, Belgium, Italy, and France as its charter members.

March 21: General George C. Marshall reports that the number of active-duty military personnel has doubled since the beginning of the Korean War, and now stands at about 2.9 million.

Pianist Dave Brubeck became arguably jazz's biggest star of the 1950s, almost despite himself. The son of a piano teacher, Brubeck resisted lessons and refused to learn to sight read, wishing instead to become a cattleman. His ambitions remained intact until a college instructor awakened him to the possibilities of applying classical modes and exotic time signatures to jazz. Further good fortune came when he met saxophonist Paul Desmond while in the Army. Together, the two would form the backbone of jazz's most dynamic and innovative quartet, scoring the genre's first million-selling album with *Time Out* by decade's end.

The Lake Shore Drive Apartments in Chicago are among architect Ludwig Mies van der Rohe's most respected works. Though designs of this sort may seem commonplace to contemporary eyes, in 1951 this was groundbreaking architecture. The 26-story luxury high-rise exemplified the steel and glass postwar aesthetic. However, Mies had first conceived of these perfectly proportioned glass-dominated structures 30 years earlier. The supporting I-beams, coupled with the floor-to-ceiling windows, bring a sense of lightness to the buildings.

New Yorkers gather at a movie theater to watch televised hearings of Estes Kefauver's Senate Special Committee on Organized Crime. The nationally televised hearings on crime families in New York City ran from March 12 to 20, 1951. Such thuggish luminaries as Frank Costello and 49 of his colleagues electrified the nation. Millions of people watched in what might be seen as an early incarnation of Marshall McLuhan's global village. According to one observer, "Never before had the attention of the nation been riveted so completely on a single matter."

Estes Kefauver was a Democratic senator from Tennessee, serving from 1949 to 1963. He rose to national prominence as the chairman of the Senate Special Committee on Organized Crime, which conducted televised investigations of the influence of organized crime and corruption in March 1951. The senator, known for wearing a coonskin cap, parlayed the exposure into campaigns for the Democratic presidential nomination in 1952 and 1956. He was the party's vice presidential nominee in 1956, nosing out Massachusetts Senator John F. Kennedy. Kefauver died in 1963 after suffering a heart attack on the Senate floor. Artwork for this *Time* cover is by Boris Artzybasheff.

Reputed mob boss Frank Costello (*left*) looks on glumly as his lawyer, George Wolf, addresses members of the Kefauver Committee during its hearings on organized crime in March 1951. Wolf convinced the committee not to allow the television cameras to show Costello's face. An ingenious cameraman improvised by focusing on the nervous witness's constantly moving hands, which mesmerized viewers. When the committee refused to let him postpone further testimony, Costello walked out and was sentenced to 18 months in prison for contempt of Congress. He survived an assassination attempt in 1957 and died of a heart attack in 1973.

March 26: The Federal Communications Commission reveals a plan to use the UHF band that would allow for as many as 2,000 television channels.

March 29: In the face of overwhelming evidence, including testimony by the brother of Ethel Rosenberg, Ethel and husband Julius are convicted of espionage for passing atomic secrets to the Soviets. *See* April 5, 1951.

March 31: President Truman signs an executive order providing draft deferment for college students with the best academic standing, as judged by their performance on an aptitude test.

April 4: At Los Alamos National Laboratory, Edward Teller submits his new hydrogen bomb blueprint.

April 5: The Joint Chiefs of Staff authorize the defensive use of nuclear weapons against North Korea. • Judge Irving R. Kaufman sentences Julius and Ethel Rosenberg to death. *See* February 11, 1953.

April 6: President Truman authorizes a Defense Department request to use nuclear weapons against Manchuria if China's support of North Korea extends to significant ground troops or air support.

April 11: President Truman relieves the popular General Douglas MacArthur of his command in response to MacArthur's disregard of the Truman Administration's Korean War policy.

April 19: General MacArthur delivers one of the most quotable lines in American history when he tells Congress in his farewell speech: "Old soldiers never die; they just fade away."

April 21: The Toronto Maple Leafs best the Montreal Canadiens in the Stanley Cup Finals, in which all five games reach overtime.

This early *Dennis the Menace* cartoon panel shows the irrepressible youngster once again getting the best of his hapless father. Created by Hank Ketchum, the comic strip first ran on March 12, 1951. It was immediately popular, with a Sunday strip added in 1952. Ketchum won the National Cartoonists' Association Reuben Prize that year at the tender age of 22. *Dennis the Menace* became the basis of a 1959 CBS sitcom and continues to run in some 1,200 newspapers worldwide. Its appeal may lie in the fact that Dennis is eternally five and a half and, in spite of his devilment, really means no harm.

"WE'RE PLAYIN' FIREMAN. YOU'RE THE HOUSE!"

Kentucky coach Adolph Rupp (*second row, second from right*) and his players celebrate a victory over Illinois on their way to winning the 1951 NCAA championship. The Wildcats dominated college basketball during much of the 1950s, winning another national title in 1959 and finishing in the top 15 every year. Kentucky went undefeated in 1953–54 but declined an NCAA Tournament bid because the association would not allow graduate students to play. The Wildcats experienced their share of controversy, as well. Center Bill Spivey was banned in 1953 because of game-fixing allegations, and Rupp refused to recruit African-American players (even through the mid-1960s).

In 1948 Minnesota postman and fishing aficionado Herb Schaper whittled his first "Cootie" out of wood. Though it was intended to be a fishing lure, Schaper soon discovered that kids delighted in taking apart and reassembling his creation. An idea formed, and by the following fall local stores were selling his homemade invention on consignment. By 1951 the W. H. Schaper Manufacturing Company was cranking out Cooties by the millions. Schaper's other insect successes included "Ants in the Pants" and "Inch Worm."

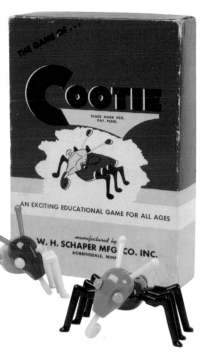

Legendary crooner Nat King Cole actually began his career as an innovative jazz pianist. Though he had always sung on occasion, his considerable keyboard abilities put him on the map as he led his trio through such hits as "Route 66" and "Straighten Up and Fly Right." But after Cole's classic take on Mel Torme's "Christmas Song," his pure vocal tone became the focus of his recordings—including his 1951 hit, "Unforgettable." Smooth, relaxed, and handsome, Cole was a natural for television. As the medium's first black host (*The Nat King Cole Show* in 1956–57), he made history, short-lived though it was.

On March 31, 1951, the U.S. Census Bureau received the first UNIVAC (Universal Automatic Computer), invented by Dr. Presper Eckert and Dr. John Mauchly. When the two inventors ran into financial trouble, Remington Rand Corporation bailed them out. The UNIVAC was superior to its IBM competitor because the magnetic tape it employed could input data much more quickly. The new computer correctly predicted the results of the 1952 presidential election, a forecast blacked out by media outlets, which feared prognostication competition.

Actor Jose Ferrer consoles Gloria Swanson in 1951 after she lost the best actress Oscar to Judy Holliday (*right*). Holliday had played dumb-but-no-so-dumb Billie Dawn in the successful Broadway play *Born Yesterday*, then reprised the role in the 1950 George Cukor film. As an uneducated but perceptive mistress of a brutal businessman, Holliday's character gradually comes to see the man's true nature. Billie is an enormously appealing character who, like Holliday herself, is no fool, but rather a natural intellect.

MacArthur's Swan Song

WHEN HOSTILITIES ERUPTED in Korea in June 1950, President Harry Truman named the former commander of Pacific Operations in World War II, General Douglas MacArthur, to head UN forces. It seemed a logical choice, despite MacArthur's reputation as a difficult, ego-driven grandstander. Within weeks of taking command, the general sized up the situation and announced an audacious plan that he coolly predicted would turn things around for allied forces.

In August 1950, MacArthur called for an assault on Inchon, South Korea, by sea. Advisers were alarmed, describing his intentions as a precise list of military "don'ts." But with MacArthur insisting that its utter unpredictability was its strength, Operation Chromite proceeded. To everyone's astonishment but MacArthur's, UN forces smashed the North Korean army and drove it back into its own territory.

Unwilling to leave well enough alone, MacArthur disregarded his orders from Washington, stretching his troops dangerously thin in pursuit of the enemy. Seizing an open-

ing, Chinese troops entered the fray in late November and blindsided American forces. The ensuing slaughter appalled the Truman Administration and the American public alike. Seeking to salvage the campaign, General Matthew Ridgway was installed to take command of the Eighth Army. Irked, MacArthur lashed out at civilian authorities, venting to the press his belief that only an expansion of the war would bring victory—a direct contradiction of U.S. policy.

At long last pushed to his limit, President Truman relieved the general of his command on April 11, 1951. Despite the demonstrable grounds for the dismissal, MacArthur was greeted as a hero by an uncritical American public. Sympathetic members of Congress gave the general a grand send-off on the floor of the Capitol. There, in a voice dripping with melodrama, MacArthur delivered his valedictory, declaring that "old soldiers never die; they just fade away." He would do just that, despite predictions by some that his showboating was preparation for a presidential run.

General Douglas MacArthur basks in a tumultuous ticker tape parade in New York City on April 20, 1951, nine days after being fired by President Truman. Hundreds of thousands of worshippers turned out for parades in San Francisco and Washington, D.C., as well as in the Big Apple, and angry letters flooded the White House. Initially, Americans overwhelmingly condemned Truman's action. A Gallup poll taken in mid-April, for example, showed that 66 percent of Americans disapproved of the dismissal. By May 16, passions had cooled, as 51 percent approved of the firing.

During World War II, Matthew B. Ridgway distinguished himself as commander of the 18th Airborne Corps. Named to lead the U.S. Eighth Army in December 1950, Ridgway used what historian Joe Dunn calls his "legendary motivational talents" to improve troop morale. For example, he ordered more hot food, warmer clothes, and better medical

units for his men. In April 1951, he assumed General MacArthur's position as commander of all U.S. and UN forces in the Far East. Noted for his organizational skills and leadership, Ridgway helped stanch the Chinese advance. In May 1952, he replaced Dwight Eisenhower as supreme commander of U.S. forces in Europe.

The F-86 Sabre jet was the most effective U.S. fighter plane during the Korean War, even though only 125 were actually in the military theater. Manufactured by North American Aviation Corporation, the F-86 was similar in appearance to the Soviet MiG-15, the main North Korean jet. Although they both had swept wings to increase speed, the MiG's stabilizer placement made it almost impossible for pilots to recover from a spin. The F-86's lower stabilizer allowed it to outmaneuver its counterpart, especially in turns. Korean War pilot Bud Mahurin described flying the Sabre as "more fun than anything else I've ever done."

Film director Edward Dmytryk testifies as a friendly witness before the House Un-American Activities Committee (HUAC) on April 25, 1951. In 1948 Dmytryk had been sentenced to a year in prison for contempt of Congress after refusing to answer questions about his alleged Communist connections. Blacklisted upon his release, he moved to England. HUAC offered to recommend he be removed from the blacklist if he would name associates with Communist ties. In his 1951 testimony, Dmytryk identified 26 colleagues as members of left-wing groups, much to the disgust of many free-speech advocates in the U.S.

From 1943 to 1950, Pittsburgh steelworker Matt Cvetic led a double life. While rising as a star within the local Communist Party, he was, in fact, reporting their activities to the FBI. Though some of his testimony actually led to espionage convictions, Cvetic's alcoholism and penchant for embellishment led to his dismissal by the bureau. Nonetheless, he managed to parlay his experiences into celebrity, first with a series in the *Saturday Evening Post,* then through this film, *I Was a Communist for the F.B.I.* Though heavily fictionalized, the documentary-style depiction provided electrifying entertainment.

April 24: The University of North Carolina at Chapel Hill admits its first black student.

April 25: HUAC extracts the names of 26 Communists from film director Edward Dmytryk. • On the Korean hill that would hereafter be named "Gloucester Hill" in their honor, the Gloucestershire Regiment is decimated at the end of a three-day battle against Communist Chinese forces.

May 1: The U.S. government-sponsored Radio Free Europe broadcasts for the first time, from Munich to Eastern Europe.

May 9: A U.S. nuclear test at Eniwetok Atoll in the Pacific Ocean proves that a fission device can provide the ignition for a thermonuclear weapon.

May 16: Communist forces launch a major spring offensive, during which they will gain up to 20 miles of Korean territory.

May 18: The United Nations moves to its new headquarters on Manhattan's East Side. • An arms embargo against China and North Korea is imposed by a unanimous vote in the UN General Assembly.

May 20: U.S. Air Force Captain James Jabara shoots down two MiGs in Korea, bringing his total to six and earning him the designation of the world's first jet ace.

May 24: The District of Columbia bans racial segregation in restaurants.

May 25: British Soviet spies Guy Burgess and Donald Maclean disappear. Both men served in the British Embassy in Washington, D.C., and had access to sensitive Anglo-American security information.

May 27: Tibet enters into a subordinate agreement with China, relinquishing sovereignty over its army and foreign affairs to Beijing.

Take science fiction writer J. W. Campbell's short story "Who Goes There?"; add veteran western/war movie director Howard Hawks; film it during an era of heightened paranoia; and what do you have? *The Thing,* of course. In this sci-fi thriller, a crew of scientists stationed in the Arctic discovers an alien spacecraft buried beneath the ice. Investigating military personnel inadvertently destroy the alien craft and unleash the title entity, played by a pre-*Gunsmoke* James Arness. Though the movie is credited to veteran film editor Christian Nyby, Hawks's directorial fingerprints are much in evidence, including superb framing and realistic overlapping dialogue.

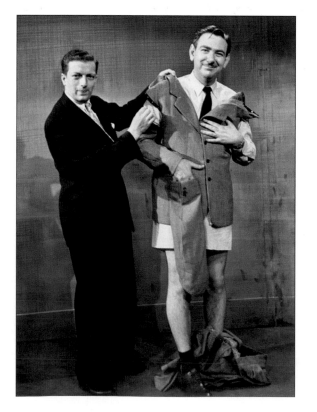

During the 1940s, a pair of staffers at WHDH in Boston serendipitously joined forces to form one of comedy's most enduring duos. Compelled to fill airtime during baseball rain-outs, disc jockey Bob Elliot (*left*) and newscaster Ray Goulding began improvising a satirical comedic act. *Matinee with Bob and Ray* premiered on radio in Boston in 1946 and moved to New York in 1951. Featuring absurdist takes on commercials, soap operas, game shows, and other broadcast staples, their intelligent brand of comedy won them a devoted fan base. A television run on NBC beginning in 1951 featured Audrey Meadows among the cast.

> **"My head was covered with several thicknesses of raincoat and my eyes were covered with my hands, yet when the blast went off I could see through all that with an unbearable light, which showed my hands as bright red and showed the outline of every bone."**
>
> —U.S. SERVICEMAN MO INGRAM, DESCRIBING A DETONATION NICKNAMED "THE BIG ONE" AT ENIWETOK ATOLL NEAR THE MARSHALL ISLANDS, SPRING 1951

In the 1940s, physicist Edward Teller worked under Robert Oppenheimer on the development of the atomic bomb. His major contribution was calculations that assured fellow scientists that the bomb's destructive force could be limited. In 1949, after the Soviets tested their first atomic bomb, Teller headed the

project to develop the hydrogen bomb. Based on nuclear fusion, rather than fission like the A-bomb, the H-bomb's destructive potential was much greater. The U.S. successfully tested the first fusion bomb in 1952. In 1954 Teller opposed renewal of Oppenheimer's security clearance. He later experienced emotional problems when he became an outcast among many fellow scientists because of his testimony.

The telltale mushroom cloud rises after the detonation of George, a U.S. nuclear bomb, on May 9, 1951. Part of a four-test series conducted in the South Pacific, George was detonated on a tower located on an island in the Eniwetok Atoll. The test series resulted in serious radioactive fallout in the atoll that affected men in nearby Navy medical research and Army communication units. The tests comprised Operation Greenhouse, one of the steps along the road to U.S. development of the hydrogen bomb.

Eugene Dennis, general secretary of the Communist Party of the USA, is taken to prison in early summer 1951, after the Supreme Court ruled that the Smith Act was constitutional. Passed in 1940, the act made it illegal to advocate the overthrow of the U.S. government by force. In 1951 Dennis and 10 others were convicted of violating the act because they had discussed the merits of such an overthrow in a secret meeting. The Supreme Court ruled that the defendants' discussion had, in fact, posed "a sufficient danger of a substantial evil," the outlawing of which did not violate the First Amendment. Many civil libertarians attacked the decision as a violation of free speech.

This Chinese soldier was killed by U.S. Marine aircraft in May 1951. Most of the Chinese forces in Korea belonged to what was called the Chinese People's Volunteer Army, as if hundreds of thousands of men had *voluntarily* left their civilian jobs to defend their North Korean comrades. In fact, the soldiers belonged to units of the regular Chinese armed forces. Initially, between 250,000 and 400,000 Chinese troops swarmed across the Yalu River in human-wave attacks. The casualty figures for Chinese forces are contested. China claims 152,400 killed, while American estimates stand at around 500,000.

"Does it bother you—"

After the outbreak of the Korean War in June 1950, Director of Selective Service Lewis Hershey reinstituted military draft calls, which had been suspended in January 1949. Male college students were given a chance to apply for a draft deferment based on their class rank and their score on a special test developed by the Educational Testing Service, which was first given in May 1951. In the first round of tests, 339,066 students (more than 60 percent) passed. A number of draft board members protested what they saw as favoritism, some even resigning en masse. While colleges generally supported the plan, Princeton President Harold Dodds feared it made college students look like they were "seeking to avoid civic duty."

In May 1951, the United Nations moved from its temporary headquarters in Lake Success, New York, to its permanent home in Manhattan, on land donated by John D. Rockefeller. Dominating the site is the Secretariat, a 39-story office tower. The building was designed by famed architect Le Corbusier (born Charles Jenneret). The Secretariat is an example of the International Style, a mode bereft of historic and culture-specific references. Although hailed for its symbolic value, its functionality left much to be desired. Cramped quarters and chronic temperature-control problems plagued the Secretariat for years.

Vietnamese General Vo Nguyen Giap (*top left*) gets together with Vietnamese leader Ho Chi Minh (*top right*). General Giap had a trying year in 1951. As commander of anti-French Viet Minh forces in Vietnam, he optimistically launched a series of large frontal attacks on French forces instead of continuing hit-and-run guerrilla tactics. Encouraged by his Chinese advisers, who believed that they had used human-wave assaults with great success in Korea, Giap attacked French forces at Vien Yen in January and the Day River in May. The French managed to beat back the Viet Minh, inflicting devastating losses on Giap's army. Morale among his troops worsened, and he returned to a more cautious approach in 1952.

Iranian Premier Mohammed Mossadegh (*left*) greets U.S. Ambassador Ernest Gross. A legal scholar and politician, Mossadegh became premier in 1951, in spite of opposition from the Iranian shah (equivalent to an emperor). Mossadegh's most controversial act came in June 1951 when he ordered British oil refineries seized as part of his nationalization plan. When British companies sued, the International Court at The Hague, Netherlands, ruled in Mossadegh's favor. The British and their American allies saw his scheme as a direct threat to their national interests, and an action that would increase Soviet influence in the region. U.S. officials began working on plans that would lead to the premier's overthrow in 1953.

Seen behind the wheel of his legendary 1951 Buick Le Sabre concept car, General Motors design chief Harley Earl almost singlehandedly sublimated function for style within the automobile industry. From his beginnings as Hollywood's premier custom body designer for car-crazy stars, Earl ventured east to work for GM in the 1920s. He soon revolutionized car design through his use of clay mock-ups. Earl's innovations included wraparound windshields, disappearing headlamps, and the ubiquitous tailfins of the '50s. His obsession with aircraft motifs would strongly influence the direction of Detroit bodywork and instrument panels.

Alfred Sloan had a lot to smile about in 1951. General Motors, the company he had headed from 1923 to 1946 and served as board chairman until 1956, continued to be the world's largest producer of automobiles, a position it had held since 1931. An organizational genius, Sloan created the annual model change and a divisional structure within the company. Customers were encouraged to "buy up," from

the inexpensive Chevrolet to the top-of-the-line Cadillac. Bill Gates, founder of computer behemoth Microsoft, claims that Sloan's memoir, *My Years with General Motors* (1964), might be the best book to read about business.

1951

May 29: Fanny Brice, famed Broadway actress, dies at age 59. • Captain Charles Blair, in a converted P-51 single-engine plane, makes the first solo flight over the North Pole.

May 29–June 18: In an early engagement of the Vietnam War, Viet Minh General Giap attempts to break through the French defensive line.

June: A devastating flood in Missouri leaves a half million homeless.

June 4: In *Dennis v. United States,* the U.S. Supreme Court rules against 11 members of New York City's Communist Party who were charged with sedition in violation of the Smith Act.

June 12: The South Korean National Assembly finds that more than 50,000 of the republic's military draftees died due to horrible conditions in the winter training camps.

June 13: UN troops capture the North Korean capital of Pyongyang.

June 14: UNIVAC, the first commercial digital computer, is unveiled in Philadelphia by its creator, the Remington Rand Corporation.

June 15–July 1: Forest fires blaze through several states, including New Mexico, Washington, Oregon, California, and Arizona, as well as the Canadian province of British Columbia.

June 16: Golfer Ben Hogan wins his third U.S. Open, at the Oakland Hills Country Club.

June 19: The Universal Military Training and Service Act is signed by President Truman. The act lowers the minimum conscription age to 18 and extends the draft to July 1, 1955.

June 20: In a New York federal court, 21 Communists are indicted for conspiring against the U.S. government.

C. Wright Mills, noted Columbia University sociologist, was no ivory-tower intellectual. He was a passionate and engaged scholar with a mission who wrote primarily about the American power structure and its threat to personal freedoms. His *White Collar,* published in 1951, examined the American corporate middle class, exposing what he saw as its grayness and conformity. Later works, most notably *The Power Elite,* would be seen as even more anti-capitalist, but Mills saw himself as an American individualist. He died in 1962 at age 45.

In 1951 the popular radio series *Amos 'n' Andy* came to the CBS television network. The cast included Kingfish (Tim Moore, *standing*), a con man; Andy (Spencer Williams, *left*), Kingfish's overly trusting friend; and Amos (Alvin Childress, *right*), a level-headed cabdriver. The fact that characters created by whites mocked blacks was not lost on the NAACP. Thus, even though the majority of the show's one-time background characters (doctors, lawyers, and others) were not portrayed as buffoons, the program was pulled in 1953, two years after the NAACP's initial protest.

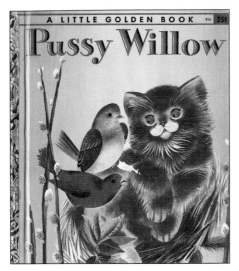

Within a decade after their 1942 introduction, Little Golden Books had
become a phenomenon of children's
literature. These durable editions,
available in hundreds of titles, broke
new ground in mass-marketing, selling
in chain stores rather than merely in
bookshops. Sales of Little Golden Books,
priced at 25 cents each, exceeded 180
million in their first decade. In addition
to featuring contemporary pop culture
figures (such as Howdy Doody), Little
Golden Books introduced many original
characters, such as Margaret Wise
Brown's Pussy Willow (art by Leonard
Weisgard). For children then and since,
these volumes became an essential
introduction to the joy of reading.

Pogo

AT THE HEIGHT OF SENATOR Joseph McCarthy's power, few in the country
dared to take him on directly. One opponent, however, came from the
most unlikely of sources: a newspaper comic strip depicting the animal population of the Okefenokee Swamp. Decades before *Doonesbury* routinely lam-
pooned the political figures of the day,
Pogo presented a devastating mockery of
the divisive senator with a character called
Simple J. Malarkey. So brutal was the parody that some dailies refused to run it.

Pogo was the brainchild of a former
Disney cartoonist named Walt Kelly.
Before becoming overseer of Okefenokee's
residents, he had worked as a political
cartoonist for a New York daily, and as a
comic book artist. The strip began running in 1948. Pogo Possum emerged as
the central figure, surrounded by such regulars as Albert the Alligator, Churchy La
Femme, Howland Owl, and many others.

Not only was *Pogo* beautifully drawn,
but it combined elements of social and
political commentary with the typical farce expected from a daily strip. Kelly
"ran" Pogo for president every four years, on the slogan of "I Go Pogo." The
astute observations and cultural references made Kelly's *Pogo* a favorite among
liberals of the day.

Among the Disney Studio's
animated movies, 1951's *Alice in
Wonderland* tends to be overlooked. While the sprawling
nature of joining two Lewis
Carroll works together (*Alice's
Adventures in Wonderland* and
Through the Looking Glass) came at
the expense of a coherent story
line, the film boasts superb
animation and 14 catchy tunes.
Though offering some memorable sequences, including the
"Mad Tea Party" (*pictured*), the
film possesses an edginess (more
fully explored in the books) and
lacks some of the warmth associated with typical Disney projects.
That said, the film's almost post-
modern sensibility amply rewards
today's viewing audience.

June 23: Jacob Malik, the Soviet Union's delegate to the UN, urges all parties in the Korean War to sit down at the negotiating table.

June 25: CBS broadcasts the first color television program, *Premiere,* with Ed Sullivan and Arthur Godfrey, on station WCBS out of New York.

June 26: The Soviets officially propose a Korean War cease-fire.

June 28: *Amos 'n' Andy,* the first network television series to feature an all-black cast, debuts on CBS.

June 30: Following orders from the Truman Administration, General Matthew Ridgway announces that the UN has agreed to discuss armistice with North Korea.

July 4: The Madison, Wisconsin, *Capital Times* reports that 99 of 100 people who were offered a petition comprised of quotes from the Declaration of Independence and Bill of Rights refused to sign, often citing the "subversive" text.

July 10: North and South Korean delegations meet in the North Korean town of Kaesong to begin the long process of negotiating a cease-fire.
• Author Dashiell Hammett is sentenced to six months for contempt, following his refusal to reveal the names of Communist sympathizers to HUAC.

July 12: More than 3,000 white protesters riot in Cicero, Illinois, near Chicago, after a black family moves into town.

July 14: The first national park in honor of an African-American, the George Washington Carver National Monument in Joplin, Missouri, opens its gates.

July 18: "Jersey" Joe Walcott wins the world heavyweight boxing championship with a seventh-round knockout of Ezzard Charles.

Fresh from the success of *Sunset Boulevard,* director Billy Wilder was ready to tackle a theme close to his heart—the public demand for news as entertainment and the press that fed into it. In 1951 such cynicism was seldom expressed in movies, much less utilized as a premise. But in the film *Ace in the Hole,* Kirk Douglas (*pictured*) stars as an opportunistic reporter who single-handedly turns a tragedy (a person trapped in a cave) into a national sensation, while personally reaping the benefits. (The story itself was inspired by spelunker Floyd Collins's 1925 mishap.) But critics and audiences alike rejected their culpability in such exploitation, and Wilder's piercing film bombed.

Singing First Daughter Margaret Truman (*left*) and comedienne Portland Hoffa share a laugh during a broadcast of NBC's *The Big Show.* Margaret's father, President Harry Truman, was proud of his daughter, who had begun her singing career in 1947. She made her first television appearance on *Toast of the Town* in 1950, and went on an extended tour in 1951. When *Washington Post* music critic Paul Hume wrote an unenthusiastic review of one of Margaret's concert performances in December 1950, the President was understandably upset. He fired off an angry letter to Hume, claiming that if he ever met the critic, he would need a new nose as well as beefsteak for black eyes.

"[W]hen I was a young man, they had a law that they called 'reckless eyeballing.' If they saw you looking at a white woman, they would arrest you for reckless eyeballing....So, when you'd see white women, you had to look the other way."

—HAYWOOD BAUGH, DISCUSSING SEGREGATION IN RICHMOND, VIRGINIA

Jim Crow

THE 1950s ARE REGARDED as an era of peace and prosperity for Americans. But for the nation's nearly 15 million African-Americans—living in a parallel but inferior society—there was no real peace and very little prosperity.

In general, African-Americans were treated as second-class citizens, even after fighting for their country in both world wars. They could go only where they were allowed to go, do only what they were allowed to do, and always on terms set by white custom, comfort level, and law.

In the "Jim Crow" (segregated) South, African-Americans attended all-black schools and all-black churches. The segregation in the region was backed by state and local laws, all-white police departments, and even white terrorist groups, most notably the Ku Klux Klan. Some African-Americans served their black communities as doctors, lawyers, teachers, and preachers. But most took jobs serving white people—as field hands, maids, porters, cooks, bellhops, and busboys. Through "poll taxes," "understanding tests," and intimidation, southern whites kept African-Americans off the voting rolls.

Public signs clearly dictated blacks' public actions in the white world: where to sit, where to go to the bathroom, where to get their food. In addition to the degradation that came with "whites only" drinking fountains, libraries, and swimming pools, blacks had to call white men "Mister" and avoid eye contact with white women.

Northern blacks also lived in segregated communities. Most attended predominantly black schools and churches in black urban neighborhoods. Away from cities' cores, northern whites created segregated, white-only school districts, locked blacks out of most high-paying jobs, and used an array of methods, including violence, to prevent black families from moving into all-white neighborhoods.

In the early 1950s, NAACP attorneys began to fight school-segregation laws. They made gradual progress before breaking through with the 1954 *Brown v. Board of Education* decision. A year later, the Emmett Till lynching and Rosa Parks's arrest in Montgomery, Alabama, encouraged African-Americans, including black veterans, to mobilize against Jim Crow. Thousands of black activists joined forces to initiate the epic civil rights movement.

1951

July 20: Anti-Communist Spanish dictator Generalissimo Francisco Franco tells his cabinet that he intends to focus on Spain's thawing relationship with the U.S. • Jordan's King Abdullah is assassinated in a Jerusalem mosque. He will be succeeded by his son, Hussein.

August 3: In *Brown v. Board of Education,* the U.S. District Court of Kansas rules that no significant discrimination exists in Topeka's school system. However, it states that segregation is detrimental to black children. The decision is a ray of hope for the NAACP, which will appeal this case to the U.S. Supreme Court. *See* December 9, 1952.

August 5: Armed North Korean troops are spotted in supposedly neutral areas, leading the United Nations to freeze armistice negotiations with North Korea.

August 14: Newspaper magnate William Randolph Hearst dies at age 88.

August 18: President Truman invokes the emergency injunction in the Taft-Hartley Act to end a copper industry strike.

August 23: In a scandal that rocks the tradition-bound U.S. Military Academy at West Point, 90 cadets are expelled for cheating.

August 30: The U.S. Navy announces that a Douglas Skyrocket has shattered the previous altitude record of 13.7 miles.

September: Tennis phenom Maureen Connolly, age 16, wins the U.S. Open.

September 1: The United States, Australia, and New Zealand cement their security alliance with the signing of the Anzus Pact, at the Presidio in San Francisco.

September 3: Television's first daytime soap opera, *Search for Tomorrow,* airs on CBS.

An American border patrolman checks the identification of a Mexican farmworker in August 1951 as part of the Bracero Program. Begun in 1942 and reaffirmed by Public Law 78 in 1951, the program allowed Mexican nationals to work in the United States on a temporary basis. Farm owners in the Southwest argued that a severe shortage of farmworkers necessitated such a policy. More than three million such workers entered the U.S. in the 1950s. The influx during a time of high demand helped the Southwest prosper economically.

Stage performer Eddie Gaedel takes another ball in one of the greatest pranks in American sports history. On August 19, 1951, St. Louis Browns owner Bill Veeck activated Gaedel for one day and one at-bat against the Detroit Tigers. Wearing number ⅛, he walked on four straight pitches (in spite of the catcher's plea for pitcher Bob Cain to "keep it low"). Gaedel said he "felt like Babe Ruth" as he sauntered to first base. Veeck was an inveterate promoter, introducing such novelties as morning games (with free cereal for fans) and a panty hose giveaway.

Charm, "the magazine for women who work," was launched in 1950 by Street & Smith Publications. The particular personality of *Charm*—up-level yet friendly—was created by Helen Valentine and Estelle Ellis, who acted upon market studies that revealed the needs and desires of educated women. The magazine targeted young white women, mainly secretaries, since there were not enough female executives to sustain this glossy production. *Charm*'s very name suggests that physical attractiveness and stylishness were the keys to advancement for women in the workplace, an attitude prevalent in its day.

Rosemary Clooney was introduced to the big time via a novelty tune, but her sheer talent and charisma enabled her to become a respected jazz interpreter. By age 17, the self-described "girl singer" had landed a gig fronting bandleader Tony Pastor's orchestra. A solo recording contract followed, but to her dismay, her handlers foisted the silly "Come On-a My House" upon her. Two million copies of the record were sold, paving the way for Clooney to tackle more fitting material, such as the show ballad "Hey There" in 1952.

U.S. Army Sergeant John R. Rice, an American Indian, was killed while fighting in Korea in 1951. Local caretakers of a private cemetery in Sioux City, Iowa, stopped his burial when they realized that he was not a Caucasian. President Harry Truman was so incensed that he ordered that Rice be interred at Arlington National Cemetery in Washington, D.C. The incident exemplified Truman's commitment to forging advances in racial equality.

West Point cadet Donald Senich testifies at a public hearing in New York City on August 31, 1951. Senich was one of 90 students at the U.S. Military Academy dismissed for cheating or "cribbing" on tests in 1951. Thirty-seven of those expelled, including Senich, were on the Army football team. An appeal went all the way to President Harry Truman, who affirmed the decision. Famed football coach Red Blaik, who thought the charges were exaggerated, retained his job. However, Americans were shocked to hear about cheating at an institution founded on the principle of honor.

1951

September 4: In the first transcontinental television broadcast in the U.S., President Truman addresses the nation from Japan.

September 6: During a game of "William Tell," author William Burroughs accidentally shoots his common-law wife, Joan Vollmer, in the head, killing her.

September 8: Forty-nine nations sign the Japanese Peace Treaty in San Francisco, officially ending World War II and reestablishing Japanese sovereignty.

September 12: Sugar Ray Robinson captures the world middleweight boxing title with a 10th-round knockout of England's Randy Turpin.

September 13: One of the longest and bloodiest battles of the Korean War begins when U.S. Army troops move against Heartbreak Ridge. The month-long battle will take 3,700 American lives.

September 17: Marshall Holloway, an American physicist, is slated to lead the development of the hydrogen bomb at Los Alamos National Laboratory.

September 20: The North Atlantic Treaty Organization (NATO) confers membership on Greece and Turkey.

September 22: The University of Pittsburgh football team hosts Duke in the first live sporting event broadcast nationally. • David Ogilvy's print ad "The Man in the Hathaway Shirt" appears in *The New Yorker,* causing a sensation and ushering in the era of creative advertising.

September 24: For the second time, following further development, the Soviets test their plutonium bomb.

September 26–28: Ash from North American forest fires in the early summer makes its way to Europe, causing the sun to appear blue over much of the continent.

Fashion model Suzy Parker poses provocatively for the cover of *Life* magazine. Parker, whose sister was also a successful model, failed to crack the industry when she was 14 because she was considered too tall. Fashion editor Diana Vreeland introduced her to famed modeling agent Eileen Ford, who launched her career. Parker helped redefine fashion during her association with designer Coco Chanel and went on to a movie career in the late 1950s, playing opposite such icons as Cary Grant and Gary Cooper.

By 1951 apartheid was established as public policy in South Africa. Blacks were officially barred from voting and had to carry passbooks to travel throughout the country. When blacks and whites had to mingle outside of the black townships, separate public facilities were established. They were marked either "Non Europeans" (for blacks) or "Europeans." Here, a police sergeant writes a summons because the railway bench is marked for the latter. (The protester is Manila Gandhi, son of Mahatma Gandhi.) The following year, the African National Congress, the nation's most prominent black organization, called for a "defiance campaign" against the apartheid regime.

An update of a Victorian-era amusement became big business when View-Masters were first marketed by Sawyer's Incorporated in 1939. Intended as an edifying diversion for grown-ups, the spring-loaded viewers enabled users to enjoy a series of full-color, three-dimensional tableaus from around the world. During the war, the viewers were used extensively for training purposes. But

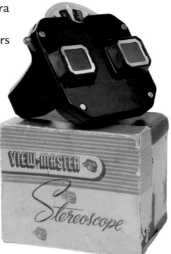

the 1951 acquisition of Tru-Vue by Sawyer came with an exclusive license to market scenes from Disney films. Kids of the '50s enjoyed viewing 3-D images of such characters as Cinderella and Peter Pan.

Trumpet player-arranger Shorty Rogers exemplified the West Coast "cool jazz" scene that arose in the late 1940s as a counterpoint to the harder sounds of bebop. The 10-inch LP *Modern Sounds* (1951) was smart and innovative, even revolutionary, because Rogers gave him-

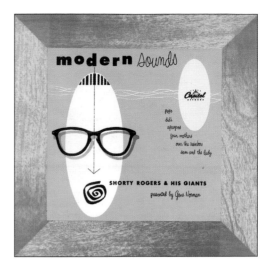

self and his "Giants" a large canvas on which to subtly meander and experiment. Personnel included Art Pepper on alto sax, Jimmy Giuffre on tenor, Shelley Manne on drums, and Hampton Hawes on piano.

The Day the Earth Stood Still was not an ordinary sci-fi film. Unlike typical space-invasion movies, director Robert Wise's film is a cautionary tale, based on the premise that humans' warring ways inevitably will lead to their own destruction. Michael Rennie stars as Klaatu, a sober emissary from deep space with a Christ-like message of peace. Making this film at the height of the Red Scare was an incredibly bold move, especially since it took place in Washington, D.C. Bernard Hermann's eerie, evocative score provides an undercurrent of suspense to this timeless classic.

The Catcher in the Rye

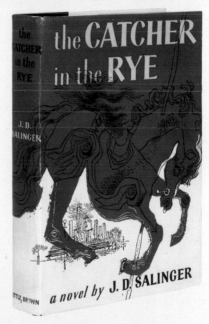

IN THE EARLY 1980S, a reclusive writer's sole novel made the news when two sociopaths sang its praises. Both John Lennon's killer and President Ronald Reagan's attacker used their moment of infamy to promote *The Catcher in the Rye* as recommended reading. Despite the sources of the advice, J. D. Salinger's book is an American classic, with particular appeal to adolescents making the rocky transition to adulthood.

In *Catcher*, 16-year-old Holden Caulfield has been kicked out of yet another prep school, this time before the Christmas holidays. Unprepared to face his parents just yet, he embarks on a bizarre odyssey from Pennsylvania to home, spending a few days in New York City en route. There, he crosses paths with all manner of humanity. With bewilderment and moments of crystal lucidity, Holden's first-person narration articulates the inherent confusion of those recognizing the world's hypocrisies. He sees himself as a savior of innocents, offering protection from the corrupting effects of "phonies."

With precision and authenticity, Salinger paints a portrait of a lonely but perceptive youth, told with compassion and understanding. His raw (by 1950s standards) language and adult themes would unnerve conservative school board members for the remainder of the century.

A zoologist and geneticist, Rachel Carson authored *The Sea Around Us* (1951). The best-selling book resonates with what Carson called "the poetry" of the sea and its interconnected systems: marine and other life; islands, beaches, and undersea mountain ranges; ocean currents; the water itself; and the delicate balance that must be maintained if the oceans and humanity are to survive. A theatrical documentary of the same name was released in 1952, the year Carson received the National Book Award. Her most widely read book, *Silent Spring,* was published in 1962.

A model looks somewhat bemused as she illustrates how to wear falsies. By 1951 the Sears department store carried more than 20 variations of the breast enhancers. With the rise in popularity of such buxom actresses as Jayne Mansfield and Marilyn Monroe, a big bosom was in style in the 1950s, and falsies seemed to provide the answer for some women. Later in the decade, slender Audrey Hepburn would offer a counterimage.

Comedian Red Skelton scores big laughs with his version of a 1950s television "test pattern." After the networks had signed off for the night, a test pattern—sporting the image of an Indian chief—served notice that it was time to go to bed (and helped station technicians keep their signals in focus). The advent of 24-hour programming eventually retired the Indian for good. As for Skelton, his long-running variety show premiered on September 30, 1951. Portraying an array of characters that included Freddie the Freeloader, the veteran slapstick comedian kept audiences laughing for nearly 30 years.

The roots of Monty Python and other absurdist British comedy acts can be traced to *The Goon Show,* an ensemble BBC radio comedy that began in 1951. The core troupe consisted of (*from left*) Peter Sellers, show originator Spike Milligan, Michael Bentine, and Harry Secombe. With each playing a multitude of characters, the Goons made their reputation by shattering comic conventions. They used outrageous wordplay and a rich array of sound effects to enact their surreal, satiric works. Frequent targets included politicians, the military, show business, and British class structure.

Marlon Brando

"METHOD" ACTING WAS PIONEERED by 19th century drama coach Konstantin Stanislavski. As embodied by alumni of Lee Strasberg's Actors Studio in New York, it demanded that thespians draw upon their own emotional experiences, thereby imbuing their roles with authenticity. No other actor in the 1950s displayed more command of this skill than Marlon Brando.

Brando's work in such films as *Viva Zapata!* (1952), *The Wild One* (1953), and *On the Waterfront* (1954) was electrifying. But he made perhaps his biggest impression with his second film, reprising a role he had played to great acclaim on the stage: Stanley Kowalski in Tennessee Williams's *A Streetcar Named Desire* (1951). His animalistic performance fully captured the primitive, inarticulate amorality of the lead character.

Brando burst onto the theatrical scene virtually fully formed in the 1940s. His Broadway debut at age 20 in *I Remember Mama* drew critical notice, as did his next three roles. By the time *Streetcar* arrived, it was like the second coming. Reviewers were beside themselves with adulation for the 23-year-old's instinctive grasp of such a demanding part. Said one, "Nothing human [is] foreign to him." Brando, said a director, had the "natural dangerousness and unpredictability that's always exciting in the theater."

Brando's first film, *The Men* (1950), delayed his film interpretation of Kowalski for one year. Elia Kazan, who had directed Brando in *Streetcar* on Broadway, brought him along to nail the part a second time, this time for the cameras. Despite the obvious antihero qualities of the role, it vaulted the actor into the Hollywood spotlight. But mass adulation was a crown that never fit Brando well. Off the set, his outspoken views and anti-stardom persona signaled that a new breed of actors had arrived, those with little use for the trappings of fame and wholly dedicated to mastering their craft.

One year after his film debut, in Stanley Kramer's *The Men,* actor Marlon Brando (*right*) sealed his fate as a legend with his performance as Stanley Kowalski in the film version of Tennessee Williams's *A Streetcar Named Desire.* Directed by Elia Kazan, the movie also starred Vivian Leigh (*left*) and Kim Hunter. It's doubtful that many audiences were prepared to experience Brando's brutal and frankly sexual performance, set in the steamy squalor of New Orleans's French Quarter. But under Kazan's brilliant direction, Williams's powerful play made for compelling viewing. The film went on to win four Oscars out of 12 nominations.

1951

October 1: The first baseball game broadcast live coast-to-coast features the New York Giants and the Brooklyn Dodgers in Game 1 of their playoff series. The Giants win, 3–1.

October 3: Bobby Thomson sends his New York Giants to the World Series with a ninth-inning home run off Brooklyn's Ralph Branca in Game 3 of their series.

October 7: Henry Gurney, British diplomat, is assassinated by Communist insurgents in Singapore.

October 10: The New York Yankees beat the New York Giants 4–3 in Game 6 of the World Series to win their third straight title.

October 15: *I Love Lucy,* starring Lucille Ball and Desi Arnaz, airs for the first time, on CBS.

October 16: Pakistan's first prime minister, Leaquat Ali Khan, is assassinated in Rawalpindi.

October 18: British military personnel in the Suez Canal Zone take control of public utilities and communications in an effort to increase security.

October 19: President Truman signs an act formally ending World War II in the Atlantic Theater.

October 22: The U.S. Navy tests a fully controllable, one-man, rocket-powered helicopter backpack, hoping to revolutionize warfare. The Navy ultimately will determine that the devices would not be cost-effective.

October 25: Armistice negotiations resume following a 63-day hiatus. The location has been moved to Panmunjom, located on the border between the two Koreas. • Conservative Winston Churchill is elected prime minister of England.

October 28: Coleman Young helps establish the National Negro Labor Council to combat unfair hiring and employment practices.

Wounded U.S. soldiers are carried to an aid station after being ambushed on October 5, 1951, while making their way to the rear. The soldiers had been part of the bloody battle of Heartbreak Ridge for the previous two weeks. While the Communists were boycotting the truce negotiations, General Matthew Ridgway had ordered a major U.S. offensive in the area to pressure their return to the peace table and to gain territory. This battle, which was only one component of the plan, resulted in 3,700 U.S. casualties, while the overall operation saw 33,665 Americans killed or wounded. However, UN forces did gain some important defensive positions.

Stymied militarily, the Communist Chinese and North Koreans agreed to open peace talks, which began on July 10, 1951. However, Chinese and North Korean leaders suspended the talks on August 22, ostensibly because the U.S. had bombed near the conference site. This editorial cartoon, created by Art Bimrose in October, shows a saddened symbol of peace amid pages torn from a calendar, symbolizing American frustration that peace still seemed so far away. The Communists came back to the table in October, but the war dragged on.

The Shot Heard 'Round the World

IN RETROSPECT, the New York Giants and Brooklyn Dodgers were perhaps too closely intertwined—their rivalry so intense as to push fans to the edge. As sportswriter Bruce Lowitt put it, only half jokingly, "people got knifed over who was a better pitcher, Carl Erskine or Sal Maglie."

The Giants and Dodgers were the only teams in Major League history to play in the same city, in the same league, at the same time. They played each other 22 times a year—half in Brooklyn's compact, quirky Ebbets Field (with its famously rabid fans) and half in the Giants' mammoth Polo Grounds.

Leo Durocher and Bobby Thomson

In summer 1951, Brooklynites did all the boasting. Led by future Hall of Famers Jackie Robinson, Duke Snider, and Roy Campanella, the Dodgers held a 13½-game lead in the National League as late as August 12. The Giants, though, refused to die. Managed by former Dodgers skipper Leo Durocher and ignited by rookie Willie Mays, New York went 39–8 down the stretch to catch their hated rivals. A three-game playoff was scheduled to determine the league champion, and the clubs split the first two contests.

Entering the bottom of the ninth of Game 3, the Dodgers felt as comfortable as they had in early August, leading 4–1. The Giants, though, had one more comeback in them. Alvin Dark and Don Mueller singled, and with one out Whitey Lockman doubled to make it 4–2. Dodgers pitcher Ralph Branca was called in to put out the fire.

With two men on, New York's Bobby Thomson stepped to the plate. On the second pitch, he rifled a shot that just cleared the left field fence—and sent fans into hysterics. "The Giants win the pennant!" blared broadcaster Russ Hodges, over and over again. Thomson's homer was soon dubbed the "shot heard 'round the world."

British Conservative leader Winston Churchill flashes his famous "V for Victory" a few weeks before the 1951 general election in Great Britain. His gesture proved prophetic, as the famed wartime prime minister was elected to that office again. According to historian Peter Clarke, a major reason for Churchill's victory was his promise to deal with a housing shortage that was especially critical for World War II veterans and their growing families. Churchill, 76 years old in 1951, retired four years later.

Based on his 1947 expedition, Thor Heyerdahl's best-selling *Kon-Tiki* documented the Norwegian's successful Pacific Ocean crossing. The biologist had long been fascinated with indigenous tales of an ancient sun god, Tiki, and his settlement of the Polynesian islands via a sea journey from the east. To Heyerdahl, this meant Peru. Eager to test whether a trip implementing primitive technology was possible, he set out with a crew of five on a balsa wood raft while facing universal derision. Braving storms and sharks, the group completed the 4,300-mile trip in just over 100 days, proving Heyerdahl's theory possible, if not likely.

1951

October 31: Princess Elizabeth and her husband, the Duke of Edinburgh, make their U.S. television debut, as their visit to Windsor, Ontario, becomes the first program broadcast internationally.

November 1: The Algerian National Liberation Front fires the first shot in its war for independence from French colonial rule. • The Johnson Publishing Company publishes its first issue of *Jet,* which offers weekly news coverage of black America. • For the first time, U.S. military training exercises in preparation for nuclear war are conducted using infantry troops.

November 7: Blue-eyed crooner Frank Sinatra marries actress Ava Gardner.

November 10: The mayor of Englewood, New Jersey, calls the mayor of Alameda, California, with the first transcontinental direct-dial phone call.

November 11: President Truman, in his capacity as head of the Democratic Party, offers to sponsor General Dwight D. Eisenhower for president, essentially guaranteeing the nomination. *See* January 7, 1952.

November 12: In anticipation of a truce with the North Koreans, the U.S. Eighth Army is ordered to cancel plans for offensive action and focus solely on defense.

November 14: The U.S. and Yugoslavia sign a pact establishing a mutual military alliance. • According to Colonel James M. Hanley of the Eighth Army, more than 5,500 U.S. prisoners of war have died at the hands of Communist forces in Korea.

November 17: Britain announces that it has developed the first heating system powered by atomic energy.

November 18: Edward R. Murrow amazes his television audience by showing live, split-screen images of both the Brooklyn and Golden Gate bridges on his CBS program, *See It Now.*

From a distance of six miles, American soldiers watch a nuclear explosion at the Nevada Test Site on November 1, 1951. This was the first time U.S. troops actually participated in such a test. The military was considering building a "penatomic" unit that could exploit the use of a tactical atomic bomb against an enemy. The troops were provided with dosimeters, which monitored radiation exposure, but the government claimed that such an explosion would have minimal fallout. A 1999 report by the National Research Council showed that, in fact, "tens of thousands" of Americans, including the soldiers in this operation, may have received excessive doses of radiation from nuclear tests.

A BLINDING, DEAFENING BLAST

THE SOUND OF THE PLANE gradually decreased and again silence returned. No one spoke. Subconsciously I made an act of contrition and realized a rapid increase in my heartbeat. Suddenly it happened. The pitch black of night turned into a blinding light 100 times brighter than the sun. We were all wearing protective eye gear but instinctively I raised my arm to shield my eyes. In doing so, I looked up and could see the plane trying to escape the inevitable shock wave that was moving rapidly towards it.

The epicenter of the blast was the color of white incandescent heat rapidly changing to a bright orange, then to a fiery crimson fading to a purple glow. The entire landscape around us was lit up in an eerie unrealistic light from horizon to horizon as far as the eye could see. The light was so intense that THERE WERE NO SHADOWS.

As the mushroom cloud began to rise—still glowing brightly—I dropped to one knee. As I did so, the first positive shock wave struck. The concussion was equal to a 100-pound bag of sand hitting me in the chest. I was knocked backward quite some distance but was able to stay on my feet. My fur-lined flight cap was blown off my head. The tremendous explosive sound was deafening, unlike any other man-made sound ever created.

—ARMY ENLISTED MAN GERALD SCHULTZ (WHO WOULD DIE OF LEUKEMIA AT AGE 68), DESCRIBING AN ATOMIC BLAST AT FRENCHMAN FLAT IN NEVADA ON FEBRUARY 5, 1951

Ills of Atomic Testing

WHEN THE ATOMIC ENERGY COMMISSION declared that the Nevada desert was "virtually uninhabitable," the U.S. government took steps to be sure it stayed that way. Above-ground detonations of atomic bombs began at the Nevada Test Site with Operation Ranger on January 27, 1951—even though many thousands of people in Nevada and Utah who lived downwind of the explosions would be contaminated by drifting fallout. A top-secret government memo dismissed those Americans as a "low-use segment of the population." Isolated and without influence, they became the first A-bomb victims located outside of Japan and the USSR (where reckless above-ground testing began in 1949).

At first, the American A-bomb tests were events of some novelty. Although locals eventually grew bored with the distant flashes and rumbles, Las Vegas hotels and casinos regarded each blast as a boon for tourism.

For some in the U.S. Army, the blasts were anything but fun. The military was curious about radiation's effects on human beings; infantrymen were routinely positioned near blast zones, sometimes as close as 2,500 yards from Ground Zero, and then ordered to leave their trenches and march toward the mushroom clouds. In 1953 sheep herders in Utah discovered their stock covered with burns, sores, and lesions. In May and June of that year, some 4,500 sheep died mysteriously. Newborn lambs were severely undersized, and many died shortly after birth.

The greater tragedy came later, when abnormal numbers of regional residents, and former soldiers, contracted exotic forms of cancer that resulted in hideous, painful surgeries and premature deaths. Leukemia took a particular toll on children.

From 1951 to 1963, 126 clouds of fallout drifted eastward from the Nevada desert. Each cloud spread levels of radiation comparable to that released during the 1986 Chernobyl disaster. No state in the continental 48 was spared exposure.

On November 7, 1951, singer Frank Sinatra married twice-divorced actress Ava Gardner. Sinatra's relationship with the star of *The Killers* came as his own film career was in a nosedive and his record sales were plummeting. Years of hard living and over-singing had strained his vocal cords to the point of hemorrhage. Sinatra's days as a bobby-soxer phenomenon long behind him, he was forced in 1950 to accept a television gig (*The Frank Sinatra Show*), a move regarded at the time as a dead-end. Hitting bottom so dramatically made his eventual comeback from oblivion all the more remarkable.

Every few months, it seemed, television producers in the early 1950s treated viewers to something new and extraordinary. On November 18, 1951, *See It Now,* hosted by Edward R. Murrow (*pictured*), premiered on CBS. Murrow told viewers, as they looked at live split-screen images of the Golden Gate Bridge (*left*) and the Brooklyn Bridge, that for the first time they were seeing the Atlantic and Pacific oceans simultaneously. In that instant, distance had been obliterated.

1951

November 27: A cease-fire line is agreed upon in talks at Panmunjom, and UN forces establish their defensive positions. This containment policy will remain indefinitely.

December 9: Viet Minh General Giap tests a successful new strategy against French forces—hit and run attacks followed by retreat. It becomes the hallmark of guerrilla warfare in Vietnam.

December 11: New York Yankees superstar Joe DiMaggio announces that he is retiring from baseball.

December 13: Colombia's 14th ratification of the Bogota Charter creates the Organization of American States. • A meeting with FBI Director J. Edgar Hoover convinces President Truman of the urgent need to purge the government of seditious employees.

December 16: New York, a city whose residents consume 1.2 million bagels in a typical weekend, is bagel-free due to a union contract dispute.

December 17: In a petition to the UN, William Patterson and Paul Robeson charge the U.S. government with genocide against African-Americans.

December 20: The nuclear reactor at Arco, Idaho, generates electricity for the first time.

December 21: A devastating coal mine explosion in West Frankfort, Illinois, kills 119 people.

December 24: With support from the UN, former Italian colony Libya becomes an independent state. • NAACP activist Harry Tyson Moore and his wife, Harriette, are killed by a bomb in their home in Mims, Florida.

December 31: Inventor Philip Edwin Ohmart announces his development of a battery that converts atomic energy to electrical energy.

By the end of 1945, Japan was occupied by more than 350,000 American troops and numerous administrators. One of the key mandates from General Douglas MacArthur was a revival of war-ravaged Japanese industry. A flood of inexpensive toys manufactured for export was perhaps the most noticeable evidence of Occupied Japan's reindustrialization. Most of these playthings were simple geegaws made of celluloid, rubber, wood, or tin. Turn the key and this felt-covered tin elephant bobs his head and twirls his tail. The factory stamping is on the bottoms of the elephant's hind feet. U.S. occupation of Japan ended in the spring of 1952.

Spanish Surrealist Salvador Dali often was called a genius—and many agreed with him! Whether viewing Dali as a groundbreaking visionary or a self-aggrandizing charlatan, few were left without strong feelings about the artist or his imaginative work. Here he shows off his controversial 1951 painting, *Christ of St. John of the Cross.* It exemplifies Dali's considerable skill at coupling Renaissance stylings with bizarre symbolism, often drawn from his dreams. Like others among the avant-garde, Dali found it impossible to separate his life from his art, at least publicly.

I Love Lucy

By 1950 actress Lucille Ball's career had stalled. Attempts at film stardom had taken as many forms as her hair color, but all led nowhere. Moreover, Ball's steady radio gig in *My Favorite Husband* kept her apart from her traveling bandleader husband, Desi Arnaz. Frantic to find a joint project that would preserve their shaky marriage, she petitioned studio bosses to retool the planned television adaptation of the radio show. Instead of making her TV husband a Midwestern banker, she insisted that he be a professional Cuban musician.

The network was loath to disturb the formula, feeling that the coupling was just too implausible. But "we *are* married," Ball protested. Eager to prove their viability as a comedic team, the couple took their act on the road, honing the characters before live audiences throughout the country. Rave reviews won over reluctant network bosses, and in 1951 *I Love Lucy* made its Monday night debut on CBS.

The domestic farce centered on nightclub performer Ricky Ricardo, and his starstruck wife Lucy's incessant attempts to enter show business over his objections. Costarring Vivian Vance and William Frawley as their landlords/best friends, the show was an immediate smash. Lucy's harebrained schemes and hilarious facial contortions kept viewers in stitches. In 1953 the unprecedented working of Ball's real-life pregnancy into the script resulted in a ratings bonanza when she gave birth.

To spare themselves a long-distance commute, Arnaz insisted on filming the shows in advance (with three cameras), rather than broadcasting them live. In bucking established practice, the lucrative concept of reruns was spawned. *I Love Lucy* would shape a generation's viewing experience, with endless repeats of episodes depicting Lucy's misadventures at the candy factory, in the deep-freeze, stomping grapes, or pitching "Vitameatavegamin." Her ubiquitous presence on the tube would endear her to audiences for decades to come.

In their only cinematic pairing, two of Hollywood's biggest stars found themselves cast as mismatched companions in director John Huston's *The African Queen*. Veteran tough guy Humphrey Bogart (*left*) stars as the gin-soaked Charlie Allnut, a river pilot who must spirit proper, high-strung missionary Rose Sayer (Katharine Hepburn, *right*) to safety on the title vessel. Circumstances lead to an "opposites attract" story line. The film gave audiences a chance to see two screen legends battling leeches, German troops, and each other. Bogie earned an Oscar for his performance.

1951

New & Notable

Books

The Ballad of the Sad Cafe
    by Carson McCullers
The Caine Mutiny by Herman Wouk
The Catcher in the Rye by J. D. Salinger
The Cruel Sea by Nicholas Monsarrat
The Day of the Triffids
    by John Wyndham
From Here to Eternity by James Jones
Lie Down in Darkness by William Styron
The Mechanical Bride
    by Marshall McLuhan
One Lonely Night by Mickey Spillane
The Rebel by Albert Camus

Movies

The African Queen
Alice in Wonderland
An American in Paris
The Day the Earth Stood Still
Death of a Salesman
The Lavender Hill Mob
A Place in the Sun
A Streetcar Named Desire
The Thing

Songs

"Cold, Cold Heart" by Hank Williams
"Come On-a My House"
    by Rosemary Clooney
"Cry" by Johnnie Ray
    and the Four Lads
"Hello, Young Lovers" by Perry Como
"Sixty Minute Man" by Billy Ward
    & His Dominoes
"Too Young" by Nat King Cole

Television

Amos 'n' Andy
Dragnet
I Love Lucy
The Red Skelton Show
The Roy Rogers Show
See It Now

Theater

Don Juan in Hell
Gigi
The King and I
The Moon Is Blue
Oklahoma!
The Rose Tattoo

In the pre-rock 'n' roll era, no singer could grab audiences by the ears and leave them emotionally drained like Johnnie Ray. The most unlikely of jukebox heroes (he did, after all, sport a hearing aid), the singer was "discovered" while performing in a Detroit R&B club. Ray was tabbed as a white man who possessed the raw dynamics of a black soul singer. He enjoyed several million-selling records, beginning with the 1951 hit "Cry"—which he did during live performances. Such histrionics led critics to dub him the "Prince of Wails," but his popularity withstood the derision.

American housewives enjoy a '50s phenomenon: the Tupperware party. These storage containers were developed by Earl Silas Tupper in 1942 after he discovered that certain plastics could be molded into flexible containers. Tupper initially sold the product through retail stores and door-to-door. But in 1951 he pulled them from the shelves when Brownie Wise, a single mother from Detroit and a top saleswoman, convinced him that having housewives give Tupperware parties would be the most effective distribution scheme. The parties became an instant hit nationwide, providing middle-class housewives with a way to earn money while remaining at home.

Born soon after Italian tenor Enrico Caruso died, Mario Lanza would live his life forever connected to his idol. Despite his modest Philadelphia origins, Lanza's gifts were nurtured early on. By his teens, he was showcasing his exceptional voice in classical concerts. After the war, the ambitious singer landed a film contract with MGM. In 1951 he starred in *The Great Caruso* while reaping the rewards of his hit singles, such as "Be My Love." Lanza's enormous talent was equaled by oversized appetites. After years of excessive eating, dieting, and alcohol consumption, he died of a heart attack at age 38 in 1959.

The self-anointed "King of the Cowboys," Roy Rogers made a smooth transition from the big screen to television in late 1951. With wife Dale Evans at his side, Rogers exemplified mythic western values, including honor, bravery, and fair play. *The Roy Rogers Show* became a staple of children's entertainment during its run, spurring sales of accoutrements ranging from plastic guitars to guns and holsters. Aboard his trusty horse, Trigger, Rogers battled the bad guys between musical interludes. No episode was properly resolved without the signature sign-off of "Happy Trails."

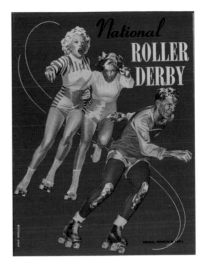

In 1935 Chicago promoter Leo Seltzer emulated the success of six-day bicycle racing and dance marathons with the roller derby. He hoped that his notion of an endurance "race" of 57,000 nonstop laps would appeal to Depression-weary audiences. He was right. By 1937 physical contact between skaters began to manifest itself, and a decade later, rough and tumble roller derby (by now distinguished by co-ed teams, with men and women who skated alternately) was embraced by early television. Officially sanctioned programs such as this one from 1951 were distributed nationally; local-city inserts had skater bios and scorekeeping grids. The cover artwork seen here is by Lon Keller, for many decades one of America's premier sports illustrators.

In 1951 Hallmark Cards approached NBC with a proposal for a series of high-quality theatrical presentations. For the first, the network commissioned composer Gian-Carlo Menotti to create a one-act opera. On Christmas Eve 1951, *Amahl and the Night Visitors* premiered. Inspired by the painting "The Adoration of the Magi," Menotti crafted the story of a crippled boy (played by Chet Allen, *right*) and his widowed mother (Rosemary Kuhlmann) who host the three wise men on their journey to see the Christ child. Both *Amahl* and the *Hallmark Hall of Fame* would become much-loved traditions.

"McCarthy first began to make himself notable during my administration, and I recognized him immediately as a fake and a phony and as a real menace to our country and our principles of freedom and decency."

—President Harry Truman

1952

McCarthyism

WILLIAM O. DOUGLAS WAS NOT a typical Supreme Court justice. He had grown up in the far reaches of the great Northwest, and an awed law student described him as a "Remington cowboy; a man of leather and rawhide tough." President Franklin Roosevelt had appointed him to the court in 1939 because he believed that Douglas had the guts and intelligence to take on entrenched interests and the stifling power of conventional wisdom. Still, Douglas surprised a lot of people in 1952 when he drew back his judicial robes to make public his disgust with what he called "the black silence of fear."

In the January 13, 1952, issue of *The New York Times Magazine,* Justice Douglas attacked the growing power of McCarthyism in the United States. Douglas was no friend of communism. He despised Soviet totalitarianism and had no sympathy for the American Communist Party. But he believed that the domestic anti-Communist crusade, led by Senator Joseph McCarthy (R–WI) and his supporters, had run amuck, crushing civil liberties and the independence of thought that made America great.

Douglas wrote: "Fear is fanned to a fury. Good and honest men are pilloried. Character is assassinated. Fear runs rampant...." He concluded: "The great danger of this period is not inflation, nor the national debt, nor atomic warfare. The great, the critical danger is that we will so limit or narrow the range of permissible discussion and permissible thought that we will become

In this 1951 photo, Senator Joseph McCarthy (*seated, left*) promises a group of reporters that he will reveal a 100-percent accurate list of 26 State Department employees who are suspected Communists, but only if they grant him immunity from libel. They refused.

Supreme Court Justice William O. Douglas pores over one of his law books. In an article he penned for *The New York Times Magazine* in 1952, Douglas used his knowledge of the law and his commitment to toleration of unpopular ideas to excoriate McCarthyism.

McCarthy makes a point about alleged Communist subversion in America in the cover photo of this 1952 publication. In it, he answered dozens of "questions" (posed by himself) and condemned those who dared to "smear" him.

victims of the orthodox school.... Our weakness grows when we become intolerant of opposing ideas, depart from our standards of civil liberties, and borrow the policeman's philosophy from the enemy we detest."

Douglas knew that Soviet spies really were in the United States and that they represented a genuine threat. But he also believed that hysterical attacks by anti-Communist zealots against anyone who dared to think outside the mainstream were destroying the moral fiber and spiritual strength of the nation.

Senator McCarthy was the most visible face of anticommunism in the United States. And it was not a pretty face. One of McCarthy's earliest and most outspoken opponents was *Washington Post* editorial cartoonist Herbert Block (Herblock), who had coined the phrase "McCarthyism" back in spring 1950—right after the senator's baseless charge that more than 200 Communist agents worked for the U.S. State Department. Block always drew the senator in his characteristic scowling pose, with heavy jowls darkened by black stubble.

Besides making general accusations that the federal government was riddled with Communist agents and supporters of the Soviet Union, McCarthy maliciously accused Secretary of State Dean Acheson (whom he called a "pompous diplomat in striped pants with a phony British accent") of being a Communist sympathizer. The entire State Department, McCarthy fumed, was nothing but a "lace handkerchief crowd" filled with "bright young men who are born with silver spoons in their mouths." Spoiled, weak, and ideologically tinted either "pink" or "red," America's diplomatic corps, McCarthy declared, had turned over China, Poland, and the rest of Eastern Europe to the iron rule of communism.

McCarthy also singled out World War II hero General George Marshall, who was secretary of defense under President Harry Truman, for opprobrium, insisting that Marshall was, at the least, a fellow traveler of the Communist cause. McCarthy loved newspaper headlines and was willing to say almost anything to get them. He targeted every branch of the federal government, including the Army, in his hunt for headlines and scapegoats. As one of McCarthy's critics would later exclaim, "Have you no sense of decency, sir?"

Washington insiders knew that McCarthy often prepared himself for his attacks by gulping a water glass full of scotch whiskey, and that once in the public eye he had little or no regard for the factual basis of his charges. Almost none of McCarthy's Senate colleagues liked or respected him, but a great many feared him. The electoral fate of Maryland Senator Millard Tydings intensified that fear. Tydings had officially reported to the Senate in July 1950 that McCarthy's charges against State Department officials were without merit. McCarthy attacked Tydings as soft on Communists, and that November Tydings lost his Senate seat. Politicians as different as President Harry Truman and General Dwight Eisenhower knew that in 1952 McCarthy and his anti-Communist crusade were riding a tidal wave of popular support.

In part, that support had been built on the reality of a genuine Communist threat to American principles and national security. In the immediate post–World War II years, Soviet ruler Joseph Stalin had dropped an "Iron Curtain" over almost all of Eastern Europe. Soviet tanks guarded Communist governments installed by the Kremlin. In 1949 Communist revolutionary Mao Zedong of China defeated the American-supported army of Chiang Kai-shek. Under Mao, China became "red."

While Acheson blandly announced that "the ominous result of the civil war in China was beyond the control of the government of the United States," many Americans refused to believe that the world's most powerful nation could not have saved its Chinese ally. Somebody in the American government, they believed, must have deliberately "lost" China to the Communists. Then, in June 1950, the military forces of Kim Il Sung began their war to unify all of Korea under Communist control.

Communist forces really were on the march in the immediate post–World War II years, and the threat of those Red armies stirred Americans' anxieties. U.S. citizens were even more frightened by the FBI's well-publicized revelations that Communist spies were hard at work right in the United States. The most sensational discovery was that America's atomic weapons program had been riddled with Soviet agents. The story had first broken in 1950 when British physicist Klaus Fuchs confessed that while he was working at the secret World War II weapons laboratories in Los Alamos, New Mexico, he had passed atomic secrets to a Soviet spy network. Those revelations led to the arrest of American Communist Party members Ethel and Julius Rosenberg. In 1951, after a spectacular trial, the Rosenbergs were found guilty of having taken part in a "diabolical conspiracy to destroy a God-fearing nation" and were sentenced to death. They were executed in 1953.

A great deal of controversy surrounded the Rosenbergs' trial, and for many years people debated their guilt. In truth, the American government had proof that the Rosenbergs were spies, and that many other Americans were involved in a Soviet atomic-secrets spy ring or in other acts of espionage.

Americans responded to the combined threat of Communist victories abroad and Communist subversion right in the United States with a great

Senator Millard Tydings (D–MD) *(center)* chairs a meeting of the Senate Foreign Relations Committee, whose July 1950 report blasted Senator McCarthy's anti-Communist crusade. In retaliation, McCarthy used such dirty tricks as a fake photograph showing Tydings talking to American Communist leader Earl Browder to help sink Tydings's 1950 bid for reelection.

deal of fear. Reckless individuals, most famously Senator McCarthy, traded on that anxiety with craven acts of demagoguery. By the end of 1952, a handful of genuine Communist spies had been rounded up and prosecuted. But the anti-Communist crusade too often punished people for what they thought— or even *had* thought years earlier—not for anything they actually did.

Schoolteachers lost their jobs. University professors were fired. Actors, writers, and others involved in the entertainment industry were blacklisted, unable to work at their trades for years. Labor unionists were forced to give up their careers. African-American champions of racial justice, such as Paul Robeson and W.E.B. DuBois, were refused passports by the State Department, as were hundreds of political radicals. Outspoken foreigners, even international celebrity Charlie Chaplin, were refused admission to the United States.

Fans of Senator McCarthy support his battle against alleged Communist subversion in the State Department and other American institutions. While the senator energized a vocal core of American conservatives, the majority of U.S. citizens viewed him unfavorably for most of his career.

As Justice Douglas wrote in 1952, the anti-Communist crusade, while mainly targeting individuals who had in some way been connected to the American Communist Party, served also to intimidate and repress a great many more Americans who were simply advocates of political reform or intellectual nonconformity. Douglas stated: "Fear has driven more and more men and women in all walks of life either to silence or to folds of the orthodox.... This fear has stereotyped our thinking, narrowed the range of free public discussion, and driven many thoughtful people to despair." It was not safe to challenge the political status quo.

In 1952 zealous anticommunism was a force throughout the United States. Cities and states had their own campaigns. In Texas, pharmacists had to swear loyalty oaths to the United States. So did professional wrestlers in Indiana, and people who wanted to fish in New York City. Local public librarians carefully policed their bookshelves and magazine racks, scouring for subversive literature. Racist politicians in the Deep South exclaimed that proponents of integration were nothing but Communists and that the National Association for the Advancement of Colored People (NAACP) was intertwined with the Communist cause. The anti-Communist crusade was far bigger than Joe McCarthy; it was a popular national campaign embraced by politicians, championed by the FBI, and cheered by a large portion of the American population.

Americans' fear of communism at home and abroad intensified popular support for a massive increase in military expenditures aimed at countering the Soviet threat. In 1950 President Truman received a secret report prepared by the National Security Council (NSC) arguing that the Soviet Union, "animated by a new fanatic faith, antithetical to our own…seeks to impose its absolute authority over the rest of the world." The NSC insisted that the Soviet threat mandated an unparalleled peacetime buildup of America's conventional military strength and of its emerging strategic nuclear arsenal.

President Truman agreed. From 1950 to the end of 1952, Truman and Congress increased defense spending in the United States from some $14 billion to nearly $45 billion—which was the lion's share of the federal budget.

America's commitment to achieving a nuclear weapons breakthrough accelerated accordingly. Just before the 1952 presidential election, Americans successfully tested the "Super," a thermonuclear weapon that was about a thousand times more powerful than the bomb that had destroyed Hiroshima. Less than a year later, the Soviets successfully tested a similar weapon.

Throughout the 1952 presidential election campaign, Republican candidate Dwight Eisenhower, while insisting that his administration would be even more anti-Communist than Truman's, did his best to dance around the specific issue of McCarthyism. Ike found McCarthy

Chicagoans crowd around a television set to watch a nuclear test. The spread of communism in Europe, the arms race between the U.S. and the USSR, and the Rosenberg spy case caused anxiety among Americans that McCarthy blatantly exploited.

personally distasteful, and he knew that McCarthy's charges were often unfounded. He also knew that McCarthy was a popular figure among Republican voters. Thus, he simply told his staff that he would not "get into the gutter with that guy." Taking on McCarthy, he added, would be like getting into "a pissing contest with a skunk."

When Eisenhower won the presidency in November, the Republican Party also took control of the Senate. Joe McCarthy was rewarded with the chairmanship of the Permanent Investigating Subcommittee of the Government Operations Committee. As 1952 ended, McCarthy's hunt for Communists was far from over. Only in 1954, when McCarthy began making wild, televised accusations that the U.S. Army was a hotbed of Communist activity did the American people begin to turn on their one-time champion. Though McCarthy was pulled down by his own recklessness and a spreading criticism of McCarthyism, the broader anti-Communist crusade continued with a vengeance throughout the 1950s.

1952

1952: Greece grants women universal suffrage. • The U.S. Justice Department files an antitrust lawsuit against DuPont. The company's relationships with General Motors, Standard Oil, and Ethyl come under heavy scrutiny during testimony. • House Resolution 698 is passed. This bill ends federal control of Indian lands, leaving the land open to purchase and exploitation by non-Indians. Some tribes are forced to sell portions of their land to survive. • Acting on a commission by the CIA, psychiatrist Henry P. Laughlin reports that lobotomy and other forms of psychosurgery have the potential to sway the thinking of Communists, or eliminate Communists as threats to American interests. Alter the brain's frontal lobes, Laughlin writes, and the patient's zeal to labor for a cause is markedly diminished.

1952: Jacques Cousteau leads the first underwater archaeological expedition, to salvage the hull of a 2,000-year-old Greek wine freighter buried in the mud off the coast of Marseilles. • Cuthbert C. Hurd and his colleague, James Birkenstock, develop the IBM 701, one of the first general purpose computers, at a cost of $3 million. • A street poll indicates that less than one in five Americans are currently reading a book, compared to 55 percent of British citizens. • The U.S. reports 300,000 cases of polio in 1952, the worst epidemic of the disease since 1916.

1952: Levittown, Pennsylvania, a planned community featuring prefabricated homes, opens. • The Gibson Les Paul solid-body electric guitar bursts onto the scene with a gold-top, nitro-cellulose lacquer finish and a $210 price tag. • Kentucky's Paducah Gaseous Diffusion Plant opens for business. In an experiment in the recycling of used nuclear reactor fuel, the Paducah facility fails to protect its employees from exposure to radiation.

In the early 1950s, Americans thought they were satisfied with their ritual of breakfast, coffee, and the morning paper. But then NBC gave them an alternative: a live version of the daily news, called *Today*. Dave Garroway (*pictured*), a proven talent at the network, was named the host of the New York City-based news and entertainment show. At 7 A.M. EST on January 14, 1952, Garroway introduced the world to what he called "a new kind of television." Audio news streamed in from Washington, D.C., London, and Germany. A remote camera in Chicago showed commuters. Just like that, Americans had a new morning habit.

International Business Machines (IBM) President Thomas J. Watson (*seated*) and Applied Science Division President Cuthbert C. Hurd examine IBM's breakthrough computer, the 701. Developed in 1952 for sale to the Defense Department during the Korean War, it was IBM's first true venture into the mainframe computer business. Although only 19 units were sold over the next three years, the 700 series ultimately catapulted IBM to the forefront of commercial computer sales. Also in 1952, the U.S. military took advantage of computer technology. The first U.S. H-bomb test was made possible because of mathematician John von Neumann's earlier development of the mathematical analyzer numerical integrator and computer (or MANIAC, for short).

In a sense, Ginny Dolls were a direct precursor to Barbie. These initially homemade creations were the first mass-produced dolls accessorized by a separate clothing line. Shown here are "Jim" and "Jan" from 1952's Brother and Sister series. The Vogue Doll Company enhanced the dolls as their popularity grew, adding "sleep eyes," walking legs, and bending knees. Today, the dolls are hugely collectible.

The first commercial jet-passenger airliner, a de Havilland Comet, taxis onto the runway at London's Heathrow Airport in February 1952. The jet was developed in 1949 by Britain's de Havilland Aircraft Company, which had had great success with the Spitfire and other fighter planes during World War II. Although the Comet was put through three years of grueling tests, it experienced numerous problems. After three crashes in 1953 and 1954, the Comet was grounded, with tests revealing cracks caused by metal fatigue. By the time the problem was solved in the late 1950s, the rival Boeing 707 and Douglas DC-8 had captured most of the market.

Crowds outside Buckingham Palace read the sad news that Britain's King George died of a heart attack on February 6, 1952. Although he had ascended to the throne in 1937 under the cloud of his brother Edward's abdication, George gained stature as the monarch who helped lead his nation through the difficult years during World War II. To mourn the king's passing, all theaters and cinemas were closed, as were pubs. According to *The Times* of London, restaurants remained open but were advised to cancel "any arrangements for music, dancing, or other entertainment."

Television viewers of the early 1950s took interest in Faye Emerson, host of *Wonderful Town,* for several reasons. First, she had been married to President Franklin Roosevelt's son, Elliott, before taking up with renowned band-leader Skitch Henderson. As a television host, Emerson earned praise for her wit, yet many men tuned in simply to ogle her considerable cleavage. Well aware of where public interest lay, Emerson willingly displayed herself. (It was said that she put the *V* in TV.) A network edict to cover up was rescinded after viewer outcry.

1952: Kraft Cheez Whiz, Pream nondairy creamer, Bird's Eye frozen peas, and Mrs. Paul's fish sticks are the latest American culinary offerings. • Pez candies, and their signature dispensers, are introduced to the U.S. • Kent cigarettes are introduced by the Lorillard Tobacco Company. According to their advertising campaign, Kents are outfitted with a unique filter that renders the cigarettes safe. In fact, the filters contain asbestos. • Legendary composer Ralph Vaughan Williams completes Sinfonia Antartica (Symphony No. 7).

January: In an early victory in the search for a birth control pill, Dr. Gregory Pincus discovers that progesterone can suppress ovulation in rabbits and rats.

January 1: Che Guevara, future Cuban revolutionary leader, leaves on a 4,000-mile motorcycle trip throughout northern Argentina. The observations he makes on this journey will help shape the course of his life.

January 2: The U.S. Supreme Court rules in favor of the plaintiff in *Rochin v. California*, forbidding unreasonable searches. This case is in response to an incident in which the Los Angeles police, in search of drugs, forced a subject to have his stomach pumped.

January 4–5: Some 500 marijuana and heroin dealers are netted in a massive, nationwide drug raid. • British Prime Minister Winston Churchill arrives in Washington, D.C., for an official state visit with President Harry Truman.

January 7: General Dwight D. Eisenhower issues a statement from his French headquarters that, were he to run for president, he would run as a Republican. However, he says that he will not actively seek the nomination. *See* April 11, 1952.

> "Mike Hammer drinks beer, not cognac, because I can't spell cognac." —MICKEY SPILLANE

Mickey Spillane

NEEDING CASH TO BUILD A HOUSE, Brooklyn-born ex-comic book writer Frank "Mickey" Spillane announced his intent to raise the funds by writing a mystery novel. With the laughter of his friends ringing in his ears, he sat down and quickly pounded out a story that had been incubating in his head for some time. Hitting the street in 1947, *I, The Jury* did more than raise the money Spillane needed; it introduced the world to forceful New York detective Mike Hammer.

The book's tremendous popularity contrasted sharply with the derision expressed by reviewers. As *I, The Jury* and successive works (including *My Gun Is Quick, Vengeance Is Mine!,* and *The Big Kill*) demonstrated, Hammer had little use for due process. Morality was a black or white proposition; honor demanded action, even if beyond legal bounds. Women were sexpots, connivers, or both.

Spillane's lurid exploitation of sex and carnage startled and intrigued readers—"violence as orgasm" was how critic John G. Cawelti described it. Moreover, Hammer's swift, heavy-handed brand of "justice" provided a cathartic release for readers in a world in which fairness seemed an arcane abstraction.

In the golden age of pulp fiction, Spillane reigned supreme. Over time, more than 200 million copies of his books were sold, making him the best-selling writer of the 20th century.

"The rod belched flame and the slug tore into my side and spun me around." Thus begins the climax of *Kiss Me, Deadly,* the sixth Mike Hammer detective novel by Mickey Spillane. In this adventure, our ferocious antihero tangles with the FBI and Mafia dope peddlers while angling to rescue his kidnapped gal Friday, Velda. It's a swift, engaging read marked by Spillane's familiarly cynical dialogue, terse, unreflective narrative voice, and a horrific final page—all of it extolling the virtues of rough justice.

A positive point of view, a bit of moral uplift, and a resolute avoidance of controversy characterized *The Saturday Evening Post,* for many years the cornerstone of the Curtis Publishing Company. The *Post*'s quietly conservative nature was established before World War I by editor George Horace Lorimer, who in 1916 commissioned cover art from a gangly 22-year-old illustrator named Norman Rockwell. The artist's relationship with the *Post* continued for more than 45 years. This 1952 painting displays not just Rockwell's astonishing technical skill, but his affinity for the humor and ironies of everyday American life.

Actress Elizabeth Taylor beams after the second of what would be many strolls down the aisle. On February 21, 1952, she married British actor Michael Wilding (*pictured, in hat*) in London. According to Taylor, who had recently divorced hotel heir Nicky Hilton, the sophisticated Wilding was "everything I admire in a man." The admiration must have waned, since the pair split up after less than five years and two children. Liz found five other men to admire and marry, including actor Richard Burton—twice.

Soviet leader Joseph Stalin is idealized in this postwar painting by Fyodor Shurpin, a proponent of the state-approved Socialist Realism school of Soviet art. In truth, Stalin was feared and despised not only in Western nations and Soviet-bloc countries but in Russia itself. His prewar policy of collective farming was strongly resisted by many peasants, and resulted in more than seven million deaths due to famine. In his Great Purge of the late 1930s, an estimated 600,000 Communist Party members died by execution, torture, or death in the Gulag. Historians believe that, all told, Stalin and his colleagues were responsible for as many as 50 million deaths inside the Soviet Union.

1952

January 10: Henrik Kurt Carlsen, captain of the American freighter *Flying Enterprise,* is rescued after spending 12 days alone, trying to save the foundering ship off the coast of England.

January 11: The UN replaces the Atomic Energy Commission with the Disarmament Commission.

January 12: Viet Minh fighters deal a blow to the French when they cut supply lines to Bin Hoa along the Black River in Vietnam.

January 14: *Today* begins on NBC starring Dave Garroway and Jack Lescoulie, the first of the show's many hosts.

February: The U.S. builds alliances in South America when it signs military aid pacts with Ecuador and Peru.
• The Mattachine Foundation forms the Citizens Committee to Outlaw Entrapment after one of its own, Dale Jennings, is charged with lewd behavior following an instance of entrapment by a Los Angeles police officer. • New York's Times Square becomes the home of the first "walk/don't walk" signs. Four are installed at the intersection of Broadway and 44th Street.

February 6: Former Communist turned FBI informant Harvey Matusow testifies before the House Un-American Activities Committee (HUAC) about the Communist affiliations of musicians, such as the Weavers and Pete Seeger. • King George VI dies. He had ascended to the British throne after his brother, Edward VIII, abdicated in order to marry an American divorcée.

February 8: Princess Elizabeth of England takes the oath of accession following the death of her father, King George VI. She becomes, at the age of 25, the fourth woman to sit on the throne of the British Empire.

A smiling Ronald Reagan looks adoringly at his new wife, actress Nancy Davis Reagan, whom he married on March 4, 1952. The popular actor was president of the Screen Actors Guild from 1947 to '52 and was noted for his growing opposition to alleged Communist influence in Hollywood. Politically, he moved from being a New Deal Democrat to a conservative who supported Dwight Eisenhower in 1952 and 1956. As Reagan became increasingly well known for his anticommunism, he laid the groundwork for his future political career.

A tornado originating from a Gulf of Mexico tropical storm touched down in Dierks, Arkansas (*pictured*), on March 21, 1952. From there, the twister proceeded to cut a swath of destruction across the state. Other tornadoes spread ruin throughout the South, including areas of Mississippi, Alabama, Kentucky, Tennessee, and Missouri. By the time the forces had spent themselves the following day, more than 200 people were dead and nearly 2,500 were injured.

Batista's Cuba

BY THE EARLY 1950S, Cuba's reputation as a playground for the rich had taken root. American mobsters first entered the country during Prohibition, and when mob boss Meyer Lansky was invited to run Havana's casinos in 1938, a working partnership was established. Fulgencio Batista *(pictured)*, who had seized control of the government during a 1933 coup, was the *de facto* leader of Cuba. He profited not only from the mob-run vice industries, but from U.S. support of his ostensible "democracy."

For years, Batista mostly ruled from behind the scenes, but in a bloodless coup staged on March 10, 1952, he achieved absolute power. With the military at his disposal, Batista's unquestioned authority made the island safe for wealthy fun-seekers and high-rolling criminals, but miserable for anyone foolish enough to challenge him. Though he was sufficiently savvy to keep the economy running through diversification, abetted by U.S.-owned businesses, Cuba's impoverished majority found little to celebrate. Batista's skimming of revenue meant little left over for such basics as schools and infrastructure.

While patrons of Cuba's casinos and nightclubs enjoyed the time of their lives, a young, charismatic Cuban lawyer found a receptive audience while railing against the corruption. Fidel Castro, backed by like-minded guerrillas, made a disastrous coup attempt in 1953, resulting in jail for Castro and his surviving supporters. (Some uncharac-teristic goodwill from Batista saw Castro freed after two years.) With unrest stirring, Batista moved quickly to stifle opposition.

However, Batista's brutal means of suppression caused him to lose the support of both Cuba's middle class and American business interests. Despite (and because of) the executions, torture, and imprisonment carried out by the government, Batista's once mighty hold started to weaken. His army, though American-equipped, was undisciplined and inept. Before the decade's end, all the elements would be in place for a successful overthrow.

While William Levitt was mass-producing suburban communities, Chicago engineer Carl Strandlund offered his own solution to the postwar housing shortage. Backed by government funding, Strandlund developed the Lustron house—a prefabricated steel structure, inside and out, coated with baked porcelain. Buyers had a choice between two- or three-bedroom models, with a starting price of $7,000. Color choices included pink, desert tan, dove gray, and surf blue. Despite Strandlund's hopes, the houses were too costly to produce for their intended market, and government shenanigans robbed the enterprise of much of its funding. Fewer than 2,500 Lustron homes were built.

1952

February 12: Fulton Sheen, auxiliary bishop of New York, airs his television show, *Life Is Worth Living,* for the first time.

February 17: Opera soprano Dorothy Maynor becomes the first black artist to perform commercially in the Daughters of the American Revolution Constitution Hall.

February 19: The Interstate Commerce Commission rules that Southern Railway dining cars can remain segregated.

February 21: Elizabeth Taylor marries British actor Michael Wilding, her second husband, in London. • American Dick Button lands the first triple loop in competition, winning a unanimous vote from the Olympic judges for the men's figure skating gold at the Oslo Winter Games.

February 22–26: Under heavy artillery fire in Vietnam, the French withdraw from Hoa Binh to the De Lattre Line.

February 26: Prime Minister Winston Churchill announces to Parliament that Great Britain has developed its own nuclear warheads.

March: In a series of joint espionage sorties, the U.S. Strategic Air Command and the British Royal Air Force begin radar and photographic reconnaissance missions over the Soviet Union. • In the scandalous "calendar caper," nude pictures of Marilyn Monroe, taken three years earlier, are released as a pin-up calendar. Marilyn confesses to posing for the photos, and her career takes off.

March 1: A "moral code" governing appearance and behavior of television scripts and personalities is officially adopted by the industry.

Wisconsin boys participate in a soapbox derby, dreaming undoubtedly of greater glory in Akron, Ohio. Akron's annual derby was a much-loved summer tradition. From origins as a local diversion in the 1930s, the derby grew into a serious international competition, with sponsorship by Chevrolet and prizes that included a college scholarship. The event was open to boys ages nine through 15, and strict criteria were applied to contestants. Most critically, the boys needed to build their cars without help from adults. Annually in the 1950s, more than 100 entrants put their abilities to the test in Akron's fierce downhill competition.

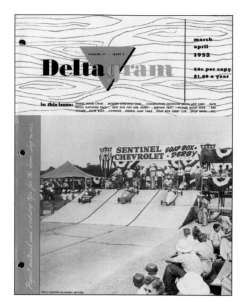

Observers, including members of the media, watch nuclear test Able at the Nevada Testing Grounds on April 1, 1952. This was the first in a series of tests designed to gather information about smaller tactical nuclear weapons. Fearing the possibility of an expanded Asian ground war growing out of the Korean conflict, the Joint Chiefs of Staff were keen on testing such weapons. Despite the extensive press coverage of this event, there was no discernable negative public reaction, probably because of the Cold War consensus in favor of defense against potential Communist attacks.

A distinguished and dapper George Kennan strolls down a London Street in April 1952, shortly before going to Moscow as U.S. ambassador to the Soviet Union. An experienced diplomat and Sovietologist, Kennan was best known as the founding father of the containment policy after World War II. As a young diplomat in Moscow in 1946, he had warned the State Department that the Soviet Union posed a serious threat to U.S. security, one that could best be contained by continued pressure. He proposed a strong Western alliance system

as well as economic and military assistance to anti-Communist countries. Kennan predicted that such pressure would ultimately cause the USSR to implode—an accurate prophecy.

Among the crop of Hollywood's Red Scare propaganda pieces, *My Son John* stands as an anomaly. Though its predictable depiction of insidious homegrown "fellow travelers" was unexceptional, its makers were not. Writer-director Leo McCarey was an Oscar-winning comedy auteur. By the late 1940s, however, he had become firmly right-wing, testifying before HUAC as a "friendly" witness. Stage legend Helen Hayes was lured back to Hollywood after a 20-year lull to play the mother of the title character. The film's heavy-handed message seems to be that nonconformity equals subversion.

Actor John Garfield *(left)* testifies before HUAC. After World War II, Garfield had become famous as the star of several movies in the *film noir* genre, such as the MGM classic *The Postman Always Rings Twice.* Garfield's left-wing views brought him to the attention of HUAC, but he refused to cooperate and name names. After this appearance, he was essentially blacklisted and found few new projects. Garfield died of a heart attack in 1952 at age 39. Many, including members of his family, believed that the coronary was a result of the stress of testifying.

A group of Columbia University students celebrates after swiping undergarments from their female counterparts at Barnard College. These so-called "panty raids," according to legend, began at the University of Michigan in March 1952. They became fairly common at institutions of higher education in the 1950s, much to the dismay of college administrators. Occasionally, women would strike back with raids of men's boxer shorts. The activity died out in the 1960s.

March 3: New York's Feinberg Law, which bans Communist teachers in public schools, is upheld by the U.S. Supreme Court. • The U.S. Supreme Court refuses to hear the appeal of Joseph Rice, a Florida man who lost a lawsuit against the Miami Springs Country Club over its restrictive policies for black golfers.

March 4: North Korea claims that UN troops are using biological weapons against them. • Actor and future president Ronald Reagan marries actress Nancy Davis, his second wife, in Southern California.

March 8: For the first time, a mechanical heart is used to sustain a patient during heart surgery. The procedure, performed at Philadelphia's Pennsylvania Hospital, is itself successful, although the patient, 41-year-old Peter During, later dies of unrelated complications.

March 10: The UN Tokyo headquarters announces that the North Korean Army is equipped with Soviet weaponry that has been channeled to the North Koreans through Red China. • Dictator Fulgencio Batista regains control of the Cuban government.

March 21: Alan Freed hosts the first rock 'n' roll show, *The Moondog Coronation Ball,* at the Cleveland Arena. The concert doesn't last long, as the crowd overwhelms the venue and the show is canceled. • More than 200 Americans are killed when more than 30 storms batter six south-central states.

Spring 1952: Gerry Mulligan and his piano-less quartet open at L.A.'s Haig Club and popularize the new "West Coast jazz" sound.

March 24: Massive anti-apartheid demonstrations are held across South Africa.

March 25: A Soviet proposal for a reunified, rearmed Germany is shot down by the U.S., Britain, and France.

What a Glorious Feeling

SINGIN' IN THE RAIN

MGM's TECHNICOLOR MUSICAL TREASURE!

starring

**GENE KELLY
DONALD O'CONNOR
DEBBIE REYNOLDS**

JEAN HAGEN · MILLARD MITCHELL and CYD CHARISSE

BETTY COMDEN and ADOLPH GREEN

ARTHUR FREED · NACIO HERB BROWN · GENE KELLY and STANLEY DONEN · ARTHUR FREED

Many film critics and fans consider *Singin' in the Rain* (1952) America's greatest movie musical. The story, built upon vintage MGM songs, takes place during the era when Hollywood made the rocky transition from silents to talkies. Dancer-actor Gene Kelly, who codirected with Stanley Donen, was at his creative peak, drawing career-making performances out of Donald O'Connor, Jean Hagen, newcomer Debbie Reynolds, and—in a stunning dance sequence—the unearthly Cyd Charisse. Kelly's performance of the title number remains one of cinema's best-loved sequences. Remarkably, the film was largely overlooked at the time of its release.

Elia Kazan was one of the finest directors of the 1950s, with such films as *A Streetcar Named Desire* (1951), *On the Waterfront* (1954), and *East of Eden* (1956) to his credit. Like many young idealists during the 1930s, Kazan had flirted with communism as an alternative to capitalism's apparent failure. In 1952 Kazan was called before HUAC to explain himself. By that time, he had grown to hate communism. Further, Hollywood executives warned him that a refusal to cooperate with HUAC could kill his career. Renouncing his past, Kazan named names, destroying careers in the process. Though he continued to work, many of his colleagues shunned him for what they felt was a self-serving and gratuitous betrayal of his former friends.

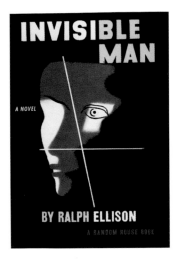

Ralph Ellison's meditation on alienation in modern society led to one of the greatest American novels of the 20th century. The naive and nameless narrator of *Invisible Man* journeys from a black college in the South to Harlem, where cynical Communists recruit him as an organizer. His eventual dismay with all of society suggests that he is invisible to *everybody,* including other African-Americans. In the following decade, Black Power advocates would claim that Ellison's work neither explained nor defined anything valuable to those fighting the Black Revolution. But those objections now are largely forgotten, swept away by the resonating power of Ellison's art.

Demonstrators in Japan take to the streets on May 1, 1952, urging that U.S. military forces leave their country. The final peace treaty between the two countries, which was ratified by the U.S. Senate in March 1952, restored Japanese political sovereignty. However, it also made the U.S. the guarantor of Japan's military security, since Japan would have no standing army. American troops could be stationed on Japanese soil indefinitely. To this, Communists and radical students vociferously objected. They also called for the ouster of Japanese Premier Yoshida Shigeru, who had negotiated the treaty.

Spock's Babies

THE PHILOSOPHY OF RENOWNED pediatrician Benjamin Spock *(pictured)* could be summed up in two words: "Trust yourself." Beginning at the start of the postwar baby boom, Spock's 25-cent treatise, *Baby and Child Care,* provided a wealth of common-sense advice to a new generation of parents-to-be. So well received was his work that only the Bible exceeded it in total book sales for the 1950s. But Dr. Spock was not without critics. Indeed, as the Baby Boomers grew into adults, some detractors blamed Spock for fostering a "permissive society."

The criticism, however, seems unfounded, since the book distinctly advocates discipline. Dr. Spock did oppose corporal punishment, which he felt was ineffective at best and cruel at worst. The doctor stood apart from some other experts on child care, who advocated such bizarre measures as refraining from displaying affection toward one's child, on the grounds that "mother-love is a dangerous instrument." The reverence felt by most Americans toward their doctors was smashed when Dr. Spock insisted that parents "know more than [they] think [they] do." Such soothing words, flying in the face of conventional wisdom, were revolutionary in their day.

Spock, an Olympic gold medalist in rowing in 1924, studied pediatrics at Yale and Columbia before securing a teaching position at Cornell in the 1930s. During that time, he studied human psychology, gleaning valuable insights into security and self-esteem issues. In his book, he advised parents not to hold back when cuddling their child, and to be free with encouragement and praise. As such counsel echoed most parents' natural instincts, it readily took root with millions.

1952

March 27: Sun Records is founded in Memphis, Tennessee, by Sam Phillips. *See* July 7, 1954.

March 29: President Truman withdraws from the presidential race, ending speculation about the likelihood of his winning a second term.

March 30: Mohammed el Amin Pasha, the Bey of Tunis, is seized by French forces as a show of power aimed at crushing the Tunisian rebellion against French rule.

April 1: The Big Bang Theory is publicly posited for the first time, in the pages of *Physical Review*.

April 3: Public Law 280 takes oversight of American Indian reservations out of the hands of the federal government and gives it to the individual states.

April 8: Invoking his war powers, President Truman orders U.S. troops to seize American steel mills in order to avert a strike over wages. *See* June 2, 1952.

April 10: In a move that will stain his reputation for years, Hollywood director Elia Kazan cooperates with HUAC when he offers the names of his comrades in the Communist cell at the Group Theater.

April 11: General Eisenhower requests permission from President Truman to resign as the supreme commander of NATO in order to pursue the Republican nomination for the presidency. *See* July 11, 1952.

April 15: President Truman signs the Japanese Peace Treaty, officially ending Japan's occupation by the U.S. ● The first bank credit card is issued by Franklin National Bank.

April 22: Operation Big Shot, a 31-kiloton nuclear detonation at the Nevada Test Site, is broadcast nationally on American television to some one million viewers.

The Korean Story

Cartoonist Reg Manning suggested that while Korean peace talks dragged on, soldiers continued to die (*left*). In spring 1952, General Mark Clark replaced General Matthew Ridgway as commander of UN forces. As negotiations went nowhere, Clark maintained pressure on the Communists. In April, the Army began a campaign of psychological warfare, broadcasting in Korean to Communist troops and exhorting them to surrender. On May 8, the U.S. staged the largest air strike of the war to that time, dropping bombs and 12,000 gallons of napalm on the ancient city of Suan (*below*).

Policy of Termination

THE INDIAN REORGANIZATION ACT of 1934, which restored to Native Americans management of their land (i.e., reservations), did not sit well with many white Americans. During post-war expansion, the real estate was becoming valuable, and many of the Indian tribal lands were resource-rich. As in earlier decades, whites went after Indian land. Congressmen demanded that the Bureau of Indian Affairs "liberate" Indians, assimilate tribal lands, dissolve tribal governments, renounce responsibility for Indian welfare, and ultimately reverse most of the benefits derived from the Indian "New Deal" of the 1930s.

A Navajo family in New Mexico

House Resolution 698 (1952), which called for the reorganization and outsourcing of several Bureau of Indian Affairs functions, jump-started what would become known as the "Policy of Termination." House Concurrent Resolution 108 (1953) ended Indians' status as wards of the United States, while Public Law 280 (1953) set a precedent for the transfer of criminal jurisdiction from tribal governments to individual states. Several similar laws enacted over the next decade would ultimately strip some 109 tribes of federal services and protection.

The termination policy would impoverish such tribes as the Klamath and Menominee, who had been enjoying relative prosperity administering tribal-owned forest industries. Urban resettlement, which sought to offset the impact of termination by assimilating Indians into America's cities, compounded the ills when racism and insufficient job training left many Indians unemployed and living in poverty. The efforts of the American Indian movement and civil rights activist groups would lead to a legislative course correction, but for many American Indians, the damage was done.

A bizarre, little-known chapter of the Korean War unfolded with the American deployment of insect-carrying bombs in a primitive attempt at biological warfare. This secret operation began in collaboration with Japanese specialists from the notorious Unit 731, a team that had experimented with an array of diseases during World War II. After WWII, a secret alliance began between Japanese and Americans, who feared Soviet superiority in chemical and biological weaponry. Bombs containing bees, flies, and spiders are now believed to have been utilized as active agents for bringing disease to the enemy during the Korean conflict. In time, captured U.S. personnel "confessed" to the charges, but only under duress.

As General Douglas MacArthur worked to bring fundamental change to postwar Japan, the 1952 edition of *A Pocket Guide to Japan* advised American Occupation troops on local customs and proper behavior. The American agenda for the conquered nation (where many in the Japanese military had been tried for war crimes during 1946–48) was ambitious and potentially touchy: democracy, a rebuilt economy that forsook militarism, and public confidence instead of the shock of defeat. The Japanese proved to be gracious, even welcoming, partly because many GIs took to heart the booklet's gentle half-truth that U.S. troops "will be in Japan at the express invitation of the Japanese government and people."

1952

April 26: *Gunsmoke,* destined to become a huge television hit in the 1960s, initially airs as a radio program.

April 27: More than 160 people die when the destroyer *Hobson* sinks after colliding with the aircraft carrier *Wasp* off the coast of the Azores.

April 28: Peace between China and Japan is affirmed with the signing of the Treaty of Taipei.

May 1: In an inaugural flight to Shannon, Ireland, Trans World Airlines introduces tourist class, bringing the luxury of air travel within the reach of most Americans. • The U.S. State Department bans all nonessential civilian travel to the Soviet Union as well as Soviet Bloc countries.

May 3: Lieutenant colonels William P. Benedict and Joseph O. Fletcher land a ski-modified Air Force C-47 at the geographic North Pole. It is the first time that an airplane has landed at the Pole.

May 8: A day following a final armistice ultimatum, Allied fighters stage a massive air strike against the city of Suan, a North Korean supply center 35 miles southeast of Pyongyang. • *Mad,* a 10-cent comic book from EC Comics, appears on newsstands for the first time.

May 12: General Matthew Ridgway cedes command of the UN forces in Korea and U.S. forces in the Far East to General Mark W. Clark.

May 13: Pandit Jawaharlal Nehru becomes premier of India. In a decisive victory, Nehru's Indian National Congress party wins 364 of 489 seats in Parliament. • In a record-setting pitching performance, minor-leaguer Ron Necciai strikes out 27 batters in a nine-inning game.

May 19: Actor John Garfield dies of heart failure at age 39.

Congressman Ezekiel Gathings (D–AR) looks disapprovingly at racy magazines at a Washington, D.C., newsstand in May 1952. That year, Gathings headed the House Select Committee on Current Pornographic Materials. He was determined to attack "sex books" that contained "artful appeals to...filth, perversion and degeneracy." Although the committee examined more than 200 books, the examples apparently weren't quite nasty enough, since no anti-pornography laws emerged from the hearings. The proceedings did, however, inspire local vigilante-type actions, including one by the Youngstown, Ohio, police chief who personally banned supposedly filthy paperbacks.

Noting how much children loved to play with their food, inventor George Lerner first conceived of a line of potato accessories during World War II. Stymied by general disinterest, Lerner took until 1951 to convince New England's Hassenfeld Brothers to take a chance on his brainchild. The following year, Hasbro introduced Mr. Potato Head to the public. Once parents got past their resistance to wasting food, a phenomenon was born. The canny use of television advertising contributed to the toy's massive success. Eventually, plastic potatoes replaced the natural ones.

Dozens of crime titles were published during the comic book boom of the early 1950s, but none were livelier than those of Lev Gleason. His flagship title was *Crime Does Not Pay*, but *Crime and Punishment* had an identically nasty allure, as this outrageous cover suggests. Although "punishment" was meted out in the Gleason crime comics, it didn't come until the stories' last panels. Until then, the bad guys had a high old time, while kids—critics contended—picked up valuable crime tips. Cover art for this issue is by Gleason staffer Charles Biro.

Better Homes and Gardens, one of the most widely circulated American magazines in the 1950s, offers its vision of the ideal home. The post-World War II period saw a suburban housing boom, as 11 million of the 13 million new homes built in the 1950s were in suburban areas. *BH&G* wielded enormous influence with the millions of people it reached. This cover focuses on large windows and the importance of the outdoor patio, components of housing simply not available in most urban areas. Light, airy, and distinctly middle-class features marked the ideal that *Better Homes and Gardens* both reflected and helped to create.

On June 2, 1952, an electrician at the Homestead Steel Works in Pennsylvania displays the first picket sign of a CIO-led strike. In spite of large profits as a result of the Korean War, steel companies had not provided raises for their workers since 1950. When the U.S. Wage Stabilization Board recommended an hourly increase of 26 cents, the industry proposed a $12 per ton hike in the price of steel. President Truman invoked emergency war powers to order the federal government to seize steel mills in April, to prevent a shutdown. He accused the companies of trying to get special treatment, and said it was his "plain duty to keep this from happening." On June 2, 1952, the Supreme Court ruled Truman's action unconstitutional, and the strike began. It lasted 53 days, but it did not harm the economy as much as Truman had anticipated.

Painter Willem de Kooning antagonized many art lovers with his "Woman" series. "Woman I" (*pictured*) exemplifies what some found disagreeable—exaggerated features and savage teeth and eyes, all depicted in a fury of blunt brushstrokes and harsh juxtapositions of colors. Many interpreted what they saw as evidence of the artist's disturbed view of femininity. Others saw it as a statement deploring society's reduction of women to commodities. In either case, de Kooning's provocative work added richness to an eventful decade for art.

1952

May 26: The U.S. Supreme Court lifts a ban on the movie *The Miracle*, reversing a lower-court ruling in *Burstyn v. Wilson*. The court determines that motion pictures are constitutionally protected free speech.

May 27: The European Defense Community is chartered by France, Italy, West Germany, Belgium, and the Netherlands.

May 31: In a nationwide operation, French police raid Communist Party headquarters across the country.

June 2: The U.S. Supreme Court rules that President Truman's seizure of U.S. steel mills was unconstitutional. A 53-day workers strike will follow the decision.

June 10: American troops suppress a massive rebellion by North Korean prisoners in the South Korean Koje prisoner of war camp.

June 14: The world's first nuclear submarine, the USS *Nautilus,* is dedicated in Groton, Connecticut.

June 16: The House Select Committee on Current Pornographic Materials, chaired by Congressman Ezekiel Gathings (D–AR), convenes, setting its sights on "salacious" magazines and paperbacks.

June 25: President Truman signs the Federal-Aid Highway Act, which earmarks federal funds for highway reconstruction.

June 27: Congress passes the Immigration and Naturalization Act, which sets immigration quotas according to a person's country of origin rather than his or her race.

June 29: The first Miss Universe Pageant is won by Finland's Armi Kuusela.

July 7–11: The Republicans get a jump on the Democrats when, for the first time, a presidential convention is broadcast on national television.

Georgia's revocation of the Ku Klux Klan's charter in 1947 was the nail in the coffin for the national organization. It had disbanded three years previously when it could not pay its federal taxes; without Georgia, the KKK splintered into local camps, still active but living up to its nickname of the "Invisible Empire." During the 1950s, however, the Klan resurfaced with a new goal: to stop the growing civil rights movement. With a mission to keep the most acidic parts of America's cultural past alive, the Klan was revitalized by, ironically, the forces it opposed the most.

"C"

1. Can the state coin money with the consent of Congress? No

2. Name one area of authority over state militia reserved exclusively to the states. The appointment of officers

3. The power of granting patents, that is, of securing to inventors the exclusive right to their discoveries, is given to the Congress for the purpose of promoting progress.

4. The only legal tender which may be authorized by states for payment of debts is U. S. Currency .

Southerners believed that a literacy test or a Constitution test was a good way to block the 15th Amendment's application to African-Americans. White registrars routinely denied the vote to black applicants who could not answer advanced U.S. civics questions, such as those on this test. The Voting Rights Act of 1965 would finally end this practice by permitting federal officials to supervise election practices at the state and local levels.

Argentinian President Juan Peron (*right*) and his equally charismatic wife, Eva, wave to supporters. Peron was elected president in 1946 after being released from prison in 1945 at the insistence of huge numbers of supporters, including the military. His wife became especially popular among the more privileged members of the working class, who affectionately called her "Evita." Juan became deeply depressed after her death in 1952. His growing authoritarianism, the nation's economic problems, and his excommunication by the Catholic Church preceded his ouster by a military coup in 1955.

For millions of kids, actor George Reeves *was* Superman, the latest incarnation in a long line of depictions that had begun in 1938. Throughout the 1940s, the DC Comics superhero and his accompanying myth took root in public imagination via comic books, radio, movie serials, and animated shorts. In 1951, after finishing work on the feature-length *Superman and the Mole Men*, Reeves resumed the part for TV. *The Adventures of Superman* made him a star, if a ghettoized one. Boasting impressive effects, imaginative story lines, and color (before most people had color sets), the program endured on television for years.

E. B. White made a name for himself as a contributor to *The New Yorker* magazine. Though he was a noted poet and essayist with a satiric bent, few could have predicted that his greatest success would come from a pair of children's books. His book *Stuart Little* (1945) was followed in 1952 by *Charlotte's Web,* which became a publishing phenomenon. The tale of an unlikely friendship between the title spider and a pig named Wilbur served as a vehicle for lessons in love and sacrifice. Sensitive illustrations by Garth Williams contributed immensely to the book's charm.

Old Gold packages dance in just one of the many cigarette commercials that appeared on television in the 1950s. Old Gold boasted that their cigarettes were made by "tobacco men," not doctors. A number of television shows, such as *Topper* and *I Love Lucy,* were sponsored by cigarette companies, whose products the actors smoked. Actor John Wayne, who later suffered from lung cancer, flogged the Camel brand.

Clergyman Norman Vincent Peale and his wife, Ruth, promote his 1952 bestseller, *The Power of Positive Thinking.* Indeed, were it not for Ruth's positive thinking, the book might never have seen the light of day at all, since her husband had pitched the oft-rejected manuscript into the trash. Her perseverance would result in sales of more than 20 million copies. Relying on inspirational scripture and true-life stories, Peale asserted that modern man was not self-contained, and could achieve his potential only by looking beyond himself for guidance.

Originally developed as a synthetic rubber during World War II, a compound dubbed "Gup" proved inadequate for its intended purpose, but ideal for frivolous uses. Intrigued by the material's elasticity, its bounciness when formed into a ball, and its ability to lift newsprint impressions, out-of-work ad executive Peter Hodgson aggressively marketed the material as a children's novelty. Using surplus plastic Easter eggs for packaging, Silly Putty®, "The Real Solid Liquid," was launched in 1950. Following some good press, sales topped 250,000 in three days, unleashing a phenomenon.

Seniors at Stevens Institute of Technology appreciate a comment made by a recruiter for General Electric Corporation in 1952. Smiles were common among college graduates that year, especially those who majored in growth areas such as engineering. In spite of an unusually large number of college graduates because of veterans who enrolled under the GI Bill in the late 1940s, the U.S. experienced an acute shortage of engineers and scientists. Companies such as GE offered bonuses and on-the-job training to lure recent graduates. Recruits often moved from technical jobs into managerial ones and became part of the growing affluence of the 1950s.

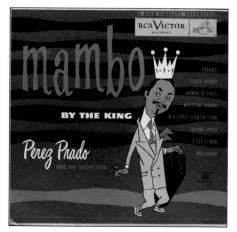

The mambo was a beat-driven, Afro-Cuban dance that originated during World War II. It superseded the rhumba and later became a favorite of orchestras and club dancers in Mexico City and on both American coasts. Whether fast or slow, a mambo tune typically established the rhythm with saxophones, with melody carried by brass. Cuban musicians Orestes Lopez and Arsenio Rodriguez laid down the form, but it was pianist-bandleader Perez Prado who pumped up the rhythm with congas. Prado became—as this lively 10-inch EP suggests—the "mambo king."

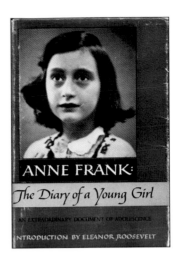

Many Americans were awakened to the Holocaust in 1952 with the English-language publication of *Anne Frank: The Diary of a Young Girl.* Anne and her family had spent two years hiding in a Dutch attic while other Jews were being rounded up by Nazis for extermination. In 1944 the hideout was raided and its occupants dispatched to a death camp—but not before the adolescent girl had chronicled in moving and articulate detail their horrific experience. The book has been translated into 55 languages, and more than 25 million copies have been sold.

Before labor costs and wholesale gasoline prices killed the concepts of courtesy and attentiveness, a "service station" meant just that. In Pennsylvania in 1952, the driver of this '51 Ford was looked after by *a pair* of attendants—one offering a helpful glance at the oil dipstick, the other filling the car's tank. You can bet that the lady's windshield was cleaned and the air pressure of her tires conscientiously checked. Attendants at some stations even vacuumed cars for free. A close look at the pump reveals that premium-grade Blue Sunoco was priced at 24^9 cents a gallon.

The Mexican film industry thrived artistically in the 1940s, but after 1950, budgets were trimmed and the industry tipped into a slight decline. Still, Mexican film studios produced an average of 110 pictures a year throughout the decade, offering comedies, horror shockers, urban thrillers, musicals, and rural dramas. Cuban-born Amalia Aguilar, showcased here in a 1952 lobby card promoting *Delirio Tropical,* originally was a *rumbera* (tropical dancer). She became a star by wowing moviegoers with her lithe figure, uninhibited footwork, and delightful flair for verbal and physical comedy. Aguilar was known throughout Latin America as *"La Bomba Atómica."*

Senator Pat McCarran (D–NV) holds up a leprechaun he bought during a trip to the Old Country. However, the senator did not smile at what he saw as Communist infiltration of American institutions. McCarran was the chief author of the 1950 Internal Security Act, which severely limited the rights of suspected Communists and "fellow travelers," as well as 1952 legislation that further tightened immigration quotas. The Immigration Act made the deportation of suspected radicals easier, and excluded immigrants with subversive connections. Less flamboyant than anti-Communist Senator Joseph McCarthy, McCarran, according to his latest biographer, was "the real force behind" the anti-Communist crusade.

1952

July 11: Dwight Eisenhower and Richard Nixon are nominated for president and vice president at the Republican National Convention in Chicago.

July 13: In a report to the UN Security Council, the U.S. government asserts that the UN is holding some 100,000 prisoners who have indicated that they do not wish to be returned to Communist countries. • The East German People's Army is formed.

July 14: General Motors announces that its cars will henceforth offer air conditioning as an optional feature.

July 16: The GI Bill, which provides funds to veterans for education and housing loans, is extended to include Korean War veterans.

July 17–August 4: U.S. forces battle Chinese Communist forces for the strategically important Hill 266, or "Old Baldy," so known because heavy artillery fire denuded the vegetation at the summit. The hill will change hands several times and ultimately end up under Chinese control. • Nationalist Chinese Taiwan boycotts the Olympic Games when it discovers that Red China has also been invited by the International Olympic Committee.

July 19: The Olympic Games open in Helsinki, Finland. For the first time, Soviet athletes participate, though they stay fenced in behind barbed wire to prevent defections.

July 19–August 3: Bringing home two gold and five silver medals, Soviet gymnast Maria Gorokhovskaya sets a record for the most medals won by a woman in a single Olympics. • American decathlete Bob Mathias leaves Helsinki with his second gold medal, having shattered the world record by 912 points. • By the close of the Olympics, the Americans bring home 41 gold medals, while the Soviets net 23.

Patricia Ryan Nixon beams for the cameras at the 1952 Republican National Convention, where her husband, Senator Richard Nixon, was nominated as the vice presidential candidate. A University of Southern California graduate and a high school teacher in Whittier, California, Pat married Richard in 1940. They had two daughters, Julie and Tricia. Although she did not particularly relish the life of a politician's wife, Pat was a tireless campaigner during her husband's many political races. In later years, she remarked, "I have sacrificed everything in my life that I consider precious to advance the political career of my husband."

Presidential hopeful Senator Robert Taft (R–OH) gives one last campaign speech outside the venue for the 1952 Republican National Convention. Elected to the Senate in 1938, Taft became a staunch opponent of the New Deal and a committed isolationist who opposed most of President Truman's foreign policy initiatives, including NATO. In 1952 he ran a spirited campaign against Eisenhower, representing the traditional conservative wing of the party. Mainly because they thought that the affable and moderate Eisenhower was more electable than Taft, convention delegates gave the former general and war hero a narrow first-ballot victory. Taft remained in the Senate and died in 1953.

Dwight D. Eisenhower

SENSING A CHANGE in public mood in 1952, Republican leaders recognized their best shot in 20 years at wresting executive rule away from the Democrats. Unfortunately, they were saddled with a front-runner, Ohio Senator Robert Taft, whose chief characteristic was a reactionary isolationist worldview. Moderates in the party, alarmed at the potential electoral disaster, began making overtures to General Dwight D. Eisenhower, who at the time served as supreme commander of NATO forces.

Though so apolitical as to have never even voted, the general was eager to promote the Communist containment policies he had engineered with President Truman, and to resolve the stalemate in Korea. Once he entered the race in early 1952, his success seemed assured.

As the American face of the Allied victory in World War II, Eisenhower was revered as a hero nationwide. Unlike the pompous Douglas MacArthur, who once derided him as "his clerk," Ike projected the image of an unpretentious and down-to-earth warrior. However, even though a decades-long military career had prepared him for a life of service, the candidate lacked a grasp of the intricacies of successful partisan politics. The education he was to receive at the hands of party professionals did nothing to change his innate distaste for politicking.

"I Like Ike" proved to be the most effective slogan in political history. Campaigning on a platform to "clean up the mess in Washington," the general refrained from directly attacking his Democratic presidential opponent, Illinois Governor Adlai Stevenson. But as the campaign wore on, Eisenhower's anti-Democrat rhetoric became increasingly pointed. Many people were further dismayed by his uncritical acceptance of Senator Joseph McCarthy's out-landish assaults on members of the Democratic administration, Truman among them. Stung by Eisenhower's apparent embrace of the destructive "gutter politics" being practiced on his behalf, Truman lashed out at his former friend, telling an audience, "I never thought the man who is now the Republican candidate would stoop so low...."

The public thought otherwise and elected Eisenhower twice, giving him 39 of 48 states in 1952 and even more in '56. With an easy grin and grandfatherly charm, he was widely viewed as an affable, decent man. Though he privately battled a furious temper, Ike and wife Mamie brought an air of decorum to Washington. The First Lady was an adept, supportive helpmate, thanks to years of practice while she followed her husband wherever the Army had assigned him.

Eisenhower's Cabinet was stacked with industry leaders, resembling less a military headquarters than a corporate boardroom. An air of businesslike efficiency drove Ike's domestic policy, as the credit-bolstered economy hummed along seemingly on autopilot. When not in Washington, the President often could be found on the golf course or indulging in a passion for painting.

Though his tenure could hardly be described as uneventful, Eisenhower's tranquility made even shocking events—such as the Soviets' introduction of intercontinental ballistic missiles in 1957—seem bearable. The nation did receive a significant jolt when the President suffered a heart attack in September 1955. Though he fully recovered, his health remained a concern. In 1956 he was stricken by ileitis and later a stroke, but he managed to remain sharp and steady throughout the final years of his presidency. By 1960, however, the country was ready for a younger, more progressive chief executive, paving the way for John F. Kennedy.

July 21: A massive earthquake rocks Southern California. Tremors can be felt over a 100,000-square-mile area.

July 23: Airstrikes cripple North Korea's hydroelectric power grid. A subsequent blackout lasts two weeks, and its effects are felt in northeastern China.

July 24: President Truman commutes the death sentence of Oscar Collazo to life in prison. Collazo is one of two Puerto Rican nationalists who tried to assassinate Truman at Blair House two years earlier.

July 25: Puerto Rico is established as a sovereign commonwealth of the U.S.

July 26: The Democrats nominate Adlai E. Stevenson and John Sparkman at their national convention in Chicago. • Eva Peron, Argentina's beloved first lady who was known to her millions of admirers as Evita, dies of cancer at age 33.

July 31: Two U.S. Air Force Sikorsky H-19 helicopters, piloted by Captain Vincent H. McGovern and First Lieutenant Harold W. Moore, land in Prestwick, Scotland, to complete the first transatlantic helicopter flight.

August–September: The First Marine Division engages North Korean forces in the Battle of Bunker Hill, the first significant Marine ground action in western Korea.

August 1: The first Holiday Inn is opened just outside of Memphis, Tennessee, by hotelier Kemmons Wilson.

August 5: A federal judge in Los Angeles convicts 14 Communist Party leaders for conspiring to overthrow the U.S. government.

August 11: Jordan's King Hussein, age 16, rises to power when his mentally ill father, Talal, abdicates the throne.

A TV cameraman zooms in on the action at the 1952 Republican National Convention, the first ever to be televised nationally. Television had a major impact on the campaign. Although radio was still more popular than the new visual medium, television received the lion's share of attention from campaign planners. According to historian Eric Barnouw, they were convinced that the "television viewers who were watching fifteen million sets were . . . 'influentials.'" Eisenhower played beautifully on television with his big grin and carefully crafted short speeches. Conversely, his Democratic opponent, Adlai Stevenson, seemed long-winded and overly convoluted on TV. While it is unclear whether the new medium significantly affected election results, presidential politics would never be the same.

Appliance maker Westinghouse saw its sales soar after casting former model and actress Betty Furness as its spokeswoman. Furness was performing on the Westinghouse-sponsored *Studio One* anthology program in 1948 when called upon to step in for the previous on-air advertising talent. Her self-assured yet down-to-earth persona impressed Westinghouse executives, who thereupon signed her for full-time work. During the 1952 presidential national conventions, Furness seemed to get more airtime than the candidates. Her key line— "You can be *sure* if it's Westinghouse"—stuck in America's consciousness.

Adlai Stevenson

BESET BY AN ARRAY of controversies in 1952, President Harry Truman was ready for retirement. After hopes to lure General Dwight Eisenhower into the Democratic fold as his successor evaporated, Truman was forced to cast about for a replacement. He found his man in Illinois Governor Adlai Stevenson, the grandson of the former vice president of the same name.

Elected governor in 1948, Stevenson proved an able, reformist magistrate. Solid liberal credentials coupled with vehement anti-Communist views made him a natural, reasoned Truman, who pushed hard for him to accept the party's presidential candidacy. But Stevenson expressed disinterest, gearing up instead for a second term as governor. The President would have none of it, and following an unprecedented six-day convention, Stevenson reluctantly emerged as his party's nominee.

In retrospect, it is hard to see how the choice could have worked. With Truman out of favor with the electorate, any Democrat would have been a hard sell. Stevenson's natural aversion to easy or simple solutions to the nation's troubles didn't help. His brand of rhetoric challenged rather than soothed. Also, he was an intellectual (or an "egghead" to detractors) at a time when being educated and articulate was viewed with distrust. Moreover, he was a divorced man— strictly taboo in the 1950s.

In truth, no one likely could have prevailed over the easygoing, unpretentious war hero, Dwight Eisenhower, who ran as a Republican. Stevenson lost twice to Ike—in 1952 and again four years later. Characteristically, his response to his 1956 loss was eloquent: "Like the little boy who stubbed his toe in the dark said: 'I'm too old to cry, but it hurts too much to laugh.'"

The 1952 Democratic presidential nominee, Illinois Governor Adlai Stevenson (*left*), and his running mate, Senator John Sparkman of Alabama, accept the plaudits of their party. Near the end of a deadlocked convention, Stevenson—thanks to support by President Truman— won the nomination on the third ballot. The Democratic platform endorsed New Deal liberalism and the concept of peace with honor. It also called for the repeal of the Taft-Hartley Act, which labor unions opposed due to the powers it gave to employers. Sparkman was chosen as the vice presidential nominee in part to appease Southerners who opposed the platform's support of federal civil rights legislation.

A sullen King Farouk of Egypt prepares for a lavish state dinner. In the 1950s, Farouk inspired an American colloquial expression about people who demanded more than they deserved: "Who do you think you are—King Farouk?" A military coup in July 1952 ended the king's reign. Upset by his pro-Western stance, a nationalist group that called itself the "Free Officers" ran him out of Egypt. Farouk continued to live extravagently while in exile.

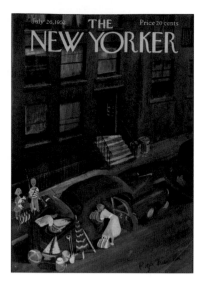

In 1952 *The New Yorker* was edited by William Shawn, a zealously dedicated manager who expanded the magazine's interest in politics, social issues, literature, dance, painting, theater—all aspects of sophisticated American endeavor. Major writers who contributed to the magazine during the 1950s included J. D. Salinger, E. B. White, John Updike, Mary McCarthy, and A. J. Liebling. Despite its liberalism, *The New Yorker* carried a faint air of privilege, subtly suggesting that institutions of real import were best appreciated by the well-born. This charming and unpretentious July 26, 1952, cover depicting a summertime getaway is by Roger Duvoisin.

By 1952 it was assumed that space travel would happen—the question was *when*. *Across the Space Frontier* is speculative science grounded in fact, and describes how an orbiting space station might be constructed and used as a jumping-off point for deeper exploration. Rocket engineers Wernher von Braun and Willy Ley contributed to the text. The jacket painting and many interior illustrations were created by prominent astronomical artist Chesley Bonestell.

Bob Mathias was America's shining star at the 1952 Summer Olympics, held in Helsinki, Finland. Four years after first winning the decathlon gold (at age 17), Mathias repeated the feat in '52, becoming the first to score back-to-back decathlon victories. The Helsinki Olympics proved to be a microcosm of the Cold War, with Russians competing in the Games for the first time since 1912. The U.S. edged its rival in total medals, amassing 76 to the Soviets' 71. Another star among the 69 participating countries was Czechoslovakia's Emil Zatopek, who set three Olympic track records.

On July 11, 1952, a member of the Air Force's 67th Tactical Reconnaissance Wing photographed a Communist troop headquarters (*top photo*) at Pyongyang, North Korea, following direct hits made during a USAF bombing raid. Located within the black rectangle are troop supply areas, which were prime targets. The UN military leadership naturally had a keen interest in Pyongyang, which was hammered on August 29 by the largest single-day air raid of the war. Also in August, along a mountain ridgeline in South Korea (*bottom photo*), the U.S. Eighth Army pounded Red positions dug in across a deep, circular valley nicknamed "Punchbowl." Here, a mortar platoon with the Fifth Infantry Regiment rains 81mm shells into the bowl.

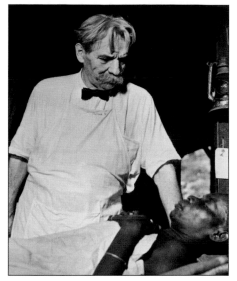

Alsatian physician Albert Schweitzer ministers to one of his patients in French Equatorial Africa. Schweitzer and his wife established a hospital in the French colony in 1913, and he continued to help poverty-stricken Africans until his death in 1965. He also was a fervent opponent of nuclear weapons from 1945 on. Because of Schweitzer's deeply felt humanitarianism and rejection of personal gain, he was awarded the 1952 Nobel Peace Prize.

As depicted in the book, film, and television series, Mobile Army Surgical Hospitals, or MASH units, proved a highly effective alternative in Korea to the portable field hospitals in use during the previous war. Despite the wartime necessity that often meant pressing inexperienced medical personnel into service, advances in arterial repair and care for hemorrhagic shock pushed the casualty survival rate up to 90 percent. Helicopters also helped by rushing victims to MASH units in minutes. Intense periods of overwork, stress, harsh weather, and battle fatigue often led the young staffers to blow off steam in a variety of ways, all well documented in Richard Hooker's novel.

August 26: The first same-day transatlantic round-trip flight occurs when a Canberra bomber takes off from Aldergrove, Northern Ireland, lands in Gander, Newfoundland, and makes it back in 7 hours, 59 minutes.

August 27: Negotiations between Israel and West Germany over the issue of war reparations come to a close in Luxembourg, with the Germans agreeing to pay three billion Deutsche marks (more than $800 million U.S.). • Suffrage is officially withdrawn from all nonwhites in South Africa.

August 28: Two Delaware Supreme Court decisions, *Belton v. Gebhart* and *Bulah v. Gebhart,* uphold the constitutionality of the practice of "separate but equal" segregated schools.

August 29: More than 1,400 planes of the Far East Air Force hammer Pyongyang, North Korea, in what will be the largest bombing raid of the Korean War.

August 30: Buckminster Fuller unveils his latest design innovation, the geodesic dome house, at New York's Museum of Modern Art.

September: Livermore, California, becomes the site of the Lawrence Livermore National Laboratory, the second U.S. nuclear weapons lab.

September 1: In the largest all-Navy raid of the war, 144 planes based on three aircraft carriers destroy a North Korean oil refinery.

September 2: Dr. Floyd J. Lewis becomes the first surgeon to use a deep-freeze technique to simulate death as an aid to heart surgery.

September 6: The Montreal area tunes in to the debut of Canadian television broadcasting. • More than 30 people die when a de Havilland 110 fighter disintegrates in midair after breaking the speed of sound, sending debris into the crowd at Britain's Farnborough Air Show.

Four unidentified flying objects appear in the sky over Salem, Massachusetts, on July 16, 1952. A Coast Guard seaman snapped this photograph, which added to the growing fascination with UFOs in the 1950s. Such B movies as *Earth vs. the Flying Saucers* (1956) hit theaters, while the phenomenon even generated its own magazine, *Flying Saucers from Other Worlds.* Many historians believe that the fear of Soviet invasion during the Cold War made Americans paranoid about extraterrestrial invaders. The origin of the "saucers" in this photo has never been determined.

Millionaire businessman Kemmons Wilson built his first Holiday Inn motel (*pictured*) outside his hometown of Memphis, Tennessee, in 1952. His intention was to make it a national chain, which he soon did. Kemmons had conceived of the idea on a family vacation in 1951 when he decided that the country needed a quality motel chain where children could stay for free. The massive growth in automobile travel, fueled by the creation of the interstate highway system in the mid-1950s, assured the success of Holiday Inn. Travelers appreciated staying in a room that was comfortable, clean, and inexpensive—and at a motel that was a known entity.

Named to head the Indian government in 1952, Pandit Jawaharlal Nehru believed that only through industrialization would his country prosper. Nehru implemented a series of five-year plans that would ultimately make India one of the most industrialized nations in the world. In foreign affairs, he advocated a policy of positive neutrality, or nonalignment, in the struggle between the Communist East and the capitalist West, a stance that often dismayed American leaders.

In order to sustain military superiority, the Pentagon tapped the technological prowess of Boeing to help achieve its aims. The Strategic Air Command sought a bomber that was capable of reconnaissance work as well as dropping nuclear weapons; that could handle long-range missions without refueling; and that could fulfill tactical speed and altitude requirements. The B-52 met all of these goals. Powered by eight Turbojet engines, this craft became a dependable mainstay for the remainder of the 20th century, and beyond. At the height of Cold War tensions, combat-ready B-52 bombers were kept airborne at all times.

The popular Betsy McCall first appeared as a paper doll in the May 1951 issue of *McCall's* magazine. It became an instant hit, and in 1952 the Ideal Toy Company created a three-dimensional, eight-inch-tall Betsy, with a vinyl head and a saran wig. Both the paper and plastic dolls remained popular throughout the 1950s, and family members were added. The paper doll welcomed a mother, father, and little dachshund, Nosy. Betsy was perky, wholesome, and feminine—an ideal 1950s girl in the eyes of many. Pictured is an official doll-clothes pattern set.

Touted as the "western for people who don't like westerns," *High Noon* told the story of one marshal's lonely stand against lawbreakers out to settle an old score. The film was seen as an allegory inspired by the blacklisting that decimated Hollywood's creative community. Politics aside, it stands as an engrossing piece of film craft. Gary Cooper, no liberal himself, shines as the increasingly desperate Marshal Will Kane. The story is told in real time, and Fred Zinnemann's taut, stark direction heightens the tension with every passing minute. Producer Stanley Kramer assembled a fine supporting cast, including Grace Kelly, Katy Jurado, and Lloyd Bridges.

1952

September 7: General Mohammed Naguib takes control of the Egyptian government following a coup that removes King Farouk from power.

September 19: Silent film star Charlie Chaplin, accused by the attorney general of "moral turpitude and Communist sympathies," is denied reentry into the U.S.

September 20: Biologists Alfred Hershey and Martha Chase confirm that the DNA molecule holds the genetic code.

September 23: In what will become known as the "Checkers" speech, vice presidential candidate Richard Nixon goes on national television to deny charges of improper campaign financing. • Rocky Marciano defeats Jersey Joe Walcott in the 13th round to claim the heavyweight boxing title.

September 26: Reclusive philosopher George Santayana, who gave the world the timeless quote "Those who cannot remember the past are condemned to repeat it," dies at age 88.

September 29: CIA Director Walter B. Smith claims to be certain that every U.S. security agency, including the CIA, has been infiltrated by Communists.

September 30: The National Council of Churches of Christ releases its Revised Standard Version of the Bible. The new version is the result of 15 years of work by more than 30 biblical scholars.

October: The Socialist Reich Party, which looks suspiciously like the Nazi Party, is banned in Germany. • George Kennan, considered the architect of the Cold War for advocating the policy of Communist containment, is recalled from his post as ambassador to the Soviet Union for making impolitic comments comparing the Soviets to the Nazis.

In 1952 a 33-year-old veteran country singer caused a stir with an "answer" to Hank Thompson's "The Wild Side of Life." Kitty Wells's "It Wasn't God Who Made Honky Tonk Angels" offered a pre-feminist assertion that unfaithful men made for unfaithful women. As record sales of the hit song exceeded 800,000, the former Muriel Deason became a star. In creating a strong, worldly female role model, Wells set the stage for the later successes of such female country stars as Patsy Cline, Loretta Lynn, and Tammy Wynette.

Vivian Vance (*left*) and Lucille Ball make a futile attempt to keep up with a speeding candy conveyor during this classic scene from *I Love Lucy*—the first episode of the 1952–53 season. Lucy's recurrent attempts to find outside employment, preferably in show business, fueled dozens of similar backfiring stunts throughout the sitcom's run. Less funny was the revelation leaked by radio commentator Walter Winchell that Miss Ball had registered to vote as a Communist back in the 1930s. Summoned before HUAC in 1953, the comedienne was looking at the possible end of her career, but a tearful, if incomprehensible, explanation won her forgiveness. Nervous execs at CBS heaved a collective sigh of relief.

One of children's literature's most beloved characters, Curious George was the creation of a married German couple, Hans and Margret Rey. In a scenario worthy of its own book, the two escaped Paris by bicycle in 1940, one step ahead of invading Nazis, manuscript in hand. By 1941 the couple had landed in New York, where *Curious George* was published. Though individual plots vary, George, a well-meaning but exceptionally curious monkey, inevitably gets into trouble by pulling naughty stunts. In *Curious George Rides a Bike,* he folds all the newspapers on his paper route into paper boats and floats them down a river. His caregiver, the Man in the Yellow Hat, is always there to bail him out.

Radio and television host Art Linkletter is shown in a familiar role—children's interviewer. His custom of querying the young in order to provoke answers that typically were humorously naive or brutally frank was a regular feature on his *House Party* series, which premiered on CBS in 1952. The program eventually became daytime TV's longest-running variety show, lasting until 1969. Linkletter's blend of easy conversation and humor, as well as audience participation, made for engaging viewing. But it was the "kids say the darndest things" segment that kept ratings high.

Catholic Bishop Fulton J. Sheen, head of the American branch of the Society for the Propagation of the Faith, delivers one of his homilies on his television show, *Life Is Worth Living.* The show, which premiered in 1951 on the DuMont Network, became a major hit, winning an Emmy and moving to the more prestigious ABC in 1952. According to his biographer, Thomas Reeves, Sheen's "humor, charm, intelligence, and considerable acting skill radiated throughout." Fifty years later, supporters of Sheen pushed for him to be canonized a saint.

Boston Red Sox slugger Ted Williams prepares to fly a F9F Panther jet while enrolled in a refresher course in September 1952. Williams, who had been trained as a fighter pilot in World War II, was recalled to active duty for service in the Korean War. He flew many of his sorties alongside his operations officer, future astronaut John Glenn. In 1953 Williams narrowly escaped death when his plane crash-landed. Due to his service in World War II and the Korean War, Williams missed nearly five seasons of play, making his career home run total (521) all the more remarkable.

1952

October 3: Videotape is born when the first video recorded on magnetic tape is created in Los Angeles. • Hurricane, the UK's first nuclear weapons test, is conducted off the northwestern coast of Australia on Monte Bello Island.

October 4: Sir Keith Murdoch dies, leaving two struggling Adelaide, Australia, newspapers in the capable hands of son Rupert. Rupert will turn his inheritance into a media empire that will generate some $20 billion in annual revenue.

October 7: U.S. Air Force pilot and espionage agent John Robertson Dunham is shot down over the Soviet Union. His remains will not be repatriated until 1994.

October 8: Two express trains crash into a commuter train in Harrow-Wealdstone, England, killing 112. • A hundred thousand supporters line the streets of San Francisco for a ticker tape parade in honor of Republican presidential candidate Dwight Eisenhower.

October 11: University of California scientists announce the discovery of a polio vaccine that can be mass-produced. • North Vietnamese General Giap attacks the French along the Fan Si Pan mountains in an attempt to draw them away from the De Lattre Line.

October 20: The British governor in Kenya declares a state of emergency when the Mau Mau begin to rise up against British colonial rule.

October 24: Promising to end the Korean War, in an election-clinching speech, Republican presidential candidate Dwight Eisenhower claims, "I will go to Korea." • The top-secret National Security Agency is founded in Washington, D.C., by a seven-page memo from President Truman to Secretary of State Dean Acheson and Secretary of Defense Robert Lovett.

Flashing his famous big grin, Republican presidential candidate Dwight Eisenhower works the crowd during the 1952 campaign. Eisenhower appealed to American voters because of his status as a war hero and also because he seemed like an honest man with small-town American values. During the campaign, he attracted enormous crowds, with many supporters wearing "I Like Ike" buttons. The use of the nickname immediately personalized the candidate. One could not imagine a similar slogan for the Democratic candidate, the cerebral Adlai Stevenson.

John F. Kennedy (*second from right*) shares a light moment with his brother and sisters as they plot strategy for his 1952 Senate campaign. The young Massachusetts congressman, aided especially by his brother Bobby (*standing, center*), ran against popular Republican incumbent Henry Cabot Lodge. Kennedy wanted to play on the larger Senate stage in part because of his growing interest in foreign affairs. Thanks to a large infusion of cash from his father, Joe, and a winning personality, JFK won a narrow but convincing victory, given the fact that Republican presidential candidate Dwight Eisenhower carried the state.

Richard Nixon

IN AN ATTEMPT TO PLACATE conservative party leaders in 1952, moderates within the GOP offered up California's junior senator as a suitable running mate for the more centrist Dwight Eisenhower. Richard Nixon's credentials as a strident anti-Communist were well established, going back to his first congressional race in 1946. Facing incumbent Jerry Voorhis, and lacking any other relevant credentials, Nixon hammered the hapless congressman by claiming he was a tool of Soviet interests.

Nixon's profile was further heightened by an assignment to the House Un-American Activities Committee (HUAC). There, the freshman congressman quickly made a name for himself as a vociferous Red-baiter, sniffing out subversive influence—real or imagined—wherever he perceived it. His reputation as a no-holds-barred campaigner was solidified during his 1950 run for Senate against Congresswoman Helen Gahagan Douglas. Through a combination of innuendo and smear, Nixon painted his liberal opponent as the "Pink Lady"—"pink down to her underwear." The slander worked, and Senator Joseph McCarthy soon found himself with a peer.

Critics branded Nixon with a sobriquet that would follow him throughout his career: "Tricky Dick." His brand of hardball did not sit well with Eisenhower, the political novice on the top of the ticket. When Nixon came under fire in September 1952 for accepting personal monetary gifts, Eisenhower did nothing to help the vice presidential candidate, secretly hoping the incident would give him opportunity to drop the would-be VP. But a flood of public support in the wake of Nixon's tear-jerking "Checkers" speech on national TV forced Eisenhower to accept the situation.

Four years later, Ike directly asked Nixon to step aside, offering him a Cabinet position, but the vice president was unmoved. He served another four years as VP before challenging Senator John F. Kennedy for the presidency in 1960.

Republican vice presidential nominee Richard Nixon pleads with the American people to support his efforts to stay on the Republican ticket in the 1952 presidential election. After he was accused by the *New York Post* of maintaining an illegal campaign slush fund created by fat-cat supporters, Nixon was dismayed when some of Dwight Eisenhower's advisers urged the presidential nominee to dump him. In a maudlin, nationally televised speech on September 23, 1952, Nixon denied wrongdoing, admitting only that his family had once accepted a little dog from a supporter—a cocker spaniel given the name Checkers by his daughter Tricia—and insisted that "we're gonna keep it." The public reacted overwhelmingly in favor of Nixon, sending more than 300,000 telegrams and letters to the Republican National Committee urging Ike to keep him on the ticket. The general did so.

THE CHECKERS SPEECH

ONE OTHER THING I probably should tell you, because if I don't they'll probably be saying this about me, too. We did get something, a gift, after the election. A man down in Texas heard Pat on the radio mention the fact that our two youngsters would like to have a dog. And believe it or not, the day before we left on this campaign trip we got a message from Union Station in Baltimore, saying they had a package for us. We went down to get it. You know what it was? It was a little cocker spaniel dog, in a crate that he had sent all the way from Texas, black and white, spotted, and our little girl Tricia—the six-year-old—named it Checkers. And you know, the kids, like all kids, love the dog. And I just want to say this, right now, that regardless of what they say about it, we're gonna keep it.

—VICE PRESIDENTIAL CANDIDATE RICHARD NIXON, IN AN ADDRESS TO THE NATION, SEPTEMBER 23, 1952

1952

October 29: In Vietnam, the French launch Operation Lorraine, which targets Viet Minh supply bases. Still, the French fail to draw General Giap away from the Black River.

November 1: The first hydrogen bomb, the massive Mike, is detonated by the U.S. at Eniwetok Atoll in the Marshall Islands.

November 2: President Truman declassifies a document detailing a 1947 Joint Chiefs of Staff recommendation that the U.S. withdraw from Korea.

November 4: The Republican ticket of Dwight Eisenhower and Richard Nixon defeats Democrats Adlai Stevenson and John Sparkman in the race for the White House. Progressive Party presidential candidate Vincent Hallinan and Charlotte Bass, vice presidential candidate and the first black woman to run for that office, pull in less than 1 percent of the vote. • John F. Kennedy unseats incumbent Republican Henry Cabot Lodge for a Senate seat from Massachusetts.

November 7: According to *Jane's Fighting Ships,* the United States Navy is "as large as all other navies of the world put together."

November 10: In a case involving the Atlantic Coast Line Railroad, the U.S. Supreme Court reaffirms the ban on segregation in passenger cars.

November 13: Harvard physician Dr. Paul Zoll pioneers the use of electric shock as a cardiac-arrest rescue technique.

November 14–17: The French fight off a Viet Minh ambush at Chan Muong while they withdraw toward the De Lattre Line in Vietnam.

November 18: Israeli Prime Minister David Ben Gurion invites Albert Einstein to become a candidate for the nation's presidency, following the death of Dr. Chaim Weizmann, Israel's first president. Einstein declines.

Ernest Hemingway has been called the quintessential 20th century American novelist. Having established himself with such works as *A Farewell to Arms* and *For Whom the Bell Tolls,* Hemingway in the postwar years felt that his best work was behind him. Years of depression and drinking further taxed his well-being, leading him to take a time-out in Cuba (*pictured*). Hemingway emerged in 1952 with his final masterpiece, *The Old Man and the Sea.* Equal parts narrative and metaphor, his tale of a past-his-prime fisherman and his struggles against nature and society mirrored the writer's own battles. Recognition came with a Nobel Prize in literature in 1954.

Hollywood struck a blow against television with Cinerama, a 1952 innovation that put viewers in the middle of the action via simultaneous three-camera projection onto a massive, deeply curved screen. Audience members did not actually sit facing each other, as in this demonstration photo, but the Cinerama effect was undeniably unorthodox. Auditorium conversion costs, however, meant that few theaters could install the technology. Further, vertical separation lines that divided the three interlocked images were often visible, and a projector that fell out of synch with the others spelled disaster. The process was introduced in *This Is Cinerama,* which was followed by a handful of travelogues and only two standard movies, *The Wonderful World of the Brothers Grimm* and *How the West Was Won* (both 1962).

Rocky Marciano

In the 1950s, blue-collar Americans, those who grumbled through their grunt work for a buck and change per hour, lived vicariously through Rocky Marciano. He was like many of them—son of immigrants, war veteran, former factory worker—but a whole lot more. The Rock was handsome, built like a god, a genuinely good guy, and the most indomitable champion the sport of boxing had ever seen.

A native of Brockton, Massachusetts, Marciano hoped to make enough money in boxing so that his father could retire from his miserable job in a shoe factory. After turning pro as a heavyweight in 1947, the powerful Rock toppled opponents like Popeye after a can of spinach. He pummeled Carmine Vingo so badly that some feared for Vingo's life.

Marciano rose to prominence in 1951 by knocking out former heavyweight champion Joe Louis. On September 23, 1952, he defeated reigning champ Jersey Joe Walcott to become the new heavyweight king. The triumph improved Marciano's record to 43–0, and—after six successful title defenses—he owned a mark of 49–0 with 43 knockouts.

On April 27, 1956, at age 32, Marciano announced his retirement, due to back pain. The Rock went out on top, the only heavyweight champion in history to retire undefeated. Like fellow '50s icons Elvis, Marilyn, and James Dean, Marciano suffered a premature death, perishing in a plane crash in 1969.

The comedy-quiz program *What's My Line?* contrasted strongly with the game show spectacles of the day. Much like its host, journalist John Daly, the show was comparatively urbane and low-key. Similarly sophisticated and erudite were the members of the show's panel (*pictured from left to right*): columnist Dorothy Kilgallen, show business fixture Steve Allen, actress Arlene Francis, and publisher Bennett Cerf. Their task was to guess the contestant's trade with 10 yes/no questions. In the final round, they were blindfolded while a celebrity was brought on as a "mystery guest." With negligible prizes awarded, the show's wit was the real draw.

Presenting "the forgotten man" was John Steinbeck's gift to literature. With a keen observational eye and an empathetic view of unsung Americans, the writer soared to fame in the 1930s on the strength of his novels *Of Mice and Men* and *The Grapes of Wrath*. *East of Eden* (1952), his most ambitious work, departed from the downtrodden theme. Instead, Steinbeck presented a sprawling exploration of the Cain and Abel parable as enacted within two ranch families, set in early 20th century Salinas Valley, California. Though his lurid book became a bestseller, few literary critics regard *East of Eden* as among Steinbeck's best works.

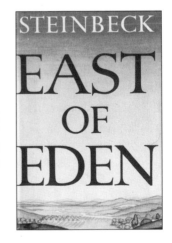

1952

November 24: Agatha Christie's first play, *The Mousetrap,* opens at London's Ambassadors Theatre. Though it will relocate once and change casts several times, it will continue to run for the rest of the century and beyond.

November 25: George Meany assumes the chairmanship of the American Federation of Labor.

November 26: The 3-D film craze of the 1950s kicks off with the premiere of *Bwana Devil,* starring Robert Stack and featuring the cinematography of Lothrop Worth.

December: Christine Jorgenson, who a couple of years earlier was a skinny GI named George, returns to the U.S. following her highly publicized sex-change operation in Copenhagen. • In preparation for his inauguration the following month, President-elect Eisenhower and his administration outline their defense policy. This new policy, which they are calling "New Look," relies heavily on atomic weaponry.

December 2: Rudolf Slansky, former secretary of the Czechoslovakian Communist Party, is executed for treason, along with 10 other party members. • Denver's KOA-TV broadcasts the first human birth seen on television.

December 2–5: Keeping his campaign promise, President-elect Eisenhower tours the front lines in South Korea.

December 4–8: A killer smog blankets London, bringing the city to a halt and causing more than 4,000 deaths.

December 8: Fifty people die when occupying French troops open fire on demonstrators in Casablanca, Morocco.

December 9: The U.S. Supreme Court begins to hear arguments in several school segregation cases, which will eventually be combined as *Brown v. Board of Education. See* May 17, 1954.

"Adventure" was hardly a word one would associate with the mild-mannered Nelson family, yet *The Adventures of Ozzie and Harriet* became one of television's most enduring sitcoms. The real-life Ozzie Nelson had been a bandleader during the 1930s, marrying singer Harriet Hilliard along the way. In the 1940s, a fictional-ized version of their domestic lives became a radio hit, with their real-life sons, David (*second from right*) and Ricky (*far right*), initially portrayed by actors. By 1952 the family's act was ready for prime-time TV, where it would remain until the mid-1960s. Ozzie masterminded the show as head writer and producer.

Soda fountains, often located in drugstores, were widespread in the U.S. from the 1920s to the 1950s. They offered soft drinks and various concoctions made with ice cream, and were popular after-school gathering places for adolescents. By the mid-1950s, fast-food restaurants with their take-out menus began to lure customers, so that by 1965, according to historian Anne Cooper Funderburg, "soda fountains could be found in only about one-third of city drugstores and about half of the drugstores in small towns."

The Beat generation's opening literary shot came in 1952, as John Clellon Holmes's *Go* chronicled the early years of the movement in postwar New York City. Holmes depicted a fictionalized view of the artistic, intellectual, and decadent atmosphere surrounding friends Jack Kerouac, Neal Cassady, and Allen Ginsberg as their philosophical and creative urges struggled to find a voice. Among their circle, Holmes was regarded as the most stable, giving his observations an air of authenticity. Though less experimental than other contemporaneous works, *Go* laid the groundwork for the Beats' contributions to American culture.

Dwight Eisenhower (*right*) and running mate Richard Nixon raise their arms in triumph after a convincing victory in the 1952 election. Ike and Nixon garnered nearly seven million more votes than their Democratic opponents and took 442 of 531 electoral votes. A number of factors contributed to the triumph: Eisenhower exploited public frustration over the Korean War by promising to go to that country if he won; Nixon managed to tar Democrats with charges of softness on communism; Democratic candidate Adlai Stevenson was perceived to be remote and excessively intellectual; and, most of all, more people just plain liked Ike.

Jordan's King Hussein bin Talal smiles engagingly on his 17th birthday in London on November 14, 1952. A year earlier, his grandfather, King Abdullah, had been assassinated by a Palestinian extremist who feared that the moderate monarch would make peace with Israel. Hussein's father succeeded to the throne but abdicated in 1952 because of mental illness. His son then became king. The young Hussein did much to improve conditions in Jordan. He helped raise the literacy rate and improved access to basic sanitary facilities. King Hussein was respected as a generally moderate force in the Arab-Israeli conflict.

This formally attired audience sports the latest in moviegoing accessories at the 1952 premiere of the African adventure *Bwana Devil,* the first 3-D movie. In a desperate attempt to pry audiences away from television, Hollywood studios began upping the technological ante in order to make the cinema an excitingly unique experience. "Cinerama" was one such innovation, while 3-D was another. Filmed in "NaturalVision," *Bwana Devil* treated audiences to thrown spears and leaping lions—that is, if the theater's projection system was just so. Far too often, 3-D films were run without the required precision, leaving the moviegoer with a headache.

1952

December 12: The nuclear reactor at Chalk River, in Ottawa, Canada, becomes the site of the world's first nuclear power plant accident. A partial core meltdown leads to the accumulation of millions of gallons of radioactive water inside the reactor.

December 14: For the first time, a surgical separation of Siamese twins is completely successful, with both twins surviving. The operation is performed at Mount Sinai Hospital in Ohio on two girls who were joined at the sternum. • The prison on Pongam Island is the site of a failed escape attempt by North Korean prisoners of war. Eighty-four die during the ensuing riot.

December 15: Las Vegas's Sands Hotel and Casino opens for business.

December 20: Eighty-four servicemen beginning their Christmas leave die when their transport plane crashes shortly after takeoff from Larson Air Force Base in the state of Washington.

December 22: The Soviet Union awards the Stalin Peace Prize to American singer-actor Paul Robeson. The State Department will make Robeson wait six years before granting him permission to travel to Russia to accept the award.

December 27: The Army Department asks the Selective Service to call 53,000 men to service, effective February 1953.

December 29: Manhattan's Sono-tone Corporation markets the first transistorized hearing aid.

December 30: According to the records of the Tuskegee Institute, for the first year out of the previous 71, no lynchings occurred in the U.S.

A Soviet nuclear weapon explodes over New York City in the 1952 film *Invasion USA*. Made in only seven days, the movie used stock footage and hammy acting to get across a serious message. The United States, the script argued, had become vulnerable to Soviet attack because, in the words of one reviewer, America's materialistic society, understaffed military, and "'let George do it' attitude" had led to terminal apathy. Clearly a product of the Cold War fear that gripped the U.S. in the early 1950s, *Invasion* argued that unless Americans became more vigilant, the country was in serious danger.

TOTAL ANNIHILATION

THE CLOUD EVENTUALLY spread 100 miles wide with a stem 30 miles across and 80,000,000 tons of soil were lifted into the air by the blast. "Mike" was more powerful than all the combined explosives used previously in the two world wars... roughly 750 times as powerful as the bomb dropped on Hiroshima. As the cloud boiled and the shock wave faded in the distance, silent thanks were given that "Mike" was not the effort of some rogue nation.

When the USS *Lipan* reached the point where the island had once stood, the island had been completely vaporized. Soundings were taken at the site to measure the bomb's crater. This was done by dropping and detonating canisters of explosives and measuring the soundings to define the scope of the crater. It measured a little over a mile in width and 164 feet in depth. "Total annihilation" stretched three miles. "Total destruction" stretched to seven miles.

—U.S. SERVICEMAN ROY ROMO, WITNESS TO THE FIRST H-BOMB BLAST

The "Superbomb"

IN AUGUST 1949, the Soviets detonated an atomic bomb. American political, military, and scientific minds concluded that deterrence required upping the ante. To that end, President Harry Truman in early 1950 announced plans for the creation of a "superbomb." Powered by hydrogen fusion, this weapon promised to unleash thermonuclear power a thousand times greater than that unleashed over Hiroshima five years earlier.

The morality of developing such powerful weaponry in peacetime sharply divided the scientific community. Some, such as atomic bomb mastermind Robert Oppenheimer, openly questioned the value of a device whose use surely would mean genocide. A report signed by like-minded researchers concluded that the hydrogen bomb (aka the H-bomb) was "an evil thing considered in any light." But a faction led by atomic physicist Edward Teller persuasively argued that it was America's duty to maintain superiority over the Soviets, lest the U.S. be left vulnerable.

Under Teller's leadership, work on the superbomb proceeded rapidly. By October 1952, the 10.4-megaton device, nicknamed "Mike" (for *m*, as in *megaton*), was ready to be assembled on Eniwetok Atoll, 200 miles west of Bikini in the Pacific. The resulting detonation on November 1 erased Eniwetok from existence, leaving a mile-wide crater.

First H-bomb test, November 1, 1952

Results of the bomb's destructive capabilities thus were revealed to the world. But the triumph would be short-lived, as the Soviets successfully tested their own H-bomb a mere nine months later. Now facing the very real danger of an accelerated arms race, the new Eisenhower Administration proposed a different sort of cooperation between the superpowers, with the "Atoms for Peace" plan. But takers would be few—even within the administration—and the plan was quietly shelved.

Members of a civil defense squad minister to a man "wounded" in a mock nuclear attack in Brooklyn, New York. This was part of the Federal Civil Defense Administration's attempts to protect against the worst effects of a nuclear attack on the United States. Along with the creation of the Emergency Broadcasting System, "duck and cover" films, and instructions on how to build fallout shelters and locate official ones, the FCDA hoped the mock attacks would prepare people for the worst. Of course, no amount of just-pretend could save people from a direct hit by a nuclear weapon.

At the end of World War II, Soviet Premier Joseph Stalin played coy with the issue of Adolf Hitler's death, reasoning that he could justify Russia's immovable presence in Berlin and the rest of the eastern zone of conquered Germany by raising the specter of a living Hitler who might lead a resurgent Nazi Party. The notion of an escaped *Führer,* ensconced (variously) in Argentina, Brazil, or Antarctica, appealed to the popular imagination and spurred speculation by pulp novelists and hack journalists. This 1952 issue of *The National Police Gazette,* a venerably disreputable tabloid founded in 1845, featured one of the earlier magazine treatments of the Hitler survival myth; the *Gazette* and many other publications would repeat the claim into the 1980s.

1952

New & Notable

Books

Anne Frank: The Diary of a Young Girl
　by Anne Frank
Charlotte's Web by E. B. White
Collected Poems by Dylan Thomas
East of Eden by John Steinbeck
Invisible Man by Ralph Ellison
The Old Man and the Sea
　by Ernest Hemingway
The Power of Positive Thinking
　by Norman Vincent Peale
Wise Blood by Flannery O'Connor

Movies

The Greatest Show on Earth
High Noon
The Member of the Wedding
Moulin Rouge
Pat and Mike
The Quiet Man
Singin' in the Rain

Songs

"The Glow Worm"
　by the Mills Brothers
"I Saw Mommy Kissing Santa Claus"
　by Jimmy Boyd
"One Mint Julep" by the Clovers
"Wheel of Fortune" by Kay Starr
"Why Don't You Believe Me"
　by Joni James
"You Belong to Me" by Jo Stafford

Television

The Adventures of Ozzie and Harriet
The Adventures of Superman
Death Valley Days
The Ernie Kovacs Show
The Guiding Light
I've Got a Secret
The Jackie Gleason Show
My Little Margie
Omnibus
Our Miss Brooks
Today

Theater

The Children's Hour
Kiss Me, Kate
The Mousetrap
Pal Joey
The Seven Year Itch

Of all the European countries devastated by World War II, none took longer to recover than the Soviet-controlled portion of Germany. For years after the Third Reich's collapse, East Germany was forced to pay reparations to the Soviet Union, overtaxing an already anemic economy. In order to keep rent low, housing was built on the cheap and then poorly maintained. East Germans also endured brutal government oppression and omnipresent secret police. Those who could fled to greener pastures in West Germany.

President-elect Dwight Eisenhower tours a UN installation in Korea in December 1952. During the 1952 presidential campaign, the former general had pledged to go to Korea if elected. By implication, he seemed to be saying that his mere presence in South Korea would somehow bring the Communists to their knees. In fact, the war dragged on for another eight months. His promise served mainly to anger President Harry Truman and destroy their previously amicable relationship.

In December 1952, the modernistic Sands Hotel opened in Las Vegas and quickly became the city's most popular casino. Initially, it was only a gambling establishment with 200 hotel rooms attached, yet it attracted thousands of visitors each year. After a large hotel and entertainment complex were added in the early 1960s, such celebrities as Frank Sinatra graced its stages. The Sands symbolized the phenomenal growth of Las Vegas, which burgeoned from a population of 24,000 in 1950 to 64,000 a decade later. The Sands crumbled in a planned implosion in 1996 to make way for a bigger and allegedly better pleasure palace.

Characteristically deadpan, TV detective Joe Friday (played by Jack Webb) prepares to keep the streets of Los Angeles safe. Beginning in 1951, actor-producer Webb brought his innovative *Dragnet* radio show to television for a highly successful run. Webb cannily exploited his own stiff demeanor to create the extraordinarily unflappable L.A. police detective. With an opening theme that can only be described as "arresting," *Dragnet* enacted cases taken from actual police files, changing the participants' names "to protect the innocent." Webb's ultra-square persona proved irresistible to parodists, but won a loyal following among viewers.

Country music's first modern superstar had created the blueprint for all that followed—good and bad—by the time he died at age 29. Hank Williams was an Alabama-born singer-songwriter who borrowed equally from blues and what was then called "hillbilly" music. His string of self-penned classics included "Move It on Over," "Hey, Good Lookin'," and "Your Cheatin' Heart." While he achieved crossover success on the pop charts, Williams's alcohol and drug abuse alienated him from the conservative country music establishment. His death on December 31, 1952, while traveling in the back of a Cadillac, ensured his iconic outlaw status.

In 1943 French Navy Captain Jacques Cousteau revolutionized undersea exploration with development of the Aqualung, essentially inventing scuba diving. In 1952 Cousteau drew widespread notice with his best-selling book, *The Silent World,* which submerged readers into the world's oceans for a fascinating glimpse at life within. A feature-length documentary based on the book followed, enthralling audiences with stunning visuals never widely seen before. It was the first of many documentaries through which Cousteau, in partnership with National Geographic, brought the "blue continent" into everyone's living rooms.

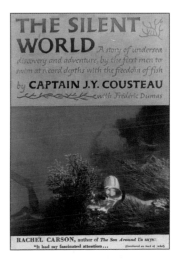

"A career is just fine, but it's no substitute for marriage. Don't you think a man is the most important thing in the world? A woman isn't a woman until she's been married and had children."

—JULIE GILLIS (PLAYED BY DEBBIE REYNOLDS), IN THE 1955 FILM *THE TENDER TRAP*

1953

The American Woman

ON JANUARY 20, 1953, Dwight D. Eisenhower took the oath of office on the East Portico of the U.S. Capitol, using two Bibles: one that had been used by George Washington at the nation's first presidential inauguration, and one given to him by his mother when he graduated from the U.S. Military Academy at West Point. The new president and former general, in his inaugural address, laid out in stark terms the challenges he saw facing the nation and the world.

"We sense with all our faculties that forces of good and evil are massed and armed and opposed as rarely before in history," he told a nationwide audience, calling attention to the dangers of the Cold War, to the continuing hot war in Korea, and to the threat of nuclear Armageddon. But viewers also saw Ike "dash over to buss Mamie on the cheek" as soon as he had completed the oath of office, in what the *Los Angeles Times* called "the most public kiss in history."

If Americans "liked Ike," as the saying went, they loved Mamie. An Army wife of 36 years at the time of her husband's election, and a woman who once estimated that she had moved 27 times during her marriage, Mamie was beloved for her charm, her femininity, and her wifely devotion. And though she has been eclipsed in historical memory by the stylish and sophisticated Jacqueline Kennedy, during the 1950s American women admired Mamie, copying her trademark bangs, her "pert" hats, and even her charm bracelet.

The woman praised by *Woman's Home Companion* as "no bluestocking feminist" and by *Ladies' Home Journal* for not trying "to become an intellec-

A homemaker enjoys lunchtime with her boys, as she plays her role of wife and mother. In the wake of the Depression and World War II, many women felt fortunate to be able to stay home with their children—although others felt unfulfilled.

First Lady Mamie Eisenhower said that women's lives "revolve around our men, and that is the way it should be." Unlike Eleanor Roosevelt, Mamie steered clear of controversial debates over policy. Here she displays her trademark charm bracelet, which includes a charm of devotion for her husband.

tual" did not hesitate to share her views on marriage and women's roles. As Mamie told *Today's Woman* magazine, "Let's face it. Our lives revolve around our men, and that is the way it should be. What real satisfaction is there without them? Being a wife is the best career that life has to offer a woman, but…it takes wit and straight thinking."

During the 1950s, following the hard decades of economic depression and global war, Americans looked to homes and families as sources of strength and stability. As historian Elaine May argues in *Homeward Bound: American Families in the Cold War Era,* the American home "held out the promise of security in an insecure world." That security, in the eyes of many during the 1950s, depended heavily upon the strength of the "traditional family," with clearly differentiated roles for men and women.

Such emphasis on male breadwinners and female homemakers countered trends in the two preceding decades. During the Depression years, many women had, by necessity, taken on all or part of the economic support of their families. During World War II, American women were encouraged to take jobs, including those traditionally performed by men, in support of the nation's war effort. Thus, notions of proper feminine and masculine behavior in the 1950s were topics of considerable interest, and young Americans were bombarded with advice.

Answering the question, "Why do boys drop girls?", the author of a 1950s advice book for teens condemned girls who were "aggressive." "The desirable boys," she wrote, "resent this buddy-buddy relationship and go in search of a

To *Life* editors in 1953, the wording of "The American and His Economy" was acceptable—never mind that women were tremendously active in the economic life of the nation. The editors also had no qualms about placing the man's wife on the same subordinate level as his daughters.

feminine girl they can master, protect, and teach. They want a girl who makes them feel like a MAN!" College students who signed up for the popular how-to "marriage" courses read textbooks that explained that the "essential differences" between men and women were the basis for a successful marriage.

Former presidential candidate Adlai Stevenson, speaking to the graduating class of Smith College in 1955, explained the higher stakes to the accomplished young women in the audience. Admitting that some might feel frustrated confining their talents to the roles of wife and mother, he insisted that the nation depended on women like them in the struggle against "totalitarian, authoritarian ideas." They needed to create in their homes and families, he said, "a vision of the meaning of life and freedom." By and large, American women did take on the roles of wife and mother. They married young, had—and wanted—a greater number of children than their mothers had, and defined themselves primarily as homemakers.

While this division of labor—woman as homemaker, man as breadwinner—was described as "natural" by many contemporary commentators, the specific possibilities of postwar American society made it possible. A major factor was financial: A strong economy and the dramatic increase in wages for blue-collar union workers meant that a large percentage of American families could live in modest middle-class comfort on one (male) salary.

During the 1950s, the great majority of households with children had two parents. Divorce rates were low—as late as 1960, only nine divorces per 1,000 married couples. Moreover, few children were born outside marriage; fewer than four in 100 births were to unmarried women in 1950 (compared to almost one-third in 2000).

Some women worked in white-collar jobs in the 1950s, such as these assistants at a brokerage house. However, relatively few women rose to positions of authority.

If a family could get by on the father's salary, then the mother typically stayed home. The move to the suburbs usually meant that grandparents or extended families were not available to help with child care, and good day care was rarely available. Because most women's jobs paid very little, it wasn't financially worth it for moms to work outside the home, especially if they had to pay for child care. In a culture that celebrated women's roles as wives and mothers and condemned "career women" for trying to "compete" with men, few women rejected "traditional" roles.

At the same time, as a collection of historical essays titled *Not June Cleaver* demonstrates, women's lives were much more varied, their experiences more diverse, than conventional images of the traditional family suggest. America's schools, charitable organizations, and religious institutions benefited greatly from the unpaid labor of married women whose talents were not confined solely to the home. Twice as many women were employed in 1960 as in 1940, and that included nearly 40 percent of women with school-age children. The employment of married women jumped 42 percent during the decade of the 1950s, rising most quickly among middle-class women.

Some did work due to financial necessity, especially women of color, who faced double discrimination on the basis of race and gender, and whose families were more likely to be poor. But many married women with children worked part-time, often to earn money toward some specific goal they saw as compatible with their primary roles as wives and mothers. Women whose goals were more ambitious had a difficult path. Medical schools commonly restricted women to 5 percent of an entering class, for example, and at the end of the decade fewer than 4 percent of the nation's lawyers and judges were female.

Many 1950s advertisements portrayed women as house cleaners, and helpless ones at that, saved only by the great detergent that came to the rescue. Vim cleaning powder was so effective that it gave the wife in this ad a chance to kick back, relax, and sing a hymn of praise . . . to Vim.

While women faced discrimination in the workplace, some did play important and visible roles on the national scene. Eisenhower appointed many women to high-level positions in his administration. He named Oveta Culp Hobby to the Cabinet-level position of secretary of Health, Education, and Welfare, and he appointed Clare Boothe Luce as ambassador to Italy, making her the first American woman ever named to a major diplomatic post.

Rosa Parks, secretary of the local NAACP, sparked the Montgomery bus boycott in 1955. And Hope Mendoza, member of the primarily Mexican-American Community Service Organization, became the official liaison between her community and Los Angeles congressman Chet Holifield in 1953. When *Woman's Home Companion* named the six most successful women of 1953, they looked to the fields of "medical science, education, literature, the theater, and the field of human rights and social betterment" for awardees. Mamie Eisenhower wrote of their accomplishments: "We can all take pride in the forward steps women have taken during our own generation. . . ."

In addition, for all the emphasis on traditional roles, there were great rumblings of discontent. Many women found suburban domesticity confining. As Barnard College sociologist Mirra Komarovsky wrote in 1953, "the status of women in our society is fraught with contradictions and confusion." And while a feminist movement would not reemerge in the United States until the 1960s, it was in 1953 that Simone de Beauvoir's *The Second Sex* was first published in the United States. Beauvoir introduced readers to the phrase "women's liberation."

Nothing published by or about American women in 1953, however, was as controversial as Alfred Kinsey's *Sexual Behavior in the Human Female*, popularly known as "The Kinsey Report." Kinsey, a driven, detail-oriented zoologist who had begun his career studying gall wasps, created a stir with his study of male sexual behavior in 1948 by reporting, among other things, that 37 percent of American men had had "some homosexual experience." Kinsey and his colleagues at Indiana University's Institute for Sex Research knew that the volume about female sexuality would be even more incendiary. They were right.

The dry, statistic-laden volume jumped to the bestseller list, and Kinsey's report was covered in virtually every important magazine and newspaper in the nation. Women's sexual behavior, Kinsey's data revealed, was not at all in line with the popular mores of a society that insisted that a woman's "value" was closely correlated with her virtue. Reverend Billy Graham greeted the report—including Kinsey's claim that half of American women had had premarital sex—by declaring that Dr. Kinsey "certainly could not have interviewed any of the millions of born-again Christian women in this country who put the highest price on virtue, decency, and modesty."

Dr. Wardell B. Pomeroy, an associate of Alfred Kinsey, interviews one of the many women whose stories formed the basis for the controversial book *Sexual Behavior in the Human Female*. After collecting thousands of sex histories, the researchers discovered that American women were not nearly as "virtuous" as the public had assumed.

The *Chicago Tribune* called Kinsey "a menace to society," and *Ladies' Home Journal* stipulated that "the facts of behavior as reported . . . are not to be interpreted as moral or social justification for individual acts." Later researchers would question the accuracy of Kinsey's data.

Nevertheless, a gap certainly existed between public codes and private behaviors, in the sphere of sex as well as in other aspects of American family life during the 1950s. These tensions made for much more complex lives than we usually associate with the 1950s "traditional family," and they provided fertile ground for the changes in gender roles and family structure that would emerge in the next generation.

1953

1953: The U.S. House of Representatives establishes the Gathings Committee, which is charged with overseeing paperbacks and periodicals the committee deems inappropriate. Its attempts to pass censorship legislation will ultimately fail. • Mexico grants women suffrage. • Japan updates its Leprosy Prevention Law, banishing lepers to remote outposts. • Harvard visiting professor Henry Kissinger opens his students' mail and hands "subversive" anti-atomic bomb materials over to the FBI.

1953: Lawrence Ferlinghetti and Peter Martin open City Lights Bookstore, San Francisco's North Beach literary mecca. • The Mattachine Society publishes *One Magazine: The Homosexual Viewpoint,* America's first wide-circulation gay magazine. • Some 20 million American families now have television sets, comprising about half of all households. In contrast, only four years earlier, fewer than one million families owned one. • The phrase "women's liberation" is popularized in America with the U.S. release of French feminist Simone de Beauvoir's *The Second Sex.* • America is introduced to two more products it will soon find it can't live without: Saran Wrap and Eggo waffles.

January 1: Superstar country singer Hank Williams, Sr., dies of a drug and alcohol overdose at age 29.

January 2: As pressure mounts to get the Equal Rights Amendment on the calendar of the 83rd Congress, former First Lady Eleanor Roosevelt aligns herself with the National Federation of Business and Professional Women, a group that is actively promoting equality for women.

January 7: In the final State of the Union address of his presidency, Harry Truman warns the Soviets that war with the U.S. in this atomic age would be their ruin.

Dwight D. Eisenhower (*right*) is sworn in as the 34th president of the United States by Chief Justice Frederick Vinson on January 20, 1953. As the first inaugural ceremony to be televised, the event was seen live by more people than all previous inaugurations put together. After bestowing a classic Ike grin, the new president talked exclusively about foreign policy. Although he recognized the threat of communism and promised to confront it, Eisenhower also emphasized the need to seek peace since "science seems ready to confer upon us, as its final gift, the power to erase human life from this planet."

The rakish Corvette was the brainchild of General Motors design chief Harley Earl and engineering gurus Ed Cole and Zora Arkus-Duntov. When the roadster made its first public appearance, as a concept car at GM's New York Motorama show in January 1953, it became a highly publicized sensation. Car nuts were pleasantly surprised when it went into production a few months later virtually unchanged. Though stylish, the two-seater possessed an under-powered engine and automatic transmission, belying Chevy's "sports car" claim. Both of those shortcomings were corrected in 1955, validating its classic status.

Playwright Arthur Miller followed his acclaimed *Death of a Salesman* with a period piece entitled *The Crucible* (*pictured*) in 1953. The Broadway production featured Arthur Kennedy (*left*) and Beatrice Straight (*right*) in the roles of John and Elizabeth Proctor. Based on the events of 1692 in Salem, Massachusetts, the play intentionally reflected the McCarthyism witch hunts of the 1950s. Miller depicted a community in which rampant fear was fueled by accusations leveled against good people. In Miller's tale, a single group was held accountable for all societal ills by a handful of powerful accusers. Only one person, John Proctor, dared to risk all by standing on principle.

Niagara, starring Marilyn Monroe, demonstrated 20th Century–Fox's commitment to making her a star. The Hitchcockian tale of betrayal and murder boasted some stunning visuals—including shots of the title locale—under Henry Hathaway's concise direction. The esteemed Joseph Cotten costarred as Monroe's ill-fated husband. Filmed in glorious Technicolor, the movie showcases the beauty of Monroe, particularly in scenes in which she wears the formfitting red dress seen here. Though the plot is fairly standard *film noir,* the real revelation was Monroe's considerable dramatic conviction as an adulteress who aspires to murder.

In 1950, on what had been 3,500 acres of flat sugar beet fields near Long Beach, California, developers Mark Taper, Louis Boyar, and Ben Weingart began construction of up to 100 tract houses a day—46 to each grid-like block. This was Lakewood, the largest postwar housing development in the USA, and the American Dream made real for blue-collar workers who aspired to the middle class. As at the similar Levittown developments in the East, the 1,100-square-foot Lakewood houses were assembled on-site from precut components. Prices ranged from $7,575 (two bedrooms) to $8,525 (three bedrooms). By 1953 Lakewood was welcoming nearly 250 new families every week.

In 1953 an English translation of *The Second Sex,* a study of the often unhappy psychological and behavioral development of women, was published in the U.S. Its French author, Simone de Beauvoir, was an existentialist who believed that existence precedes essence, and therefore so-called "female characteristics" are constructed by culture, not biology. She was particularly concerned with the isolation of mothers, who were prized for their maternal duties but little else.

1953

January 9: Some 249 people are reported dead when a passenger ferry sinks off shore in Pusan, South Korea.

January 13: Communist strongman Josip Broz Tito is elected to the Yugoslavian presidency by Parliament. • In a scandal that rocks the Kremlin, nine Jewish doctors are arrested for plotting to kill members of the Soviet Politburo. *See* April 1953.

January 19: The *I Love Lucy* episode in which Lucy Ricardo gives birth to Little Ricky airs on the same night that actress Lucille Ball gives birth to Desi, Jr.

January 20: Dwight Eisenhower is inaugurated as the 34th president in Washington, D.C. •Eisenhower names anti-Communist crusader John Foster Dulles to the post of secretary of state.

January 21: Marilyn Monroe shines in her first important starring role, as housewife Rose Loomis, with the release of *Niagara*.

January 31: The motor vessel *Princess Victoria* founders in a strong storm off the coast of Northern Ireland, killing 133 passengers and crew.

February: The Congress of Racial Equality (CORE) begins sit-in protests in Baltimore restaurants.

February 3: President Eisenhower lifts the Seventh Fleet's naval blockade of Taiwan, allowing the Nationalists to invade Red China.

February 6: In an effort to reduce federal control over the economy, President Eisenhower suspends wage controls and rolls back price controls on consumer goods.

February 9: Allen W. Dulles succeeds General Walter Bedell Smith as director of the CIA.

February 11: Denying them clemency, President Eisenhower allows the death sentences of traitors Julius and Ethel Rosenberg to stand. *See* February 13, 1953.

The concept for "morning zoo" entertainment may have originated in spirit with the antics of chimpanzee J. Fred Muggs on NBC's *Today* show. After being spotted dunking doughnuts in the studio commissary by a network executive, Muggs became a gimmick that NBC hoped would attract viewers to the struggling show. The chimp soon became a regular feature. Following a ratings surge, a female counterpart, Phoebe B. Beebee, was added. Fred was forced into retirement in 1957 due to multiple biting incidents.

Beat writer William S. Burroughs established his literary reputation in 1959 with *Naked Lunch*. Prior to that, his experiences as a heroin user were chronicled in *Junkie* (1953), his first book. Bolstered by shots of morphine, Burroughs completed the manuscript and eventually found a pulp publisher that issued the work under the pseudonym William Lee. Despite disclaimers inserted at the publisher's insistence, Burroughs presented a harrowing but unapologetic account of life within the postwar drug culture.

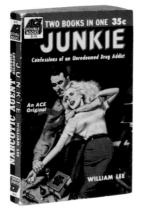

French actor-filmmaker Jacques Tati created an indelible comic character, the diffident, disaster-prone Monsieur Hulot, for his 1953 release, *Mr. Hulot's Holiday*. Rich in visual humor and essentially without plot, the film observes the middle-aged Hulot as he undertakes a beach vacation. The trouble is that everybody around him suffers because of his innocent carelessness. Hulot accidentally sets off a fireworks display and allows a running automobile to slip from his grasp. He plays a maladroit game of tennis and destroys a small boat. He's a skinny hurricane, a force of nature who recalls both Chaplin and Keaton. Tati reprised the role four times, to considerable acclaim.

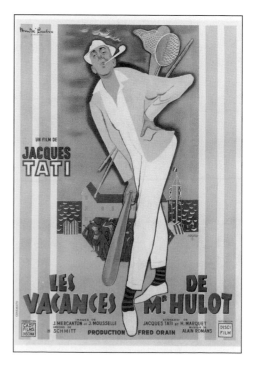

Juvenile Delinquents

FREED FROM YEARS of shared deprivation caused by the Great Depression and World War II, Americans turned inward as the 1950s commenced. A surge of me-ism and materialism was accompanied by an increase in crime that included an alarming uptick in juvenile arrests.

The FBI reported in 1953 that more than half the car thefts and nearly half of all burglaries were committed by offenders under the age of 18. Alongside the "Red Menace," the specter of juvenile delinquency ran like an undercurrent throughout the decade, fueling public anxiety while providing fodder for B movies. In spring 1954, Senator Estes Kefauver chaired a Senate subcommittee on juvenile delinquency.

Although no one could determine precisely the reasons for the rise in criminality among the young, too many opportunistic politicians simplistically pointed the finger at the entertainment and publishing industries. "Many radio and television programs, as well as certain scurrilous books and comics, are corrupting the minds and morals of the American people," declared Congressman E. C. Gath-

A 1958 paperback

ings (D–AR). "Juvenile delinquency...has increased in this country because of the laxity in which these problems have been dealt with." Psychiatrist Dr. Fredric Wertham echoed that sentiment in *Seduction of the Innocent,* his widely read 1954 attack on the supposed link between youth crime and comic books. A publishers' code put many comics publishers out of business by 1956, but youth crime continued.

Other seers blamed juvenile delinquency on the absence of strong father figures because of divorce, wartime casualties, or a perceived "feminization" of adult males. Similarly, as women entered the workforce in record numbers, many believed that teens were going astray due to lack of a mother's care. Some observers saw evidence of youth "acting out" against a generation that had spawned the atomic bomb and a nihilistic Cold War.

Youth crime may have been caused by some, none, or all of these. Whatever the truth, the problem was real (if exaggerated), and drove a wedge between teenagers and the grownups whose job it was to respect and understand them.

Streetcars were common means of public transportation in most American cities from the turn of the century through the early 1950s. This sort of rail transit vehicle, powered by an overhead electric wire, was first employed in Richmond, Virginia, in 1888. Because streetcars could not deviate from fixed tracks, combustion-engine buses and automobiles began to replace them, particularly when oil and gas interests wanted the streetcars to disappear. The car seen here operated in Philadelphia.

1953

February 13: Pope Pius XII appeals for mercy for the Rosenbergs. *See* June 19, 1953.

February 15: Polio survivor Tenley Albright becomes the first American woman to win a world figure skating title.

February 19: The Georgia state legislature launches an offensive against "obscene" literature when it establishes the Georgia Literature Commission.

February 24: Robert M. La Follette, Jr., who along with his father and brother was part of a long-running Wisconsin political dynasty, dies at age 58 from a self-inflicted gunshot wound.

February 28: Francis Crick and James Watson discover the double-helix structure of the DNA molecule.

March 3: Clare Boothe Luce, playwright and former congresswoman from Connecticut, becomes the first woman to represent the U.S. in a major diplomatic post when she is appointed ambassador to Italy.

March 5: Joseph Stalin, the leader of the USSR, dies at age 73, four days after suffering a brain hemorrhage. • Sergei Prokofiev, prolific Soviet composer who gave the world *Peter and the Wolf*, dies at age 62.

March 6: Georgi Malenkov becomes premier of the Soviet Union following the death of Joseph Stalin.

March 8: A census report reveals that there are some 239,000 fewer farmers in the U.S. than there were just two years ago.

March 9: In *U.S. v. Reynolds,* the U.S. Supreme Court establishes that the government has the right to invoke the "state secrets" privilege when national security is at stake.

The Hoxsey therapy for cancer was developed by John Hoxsey, who noticed a horse that seemed to cure itself of cancer by grazing on certain plants. This folk remedy was passed down to his great-grandson, Harry, who opened clinics in 17 states by the 1950s. Although many patients claimed that the Hoxsey method—a combination of dietary and herbal approaches—worked, these clinics were bitterly opposed by the American Medical Association. Under AMA pressure, all the clinics were shut down except one in Tijuana, Mexico, which still remains. The one seen here was in Portage, Pennsylvania.

Newspapers chronicle the death of Soviet leader Joseph Stalin, who died of a brain hemorrhage on March 5, 1953. Following an intense power struggle after the death of Vladimir Lenin, Stalin had emerged as the head of the USSR in 1928. In the 1930s, he consolidated power through a series of massive purges and instituted forced industrialization in his five-year plans. Stalin led his country to a bloody victory over Nazi Germany in World War II at a cost of millions of lives. After the war, he suffered an almost paranoid fear of capitalist encirclement and oversaw the installation of Communist governments in most of Eastern Europe. He also pushed Soviet scientists to develop nuclear weapons.

In March 1953, a nuclear weapons test at the Nevada Test Site demolished a house and a family of mannequins living in it (as well as their car). The bomb was exploded 3,500 feet from the house, and the heat wave set the structure on fire within one-third of a second. The blast wave lifted the roof, then turned the dwelling to matchsticks within three seconds. The high-speed camera's only source of light was from the blast itself. The Atomic Energy Commission hoped the test would illustrate the nature and extent of damage to "average" family houses. Obviously, they learned that it was considerable. The infamous film sequence would be used to great effect in the antinuclear documentary film *Atomic Café* in 1982.

The Race for the Code

Dr. James Watson

HUMAN UNDERSTANDING OF DNA, the greatest scientific milestone of the last half of the 20th century, was achieved by an unlikely pairing of men. One was American and the other British, and both were brash, boisterous, and ambitious. But once paired up at the University of Cambridge in Britain, they proved they were more than just the "Laurel and Hardy" of science. True, Britain's Francis Crick was almost as wholly ignorant in biology as American James Watson was deficient in chemistry. Yet together, the two possessed a gift for detecting the flaws in the work of others while drawing unlikely but accurate conclusions.

By the early 1950s, the rush to discover molecular biology's Holy Grail was under way. Some unsung heroes made sig-nificant contributions to the eventual discovery, but fundamental errors stopped them short of the finish line. Both Cal Tech's Linus Pauling and British scientist Rosalind Franklin provided important clues to the path that Watson and Crick eventually followed to success.

Their cracking of the DNA code, which they announced in February 1953, led to an understanding of how genes are duplicated and passed along from one generation to the next. Uncovering the building blocks of life led to great breakthroughs in later years. The understanding of DNA helped scientists find cures for diseases, delve into biological engineering, and help prosecutors identify perpetrators of crimes.

1953

March 11: A nuclear bomb is accidentally released from a B-47 bomber over South Carolina. Fortunately, safety measures prevent the bomb from detonating.

March 17: The Boston Braves of baseball's National League relocate to Milwaukee. • A fabricated American city is hit by nuclear warheads in a test dubbed "Annie" at the Nevada Test Site. Annie helps scientists understand the potential effects of a nuclear blast on a typical American city.

March 19: *Camino Real,* considered by some to be Tennessee Williams's best play, makes its debut on Broadway. •Comedian Bob Hope hosts the first Academy Awards telecast.

March 20: Hamilton E. Long's booklet *Permit Communist-Conspirators to Be Teachers?* is published. The booklet will be distributed to more than 35,000 New York teachers.

March 24: Queen Mary, widow of King George V and grandmother of Queen Elizabeth II, dies at age 85.

March 26: President Eisenhower offers the French an increased aid package to help in their fight against Communist North Vietnam. • Dr. Jonas Salk reports that his experimental polio vaccine has tested successfully in a small sample population. *See* February 23, 1954.

March 28: Jim Thorpe, who excelled as an amateur and a professional in three sports—track and field, baseball, and football—dies at age 64. • General amnesty is granted to Soviet gulag prisoners while the penal system is revised following Stalin's death. Excepted are anarchists, thieves, and murderers.

March 30: Albert Einstein announces that he has revised his Unified Field Theory.

Continuing its tradition of "Disneyfying" children's classics, Disney Studios produced a feature-length telling of J. M. Barrie's *Peter Pan* in 1953. As usual, the animation is first-rate, as are the supporting musical numbers. Captain Hook, the story's heavy, is presented as vengeful without being frightening to children. Moreover, little Tinkerbell took her place alongside Jiminy Cricket as a popular Disney icon. But Walt Disney himself took issue with the title character, feeling his duplicitous nature made him unlikable. Nonetheless, the film was a box office hit, with a domestic lifetime gross of more than $87 million. The *Peter Pan* character would become firmly connected to future Disney projects.

Baby Boomers were still toddlers and preschoolers when Nancy Claster (*pictured*) and her husband, Bert, came up with an idea: Put a TV version of preschool on the air. In *Romper Room,* which was first broadcast in Baltimore in 1953, Nancy read and sang with children, taught them simple lessons, and introduced fantasy characters. This was during an era in which many kids didn't start school until first grade. The show was so popular that the Clasters turned it into a franchise, with local *Romper Rooms* broadcast in many major cities. The program lasted until the 1990s.

Dr. Salk's Miracle

THE SCOURGE OF POLIOMYELITIS (or infantile paralysis) struck horror into the hearts of parents throughout much of the 20th century. Lacking real understanding of the disease, parents placed children under severe restrictions, especially during summer. Recalled a child of the times: "I was bending over to take a drink from a fountain. . . . I heard my mother's voice saying, 'Don't drink that—you'll get polio.'" (Ironically, it was modern improvements in sanitation that *spurred* outbreaks, as people no longer acquired natural immunity through early exposure.) The prospect of death or a life spent helplessly immobile in an iron lung hung over kids like a dark cloud.

Initial symptoms were deceptively flu-like: fever, sore throat, headache. But when lungs forgot to breathe or limbs stopped working, polio's presence became known. Although termed "infantile," no adult was immune, as the afflicted Franklin Roosevelt proved. The year 1952 was the worst of all, with 58,000 new cases. But on March 26, 1953, University of Pittsburgh researcher Dr. Jonas Salk announced a breakthrough.

Backed by heavy funding, Salk had fast-tracked a vaccine using dead polio strains, which triggered antibodies upon injection. With early trials proving successful, he trumpeted his findings in a most unscientific way, via radio and television, alienating his peers in the process. But an eager public quickly embraced the miracle, and Salk

Dr. Jonas Salk

was hailed across the United States as "The Man Who Saved the Children."

The victory, however, was tempered by several factors. An improperly prepared batch of Salk vaccine caused 11 deaths, and newsman Walter Winchell reported that during the trials, Salk's benefactors were stockpiling children's caskets—just in case. Finally, a rival vaccine developed by Dr. Albert Sabin became available. Sabin's oral vaccine, which contained a live virus in weakened form, provided stronger protection than Salk's vaccine. By the early 1960s, Sabin's vaccine would become standard in the United States.

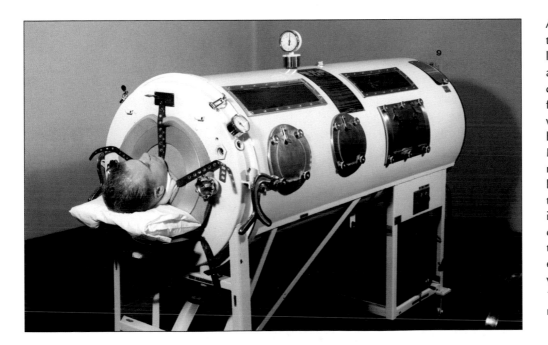

According to one manufacturer, the artificial respirator (or "iron lung") was "a symbol of victory" against the scourge of polio. The device operated as a mechanism for breathing, enabling sufferers whose chests were paralyzed to breathe until they recovered. Most of those who needed the machine eventually resumed breathing unaided. Though the thought of being confined to an iron lung was nightmarish, the contraption saved the lives of thousands at the peak of the epidemic. Thankfully, polio vaccines developed during the 1950s eventually reduced the machine to a relic.

1953

April: Nine Jewish doctors are released in the Soviet Union after it is determined that their confessions, concerning a plot to kill members of the Soviet Politburo, were coerced.

April 1: Soviet Foreign Minister V. M. Molotov agrees with a set of proposals developed by the Chinese and North Koreans that will end the Korean War and repatriate POWs. •The Department of Health, Education, and Welfare is established by an Act of Congress.

April 2: A 10-year, U.S.-Japanese treaty of friendship is signed.

April 3: *TV Guide* is published nationally for the first time.

April 4: CIA Director Allen Dulles approves the allocation of $1 million to help destabilize the government of Iranian Prime Minister Mohammed Mossadegh. •The premiere issue of *I. F. Stone's Weekly,* a left-wing newspaper founded by its namesake, hits the newsstands.

April 7: Swede Dag Hammarskjold is elected UN secretary-general by the General Assembly.

April 8: Jomo Kenyatta, chief of the Mau Mau people of Kenya, is convicted of leading the rebellion against the occupying British government. He will be incarcerated for seven years.

April 10: *House of Wax,* starring Vincent Price, premieres. Directed by Andre de Toth, it's the first 3-D horror movie ever made.

April 15: The Kingdom of Laos asks the United Nations General Assembly to formally condemn the aggression of the Viet Minh Communists against Laos.

April 18: In Korea, the three-day battle of Pork Chop Hill ends with an American victory. *See* July 6–10, 1953.

Philadelphia publishing heir Walter Annenberg became one of the first to recognize the possibilities of a national digest of TV listings bookended by articles about television personalities. Premiering in April 1953, *TV Guide* became *the* source for industry information, reviews, and relevant articles by prominent writers, including Cleveland Amory. The first national issue (*pictured*) discussed the birth of Desi Arnaz, Jr.—a television milestone that cleverly wove Lucille Ball's real-life pregnancy into *I Love Lucy*'s story line. *TV Guide* quickly became America's biggest-selling weekly magazine.

Confession magazines suggested that not all was quiet on America's home front, particularly in the lives of women. *True Story* was created in 1919 by Bernarr Macfadden, who amassed a vast fortune with magazines devoted to physical fitness, detective fiction, and women's "confessions." *True Story* reflected Macfadden's belief in emotional honesty, not least because the articles drew from manuscripts submitted by "real women." Although Macfadden sold his publishing empire in the 1940s, *True Story* continued to follow the course he had set, and was one of the most widely read women's magazines of the 1950s.

Publisher William Gaines became most famous for *Mad* magazine. But when Gaines inherited the kiddie-oriented EC Comics from his father in the late 1940s, he and writer-editor Al Feldstein crafted a line of crime, horror, war, and science fiction comics aimed at older readers. *The Vault of Horror* was one of EC's mainstay spook titles; the others were *Tales from the Crypt* and *The Haunt of Fear.* Caption heavy and unusually literate, EC stories also had plenty of sick humor, as this 1953 cover by Johnny Craig suggests. Craig was just one of many top illustrators who found their way to EC. Others included Jack Davis, Wallace Wood, and Reed Crandall.

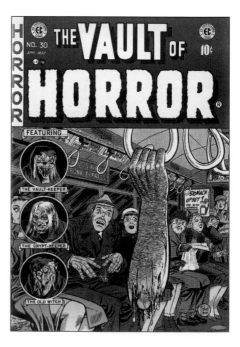

Just when the public's preoccupation with spies and foreign intrigue was at its zenith, a literary franchise premiered. *Casino Royale* introduced readers to Agent 007, James Bond, a suave, sexy British super-spy. Bond possessed a fondness for gambling, gadgets, fast cars, and women. His tastes mirrored those of creator Ian Fleming, who had been in Britain's Naval Intelligence during the war. On the eve of marriage after a prolonged bachelorhood, Fleming set to paper a story that had been incubating in his head for some time, drawing on a variety of experiences and acquaintances.

Of all the Communist bloc leaders, Yugoslavia's Marshall Tito operated the most independently, shaking off Stalinist domination while adhering to Marxist doctrine. With the adoption of a new constitution after the war, Tito consolidated his power by amassing a secret police force while purging political opposition. However, his continued defiance of Kremlin edicts led to a break with the Soviets. Undeterred, Tito began organizing an alliance with nonaligned nations. Cultivating such leaders as Egypt's Nasser and India's Nehru, he pursued a middle path between the two superpowers. The resulting bloc made Tito a major player on the world's stage.

Depending on one's disposition, *Invaders from Mars* (1953) is either low-tech sci-fi schlock or a sophisticated depiction of the period's political paranoia. With a shoestring budget, director-art director William Cameron Menzies displayed great resourcefulness in presenting his nightmarish tale. Extraterrestrials who have landed their saucer in a sand pit near a government rocket installation subvert the personalities of local people, turning them into ill-tempered spies and saboteurs. In a clever stroke, the adventure is told from the point of view of 12-year-old David (Jimmy Hunt, *right*), who is terrified when his parents are among those "taken over" by the aliens. The boy enlists the aid of Dr. Pat Blake (Helena Carter, *left*) to combat the title creatures.

Alan Ladd (*right*) starred as the title character in George Stevens's classic western, *Shane*. Featuring (*left to right*) Brandon De Wilde, Jean Arthur, and Van Heflin, the story centers on a boy's innocent hero-worship of a violent gunfighter. Weary of his bloody past, Shane attempts to put the gunplay behind him but finds his history—and a vicious dispute between homesteaders and cattlemen—will not let go. The film's poignant depiction of the closeness that develops between him and young Joey reaches an emotional climax with the latter's plaintive cry of "Shane—come back!" at the conclusion. The film garnered six Oscar nominations.

April 20: The U.S. Communist Party is ordered to register with the Justice Department by the U.S. Subversive Activities Control Board. • In Korea, Operation Little Switch, a POW exchange for sick and wounded prisoners, gets under way.

April 22: The televised Army-McCarthy hearings, Senator Joseph McCarthy's investigation of Communist infiltration of the Army, begin.

April 26: Korean War peace negotiations resume at Panmunjom. • The U.S. Air Force drops leaflets behind North Korean enemy lines, offering $50,000 for the delivery of a Soviet MiG-15. *See* September 21, 1953.

April 27: In a move designed to keep homosexuals out of the federal workforce, President Eisenhower signs Executive Order 10450, which makes "sexual perversion" a firing offense.

April 29: Triangle Publications, a publisher of horse racing magazines, asserts that nearly 46 million spectators attended horse races in 1952.

April 30: Leaders of the British West Indies colonies, meeting in London, plan to unite as the British Caribbean Federation.

May: General Omar Bradley retires from his position as chairman of the Joint Chiefs of Staff, and Admiral Arthur Radford steps in. President Eisenhower will butt heads with Admiral Radford often, over what Ike perceives to be Radford's overly hawkish approach.

May 2: Prince Hussein of Jordan joins his cousin, Faisal II of Iraq, in monarchy when he ascends to the throne following his father's abdication. • The crash of a De Havilland Comet, the first commercial jet aircraft, marks the third time since October 1952 that a Comet has gone down. Evidence points to mechanical failure in all three cases.

The Cadillac Division of General Motors unveiled the Eldorado model in 1953. Its name meant "The Gilded One" in Spanish, an appropriate designation for a vehicle with so much chrome. The Eldorado weighed nearly two and a half tons and cost $7,750—almost the price of a small house at the time. Americans got their first glimpse of the new machine when President Eisenhower rode in one in his inaugural parade on January 20. Only 532 were made and sold in 1953, but in 1955 sales quadrupled. For some Americans, the Eldorado symbolized the epitome of luxury; for others, it represented the acme of tacky, conspicuous consumption.

Local legend held that the Texas city of Waco, situated on the banks of the Brazos River, was immune to a tornado strike. That faith proved tragically misplaced on May 11, 1953, when an F5 storm buzzed through downtown on a workday. This view captures some of the devastation of the tornado, which claimed 114 lives. Twisters killed many more Americans that spring. On June 8, an F5 tornado flattened parts of Flint, Michigan, taking 115 lives. The next day, Worcester, Massachusetts, was blindsided by a rare New England tornado, which killed 90 people.

In 1953 the Pentagon sanctioned the testing of an atomic cannon, which would be deployed by ground troops to exact maximum casualties with minimum risk (to themselves). On May 25, 1953, at a Nevada testing range, the cannon known as Atomic Annie fired a 280mm shell containing a fission warhead (*pictured*). The projectile detonated aboveground seven miles away. As part of the exercise, more than 2,000 soldiers huddled in trenches, as close as 2.3 miles from the blast, then charged toward the mushroom cloud minutes after the explosion. The atomic cannon was fired only once, but it did put the Soviets on notice.

With a revolutionary approach to melody and harmonics in his soloing, saxophonist Charlie Parker laid the groundwork for all that followed in modern jazz. "Bird," as he was known, had begun recording at age 20, developing a style that built upon work by such masters as Lester Young. Subsequent collaborations with trumpeter Dizzy Gillespie in the mid-1940s broke new ground, as such recordings as "Ko Ko" created the blueprint for bop jazz. Tragically, Parker's serious heroin addiction sapped his creativity, and hastened his death at 34 in 1955.

The Idaho National Laboratory, located in an isolated area near Idaho Falls, boasted one of the first nuclear reactors designed specifically to produce power. In 1951 workers at the lab produced significant amounts of electrical energy from nuclear power for the first time. Two years later, they demonstrated that a reactor could actually "breed" by producing more electricity than it consumed. This established the principle on which future nuclear power plants operated.

1953

May 4: In *Terry v. Adams,* the U.S. Supreme Court rules that primary elections that exclude black voters violate the 15th Amendment.

May 5: Chicago-based Vee-Jay Records is launched with the recording of its first album, by the Spaniels. Founders Vivian and James Bracken and Calvin Carter will soon shape Vee-Jay into the nation's biggest black-owned record label.

May 11: Tornadoes devastate the Waco, Texas, area, killing 114 people. • British Prime Minister Winston Churchill challenges John Foster Dulles's "domino theory," which has become the cornerstone of U.S. foreign policy in Asia. • Oveta Culp Hobby is named secretary of the newly created Department of Health, Education, and Welfare.

May 13: A U.S. air raid on North Korea's Toskan Dam results in the destruction of several miles of roads, railroad tracks, and rice crops.

May 18: Jacqueline Cochran becomes the first woman to shatter the sound barrier when she pilots her F-86 at 652 mph over Rogers Dry Lake, California.

May 19: An A-bomb test, nicknamed "Dirty Harry," produces levels of radiation in St. George, Utah, that are thought to be hundreds of times greater than "safe" levels of exposure.

May 25: Houston's KUHT, the first educational, commercial-free television station, begins its regular programming schedule. • The U.S. conducts its only nuclear artillery test at the Nevada Test Site. A 280mm atomic cannon fires a projectile seven miles.

May 27: Following a meeting with President Eisenhower, Atomic Energy Commission Chairman Gordon Dean notes in his diary that Eisenhower has told him to "keep them [the public] confused as to 'fission' and 'fusion.'"

Queen Elizabeth II and her husband, Philip, the Duke of Edinburgh, wave happily to the masses of people who gathered in London for her coronation on June 2, 1953. The rainy weather didn't dampen the enthusiasm of British citizens, who lined the streets. When it had been announced that the ceremonies would be shown on television, sales of TV sets skyrocketed. As a young woman, Elizabeth had studied constitutional history at Eton, had served as a model of composure during World War II, and had been a patron of numerous charitable organizations, especially those helping children.

The famous 1955 bus boycott in Montgomery, Alabama, was not the first of its kind. A similar but less publicized boycott played out in Baton Rouge, Louisiana, in June 1953. That month, black citizens were angry that white bus drivers refused to obey a local ordinance that provided for "first-come, first-served" seating. The black community, led by Reverend T. J. Jemison, responded with a five-day boycott that included free car service for protesters. The boycott ended successfully when city officials reaffirmed the ordinance. Martin Luther King, Jr., later wrote that Montgomery's boycott leaders had learned much from the protest in Baton Rouge.

Conquering Mt. Everest

"**W**ELL, WE KNOCKED THE BASTARD off!" So said Edmund Hillary (*left*) after reaching the top of Nepal's Mt. Everest. On May 29, 1953, the New Zealand beekeeper and Sherpa climber Tenzing Norgay (*right*) became the first men to successfully scale the world's highest summit. Why anyone would attempt such a dangerous stunt had been answered in the 1920s by British climber George Mallory (who died trying): "Because it's there."

The exercise represented a last gasp of glory on behalf of the British Empire, now in its inexorable sunset. Though other nations had made attempts (with the Swiss coming closest to the summit one year before), the British maintained a sort of proprietorship toward the mountain. With a new monarch about to be crowned, the pressure to succeed was enormous.

The drive to conquer the 29,028-foot peak was very much a team effort, with Colonel John Hunt providing superb planning that was essential to the successful outcome. Norgay, a member of the most recent viable attempt to scale Everest, offered important experience. Alas, the Empire stayed true to form: British subjects Hunt and Hillary were knighted, while Nepal's Norgay received a lesser honor from the Queen.

Native Dancer (*left*), arguably the greatest racehorse of the 1950s, defeats Jamie K. by a neck at the 1953 Belmont Stakes. Owned by Alfred G. Vanderbilt, Jr., the "Gray Ghost," as he was nicknamed, also won the Preakness Stakes in 1953. Although he lost the 1953 Kentucky Derby, film of the race shows that he was fouled twice. Voted Horse of the Year in 1954, when he won all three of the races he entered, Native Dancer appeared on the cover of *Time* magazine. A foot injury that same year cut short his brilliant career.

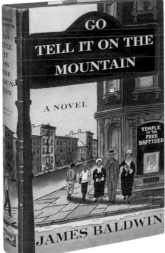

James Baldwin felt a need to write about his difficult early years in Harlem. He had spent his whole young life there, serving three years as a boy preacher. But in 1953, he published an autobiographical novel, *Go Tell It on the Mountain,* in which truth and (self-) love "saves" a black boy preacher from being crushed by the pain of his family and his environment. "The morning I typed *the end* to my manuscript, I knew I had gone through something," he recalled. Henceforth, Baldwin dedicated himself and his art to the purpose of making whites and blacks face their history, themselves, and each other.

1953

May 29: Mountain climbers Edmund Hillary of New Zealand and Tenzing Norgay of Nepal become the first to reach the summit of Nepal's Mount Everest, which at 29,028 feet is the tallest mountain in the world.

May 31: The first nuclear reactor designed with the sole goal of producing energy is fired up near Idaho Falls, Idaho. Called the Submarine Thermal Reactor, it is actually built from the hull of a submarine.

June: The Crows release "Gee," considered one of the first rock 'n' roll records.

June 4: The U.S. tests a giant A-bomb, nicknamed Climax, at Yucca Flats, Nevada. Equal to 50,000 tons of TNT, the bomb explodes with twice the force of the bomb that was dropped on Hiroshima.

June 7: President Eisenhower announces that the U.S. has decided to accept North Korean truce proposals.

June 8: Operation Alert, a three-day, nationwide civil defense training exercise, begins. It exposes inadequacies in several areas, including urban evacuation and government relocation procedures. • The U.S. Supreme Court upholds an 1873 law that bans segregation in Washington, D.C., restaurants. • A tornado strikes Flint, Michigan, killing 115 people.

June 9: A devastating tornado claims 90 lives in Worcester, Massachusetts.

June 15: President Eisenhower addresses a crowd at Dartmouth College, speaking out against "book burners" who would purge libraries of books that even mention communism. • Aircraft carrier USS *Princeton* sets a record for the greatest number of combat sorties, 184, carried out in a single day from a single carrier.

Despite the end of both the Rosenberg case and the Korean War in 1953, Senator Joseph McCarthy scarcely let up in his pursuit of targets for persecution. He no longer confined his rhetoric to the opposing party; his indiscriminate charges of disloyalty drew increasingly closer to the administration. With President Eisenhower avoiding direct confrontation, underlings such as Secretary of State John Foster Dulles (featured in this Reg Manning cartoon) were forced to respond. McCarthy's subsequent attack on the Army in 1953 set the stage for a showdown the following year.

Hundreds march in Washington, D.C., to protest the impending execution of Julius and Ethel Rosenberg. In 1951 the couple had been sentenced to death for conspiring to transmit classified military material to the Soviet Union. Various voices demanded a new trial, citing McCarthyite hysteria as the reason for the "witch hunt." Most Western European newspapers called for mercy in the case. In France, even the right-wing *L'Aurore* pleaded for clemency, while *Le Monde* referred to the decision not to retry the case as "barbaric."

American GIs celebrate the June 19 execution of atom spies Julius and Ethel Rosenberg. In spite of pleas for a new trial, or clemency from President Eisenhower, the executions were carried out as scheduled. Millions of Americans took a grim satisfaction in seeing the couple die, given the level of anti-Communist sentiment and fear of internal subversion in the early 1950s. They no doubt agreed with presiding Judge Irving Kaufman, who said he considered the Rosenbergs' crimes "worse than murder."

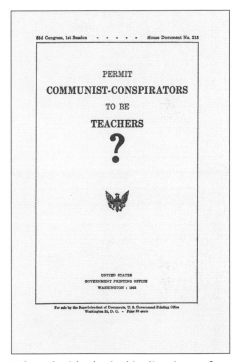

When the ideological inclinations of American teachers became a flash point for Red-baiting politicians, one result was the 83rd Congress's House Document No. 213, *Permit Communist-Conspirators to Be Teachers?* Although the 47-page pamphlet admitted that "comparatively few Communists" worked as teachers, it nevertheless described a "Kremlin-controlled conspiracy" to place a Red in front of every classroom in the U.S. A particularly provocative recommendation was that teachers be dismissed on mere suspicion of Communist sympathy, whether or not they actually promulgated Communist thought on the job.

Dissatisfied workers in East Berlin hurl stones at a Soviet tank during a 1953 rebellion against the Communist government of East Germany. Officials had recently implemented a stringent centralized economic strategy that resulted in wage reductions. On June 17, more than a million workers went on strike, and violence ensued. Although the brief rebellion was put down easily by the Soviet Army, it signaled to the world that many in East Germany despised the Communist government.

June 18: Some 27,000 North Korean POWs refuse repatriation upon their release by South Korean forces. • A transport plane crashes near Tokyo, killing 129 U.S. servicemen.

June 19: Julius and Ethel Rosenberg die in the electric chair at Sing-Sing prison. • In Baton Rouge, Louisiana, Reverend T. J. Jemison initiates the first successful bus boycott by southern blacks. After five days, the city agrees to an open seating policy, excluding the first two seats (which will be reserved for whites) and the two rear seats (for blacks). • Lieutenant Colonel Gamal Abdul Nasser becomes premier of Egypt following its proclamation as a republic.

June 21: A four-day uprising by East German workers is crushed by Soviet troops.

June 25: The two Koreas are one step closer to armistice with the success of the "Little Truce Talks." However, the Chinese Communists launch fresh attacks against South Korea.

June 26: Soviet official Nikita Khrushchev calls for the arrest (and eventually the execution) of Lavrenti Beria, head of the Soviet bomb project.

June 30: The first Corvette is manufactured at the Flint, Michigan, Chevrolet plant. It will retail for $3,250. • The skies over Korea see their busiest day yet, with 16 MiGs destroyed by U.S. forces.

July 1: General Alfred Gruenther succeeds General Matthew Ridgway as supreme allied commander in Europe. • The U.S. Treasury Department announces a federal budget deficit of nearly $10 billion.

July 4: Imre Nagy, a moderate Communist reformer, becomes premier of Hungary.

July 6–10: A second battle for Pork Chop Hill in Korea ends with the U.S. withdrawing from the hill.

Age and a thickening middle removed Johnny Weissmuller from the Tarzan role in 1949, and the character was handed to a younger, more noticeably fit actor, Lex Barker (*pictured*). The five films that resulted were competent adventures with solid supporting casts and nice work by Barker, whose Tarzan was educated and articulate. In this scene from *Tarzan and the She-Devil*, Jane (Joyce MacKenzie) looks on as Tarzan prepares to cuff perennial heavy Raymond Burr.

KING OF THE ROAD

In the years prior to World War II, well-off Americans engaged in "touring." These were pre-superhighway pleasure trips in which the local color along the way was as important as the destination. Bringing comfort and amenities to the less hardy was Wally Byam, who introduced the Airstream line of campers to the well-heeled. These aluminum-bodied trailers captured the public's imagination with their futuristic design and the promise of smooth, relaxed traveling. Although business plummeted during the war, Airstream bounced back in the 1950s to ride the waves of highway construction, prosperity, and increased leisure time.

No Gays Allowed

NEWS THAT SENATOR LESTER Hunt (D–WY) had shot himself to death stunned Washington in June 1954. While shocked constituents could only guess at his reasons, insiders guessed at his motivation: Political enemies had threatened to go public with the story of his grown son's arrest on a "morals charge." In an ugly climate where the taint of "perversion," if only by association, could bring shame and derail a career, even a senator as conscientious and popular as Hunt (an ardent foe of Joseph McCarthy) might decide to take his own life.

The tragedy occurred just over a year after President Eisenhower signed Executive Order 10450, which expanded grounds for dismissal from federal jobs to include the purposely amorphous "sexual perversion." The order declared that homosexuals were not to be hired for government work. The mandate soon spread to state and local jurisdictions as well as to quasi-governmental agencies, such as the American Red Cross.

The reasoning behind such a measure was spelled out in a 1950 Senate subcommittee report entitled "Employment of Homosexuals and Other Sex Perverts in Government." The report concluded that gays, being subject to blackmail due to their "immoral behavior," posed security risks. In recommending a purge, the committee noted that "to pussyfoot or to take half measures will allow some known perverts to remain in Government."

These conclusions reflected prevailing public sentiment. Homosexuality was regarded as a mental disorder, akin to criminality or alcoholism. "Cures," through hormone treatments, electroshock, or counseling, were believed possible. Many gays concluded that "voluntary" repression or even suppression of their natural sexuality could be acts of self-protection. Some gays entered into traditional marriages and pursued their true sexual natures in secret, if at all.

The public acquiesced to the charade, willfully overlooking the obvious. Flamboyant pianist Liberace enjoyed widespread adoration throughout the 1950s, as did actor Rock Hudson, the subject of many rumors. Conversely, closeted gay attorney Roy Cohn, Senator Joe McCarthy's right-hand man, persecuted homosexuals with a vengeance.

In the 1950s, *Holiday* magazine targeted middle- and upper-middle-class Americans with aggressive, splashy covers and enticing stories of faraway travel destinations. Aware of increasing affluence and leisure time engendered by the postwar economic boom, Curtis Publishing's editors tried to show readers how exciting holiday travel could be. Featured locales varied greatly. One issue profiled travel destinations in Minnesota, the Philippines, and Buffalo. This issue's cover is by designer Robert Geissmann.

Looking the worse for wear, actor William Holden starred as Sergeant Sefton in director Billy Wilder's 1953 film, *Stalag 17.* Adapted from Donald Bevan and Edmund Trzcinski's Broadway play, the comedy-drama examined circumstances befalling a group of Allied soldiers imprisoned in a German POW camp during World War II. With Otto Preminger as the camp's heavy-handed commandant, the ensemble enacted the boredom, suspicion, and occasional brutality experienced by captive troops. *Stalag 17* was a commercial success and garnered Holden a best actor Academy Award.

July 10: The Communists return to the negotiating table as both sides continue to work toward a cease-fire agreement in Korea. • Ben Hogan wins the British Open, capturing his third major golf championship of the year.

July 13–20: The Battle of Kumsong River Salient, the largest Chinese offensive in two years and the last battle of the Korean War, lasts a week and establishes the boundaries of the permanent demilitarized zone.

July 26: A massive raid against polygamists puts nearly the entire adult population of Short Creek, Arizona, behind bars. • Insurgents, Fidel Castro among them, stage an unsuccessful revolt against self-appointed Cuban President Fulgencio Batista, attacking the Moncada army barracks. *See* October 16, 1953.

July 27: The cease-fire that ends the Korean War is signed in Panmunjom. More than 33,000 U.S. soldiers were killed in action, more than 100,000 were wounded, and more than 7,000 became prisoners of war.

July 29: A U.S. Air Force RB-50 reconnaissance plane is shot out of the sky by two Soviet MiGs, about 100 miles southeast of Vladivostok, USSR. Only one of the 16 crew members on board survives.

July 31: Republican Senator Robert A. Taft of Ohio dies at age 63.

August: Operation Big Stick, which involves moving 20 B-36s armed with nuclear warheads to Okinawa, Japan, gets under way.

August 7: Eastern Airlines unveils the prop-jet Electra, its first commercial jet airplane.

August 8: The U.S. signs a mutual security pact with South Korea. • Soviet Premier Georgi Malenkov announces that the Soviets have developed the H-bomb.

A beardless Fidel Castro (*standing, center*) smiles with fellow guerrilla fighters in July 1953. The young Cuban lawyer joined radical activists in 1952 to plan the overthrow of dictator Fulgencio Batista, who had staged a military coup that year. On July 26, 1953, Castro's forces launched an unsuccessful strike on two army garrisons. Fidel and his brother, Raul, were captured, tried, and sentenced to prison. While in jail, Fidel began teaching an informal class on politics, philosophy, and weapons training, attracting a number of anti-Batista prisoners. This marked the birth of the July 26 Movement, which would spearhead the overthrow of Batista in the late 1950s.

American troops march on a North Korean mountain road toward Pork Chop Hill, site of the war's last big clash. As peace talks at Panmunjom proceeded in 1953, both sides recognized the propaganda value of demonstrating their willingness to carry on fighting if necessary. Though of little strategic significance, the American-held outpost at Pork Chop Hill was chosen for a series of bloody showdowns. Amid brutal artillery exchanges and ferocious hand-to-hand combat, turf changed hands several times before being evacuated by UN troops in July.

Marines carry a dead body from the field of battle during the Korean War in July 1953, shortly before the armistice ending the conflict was signed. Although no completely accurate figures exist for casualties, official estimates indicate that 33,667 Americans were killed or are missing in action, 3,249 died of non-hostile causes, and 103,284 were wounded. UN allies accounted for another 3,360 killed and 11,886 wounded. There are simply no valid statistics for South Korean, North Korean, or Chinese losses, but casualties, including civilians, probably were in the millions.

On July 27, 1953, General Mark Clark, commander of UN forces in Korea, signs an armistice agreement previously agreed to by Communist leaders three days earlier. The pact called for the halt of hostilities and establishment of a four-kilometer-wide demilitarized zone between the two Koreas near the original 38th parallel (which had separated North and South Korea). POWs willing to be repatriated would be so within 60 days, while those who opposed would be interrogated by both sides under the supervision of a neutral repatriation commission. Although this armistice ended military hostilities between UN forces and Communist North Korean and Chinese forces, a state of war technically still existed between the two Koreas well into the 21st century.

Not until four years after Hiroshima did the Soviets respond with their own atomic bomb, in 1949. But with a successful hydrogen bomb test *(pictured)* in August 1953, less than a year after America's first H-bomb detonation, the western world was put on notice that Russian technology was not to be underestimated. Physicist Andrei Sakharov's "layer cake" design, though less powerful than the first U.S. H-bomb, had the distinct advantage of being deployable from a plane, and therefore practical. Deeply concerned, President Eisenhower proposed the "Open Skies" policy to the Soviets in 1955: a mutual information exchange intended to prevent a "nuclear Pearl Harbor." Moscow rejected the proposal.

Operation Ajax

BY MID-AUGUST 1953, events in Iran had reached a boiling point. Amid great violence, those protesting the rule of Iranian Prime Minister Mohammed Mossadegh were filling the streets of Tehran, clashing with government forces struggling to maintain order. Reza Shah Pahlavi, ruler since 1941, had dismissed the democratically elected prime minister over fears that he had assumed too much power and would soon turn the country into a republic with himself as head. Bypassing the Parliament, Pahlavi named General Fazlollah Zahedi as new prime minister.

But Mossadegh was no pushover, and he quickly forced the Shah into a humiliating flight—first to Baghdad, then to Rome. Said Foreign Minister Hossein Fatemi to Shah Pahlavi in exile: "A traitor is afraid. The day when you...heard...that your foreign plot had been defeated, you made your way to the nearest country where Britain has an embassy." But within 48 hours, General Zahedi arrested Mossadegh and his aides, paving the way for the Shah's triumphant return three days later.

What Foreign Minister Fatemi knew that the rest of the world did not was that Prime Minister Mossadegh had been the victim of a coup d'état, instigated by the British and American governments and stage-managed by the CIA. Kermit Roosevelt, Jr., helped draft what was called Operation Ajax, the CIA's first successful overthrow of a democratically elected government. General H. Norman Schwarzkopf, Sr., an intimate of the Shah, was another major player. Months of propagandizing laid the groundwork for inciting the "spontaneous" anti-Mossadegh demonstrations that peaked in August, with crowds that included CIA operatives and paid hooligans wreaking havoc.

The West's displeasure with Mossadegh stemmed from his seizure of assets of the British-owned Anglo-Iranian Oil Company and nationalization of Iran's petroleum industry in 1951. Unwilling to cede control of lucrative oil contracts, Britain approached U.S. intelligence with its plan to overthrow the prime minister. President Harry Truman rebuffed the overtures. But President Dwight Eisenhower, fearful that Mossadegh's socialist reforms could move the country toward a Soviet alliance, agreed to support the effort. Shah Pahlavi was persuaded to go along with the outsiders' designs, but his vacillating nature made him an unreliable figure in the plot. Nevertheless, the coup was a great success for the U.S.

Reza Shah Pahlavi

Buoyed by triumph (and its relatively low cost), the CIA enacted similar endeavors in other countries. While Ajax was unfolding in Iran, Eisenhower approved plans for Operation Success in Guatemala. There, a duly elected government seen as hostile to American business interests was subverted, although the operation in Guatemala did not go as smoothly as the coup in Iran. Nevertheless, the operations emboldened the American high command. The CIA under Allen Dulles (brother of Secretary of State John Foster Dulles) would set a policy course far beyond intelligence gathering—one that would include psychological warfare and assassinations. Future adventurism would occur in other Central American countries as well as in Cuba and Vietnam.

Meanwhile, the Iranian escapade would, over time, prove to be a Pyrrhic victory. The Shah, whose position was bolstered by an influx of foreign funding, assumed dictatorial powers. All dissent within his borders was crushed, as the Iranian military and secret police carried out kidnappings and torture under his direction, with America's tacit approval. The Shah's reign of brutality fomented the seeds of revolt, and would prompt Islamic radicals to seize control a quarter-century later.

> "Our agent there, a member of the CIA, worked intelligently, courageously, and tirelessly! I listened to his detailed report and it seemed more like a dime novel than an historical fact."
>
> —PRESIDENT EISENHOWER, WRITING ABOUT THE IRAN COUP IN HIS DIARY

WHY MOSSADEGH HAD TO GO

THE AMERICANS were seriously looking for a qualified military officer to replace Mossadegh. But we convinced them that after detailed study and search we had come to the conclusion that there was no officer qualified for the job. Therefore it was better for the Shah to return. The Americans accepted, met with him in Rome, and arranged the trip back to Tehran. It was us who encouraged the Americans to go ahead with the coup. If we had delayed, a Communist coup would have stolen the show. Therefore, in order to rescue Iran from the grip of communism, we decided that Mossadegh had to go and the Shah must return.

—A BRITISH M16 STATION CHIEF IN IRAN

A Tehran native removes graffiti that expresses local resentment in the wake of the CIA-sponsored coup that toppled Prime Minister Mohammed Mossadegh. After initially fleeing the country, Reza Shah Pahlavi returned as Iranian leader. The Shah's warm relationship with the United States would endure for a quarter century. In exchange for military and financial aid from the U.S., Iran would provide a Middle Eastern bulwark against Soviet expansionism. Foreign observers, recognizing America's interference in Iran's affairs for what it was, articulated the suppressed sentiments of Iranian citizens.

American prisoners of war are repatriated during Operation Big Switch, which lasted from August 4 to September 6, 1953. During that period, nearly 3,600 Americans returned from Communist camps. Accusations of torture and murder of American prisoners were undoubtedly accurate. Although the exact number of American prisoners who died as prisoners of war will never be known, the best estimate is about 3,000. More than 20 U.S. POWs chose to remain in North Korea or China.

Stunned by the revelation of Soviet H-bomb development, President Eisenhower responded with saber rattling intended to one-up the Reds' show of strength. Operation Big Stick in August 1953 called for the deployment of 20 Convair B-36 bombers, each carrying nuclear weapons, to Okinawa, Japan. With these lumbering but deadly behemoths staged so close to the Chinese and Soviet borders, no one could miss the point. The operation's apparent success reinforced the administration's belief that nuclear deterrence was good policy.

1953

August 12: The Soviets test Joe 4, their first fusion bomb, at the Semipalatinsk test site. • Ann Davidson arrives in Miami on the 23-foot *Felicity Ann,* becoming the first woman to single-handedly sail across the Atlantic.

August 17: Narcotics Anonymous, developed on the same 12-step platform as Alcoholics Anonymous, convenes its first meeting, in Southern California.

August 19: In a coup that takes some 300 lives, General Fazlollah Zahedi becomes the prime minister of Iran, deposing Mohammed Mossadegh. *See* August 25, 1953.

August 22: The last prisoner leaves the now-closed penal colony on Devil's Island, French Guiana.

August 25: Reza Shah Pahlavi assumes power in Iran.

August 30: The *Kukla, Fran, and Ollie Show* is broadcast in color on NBC.

September: Stefan Cardinal Wyszynski, primate of Poland and mentor of Pope John Paul II, is arrested in Warsaw for speaking out against the occupying Soviets. • Prompted by U.S. and USSR tests of thermonuclear devices within nine months of each other, the editors of the *Bulletin of Atomic Scientists* move the hands of their "doomsday clock" to two minutes before midnight.

September 4: Prisoners of war begin the process of repatriation at Panmunjom's Freedom Village. • The journal *Science* reports that a team of scientists at the University of Chicago, led by Dr. Nathaniel Kleitman, has observed rapid eye movement, or REM, in the sleep laboratory.

September 6: In the final act of the Korean War, Operation Big Switch winds down with the last few POW exchanges.

Celebrants take part in Chicago's annual Bud Billiken Day Parade, a Bronzeville fixture since 1929. (The fictional "Billiken" was created by the *Chicago Defender* newspaper.) Originally begun as an event for underprivileged children, the parade hosted luminaries ranging from radio's Amos 'n' Andy to President Harry Truman. Bronzeville was "the Harlem of Chicago," a thriving South Side community empowered by black-owned businesses, including banks and insurance companies. Boasting such important venues as the Regal Theater and the Savoy Ballroom, the area drew the country's top entertainers. Beginning in the 1950s, however, freeway construction sliced up Bronzeville and contributed to its demise.

Steve Allen (*left*) was a composer, musician, and comedian who also just happened to be a great straight man. That's why WNBC-TV, NBC's New York affiliate, asked him in 1953 to host a local nighttime talk show, which the network turned into *The Tonight Show* in '54. Allen showed later generations of talk show hosts how to display their talent by letting others display theirs. For example, Jonathan Winters (*right*) became famous for his uproarious, often ad-libbed appearances with Allen. The format of an unflappable host, in-house band, famous and soon-to-be famous guests, bits and gags—it was all there, right at the beginning.

Fran Allison (*right*) was the voice of reason, and Burr Tillstrom (*left*) was the show's creator. But puppets Kukla (*left*) and Ollie (*right*) took on lives of their own for generations of kids. Tillstrom's idea for a live puppet show, with former schoolteacher Allison as the host, was a big hit. The limited action of *Kukla, Fran and Ollie* encouraged children at home to *listen* to the dialogue, and how the trio talked to each other made kids feel they were *listened to.*

Love comics were hugely popular in the 1950s, exemplified by this 1953 issue of *Wartime Romances* from the St. John company. *WR* linked romance to the Korean War, and further spurred sales with an air of working-class frankness. The assured cover art is by Matt Baker, who built a reputation as the best of comics' "good girl" artists—a cartoonist with a gift for drawing extraordinarily desirable women.

An African-American in an industry populated almost exclusively by whites, Baker was prolific and hardworking to a fault. He died of a heart ailment in 1959, at age 37.

In 1953 Paramount Pictures adapted H. G. Wells's *The War of the Worlds* with grim realism and an update to 1950s Southern California. Producer George Pal had scored in 1950 with *Destination Moon,* but he went all out this time, assigning *The War of the Worlds* a $2 million budget and allocating $1.6 million for Gordon Jennings's special effects. When the sinister yet graceful Martian war machines (designed by Albert Nozaki) glide into downtown L.A., the carnage that follows is mind-numbing.

American tennis star Maureen Connolly launches one of her feared baseline bombs during a 1953 match. The diminutive Connolly, nicknamed "Little Mo," won 56 consecutive matches at the age of 14 and won her first of three U.S. Open titles in 1951. In 1953 she achieved tennis immortality by winning her sport's Grand Slam: the Australian, French, and U.S. Opens as well as Wimbledon in Britain. Tragically, Connolly's career was cut short in 1954: While she was horseback riding, her right leg was crushed when she was hit by a truck.

1953

September 7: With her victory in the U.S. Open, 16-year-old Maureen Connolly becomes the first woman to win the coveted Grand Slam of tennis (all four major tournaments).

September 10: Swanson sells its first "TV dinner."

September 12: Massachusetts Senator John F. Kennedy marries Jacqueline Lee Bouvier in Newport, Rhode Island.

September 13: Nikita Khrushchev is named first secretary of the Soviet Communist Party.

September 14: Alfred Kinsey releases the highly controversial *Sexual Behavior in the Human Female*.

September 21: Lieutenant Ro Kim Suk, a North Korean pilot, collects a $50,000 bounty for delivering a Soviet MiG-15 to South Korea's Kimpo airfield.

Fall: The FBI publication *Crime in the United States* reveals an alarming trend: During the previous 12 months, 54 percent of car thefts, 49 percent of burglaries, 18 percent of robberies, and 16 percent of rapes were committed by juveniles. • Public Health Workers collect milk samples in Utah that show dramatically elevated levels of radioactive iodine. • Lucille Ball testifies before HUAC. She is asked to explain why she signed a petition for a Communist Party candidate in 1936. She blames her youthful naïveté.

September 22: Twenty-three American prisoners of war, deciding they'd rather stay in North Korea, refuse repatriation.

September 28: An agreement is reached that will send the St. Louis Browns of baseball's American League to Baltimore. They will be renamed the Orioles.

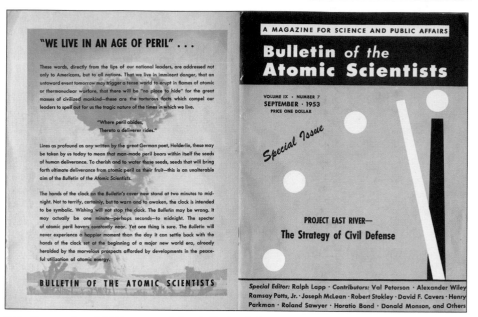

This September 1953 cover of the *Bulletin of the Atomic Scientists* features its famed doomsday clock. First published in 1945, the *Bulletin* became a vehicle for nuclear scientists to express their dismay over the growing arms race between the U.S. and the USSR. The doomsday clock first appeared in the journal in 1947 as a graphic representation of the growing shortness of time before a nuclear catastrophe. The successful Soviet H-bomb test in August 1953 moved the clock up to two minutes to midnight—the closest it had ever been.

Though introduced at a 1951 dinner party, U.S. Congressman John F. Kennedy and debutante-cub reporter Jacqueline Bouvier did not begin dating until almost a year later. The latter had been engaged until then, while the former was pursuing bachelorhood with a vengeance. Nonetheless, the ambitious Massachusetts politician was drawn to the cultured, intelligent beauty. Since they shared many interests, it was only a matter of time before the newly elected senator proposed. On September 12, 1953, 750 guests gathered at Newport, Rhode Island, to witness what the press dubbed "the wedding of the year," which rivaled anything in Hollywood for glamour and star appeal.

Alfred Kinsey

DR. ALFRED KINSEY, whose academic training in zoology and entomology prepared him for a study of gall wasps that occupied him during much of his adult life, was neither a sociologist nor a "sexologist." Yet his name was synonymous throughout the 1950s with intense study and taxonomy of the varieties of human sexuality.

While a professor at Indiana University in 1938, Kinsey taught a course on marriage, and soon after he undertook his concerted examination of human sexuality. Kinsey was fortunate to have two powerful patrons at Indiana: Department of Zoology Chairman Fernandus Payne and university President Herman B. Wells. Because of their support, Kinsey was able to outfit and staff an on-campus facility, travel, conduct research interviews, and collate his findings.

Throughout the years of his inquiry, Kinsey hoped to collect 10,000 individual sex "histories" of men and women. He ultimately collected nearly 8,000, including his own, his wife Clara's, and those of his young male associates and their spouses. Indeed, Kinsey, Clara, and many of his inter-

viewers and their spouses regularly engaged in roundabouts of straight and same-sex activity—notating, photographing, and filming as they went.

Clearly, Kinsey's powers of persuasion were enormous. He remained confident in his path, even when his first book, *Sexual Behavior in the Human Male*, was criticized (often on moral, nonscientific grounds) upon publication in 1948.

A bigger firestorm hit in 1953 with the release of *Sexual Behavior in the Human Female*. Both books were surprise bestsellers but the second, in particular, inflamed conservative moralists. They were horrified by Kinsey's contention that women were far more sexually active—and varied in their practices—than had been assumed.

Although the unrelenting criticism contributed to a deterioration of Kinsey's health, and a falling away of his patrons, he pushed himself mercilessly. The workload took its toll: Kinsey died of an embolism on August 25, 1956. This giant of research and public information was only 62 years old.

Stung by criticism of his earlier work on male sexuality, Dr. Alfred Kinsey refined his approach somewhat for 1953's *Sexual Behavior in the Human Female*. Still, when his data pointed to women being more promiscuous than was generally thought, he faced a public outcry. Kinsey found that more than 90 percent of females engaged in sexual "petting," while half of the subjects surveyed participated in premarital sex. His finding that such women were more likely to have gratifying marriages surprised many, as did the revelation that 26 percent of married women had engaged in extramarital affairs.

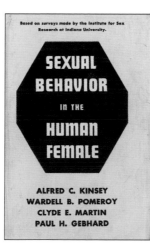

Writer Saul Bellow hit his artistic stride with his 1953 novel, *The Adventures of Augie March*. Possessing a free-form exuberance that his previous two works lacked, Bellow's story traces the title character's life, beginning with his Depression-era upbringing in Chicago. Augie's efforts at finding his place in the world are depicted through an episodic series of comic adventures. Bellow cast an assortment of colorful characters in support of the free-spirited Augie, who by novel's end recognizes the inherent contradictions between love and freedom. The novel earned its author a National Book Award in 1954.

1953

September 30: President Eisenhower appoints Earl Warren as the 14th chief justice of the Supreme Court. Warren will be sworn in on October 5.

October: The U.S. Supreme Court hands down an injunction intended to shutter Harry Hoxsey's cancer clinics. The injunction won't take effect until October 1954. • The UNIVAC 1103, the first commercial computer to use RAM (random access memory), is introduced.

October 1: Japan Airlines is restructured as a government-owned airline.

October 5: The New York Yankees win their record fifth straight World Series, defeating the Brooklyn Dodgers in six games.

October 9: West Germany elects its first federal chancellor, Conrad Adenauer.

October 12: The U.S. and Greece sign their first defense cooperation agreement.

October 14: President Eisenhower says that he will fire any federal employee who pleads the Fifth Amendment while attempting to circumvent the law requiring disclosure of Communist association. • A young Ariel Sharon leads his Israeli commando unit in a raid on the Jordanian village of Qibya.

October 16: Fidel Castro is sentenced to 15 years in prison for his role in the Moncada uprising. • An accidental explosion aboard the aircraft carrier USS *Leyte* in Boston's Charlestown Naval Shipyard kills 37 people and injures 28.

October 19: • TWA becomes the first commercial airline to offer nonstop service between New York and Los Angeles.

Earl Warren had been a highly successful Republican governor in California and had played a major role in securing the presidential nomination for Dwight Eisenhower. On September 30, 1953, Ike appointed Warren chief justice of the U.S. Supreme Court. If Eisenhower expected a conservative, he was greatly mistaken. The Warren court was one of the most interventionist in U.S. history, especially in expanding civil rights for African-Americans, protecting the rights of prisoners, and extending the coverage of the First Amendment. Eisenhower once said that his biggest mistake was to appoint "that dumb son of a bitch Earl Warren."

Frank Sinatra (*left*) and Burt Lancaster flank Montgomery Clift in a scene from director Fred Zinnemann's *From Here to Eternity,* winner of eight Academy Awards. While James Jones's novel was a bestseller, many thought that its negative depiction of army life at Pearl Harbor wouldn't make for a successful film. But despite a few changes, most of the drama's themes—including adultery, prostitution, and murder—survived intact. Deborah Kerr and Donna Reed both played against their wholesome type, while Sinatra's hard-won role put him back on top. The film's memorable beach scene with Kerr and Lancaster was a last-minute inspiration.

As depicted on this vintage collector's plate, the painting entitled *Jack and Jill* exemplifies the primitive charm of American folk artist Anna Mary "Grandma" Moses's work. Born in rural New York in 1860, Moses didn't begin her career until her 70s, when arthritis curtailed her embroidery activities. She put her artistic impulses to work, channeling memories of her bucolic 19th century upbringing. After an art collector noticed her work in a local drugstore window, the self-effacing widow was on her way to national celebrity.

Ray Bradbury's *Fahrenheit 451* remains one of American literature's most-read novels. The story unfolds in a future society in which books are banned (the title refers to the temperature at which they burn) and thinking is discouraged. The populace inhabits a world of passive pursuits in which intellectualism is characterized as "melancholy." Bradbury, under deadline pressure to script-write John Huston's *Moby Dick,* turned out the book manuscript quickly, building upon a short story he had completed previously. Despite its short gestation, the book was a bold exploration of censorship and conformity, coming at a time rife with both.

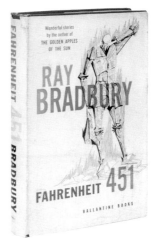

New York Yankees greet outfielder Mickey Mantle (*center*) after one of his many home runs. The "Bronx Bombers" established a baseball dynasty in the late 1940s and early 1950s that has never been matched. Led by wisecracking manager Casey Stengel and such brilliant ballplayers as Mantle and catcher Yogi Berra, the Yankees won five consecutive World Series from 1949 through 1953, and two more in the late 1950s. Combining power hitting, smart play, and dominating pitching, the Yanks were the team that other contenders, especially the Brooklyn Dodgers, loved to hate.

Seldom had such qualities of virtuosity and high camp coexisted within the same performer, but such was the appeal of "Mr. Showmanship," Liberace. A piano prodigy, he played with the Chicago Symphony at age 17. After discovering the crowd-pleasing trick of rendering pop fluff in a classical style, he changed his musical course. From club performances to television, Liberace's brand of ostentatious glitter coupled with a self-effacing manner won him millions of fans. In 1957 he sued a British tabloid that had implied he was gay, and won. Only on his deathbed 30 years later was the long-suspected truth confirmed.

1953

October 23: After years of conflict, France finally grants Laos full sovereignty. • The White House announces that since the Eisenhower Administration stepped up its internal anti-Communist security, more than 800 federal employees have been let go and nearly 600 have resigned.

October 28: According to the Department of the Army, more than 6,000 U.S. POWs were subjected to inhumane treatment at the hands of the Chinese and North Koreans.

October 30: President Eisenhower approves *National Security Council Paper No. 162/2*, asserting that the U.S. must expand its nuclear arsenal to ward off the threat of Communist world domination.

November: Hugh Hefner's inaugural issue of *Playboy*, created with $600 seed money out of his own pocket, features a nude center spread of Marilyn Monroe. • Over a six-day period, New York City is engulfed in a smog so thick that it kills more than 100 people.

November 2: Pakistan is declared the Islamic Republic of Pakistan by its parliament.

November 7: In a letter to FBI Director J. Edgar Hoover, attorney William L. Borden accuses Manhattan Project chief Robert Oppenheimer of being a Soviet spy.

November 9: France agrees to withdraw from Cambodia. •Welsh poet Dylan Thomas, best known for his poem "Do Not Go Gentle into That Good Night," in which he implores his father to fight death, himself dies of alcohol poisoning at age 39.

November 15: Testing begins on the "Drunkometer," an early breathalyzer, which was invented by Robert Borkenstein in collaboration with R. N. Harger at the Indiana School of Medicine.

The Robe fell within the genre of "sword and sandal" pictures—cinematic epics set in biblical times. Filmmakers found that they could depict violence and bare skin with impunity, so long as the stories conveyed a modicum of religiosity. The first film shot in CinemaScope, the widescreen, larger-than-life spectacle proved a successful draw, prompting such similar projects as *The Ten Commandments* and *Ben-Hur*. In *The Robe*, Richard Burton *(left)* starred as a Roman Centurion whose contact with a robe belonging to Jesus Christ makes him a true believer. Supporting cast included Victor Mature *(center)*, Jean Simmons, and Jay Robinson, as a scene-stealing Caligula.

One of the nation's preeminent physicists, J. Robert Oppenheimer was picked to head the Manhattan Project during World War II, earning him the sobriquet "Father of the Atomic Bomb." Though both husband and brother to known Communist Party members, those associations went overlooked at the time. Following the war, Oppenheimer chaired the General Advisory Committee of the Atomic Energy Commission. Soon after, he became increasingly outspoken in his opposition to development of the hydrogen bomb. With his loyalties called into question, Oppenheimer was stripped of his security clearance.

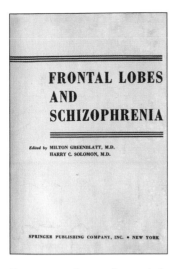

The introduction of chlorpromazine in 1952 led to the gradual abatement of modern-day medicine's most barbaric practice, the frontal lobotomy. Before the advent of chemical treatments for depression, anxiety, and schizophrenia, a "cure" for such mental maladies was believed achievable through judicious mutilation of the brain's frontal lobes. The procedure's biggest champion was psychiatrist Walter Freeman, who performed the surgery more than 3,400 times during a 30-year period. Patients deemed unmanageable and "difficult" were referred to Freeman, who sometimes left his subjects as inert, emotionless automatons. By mid-decade, the medical profession began reexamining its previous approval and quietly abandoned the practice.

The Big Heat, starring Glenn Ford and Gloria Grahame, was based on a popular crime novel by William McGivern. It's an unusually hard-edged revenge tale in which the police detective played by Ford maniacally breaks the law to crush the mobsters who killed his wife. Audiences were shocked when Grahame, playing the smart, sultry girlfriend of a psychotic hood (Lee Marvin), is disfigured by boiling coffee that her lover dashes in her face; the lady's revenge is hardly less startling. Today, *The Big Heat* is revered as a masterpiece of *film noir,* and one of the best achievements of director Fritz Lang.

Those "thrilling days of yesteryear" were well represented each week through the exploits of *The Lone Ranger,* enacted by longtime movie-serial star Clayton Moore (*left*) in the title role and Jay Silverheels (*right*) as his Comanche companion, Tonto. Conceived for radio back in the early 1930s, the show told the story of Texas Ranger John Reid, sole survivor of an ambush that killed five others. Nursed back to health by Tonto, he vowed to devote his life to fighting injustice. With a hearty "Hi-ho, Silver," the ranger and his partner attracted millions of TV viewers throughout the 1950s.

This 1953 advertisement for Minute Rice highlights the growth of the instant food phenomenon in the 1950s. The ad promotes quickness, emphasizing that the busy housewife is now liberated from the troubles of cooking rice. Just boil water and plop! The increasing popularity of such culinary solutions probably grew out of the postwar baby boom, as larger families and houses meant more work and less time for homemakers. Relentless marketing also helped Minute Rice and other convenience foods fly off store shelves.

1953

November 20: The French begin Operation Castor, the construction of defensive outposts at Dien Bien Phu in Vietnam.

November 21: Paleontologists and anatomists reexamine the bones of 1912's "Piltdown Man" discovery, and determine that there are obvious signs of a hoax.

November 22: An episode of *The Colgate Comedy Hour* puts RCA's color system to the test for the first time.

November 23: In Beijing, China and North Korea sign a 10-year economic assistance agreement.

November 24: In a nationally televised speech, Senator Joseph McCarthy asserts that former President Truman aided and abetted Communists.

November 28: Frank Olson, an undercover CIA employee, jumps from a hotel window after being secretly given LSD as part of the MK ULTRA research into human mind control. More than 20 years later, Congress will approve a compensatory payment to his widow. • Eugene O'Neill, considered by many to be America's greatest playwright, dies at age 65.

December: For the first time, a baby conceived with frozen sperm is born. The pioneering research will revolutionize the science of fertility.

December 1: AT&T reveals a plan to revolutionize worldwide communication with the first transatlantic telephone cable.

December 2: The Senate censures Joseph McCarthy, condemning his conduct as an anti-Communist crusader. This is the beginning of the end for McCarthy, whose star will quickly fade with diminished media attention.

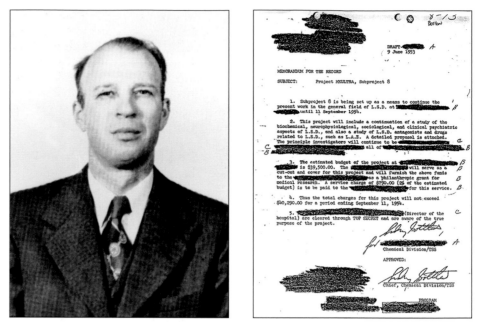

On November 28, 1953, Dr. Frank Olson became a tragic victim of the CIA's secret MK ULTRA operation after plunging from a 13th floor window of Manhattan's Statler Hotel. Though the death was reported as a suicide at the time, the 1975 Rockefeller Commission inquiry into the agency's excesses revealed that the scientist had been involuntarily dosed with LSD by the CIA. It was all part of a mind-control program that was implemented in response to reports of "brainwashing" of POWs in Korea. Specifics of the MK ULTRA project remain murky, although the pictured memo offers a few details.

For an all-too-brief time, two stars of "cool jazz" joined forces, scoring a hit record in 1953 with their rendition of "My Funny Valentine." Trumpeter Chet Baker (*left*) and baritone sax man Gerry Mulligan (*right*) formed the core of an uncommon piano-less outfit, the Gerry Mulligan Quartet. Mulligan was a musical wunderkind, playing numerous instruments and arranging while still a teen. Baker, with his movie-star looks and an air of mystery, had the makings of a superstar, but drug addiction eventually destroyed his promise.

When the *Winky Dink and You* cartoon show premiered in 1953, mail order outlets were ready with 50-cent Winky Dink kits consisting of a clear plastic sheet to be placed over the TV screen, and five "magic" crayons. During each adventure of Winky and his dog, Woofer, host Jack Barry asked young viewers to help out by drawing whatever it was that Winky needed at the moment—a ladder, perhaps, or a fire hose. Of course, not every kid had the plastic sheet, which led to a lot of marked-up TV screens and unhappy parents.

Clark Gable became the "King of Hollywood" in the 1930s, and never relinquished the honorary title. Appealing to men as well as to women, he brought virility and humor to more than 60 films. Director John Ford's steamy jungle adventure-romance *Mogambo* (1953) teamed Gable with two of the biggest female stars of the 1950s, Grace Kelly and Ava Gardner. The box-office smash was a remake of *Red Dust* (1932), which had featured Gable, Mary Astor, and Jean Harlow.

Intrigued with the lyricism of the commonplace and issues of mortality, Welsh poet Dylan Thomas first gained wide recognition during World War II. Because he believed his works should be heard as well as read, Thomas became a fixture on the BBC. With his romantic stylings set to Welsh speech rhythms, Thomas worked against the prevailing 20th century poetry trends. His best known works included *Portrait of the Artist as a Young Dog* and *Under Milkwood,* both set in his native country. Chronically broke though widely celebrated, he died in 1953 following a drinking binge while on tour in America. He was 39.

French troops watch their comrades parachute into Dien Bien Phu in northwest Vietnam in late November 1953. General Henry Navarre, the latest commander of French forces, wanted to establish a position near the point at which Communist Viet Minh troops were most likely to invade Laos. Some 2,200 elite paras, as they were called, created the base and prepared to battle the Communists. Navarre hoped a large Communist army would attack since he assumed that airpower and superior French artillery would easily defeat the Viet Minh. As events in the spring of 1954 would prove, Navarre was dead wrong.

1953

December 3: President Eisenhower, concerned that Manhattan Project chief Robert Oppenheimer has Communist associates, orders a figurative "blank wall" placed between Oppenheimer and nuclear secrets. *See* December 23, 1953.

December 8: In an address to the UN, President Eisenhower proposes "Atoms for Peace," in which the U.S. would give aid to countries that limit their nuclear research to peaceful aims.

December 9: Management at General Electric headquarters announces that the company will no longer employ Communists.

December 10: Sir Winston Churchill is awarded the Nobel Prize in Literature for his lifetime body of work. • The Nobel Peace Prize is awarded to Alsatian theological scholar and medical missionary Albert Schweitzer, who built Lambarene, a 500-bed, free hospital in equatorial Africa.

December 12: Flying legend Chuck Yeager shatters the speed record when he attains Mach 2.43 in a Bell X-1A rocket plane.

December 16: With an audience of some 160 journalists, President Eisenhower holds the first White House press conference.

December 17: The FCC approves the RCA/NTSC color television system, in a reversal of its 1951 decision.

December 23: Robert Oppenheimer receives a letter from the Atomic Energy Commission stating that his security clearance is suspended. He will request, and be granted, a hearing, but reinstatement of his clearance will be denied.

December 30: The first consumer color television sets hit the market, retailing for a staggering $1,175. It will be some 15 years before the cost will drop enough to appeal to the average American family.

During the course of his cockpit career, pilot Chuck Yeager set aeronautic records while demonstrating grit and guile in the face of overwhelming adversity. Enlisting in the Army Air Corps just before Pearl Harbor, he made a name for himself as a flying ace before being shot down. In 1947 he became the first pilot to break the sound barrier (nursing two broken ribs at the time). On December 12, 1953, he surpassed Mach 2 (reaching a record 1,650 mph) in a Bell X-1A rocket plane. Larger than life, Yeager embodied what writer Tom Wolfe called "the right stuff."

Mighty Mouse (*top right*) became the franchise character of Paul Terry's Terrytoons, an energetic, low-budget outfit that began cranking out animated shorts in 1929. The super rodent was introduced in a 1942 cartoon called *Mouse of Tomorrow,* in which a sickly mouse who eats "Super Cheese" is transformed into a cat-slugging superhero. Mighty remained a mighty box office attraction into the 1950s. Smart-aleck magpies Heckle and Jeckle (*lower right*) also achieved considerable popularity. In 1955 Terry sold his company to CBS-TV, where Mighty Mouse and friends thrived for another decade.

Going *Mad*

DURING A TIME OF HEAVY-HANDED censorship of comic books, some light relief arrived on newsstands with the magazine debut of *Mad* in July 1955. Originating as a comic book three years earlier, it was one of many titles offered by industry innovator EC (Entertaining Comics). Among such lurid titles as *Tales from the Crypt* and *The Vault of Horror,* *Mad* stood out as a surprisingly literate, if sometimes juvenile, parody of other comic books. After the passing of the Comic Code, which placed severe restrictions over content viewed by children, publisher William Gaines's EC empire crumbled. Only *Mad* was left standing by 1956.

But for Gaines, his real work was just starting. Ably aided by editors Harvey Kurtzman (initially) and later Al Feldstein, *Mad* parodied movies, television, advertising—indeed, all aspects of popular culture. (Some targets regarded it as a badge of honor to endure the magazine's barbs.) Iconoclastic and fearless, *Mad* accepted no ads, ensuring that the recipients of their lampoons could not pressure them economically.

A brilliant assemblage of writers and illustrators comprised "the usual gang of idiots," including Don Martin, Bill Elder, Wallace Wood, and Jack Davis. Occasionally, big-name wits also contributed material, including Ernie Kovacs, Bob and Ray, and Roger Price. The magazine's relentlessly irreverent tone found a solid audience among young, primarily male, readers. For many, it would be their first exposure to irony and satire.

A generation became acquainted with *Mad*-speak, which included such words as "Potrzebie," "furshlugginer," and "Kaputnik." The magazine's gap-toothed mascot, Alfred E. Neuman, became a fixture of *Mad*'s covers, sporting his vacant, "What, me worry?" grin. Other regular features included Dave Berg's "The Lighter Side of…" pieces and Antonio Prohias's "Spy vs. Spy," a Cold War-era mainstay of *Mad* that would run for decades.

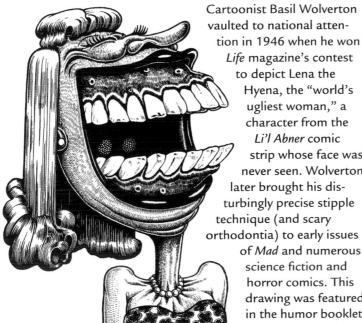

"YOU WOULD ORDER AN ANGEL'S KISS"

Cartoonist Basil Wolverton vaulted to national attention in 1946 when he won *Life* magazine's contest to depict Lena the Hyena, the "world's ugliest woman," a character from the *Li'l Abner* comic strip whose face was never seen. Wolverton later brought his disturbingly precise stipple technique (and scary orthodontia) to early issues of *Mad* and numerous science fiction and horror comics. This drawing was featured in the humor booklet *Common Types of Barflyze.*

The daughter of European aristocrats, Audrey Hepburn found stardom almost overnight. After working in musical theater and appearing in a few British films, she was cast as the lead in the Broadway production of *Gigi* at age 22 in 1951. Possessing alluring, waiflike features, Hepburn stood in contrast to the voluptuous screen goddesses of the day. Stardom came with her Hollywood debut, 1953's *Roman Holiday,* for which she won an Oscar for best actress. Hepburn continued to delight audiences with a series of light comedies and dramas, including *Sabrina* (1954), *Funny Face* (1957), and *Love in the Afternoon* (1957).

1953

New & Notable

Books

The Adventures of Augie March
  by Saul Bellow
Casino Royale by Ian Fleming
Fahrenheit 451 by Ray Bradbury
Go Tell It on the Mountain
  by James Baldwin
Junkie by William Lee
  (William S. Burroughs)
Life Is Worth Living by Fulton J. Sheen
The Power of Positive Thinking
  by Norman Vincent Peale
Science and Human Behavior
  by B. F. Skinner
Sexual Behavior in the Human Female
  by Alfred Kinsey

Movies

The Band Wagon
The Big Heat
From Here to Eternity
Gentlemen Prefer Blondes
Mogambo
The Robe
Roman Holiday
Shane
Stalag 17
The Wages of Fear

Songs

"The Doggie in the Window"
  by Patti Page
"I've Got the World on a String"
  by Frank Sinatra
"Oh! My Papa" by Eddie Fisher
"Rags to Riches" by Tony Bennett
"That's Amore" by Dean Martin
"You Belong to Me" by Jo Stafford
"Your Cheatin' Heart"
  by Hank Williams

Television

Candid Camera
The Loretta Young Show
Make Room for Daddy
Person to Person

Theater

Can-Can
The Crucible
Tea & Sympathy
Teahouse of the August Moon

A 1947 confrontation in Hollister, California, between unruly bikers and the local townsfolk inspired 1953's *The Wild One.* Though the real story was embellished beyond recognition, the film's ring of authenticity came from the casting of certified Hollywood rebel Marlon Brando (*pictured,* with Mary Murphy) in the lead role. The misunderstood-misfit theme was hackneyed even then, but the film's evocative imagery—featuring the leather-clad Brando astride his Triumph—struck fear into the hearts of those unfamiliar with biker culture. The mythologizing of biker gangs established an archetype of lawlessness that persists to this day.

Following World War II, Indiana's venerable Studebaker Company was the first automaker to unveil new car designs. This helped Stude become the most robust postwar independent manufacturer. Showcasing Raymond Loewy's innovative designs, the company pioneered such features as wraparound glass, limited chrome, and the famous "bullet nose." But by 1953, Studebaker's finances were in serious disarray, and not even the sleek *Commander* model (*pictured*) could reverse the trend. A 1954 merger with Packard and the later introduction of the Lark merely delayed the inevitable, though Studebaker managed to hang on until 1966.

Hefner's *Playboy*

IN 1957 *ESQUIRE* MAGAZINE paid copywriter Hugh Hefner a mere $60 a week. When Hefner requested $65 and was refused, he decided to go off on his own—"to publish a magazine that would thumb its nose at all the restrictions."

Hefner decided to target his periodical to an audience not properly recognized at the time: an urban, single male aspiring to sophistication—not one interested in hunting, fishing, and the great outdoors. The magazine would feature fiction as well as articles about jazz, fine wines, and even fashion. One more feature would set Hefner's wares apart: a monthly photo spread of an unclothed young woman. He would call the magazine *Stag Party*.

A social revolutionary and naive romantic, Hefner succeeded beyond his wildest dreams when the venture, retitled *Playboy,* hit newsstands in December 1953. Uncertain that there would be a second issue, Hefner did not date the first one. But he needn't have worried. Shrewdly placing starlet Marilyn Monroe's picture on the cover and resurrecting as his first centerspread the nude calendar shot she had done four years earlier, the issue (approximately 54,000 copies) sold out.

That Hefner's creation would find less savory usage than he would admit to was beside the point. He was eager to score points against what he regarded as an oppressive, unhealthy society. Airing his sociological musings in rambling essays he later entitled "The Playboy Philosophy," Hefner envisioned a world where sexuality was a source of celebration rather than shame—even for women. Hefner said he wanted to put forth the message "that nice girls like sex, too." In the early 1950s, this was radical stuff. At the time, what consenting adults did behind closed doors was barely acknowledged, let alone exalted.

Hefner's impact on popular culture would become indelible, surviving attacks from cultural conservatives on one side and feminists on the other. By 1972 *Playboy*'s monthly circulation would peak at 7.2 million.

The 1950s marked the final glory days of men's hats. Other than the familiar hunter's cap with earflaps, few men's hats were truly utilitarian. However, they remained important in America as symbols of decorum and status, a notion that dates to the second half of the 19th century. Hats were instant identifiers of one's place in the social order. In the 1950s, few men over 40 felt dressed without a hat, and men just beginning to make their way in business coveted "young executive" styles. This advertisement for Adam Hats, a division of Miller Bros. Hat Co., appeared in *Esquire* magazine.

Hathaway offers English shirtings ready-made

One of the decade's most memorable advertising campaigns brought with it a mysterious, urbane figure—the man in the Hathaway shirt. This graying, mustachioed, eye-patched gentleman was pictured in a variety of settings, usually engaged in some cultured pursuit. Without saying anything at all about the product itself, the mere suggestion of the lifestyle that the shirt's wearers could expect resulted in a tripling of sales within two years of the ads' debut. The campaign was the brainchild of David Ogilvy, who built his agency into the world's eighth largest on the strength of his uncanny knack for connecting with consumers.

"[The suburbs were] inhabited by people who didn't know one another, let alone their neighbors' parents, who had never lived in such a place before and weren't quite sure how to do it."

—AUTHOR THOMAS HINE, *POPULUXE*

1954

Suburban America: Who Belongs?

WITH THEIR THIRD CHILD on the way in late 1956, William and Daisy Myers decided they needed a larger house for their growing family. They began looking in the new suburb of Levittown, Pennsylvania, about 25 miles northeast of Philadelphia and adjacent to the integrated suburb in which they had lived for several years. They found a house they liked in the Dogwood Hollow section of Levittown, a pink, ranch-style three-bedroom for $12,500—affordable on the $5,000-a-year salary Mr. Myers earned as a laboratory technician.

But before purchasing the house, William Myers—an African-American veteran of World War II and a graduate of Hampton University—took the precaution of talking to some of his potential neighbors. As he said later, "I knew all the reaction wouldn't be favorable" when neighbors learned that a black family was moving into the previously all-white suburb. However, he was encouraged to find the closest neighbors "cordial, even warm."

But in August 1957, the night after the Myers moved into their new home on the corner of Deepgreen and Daffodil, a crowd of angry protesters gathered. By 9 P.M. the next night, the mob, mostly teenagers, had swelled to almost 300 people, held back from the Myers's property by 20 state troopers and 10 township police officers. Soon, a vacant house behind the Myers's property was taken over by a "social club" devoted to driving the family out of Levittown.

After World War II, people of varied ethnic and religious backgrounds converged on the American suburbs. In some ways, suburbanites were more open to diversity than residents of small towns and ethnic urban enclaves. However, the homogenous suburban culture had its own restrictive code of conduct.

These men began what Myers called a "war of nerves"; their most inventive tactic was playing "Old Man River" over outdoor loudspeakers at all hours of the day and night. William and Daisy Myers sent their children to stay with their grandparents in York, Pennsylvania. Then someone burned a cross on the lawn next door.

More than two million African-Americans moved out of the rural South during the 1950s, and very, very few of them moved to the suburbs. They were not legally excluded, but social resistance combined with economic pressures ensured that suburban developments remained racially segregated.

Though the Supreme Court had decided in 1948 that state courts could not enforce "restrictive covenants" (agreements that restricted homeowners from selling to members of another race or religion) against the will of the seller and buyer, nothing prevented sellers from adhering to restrictive covenants voluntarily. In fact, the Federal Housing Administration recommended and sometimes required racially based restrictive covenants as a precondition for approving a loan. (Such policies would have a long-term impact: Those new houses would appreciate in value enormously over the following decades, and most African-Americans and many Latinos were closed out of that wealth.)

While new subdivisions carved out of farms and fields surrounding America's cities in the 1950s were almost always racially segregated, that does not mean that they were homogenous. It was in the postwar suburbs that many Americans met people who were not like themselves. New suburbanites came not just from cities but from small towns and farms. They came from different ethnic backgrounds and practiced different religions.

Attractive and affordable, Levittown homes were sought by many Americans eagerly searching for an escape from city life. However, in the 1950s and beyond, William Levitt and many other developers limited their suburban dwellings to white buyers only.

The postwar suburbs were, in many ways, a frontier. The people who moved there had to forge a new way of life in a new landscape. European-Americans left behind much of their ethnic identity and embraced a "white" suburban culture. Ethnicity became less important, in part, because fewer and fewer Americans had any direct ties to a homeland outside the United States. Immigration quotas imposed in the 1920s had all but shut down large-scale immigration (immigration restrictions would be relaxed in 1965), so the nation was much more racially and ethnically homogenous in the 1950s than before or since. In the mid-1950s, about 88 percent of Americans were of European descent (as compared to 69 percent in 2000). Most of the rest were African-Americans. Latinos, Native Americans, and Asian-Americans comprised well less than 3 percent of the population—combined.

The young suburban couples starting families during the 1950s were likely to be at least third-generation American, and there was no steady flow of people from Italy or Ireland or Germany strengthening and replenishing the ethnic cultures they were leaving behind. While most of those who lived in the new suburbs thought of themselves as middle class, that category included unionized blue-collar workers whose income rose substantially in the postwar years and often rivaled that of salaried professionals in the 1950s.

On the one hand, suburban life was constrained by fewer rules and expectations than the urban ethnic enclaves or small towns from which many of the residents came. But in trying to make sense of a new place, many suburbanites traded the confines of ethnic or small-town cultures (which were usually quite homogenous and not especially tolerant of difference) for a new set of standards—a suburban middle-class culture.

The uncharted waters of the suburbs sometimes led to funny misunderstandings. Sociologist Herbert Gans, who in 1958 moved into the Levittown development in Willingboro, New Jersey, described a minor suburban crisis. A couple who had recently moved to Levittown from New York City invited some of their new neighbors over for cocktails. The first couple to arrive saw, through the house's front window, the hostess, who was wearing fashionable capri pants. Mistakenly thinking she was in her pajamas, they went home and called the other neighbors to confer about what they should do. The party eventually happened, but the capris were retired to the back of the closet.

Father Knows Best starred Robert Young (*center*) and Billy Gray, Elinor Donahue, Jane Wyatt, and Lauren Chapin (*clockwise from lower left*). Antiseptic and idealized, '50s sitcoms such as this and *Leave It to Beaver* portrayed the new middle-class family as a flawless bunch. They were nonethnic, with such Anglo-Saxon names as Anderson, Cleaver, and Nelson.

After moving to the suburbs, many couples lived apart from their families for the first time. In a sense, neighbors became surrogate family members, keeping an eye on each other's children, lending tools, and celebrating special occasions together. Cocktail parties were a regular ritual, as were Tiki parties, barbecues, and bridge games.

After the Rosenberg trial in 1951, many American Jews felt wary of right-wing nationalists. Jews who moved out of big cities tended to choose suburbs heavily populated by Jews, such as Skokie, Illinois, and Oak Park, Michigan. Rabbi Jacob Rothschild (*pictured*) saw his Atlanta synagogue bombed, not by anti-Semites, but by racists who opposed his civil rights activism.

As suburbanites looked to one another for clues, they also found a wealth of advice from a growing national media. Magazines such as *Redbook* and *Ladies' Home Journal* offered "American" recipes—including the ubiquitous casseroles made with canned cream of mushroom soup and canned onion ring toppings. Television also played a critical role in instructing people about the new middle-class culture. One of the classic family sitcoms, *Father Knows Best,* premiered on CBS in 1954. But perhaps no '50s series had the iconic power of *Leave It to Beaver,* which premiered in 1957. In each episode of *Leave It to Beaver,* a small domestic problem is resolved—after a series of mishaps—and a moral lesson is administered, typically by the father, Ward. In addition, the producers of the show, as with other sitcoms, purposely tried to teach their viewers how to be middle class.

During an episode in which Wally and the Beaver accidentally have broken the window of the family car, the Cleavers gather for dinner. The table is properly set, with tablecloth and napkins. June (the mom) reminds the boys to wash their hands before dinner and enforces the use of "please," "thank you," and "may I be excused." When Ward and June begin to argue during dinner, no one yells. Emotion is signaled by raised eyebrows and wry comments. When the discussion threatens to get out of hand (as Beaver says, "It was just getting good!"), the parents agree to change the subject. And when it comes to the window, the boys are not preoccupied with physical punishment. Though Wally's friend, Eddie Haskell (clearly working class in the early episodes), says that his father would have "smacked" him for breaking the window, Beaver and Wally had worried that their father would "give [them] that look."

Critics of the middle-class culture that was promoted so strongly in the 1950s pointed to a strangling conformity and a culture of intolerance. They were half right. The white middle class of 1950s America drew strict lines between the races, but it was otherwise willing to accept a wide variety of (white) Americans into its embrace—so long as they played by its rules. In some ways it was a more inclusive culture, with room for people from different ethnic, religious, and class backgrounds. But to fit in, one had to conform to the norms. There was not much tolerance for those who violated the rules, whether it was young women who "went too far" sexually, men who didn't marry, or intellectual and political dissidents.

During the 1950s, a woman who became pregnant outside of marriage was publicly shamed. Unwed pregnancy meant her expulsion from school or college; it meant being whispered about by her peers. Homosexuality was more dangerous; homosexuals reported or discovered faced not only expulsion from school or loss of a job, but possible arrest.

Those newest to the white middle class faced great suspicion. Jews, for example, found new opportunities for assimilation during the 1950s, but they often were judged harshly by the rigid standards of white suburban culture. The treason charges against Ethel and Julius Rosenberg and the public associations of Jews with communism in the HUAC investigations of the 1950s compounded lingering suspicions that Jews were somehow un-American.

Such intolerance, compounded by Cold War fears, often produced a sense that the world was composed of "us" and "them." "Them" was, most often, Communists. Congress added the phrase "under God" to the Pledge of Allegiance in 1954 to emphasize the difference between the United States and the "godless Communists" of the Soviet Union. This change, according to the act's legislative history, would "acknowledge the dependence of our people and our Government upon . . . the Creator . . . [and] deny the atheistic and materialistic concepts of communism."

Communists, of course, also might threaten the United States from the inside. Such films as *Invasion of the Body Snatchers*—in which emotionless but otherwise indistinguishable aliens replace the town's citizens, one by one—reflect a suspicion of internal subversion. Suspicion translated into intolerance of difference and, often, into anti-intellectualism. In 1954 a major survey found that 60 percent of Americans would ban from public libraries books by atheists. Communists fared worse. Only 11 percent of Americans would allow Communists to teach in the nation's universities.

Just as America sent more and more of its youth to college, Americans worried about what their children would learn there. Just as ethnic differences became less important, lines were drawn more clearly between races. Just as more Americans were accepted into a broad middle-class culture, intolerance grew toward those who would not accept its rules and customs. The rapidly changing nation struggled over who belonged, and on what terms—and in its answers, often came up wanting.

Though Americans had the freedom to espouse their religious and political beliefs, they did so at their own risk. A small segment of Americans viewed non-Christians and socialists as threats. Editors of this publication believed in a sinister Jewish/Communist conspiracy that had the potential to dominate the world.

1954

1954: In an effort to broaden its sphere of influence, the Soviet Union begins a wide-reaching program to distribute foreign aid to non-Communist Third World nations. • White America, Inc., a racist, segregationist group, is formed in response to *Brown v. Board of Education.* • The Cuban-inspired cha-cha and mambo become popular dances across the U.S. • Irving Howe and Lewis Coser cofound the Socialist *Dissent* magazine. • The Boy Scouts of America become desegregated by integrating their "Colored Troops."

1954: The Gross National Product (GNP) of the United States hits a record $364.8 billion, or almost $1 billion per day. • The Uzi submachine gun, named for its inventor, Uziel Gal, is first manufactured by Israel Military Industries and distributed to Israeli special forces. • The American Cancer Society's Hammond-Horn study is the first to reveal a causal connection between smoking and poor health. Almost simultaneously, a British study reaches the same conclusion. • The highly acclaimed film *Salt of the Earth,* about striking Mexican-American zinc miners in New Mexico, is seen in just 13 theaters nationally due to its anti-capitalist theme.

1954: Labor union membership peaks at 35 percent of the workforce. The subsequent decline reflects the fact that while some unions have protected workers' rights, others have been accused of associating with organized crime syndicates and driving jobs overseas. • Ray Kroc signs a franchising deal with the McDonald brothers in San Bernardino, California. By the end of the century, more than 13,000 McDonald's restaurants will exist worldwide. • Gross revenue for television broadcasters reaches $593 million, exceeding that of radio broadcasters for the first time.

Though most U.S. television broadcasting remained black and white into the 1960s, the technology for color TV existed as early as 1950. The Korean War sidelined development until 1954, when RCA introduced the first commercially available sets, priced at $1,000. Buyers with the wherewithal to afford them were not given much choice of color programming. Only NBC, owned by RCA, offered any. (CBS and ABC resisted, so as not to encourage color purchases and help NBC's bottom line.) RCA moved 5,000 color sets in '54, although most were greatly discounted or even donated.

Not long before the two married, Marilyn Monroe described her relationship with retired New York Yankees great Joe DiMaggio. "I don't know if I'm in love with him yet," she said, "but I know I like him more than any man I've ever met." After a two-year courtship, Monroe and DiMaggio eloped and married at San Francisco's City Hall on January 14, 1954. It didn't take long for homebody DiMaggio to become jealous of his wife's role as America's hottest sex symbol. The problems in the marriage came to a head nine months later when Monroe sought a divorce on grounds of "mental cruelty."

Dulles's Nuclear Threats

IN THE POSTWAR YEARS, American foreign policy sought to "contain" hostile forces within established borders. Rather than risk setting off another war, the United States poured aid into countries that served as bulwarks against Communist encroachment. Germany was a microcosm of this practice, with the western half of the country acting as a critical counterweight to any potential Soviet expansionism.

Such philosophy was strenuously tested when President Dwight Eisenhower tapped hard-liner John Foster Dulles to be secretary of state. Dulles's impeccable credentials in law and international affairs made him an obvious choice. Though he had helped shape foreign policy under previous Democratic administrations, Dulles was clearly a hard-line Republican. Given to moralizing (his father had been a Presbyterian minister), he projected a stern, humorless image—alienating many in the process.

John Foster Dulles

The President, however, valued his expertise.

According to Dulles, negotiation with the Soviet Union was a folly to be avoided. Peace would come through his strategy of "brinksmanship"—that is, playing chicken with nuclear weapons, just shy of actually using them. Said Dulles in an interview with *Life* magazine, "The ability to get to the verge without getting into war is the necessary art." He put the world on notice in a speech on January 12, 1954, alarming friends as well as enemies.

Three months later, Dulles (under Eisenhower's authorization) offered two atomic bombs to the French for use in their war against Vietnam, a proposal that France turned down. Nuclear saber rattling also arose in 1954 and 1958 when Red China attacked the Nationalist forces in Quemoy and Matsu. By demonstrating a willingness to employ such weaponry, Dulles exacerbated already-high Cold War tensions.

On January 21, 1954, First Lady Mamie Eisenhower christened the USS *Nautilus,* the world's first atomic-powered submarine. Nuclear power enabled the *Nautilus* to remain submerged for weeks at a time, as there no longer was a need to surface and recharge batteries. Over the next few years, the *Nautilus* shattered all submerged speed and distance records. The successful shift to nuclear power with the *Nautilus* set off a larger transition to nuclear power throughout the Navy's fleet.

1954

1954: Dr. Gregory Pincus begins drug trials of his experimental oral contraceptives on volunteers in Massachusetts. • Electronics manufacturers begin to replace glass vacuum tubes with transistors. • Stop signs are redesigned to feature white lettering on a red background. The old style used yellow and black—the same colors on many other less-critical road signs.

1954: Gil Lamb stars in a 30-minute *Bozo the Clown* TV pilot, produced by Hal Roach, Jr., for Capitol Records. • American International Pictures, which will produce such classic B movies as *I Was a Teenage Werewolf,* is founded by Samuel Z. Arkoff and James H. Nicholson. • Jacques Cousteau's first underwater films are broadcast on the television series *Omnibus.*

January: French filmmaker François Truffaut publishes *A Certain Tendency in the French Cinema,* promoting the *auteur* theory. He asserts that only directors who leave a "signature" on each of their films are worthy of consideration.

January 5: The Soviets unveil their MiG-19, a highly maneuverable, supersonic fighter jet.

January 7: In his State of the Union address, President Dwight Eisenhower confirms that 2,200 federal government employees have been dismissed due to security concerns.

January 12: Within 10 hours, two avalanches kill hundreds of people in the Austrian Alps. • Secretary of Defense Charles E. Wilson orders the integration of military post schools. • Secretary of State John Foster Dulles announces his doctrine of massive retaliation. He states that enemy aggression will be met with a nuclear response.

A teacher at Milwaukee's Palmer School poses with his 30 young students. A troubling effect of the postwar baby boom was the subsequent overcrowding of classrooms. Typical class sizes ballooned to an average of 30 students per teacher, a number that remained steady throughout the next decade. Set into motion by this reality was an ongoing debate as to whether large classes led to inferior education.

In the early 1950s, the New York City Board of Education mandated that the metropolitan public schools issue personalized, military-style dog tags to schoolchildren. The board's decision was prompted by the grim possibility of enemy nuclear attack: If a strike were to occur, the metal tags might be sufficient to reunite lost or injured children with their families, or to identify the remains of those who died. One former student, Laura Kunstler Graff, held on to her tag as a keepsake.

With the consolidation of the beer industry in the 1950s, such companies as Schlitz, Pabst, and Anheuser-Busch bought out smaller regional breweries such as New York's Ballantine Ale. In the process, large companies aggressively marketed some regional brands as specialty brews. Their target audience: prosperous suburbanites, who comprised an expanding demographic. Marketing execs wanted the well-to-do to think that beer was an acceptable upscale drink, and not just for the working class.

One of television's earliest outer space adventure shows was *Space Patrol*, which began its run on KECA in Los Angeles in 1950. Adapted from radio, it initially aired in a 15-minute serial format before becoming syndicated by ABC in half-hour episodes. Stories revolved around the exploits of Commander Buzz Corey (Ed Kemmer, *left*) and Cadet Happy (Lyn Osborn, *right*) as they kept the peace on behalf of the United Planets of the Universe in the 30th century. Though the program's "effects" were something short of "special," its themes—such as cloning and suspended animation—were surprisingly sophisticated.

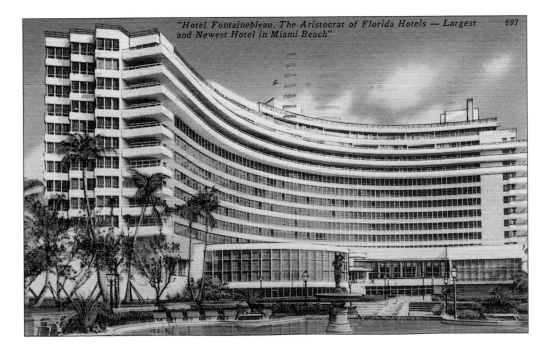

Architect Morris Lapidus helped define the Miami Beach style. His glorious—and to many critics at the time, tacky—style was best expressed in his design of the luxurious Fontainebleau Hotel, which opened in 1954. Lapidus built the 17-story, semicircular Fontainebleau on the site of the old Harvey Firestone estate on Collins Avenue. Many Modernists disdained his flourishes, which included curving staircases, "floating" ceilings, and theatrical lighting. Only later would his decorative choices be seen as a precursor of postmodernism.

1954

January 14: Concert promoter Alan Freed fuels the new music craze by staging the Rock 'n' Roll Jubilee. Freed's efforts to copyright *rock 'n' roll* will be rebuffed. • Marilyn Monroe marries Joe DiMaggio.

January 19: The United States signs a mutual defense pact with South Korea.

January 20: More than 20,000 anti-Communist prisoners of war are repatriated when they are delivered into the hands of United Nations forces. • The CIA begins construction on a tunnel connecting East and West Berlin in an effort to intercept Soviet and East German communications.

January 21: First Lady Mamie Eisenhower christens the first nuclear submarine, the USS *Nautilus*.

January 31: Foreign ministers from the U.S., the Soviet Union, France, and Great Britain meet in Berlin to hammer out agreements on arms control and other issues. No significant consensus is reached.

February 2: Soviet scientist Vladimir Demikhov, author of *Experimental Transplantation of Vital Organs*, creates a two-headed dog by grafting the head of a puppy to the neck of an older dog. The new creation reportedly survives as long as 29 days.

February 7: The first flight of Lockheed's F-104 prototype is a success. Called Starfighter, this high-performance jet fighter is capable of reaching Mach 2.

February 10: At a news conference, President Eisenhower says that he "cannot conceive of a greater tragedy" than to become involved in a war with Vietnam.

February 15: President Eisenhower signs a bill authorizing the construction of the Distant Early Warning Line across Canada. The DEW Line will warn of an invasion of North America from over the North Pole.

"It was so wonderful, Joe. You never heard such cheering."

"Yes, I have."

—EXCHANGE BETWEEN NEWLYWEDS MARILYN MONROE AND JOE DIMAGGIO AFTER MONROE'S RETURN FROM KOREA, WHERE SHE HAD ENTERTAINED SOME 100,000 ARMY TROOPS

In February 1954, Marilyn Monroe was honeymooning in Japan with her new husband, baseball great Joe DiMaggio. Monroe decided to take a side trip to visit troops in Korea. In front of crowds that reached 13,000, Marilyn sang songs and posed for photographs during 10 shows over four days. By the end of her stop, more than 100,000 happy soldiers and Marines had caught a morale-boosting glimpse of the glamorous sex symbol.

Auto designer Howard "Dutch" Darrin was intrigued by the 100-inch wheelbase of Kaiser-Frazer's Henry J compact. That was the starting point for the '54 Kaiser Darrin, a novel, fiberglass-bodied convertible with lively performance, a high, shell-shaped grille, and doors that slid forward into the bodysides. At $3,668, however, the Kaiser Darrin cost nearly as much as a Cadillac or Lincoln, and although the public admired the car, sales were almost nonexistent; production was halted after just 435 units. Remarkably, close to 400 survive.

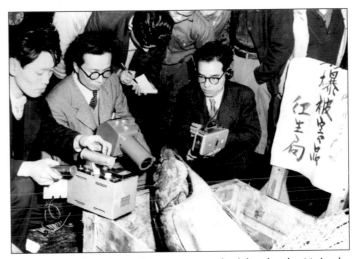

On March 1, 1954, a group of four Puerto Rican Nationalists attacked the U.S. House of Representatives. The assailants, led by Lolita Lebron (*second from right*), shouted "free Puerto Rico" just before they opened fire on members of the House. Five congressmen sustained wounds as they scrambled on the House floor, although none were killed in the attack. The four assailants later were found to be part of a larger conspiracy to overthrow American influence in Puerto Rico by revolutionary means, which included a planned assassination of President Eisenhower. The U.S. government convicted Lebron and her compatriots along with eight others.

After evacuating the residents on nearby islands, the United States dropped a 15-megaton thermonuclear bomb—the H-bomb—on Bikini Atoll in the South Pacific on March 1, 1954. The "controlled test," which included intentional contamination of farm animals and placement of unmanned ships dangerously close by, went awry when fallout from the explosion spread radioactive pollution far beyond the test site. Ash showered down on Japanese fishermen aboard the *Fukuryu Maru* ("Lucky Dragon") more than 80 miles away. At least 23 fishermen were exposed to fallout, and one crew member, radioman Aikichi Kuboyama, died months later. In Japan (*above*), scientists used Geiger counters to measure radiation levels emitted by tuna that were in the area. The troubling episode fueled anti-American sentiment in Japan.

Americans were intrigued by nuclear testing in the Nevada desert. So was the Warner Bros. film studio, which produced *Them!*, a shocker about irradiated mutant ants. A terse, adult script treated the story as a murder mystery rather than a monster thriller, and Gordon Douglas directed with the smart, "police procedural" style that had come into vogue with such films as *The Naked City* and *Call Northside 777*. The startling moment captured here is the audience's first glimpse of the gi-ants. The actress is Joan Weldon. *Them!* was WB's biggest box-office grosser of 1954, and inspired a multitude of imitators.

February 16: Marilyn Monroe kicks off her tour of Korea. She will entertain troops at 10 stops throughout the former war zone.

February 17: Cigarette manufacturers announce the formation of the Tobacco Industry Research Committee in response to a recent rash of reports blaming smoking for lung cancer.

February 18: L. Ron Hubbard founds the Church of Scientology in Los Angeles.

February 23: The first mass inoculation of children with the Salk polio vaccine takes place in Pittsburgh.

February 24: The proposed Bricker Amendment, which seeks to limit the federal government's power to make treaties, is rejected by the Senate.

February 26: Michigan Representative Ruth Thompson attempts to interrupt the growing popularity of rock 'n' roll by introducing legislation that would ban the mailing of "obscene, lewd, lascivious, or filthy" records.

March: The siege at Dien Bien Phu, one of the defining events in the history of Southeast Asia, begins. Some 10,000 French troops are surrounded by 50,000 Viet Minh, and soon run out of supplies. *See May 7, 1954.*

March 1: Dave Edgerton opens Insta Burger King in Miami, selling 18-cent burgers as well as shakes. • Residents of two islands and those aboard the Japanese fishing boat *Lucky Dragon* are contaminated by fallout from the test of Bravo, a hydrogen bomb detonated by the U.S. at Bikini Atoll. Atomic Energy Commission head Lewis Strauss downplayed the accidental irradiation, claiming that the Japanese fishermen were part of a "Red spy outfit." • Five Congressmen are wounded when four Puerto Rican Nationalists open fire on the House floor from the gallery.

Edward R. Murrow's commentaries on American social and political issues broke new ground in the 1950s. On his CBS prime-time show, *See It Now,* on March 9, 1954, Murrow exposed Red-baiting Senator Joseph McCarthy as a fanatic. Murrow concluded that McCarthy's accusations had caused alarm and dismay among America's allies and had pleased the nation's enemies. Murrow blamed McCarthy not for creating the Red Scare but for exploiting it, adding that the "fault...is...in ourselves." CBS received literally thousands of calls and letters applauding the program.

Juan Chacon (*left*) and Rosaura Revueltas (*right*) are featured in *Salt of the Earth,* a film depiction of the famous strike by Mexican-American mine workers against the Empire Zinc Company in Bayard, New Mexico, in 1950–51. The movie honestly portrays the gender, ethnic, and class divisions among workers at the time, and offers an uplifting story about the role of the community—especially strong-willed women—in the labor struggle. But the project faced difficulties. The creation of director Herbert J. Biberman and other blacklisted film workers, the movie itself was blacklisted. The projectionists union refused to screen the film, and the American Legion called for a boycott. Even the FBI got involved, investigating the film's financing.

France's Debacle in Vietnam

FOLLOWING WORLD WAR II, the withdrawal of Japanese troops from what had been called Indochina paved the way for France to rebuild its Southeast Asia colonial holdings. But Communist insurgents—the Viet Minh—had other ideas.

Led by Ho Chi Minh, these rebels sought to expel France from Vietnam once and for all. By late 1953, six years of fighting had taken their toll on French morale, and support for the French effort was eroding at home. Meanwhile, hard-liners within the U.S. State Department were distressed to see another Asian country about to fall to communism. Yet they could not agree on a way to help without being dragged into the conflict.

In November 1953, French Gengeral Henri Navarre began a buildup of troops in a valley hamlet called Dien Bien Phu. Located in the northwest, it served as a gateway to Laos, which the general was anxious to protect. Strategically, it was a poor place to set a trap for the enemy; ringed by hills, the outpost made the French troops stationed there vulnerable to guerrilla attack. But Navarre's intent was to demonstrate military might in order to broker a settlement from a position of strength.

The Viet Minh, under the command of General Vo Nguyen Giap, stealthily installed captured U.S. heavy artillery (courtesy of the Chinese, who confiscated it during the Korean War) in the elevated points surrounding the French position. Not only could the Viet Minh bombard the French with impunity, but they were well positioned to destroy reinforcements arriving by air. On March 13, 1954, the Viet Minh attacked, launching a furious assault that convincingly demonstrated their military superiority. France's decisive defeat in the battle, coming just as peace talks were to begin in May, cost 2,200 lives (to the Viet Minh's 8,000). Dien Bien Phu offered a lesson that would go unheeded by Western powers intent on later involvement with Vietnamese affairs.

Communist Viet Minh troops storm one of the so-called "strong points" set up by the French at Dien Bien Phu in spring 1954 (*left photo*). French military leaders arrogantly had assumed that the Viet Minh would be unable to move heavy artillery up the steep hills surrounding French positions. Buttressed by General Vo Nguyen Giap's military genius and inspired by admiration for their political leader, Ho Chi Minh (*pictured on poster in above photo*), the Communists shelled the French mercilessly, then overran the base after 56 days of fighting. The battle effectively confirmed the end of French colonial rule in Southeast Asia.

March 4: An oil pool is discovered at Uthmaniyah, Saudia Arabia. It is believed to hold as much oil as all U.S. reserves combined.

March 8: As part of a mutual aid pact, the U.S. offers Japan $100 million in financial assistance, payable over the next three months.

March 9: Television journalist Edward R. Murrow condemns Senator McCarthy on his popular show *See It Now*. See April 6, 1954.

March 10: Ira C. Lowe, a smoker stricken with lung cancer, files the first tobacco-industry liability lawsuit. It will be dropped after 13 years.

March 11: The Army asserts that Senator McCarthy and Roy Cohn, his chief counsel, improperly attempted to influence the Army career of Private G. David Schine, a McCarthy consultant. The investigation of these charges will develop into the Army-McCarthy hearings. *See* April 22, 1954.

Spring: The Senate Subcommittee on Juvenile Delinquency, chaired by Senator Estes Kefauver, holds hearings on comic books in New York City. • The *London Daily Mail* sponsors a 15-week expedition to the Himalayas in search of the Yeti, the Abominable Snowman.

March 22: Southfield, Michigan, becomes the site of America's first shopping mall when the Northland Mall opens its doors.

March 23: Moscow formally grants sovereignty to East Germany.

March 25: RCA begins mass production of its new color television set. The 12-inch model sells for $1,000.

March 26: Another American H-bomb test at Bikini Atoll contaminates the island of Rongelap and other atolls downwind of the blast site. The bomb is 750 times more powerful than the one dropped on Hiroshima.

With only four American clubs in the six-team NHL in the 1950s, hockey lagged far behind baseball and football in popularity in the United States. Detroiters, however, were hockey-mad, and Gordie Howe—"Mr. Hockey"—was their favorite son. Prior to Wayne Gretzky, Howe was universally regarded as the greatest hockey player of all time. Rugged, durable, and immensely talented, Howe finished among the top 10 in NHL scoring for 21 consecutive seasons. He also recorded 19 career "hat tricks"—three goals in one game. Only Gretzky has surpassed his 801 goals. In 1954 Howe led the league in scoring while guiding the Detroit Red Wings to the Stanley Cup championship.

Seven-year-old Mimi Meade receives a dose of the new Salk polio vaccine on April 26, 1954. Though the vaccine was still in the testing stage, federal approval would be granted in April 1955. Despite some early apprehension about the vaccine in some communities—broadcaster Walter Winchell warned his audience that the vaccine "might be a killer"—most people believed, correctly, that the cure had arrived.

Writer-illustrator Robert Lawson created a series of award-winning books that included animal characters and scenes based on the surroundings of his Connecticut countryside. As he wrote, Lawson followed a philosophy of not condescending to children or adults. *The New York Times* welcomed *The Tough Winter* (1954), a follow-up to the successful *Rabbit Hill* (1944), for its "gentle humor" and "sensitive, beautiful drawings." Readers were enchanted by Lawson's regard for nature and his special fondness for animals.

Blues shouter "Big" Joe Turner was one of rock 'n' roll's most formidable pioneers. Possessing an oversized voice and a piano-pounding persona, Turner wrote and performed the lascivious "Shake, Rattle and Roll," which was released in April 1954. The song became a rock standard, albeit through Bill Haley's bowdlerized version. The 1950s saw Turner hit his artistic stride via a series of singles for the premier R&B label, Atlantic. "Chains of Love," later covered by Pat Boone, was among his hits. Though he was never a household name, Turner's influence on early rockers was incalculable.

Artist-designer Jim Flora created many memorable album sleeves in the 1940s and '50s. Few were as extraordinary—or as representative of Flora's zany but sophisticated sensibility— as this 1954 illustration for an LP by the Sauter-Finegan jazz-pop orchestra. Many of Flora's best sleeves are dominated by just two colors, and manage to mix the visual grotesqueness of Weimar Germany with the bohemian attitude of Greenwich Village. The artist's cool-kitty approach was widely imitated.

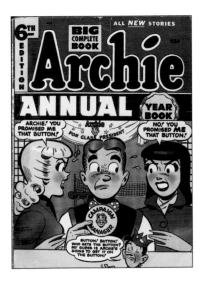

The red-headed teenage comic book character Archie (Archibald Andrews) first appeared in 1941, and enjoyed increasing popularity in the 1950s. Bob Montana's comic, set in the fictional town of Riverdale, followed the innocent escapades of Archie and his friends Jughead, Reggie, Betty, and Veronica. Most of the plots revolved around Betty and Veronica's rivalry for Archie's attention, conflict with authority figures (such as Principal Weatherbee), and visits to Pop Tate's Chock'lit Shoppe for malteds.

1954

April 1: The U.S. Senate votes 57 to 28 to grant statehood to Alaska and Hawaii. *See* January 3, 1959. • President Eisenhower signs a bill that establishes the Air Force Academy in Colorado. The first class will be sworn in on July 11, 1955.

April 5: Nicaraguan President Anastasia Somoza enacts martial law following an attempt on his life.

April 6: Senator Joseph McCarthy answers Edward R. Murrow's on-air charges with his own denunciation of Murrow as someone who has "engaged in propaganda for Communist causes."

April 7: Speaking at a press conference, President Eisenhower outlines the Domino Theory—the concept that if one nation falls to communism, others soon will follow. The Domino Theory will drive U.S. policy in Southeast Asia in the 1950s and 1960s.

April 10: For the first time since Iran nationalized its oil production in 1951, eight American and European oil firms announce that they will work in Iran. • On orders from President Eisenhower, Secretary of State John Foster Dulles offers two atomic bombs to the French for use in Vietnam, but the French decline the offer.

April 12: The occupying British arrest some 700 of Kenya's Mau Mau activists after independence negotiations break down.

April 18: Colonel Gamal Abdel Nasser becomes prime minister of Egypt.

April 22: The televised Army-McCarthy hearings convene in Washington. *See* June 9, 1954.

April 25: In a press conference in front of company headquarters, Bell Lab scientists unveil their new invention, the solar (photovoltaic) cell.

Japanese director Akira Kurosawa's *The Seven Samurai* (1954) tells the story of samurai swordsmen hired by farmers for protection against marauding thieves. The 160-minute epic, starring Toshiro Mifune (*pictured*), helped to create a new style of action film, both in its strong character development and its use of new techniques such as slow motion and panning shots of battle scenes. *The Seven Samurai* is considered one of the best films of all time and the most popular and well-known Japanese film ever. It later served as the model for the successful Hollywood American western *The Magnificent Seven*.

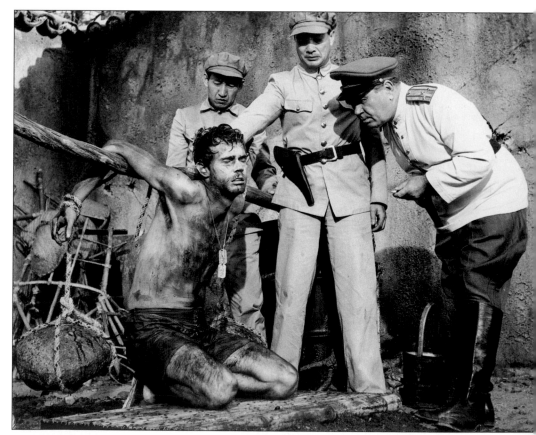

At the conclusion of the Korean War, a small but highly publicized group of American soldiers chose not to return to the United States. *Prisoner of War,* a fictional treatment that premiered a year after the war's end, helped to explain how such a thing might happen while painting a vivid picture of Communist brutality. The film follows a U.S. Army officer (Ronald Reagan) who investigates the treatment of POWs in North Korean prison camps. He finds rampant torture (the victim seen here is played by actor John Lupton), brainwashing, beatings, and starvation, with Russian interrogators leading the process. Though a propaganda film, *Prisoner of War* realistically depicts some of the hardships that American soldiers endured.

Comic Book Wars

BY 1954 COMIC BOOK STORIES were aswirl in an ever quickening spiral of violence, sexual suggestiveness, gore, and terror. In part, this happened because comics had been widely read by GIs during World War II and in Korea; after 1945, the general comic book readership skewed considerably older than before.

By 1950 superheroes were in serious decline, as comic book publishers focused on crime, horror, and war. For young women and girls, there was a generous complement of surprisingly frank romance comics. The industry produced an abundance of quality art and some good writing during 1950–54, most famously at the ever innocuous DC (home to Superman) and EC, publisher of *Mad, Tales from the Crypt, Crime SuspenStories,* and other titles. Another company, Lev Gleason, struck a chord with the bluntly competent *Crime Does Not Pay* and similar titles. Meanwhile, Marvel (called Atlas during this period) and dozens of smaller publishers issued so many mediocre "me-too" horror and crime titles that newsstands groaned beneath the weight.

Overall annual sales were in the hundreds of millions, but it was the industry's bad luck that the creative excesses inspired by competition and the endless battle for rack space coincided with a national rise in juvenile delinquency. Enter such self-styled reformers as Senator Estes Kefauver (D–TN) and New York psychiatrist Fredric Wertham, whose well-publicized anti-comics campaigns provided parents with what many had been looking for: a scapegoat to explain their kids' awful behavior.

In 1954–55, alarmed comics publishers agreed to join the new, "voluntary" Comics Code Authority. Ghouls, crime, sexy women, and other images deemed objectionable were prohibited. Without the Code seal (conferred under the auspices of New York judge Charles Murphy), no comic had a hope of being distributed to retailers. EC, Lev Gleason, and other companies sank in financial ruin. Others, including Fawcett and Avon, left the field voluntarily. The postwar comics boom was over, and the industry would not completely recover until Spider-man and other Marvel heroes appeared in the early 1960s.

Publisher Bill Gaines and writer-editor Al Feldstein turned EC Comics into a minor publishing phenomenon, but competition from other publishers encouraged creative excess. This 1954 cover by Johnny Craig, while very well drawn, is exorbitant in its unpleasantness. When Gaines volunteered to appear before a Senate subcommittee to explain himself, he unwisely engaged Senator Estes Kefauver in debate. Kefauver asked whether Gaines thought the cover was in good taste. Gaines replied, "Yes, sir, I do, for the cover of a horror comic." The senator was not persuaded. Time was running out for EC, and for the comics industry in general.

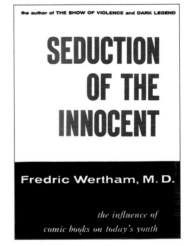

Psychiatrist Fredric Wertham was director of the mental hygiene clinic at New York's Bellevue Hospital when he wrote *Seduction of the Innocent,* a faintly hysterical screed about the deleterious effect of comic books on children. Many of Wertham's claims about the industry's excesses remain difficult to argue against, but numerous contentions (famously, that Batman and Robin are homosexuals) are absurd. Because Wertham treated disturbed children, many of whom had committed crimes of violence, he concluded that comic books were the cause—because each of those children enjoyed them. His book was widely read, and was a major factor in the 1954–55 implosion of comic book publishing.

1954

April 26: Delegates from the U.S., Vietnam, Laos, Cambodia, France, the Soviet Union, China, and Britain convene the Geneva Conference on Indochina, in an effort to reach consensus on the unrest in Southeast Asia.

April 28: In a statement made at the Geneva Conference, U.S. Secretary of State John Foster Dulles accuses China of exacerbating the hostilities in Southeast Asia.

April 29: India signs an eight-year peace pact with Red China.

May: Some 60,000 Honduran workers begin a two-month strike against United Fruit, seeking improved working conditions. It is the largest strike in Honduran history.

May 1: Sun Myung Moon founds the Unification Church in Korea. • Nash-Kelvinator and Hudson Motors merge to form American Motors Company. • Legos, founded by Ole Kirk Christiansen in the 1930s, becomes a registered trademark.

May 5: General Alfredo Stroessner becomes dictator of Paraguay following his successful military coup. Under his leadership, Paraguay will become a haven for Nazi war criminals.

May 6: President Eisenhower signs the Federal-Aid Highway Act, authorizing $175 million for the interstate highway system. • British medical student Roger Bannister breaks the four-minute mile (3:59.4).

May 7: Dien Bien Phu falls to the Viet Minh, ending French occupation in Vietnam and taking the lives of more than 2,200 French and 8,000 Viet Minh troops. • The U.S., Britain, and France reject Moscow's attempts to join NATO.

May 13: The Wiley-Donder Act, which paves the way for the construction of the Saint Lawrence Seaway (connecting the Great Lakes with the Atlantic Ocean), passes Congress.

English medical student Roger Bannister breaks the tape to become the first person ever to run a mile-long race in under four minutes. Bannister had refused to run in the 1948 Olympics, preferring to concentrate on his studies, and finished a disappointing fourth in the 1,500 meters in the 1952 Games. He redeemed himself with this record-shattering effort on May 6, 1954, finishing with a time of 3:59.4. Bannister was aided by two runners who had agreed to set the pace that he wanted. Less than a month later, Australian John Landy broke Bannister's record.

In 1953 President Eisenhower appointed Arthur Summerfield (*pictured*), former head of the Republican National Committee, the postmaster general of the United States. In May 1954, with Eisenhower's support, Summerfield approved a CIA mail-opening project that sought to root out smut and obscenity in the mail system. The project also set a precedent for future government intrusion as part of the anti-Communist crusade during the 1950s. In late 1954, civil liberties groups began to successfully challenge Summerfield's activities in the lower courts—especially his attempts to prevent future mailings, and thus future publication, of nudist magazines.

Universal struck box-office gold in 1954 with *Creature from the Black Lagoon,* a moody Amazon thriller (shot in California and Florida) about a humanoid sea creature who has unwholesome designs on a young scientist (Julie Adams, *pictured*). Jack Arnold's direction was subtle and intelligent, with judiciously placed shock sequences. The ornate monster suit was created by Bud Westmore, Jack Kevan, Millicent Patrick, and others, and remains a marvel of the art. As seen here, the Creature is played by Ben Chapman; Ricou Browning took the role in underwater sequences.

Those who criticize the 1950s as devoid of individual expression frequently cite the decade's paint-by-numbers craze to prove their point. The kits supplied paintbrushes and canvases with numbered shapes that corresponded to pre-chosen colors. As new painters developed their hobby, they could take great satisfaction as their composition came into view. Regardless of its lack of creativity, painting by numbers put brushes in many American hands for the first time, helping to foster an appreciation for the arts.

For fans of sci-fi pulps, the early 1950s represented a golden age, with dozens of titles populating the newsstand. The more highly regarded included *Astounding, Fantasy and Science Fiction, If,* and *Galaxy.* Featuring the work of such acclaimed writers as Robert Heinlein, Theodore Sturgeon, Frederik Pohl, and Isaac Asimov, the genre readily lent itself to speculative explorations of political, social, and technological themes. Yet, adolescent males made up the largest segment of their readership. With the collapse of independent distributors halfway through the decade, many digests folded, and the remaining handful reinvented themselves to survive. The provocative *Galaxy* cover seen here is the work of Ed Emshwiller.

At the beginning of the 1950s, more than 44 percent of American adults smoked cigarettes and about 33 percent of the nation's women smoked. In part, the high rate of smoking could be attributed to advertising. During the decade, Americans saw beautiful people smoking on television, in the movies, and in lush magazine advertisements, such as this one rendered for Philip Morris by Edwin Georgi. Ironically, the advertising ran concurrently with a series of high-profile medical studies that strongly linked lung cancer to cigarette smoking.

May 14: The Defense Department introduces Nike guided missiles, as well as its plan to protect 13 vulnerable sites with them, at San Francisco's Presidio.

May 15: The Defense Department charges the Soviets with masterminding the Korean War.

May 17: In *Brown v. Board of Education*, the U.S. Supreme Court unanimously declares school segregation unconstitutional, overturning the decades-old "separate but equal" doctrine.

May 19: Postmaster General Arthur Summerfield authorizes a CIA mail-opening project designed to intercept communications between the U.S. and the Soviet Union.

May 24: IBM unveils its vacuum-tube electronic "brain," capable of performing 10,000 functions per hour.

May 25: Legendary war photographer Robert Capa dies in Indochina when he steps on a landmine while following a French regiment through the jungle.

May 26: An explosion ignites a fire on board the aircraft carrier *Bennington,* off Quonset Point, Rhode Island, killing 103 sailors.

June 2: Senator Joseph McCarthy asserts that both the CIA and U.S. atomic weapons plants have been infiltrated by Communists.

June 9: Joseph Welch, Army attorney, famously confronts Senator Joseph McCarthy with the question "Have you no sense of decency, sir? At long last, have you left no sense of decency?" *See* June 17, 1954.

June 10: At a meeting in Richmond, Virginia, southern governors vow to defy the Supreme Court's *Brown v. Board of Education* ruling.

June 12: The song "Rock Around the Clock" by Bill Haley and His Comets is released.

Brown v. Board of Education

IN 1950 REVEREND OLIVER BROWN of Topeka, Kansas, was incensed that his young daughters could not attend the Sumner Elementary School, an all-white public school close to their home. Instead, they had to walk nearly a mile through a dangerous railroad switchyard to reach a bus that would take them to an inferior all-black school.

In the early 1950s, this sort of school segregation was commonplace in the South and certain border states. By law, all-black schools (and other segregated public facilities) were supposed to be as well-funded as whites'—but they rarely were. States typically spent twice as much money per student in white schools.

Classrooms in black schools were overcrowded and dilapidated.

In 1951 NAACP lead counsel Thurgood Marshall filed suit on behalf of Oliver Brown. By fall 1952, the Brown case and four other school desegregation cases had made their way to the U.S. Supreme Court, all under the case name *Brown*

Plaintiffs (and their children) in the *Brown* case.

v. Board of Education of Topeka. Marshall argued that the Supreme Court should overturn the "separate but equal" ruling of *Plessy v. Ferguson* (1896), which had legitimized segregation. Marshall believed that even if states spent an equal amount of money on black schools, the segregated system would still be unfair because the stigma of segregation damaged black students psychologically.

Chief Justice Earl Warren, who was moderately progressive in his social philosophy, sided with Marshall. On May 17, 1954, Warren declared: "We conclude, unanimously, that in the field of public education, the doctrine of 'separate but equal' has no place. Separate educational facilities are inherently unequal."

The Supreme Court's ruling specified that states needed to integrate their schools—not at once but "with all deliberate speed." Some southern leaders, shaken by the verdict, quickly passed legislation declaring they would not integrate at all. Whites throughout the South feared the end of their centuries-old white caste system. Stated the *Jackson* (Mississippi) *Daily News:* "White and Negro children in the same schools . . . leads to mixed marriages and mixed marriages lead to mongrelization of the human race."

Despite monumental attempts to resist school integration—most notably in Little Rock, Arkansas, in 1957—subsequent Supreme Court rulings and federal enforcement eventually ensured desegregation. The process, however, took many years. By 1973, about half of southern black schoolchildren were attending formerly all-white public schools.

Nathaniel Steward, 17, recites his lesson in a Washington, D.C., high school on May 21, 1954, four days after the Supreme Court ordered the desegregation of American public schools. The school districts in Washington and Baltimore were among the few to make desegregation mandatory by fall 1954. For Washington, the implementation wasn't hard; the Congress controlled the city and the law was the law, even if many in Congress disagreed with it. But the white backlash in the Mid-Atlantic was apparent. Many whites in Washington and Baltimore responded to the *Brown* decision by moving to the suburbs, enrolling their children in all-white schools.

THE SHAME OF SEGREGATION

I REMEMBER PLAYING stickball as a boy and watching white women driving into the neighborhood to pick up black women to work in their house. One time in particular, I can see it almost in slow motion, when a white woman came to pick up Mrs. Bertrand, a prominent member of our church, a highly regarded member of our community, who raised smart children of her own, was a good grandmother...that white woman made Mrs. Bertrand sit in the back seat of the car because her dog was in the front seat. I can still see Mrs. Bertrand today, standing there, thinking about it before she got in the car, with her head hanging down.

And men that we had a lot of respect for, most of whom were World War II veterans, were completely humiliated by the police. One time, when our scoutmaster was driving six or seven of us somewhere, a cop stopped him for a broken taillight and referred to him as "boy," to which he was compelled to duck his head and respond, "yes suh, yes suh." At other times, even our dad, in front of us, had to say it.

—LESTER MONTS, WHO WAS A SEVEN-YEAR-OLD STUDENT IN LITTLE ROCK, ARKANSAS, IN 1954

The *Brown v. Board of Education* decision outraged whites in Mississippi, some of whom formed a Citizens' Council to defend their segregated way of life. (White Citizens' Councils eventually would spread throughout the South.) Segregationists called the day of the *Brown* decision "Black Monday." Soon afterward, Mississippi Circuit Court Judge Tom P. Brady wrote a Jim Crow manifesto explaining that desegregation advanced the Communist agenda and would lead to race-mixing, which would ruin the nation. His treatise was published in book form later in the year. The blatantly racist Brady claimed that the personal "preferences of the Negro remain close to the caterpillar and the cockroach...proper food for a chimpanzee."

To millions of Americans throughout the baby boom years, broadcast journalist Walter Cronkite was "the most trusted" man in the country. Whether anchoring the *CBS Morning Show* (*pictured*) or hosting the historical reenactment program *You Are There,* Cronkite projected a plainspoken yet nuanced sincerity, which viewers came to rely upon. After working as a United Press correspondent during the war, Cronkite moved to CBS in 1950. In 1962 he took over the CBS anchor desk, where he remained until 1981.

June 14: The U.S. conducts its first nationally coordinated nuclear attack preparedness drill. • The congressional resolution that adds the words "under God" to the Pledge of Allegiance is signed by President Eisenhower.

June 16: Vietnamese Emperor Bao Dai names Ngo Dinh Diem as prime minister of South Vietnam. The U.S. hopes it has found a strong ally in Diem.

June 17: The Army-McCarthy hearings conclude. *See August 31, 1954.*

June 27: Operation PBSUCCESS, a CIA-sponsored military coup that deposes Guatemalan President Jacobo Arbenz Guzman, triggers a civil war that will last for several decades. • The Soviets fire up their first nuclear energy plant at Obninsk, about 60 miles southwest of Moscow.

June 28: Robert Oppenheimer's appeal of the revocation of his security clearance is denied by the Atomic Energy Commission.

July 3: Nine years after the end of World War II, food rationing finally comes to an end in Great Britain. • One year after undergoing cancer surgery, golf legend Babe Didrikson Zaharias wins the U.S. Women's Open by 12 strokes.

July 4: In a story that will grip the nation for the rest of the century and beyond, Ohio housewife Marilyn Sheppard is murdered. Dr. Sam Sheppard, her husband, will go to prison proclaiming his innocence.

July 6: The first Newport Jazz Festival opens. The festival will become one of the premier jazz events in the U.S.

July 7: Elvis Presley is heard on the airwaves for the first time when Memphis station WHBQ plays his first studio recording, "That's All Right (Mama)." The song was produced by Sam Phillips at Sun Records in Memphis.

> "[U]ntil this moment, Senator, I think I never really gauged your cruelty or your recklessness. . . . You have done enough. Have you no sense of decency, sir? At long last, have you left no sense of decency?"
>
> —ATTORNEY JOSEPH WELCH, REPRESENTING THE U.S. ARMY AT THE 1954 ARMY-MCCARTHY HEARINGS

McCarthy Takes on the Army

EMBOLDENED BY A SERIES of confrontations with virtually anyone who displeased him, Senator Joseph McCarthy crossed the line by declaring war on the U.S. Army. The conflict started when G. David Schine, an intimate of McCarthy's right-hand man, Roy Cohn, had been drafted—over McCarthy's and Cohn's strenuous objections. Failing to get Schine into a less dangerous line of service, McCarthy, at Cohn's behest, exerted tremendous pressure on the military to grant Schine special privileges. Less than satisfied with the response, McCarthy trained his sights on the Pentagon, accusing officials of harboring known Communists.

Not about to see his beloved Army impugned, President Dwight Eisenhower tacitly approved the military's demand that McCarthy put up or shut up. Thus, the Army-McCarthy hearings began on April 22, 1954. Television brought gavel-to-gavel coverage of the drama into people's homes, giving Americans an opportunity to see the senator in action at last.

Army attorney Joseph Welch banked on winning public opinion by essentially giving McCarthy enough rope with which to hang himself. This McCarthy did on June 9 by launching into a gratuitous slander of one of Welch's colleagues (who was not even involved in the proceedings). The event climaxed with an incredulous Welch inquiring, "Have you no sense of decency, sir?" McCarthy replied, "I know this hurts you, Mr. Welch," to which the attorney responded, "I'll say it hurts!"

The clash achieved what President Eisenhower and others had lacked the will to do: confront McCarthy head-on and break his untouchable status. Emboldened by the public shift in mood, Senator Ralph Flanders (R–VT) introduced a resolution in July to censure the senator. This sealed his *persona non grata* status among his peers. Though McCarthyism's most infamous practitioner was out of business, the Red Scare continued with others carrying on the antisubversive banner, most notably FBI Director J. Edgar Hoover.

As a young prosecutor in the U.S. Attorney's office, Roy Cohn (*right*) played a pivotal role in the espionage trial of Julius and Ethel Rosenberg. Cohn's aggressive anticommunism drew the attention of Senator Joseph McCarthy (*left*), who soon made Cohn his chief counsel in the Senate Subcommittee on Investigations. Cohn helped shape the committee's strategy of using blackmail to gain informants in the mission to root out Communists from the State Department. Ultimately, it was Cohn's effort to arrange a leave for his friend, David Schine (most likely his lover), from the Army that led to the intense clashes between the committee and Army attorney Joseph Welch.

Boston lawyer Joseph Welch acted as special counsel for the U.S. Army during the famous Army-McCarthy hearings in spring 1954. Earlier in the year, Senator Joseph McCarthy had begun to attack the Army because it had refused to give a member of McCarthy's staff preferential treatment. In the standoff, the senator upped the ante by directly pursuing a lawyer on Welch's staff, accurately pointing out his past involvement in the Lawyers Guild, a group with ties to the Communist Party. Welch's anger bubbled over on live television during the hearings, and he said what many fearful people had long been thinking about McCarthy.

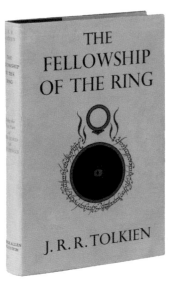

By 1954 American workers found themselves in a strong bargaining position. The economy was booming, and union membership that year reached an all-time high of 35 percent of the workforce. In many instances, union leaders were able to secure healthy raises for the rank and file. Union members who worked in factories or in various trades no longer were confined to urban, working-class neighborhoods; many joined the suburban middle class. Moreover, with fatter weekly paychecks, union members spent more than they had in the past—which further bolstered the national economy. Never before had the "American system" worked so well.

J. R. R. Tolkien was an English academic fascinated with Anglo-Saxon and Norse myths. Tolkien drew upon these sources to create his own legends, beginning with 1937's *The Hobbit*. The book's imagination, humor, and rich detail led to demands for a follow-up. Twelve years in the making, the Middle-Earth saga resumed with the sprawling *Lord of the Rings* trilogy. The first two volumes, *The Fellowship of the Ring* and *The Two Towers,* arrived in 1954, followed by *The Return of the King* one year later. Decades would pass before these immensely popular tales would receive a successful Hollywood treatment.

1954

July 10: The Alabama Board of Education votes to maintain segregation in public schools.

July 11: Upset by the *Brown v. Board of Education* decision, segregationists in Indianola, Mississippi, form the first of many White Citizens' Councils. The councils will oppose integration, often by economically attacking African-Americans active in voter rights.

July 13: Frida Kahlo, a Marxist Mexican artist and the wife of renowned artist Diego Rivera, dies at age 47.

July 15: Boeing introduces the 707 passenger jet with a 90-minute maiden voyage. The 707 will become a commercial success, with more than 3,000 sold. • In what will be known as Operation Wetback, federal and state authorities begin a program of forced repatriation of Mexican workers from U.S. cities in the lower Rio Grande Valley.

July 18: In an effort to maintain the British presence in the Suez Canal, coded messages are delivered to Israeli agents instructing them to sabotage several buildings in Egypt.

July 19: Roy Cohn resigns as Senator Joseph McCarthy's chief counsel.

July 21: The Geneva Accords agreed upon at May's Geneva Conference go into effect, dividing Vietnam into North and South at the 17th parallel. The accords call for reunification in two years.

July 22: The Revised Organic Act is passed by Congress to serve as a charter of civic government for the U.S. Virgin Islands.

July 28: President Syngman Rhee of South Korea addresses a joint session of Congress. He asks the U.S. to ally with South Korea and other Asian nations in a war against Communist China.

In 1954 these workers in Honduras went on strike against the American-owned United Fruit Company. Established in 1899, the giant agricultural conglomerate virtually controlled the economies of many Caribbean countries for much of the first half of the 20th century. United Fruit maintained its monopoly on banana production in such places as Honduras by preventing the governments from distributing land to peasants. It often used intimidation and threats to keep governments in line, even on occasion overthrowing recalcitrant regimes. The company began to lose its stranglehold over the Caribbean in 1958 when an antitrust decision forced it to sell one of its operating divisions.

In 1954 Guatemalan President Jacobo Arbenz Guzman (*right*) worked with Communists on land reform, including the expropriation of more than 200,000 acres of land owned by the very powerful United Fruit Company. In June 1954, the CIA—with full approval of the Eisenhower Administration—sponsored a successful coup against Arbenz, led by pro-American Colonel Carlos Castillo Armas (*left*). The CIA wanted to both restore the American corporate giant's holdings and stem the potential spread of communism. The U.S. even supplied Armas with World War II bombers. Apparently for the Eisenhower Administration, the threat of communism and American business interests were more important than respecting the sovereignty of a democratically elected government.

Babe Didrikson Zaharias celebrates after winning the 1954 U.S. Women's Open Golf Championship by a whopping 12 strokes. The performance inspired millions of Americans, as Zaharias had undergone surgery for colon cancer just 14 months earlier. As a younger woman, Didrikson had excelled in more than a dozen sports. She was an All-American basketball player in the early 1930s, broke two world track-and-field records at the 1932 Olympics, and even pitched against Major League batters in spring training games. She died of cancer on September 27, 1956, at age 45.

During her short life, Mexican Frida Kahlo's artistic contribution was over-shadowed by her larger-than-life husband, muralist Diego Rivera. Only recently has her artwork been accorded its due. Kahlo suffered years of debilitating back and leg pain as the result of injuries from a bus accident in her youth. Out of her life of chronic discomfort, and from her commitment to personal liberation and political revolution, Kahlo pioneered a radically new mode of artwork. She often placed her own image in her vivid paintings while exploring diverse themes, including gender identity and indigenous Mexican history. Kahlo died on July 13, 1954, at age 47.

In the summer of 1953, Elvis Presley (*far left*) walked into the studio of Sun Records owner Sam Phillips (*far right*) to record his voice professionally for the first time. Phillips, who saw himself as a bridge between the races with his role as producer of such musicians as BB King and Roy Orbison, found his crossover success with Presley. The following year, Phillips brought Elvis back to the studio to create a new sound with bassist Bill Black (*second from left*) and guitarist Scotty Moore (*second from right*). On July 5, 1954, Black and Moore helped Elvis record his first hit single, "That's All Right (Mama)." The record set the groundwork for the new rock 'n' roll sound.

"Why Isn't Sam Sheppard in Jail? Quit Stalling—Bring Him In"

—EDITORIAL HEADLINE ON THE FRONT PAGE OF *THE CLEVELAND PRESS* ON JULY 30, 1954, JUST HOURS BEFORE SHEPPARD WAS ARRESTED

The Sheppard Murder Case

DAWN ARRIVED PEACEFULLY for the lakefront community of Bay Village, Ohio, on the Fourth of July, 1954. But the idyll was short-lived when word of a brutal murder reached residents of the Cleveland suburb. Marilyn Sheppard, 31 and pregnant, was found bludgeoned to death in her bed, as her son slept in a nearby room. Her husband, Dr. Sam Sheppard—after regaining consciousness following an injury that had laid him out—notified the authorities.

Sheppard told police that, having dozed off downstairs while watching TV, he awoke to the sounds of his wife's screams. Rushing to her aid, he was felled by a blow to the head by an unseen assailant. Blacking out momentarily, he came to and immediately checked his family. While Sam Jr. remained sound asleep, Marilyn was dead, beaten beyond recognition. A noise from downstairs caught his attention, and he pursued it, finding what he described as a "bushy-haired" stranger fleeing the scene. Grappling with the intruder outside near the lake, he was again assaulted and passed out.

Despite his testimony, police attention soon reverted to the doctor. Though he was badly injured, Sheppard lost credibility when word of an extramarital liaison leaked out. Thereupon, and with little pretext of objectivity, a frenzy of screaming headlines began, most ferociously in *The Cleveland Press*. The drumbeat continued throughout the trial. With Sheppard's defense out-shouted, "Dr. Sam" was convicted in December and sentenced to life in prison.

Sheppard being returned to his cell, December 21, 1954

The case, however, would remain in the public eye for years afterward. Sheppard's conviction would be thrown out on the grounds of an unfair trial, and subsequent court action acquitted him. Meanwhile, television parlayed details of the case into the popular 1960s series *The Fugitive*. Years later, son Sam Reese Sheppard would continue the fight to clear his father's name, introducing DNA evidence that suggested a frame-up.

The Boeing Aircraft Company unveiled its 707 aircraft on July 15, 1954, initiating the "jet age." The 707 was not the first jet airliner; the De Havilland Comet was. However, with its six-seat-wide fuselage and large carrying capacity, the 707 quickly became the most cost-efficient and comfortable way to fly. Pan Am was the first airline to adopt the plane as part of its fleet. By the end of the 1950s, the 707 was making transcontinental flights within the United States as well as regular flights from the U.S. to Europe.

In the 1950s, John Wayne starred in many of his most famous films, including *The Searchers* (1956) and *Rio Bravo* (1959). *The High and the Mighty* (1954) allowed this symbol of American manliness to depart from his usual specialties of war movies and westerns. In the adaptation of Ernest K. Gann's novel, Wayne plays a heroic copilot who must save the day when engine trouble threatens the passengers' survival. Following decades of legal wrangling, *The High and the Mighty* came to home video and DVD in 2005.

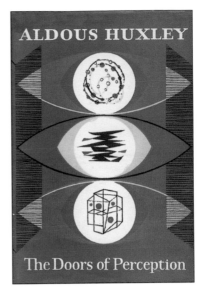

Aldous Huxley's 1954 book, *The Doors of Perception,* offered insight into the effects of mescaline on one's mind. At a time when society could scarcely come to terms with marijuana, this was heady stuff. The author of *Brave New World* advocated the removal of "culture-conditioned prejudices" in order to experience transcendental contact with the world. His call for the use of hallucinogens in the cause of self-liberation found a receptive audience among intellectuals. Critics, of course, ridiculed his profundities as the intoxicated ramblings of a dangerous crank.

Innovative graphic designer Paul Rand worked at four careers: media promotion and cover design, advertising design, corporate logos and trademarks, and teaching (at Cooper Union, Pratt, and Yale). This 1954 ad for Dubonnet wine is a perfect example of Rand's belief that effective advertising is driven not by the copywriter but by the designer. When he found copywriters who agreed, the results were memorable.

At New York's Palladium Ballroom, professional Cuban dancers Pete and Millie show off their moves at the height of the mambo dance craze. During the 1950s, artists such as the Mambo Aces, Tito Puente, and Cuban Pete brought mambo mania to a boiling point throughout the United States. In 1954 Cuban violinist Enrique Jorrin created a simplified mambo called the cha-cha, making the style accessible to an even broader audience. By the late 1950s, the music appealed to ethnically diverse audiences, and influenced the shape of jazz and other popular art forms.

1954

August: Approximately 30,000 Chinese die due to a flooding of the Yangtze River. • Arnold Palmer, 24, wins the U.S. Amateur Championship at the Country Club of Detroit.

August 2: The Housing Act of 1954 is passed in an effort to curb the spread of urban blight.

August 5: The B-52A Stratofortress, featuring external fuel tanks and midair fueling capability, is test-flown for the first time. Ultimately, only three will be built. • More than 10,000 people die following torrential rains that flood the Iranian capital of Tehran.

August 7: Charles H. Mahoney is confirmed as a permanent delegate to the United Nations, becoming the first black American to hold the position.

August 12: The last United Nations forces leave North Korea.

August 16: The first issue of *Sports Illustrated* is published, with Eddie Mathews of baseball's Milwaukee Braves on the front cover.

August 23: Lockheed tests "Hercules," a YC-130 turboprop, for the first time. The YC-130 will become one of the most widely used transport planes in history due to its ability to take off and land on short runways.

August 24: In an effort to eradicate the American Communist Party, President Eisenhower signs the Communist Control Act. • Amid mounting criticism of his administration, Brazilian President Getulio Vargas dies of a self-inflicted gunshot wound.

August 30: The Atomic Energy Act of 1954 is passed, giving the Atomic Energy Commission the power to develop standards to protect the environment from radioactive waste.

With a booming economy and easy credit, the "good life" was within reach for large numbers of Americans in the 1950s. Many escaped urban crowding by moving to the burgeoning suburbs. There, ranch homes were designed for the domestic pleasures of indoor/outdoor living. Sliding glass doors often overlooked a patio and (possibly) an in-ground swimming pool. Barbecue grills were a must. Life for Mom was hardly easy, however, as she was expected to run the domestic show, attend to everyone's needs, and keep a fresh face.

MOVING UP

LATER WE MOVED out a little further. It was still a suburb, but we had a larger house that was a little more idiosyncratic than our old house. This was the time when people were very concerned about bomb shelters. This house had a large backyard, the largest plot on the block, and it had a swimming pool.

Well, after we'd moved in, we were approached by the neighbors, who said, you've got the big backyard so we should put the bomb shelter in your yard. We thought this was dumb—we didn't think a bomb shelter was going to save any lives. And of course, no one was interested in sharing the costs of building this air-raid shelter! We did a lot of backyard entertaining—big brunches, swimming parties, barbecues. You were trying to live out this ideal of life in the suburbs, in a way, that you saw in *Life* magazines. But you always considered yourself just a little above it.

—CAROL FREEMAN, *THE FIFTIES: A WOMEN'S ORAL HISTORY*

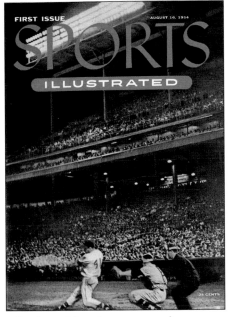

After launching the enormously successful *Time, Fortune,* and *Life* magazines, publisher Henry Luce took a chance in 1954 with a national sports magazine, *Sports Illustrated.* The initial cover (*pictured*) of the four-color publication featured Milwaukee Braves slugger Eddie Mathews. At first, *SI* was too elevated for the masses, with stories on polo and yachting. In time, the magazine focused more on spectator sports, which boomed in popularity in the late 1950s due to television and general economic prosperity. With brilliant color photography and lively, literate articles, *Sports Illustrated* eventually boasted three million subscribers.

In *On the Waterfront,* Marlon Brando (*center*) plays a disillusioned, washed-up fighter who labors as a New York City longshoreman. Disgusted with his corrupt union and inspired by his love for a good woman, he finally exposes the well-dressed thugs who rule the docks. Writer Budd Schulberg and director Elia Kazan fashioned the movie into a powerful statement about morality and the capacity of the individual to smash injustice. However, many in Hollywood believed that Kazan, a Communist Party member in the 1930s who had recently named names for HUAC Red-baiters, was hypocritical. Regardless, *On the Waterfront* is unquestionably powerful. It earned eight Academy Awards, including Oscars for Brando and Kazan.

The Mercedes-Benz 300SL was nicknamed "Gullwing" for its distinctive doors, which swung up on hinges from the roof like the wings of a bird. The unique entry captivated the public. Engineers based the 300SL on the similar SLR racing car, which had a tubular chassis that required race drivers to climb into the car over a tall sill. The street version of this racing car was the first gasoline-powered automobile with fuel injection. Its powerful engine and aerodynamics put it among the faster vehicles on the road in 1954.

1954

August 31: The Senate subcommittee on investigations censures both the Army and Senator Joseph McCarthy. *See* December 2, 1954. • Hurricane Carol makes landfall near Old Saybrook, Connecticut. Carol's path of destruction reaches from the Carolinas to New England and leaves more than 60 people dead.

September: Harry Winston's flawless 62.05 carat Winston Diamond is unveiled at the Texas State Fair.

September 1: President Eisenhower signs a bill extending Social Security benefits to 10 million additional Americans.

September 3: President Eisenhower signs the Espionage and Sabotage Act of 1954, which further defines acts of espionage that are subject to penalties of death or imprisonment. • In its ongoing effort to reclaim sovereignty over Taiwan, Red China shells the islands of Matsu and Quemoy.

September 6: President Eisenhower establishes a global "atomic pool," whereby nations join their atomic resources, to be used for peaceful purposes only. The Soviets are not invited to participate. • A U.S. Navy patrol bomber is shot down by two Soviet fighter jets more than 40 miles off the coast of Siberia.

September 7: School desegregation begins in Baltimore and Washington, D.C.

September 8: The Manila Pact is signed. It establishes the Southeast Asia Treaty Organization, a mutual defense pact among the U.S., Great Britain, Australia, New Zealand, the Philippines, Thailand, Pakistan, and France.

September 9: Canadian Marilyn Bell, 16, touches the seawall in Toronto to become the first person to swim Lake Ontario. She had left Youngstown, New York, more than 21 hours earlier.

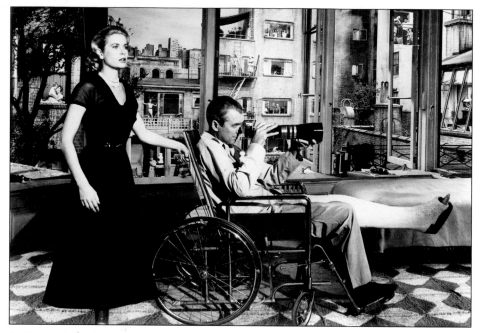

In *Rear Window* (1954), Alfred Hitchcock placed leading man Jimmy Stewart in a wheelchair and limited his movements to a small apartment. Stewart's character, a sidelined photojournalist, can't help but spy on his neighbors through his rear window. With his girlfriend (actress Grace Kelly, *pictured*) as his proxy, Stewart investigates a possible murder that he saw in one of the apartments. In this taut thriller, Hitchcock explored themes of repressed sexuality, fear of commitment, and postwar male angst. But he also invited his audience to partake in the voyeurism of the picture window, and to consider its relationship to film.

Necessitated by clogged roads and spurred by an influx of federal money, large U.S. cities instituted major intercity highway construction projects in the 1950s. Linking the downtowns to the suburbs meant cutting swaths through decades-old infrastructure, gutting communities while in effect barricading one block from the next. As seen in this under-construction view of Chicago's Congress Street Expressway, city planners invariably chose corridors through the poorer neighborhoods, easily brushing aside any grassroots resistance. In creating a direct path from downtown to the suburbs, the process of cultural homogenization was hastened while sleepy outlying areas became bustling population centers.

Rock 'n' Roll

DURING THE GREAT MIGRATION from the South in the 1940s, many itinerant musicians settled in such urban centers as Chicago. Among them was McKinley Morganfield, better known as Muddy Waters. Along with others, Waters brought electric amplification to rural blues, laying the groundwork for the cultural tsunami that would define an era.

Though the phrase "rhythm and blues" came to describe the sound emanating from cities hosting large black populations, "rock 'n' roll" would be a hybrid—a mix of R&B, country, and jazz boogie. It is not coincidental that so many of the genre's earliest practitioners were of southern origin, as they were ideally placed to absorb the musical crosscurrents.

The phrase itself, rock 'n' roll, had existed as a euphemism for carnal relations dating back to the 1920s (or earlier), but it took white disc jockey Alan Freed to popularize it. As host of the Cleveland radio show *Moondog Rock 'n' Roll Party,* Freed began showcasing the underground craze in 1951, drawing listeners from several states. In 1954 rock 'n' roll entered the mainstream with Bill Haley and His Comets' hit song, "Rock Around the Clock."

The energetic sound of rock 'n' roll demanded nothing more profound from its listeners than dancing, but its

Little Richard

unmistakably African-American origins made it a lightning rod for controversy among reactionaries. Feeling that the music was steeped in sexual connotation and associated with youthful lawlessness, authorities moved to outlaw both airplay and public gatherings. But by doing so, they simply gave teen fans something to rebel against; by the end of the decade, rock 'n' roll would essentially co-opt the popular music industry.

In 1954 New York radio station WINS hired a popular Cleveland disc jockey named Alan Freed. In Ohio, the radio host and promoter had begun to shape a new audience for rhythm and blues music, bringing an increasing number of white listeners to the genre. In fact, Freed is credited with coining the term "rock 'n' roll." The deejay helped to introduce the music of Bo Diddley and Chuck Berry to a white audience—and helped those artists sell many more records in the process. In 1955 Freed began emceeing wildly popular events in Brooklyn and New York that he promoted as rock 'n' roll shows. He also reached a national audience on CBS radio.

1954

September 12: The Joint Chiefs of Staff recommend using atomic weapons against Red China in order to secure a victory for Chiang Kai-shek's Nationalists.

September 14: Hurricane Edna rips into New York City, causing more than $50 million in damages. • The Soviet Union gathers about 45,000 soldiers at the Totskoye test range in Kazakhstan and explodes a nuclear weapon in their midst. The purpose is to observe the effects of fallout on the battlefield.

September 17: Some 250,000 refugees recently have fled into South Korea from the North.

September 20: The first program using the FORTRAN computer language is run.

September 23: The Joint Chiefs of Staff reiterate their call for nuclear attacks on China following that nation's sentencing of 13 American pilots shot down over Chinese skies during the Korean War. • The East German police take more than 400 people into custody, accusing them of spying for the United States.

September 25: François "Papa Doc" Duvalier wins Haiti's presidential election and begins his 14-year dictatorship.

September 26: Actor Ronald Reagan becomes the host of TV's *General Electric Theater.* He will appear on the program for eight years. • A killer typhoon hits Japan, sinking several ferryboats and claiming more than 1,000 lives.

September 27: *The Tonight Show* with host Steve Allen premieres on NBC.

October: Ho Chi Minh returns to Hanoi to lead North Vietnam after eight years of self-imposed jungle exile during the French occupation. • Thick smog forces the closing of schools and industry in the Los Angeles basin for much of the month.

Chinese Nationalist troops prepare defensive caves on the island of Quemoy in 1954. Chinese Communists had begun shelling the island, claimed by both Chinese Nationalists and the Communist People's Republic of China, shortly after the Eisenhower Administration removed warships that had prevented a Nationalist assault on the mainland. The Communists took advantage of the American departure by attacking the Nationalists. In spite of pressure at home, Eisenhower refused to use military might to resolve the crisis, which continued for the next three years.

Zampanò (played by Anthony Quinn) is consoled by Gelsomina (Giulietta Masina) in Italian director Federico Fellini's film *La Strada* (*The Street*). Part allegory, part pantomime, the movie tells the story of the unlikely coupling between a brutish, professional strongman (Quinn) and his devoted, if simple, "assistant." (He in fact has purchased her from her impoverished mother.) Shot in the famous neorealist style of the era, *La Strada* furthered Fellini's reputation as a distinctive filmmaker. Indeed, "Felliniesque" entered common parlance, denoting cinema rife with abstract imagery and bizarre characters.

"Havana's Fabulous Night Club and Casino"

From the late 1940s through the mid-1950s, nightlife in Havana was a major draw for well-off American tourists. In 1954 more than 200,000 Americans visited Cuba, with most of them headed for the capital. The Cuban government welcomed American mobsters, such as Meyer Lansky, to oversee the casinos. The Tropicana (*pictured*) was the largest nightclub in the city, offering lush gardens as well as a casino, restaurants, and show areas. More than a thousand customers thronged to its pleasures nightly, including celebrities ranging from Marlon Brando to Senator Joseph McCarthy. In the words of journalist Jay Mallin, Havana was celebrated for its "Rum, Rhumba, and Roulette."

Superstar Willie Mays of the New York Giants makes what became known simply as "The Catch" during Game 1 of the 1954 World Series. The Cleveland Indians were threatening to break open a tie game in the top of the eighth, with runners on first and second and nobody out, when Vic Wertz blasted a towering drive to deep center field in New York's cavernous Polo Grounds. Mays made the spectacular catch while running full speed toward the wall, then whirled and made a perfect throw to prevent a run from scoring. The Giants went on to sweep the favored Indians, who had won an American League record 111 games.

By October 15, 1954, Los Angeles citizens had endured nine days of throat-burning and eye-stinging smog. The foul air smothered the city, killing a child and shutting down schools and businesses for most of October. A gas mask seemed a sensible precaution. Pollution had become a serious problem in the city after World War II, as the number of automobiles and highways grew precipitously. The smog actually was a combination of sea air, car exhaust, and other pollutants sealed into the valley by temperature inversions and the surrounding mountains. The October crisis set off public outcry and a round of grand jury investigations.

1954

October 1: Automobile manufacturers Studebaker and Packard merge to form the Studebaker-Packard Corp.

October 2: The New York Giants sweep the favored Cleveland Indians in the World Series. For the first time, the Series is broadcast in color.

October 15: Hurricane Hazel hits the Carolinas and begins its trek north through New York and into Canada. The death toll will reach 500 in Haiti, 95 in the U.S., and 78 in Canada.

October 19: Egypt and Great Britain reach a consensus on terms to end the 72-year British occupation of the Suez Canal.

October 22: In response to the division of Vietnam and the ceding of the North to the Communists, President Eisenhower authorizes a quick and intensive training course for the South Vietnamese army. • West Germany gains full membership in NATO. • The 1955 Thunderbird, an answer to General Motors' Corvette, rolls off the Ford Motor Company assembly line.

October 25: President Eisenhower presides over the first Cabinet meeting broadcast on television.

October 27: Reverend Martin Luther King, Jr., takes the pulpit as the new pastor of the Dexter Avenue Baptist Church in Montgomery, Alabama. • "The Disneyland Story," the first episode of the *Disneyland* television series (which takes its name from the unfinished theme park), airs on ABC.

October 30: Six years after President Harry Truman banned segregation in the U.S. Armed Forces, the last of the Army's segregated units are finally integrated.

October 31: Algerian nationalists revolt against French rule.

November 1: Fulgencio Batista is elected president of Cuba.

To weather a crisis, a family sometimes needs an example of fortitude, bravery, and selflessness. Absent any better model, it may turn to the family dog. At least that was the case with the Miller clan, who found Lassie to be their guiding light. The Millers included (*clockwise from top*) Mom (Jan Clayton), Gramps (George Cleveland), and Jeff (Tommy Rettig). The *Lassie* series saw several cast overhauls and lasted from 1954 to 1974, with the first episodes entitled *Jeff's Collie*. The show was an American adaptation of a popular dog character depicted in books and in film, originally set in wartime England.

Godzilla, King of the Monsters premiered in the United States in 1956, but it had opened in Japan as *Gojira* in 1954. The Ishiro Honda film resonated deeply with Japanese audiences. The fire-breathing giant beast is disturbed from its slumber by an atomic test (presumably American) in the ocean and then rampages through Tokyo, crushing people and laying waste to the city—a monstrous allegory for radiation and American hegemony run amok. The film's special effects, created by Eiji Tsuburaya, set a new standard for monster movies. Japanese and American production companies would crank out Godzilla movies for the next half-century.

Egyptian President Gamal Adbel Nasser (*right*) shakes hands with Sir Ralph Stevenson, the British ambassador to Egypt. On October 19, 1954, the two nations agreed to the withdrawal of all British troops from the Suez Canal Zone. This event enhanced Nasser's reputation in Egypt and in other Arab nations, as he became a leading spokesman for Arab unity. The relative stability in the region would be shattered in 1956 when Nasser nationalized the canal, provoking military intervention by Britain, France, and Israel.

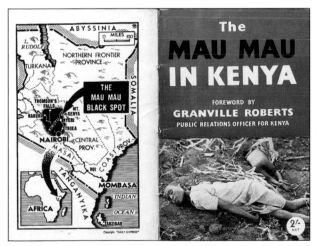

Kenya became a British protectorate in 1920, and the colonial government welcomed large numbers of British settlers. But Kenyan nationalism asserted itself after 1950, most famously as the Mau Mau, whose members dedicated themselves to retaking their country. Dozens of whites and many thousands of Kenyans were slaughtered in the turmoil that followed. The British government was determined to hang on and encouraged anti-Mau Mau propaganda, such as this 1954 volume written by a minor functionary of the British government. Filled with atrocity photos, the book paints Britain as Kenya's best hope for peace and prosperity.

The Mau Mau Uprising

EVEN 50 YEARS LATER, authorities disagree on whether the term "Mau Mau" originated with Kenya's Kikuyu rebels themselves or by those they sought to forcibly expel from their country. What is agreed is that the Kenyan struggle for independence was marked by bloody brutality on both sides, although Kikuyu force tended to be magnified in the press while white atrocities were swept under the journalistic rug.

Mau Mau was an acronym for Mzungu Aende Ulaya-Mwafrika Apate Uhuru, which is Swahili for "let the white man go back abroad so the African can get his independence." In Great Britain and other Western countries, Mau Mau became shorthand for uncivilized savagery enacted against Anglos by nonwhites.

European settlers began colonizing Kenya in the early 20th century, appropriating lands that had been homesteaded by families for centuries. After years of ill treatment, tensions came to a head in 1951, when Mau Mau members, meeting in secret, launched a campaign to retake their homeland from colonialists bent on subjugation. The rebels also targeted Kenyans who supported British rule.

By the time the rebellion spent itself in the late 1950s, more than 11,000 guerrillas were dead, 1,090 of them hanged by the British. Tens of thousands were imprisoned, including Mau Mau leader Jomo Kenyatta. By contrast, only dozens of whites were killed. In 1963 Britain finally granted Kenya its independence. On December 12, 1963, the last Mau Mau fighters turned over their weapons to Kenyatta, Kenya's new prime minister.

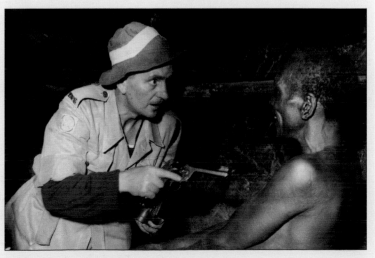

British soldier and Kikuyu rebel

1954

November 2: Strom Thurmond of South Carolina becomes the first senator elected by a write-in vote. He will hold office for 48 years, retiring at age 100.

November 4: Democrats regain control of Congress, despite Republican efforts to portray the Democrats as a party infiltrated by Communists.

November 7: Soviet fighters shoot down a USAF RB-29 north of Japan, off the Kurile Islands. One airman is killed. • The American League approves the move of the Athletics baseball team from Philadelphia to Kansas City.

November 10: President Eisenhower dedicates the Iwo Jima Memorial sculpture by Felix de Weldon. Located near Arlington National Cemetery, the sculpture is based on a Pulitzer Prize-winning photograph by Joseph Rosenthal.

November 12: The Ellis Island Immigration Station closes. Since opening in 1882, it processed more than 20 million immigrants.

November 15: Scandinavian Airlines begins the first regularly scheduled commercial flight over the North Pole, from Copenhagen to Los Angeles.

November 22: The Humane Society, dedicated to the protection of animals, is founded. Fifty years later, it will have field offices on every continent.

November 23: The 50 millionth General Motors vehicle rolls off the assembly line.

November 24: France sends 20,000 soldiers to Algeria in an attempt to quell guerrilla revolt.

November 27: Soviet spy Alger Hiss leaves prison after completing his 44-month term for perjury.

November 28: Physicist Enrico Fermi, who produced the first nuclear fission reaction, dies at age 53.

Actress Dorothy Dandridge was a gorgeous descendant of African slaves. Throughout her career, she was trapped between her glamorous image and her troubled past, between black men and white men, between Hollywood's desire to be bold and its penchant for racism, and between demeaning "jungle girl" roles and her great acting talent. Her most prominent role came opposite Harry Belafonte (*pictured*) in the 1954 film *Carmen Jones,* for which Dandridge became the first African-American to be nominated for a best actress Oscar. Unable to fight her internal and external demons, Dandridge overdosed on antidepressant pills in 1965, entering into legend at age 41.

Anti-French Algerian guerrillas march to show their opposition to French colonial rule. On November 1, 1954, members of the *Front de Libération Nationale* (FLN) launched coordinated attacks on French military and communications installations throughout Algeria. While FLN leaders called for "the restoration of the Algerian state," French Prime Minister Pierre Mendès-France pledged that Algeria would remain "irrevocably French." The armed rebellion dragged on until 1962, when France finally granted independence.

Life magazine, which began publication in 1936, rose to prominence in the 1940s with its stunning photographs of World War II. In the 1950s, the magazine remained an influential interpreter of the American experience. *Life* introduced readers to everything from SpaghettiOs to the civil rights movement. With issues such as this one,

which contrasted beauties with hard-hitting news stories and photo essays by important writers and photographers, the magazine helped to shape opinion as well as cover the world.

Clever, ringlet-haired Little Lulu was created by Marjorie Henderson Buell ("Marge") in 1935 for *The Saturday Evening Post*. The feature was a success as a single-panel gag strip, but when Lulu moved to comic books and was taken over by writer-pencil artist John Stanley and inker Irving Tripp, she blossomed, and became a favorite of girls—and smart boys— across America. Sweet but feisty, she delighted in

foiling the selfish schemes of her pal Tubby, who never learned that the good-natured Lulu was just too sharp to be outwitted.

Unlike comic book critic Dr. Fredric Wertham, British poet, novelist, and academic Geoffrey Wagner brought a jaundiced sense of humor to his critique of comics and other popular American media. *Parade of Pleasure* laments the tawdriness of the pulp mind-set (encompassing comics, movies, paperbacks, girlie magazines, and TV), but is less concerned with possible

spurs to violence than with the gross simplification of human motivations and behavior. Wagner objected, for example, to war comic books' portrayals of Communist soldiers as inept clods, and magazines' insistence that the only attractive women are young ones who look like brassiere models.

Throughout the 1950s, the neon signs of Las Vegas's "Glitter Gulch" lit the night sky, beckoning gamblers and tourists and providing top-paying venues for Frank Sinatra, Dean Martin, Sammy Davis, Jr., Louis Prima & Keely Smith, and many others. This also was the classic era of Vegas architecture, highlighted by such distinctive Fremont Street casinos and hotels as the Pioneer Club (*pictured*), the Desert Inn, the Sands, the Tropicana, and, by 1955, the Riviera, which rose to a then-impressive nine stories. A new convention center that was built during the decade opened up "Sin City" to year-round trade. Vegas offered all this, plus the appeal of no sales tax, no speed limit, and no waiting time for divorce.

1954

December: The FBI "Security Index," a secret list of people considered dangerous to national security (who could be detained without warrant during a crisis), includes 26,174 names—the most it will ever have.

December 2: The full Senate votes to censure Senator Joseph McCarthy for "conduct that tends to bring the Senate into dishonor and disrepute." • The U.S. enters into a mutual defense agreement with Nationalist China.

December 3: The opera *Troilus & Cressida* by William Walton opens at London's Royal Opera House.

December 7: Senator Joseph McCarthy verbally attacks President Eisenhower for his supposed soft stand against Communists.

December 10: The first rocket-powered sled is driven by Air Force Lieutenant Colonel John Paul Stapp in Alamogordo, New Mexico. It accelerates to 632 mph.

December 18: British soldiers open fire on rioting Cypriots during a revolt against British colonial rule.

December 21: Speaking at a press conference, Secretary of State John Foster Dulles implies that any enemy aggression in Western Europe would be answered with tactical nuclear weapons. • Citizens in Jackson, Mississippi, vote to continue school segregation.

December 23: The first successful live-donor kidney transplant is performed in Boston when a kidney is removed from Ronald Herrick and placed in his ailing twin brother, Richard, in a 5½-hour operation.

December 29: Twenty-five years after the stock market crash, the Dow Jones finally rises above precrash levels, breaking the 400 barrier for the first time.

Ann Hodges displays an 8.5-pound meteorite that came crashing through the roof of her Sylacauga, Alabama, home before striking her on November 30, 1954. Suffering a large bruise, Hodges became the only confirmed human casualty of an exceedingly rare event: a meteor surviving the trip through Earth's atmosphere. The incident caused a media sensation, with carloads of tourists descending upon the sleepy hamlet. Also arriving were scientists and Air Force personnel, who made sure the object wasn't part of an insidious Communist plot. The meteorite was eventually donated to the Alabama Museum of Natural History.

Of all the radio program genres created in the 1920s, '30s, and '40s, soap operas (so named because their original sponsors were soap companies) most easily made the transition from radio to television. With their slow, melodramatic plots, emphasis on dialogue, and extended story lines, the programs allowed American housewives to center their day around their favorite show. *Search for Tomorrow* (*pictured*) was created for television in 1951 and aired on CBS. The performers seen here are Mary Stuart and Terry O'Sullivan.

In God We Trust

AT THE HEIGHT OF THE RED SCARE, measures were implemented to codify an official federal position on religion. Through heavy lobbying by the Knights of Columbus, the words "under God" were inserted into the Pledge of Allegiance and signed into law on Flag Day, 1954.

Though the Pledge of Allegiance had originated as an 1892 Columbus Day recitation, its author, a Christian Socialist named Francis Bellamy, had kept it scrupulously nondeistic. Nevertheless, President Dwight Eisenhower approved the change, asserting that "from this day forward...millions of our schoolchildren will daily proclaim...the dedication of our nation and our people to the Almighty." In a country that was predominantly Christian, the new addition was widely applauded.

After altering the pledge, lawmakers turned their attention to federal currency. In 1955 the President signed a bill mandating the addition of "In God We Trust" to all coins and paper money. Though dissenters could have argued that the laws violated the separation of church and state,

Students reciting the revised Pledge of Allegiance

few dared to buck the prevailing tide during the McCarthy era. As such, it would remain for future generations to address concerns over the laws' legitimacy.

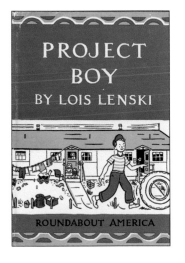

Lois Lenski was a major writer-illustrator of children's books who produced nearly 100 titles during six decades of activity. *Project Boy* is one of 11 "Roundabout America" books by Lenski. Its depiction of young Teddy Parker and his life in a sometimes rough-and-tumble government housing project is charming but surprisingly frank, even blunt. Teddy and his friends play in a dump, and adults scold and quarrel. But when another boy is shot in the eye during a game of bow-and-arrow, the community comes together to tend to him.

British composer, pianist, and conductor Benjamin Britten is considered one of the most significant composers of the 20th century. Britten produced creative and accessible compositions and had a special talent for putting words to music. His popular operas included *Peter Grimes* (1945) and *Billy Budd* (1951). At the height of his fame in 1954, Britten introduced his operatic interpretation of Henry James's *Turn of the Screw* in Venice at the International Festival of Contemporary Music.

Fallout Shelters

BY THE EARLY 1950S, the U.S. government had yet to create sufficient guidelines for its citizenry in the event of a nuclear attack. Although CONELRAD, a warning system in place since 1951, was designed to alert the country of impending doom via radio, exactly what to do next was less clear.

A Civil Defense pamphlet entitled "Facts About Fallout" advised, rather casually, for the populace to seek shelter, ideally in "an old-fashioned root cellar." Clearly, more substantial guidance was needed. In the absence of an official mandate, a growth industry soon mushroomed.

Amid extensive media coverage, fallout shelter contractors began marketing their wares to American citizens, offering an array of choices ranging from Spartan to lavish. While touting their shelters' ability to ensure survival, contractors also pointed out the peacetime purposes of the underground rooms. Brochures depicted homey bunkers as oases of calm, sort of like well-fortified rec rooms. In 1959 *Life* magazine ran a feature about a Florida couple who spent their first two weeks of wedded bliss underground, having won a contest sponsored by Bomb Shelters, Inc.

Despite the shelters' rather peculiar place in Boomer memory, by 1960 only 1,565 homeowners had actually opted for the rather expensive additions. Many made do with existing basements, securing enough supplies, foodstuffs, and water to hole up for the presumptive weeks needed until the radiation contamination abated. More people might have prepared themselves if they had heeded the 1957 findings of the Gaither Committee, a government task force charged with exploring the survivability of a nuclear apocalypse.

The Gaither Committee report suggested that billions of dollars be set aside for the creation of a national network of fallout shelters. But President Eisenhower declined, believing that turning the country into a garrison state would signal fear and create a self-fulfilling prophecy.

After successful tests in the early 1950s, the U.S. Army began deployment of Nike missiles in heavily populated areas, such as these in Lorton, Virginia, near Washington, D.C. The Nike was a strictly defensive, surface-to-air missile designed to protect America's urban centers against attack by Soviet nuclear-armed bomber aircraft. Scores of sites were established, including 19 around New York City. However, when the Soviets moved away from bombers to embrace intercontinental ballistic missiles (ICBMs), the rationale for the Nike diminished sharply. The U.S. government began to dismantle Nike sites in the early 1960s.

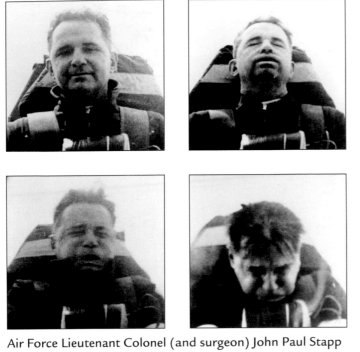

Air Force Lieutenant Colonel (and surgeon) John Paul Stapp became known as the "Fastest Man on Earth." In this rocket sled experiment in March 1954, he was accelerated on tracks to 421 mph. Stapp, who headed an annual conference for surgeons and engineers on car crashes, participated in many such tests of human tolerance. On December 10, 1954, he rocketed to 632 mph in just five seconds, and then slowed to a halt in 1.4 seconds. Stapp never lost consciousness during his rides, and although he fractured his ribs and wrists and experienced retinal hemorrhaging, he sustained few permanent injuries. He lived to be 89.

With amateur photography a thriving pastime, it seemed inevitable that someone would create a way to apply the "instant" ethos to the pursuit. That someone was Edwin Land, who in 1947 invented the Polaroid Land Camera for 60-second development of photographs. Inspired by his daughter's impatience to see the results when he photographed her, Land created a system that combined film negative with finished print. This 1954 Highlander model typified the company's offerings, which became popular at parties and other social events.

After the Great Depression and food rationing during World War II, the 1950s saw the floodgates of consumption flung wide open—like the door of this Amana "Stor-Mor Door Freezer." Along with the increased sales of new appliances came the advertised and government-approved encouragement to stuff them full of new processed and packaged foods. The image of abundance also carried with it a sense of patriotism, as Americans defined themselves in part by their newfound material riches.

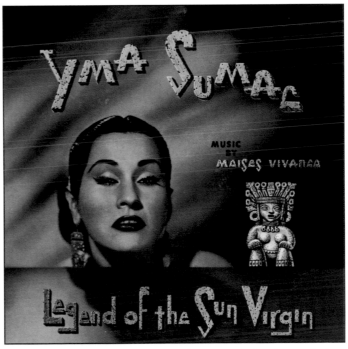

In the mid-1950s, musician Martin Denny helped popularize the new "exotica" sound. Exotica blended kitschy lounge music with Latin American rhythms and Hawaiian strains to create a unique brand of otherworldly music. The sounds exploited the new stereo technology and enchanted a postwar audience. Singer Yma Sumac epitomized the exoticism and questionable authenticity of the genre. All critics agreed that Sumac's voice was extraordinary, with a five-octave range that soared to eerie heights. But her identity was shrouded in mystery. Was she truly an Incan princess, born in the highlands of Peru, a descendent of Atahualpa, as her record covers said? Or was she Amy Camus from Brooklyn?

1954

New & Notable

Books
Bonjour Tristesse by Francoise Sagan
The Fellowship of the Ring by J.R.R. Tolkien
Lord of the Flies by William Golding
Lucky Jim by Kingsley Amis
Under Milk Wood (poetry)
    by Dylan Thomas

Movies
The Country Girl
The High and the Mighty
Magnificent Obsession
On the Waterfront
Rear Window
Sabrina
Salt of the Earth
The Seven Samurai
A Star Is Born
La Strada
20,000 Leagues Under the Sea

Songs
"Little Things Mean a Lot"
    by Kitty Kallen
"Mambo Italiano"
    by Rosemary Clooney
"Mr. Sandman" by the Chordettes
"Rock Around the Clock"
    by Bill Haley and His Comets
"Sh-Boom (Life Could Be a Dream)"
    by the Chords
"Shake, Rattle and Roll" by Joe Turner
"That's All Right (Mama)"
    by Elvis Presley
"Three Coins in the Fountain"
    by the Four Aces

Television
The Adventures of Rin Tin Tin
Disneyland
Face the Nation
Father Knows Best
Lassie
The Secret Storm

Theater
The Bad Seed
Fanny
The Pajama Game
The Rainmaker
Separate Tables
Witness for the Prosecution

In 1946 at Atlantic City's 500 Club, a laid-back crooner named Dean Martin teamed with a skinny, hyperactive kid comic named Jerry Lewis, electrifying audiences and laying the groundwork for one of the most successful showbiz partnerships of all time. Dean was the handsome straight man; Jerry the self-described "monkey." By 1954 they had starred in 12 pictures, and would go on to make four more before their breakup in 1956. During the remainder of the decade, Jerry thrived as a solo, while Dean proved himself a solid dramatic actor.

Bill Haley and His Comets helped spark a revolution in 1954. Their hit single "Rock Around the Clock" jumped to the top of the charts that year and helped make rock 'n' roll popular and acceptable to white audiences. Haley (*center*) had begun as a country performer, but after an early hit in 1951 with "Rocket 88," he turned his attention to rock 'n' roll. He and his bandmates captivated audiences with their matching plaid jackets and swinging stage presence. "Rock Around the Clock," released in the spring of 1954, would sell more than 25 million copies.

A pioneering celebrity magazine, *Photoplay* began publishing stories about the movies in 1911. During the 1950s, the magazine's audience grew along with the cult of celebrity. The biggest-selling movie magazine of the day, it provided entertainment news, in-depth articles, gossip, and photographs of such movie stars as Elizabeth Taylor (*pictured*). *Photoplay* was famous for its

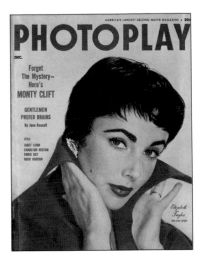

Gold Medal awards for the best films and actors of each year. The popular annual awards, which predated the Oscars, allowed readers to pick their favorite stars.

In the 1950s, Ralph Edwards (*pictured*) kept audiences and TV viewers on edge with *This Is Your Life*. The idea was simple: A member of the audience—most often a celebrity, such as Dorothy Lamour (*pictured*)—would be surprised as the guest of honor on a televised tribute. The show's producers would fly in everyone from old friends and family to retired teachers, each of whom would talk about the guest to the audience. Not surprisingly, some celebrities—such as Stan Laurel—were not pleased with the unexpected public airing of their personal lives.

The singing McGuire Sisters—Christine (*left*), Dorothy (*top*), and Phyllis (*bottom*)—began charming American audiences in 1952 when they first appeared on TV's *Arthur Godfrey's Talent Scouts*. In 1954 they enjoyed their first big success on the pop charts with "Goodnight Sweetheart, Goodnight" and "Muskrat Ramble." With their matching dresses and sweetened cover versions of R&B favorites, the McGuire Sisters became a highly lucrative recording group. In fact, Coca-Cola signed them to the largest endorsement deal ever at the time. In the 1960s, Phyllis would have a love affair with infamous mob boss Sam Giancana.

The evolution of a distinct teen culture inevitably led to advice books aimed at the younger crowd. *Your Dating Days* offers suggestions for amicable dating with an eye toward happy marriages. Heavy emphasis is given to drearily practical matters such as money management, the dynamics of the engagement period, and marriage during military service. The book is laudably honest about some difficult topics, such as "mixed-race" mar-

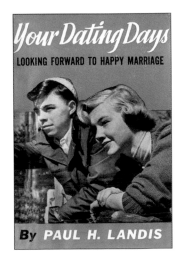

riage (no reason not to enter into one, but day-to-day life won't always be easy), but devotes just four sentences to what interested many teens the most: "the sex act."

"[W]e are not wrong in what we are doing. If we are wrong, the Supreme Court of this nation is wrong. If we are wrong, the Constitution of the United States is wrong. If we are wrong, God Almighty is wrong."

—Martin Luther King, Jr., on the first day of the Montgomery bus boycott

1955

The Fight for Civil Rights

ROSA PARKS DID NOT wake up on December 1, 1955, planning to overthrow the rule of Jim Crow in the American South. And when she boarded a Montgomery city bus that day after work, she intended only to go home. But when the bus driver ordered the 42-year-old seamstress to give up her seat so a white man could take it, Rosa Parks chose to act. She refused to move, preferring to be arrested than to submit once more to Montgomery's racist system of segregation.

As a child on a small farm in Alabama, Rosa had heard the Ku Klux Klan (KKK) nightriders terrify her community. In later years, she chose to fight that terror by joining the National Association for the Advancement of Colored People (NAACP). She became secretary of the Montgomery NAACP chapter and then, later, its youth leader. Her husband, too, was a stalwart advocate of civil rights. Both of them challenged Alabama's rigid policy of disenfranchising African-Americans by repeatedly trying to register to vote.

In summer 1955, Parks attended a civil rights workshop at the Highlander Folk School in Tennessee, which had been founded in 1932 to train progressive labor organizers but which recently had changed its mission to civil rights work. Furious segregationist state officials in Tennessee attacked the integrated institution as a "Communist training school," but Parks and others dedicated to racial justice refused to be "Red-baited." Parks emerged from her Highlander training ever more committed to the cause of civil rights. When

During a boycott of buses following the arrest of Rosa Parks, African-American citizens of Montgomery, Alabama, head to work in the icy rain without the help of public transportation. The yearlong mass protest ended successfully in December 1956 after the U.S. Supreme Court declared public bus segregation unconstitutional.

Following the initial success of the Montgomery boycott, local leaders voted to form the Montgomery Improvement Association (MIA) with 26-year-old Martin Luther King, Jr., as president. King directed the group to prepare a modest list of demands and eventually a lawsuit against Montgomery's bus segregation law.

Clinton High School, the first Tennessee state school ordered to integrate, did not do so eagerly. Violence erupted throughout the city of Clinton in September 1956 as enraged whites carried pro-segregation signs, threatened African-Americans, and eventually rioted.

Rosa Parks refused to yield her seat to a white man, she knew exactly what she was doing.

Once arrested, Parks immediately got word to E. D. Nixon, her NAACP colleague and the local head of the Brotherhood of Sleeping Car Porters. Nixon made sure that news of her arrest flashed through Montgomery's black-activist community, which had long debated how best to fight racial injustice. They began planning a bus boycott—an idea that had been under consideration for some time. That very night, Jo Ann Robinson, an English professor at Alabama State College and the head of the Montgomery Women's Political Council, mimeographed thousands of handbills that read: "We are . . . asking every Negro to stay off the buses Monday in protest of the arrest and trial. . . . [P]lease, children and grown-ups, don't take the bus at all on Monday."

That Monday, the bus boycott began. No one would have believed that it would last for 381 days. Black residents of Montgomery formed a new organization, the Montgomery Improvement Association (MIA), to oversee the boycott. All the while, E. D. Nixon and other experienced activists pushed forward a new minister in town, 26-year-old Martin Luther King, Jr., to lead the group. At the first major public meeting of the MIA, King showed why his elders thought so highly of him.

Combining ministerial eloquence with compelling erudition, King asked his brethren to join him in a noble crusade: "The only weapon that we have in our hands this evening is the weapon of protest. . . . [T]his is the glory of America, with all of its faults. This is the glory of our democracy. If we were incarcerated behind the iron curtains of a Communistic nation, we couldn't do this. . . . But the great glory of American democracy is the right to protest for right."

Reverend King then called on the core principles of American constitutionalism and Christian morality: "[W]e are not wrong in what we are doing. If we are wrong, the Supreme Court of this nation is wrong. If we are wrong, the Constitution of the United States is wrong. If we are wrong, God Almighty is wrong. If we are wrong, Jesus of Nazareth was merely a utopian dreamer that never came down to Earth."

The boycott was the last of several historic events in 1955 related to civil rights. In May, the Supreme Court finally decided how to implement the decision on school integration that the justices had unanimously issued a year earlier. In the 1954 *Brown v. Board of Education* ruling, Chief Justice Earl Warren had unequivocally stated: "We conclude that in the field of public education, the doctrine of 'separate but equal' has no place. Separate educational facilities are inherently unequal."

The ruling had been clear enough—laws that mandated racial segregation in schools were unconstitutional. But Warren knew how explosive the court's decision would be among white Southerners. Counseled by U.S. Attorney General Herbert Brownell, the court chose to wait a year before outlining how racial desegregation should be carried out in the likely event that southern states refused to comply voluntarily.

The court asked the key parties involved in the *Brown* decision to prepare briefs on the issue and to present their arguments orally to the court in April 1955. After permitting 14 hours of oral argument (usually the court gave each side just one hour to make its case orally), the court ruminated over its decision for another month before it issued a somewhat Delphic enforcement order. Chief Justice Warren stated that local federal district courts would oversee the desegregation process and that those courts should ensure that school districts integrate "with all deliberate speed." The exact meaning of that fuzzy phrase was intentionally left undefined.

African-American children gaze longingly at a whites-only playground in Mobile, Alabama, the hometown of baseball great Hank Aaron. Segregation of public places was commonplace in the South until the early to mid-1960s.

The *Brown* school desegregation case was a great victory for the cause of equal rights in the United States, but it was far from a finishing blow to Jim Crow segregation and legal racism. A few school districts did desegregate almost immediately, including those in Kansas, Delaware, and Washington, D.C. But throughout the old Confederate states, an organized campaign of massive resistance by whites began. White Citizens' Councils and the KKK saw their numbers swell as they intensified their efforts, some of them peaceful and some of them violent, to stop racial integration.

Less than a year after the Supreme Court issued its implementation order, almost every southern member of the Senate and House of Representatives (Texas Senator Lyndon Johnson was a notable exception) signed the "Declaration of Constitutional Principles: The Southern Manifesto." The congressmen baldly challenged the Supreme Court's ruling by stating, "We regard the decision of the Supreme Court in the school cases as a clear abuse of judicial power."

They further argued: "This unwarranted exercise of power by the Court, contrary to the Constitution, is creating chaos and confusion in the States principally affected. It is destroying the amicable relations between the white and Negro races that have been created through 90 years of patient effort by the good people of both races."

Citizenship schools were a mass literacy program—the largest and most effective such program ever undertaken in the United States—designed to teach African-Americans to read and write so they could register to vote. The schools were organized between 1953 and 1961 by the educators of Highlander Folk School in Monteagle, Tennessee.

As Rosa Parks and Martin Luther King knew firsthand, segregationists would not give up their fight to maintain white supremacy—no matter what the Supreme Court had decided. Citizens throughout the country were able to observe this lesson, as well, especially in late summer 1955 when the national spotlight focused on racial tensions in Money, Mississippi.

In August, the body of Emmett Till, a 14-year-old black boy from Chicago who had been visiting relatives in the Mississippi Delta, was pulled out of the Tallahatchie River. Two white men, Roy Bryant and J. W. Milam, had murdered the boy for flirting with Bryant's 21-year-old wife. At first they had intended only to beat Till, but after the boy told the white men—who already had brutally battered him—that he was as good as them, Milam shot him dead. They then threw his body, weighted down with an old cotton-gin fan, into the river.

The body was eventually recovered and shipped back to Till's mother, Mamie Till Bradley, in Chicago for burial. Mrs. Bradley ordered an open-coffin funeral so that the whole world could see what had been done to her child: "Have you ever sent a loved son on vacation and had him returned to you in a pine box so horribly battered and waterlogged that this sickening sight is your son—lynched?"

In Chicago's black neighborhoods, swelled by massive migration of African-Americans out of the South during World War II to find work in the city's booming defense plants, thousands turned out to witness what had been done to Emmett Till. Unlike so many previous lynchings of black Americans, this murder received headline coverage throughout the United States; it was even covered internationally.

The attention was due largely to the age of the victim, the gruesome pictures of his butchered face, and the outspokenness of his courageous mother. It also was due to the increasing numbers and political strength of northern

African-Americans, as well as to the growing number of whites who in the aftermath of World War II and the defeat of the Nazis were shamed by the brutal racism that went on in their own midst. Finally, the Cold War background against which the murder and trial took place played a role. It brought national and international attention to a racist murder that challenged America's claim to being a free society in which all people were treated equally.

Under massive press scrutiny, the state of Mississippi brought Bryant and Milam to trial. Till's great uncle, Mose Wright, risked his life by testifying in open court against the two men who had come to his house and taken his nephew away. The evidence left no doubt that Milam and Bryant had murdered Till. However, in his final summation, one of the defense attorneys made an effective appeal to the all-white jury: "Your ancestors will turn over in their graves [if the two white defendants] are found guilty, and I'm sure every last Anglo-Saxon one of you has the courage to free these men in the face of that pressure." The jury agreed, and the men were acquitted. (Milam and Bryant quickly sold their story to *Look* magazine; in it, they detailed their crime against Emmett Till.)

The cold-blooded killing of Emmett Till in Mississippi in 1955 raised awareness among northern whites to the severity of racial injustice in the South. The all-white, 12-man jury *(pictured)* took an hour and five minutes to return a not-guilty verdict, exonerating defendants J. W. Milam and Roy Bryant.

Few black Southerners were surprised by the verdict. They had been living with gross injustice all their lives. But what was unique was that the murder of Emmett Till captured the attention of the nation. The mainstream white press and many white people in the North (and even some in the South) were acknowledging the barbaric face of racism and the insufferable cruelty of the nation's racists. This new focus by whites on blacks' plight gave new hope to those African-Americans who were struggling to create a mass movement for civil rights. Perhaps, they thought, racial justice could be achieved in the United States.

The Montgomery bus boycott, begun as 1955 drew to a close, was the first major salvo in that fight. Looking back, Martin Luther King declared: "[The Montgomery bus boycott] would ring in the ears of people of every nation ... would stagger and astound the imagination of the oppressor, while leaving a glittering star of hope etched in the midnight skies of the oppressed." The fires of change were stirring in the very heart of the Ike age.

1955

1955: The Air Pollution Control Act is enacted in response to a 1948 incident in which an atmospheric inversion trapped smog and killed 20 people in Donora, Pennsylvania. The act calls for cleaner air, but gives no guidelines on how to reach that goal. • The U.S. government establishes air bases in Taiwan as military staging areas while it monitors the uneasy Sino-American relationship. • "Grandma's Pantry," a civil defense campaign that encourages Americans to stockpile foodstuffs, medical supplies, first aid items, hygiene products, and water, asks, "Grandma's pantry was ready, is your 'pantry' ready in the event of an emergency?"

1955: According to the U.S. Civil Service Commission, more than 3,000 federal employees lost their jobs after being deemed security risks from May 28, 1953, to September 30, 1954. • Eight women organize the Daughters of Bilitis, the first national organization for lesbians, in San Francisco. • In the "Boys of Boise" scandal, as many as 1,500 gay men are arrested when homophobia grips the Idaho city. An incident of alleged solicitation of a minor sparks the controversy, but the vast majority of the accused are adults in consensual relationships. • Urban flight is changing the shape of America, as some 4,000 U.S. families move from the cities to the suburbs every day.

1955: The magazines *Dig* and *Teen*, both aimed at the young members of the baby boom generation, debut. • Quaker Oats Instant Oatmeal, Kellogg's fat-free Special K, Kraft processed cheese, and frozen pizza all hit U.S. supermarket shelves. • The Foodarama side-by-side refrigerator is introduced by appliance manufacturer Kelvinator. • The Davy Crockett fad sweeps America. The television program and attendant merchandising gross more than $100 million.

This Office of Civil Defense advertisement reflects and fuels the great fear of "The Bomb" that swept the United States in the 1950s. The ad tells mothers how to protect their children in case of nuclear attack, listing "must have" first aid supplies, including bandages, water purification tablets, castor oil eyedrops, and tongue depressors. It also includes information about a free booklet, *Emergency Action to Save Lives,* which was based on a 1955 government film.

"Mummy, what happens to us if the bomb drops?"

With the same off-handed casualness one might apply to a soiled diaper, a student at the University of Michigan disposes of radioactive waste in 1955. At the time, with the long-term implications still more intuited than known, the Atomic Energy Commission sought convenient yet effective ways to deal with what was sure to become a growing problem. Many reasoned that simply loading waste into 55-gallon steel barrels and dropping them into the deep sea was sufficient. Others advocated on-site landfills or cooling ponds, although both methods carried the risk of contaminating local water supplies.

The Family of Man, a photography exhibit curated by Edward Steichen, opened at New York's Museum of Modern Art on January 26, 1955. The exhibit earned international attention due to the quality of the photography. Steichen and his aides had reviewed two million photographs before narrowing the number down to 10,000. From there, they chose a little more than 500 images of humanity, taken by more than 270 photographers, for the exhibit. After New York, The Family of Man was showcased on a worldwide tour, which lasted nine years.

Mark Rothko's 1955 work, *Untitled*, gives a pretty good idea of the style with which he made a name for himself. The Yale dropout had toiled in relative obscurity for decades, rendering realistic depictions of New York subways before shifting to a simpler, more primal approach. As the "New York School" of painting exploded in the early 1950s, Rothko suddenly became well known for his sparse but intense use of color, and pleasing sense of design. Seeking to apply raw emotion to canvas, he relied increasingly on broad brushstrokes as his career progressed. Acclaim never sat well with the artist, who took his life in 1970.

Diabolique, which premiered in France in 1955 and a year later in the United States, starred Simone Signoret (*right*) as a woman who plots to kill her cruel lover. The man's wife (played by Véra Clouzot, *left*) conspires with her, and the plot thickens when the husband's body disappears. This emotionally bleak shocker explores the dark depths of human nature, and slaps the viewer with a remarkable climax. Director Henri-Georges Clouzot's ability to convey atmospheric creepiness on a low budget caught the eye of Alfred Hitchcock, inspiring his work in *Psycho* (1960).

Freelance author and self-styled educational expert Rudolf Flesch made a big splash in 1955 with his bestselling polemic, *Why Johnny Can't Read.* Flesch was an evangelical advocate of phonics as the best way to teach reading to youngsters. Through phonics, beginning readers learn to read and pronounce words by learning the sound of letters, letter groups, and syllables, as opposed to the "see and say" method commonly used in the 1950s. The debate between those who followed Flesch and those who opposed him has raged with all the fervor of a religious war. Most educators now advise a combination of methods.

1955: Procter & Gamble introduces Crest toothpaste with fluoride. • Nearly eight million passenger cars, a new record, are manufactured this year.

January: U.S. involvement in Vietnam officially begins with the first shipment of military aid to Saigon, along with an offer to help train South Vietnam's army.

January 2: Panamanian President Jose Antonio Ramon is gunned down in Panama City.

January 3: According to the U.S. State Department, Soviet citizens are prohibited from visiting 27 percent of the United States.

January 5: Dacron, a wrinkle-free synthetic fabric, hits the market.

January 7: Marian Anderson becomes the first African-American to perform at Manhattan's Metropolitan Opera House.

January 19: Milton Bradley introduces Scrabble. • President Dwight Eisenhower holds the first televised presidential press conference in the Indian Treaty Room at the White House.

January 23: With a vote of 42–0, the Georgia Senate approves a bill that bars state funds to integrated schools. • The Presbyterian Church USA votes to allow women to become ordained ministers.

January 25: Scientists at New York's Columbia University unveil an atomic clock that keeps accurate time to within one second every 300 years.

January 26: The Family of Man, an exhibit of photographs, opens at New York's Museum of Modern Art.

January 28: The Formosa Resolution, which pledges that the U.S. will come to the defense of Taiwan against Communist China, passes both houses of Congress.

Part of South Africa's apartheid policy was to relocate black people from predominantly white communities to "black" areas. In February 1955, white workers razed blacks' homes in Johannesburg after black residents (*seen here*) were relocated to Meadowlands, a suburb of Soweto. The African National Congress (ANC), the nation's most prominent black-rights organization, could do little to stop the action. Wrote ANC leader Nelson Mandela in his autobiography: "The army and the police were relentlessly efficient. After a few weeks, our resistance collapsed."

South Vietnamese anti-Communist leader Ngo Dinh Diem (*seated*) had a very good year in 1955. In January and February, his U.S. allies sent extensive military aid and advisers to help train the South Vietnamese army (ARVN). In May, his troops waged a successful crackdown on the Binh Xuyen, an organized crime cartel vying for power with Diem. In October, he was elected president, although the process was suspect: He won 98.2 percent of the vote, including 605,000 of Saigon's 405,000 registered voters! Shortly afterward, Diem declared the birth of the Republic of Vietnam (RVN), to which President Dwight Eisenhower pledged support and military aid.

Ready to heat and serve

a frozen beef pot roast dinner
complete, with little browned potatoes

Swanson TV Dinners

In a decade that introduced pot pies, frozen pizza, and other convenience foods, it was not unreasonable to expect that someone might create an entire meal that could be whipped up in a jiffy. That someone was Gerry Thomas, a marketing expert with the C. A. Swanson poultry company.

Thomas's deathless innovation was less the result of planning than serendipitous inspiration. Stuck with 10 boxcars of surplus turkeys after Thanksgiving, Swanson decided to sell them as entrées, complete with sides and dessert, in airline-style aluminum serving trays. Applying "TV" to the creation proved to be marketing genius.

Supermarkets made their first appearance in the early 20th century but did not become common on the American scene until the 1950s, when they mushroomed. By 1955 such outlets accounted for 60 percent of American grocery sales. These self-serve stores burgeoned in large measure because of suburbanization, postwar affluence, and the baby boom. One economic side effect of their dominance, mourned by many traditionalists, was the rapid demise of mom-and-pop local stores and the personal attention they provided.

In 1947 Hughes Aircraft was contracted by the U.S. Air Force to develop a self-guided air missile, initially as a defense weapon for bombers. By the time the rocket, dubbed the Falcon, went into production in 1954, its purpose had changed to an offensive weapon for use *against* bombers, launched from faster fighter planes. The change signified a more aggressive posture against enemy aircraft in the event of an armed show-down. Early Falcons were radar-guided and exploded on impact; later versions used infrared to track aircraft exhaust.

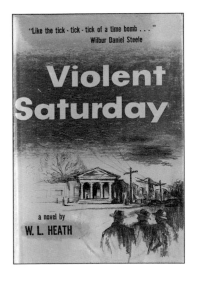

"Like the tick - tick - tick of a time bomb . . ."
Wilbur Daniel Steele

Violent Saturday

a novel by
W. L. HEATH

When a sleepy Alabama town is infiltrated by a trio of killers intent on taking the local bank, the strengths and weaknesses of various residents are revealed, in W. L. Heath's linear and exciting *Violent Saturday*. A young businessman rises to the challenge, but other citizens are useless because they have fallen prey to infidelity, alcoholism, petty thievery, and even window peeping. Very much a novel of the Cold War, the book suggests not just that normal life can be subverted by an insidious outside influence, but that the seeds of our own destruction may lie within us.

February 8: Nikolai Bulganin succeeds Georgi Malenkov as Soviet premier.

February 12: The first U.S. military advisers are sent to Vietnam by President Eisenhower. • Dorothy Dandridge, star of *Carmen Jones,* becomes the first black woman nominated for an Academy Award for best actress.

February 13: Israel takes possession of four of the Dead Sea Scrolls, found in caves near Qumran in the late 1940s and early 1950s.

February 17: Great Britain reveals that it has the technology to build a hydrogen bomb.

February 22: President Eisenhower submits a $101 billion highway construction proposal to Congress.

February 23: President Eisenhower claims that a Democratic proposal for a $20 per capita income tax break is irresponsible.

February 24: In a conversation with Scripps-Howard newspaper head Roy Howard, President Eisenhower expresses his concerns regarding sending U.S. troops to Vietnam. • Iraq and Turkey sign the Baghdad Pact, an agreement among Britain, Iran, Iraq, Turkey, and Pakistan to guard against Communist infiltration in the Middle East. Iran, Britain, and Pakistan will sign later in the year. *See* April 1, 1955.

February 26: Nobel Prize-winning British physicist Cecil F. Powell estimates that the United States has four times as many atomic bombs as the Soviet Union has.

March: Fallout from atomic weapons testing dusts Las Vegas. According to the *Las Vegas Review-Journal,* "Fallout on Las Vegas and vicinity . . . was very low and without any effects on health."

> "[M]arrying young was like getting to a sale on the first day. God knows what, if anything, would be left if you waited until you were twenty-five or -six."

—Author Mary Cantwell

The Race to the Altar

"Not so long ago," stated a 1955 *New York Times* article, "girls were expelled from college for marrying; now girls feel hopeless if they haven't a marriage at least in sight by commencement time."

In the 1950s, society encouraged and, in effect, pressured women to marry young. Because of the well-defined roles of the time, with a woman expected to serve as homemaker and mother, it wasn't deemed necessary for her to pursue a college degree and start a career. While 47 percent of college students in 1920 were women, that figure dropped to about 30 percent by 1958—largely because many women dropped out of college to get married. In the '50s, many women went to college simply to find a fast-tracking mate who would become a good provider.

Society benefited economically from a high marriage rate, because that led to an increase in home construction, home furnishings, and—inevitably—production of family-related goods. Advertising agencies targeted young couples as potential buyers. Even *Seventeen* magazine printed stories and ads about purchasing wedding dresses and bedroom furniture.

Many teenage girls were eager to realize the "fantasy" of a white wedding, a new house, dreamy furnishings, and state-of-the-art appliances. Other girls felt peer pressure; since their friends and sisters were getting married at a young age, they felt obligated to do the same. As the decade progressed, many women figuratively "raced to the altar." They felt compelled to snag one of the good men quickly before all were taken.

Sexual intercourse also was an issue. In the 1950s, premarital sex was considered sinful, while unprotected sex—in an era before the birth control pill—was a gamble few unmarried couples were willing to take. (A woman would be ostracized by society and perhaps by her family for getting pregnant out of wedlock.) Thus, marriage offered the only acceptable opportunity for young lovers to consummate their relationships. Due to a combination of all these factors, nearly half of all American brides by 1959 were younger than age 19.

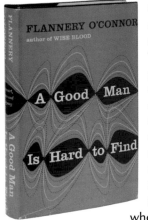

Georgia-born writer Flannery O'Connor specialized in dark explorations of the lives and motivations of unusual Southerners. Though not bereft of wit, her stories often projected an air of impending doom, which could arrive in unexpected ways. *A Good Man Is Hard to Find* (1955), her first collection of short stories, demonstrated her mastery of engaging storytelling. Though she often was described as "Faulknerian" for her depictions of southern culture and characters, O'Connor's haunting authenticity, in which she fused the commonplace with the mystical, was wholly her own. Following her death in 1964, the Flannery O'Connor Award for short fiction was established.

During the 1930s, an unemployed architect named Alfred Butts invented a board game that combined vocabulary with chance. After enjoying slim success under several names (including Lexico and Criss-Cross Words), the game underwent some fine-tuning by James Brunet (*pictured*) and a name change. As Scrabble, the game finally took off, scoring big after department store giant Macy's placed a huge order. Sales of more than a million sets in 1953 nearly quadrupled the following year, as Americans couldn't get enough of the addicting pursuit. Vice President Richard Nixon and Queen Elizabeth were among the notables who succumbed to the craze.

Actress Mary Martin takes choreographer-director Jerome Robbins on a spin during rehearsals for NBC's 1955 television production of *Peter Pan*. Drawn from the hit Broadway show, it marked the latest version of J. M. Barrie's timeless play. As Peter, stage veteran Martin shone in her signature role, benefiting from the special equipment that provided a marvelous illusion of flight. Robbins had begun as a dancer before graduating to choreography with 1944's *On the Town*. His other successes included *The King and I* and *West Side Story*.

During the post-big band, pre-rock 'n' roll era, four-man harmony units enjoyed a brief heyday. The Four Freshmen epitomized the white-bread hipness of such quartets with their smooth, sentimental sounds. Members included brothers Ross and Don Barbour, Bob Flanagan, and Ken Errair. Discovered by jazz bandleader Stan Kenton, the group produced a slew of hits during the decade, most notably "Graduation Day." Others of a similar stripe who scored big included the Four Lads, the Four Aces, and the Four Preps.

1955

March 1: Nearly 50 Palestinians die in an Israeli assault on the Gaza Strip.

March 2: Claudette Colvin, a 15-year-old black girl, is arrested after refusing to move to the back of a city bus in Montgomery, Alabama. *See* December 1, 1955.

March 3: Elvis Presley makes his first television appearance, on a program called *Louisiana Hayride*. Though he receives some attention from talent scouts, it will be another year before his star will rise.

March 4: The first fax is sent across the U.S. It is sent by a transmitter that is based on technology patented in 1843 by Scottish mechanic Alexander Bain.

March 9: A $100 million aid package to Southeast Asia is approved by the U.S. Foreign Operations Administration.

March 13: NHL President Clarence Campbell suspends Montreal hockey star Maurice "Rocket" Richard for the season for fighting in a game against the Boston Bruins. Montreal fans object, and will riot when Campbell tries to take his seat at a Montreal-Detroit match on St. Patrick's Day.

March 15: Secretary of State John Foster Dulles announces that the U.S. is contemplating using nuclear weapons against China in an effort to resolve the dispute over Quemoy-Matsu.

March 16: President Eisenhower causes an international uproar with his statement that "A-bombs can be used . . . as you would a bullet."

March 17: The 400,000-word account of the negotiations among Roosevelt, Churchill, and Stalin as they reshaped the world at Yalta in 1945 is finally released.

March 24: For the first time in 20 years, the British Army pulls its soldiers out of Belfast, Northern Ireland.

Tennessee Williams's *Cat on a Hot Tin Roof* marked the playwright's return to form, eight years after *A Streetcar Named Desire* first hit the stage. The plot, concerning the conflicts arising among family members in the wake of their patriarch's terminal illness, was a sophisticated exploration of the meaning of truth. Some critics, including director Elia Kazan, objected to Williams's original ambiguous ending, preferring something more clearly resolved. The Broadway production, however, was a smash. Actors Studio alumnus Ben Gazzara (*foreground*) was handpicked for the complex role of Brick, while Barbara Bel Geddes dazzled as the sensual Maggie (the "cat").

The denizens of New York's nightlife had much to take in, as this shot of Times Square illustrates. By the early '50s, the Great White Way's theatrical offerings were back in full swing, after diminishing somewhat during wartime. Theater aficionados found much to celebrate, with many showbiz legends at the top of their game performing nightly on stage. In addition, a plethora of weekly television broadcasts originated from the Big Apple, among them *The Jackie Gleason Show,* Ed Sullivan's *Toast of the Town,* and *Texaco Star Theater* (with Milton Berle).

The cover story of this 1955 issue of *Popular Mechanics* illustrates both the need for affordable housing and Americans' growing fascination with prefabrication and do-it-yourself projects. *Popular Mechanics,* founded in 1902, became immensely popular in the 1950s as it combined practical advice, adventure stories grounded in technology, and predictions about the future. Its most famous prophetic gaffe came in February 1951 when its cover showed a man cramming a helicopter into the family garage.

Following a successful career in radio, actor Jeff Chandler made his movie debut in *Johnny O'Clock* in 1947. By 1955 Chandler was a Universal-International contract player who had taken his place alongside Rock Hudson and Tony Curtis as one of the studio's top male stars. Four Chandler films were released in '55, including one with Joan Crawford (*Female on the Beach*) and another with Jane Russell (*Foxfire*). Chandler died in 1961 at age 43 following botched back surgery.

An essential element of rock 'n' roll's eventual takeover of youth culture was the jukebox, a source of exposure for songs and artists that often were afforded very little airtime by radio. In a jukebox, rhythm & blues and country & western tracks coexisted side by side, leaving patrons of the machines, in essence, color-blind. With jukeboxes plugged into restaurants across the country, otherwise obscure artists were able to find an audience. Seeburg led the way with machines that could not only handle the newly minted 45s but also play both sides. The company's 1955 V200 model (*pictured*) became the industry standard.

In 1952 former St. Louis hairdresser Chuck Berry (*pictured*) hooked up with pianist Johnnie Johnson, forging a unique sound that fused boogie/blues rhythms with country influences. As perhaps rock's first guitar hero, Berry possessed a readily recognizable style that provided the map for many a struggling musician ever after. His lyrics were equally exceptional, encapsulating the teenage experience through a series of witty, anthemic originals, including "Rock and Roll Music," "Johnny B. Goode," and "Sweet Little Sixteen." Berry's first big hit, "Maybellene" in 1955, launched him on his path to stardom.

1955

- The first oil rig capable of drilling in more than 100 feet of water is installed in the Gulf of Mexico, south of New Orleans. Manufactured at Bethlehem Steel, the rig is capable of driving piles with 827 tons of force.

March 27: The first drive-in church service takes place when Reverend Robert Schuller rents the Orange Drive-In in Garden Grove, California, and delivers a sermon from the roof of the snack bar.

March 31: In a move that will create one of the world's largest banking interests, Chase National Bank and Bank of Manhattan Company merge to form Chase Manhattan.

April: Richard J. Daley is elected mayor of Chicago. He will remain in office until his death in 1976.

April 1: British government buildings on the island of Cyprus are bombed by EOKA, the National Organization of Cypriot Fighters. • The Baghdad Pact, a mutual defense treaty among Great Britain, Iran, Iraq, Turkey, and Pakistan, is completed. Though instrumental in establishing the pact, the United States itself does not join. • The DuMont Television Network, active in the late 1940s and early 1950s, drastically cuts its programming. By September, only a couple of weekly sporting events will remain.

April 5: Winston Churchill, one of the most influential political figures of the 20th century, steps down as prime minister of Great Britain.

April 12: The Salk polio vaccine is declared safe and effective by the U.S. surgeon general.

April 15: Ray Kroc, the man behind the McDonald's franchising empire, opens his first McDonald's restaurant, in Des Plaines, Illinois.

April 18: Physicist Albert Einstein dies at age 76.

With white media largely ignoring news pertinent to African-Americans, John H. Johnson filled the gap. In the 1940s, the Chicago-based publisher launched *Negro Digest* (a takeoff of *Readers Digest*) and *Ebony* magazine (similar to *Life*). His pocket-sized weekly, *Jet,* which first hit the stands in 1951, offered a mix of news, politics, entertainment, sports, and business. In September 1955, *Jet* made history as the magazine that carried the picture of Emmett Till's badly disfigured body after his lynching by whites—a photo that outraged the national black community.

In 1955 local Democratic Party Chairman Richard J. Daley elbowed aside all opposition to win his first of six Chicago mayoral races. For many, he was the last of the big city "machine" politicians, the party general who could command a patronage army to do his political bidding. Once in City Hall, Daley reduced the city council to a rubber stamp. He pushed through ambitious projects that revitalized Chicago as other cities went into decline. His victories came at the expense of minorities and the poor, however, as his adherence to his segregationist base shut out those who lacked "clout."

"If they were drowning to death, I'd put the hose in their mouth."

—RAY KROC, ON THE FAST-FOOD COMPETITION

McDonald's

By 1948, after more than a decade in the restaurant business, brothers Dick and Mac McDonald had perfected their formula for maximizing profits with a minimum of effort. By limiting their menu and applying assembly line techniques to the entire process, their brand of burgers could be served hot, fresh, and—most importantly—fast.

The McDonald brothers' efficient ways did not go unnoticed by milkshake-machine salesman Ray Kroc. Driven by curiosity to investigate the businessmen who had purchased *eight* Multimixers, Kroc paid a visit in 1954 to their restaurant in San Bernadino, California. What he saw enthralled him.

Ray Kroc

Each employee was assigned a single task, streamlining production time while cutting overhead. Customers loved the quick service, returning to the restaurant time and again for "a quick bite." Kroc, a neat freak and a penny-pincher, found the restaurant's cleanliness, economy, and profitability irresistible. He saw the potential for exploitation on a grand scale.

Initially, the McDonald brothers did not want to expand beyond their eight restaurants. But Kroc offered, in partnership, to spread their pioneering methods far and wide. They acquiesced, and in April 1955 Kroc's first franchise opened in Des Plaines, Illinois.

The monumental success of Kroc's efforts was emblematic of two coalescing trends in America: that of efficiency foods and the rise of car culture. With the tradition of family meals at the dinner table slowly eroding, the quick, cheap, kid-friendly dining offered by the restaurant seemed a positive alternative. Moreover, the rise of the demographic known as the "teenager" neatly dovetailed with what McDonald's had to offer. With teens on wheels becoming an economic force, the chain chose a fortuitous moment to go national. Kroc, who bought out the brothers for nearly $3 million in 1961, would take his empire to ever greater heights in the ensuing years.

In 1955 France's Dassault Mirage became one of the world's most successful supersonic fighter jets. A later model would be equipped with after-burning turbojets that pushed the plane beyond Mach 1. Though the initial version seen here boasted an air-to-air missile, this feature eventually was dropped as impractical. Following other design changes, the Mirage III was introduced in late 1956. Its speed, simple design, and ease of operation made it a highly prized addition to the air forces of many nations, including Egypt, Pakistan, and the Congo.

1955

April 22: Congress decides that the words "In God We Trust" will appear on all U.S. coins. *See* July 11, 1955.

April 23: An African-Asian summit is held at Badung, Indonesia, with the goal of promoting cooperation and ending Third World colonialism.

April 29: South Vietnamese Prime Minister Ngo Dinh Diem orders police action against organized crime factions in Saigon.

May 5: The military occupation of Germany by the U.S., France, and Great Britain, officially ends. • Operation Cue, a test designed to show the effects of an atomic blast on a model town, is carried out at Yucca Flats, Nevada. It yields amazing footage that reveals the horrific destructive capabilities of nuclear weapons.

May 8: Twenty-five female victims of the Hiroshima bombing are brought to New York's Mount Sinai Hospital for reconstructive surgery.

May 10: Surprising the international community, the Soviets agree to the UN's plan for nuclear disarmament.

May 14: As an answer to NATO, the Soviets establish the Warsaw Pact with Bulgaria, Albania, Romania, Czechoslovakia, East Germany, Poland, and Hungary.

May 15: The Vienna Treaty calls for the withdrawal of Allied troops from Austrian soil, restoring the country's autonomy for the first time since the Nazi occupation.

May 16: Pulitzer Prize-winning writer James Agee dies of a heart attack in a New York City cab at age 45.

May 18: The U.S. Patent Office issues the first patent for a nuclear reactor. The recipient is the Atomic Energy Commission, and the patent is for the technique used by Enrico Fermi and Leo Szilard to achieve the first fission reaction in 1942.

A young tyke enjoys some of the Davy Crockett paraphernalia that inundated the American market in the mid-1950s. Actor Fess Parker portrayed the "king of the wild frontier" in three episodes of the Walt Disney television show *Disneyland* in early 1954. They were so well received that Disney spliced them into a feature film in 1955, featuring Parker singing the wildly popular "Ballad of Davy Crockett." For the 1954–55 TV season, the Disney show featured several "prequels" about Davy's life before he died at the Alamo. *Disneyland* rode Crockett to an Emmy Award for best variety show, and Crockett merchandise grossed more than $300 million.

Teenagers enjoy deejay Alan Freed's "Easter Jubilee of Stars" at the Brooklyn Paramount Theater in 1955. Featuring such artists as the Penguins ("Earth Angel"), the Moonglows ("See-Saw"), and LaVern Baker ("Tweedlee Dee"), the event put the nation on notice that rock 'n' roll (a term Freed appropriated as a handle for the upstart phenomenon) had arrived. The one-week extravaganza played to packed houses, rousing teenagers while instilling anxiety in parents.

Betsy Blair and Ernest Borgnine portrayed a pair of social underachievers in director Delbert Mann's sympathetic character study, *Marty* (1955). Adapted from Paddy Chayefsky's television drama, the film tells the story of the title character (Borgnine), a lonely mama's boy fast approaching middle age who is unwittingly being held back by those closest to him. Shot mostly on location in New York City, the film had a realistic poignancy that many moviegoers could relate to. Borgnine, who previously was known for his antisocial "heavy" roles, won a best actor Oscar for his sensitive performance. The film scored three other wins, including best picture.

Physicist Albert Einstein lived long enough to see his legend take hold. The recipient of worldwide honors for his Special Theory of Relativity, his work on the atomic bomb, and his humanitarian efforts, Einstein spent his final years at his Princeton, New Jersey, home in semiretirement. When not pushing for a breakthrough in his Unified Field Theory, he received visitors and read mail from admirers. Though unnerved by Cold War politics and his role in unleashing the power of the atom, Einstein believed that his pacifist views would one day be vindicated. He died on April 18, 1955, at age 76.

The Platters (*left to right*: Herb Reed, Tony Williams, Zola Taylor, David Lynch, and Paul Robi) were reliable hit-makers during rock's first era. The group's songwriter-manager, Buck Ram, wrote "Only You," the act's first hit. The Platters excelled at slow-dance numbers, thanks largely to Williams's soaring tenor. Seeking longevity for his protégés, Ram steered the group toward a repertoire of smoothly produced standards from the '30s and '40s, including "Smoke Gets in Your Eyes," which soared to No. 1 in 1959. The Platters' polished, "adult" image contrasted strongly with other popular doo-wop groups of the day.

1955

May 21: Lieutenant John M. Conroy pilots an F-86 round-trip from New York to Los Angeles in 11:33:27 for the first same-day transcontinental round-trip.

May 25: Tornadoes rip through Udall, Kansas, killing 80 people.

May 26: USSR First Secretary Nikita Khrushchev travels to Yugoslavia to visit with President Josip Broz Tito, ending the rift between the two nations.

May 31: In *Brown II*, the U.S. Supreme Court establishes guidelines for desegregating public education, although it fails to establish a timetable.

June 3: Tunisia is granted internal autonomy at the Franco-Tunisian Conventions, while France reserves authority over Tunisia's foreign affairs and international relations. • Barbara Graham is executed in California's gas chamber for the brutal murder of elderly widow Mabel Monohan.

June 7: The broadcast of President Eisenhower's commencement address at the U.S. Military Academy at West Point is the first time a president appears on color television.

June 11: In one of history's worst sports disasters, a three-car collision ends with a race car careening into the stands at Le Mans, France, killing 82 people.

June 15: Operation Alert, a massive nationwide nuclear attack preparedness drill, is staged. President Eisenhower and other government officials participate in the mock evacuation plans.

June 16: A vote in the U.S. House of Representatives approves the extension of the Selective Service Act until 1959.

The postwar baby boom and increased leisure time made inevitable the surge of Little League as a childhood pursuit. The pastime proved conducive to community bonding, as local businesses provided sponsorships while suburban moms traded off car-pool duties. The perceived character-building quality of competitive sports was widely seen as a long-term benefit of Little League. Occasionally, realities of the times intruded into the otherwise amenable spirit. In 1955, for example, 61 all-white leagues in South Carolina refused to play in tournaments with an all-black league.

After World War II, interest in car customizing swelled, particularly in the car-culture capital, L.A., where brothers Sam and George Barris cut and shaped showroom-stock cars into unique rolling sculpture. The Catholic priest who brought his '51 Chevy Bel Air to the Barris shop drove out with this creation, which had a chopped (lowered) roofline; radiused hood; a sharply raked '51 Olds windshield; Canadian-Ford grillework; '50 Ford taillights and skirts; and elongated, custom-fabricated rear fenders (to subdue the continental spare, which the Barrises disliked). Posing with the car is actress-model Jean Moorehead.

Screenwriter A. I. Bezzerides and director Robert Aldrich transformed Mickey Spillane's pulp novel about heroin smuggling into a blistering, anxiety-riddled thriller, *Kiss Me Deadly* (1955). In the film version, private detective Mike Hammer unwisely searches for "the great whatsit," something so terrible that it could destroy all of Los Angeles. Aldrich's fondness for bizarre camera angles, starkly lit nighttime sequences, and grotesque characters, plus Bezzerides's elliptical dialogue, profoundly influenced François Truffaut and other filmmakers of the French *Nouvelle Vague* (New Wave).

In 1955 prolific British writer Graham Greene published *The Quiet American*. Informed by Greene's own experiences living in southern Vietnam in the early 1950s, the novel focuses on Fowler, a cynical British journalist, and Alden Pyle, an idealistic young American official-secret agent. Pyle wants to find a way to help an anti-French and anti-Communist "third force" achieve power in the war-torn French colony, but is killed in the process. At the time, many saw the work as an anti-American polemic. But recent scholars have found it a powerful and prophetic comment on the limits of American idealistic interventionism in Vietnam.

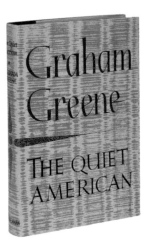

The dead and injured litter the ground after a horrific crash during the Le Mans endurance automobile race in France on June 11, 1955. Pierre Levegh, unable to stop during a slowdown in front of him, smashed his Mercedes into an earthen bank. The car disintegrated over a grandstand packed with spectators, killing 82 and maiming 76. Levegh, who was killed in the crash, had complained earlier that the cars were too fast and that the track needed some kind of signaling system. After the accident, officials allowed the race to continue, claiming that stopping it would have caused panic and impeded rescue efforts.

Bettie Page was a Tennessee high school salutatorian who went on to teacher's college. She dabbled in modeling and was invited to Hollywood for screen tests in the late 1940s. Those didn't pan out (her drawl was too thick), so she settled in New York City, where she posed for numberless "girlie picture" shoots. Her voluptuous figure, trademark bangs, and saucy charm endeared her to millions of men. She became, arguably, the preeminent pin-up girl of the 1950s.

Ten years after their lives were changed forever, a group of 25 Japanese women journeyed to America for surgical treatment of disfiguring scars suffered during the first atomic bombing. In an event instigated by *Saturday Review* editor Norman Cousins, the "Hiroshima Maidens" caused a stir, eliciting hospitality from some and suspicion from others (who feared a "subversive" Trojan horse). During their stay, the young women took in American life in a PR effort to promote better relations between the two countries. In a bizarre interlude, a televised meeting on *This Is Your Life* was staged between the group and the copilot of the Hiroshima bombing.

Artist Jasper Johns's work served as a bridge between Abstract and Pop art. Working largely with familiar visuals, such as targets (*seen here*) or American flags, Johns attempted to force fresh perceptions of the everyday, leading beholders to question his intent and their own sensibilities. This "art as object" theme would influence sculptors and artists who followed. Johns often worked by combining pigment with molten beeswax and adding bits of newspaper, thereby producing a textured effect. Juxtaposing apparently unrelated objects (such as the four faces and the target in this piece of art) compelled investigation for hidden meaning.

A 1954 Supreme Court ruling that made quiz shows exempt from gambling laws paved the way for one of the decade's most popular television programs. Adapted from the 1940s radio show *Take It or Leave It, The $64,000 Question* increased the former's top prize a thousandfold while challenging contestants who possessed deep knowledge of a given subject. These ranged from Shakespeare (championed by a New York policeman) to boxing (mastered by a young psychologist named Joyce Brothers, who explained her "expertise" as simple memorization of a reference book). Hosted by Hal March (*pictured*), the show utilized an "isolation booth" to help build suspense.

The Big Three

PRODUCTION OF AMERICAN automobiles was halted early in February 1942 and remained suspended for the duration of World War II. Immediate postwar models were little changed from the '42s, and although Studebaker and other independent makes were first with all-new models, the U.S. auto industry would continue to be dominated by Detroit's Big Three: General Motors, Ford Motor Company, and Chrysler Corporation.

By 1950, when production caught up with demand (6.7 million cars rolled off U.S. assembly lines during the calendar year), automakers were no longer able to effortlessly sell everything they produced, as in 1946–49. Instead, the new bywords were competition and innovation, and the Big Three plunged into the fray. They spent hundreds of millions of dollars to develop bigger, more powerful V-8 engines; new body styles; tailfins and lavishly chromed bumpers; boggling lists of options; and many other money-spinners.

The Big Three had the capitalization needed to compete and grow. When GM and Ford engaged in a bitter price war during 1953–54, both companies survived, but smaller automakers were crippled. Hudson, Packard, Kaiser, Frazer, and Nash were gone by 1959. The Big Three had achieved a commanding position of market dominance; General Motors alone flirted with a 50 percent market share each year during the decade, and occasionally topped it.

Cars had never been as closely linked to status as they were in the 1950s. Virtually everybody in the middle class could afford a new car, so even if your dreamboat was a Dodge instead of a Cadillac, it was *new* and it was *yours*.

Key to the bottom line was the annual model change, which became a ritualized national mania that struck every autumn. Buyer anticipation was feverish. What would the new models look like? Dealers played it cagey, soaping or papering their windows before the official rollout dates. Americans bought new cars because they were made to believe that they had to buy them. This marketing approach— the work of highly skilled conjurers—was the special genius of the Big Three.

This 7-Up advertisement targets new parents, urging them to "add 7-Up to [the toddler's] milk in equal portions" to encourage recalcitrant tykes to drink up. The combination was "wholesome" and "it works," claimed the ad. The 7-Up company, with its caffeine-free lemon-lime drink, had to try harder since it was a distant third to Coca-Cola and Pepsi-Cola in the great battle for thirsty customers in the 1950s. From a broader perspective, this ad illustrates the manic attempts by companies in the '50s to market products for children, a huge demographic at the time.

Its popularity slipping among car buyers, Chevrolet redeemed itself with all-new cars for 1955. Former Cadillac engineer Ed Cole was recruited to design the top-level Bel Air (*right*), and the result was a marked departure from the bulky, utilitarian vehicles the brand was known for. The all-new model introduced the classic "small block" V-8, which transformed the car into a formidable street rod, even without the optional "power pak." Sporting modest chrome and subdued tailfins (which burst forth fully in the 1957 offering), the Bel Air coupled classic good looks with motoring muscle, resulting in sales of 1.8 million.

June 20: A total eclipse of the sun is visible in Southeast Asia for seven minutes and eight seconds. It will be one of only seven solar eclipses that last more than seven minutes in totality during the entire millennium.

Summer: Operation Midnight Climax begins. CIA operative George White moves to San Francisco and sets up CIA-outfitted houses of prostitution, complete with two-way mirrors and LSD-laced cocktails. The CIA pays prostitutes $100 a night to bring men in, and Agent White observes the effects of LSD on the unsuspecting clients.

June 24: The Soviets shoot down a U.S. Navy aircraft over the Bering Strait. *See* June 25, 1955.

June 25: In response to the downing of a U.S. Navy plane the previous day, Soviet Foreign Minister Vyacheslav Molotov apologizes to the U.S. and says the USSR will pay for half the damage.

June 27: For the first time in the U.S., legislation mandating car seat belt use goes into effect, in Illinois.

June 29: The Air Force Strategic Air Command accepts delivery of its first B-52, to the 93rd Bomb Wing at Castle Air Force Base, California. ● Soviet tanks put a stop to anti-Communist protests in Poznan, Poland.

July: Beverly Hanson shoots a 220 to win the first-ever LPGA Championship. ● IBM introduces the 702, the company's first computer designed specifically for business applications. ● On a visit to Moscow, North Vietnamese Premier Ho Chi Minh accepts the Soviets' offer of aid.

July 9: The Bill Haley and His Comets hit, "Rock Around the Clock," becomes the first rock 'n' roll single to hit No.1, where it will stay for eight weeks.

Marilyn Monroe

THE 1950S GENERATED its share of pop culture icons, but next to Elvis Presley, Marilyn Monroe was undoubtedly the biggest. In an era in which robust sexuality was veiled, if not overtly suppressed, Marilyn combined childlike playfulness with an unabashed libido. Her appeal transcended gender: Many women desired her glamorous qualities, while men simply desired her.

From her earliest modeling days, something magical seemed to radiate from the former Norma Jeane Baker whenever a camera was pointed her way. Ordinarily shy, sometimes painfully so, Marilyn transformed herself for photographers. To the end of her life she understood that "Marilyn Monroe" was an invention that existed separately from Norma Jeane; once while with a friend in Manhattan, Marilyn walked the crowded sidewalks unnoticed. She said to her companion, "Watch this," and a switch seemed to have been tripped inside her, soundlessly, effortlessly. In an instant, she was "Marilyn," and the passersby knew it immediately. She was mobbed.

Although some critics derided her dramatic abilities, she improved rapidly in a very few years. By the time of *Bus Stop* in 1956, she had brought her acting very near to the level of her astonishing screen presence. But early in her career, Marilyn was called upon merely to perform variations of a marketable type: a sensitive, good-hearted woman-child in need of protection and love—and possessed of physical qualities that suggested a need for something else entirely.

This dichotomy reflected the 1950s' gestalt in male-female relationships: While gender roles during the era remained as clearly defined as ever, Marilyn represented the embodiment of male fantasy. But any man who mistook that illusive ideal for reality soon found himself in trouble. For example, Monroe's second husband, baseball legend Joe DiMaggio—who wanted Marilyn to be his homebody wife—quickly opted out of the marriage when he realized he had to share her with an avid public.

As an actress in a series of light comedies, farces, and occasional dramas, Marilyn worked hard to please her peers. Given good material and sympathetic direction, her films hold up well. Highlights include *The Seven Year Itch* (1955)—with MM's skirt famously billowing above the subway grate—and the American Film Institute's No. 1 comedy of all time, *Some Like It Hot* (1959). Ditzy facade notwithstanding, Monroe took her craft seriously, studying Method acting under Lee Strasberg in New York. But more lasting than her body of work is the unique persona she created; it is for this that she is rightly remembered.

Although the term and concept "hot rod" had existed prior to World War II, not until the postwar era did the culture come into its own. With '20s and '30s jalopies abounding, young men—many of them ex-GIs with disposable income—were able to buy an old car and, with their own skill and ingenuity, turn it into a head-turning road burner. The hot rod was above all a means of self-expression. Though some hot-rodders engaged in extralegal racing, *Hot Rod* and similar magazines promoted the inherent qualities of craftsmanship and engineering know-how.

Marilyn Monroe's image as a just-beyond-reach sex goddess was preserved for all time in director Billy Wilder's *The Seven Year Itch* (1955). Lacking even a name (she is credited as "The Girl"), Monroe's sensual, bubbly character was every man's fantasy, made flesh. Tom Ewell, cast as the eternally frustrated everyman (who discovers that the girl is his new neighbor), reprised his role from George Axelrod's Broadway play. The film contains the immortal image of Monroe astride a subway grate, skirt billowing. Public gawking during that scene's filming was the final straw for Marilyn's husband, Joe DiMaggio; their marriage broke up in 1955.

A young Londoner strikes a blasé pose as a "Teddy Boy." During the early and mid-1950s, many working-class young people in Britain rebelled against societal norms by adopting the formal dress of the Edwardian period. Their attire included jackets with velvet trimming, waistcoats (vests), and narrow drainpipe trousers—a marked contrast to the blue jeans and leather jackets that defined rebellious youth in the U.S. Rival gangs of Teddies often fought in public places, leading historian Dominic Sandbrook to refer to them as "the real folk devils of the fifties." The Teddy style died out in Britain after 1955, replaced by a more chic Italian look.

1955

- The Russell-Einstein Manifesto is issued in London, with the signatories expressing fear of the annihilation of the human race. They write, "Shall we put an end to the human race; or shall mankind renounce war?"

July 11: President Eisenhower signs a bill calling for the phrase "In God We Trust" to appear on all U.S. currency.

July 17: Walt Disney's vision is realized as Disneyland opens its gates. • For the first time in America, electricity generated by a nuclear power plant supplies an entire town, as the Utah Power and Light Company lights Arco, Idaho, and its 1,200 residents for more than an hour.

July 18–23: Leaders of the United States, Great Britain, France, and the Soviet Union meet in Geneva. Despite a seemingly magnanimous proposal by President Eisenhower that the four powers open their airspace to each other, little is accomplished.

August: Hurricane Diane slams into the eastern seaboard, killing 184.

August 1: The first Lockheed U-2, a prototype named Angel, is test-flown at Groom Dry Lake, Nevada. • The state of Georgia demands that black teachers leave the NAACP or forfeit their teaching licenses.

August 2: Pulitzer Prize-winning poet Wallace Stevens dies at age 76.

August 4: Eisenhower earmarks $46 million for the CIA to build a new headquarters complex in Langley, Virginia.

August 8: Cuban guerrilla Fidel Castro forms the "July 26th Movement" to foment revolution against Cuban dictator Fulgencio Batista's government. • The International Conference on the Peaceful Uses of Atomic Energy convenes in Geneva with 73 countries and nearly 1,500 delegates participating.

On July 13, 1955, 28-year-old Ruth Ellis, who had been a London bar hostess, prostitute, and nude photographers' model, became the 16th and last woman to be hanged in Britain in the 20th century. On Easter Sunday, April 10, 1955, she ambushed her lover in the street and shot him five times. The victim was David Blakely, 25, a well-educated race car enthusiast who had angered Ellis by avoiding her. At trial, the jury deliberated 23 minutes. Ellis's hanging stimulated the capital punishment debate in Britain, where 1957 legislation reserved execution for special circumstances only. The punishment was abolished altogether in 1965.

Citizens of Arco, Idaho, took a leap into the future on July 17, 1955, when a flick of the switch made them the first community in America to be powered by nuclear-generated electricity. Though the demonstration lasted less than two hours, Arco showed the country the *positive* uses of atomic power. (In fact, a film of the event was shown at the United Nations.) The Atomic Energy Commission had begun exploring the possibilities of nuclear energy after World War II, producing the first usable power in 1951. The Idaho site witnessed the country's first nuclear accident in 1961, when three workers were killed.

Disney's Dream

BEGINNING IN 1928 with a cartoon entitled *Steamboat Willie,* Walt Disney proved himself a man of considerable ambition and imagination. The former was demonstrated with 1937's *Snow White,* while *Fantasia* (1940) gave proof of the latter. Still, cinematic triumphs were not enough for Disney. His long-held dream of a recreational park for his employees ballooned into grandiose plans for a full-scale entertainment "kingdom" by the 1950s.

With a team of studio-effects wizards at his command, any fancy could be readily realized. Funding the project was a different matter. After selling his vacation home to purchase an Anaheim orange grove, Disney shrewdly arranged a deal with the burgeoning ABC network to produce a television show that would generate publicity *and* cash for his baby. Both the show and the park would be called Disneyland.

Premiering in October 1954, the TV show highlighted particular aspects of the coming park. For Frontierland, a trilogy of tales focused on the legendary Davy Crockett. With a catchy tune for its theme, the Crockett stories connected with the public beyond anyone's wildest dreams, most commonly in the form of the millions of coonskin caps sold over an 18-month period. Other "historic" heroes followed, as Disney attempted to corner the market on Americana.

Broadening his television domain, Disney launched an after-school TV show comprised of serials, songs, and a group of well-scrubbed kids sporting the requisite mouse ears. Standing out among her fellow "Mouseketeers" on *The Mickey Mouse Club* was a telegenic 13-year-old named Annette Funicello, who quickly became a fan favorite.

Within two months of its July 1955 opening, attendance at Disneyland surpassed one million. The savvy Disney had pioneered the use of television as a tool for merchandising. His aggressive cross-promotion forever changed the landscape of kids' entertainment.

A dream long in the making finally arrived for Walt Disney on July 17, 1955, with the unveiling of the Disneyland theme park in Anaheim, California. Though opening day itself was a nightmare—unseasonably hot, long lines, malfunctioning rides, and thousands of gate-crashers—approval by the masses ensured that the Disney company's $17 million investment would be recouped. In a shrewd cross-promotional move, Disney had committed his studio to a weekly television series (entitled *Disneyland*) on ABC in 1954, therein publicizing his venture while raising capital. The finished park gave visitors a chance to step into a fantasy world featuring attractions that embodied everything Disney.

Sparked by a decline in rail ridership (due largely to the development of interstate highways), the industry turned to General Motors to shore up its sagging fortunes. The result was a "concept" train, the Aerotrain, conceived by Harley Earl's design team under Chuck Jordan. Aiming for speed, comfort, and low cost, the resulting LWT-12 (for lightweight-1,200 horsepower) was fashioned from modified city bus bodies and much aluminum. While the futuristic styling was certainly pleasing, little else was. The Aerotrain was underpowered and dangerously rough to ride in at top speed. The concept was quietly abandoned after three were built.

President Dwight Eisenhower talks with Soviet Premier Nikolai Bulganin at a July 1955 summit meeting in Geneva, Switzerland. Fearing the prospect of a mutually destructive nuclear war now that the Soviets had developed the H-bomb, and pressured by NATO allies, Ike hoped to reach some sort of agreement that would lessen the chances of such a war. He called for an "open skies" treaty that would allow both sides to monitor the other's nuclear weapons development from the air, a proposal rejected by the suspicious Soviets as a clumsy American attempt to spy on them. Even without concrete results, this first summit since 1945 did create at least the possibility of future negotiations.

In 1955, 20-year-old Elvis Presley (*center*) rose from local phenomenon to the verge of national stardom. Throughout the year, Presley toured the South, working the established country music circuit. Sun Records continued to issue a series of Elvis singles, including "Baby, Let's Play House" and "I Forgot to Remember to Forget." But an association with a former carnival shill named "Colonel" Tom Parker (*left*) accelerated his progress. Recognizing Presley's explosive potential, Parker brushed aside his then-manager, Bob Neal, and pursued an aggressive strategy to gain maximum exposure. By year's end, a $40,000 deal had been inked with RCA.

The trend toward making every aspect of American life car-friendly reached the point of ridiculousness with the opening of this drive-in chapel in New York City. With the rise of the car culture and the parallel movement toward making everything faster and more efficient, entrepreneurs explored new ways to engage a country on wheels by offering any number of services with "drive-in" capabilities. While movies, fast-food, and banks readily lent themselves to the set-up, others, like the one seen here, proved to be passing fancies.

During the 1950s, Italian actress Sophia Loren burst onto American screens in a number of cinematic imports. Born to a single mother, Loren had attempted to escape poverty by appearing in beauty contests, where her earthy sensuality and ambition caught the attention of producer Carlo Ponti, her future husband. Ponti steered her into a project directed by Federico Fellini, setting her on the path to Hollywood. The iconic image of her emerging from the surf in 1957's *Boy on a Dolphin* became one of the decade's best-known images, securing immortality for the future Oscar winner.

By the time Piaggio of Italy manufactured its first Vespa-brand scooter in 1946, the company had been in business for more than 60 years, producing rail carriages, ship fittings, truck bodies, engines, and heavy aircraft. Italy's roads had been badly damaged during World War II, and Enrico Piaggio, the son of the company's founder, perceived a need for a small, economical vehicle to give practical transport to everyday buyers. Demand grew quickly, and by the time of this 1955 advertisement, the aerodynamic scooters were being produced in Italy and under license across Europe. Lighter and less noisy than motorcycles, the nimble Vespa became a symbol of carefree youth.

1955

August 11: President Eisenhower signs the Housing Amendment of 1955, which provides for the construction of 45,000 public housing units.

August 12: The Poliomyelitis Vaccination Act earmarks some $30 million for states to purchase polio vaccines for their residents. • Congress passes a law increasing the federal minimum wage from 75 cents to one dollar an hour.

August 15: Elvis Presley hires Tom Parker to manage his skyrocketing career.

August 18: Folk singer Pete Seeger appears before HUAC, but he refuses to testify.

August 20: "Maybellene," Chuck Berry's hit song, is released. • A raiding party of Algerian Berbers from the Atlas Mountains (which straddle Morocco and Algeria) kills 77 French nationals in a Moroccan settlement.

August 24: Emmett Till, a 14-year-old African-American from Chicago, makes a flirtatious remark to Carolyn Bryant, a white woman, in Bryant's Grocery and Meat Market in Money, Mississippi. *See* August 28, 1955.

August 27: Including records both mundane and bizarre, the first edition of the *Guinness Book of World Records* is released.

August 28: Roy Bryant, husband of Carolyn Bryant, and his half-brother, J. W. Milam, kidnap and murder Emmett Till, then dump his body in the Tallahatchie River. *See* September 3–6, 1955.

August 31: Egyptian President Gamal Abdel Nasser announces that Egypt is sending terrorists to conduct raids on Israel from Jordanian territory, claiming that "there will be no peace on Israel's border because we demand vengeance, and vengeance is Israel's death."

> "Before Emmett Till's murder, I had known the fear of hunger, hell and the Devil. But now there was a new fear known to me—the fear of being killed just because I was black."
>
> —ANNE MOODY, A MISSISSIPPIAN WHO WAS TILL'S AGE, 14, WHEN HE WAS MURDERED

Mamie Till Bradley collapses in grief as the boxed remains of her son, Emmett Till, arrive via train in Chicago on September 2, 1955. Bradley's emotional and spiritual strength helped her bring the story of her son's lynching to the world. On August 31, Mississippi officials were about to bury Till's body (and the story) when Bradley demanded that the battered remains be shipped back to Chicago. Against the advice of many, she insisted that Emmett's corpse be put on display for public viewing at the A. A. Rayner funeral home. The spectacle triggered national outrage against the South's insidious brand of racism. Bradley also maintained her composure amid hostile glares as a witness during the Mississippi murder trial.

In summer 1955, sharecropper Mose Wright invited great nephew Emmett Till to visit him and his family in Money, Mississippi. At 2 A.M. on August 28, J. W. Milam and Roy Bryant kidnapped Emmett from Wright's home, telling the 64-year-old to keep his mouth shut or else he "wouldn't live to be 65." During the murder trial, District Attorney Gerald Chatham asked Wright, "Do you see Mr. Milam in the courtroom?" Wright stood up and, in an action believed to be unprecedented for a black Southerner, pointed an accusatory finger at the white defendant. "Thar he," Wright declared. He then pointed to the other defendant, adding, "And there's Mr. Bryant." Soon after, Wright was spirited out of Mississippi for his own safety.

The Murder of Emmett Till

FOURTEEN-YEAR-OLD Emmett Till grew up on the South Side of Chicago. An only child, he was a smart dresser, brash, and a practical jokester. In August 1955 he and his two cousins traveled to Money, Mississippi, to stay with Emmett's great uncle, Mose Wright. One evening while hanging out at a local general store, Emmett took a dare to speak to Carolyn Bryant, the pretty, white wife of the store owner. He went into the store, flirted with her, and as he was leaving said, "Bye, baby."

Four days later, the woman's husband, Roy Bryant, and his half-brother, J. W. Milam, drove to Mose Wright's cabin and dragged Emmett into Milam's truck. Three days after that, Emmett's body was found in the Tallahatchie River. One of his eyes was gouged out, his forehead was crushed on one side, and a bullet hole was found in his skull.

Emmett's mother, Mamie Till Bradley, demanded that her son's body be sent home to Chicago immediately. When she saw the brutalized corpse, she ordered an open-casket funeral. *Jet* magazine published a photograph of the body, and the shocking case made headlines around the country.

The two accused murderers were tried in a segregated courtroom before an all-white, all-male jury. Mose Wright testified. Asked to point out the man who kidnapped Till, Wright stood up, pointed to Bryant, and—in spite of death threats against himself and his family—said, "Thar he." Other witnesses came forward after Wright testified, but the two men were found not guilty.

The brutal murder, the photograph, and the gross injustice of the trial infuriated many northern whites as well as African-Americans nationwide. Some consider Emmett Till a martyr, as his murder inspired many—including Rosa Parks—to join the fight for civil rights. In May 2004, the U.S. Justice Department announced it would reopen the case and search for others who may have been involved.

MILAM'S MOTIVE

WHAT ELSE COULD we do? He was hopeless. I'm no bully; I never hurt a nigger in my life. I like niggers in their place. I know how to work 'em. But I just decided it was time to put a few people on notice. As long as I live and can do anything about it, niggers are going to stay in their place. Niggers ain't gonna vote where I live. If they did, they'd control the government. They ain't gonna go to school with my kids. And when a nigger even gets close to mentioning sex with a white woman, he's tired of livin'. Me and my folks fought for this country and we've got some rights. I stood there in that shed and listened to that nigger throw that poison at me and I just made up my mind. "Chicago boy," I said, "I'm tired of 'em sending your kind down here to stir up trouble. Goddamn you, I'm going to make an example of you—just so everybody can know how me and my folks stand."

—J. W. MILAM, IN AN INTERVIEW WITH WILLIAM BRADFORD HUIE

Roy Bryant (*left*) and his half-brother, J. W. Milam (*center*), were the men who killed Emmett Till. Bryant and his wife, Carolyn, had operated a store in Money, Mississippi, that catered to black field hands. Till's offhand flirtation with Carolyn angered Bryant and Milam so much that they kidnapped, tortured, and murdered Emmett on August 28, 1955. After being freed by an all-white jury in Mississippi, Bryant and Milam sold their story to *Look* magazine, in which Milam confessed to the murder and explained why he killed Till.

August 31–September 7: An eight-day heat wave claims nearly 1,000 lives in Los Angeles.

September: For the first time, the Southeast Asian island nation of Indonesia holds open parliamentary elections. • French military draftees protest war with Algeria by refusing to deploy.

September 3–6: In Chicago, thousands view the mutilated body of Emmett Till in an open casket at A. A. Raynor Funeral Home and Roberts Temple Church of God in Christ. These visitors, as well as African-American citizens who see pictures of the body in *Jet* magazine, are outraged. *See* September 23, 1955.

September 6: Harold Stassen, the U.S. delegate to the United Nations, announces that the U.S. has decided not to honor the UN's plan for total, bilateral nuclear disarmament.

September 18: Researchers with the National Geographic Society reveal that they have discovered a blue-green spot on Mars that they believe to be plant matter.

September 19: Argentinian President Juan Peron is deposed in a military coup. Bizarrely, the victors confiscate Evita Peron's body as a bargaining chip.

September 22: Some 500 people die and 75 percent of the island's nutmeg trees (much of the world's supply) are lost when Hurricane Janet slams into Grenada in the British West Indies.

September 23: In Sumner, Mississippi, an all-white, all-male jury acquits Roy Bryant and J. W. Milam of the murder of Emmett Till even though the two defendants admit to abducting Till. In response, black citizens will hold large rallies in Chicago, New York, and other major northern cities.

September 24: President Eisenhower suffers a heart attack in Denver. He will spend seven weeks in the hospital.

Broderick Crawford (*pictured*) took home the best actor Oscar for the 1949 drama *All the King's Men,* but his coarse manner and beefy frame limited his roles. The syndicated TV drama *Highway Patrol* (1955–59) made the actor a wealthy man, primarily from residual payments he earned via never-ending reruns. Crawford was gruff and commanding as Captain Dan Matthews, whose barked "10-4! 10-4!" inspired a generation of impressionists.

This September 1955 cover of *Fortune* magazine features the semi-abstract art of Antonio Frasconi, an uncharacteristic choice for America's most famous periodical devoted to business. With such popular features as the Fortune 500 companies, the magazine charted the phenomenal growth of big business in the 1950s. The decade saw a wave of mergers so powerful that by 1960, according to historian George Moss, "America's 200 largest industrial corporations owned over half of the nation's industrial assets." Unlike previous periods of merger mania, '50s mergers, such as the ones that created International Telephone & Telegraph (ITT), brought together businesses in unrelated fields.

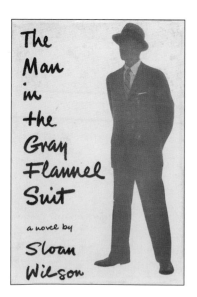

Sloan Wilson's 1955 novel, *The Man in the Gray Flannel Suit,* presented a stinging indictment of the culture of conformity and corporate servitude embraced by so many. Published to high acclaim, the book became a bestseller and, later, a successful film. In fact, its very title entered common parlance as shorthand for soulless anonymity. The book's theme—that pursuit of material success does not lead to fulfillment—reflected the experiences of its writer, who had left the corporate world to teach creative writing. Like the novel's protagonist, Wilson also was a war veteran. Indeed, war flashbacks provide a subtext throughout the story.

Joi Lansing brought sparkle and a pleasing flair for comedy to TV's long-running *Love That Bob* show, in which she costarred as Shirley Swanson, a gal whose dogged pursuit of confirmed bachelor Bob Cummings was a surefire laugh getter. A Mormon who neither smoked nor drank, Lansing had showy recurring roles in the last of Hollywood's one-reel (10-minute) movie franchises, the "Joe McDoakes" *Behind the 8-Ball* comedies. She also was a protégée of Orson Welles, appearing in the director's 1958 masterpiece, *Touch of Evil,* and in a Welles TV film, *Fountain of Youth.*

Russian expatriate Vladimir Nabokov assured himself literary immortality with the publication of his controversial novel, *Lolita,* in 1955. The story of a middle-aged intellectual's seduction of a 12-year-old girl shocked many with its sensitive depiction of an apparent pervert. In fact, the book is an allegorical paean to America—a tragic love affair between the cultured Old World and the sparkling but vulgar New World. *Lolita* is rich in literary references and adroit wordplay, and it skillfully sways between sad and comic. The book was banned for two years in France following its publication (in English) by Olympia Press, but—after a brief embargo—it went on to sell more than 100,000 copies in America during its first three weeks in print.

Miss America

A CURIOUS BLEND of civic boosting and cheap titillation resulted in the creation of the Miss America Pageant in 1921. The contest was originally conceived as a means of extending tourist season past Labor Day in Atlantic City, New Jersey. But once the event began airing nationally on television in 1954, it became an American institution. In 1955 TV personality Bert Parks began a quarter-century run as the host of the show. Millions of girls dreamed of donning the crown while Parks crooned the Miss America theme song, "There She Is."

Though envisioned as a means of choosing the "ideal" woman from among the ranks of state beauty contest winners, the showcasing of 48 beauties made the event ideal for armchair ogling. While a scholarship was the osten-

Lee Meriwether

sible prize, some winners, like 1955's Lee Meriwether, parlayed their exposure into successful showbiz careers.

Decades passed before minorities were allowed to compete, but other controversies plagued the pageant, too. In 1951 winner Yolande Betbeze balked at appearing scantily clad in public. "To . . . go into Milwaukee in the middle of the winter and walk around . . . in a bathing suit is not my idea of Miss America," she asserted. Contest officials supported her stance, while sponsor Catalina Swimwear withdrew its support and created the Miss USA Pageant instead.

The Miss America Pageant was popular until the mid-1990s, despite frequent attacks from women's rights groups. Interest in the pageant declined steadily in the 2000s.

1955

September 26: Following the news of President Eisenhower's heart attack two days earlier, the New York Stock Exchange suffers the heaviest loss in a single day to date, at $44 million.

September 30: The French delegation to the UN General Assembly walks out after the Assembly decides to discuss the Algerian independence movement. • Movie star James Dean is killed in a car accident near Paso Robles, California, at age 24.

October: NATO leaders vote to pull occupying forces from West Germany.

October 4: The Brooklyn Dodgers triumph over the New York Yankees in seven games to win their first World Series. • The first field trial of a telephone powered by Bell Labs's new solar battery is held in Americus, Georgia.

October 6: Sixty-six people die when a United Airlines DC-4 en route from Denver to Salt Lake City crashes into Wyoming's Medicine Bow Peak.

October 7: Beat poet Allen Ginsberg recites his magnum opus, *Howl,* at San Francisco's Six Gallery.

October 12: The State Department publicizes a letter sent by President Eisenhower to Soviet Premier Nikolai Bulganin in which Eisenhower suggests he would be willing to consider the Soviet proposal for bilateral arms inspections.

October 16: Esther Friedman begins her "Ann Landers" advice column. Three months later, sister Pauline will launch her own column, "Dear Abby."

October 23: In South Vietnam, Prime Minister Ngo Dinh Diem ousts Chief of State Bao Dai with considerable assistance from the U.S. intelligence community.

October 24: The South African delegation walks out of the UN General Assembly following a UN rebuke of South Africa's apartheid policy.

Born into poverty in rural Texas, Congressional Medal of Honor winner Audie Murphy became World War II's most decorated combat soldier. Credited with nearly 250 enemy kills, he parlayed his experiences into a best-selling autobiography, 1949's *To Hell and Back.* With his self-effacing persona and boy-next-door good looks, Hollywood beckoned, and the diminutive Murphy soon found a niche for himself in westerns. In 1955 he played himself in a big-screen treatment of his memoirs (*pictured*). Despite the honors and acclaim, Murphy suffered from posttraumatic stress disorder, which manifested itself in paranoia (he frequently carried a gun), depression, and addiction problems.

Robert Mitchum starred as a less than holy preacher in actor Charles Laughton's sole directorial effort, 1955's *The Night of the Hunter.* This gothic fantasy-thriller depicts a psychotic (Mitchum) in pursuit of a small fortune he believes has been hidden by a pair of children. Laughton had studied the silent films of F. W. Murnau and D. W. Griffith (and went so far as to cast 1910s star Lillian Gish in a key role), creating a film that resembles nothing less than an extended nightmare—even during the daytime scenes. Despite Mitchum's chilling portrayal and the obvious artistry of other elements, the film was largely ignored upon its release.

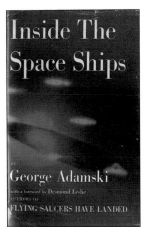

Inside The Space Ships

by George Adamski

with a foreword by Desmond Leslie

AUTHORS OF

FLYING SAUCERS HAVE LANDED

Polish immigrant and onetime mystical cult leader George Adamski also was an amateur stargazer. He lived in the Mount Palomar, California, valley, below the famed government observatory and its 200-inch telescope. Adamski claimed not merely to have photographed numerous flying saucers (he owned a six-inch telescope with a plate-camera attachment), but to have met and flown with the occupants. This—with fuzzy photographs intended to cement his point—is the gist of *Inside the Space Ships,* a 1955 follow-up to Adamski's 1953 best-seller, *Flying Saucers Have Landed.*

Regarded as a "singer's singer," Sarah Vaughan had an exquisite, sultry quality to her expressive, pitch-perfect voice. Steeped in gospel, she first drew attention in 1942 by winning a contest at Harlem's Apollo Theater, which led to a stint with Earl Hines's outfit. By the mid-1950s, Vaughan had hit her artistic stride, demonstrating superlative Bop jazz vocal chops as well as a command of pop material. Torch ballads, like those found on this 1955 release, were a specialty.

Pictured alongside her loyal sidekick, "Chim," actress Irish McCalla starred in *Sheena of the Jungle* during the show's one-season run. Based on the comic book heroine of the 1940s, Sheena was conceived as a female counterpart to Tarzan. Over the course of her adventures, she protected the interests of her jungle and its inhabitants against unscrupulous intruders. A statuesque beauty, McCalla served as a rare strong-female role model during the decade. She even performed her own stunts for the show, which ran in syndication for years.

Until the construction of Interstate 75 forced its closing, Harland Sanders ran a successful service station in Corbin, Kentucky. What made his business exceptional was the home-cooked fried chicken he offered to hungry travelers passing through. (Indeed, it was his culinary skills that had earned him the honorary "colonel" title back in the 1930s.) After "retiring" in the early '50s, Sanders set out to franchise his "secret blend of 11 herbs and spices" across the country on a handshake basis. Employing his own considerable southern charm, Colonel Sanders was the perfect spokesman for what became one of fast-food's biggest successes.

This advertisement typifies Madison Avenue's narrow view of women as housewives in the 1950s. Many ads for cleaning products emphasized this role and promised that their products would ease the burden. Ironically, in 1955 more women were in the workforce than at any previous time in U.S. history. But advertisers correctly assumed that women still did the lion's share of the housework. In the words of scholar Susan Douglas, the "real job" of women, especially wives, "was to wash diapers, make meatloaf, and obey their husbands no matter how brutish, dumb, or unreasonable they were."

Frozen here in characteristic expressions, the cast of *The Honeymooners* included (*left to right*) Jackie Gleason, Art Carney, Audrey Meadows, and Joyce Randolph. Coupling magnificent farcical dialogue with sentimental resolutions, the sitcom presented the quixotic attempts of bus driver Ralph Kramden (Gleason) and dim pal Norton (Carney) to rise above their lowly social station. Whether peddling the "Handy Housewife Helper" on TV, marketing dog food as a "mystery appetizer," or cramming to win the "$99,000 Answer," Ralph's everyman dreams inevitably fizzled, taxing the patience of his saintly but sarcastic wife, Alice (Meadows). From origins as a sketch on Gleason's variety show, *The Honeymooners* premiered in 1955 and endured in syndication for decades.

Jackie Robinson of the Brooklyn Dodgers steals home during the 1955 World Series against the Dodgers' nemeses, the New York Yankees. The Dodgers had lost to the Yankees in five previous World Series, but they had never lost the support of their vocal fans at intimate Ebbets Field. Robinson, Duke Snider, Don Newcombe, and Pee Wee Reese were among the Dodgers' "Boys of Summer," immortalized by author Roger Kahn. When Brooklyn pitcher Johnny Podres won the seventh game of the 1955 Series 2–0, Brooklynites rejoiced at last.

The "Tiki" mug stands as evidence of a once-flourishing vogue in America. Some time after World War II, a movement characterized by exotic effigies, bamboo torches, artificial palms, and carved coconuts took root, embraced chiefly (but not exclusively) by young adult males. The ersatz Pacific-rim *Objets d'Art* provided the perfect touch to a bachelor pad or suburban patio, environs enhanced by "exotica" instrumental music and a ready supply of rum-based drinks. This so-called Tiki culture extended to backyard parties, where celebrants wore leis and danced the limbo.

James Dean

ON THE HEELS OF Marlon Brando, another product of the Strasberg Actors Studio burst onto the national scene in the 1950s—a moody Indiana native named James Dean. The young actor's sullen disposition and put-upon persona endeared him to females, who wanted to mother him, and adolescent males, who wanted to be him.

Once he had mastered "the Method," Dean scored some success in small television dramas and on the stage. Though his first major film, *East of Eden* (1955), won him rave reviews, Nicholas Ray's *Rebel Without a Cause* (1955)—released after Dean's death—made him immortal. (*East of Eden* and 1956's *Giant* would garner him Academy Award nominations.) Unlike performances by youth idols of an earlier era, Dean's characterizations weren't larger than life (though his legend soon would be), enabling teens that made up a large part of his following to readily identify with him.

Dean's premature death behind the wheel of a Porsche Spyder in 1955 sealed his status as an icon. Though some of his performances may now seem histrionic, Dean projected a vulnerability that, combined with his inarticulate rebelliousness, made for compelling viewing. His misunderstood-youth archetype stands, along with Brando's, as a prime example of the American antihero in 1950s popular culture.

Exhibit A in the deification of actor James Dean (*left*) is his portrayal of the misunderstood youth in director Nicholas Ray's *Rebel Without a Cause* (1955). Costarring Natalie Wood (*right, in her first "adult" role) and Sal Mineo, *Rebel* tells the tale of three well-off but disaffected teens grappling with issues of identity and acceptance. Ray's full-color, CinemaScope treatment only enhanced Dean's vivid performance. Several scenes became enshrined in cinematic immortality, particularly the "chickie run" drag race. Released one month after Dean's fatal car crash, the film resonated with angst-ridden young audiences.

1955

October 26: The inaugural issue of *The Village Voice,* cofounded by Norman Mailer, hits New York newsstands. • South Vietnam is proclaimed a republic, and Ngo Dinh Diem is named its first president.

October 31: Moroccan Sultan Mohammed V returns from exile, although the French retain their colonial rule of his country.

November 1: Jack Gilbert Graham kills 44 people, including his own mother, when a bomb that he placed in her suitcase detonates on a DC-6 over Longmont, Colorado. • Dale Carnegie, author of the self-help classic *How to Win Friends and Influence People,* dies at age 64. • Tucson, Arizona, hosts the first international conference on solar energy.

November 7: The U.S. Supreme Court rules that segregation in public recreational facilities is unconstitutional.

November 12: Germany reconstitutes its army, inducting 101 men in a garage in Bonn. • *Billboard* begins its "Top 100" chart, which will track song popularity in three categories: sales, most airplay, and most jukebox play. These three categories will be merged in 1958 when *Billboard* inaugurates its "Hot 100."

November 19: Writer, orator, and conservative icon William F. Buckley, Jr., publishes the first issue of *National Review.*

November 22: RCA Victor buys the rights to Elvis Presley from Sun Records and Sam Phillips for the bargain price of $40,000.

November 25: The Interstate Commerce Commission bans segregation on interstate bus and rail travel.

November 26: The Soviets explode their first hydrogen bomb, dropped over Kazakhstan, with a reported force of 1.6 megatons.

Overjoyed Moroccans celebrate the return of their leader, Sultan Mohammed V, in November 1955. The country had been a French protectorate since 1912, and when Mohammed showed an independent streak by fostering a nationalist party, he was deposed by the French in 1953. Suffering the effects of a military defeat in Southeast Asia and combating the beginnings of a rebellion in its crucial Algerian colony, the French allowed Mohammed to return, and recognized the independence of Morocco under its sultan in 1956. Mohammed took the title of king in 1957; he died in 1961.

Jack Gilbert Graham, 23, awaits arraignment on charges of blowing a DC-6 passenger plane out of the sky. On November 1, 1955, United Airlines Flight 629 had left Denver's Stapleton Airport bound for Portland, Oregon. Aboard was Graham's mother, along with a bomb the young man had planted in her suitcase. Nine minutes into the flight it detonated, killing all 44 passengers and crew. FBI investigators focused on Graham, who was discovered to have taken out a $37,000 insurance policy on his mother's life just before the plane's departure. Following his conviction, Graham was executed.

Kay Thompson's first volume in the wildly popular series of *Eloise* books appeared in November 1955. Although technically books for children, they appealed to adults as well. The heroine was a precocious six-year-old girl who lived in New York's Plaza Hotel with her wealthy guardians. Refusing to be bored, she embarked on numerous adventures, such as braiding her pet turtle's ears. Thompson accurately captured the frenetic nature of children's speech by writing without the use of periods.

Back when sugar meant "energy" (and not obesity) in breakfast cereals, the makers found the perfect target for their goods: children. Taking note of the captive audiences that television drew, manufacturers deliberately retooled their packaging, making it more colorful and engaging. They also introduced cartoon characters as spokespersons, such as Tony the Tiger (*pictured, with Groucho Marx*). Saturday morning programming became the primary showcase for lively ads that pushed Sugar Frosted Flakes, Sugar Pops, Sugar Smacks, and other glucose-laden breakfast foods.

James Arness starred as U.S. Marshal Matt Dillon in CBS's *Gunsmoke,* television's longest running western (1955–75). As one of the first "adult westerns," the drama relied less upon shoot-'em-ups than on complex character studies of the town's mainstays. Rounding out the principals were Milburn Stone as Doc; Amanda Blake as Miss Kitty, owner of the town's saloon; and Dennis Weaver as Chester Goode, Dillon's simple but loyal deputy. The lanky Arness reportedly was cast on actor John Wayne's suggestion to replace radio's Matt Dillon, the portly William Conrad, who, while possessing a strong voice, was viewed as untelegenic.

For 30 years, beginning in 1955, kids woke to the strains of "Puffin' Billy," the theme song for the weekday morning show *Captain Kangaroo*. Television's longest-lasting children's show was anchored by the unflappable Captain (Bob Keeshan), so named for the large pockets of his coat. With an ensemble that included Bunny Rabbit (*pictured*), Mr. Moose, Grandfather Clock, and the inimitable Mr. Green Jeans (Hugh Brannum), the show offered a gentle form of entertainment. Viewers grew accustomed to repeat gags, including the rain of Ping-Pong balls following a knock-knock joke, and Bunny Rabbit tricking the Captain out of carrots.

1955

November 29: An accident involving Experimental Breeder Reactor #1 in Arco, Idaho, kills several researchers and destroys the reactor.

December: In North Vietnam, Ho Chi Minh begins his campaign of land reforms and ideological "cleansing," arresting and murdering thousands of landowners. • A massive northern California storm causes catastrophic flooding and the deaths of 76 people.

December 1: In defiance of the bus segregation law in Montgomery, Alabama, Rosa Parks refuses to yield her seat to a white man. She is thus arrested. *See* December 5, 1955.

December 5: Black citizens in Montgomery begin a one-day bus boycott of the city's segregated bus system. The Montgomery Improvement Association (MIA) is formed to coordinate the boycott, and Reverend Martin Luther King, Jr., the 26-year-old pastor of Dexter Avenue Baptist Church, is elected president. Meanwhile, Parks loses her case and is fined $14 for violating Montgomery's bus segregation law. In support of the Montgomery bus boycott, Martin Luther King delivers his first civil rights speech, at the Holt Street Baptist Church in Montgomery. • The American Federation of Labor and the Congress of Industrial Organizations join forces to form union giant AFL-CIO. George Meany, the first president of the organization, will serve until 1979.

December 6: Dr. Joyce Brothers, a psychologist, wins the top prize on the highly rated game show *The $64,000 Question.* Her subject category is boxing.

December 11: Israeli forces attack Syria along the Sea of Galilee.

December 31: General Motors announces that it has exceeded more than $1 billion in annual sales, becoming the first American corporation to do so.

George Meany (*left*), head of the American Federation of Labor (AFL), and Walter Reuther, president of the Congress of Industrial Organizations (CIO), celebrate the 1955 merger of the two organizations on December 5. Not only did the merger solidify the power of labor, but the two organizations developed a set of common standards, including a strong stand against Communist infiltration of unions. Meany was the more conciliatory of the two leaders, claiming he had "never walked a picket line." Reuther was more militant. His demands for worker rights had transformed industrial relations, but not before he narrowly escaped two assassination attempts.

Prior to the arrival of William F. Buckley, Jr.'s *National Review* in November 1955, right-wing conservatism was largely viewed as the domain of bitter, reactionary cranks. But the erudite, Yale-educated Buckley saw an opening for framing the conservative viewpoint in intellectual terms (though in practice, Buckley was no less critical of President Eisenhower than he was of liberals). Buckley's haughty, patrician manner made him an easy target, but it belied a genuine wit. The *National Review*'s existence gave right-of-center Republicans a platform and legitimacy that led to future political successes.

Rosa Parks

SHE WAS INDEED TIRED on that historic day in December 1955. But that is not the full story behind Rosa Parks's arrest for refusing to give up her bus seat to a white man, as was law in the Jim Crow South.

Parks was more than just a weary seamstress. She was a serious, committed civil rights activist *before* making her historic move on that Montgomery, Alabama, bus on December 1. She was secretary of the Montgomery chapter of the NAACP. Moreover, she had spent the previous summer under the tutelage of Septima Clark, whose work in training African-Americans to fight against Jim Crow inspired Parks to enter the fray.

Parks explained what happened on the bus after the driver told her to yield her seat to a white man: "When the driver saw me still sitting, he asked if I was going to stand up and I said, 'No, I'm not.' And he said, 'Well, if you don't stand up, I'm going to call the police and have you arrested.' I said, 'You may do that.'"

Parks was arrested, and E. D. Nixon, a longtime movement activist in Montgomery, made bond. It wasn't the first time an African-American had refused to get up from a Montgomery bus seat, but Nixon and other black leaders were looking for the right person to be a symbol of resistance. The upstanding Parks, they believed, was the one.

Soon after her arrest, the city's black leaders met at Dexter Avenue Baptist Church, where a young preacher named Martin Luther King, Jr., had just begun serving as pastor. Nixon, King, and others initiated a bus boycott that became a rousing success. Montgomery's African-Americans car-pooled and walked to work. The boycott lasted 381 days, costing the bus company more than $750,000. It ended after the U.S. Supreme Court ruled that segregation on intrastate buses was unconstitutional. Somewhat ironically, Parks's refusal to stand up inspired African-Americans nationwide to stand up for themselves.

After the initial success of the Montgomery bus boycott on December 5, 1955, black leaders decided to maintain the boycott until the city agreed to end its system of segregated buses. Because African-Americans still needed to get to work, a car-pool network was coordinated by the Montgomery Improvement Association (MIA). Recalled Rufus Jones, an MIA founder, "[T]hose folks who had cars would register them in the pool, and register the time they would be usable, and from that we could serve the people." The car-pool system worked so well that the boycott lasted 381 days.

John Agar draws a bead on *Tarantula* (1955) in this composite image from Brazil's *Ultra Ciencia* magazine. A scion of a Chicago meatpacking family, Agar became world famous when he married teenager Shirley Temple in 1945. He also found himself in the movies, enjoying excellent supporting roles in top pictures by John Ford and others. As a leading man in mid- and low-budget westerns and science fiction thrillers throughout the 1950s, he was stalwart and competent. Besides *Tarantula,* other pictures that cemented Agar's B-movie stardom include *Revenge of the Creature, The Mole People, The Brain from Planet Arous,* and *Invisible Invaders.*

Long the subject of misapprehension and denial, the April 14–15, 1912, sinking of the *Titanic* received its first authoritative treatment in Walter Lord's 1955 book, *A Night to Remember.* Lord studied the ship's original blueprints; contacted scores of survivors, rescuers, and relatives of victims; and pored over thousands of pages of testimony given at official investigations in London and Washington. Although portions of Lord's account have been superseded by information discovered years later (notably, that the ship broke in two as it sank), the book's balanced, minute-by-minute treatment remains vivid and important. It inspired a superior 1958 British film of the same name. The first-edition jacket design seen here is by Ben Feder.

The Ladykillers (1955) represented the sunset of England's cinematic comedy factory, Ealing Studios. Hitting their stride in the postwar years, Ealing's producers were responsible for such droll, prototypical English comedies as *Kind Hearts and Coronets* and *The Man in the White Suit.* Actor Alec Guinness (*back row, left*) was one of the studio's mainstays. Before graduating to more serious roles, such as in 1957's *The Bridge on the River Kwai,* Guinness was noted for his chameleonic ability to alter his appearance. *The Ladykillers,* which also starred Peter Sellers (*bottom row, right*), was a darkly sinister black comedy about robbers who are undone by an old lady (Katie Johnson, *center*).

With her brassy vocals and dynamic stage presence, LaVern Baker more than held her own against the male singers who dominated early rock 'n' roll. Pioneering a niche later filled by Tina Turner, Baker hit the charts with such tunes as "Jim Dandy," "See See Rider," and "I Cried a Tear." Baker had been discovered as a teenager by big-band arranger Fletcher Henderson, who steered her to the star-making producers at Atlantic Records. Atlantic quickly launched R&B's newest sensation with "Tweedlee Dee" (1955), which became a million-seller.

The Miss Rheingold contest was inaugurated in 1941, and soon became a New York-area balloting ritual for thousands of beer drinkers. The annual competition drew aspiring models from across America, including future movie stars Tippi Hedren and Grace Kelly. Meanwhile, Rheingold Brewing Company benefited tremendously

from the publicity surrounding the pretty winners who became the company's spokeswomen. Alas, the tradition came to a sour end in 1965 when the brewery, fearing a backlash by opening the contest to minorities, quietly discontinued it.

Director Phil Karlson's fact-based *The Phenix City Story* forcefully exposes the vice and murder that dominated Phenix City, Alabama, where a footbridge was all that separated the town from Fort Benning, Georgia, and its partying GIs. The movie is Hollywood melodrama informed by the better principles of muckraking jour-

nalism. Indeed, complete prints have an intriguing, 13-minute documentary prologue in which Los Angeles TV newsman Clete Roberts interviews Phenix City locals about the 1954 murder there of the Democratic nominee for Alabama attorney general, and the town's subsequent cleanup.

Though widely believed to be Ford's answer to Chevrolet's Corvette, the 1955 Thunderbird was less a performance car than a stylish set of wheels, patterned after European "personal" cars. The T-bird was certainly a looker, boasting hooded headlights, distinctive "porthole" rear side windows, and a wraparound windshield. Though its Mercury V-8 provided nearly 200 horsepower, not until the 1957 models did the engine deliver what the car's checkered-flag logo promised. Amenities included a removable hardtop and an assortment of power goodies, including windows and seat. Despite a nearly $3,000 price tag, more than 16,000 T-birds were sold during its first year.

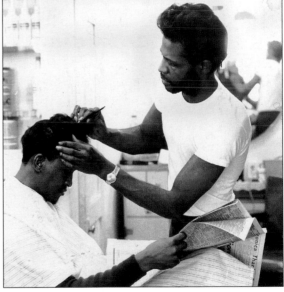

A patient customer gets his hair "conked" at a barbershop in the mid-1950s. This style, sometimes called a "process," was popular among many black Americans during the decade. It involved straightening the hair and then waving it. For some, it represented the height of status and style. For others, like black militant Malcolm X (who himself had worn a conk in the late 1940s and early 1950s), it was a lamentable sign of African-Americans rejecting their heritage. As Malcolm put it in one speech, conking was "more ridiculous than a slapstick comedy."

1955

New & Notable

Books

Andersonville by MacKinlay Kantor
A Good Man Is Hard to Find
   by Flannery O'Connor
Lolita by Vladimir Nabokov
The Man in the Gray Flannel Suit
   by Sloan Wilson
Notes of a Native Son by James Baldwin
The October Country by Ray Bradbury
The Quiet American by Graham Greene
The Strange Career of Jim Crow
   by C. Vann Woodward
Ten North Frederick by John O'Hara

Movies

Bad Day at Black Rock
Blackboard Jungle
East of Eden
Kiss Me Deadly
Lady and the Tramp
Marty
The Night of the Hunter
Picnic
Rebel Without a Cause
The Seven Year Itch

Songs

"Ain't That a Shame" by Fats Domino
"Cry Me a River" by Julie London
"The Great Pretender" by the Platters
"Love and Marriage" by Frank Sinatra
"Maybellene" by Chuck Berry
"Moments to Remember"
   by the Four Lads

Television

Alfred Hitchcock Presents
Captain Kangaroo
Gunsmoke
Highway Patrol
The Lawrence Welk Show
The Mickey Mouse Club
The $64,000 Question

Theater

Cat on a Hot Tin Roof
Damn Yankees
The Diary of Anne Frank
A Hatful of Rain
Inherit the Wind
No Time for Sergeants
A View from the Bridge

A brutal war between planets propels the action of director Joseph Newman's *This Island Earth* (1955), one of the most opulent science fiction thrillers of the 1950s. In an intriguing twist, neither of the planets is Earth. Instead, human scientists become unwilling recruits of Metaluna, whose people are losing their battle with Zahgon. Imaginatively mounted, the film is a deft parable about total war, and about Americans' fears of being manipulated by forces beyond their control. The declarative promotional art is by Reynold Brown.

"Audacious" fittingly describes the work of jazz pianist Thelonious Monk. His improvisational style, rooted in Bop but extending far beyond, explored uncharted musical territory, winning the introverted musician international renown. Some of his fame came from compositions such as "Round Midnight" and "Straight No Chaser," which quickly became jazz standards. Recording prolifically, Monk took his musical influence into other spheres with such albums as *Brilliant Corners* and *Thelonious Himself* (as well as a series of collaborations with such luminaries as Art Blakey and John Coltrane). Monk inhabited a self-made world, complete with a logic, language, and atmosphere all its own.

Public interest in uranium, a key A-bomb ingredient, was given a kick-start at the end of World War II when the Atomic Energy Commission (AEC) offered bounties to successful ore prospectors—professionals and amateurs alike. A brisk trade in "penny stocks" to finance new mines (most of them busts) began in 1953, and then came four early strikes near Moab, Utah. By 1955 the region was home to some 800 operating mines, and the "uranium boom" of 1955–56 was on. Unfortunately, the AEC issued no warnings about radiation hazards, so while moviegoers laughed at the Bowery Boys in *Dig That Uranium!* (1956), unsuspecting prospectors were working with materials that would sicken and even kill them years later.

Huntz Hall (*left*) and Leo Gorcey (*right*) were Broadway veterans who journeyed to Hollywood in 1937 to reprise their roles as boyish New York City street thugs in *Dead End*. By 1955 the pair and others who floated in and out of the group had been billed as the Dead End Kids, the East Side Kids, the Little Tough Guys, and the Junior G-Men. The earliest Bowery Boys pictures, which date from the late 1940s, were hard-bitten, even noirish. But slapstick comedy soon dominated this low-budget, enormously popular film series. In this entry, the Boys help a European king and his daughter battle sinister (read: Red) revolutionaries.

In 1955, with only 1 percent of the cigarette market, the Marlboro Company launched one of the most successful and ultimately controversial advertising campaigns in history. The first Marlboro Man (*pictured*) was designed to show that respectable men (signified by the tuxedo) could smoke filtered cigarettes without compromising their masculinity (implied by the tattoo). In 1955 Marlboro sales skyrocketed to $5 billion. After scientists confirmed the link between smoking and cancer, many antismoking groups condemned the Marlboro Man ads precisely because they were so effective.

Long associated with intrigue throughout his film career, director Alfred Hitchcock turned to television with the mystery anthology *Alfred Hitchcock Presents,* which premiered on CBS in 1955. Although he directed a handful of episodes, Hitchcock is mostly remembered for his droll introductions, which offered wry commentary on the evening's story. Featuring adaptations and original scripts by top writers, the show was rife with irony and black humor. For example, Roald Dahl's "Lamb to the Slaughter" (directed by Hitchcock himself) depicts a vain police search for a murder weapon at a woman's home. Unbeknownst to the officers—who soon sit down to dinner with the lady—the weapon is the once-frozen leg of lamb, which the policemen devour with great gusto.

"The adolescent society depended on affluence—on time and money of
its own to spend—but it also flirted with the harmless part of the culture
of delinquency: the spirit of fun and adventure, the disdain for studies,
the drinking, smoking, making out, swearing, staying out late."

—AUTHOR TODD GITLIN, *THE SIXTIES*

1956

Teen America

COUNTRY SINGER BOB LUMAN recalled the day he saw a young Elvis Presley in concert. "This cat came out in a coat and pink shirt and socks, and he had this sneer on his face and he stood behind the mike for five minutes, I'll bet, before he made a move," Luman remembered. "Then he hit his guitar a lick and he broke two strings. I'd been playing for ten years and I hadn't broken a total of two strings. So there he was, these two strings dangling, and he hadn't done anything yet, and these high school girls were screaming and fainting and running up to the stage, and then he started to move his hips real slow like he had a thing for his guitar...." "When he does that," a 15-year-old girl told a reporter for *Life* magazine, "...I just get down on the floor and scream."

By 1956, the year that saw Elvis's meteoric rise to fame, there already were clear signs that an increasingly powerful teenage culture was pulling farther and farther away from the culture of adults. Teens had their own language, magazines such as *Life* reported to their readers in alternating tones of alarm and reassurance. They had arcane dating rituals; they listened to their own music; they had their own fashions. And while teens themselves would have been appalled that anyone might not notice the vast social gulf that separated poodle skirts and sweater sets from tight pencil skirts and leather jackets, or ducktail haircuts from crewcuts, what the whole variety of teen cultures had in common was that they were for teens, not for adults.

Two teens share a snack at the local malt shop. A by-product of the newly emerging middle class, teenagers became a socioeconomic powerhouse. By 1956 America boasted more than 13 million teens, whose cumulative buying power was $7 billion per year.

In this emerging generation gap, perhaps nothing created more distance than the motion of Elvis Presley's hips. When Elvis first appeared on American TV in January 1956, there were no particular venues for teen culture. His first foray into America's living rooms—before Steve Allen dressed him in a tux and had him sing "Hound Dog" to a basset hound—came through CBS's Saturday night variety program, *Stage Show,* produced by Jackie Gleason. The other options in that time slot were NBC's *Perry Como Show* and ABC's hour-and-a-half "country-style variety show," *Ozark Jubilee.* None of the three was aimed at a teen audience. And the kids who waited eagerly for each of Presley's 11 television appearances that year more than likely watched him with their parents.

Elvis "The Pelvis" gives his fans what they want during a concert at the Olympia Theater in Miami on August 14, 1956. By spring of that year, Presley had become rock's first superstar, selling $75,000 worth of records a day. His sexually charged "Heartbreak Hotel" hit No. 1 on the pop singles charts on April 21.

As Elvis became more and more of a phenomenon, eventually reaching what some estimate as more than 80 percent of the American television audience in his appearances on Sunday evening's *The Ed Sullivan Show,* America's cultural arbiters expressed disdain and outrage. A "sexhibitionist," sneered *Time,* while a television reviewer ranted against Elvis's "'grunt and groin' antics...that should be confined to dives and bordellos."

Another critic got to what he saw as the heart of the matter: Teenagers liked Elvis, he argued, because their parents didn't. Gathered around the television in living rooms across the nation, parents and teens staked out their different positions on the singer, whom some critics called "Elvis the Pelvis."

The kids were going to win. In April 1956, Elvis was selling $75,000 worth of records every day. "Don't Be Cruel," No. 1 on the pop charts that year, sold three million copies. In 1950, by contrast, the folk song "Good Night, Irene" had topped the pop charts; in 1951, it was Patti Page's "Tennessee Waltz." Teenagers were showing their power, transforming American culture through the marketplace. By 1955 teenagers bought about 80 percent of pop music, and what they bought was their own.

Technology helped to create this distinct teen culture. Though families still gathered around television sets, the invention of small transistors made music portable in the 1950s. Transistor radios sold for $25 to $50 (roughly equivalent to the cost of an iPod in early 21st century dollars), and radio stations began to court a teen market. An Elvis Presley record player was even available, for $47.95. Elvis merchandise, in fact, pumped about $22 million into the American economy—not counting the money generated by his records. Teens bought 120,000 pairs of Elvis black jeans with emerald stitching. Girls wore

Hound Dog Orange lipstick, and boys paid an extra quarter to local barbers for haircuts that were christened "The Elvis."

In 1956 the first of the World War II babies were becoming teenagers. America boasted about 13 million teens that year—a small cohort compared to the baby boom quick on their heels. But, according to *Sr. Scholastic* (a weekly national high school magazine), they had a total combined income of $7 billion a year, and it was rising rapidly. That worked out to about $10 a week for the average teenager.

Such figures translated into influence. As *Seventeen* magazine editorialized in 1961, looking back on the decade of the 1950s: "When *Seventeen* magazine was born in 1944, we made one birthday wish: that this magazine would give stature to the teen-age years, give teen-agers a sense of identity, of purpose, of belonging. In what kind of world did we make our wish? A world in which teen-agers were the forgotten, the ignored generation.... In 1961... the accent everywhere is on youth. The needs, the wants, the whims of teen-agers are catered to by almost every major industry."

It was, in fact, advertisers, marketers, and the mass media who served as midwives to the birth of the American "teenager," dating back to the 1920s. As more and more young people went to high school, beginning in earnest in the '20s, a peer-centered youth culture emerged, characterized in part by shared tastes in music, distinctive styles, and courtship rituals. The Great Depression, paradoxically, strengthened this emerging youth culture, for youth who normally would have left school at 14 to take jobs faced grim employment prospects and were much more likely to continue through high school. By 1940, with national prosperity increasing as the nation began its buildup toward war, advertisers and marketers named a new social group: "teeners," or "teensters." A year later, they were called "teenagers." The teenagers of the 1950s, unlike their pioneering peers in the 1940s—or, even more significantly, their parents—did not remember the days of economic depression.

One of the first to recognize and exploit the possibilities of teen identity—and thus, the teen market—was an entrepreneurial young man named Eugene Gilbert. Gilbert grew up in Chicago, graduating high school right at the end of World War II. In 1945 the 19-year-old Gilbert glimpsed the potential of the teen market. Convincing store managers of his idea to appeal directly to teenagers, he began market research on teen tastes. Within the year, he had hired a network of hundreds of popular teenagers

Be Chewsy
CHOOSE THE ONE THAT "BELONGS"

BEECH-NUT...the quality gum   the 5¢ luxury

Teenagers of the 1950s began to form a community of their own, and the advertisers of Madison Avenue took heed. Ads such as this one suggested that teens would become more popular if they purchased the featured products. Advertisers typically portrayed teens as wholesome and unthreatening in order to secure the approval of parents.

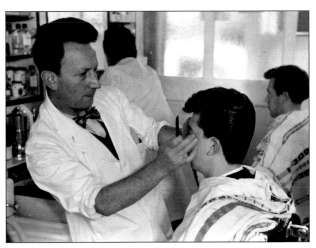

Mr. Rose puts the final touches on his famous haircut, "The Quiff," a popular '50s style he claimed he invented. Also popular with teens of the era were leather jackets (with the collars turned up), poodle skirts, and cashmere sweaters.

("Joe Guns") to survey their peers. His research won him accounts with major corporations and institutions ranging from Maybelline to the U.S. Army. In September 1956, barely in his 30s but established as the foremost expert on American teens, Gilbert launched a syndicated column, "What Young People Think," which ran in more than 270 newspapers in the U.S. and Canada.

Beginning with his first column (titled "Rock 'n' Roll Can't Ruin Us"), Gilbert laid out a defense of teen culture. Although it was universally acknowledged that teens exerted great influence in American society, many Americans found that influence pernicious. In the years following World War II, statistics revealed rising rates of crime committed by young people. In part, that was due to enforcement of laws regarding "status" crimes, in which the act was criminal because of the juvenile status of the offender—curfews, for example, or possession of alcohol.

In 1956 mega-popular deejay Alan Freed hosted a 12-day Christmas Jubilee at New York's Paramount Theater, featuring some of the day's biggest rock 'n' roll acts. In this new musical subculture, concertgoing became an increasingly popular activity among teenagers.

But many adults looked at teen culture and saw danger. They were alarmed by the sexual rhythms of rock 'n' roll, the seemingly ubiquitous jeans and leather jackets, and teens' devotion to the norms of their peer group and seeming disregard (or defiance) of adult authority. In 1953 the U.S. Senate began a series of major hearings on juvenile delinquency that lasted for the better part of a decade. In 1955 alone, close to 200 bills somehow related to juvenile delinquency were pending in Congress.

Hollywood, predictably, saw an opportunity in the controversial figure of the American teen, and produced at least 60 films on delinquency during the 1950s. As historian James Gilbert argues, the "film industry quickly developed a special genre that simultaneously portrayed delinquents as attractive and misguided . . . present[ing] an intriguing, energetic youth culture, but sternly moraliz[ing] about carrying rebellion too far."

The era's most attractive Hollywood rebel was James Dean. Famously sullen and narcissistic, Dean's characters projected what film critic Pauline Kael described as "beautiful desperation." He starred in only three films before he died at age 24, crashing his new Porsche Spyder into another vehicle on September 30, 1955. But his performance in director Nicholas Ray's *Rebel Without a Cause* already had established him as the model for the tragically misunderstood teenage rebel, the alienated youth doomed by the failings of adult society.

Years later, film director Elia Kazan, who had discovered Dean but never liked him, criticized the image of what writer David Halberstam called "self-pitying, self-dramatizing youth" that Dean had fostered. "Its essence was that all parents were insensitive idiots, who didn't understand or appreciate their kids," Kazan stated. "In contrast to these parent figures, all youngsters were supposed to be sensitive and full of 'soul.'"

In fact, there was an enormous gulf between the experiences of most '50s teens and those of their parents, the majority of whom had been teenagers in the 1930s and young adults during World War II. It was difficult for a generation that had seen or felt so much hardship not to worry about the next generation, even more than parents normally worry about their kids. Teens' spending seemed imprudent; their assumptions of economic and physical security dangerous.

Even the teenage practice of going steady seemed suspect to many adults, not only because steadies were more likely to "go further" sexually, but because it would prevent them from developing the competitive skills necessary for adult success. If young steadies could take for granted things as fundamental as companionship and social success, could they develop the gumption they would need later to earn good jobs and positions of community leadership? As a 1952 advice book warned: "To be sure of anything is to cripple one's powers of growth. To have your girl always [available] at the end of a telephone line without having to work for her ... is bound to lessen your powers of personal achievement."

Going steady for '50s teens meant slow-dancing, "necking" at the drive-in, and sometimes "parking." In a departure from previous decades, going steady was a term used more loosely in the 1950s. It no longer meant that the young man and woman were necessarily on the path to marriage; it meant only that they were an exclusive couple.

Middle-class parents and elite policy makers worried that the new generation would not prove tough enough for a harsh world. Educators throughout the nation's colleges and universities began creating curricula and extracurricular programs aimed at fostering the qualities necessary for democratic citizenship in the Cold War world.

Despite the romance of the rebel and the celebration of youth that surrounded '50s teens, most kids were shockingly eager to take on the responsibilities of adulthood. As a group, they married younger, had children younger, and "settled down" younger than had their parents—or than did any generation of American youth in the half century that has followed. Yet, they were the initial model for the American teen. The U.S. youth cultures that have flourished since owe much to their enthusiasm.

1956

1956: The CIA begins its long involvement in a project code-named MK ULTRA, in which unsuspecting subjects are given hallucinogenic drugs in an attempt to determine if such drugs might have practical brainwashing applications. • Soviet First Secretary Nikita Khrushchev, fearing assassination by members of the old regime unhappy with his reforms, purges his government of Stalinists.

1956: Atoms can be seen for the first time, thanks to an ion microscope created by inventor F. W. Muller. • Detroit's Fermi nuclear power plant is the site of the first U.S. nuclear protests. • Thirteen million women are part of the American workforce this year, compared to 8.5 million in 1947. • Future Iraqi dictator Saddam Hussein joins his country's Baath Socialist Party.

1956: The leftist tome *The Power Elite* is published. Author C. Wright Mills asserts that a system in which a small group drives policy for the masses is inherently flawed. • William Hollingsworth Whyte publishes *The Organization Man,* a statement about the corporate rat race in America. • *The Exploration of Mars,* written by Wernher von Braun, is published. • Forrest E. and Gloria Fickling (aka G. G. Fickling) publish the first of their popular Honey West detective novels.

1956: *Life* magazine publishes interviews with five male psychiatrists who assert that ambition in women leads to ill social effects, including divorce, mental illness among wives, and homosexuality among boys. • La Leche League International, a support group for mothers and an advocate organization for breast-feeding, is founded. *See* October 17, 1956. • John Lennon and three of his schoolmates at the Quarry Bank School in Liverpool, England, form a band called the Quarrymen. • Pampers disposable diapers hit the market.

In 1956 Margaret Ellen Towner became the first woman ordained by the Presbyterian Church. After receiving a bachelor's degree at New York's Union Theological Seminary, Towner accepted a commission in Allentown, Pennsylvania, as a minister of education. Her rise coincided with an ongoing debate within the Presbyterian Church regarding women's roles. After voting down the issue of Word and Sacrament ministry for women several times, the General Assembly was at last persuaded to accept societal realities in 1956.

Rabbits are held fast while undergoing a pyrogens test at a chemical research center. Animal testing was generally accepted in the United States in the 1950s, although in 1959 British scientists adopted a protocol that called for a reduction in the number of animals used in research. According to science writer Julian Groves, animal research did not become an issue in the States until the mid-1960s.

American figure skater Tenley Albright practices for the 1956 Winter Olympics in Cortina, Italy. Albright had overcome polio as a young girl to win the silver medal in women's figure skating in the 1952 Winter Games. Even though a serious accident two weeks before she was to compete at Cortina caused her considerable pain, Albright courageously skated through it and became the first American woman to win a gold medal in the event. After graduating from Harvard Medical School, she became a famed surgeon, specializing in sports injuries.

First launched in the 1930s, the "Breck Girls" advertising campaign became one of the best known and longest running ad campaigns in history. The Breck Girls presented an idealized version of American womanhood—desirable, but projecting a classic purity. Though the faces changed throughout their decades-long run, these iconic images intrigued the public. Typically, the ads were positioned on magazine back covers, boosting their prestige. At a time when gender roles were clearly defined, the Breck Girls reflected a cultural touchstone of domestic femininity. This illustration is by Charles Sheldon, who rendered every Breck Girl until his death in 1960.

With his trademark bent trumpet and puffed-out cheeks, and complex yet exciting solos, Dizzy Gillespie was among the best-loved giants of music. Though rightly associated with bop, to which he was a key contributor, Gillespie's musical scope knew no limits, encompassing Afro-Cuban influences, Latin percussion, and scat singing. Following in the footsteps of Roy Eldridge, Gillespie by 1945 had carved out his own identity with his harmonically complex soloing. His associations with the equally innovative Charlie Parker put him at bop's forefront. Avoiding the scene's bad habits, Gillespie made an ideal goodwill ambassador when President Eisenhower sent him around the world in 1956.

1956

January: About 1,000 people die due to a wave of smog in London, the latest in a series of smog incidents that will prompt Britain's parliament to pass a clean-air act. • Pauline Friedman Phillips contributes her first "Dear Abby" advice column to the *San Francisco Chronicle* under the pen name Abigail Van Buren. • South Vietnam Premier Ngo Dinh Diem orders the arrest of Viet Minh suspects throughout the country. Detainees are denied counsel, and many are tortured and executed.

January 1: The Sudanese declare independence from joint Egyptian and British rule. Muslims from the north seize power, and civil war breaks out.

January 2: Undefeated Oklahoma beats Maryland 20–6 in the Orange Bowl.

January 12: The FBI arrests six suspects in the 1950 Boston Brinks heist.

January 13: Lebanon and Syria sign a mutual defense pact to protect themselves against an attack by Israel.

January 16: Egyptian President Gamal Abdel Nasser vows to take Palestine back from Israel.

January 19: Citing Israel's violation of the Palestinian cease-fire, the United Nations Security Council votes unanimously to censure Israel for aggression against Syria.

January 24: Governors of Virginia, South Carolina, Mississippi, and Georgia agree to band together in opposition to *Brown v. Board of Education.*

January 26–February 5: The first televised Olympic Winter Games are held in Cortina d'Ampezzo, Italy. The Soviets win the most medals in their first-ever Winter Games. American polio survivor Tenley Albright captures the women's skating title, while Austrian skier Toni Sailer wins an unprecedented three gold medals.

Identical twin sisters Ann Landers (born Esther Pauline Friedman; *left*) and Abigail Van Buren (born Pauline Esther Friedman; *right*) work on their rival advice columns. In 1955 Landers replaced the advice columnist at the *Chicago Sun-Times.* Around the same time, Van Buren wrote the editor of the *San Francisco Chronicle,* claiming she could write a better advice column than the one currently appearing in that newspaper. The editor agreed, and "Dear Abby" premiered in January 1956. Both columns were immensely popular in the 1950s and afterward. The two sisters, however, did not have a happy relationship, and were barely on speaking terms in their later years.

Courtship rituals changed considerably throughout the 20th century, from the arcane practice of "calling" to the refinement of modern dating as known today. Youth of the 1950s effectively rewrote the rules: Dating became less a means of choosing a life partner than a social activity pursued for fun and experience. But when a relationship deepened past the point of "going steady," a token—such as a fraternity pin (as seen with this couple on New Orleans' Tulane University campus) or class ring—signified that the girl was off-limits to casual pursuit, and possibly on the way to engagement.

Sci-Fi Paranoia

THE POLITICAL REALITY of the 1950s encouraged an impressive number of science fiction movies rooted in paranoiac plots of alien takeover and domination. Most alarmingly, the interlopers frequently walked among us in disguise, waiting for propitious moments to conquer, and subvert the American way of life. Who was the enemy? Your boss? Your spouse? You? All of this was America's Red Scare mentality writ large on 20-foot movie screens.

Director Don Siegel's *Invasion of the Body Snatchers* is an especially stark example of the concealed enemy: When ordinary people fall asleep, they are replaced by pod-bred, extraterrestrial duplicates that exist only to survive, without joy or other emotions. Even family wasn't sacrosanct, as expressed in *I Married a Monster from Outer Space* and *The Space Children*.

Invasion of the Body Snatchers

Much of the public's uneasiness arose not just from a general dread of communism, but from attitudes about science that were radically altered by the atomic bomb. Some films, such as *Day the World Ended* and *Invasion U.S.A.*, show the horrifying consequences of atomic war. Other sci-fi shockers paint scientists as heedless dreamers who might sacrifice Earth in naive or unscrupulous attempts to stretch the boundaries of research (*Beginning of the End*), commu-

nicate with aliens (*It Conquered the World*), or secure personal gain (*The Man from Planet X*).

In Howard Hawks's *The Thing from Another World*, a scientist at an isolated Arctic outpost imperils all of his companions when he tries to "understand" the savage humanoid vegetable whose main preoccupation is human blood. Only the intervention of an Air Force captain and his men (that is, an alert, prepared military) destroys the creature and ends the threat.

An assured, intelligent storyteller equally at home with short stories, novels, and screenplays, Richard Matheson contributed to folklore with his fourth novel, a paperback original entitled *The Shrinking Man.* Although the springboard is science fictional (the protagonist begins to shrink in size after exposure to radioactive mist), the book is best read as a parable of the diminishment of individual—particularly male—control in an increasingly complex and hostile world. Cover art is by Mitchell Hooks. Matheson wrote the screenplay for the highly regarded 1957 film adaptation, *The Incredible Shrinking Man.*

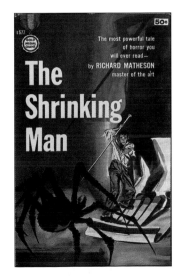

The Search for Bridey Murphy became an unexpected bestseller in 1956, telling the purportedly true story of a Colorado housewife's past life as a 19th century Irish woman. Amateur hypnotist Morey Bernstein had drawn from Virginia Tighe's "memories" that predated her current life. While in an induced trance, Tighe recounted (in a rich brogue) details of a mundane life in County Cork. The case's popularity sparked a faddish embrace of all things reincarnate, with thousands holding "come as you were" parties. However, interest subsided following an investigation of Tighe, who in reality had simply recounted stories of a forgotten Irish neighbor.

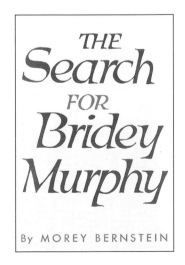

1956

January 28: Soviet Premier Nikolai Bulganin's 20-year friendship pact proposal with the U.S. is rejected by President Dwight Eisenhower. *See* October 21, 1956.

January 29: *Baltimore Sun* journalist and author Henry Louis Mencken dies at age 75.

January 30: Martin Luther King, Jr.'s home in Montgomery, Alabama, is bombed. *See* February 1, 1956.

February 1: Development of the Jupiter intermediate-range ballistic missile (IRBM), which has been a joint U.S. Army-U.S. Air Force project, is consolidated under Army control with establishment of the Army Ballistic Missile Agency (ABMA). Based at the Redstone Arsenal in Huntsville, Alabama, ABMA inherits the Wernher von Braun scientific team and ballistic missile projects already under way there. *See* November 26, 1956. • Challenging the bus segregation law in Montgomery, attorney Fred Gray files a lawsuit, *Browder v. Gayle,* in a U.S. district court. *See* February 21, 1956.

February 4: George Wright, a 14-year-old contestant on the game show *The Big Surprise,* wins $100,000 for correctly identifying the song *Me and My Shadow.*

February 6: Students at the University of Alabama riot against the admission of Autherine Lucy, the school's first black student. Lucy is suspended during the evening for "her own safety." The NAACP will pressure the university to drop the suspension, which will prompt the school to expel Lucy.

February 14: At the opening of the 20th Party Congress in Moscow, Soviet First Secretary Nikita Khrushchev asserts that communism can exist without violence.

A popular-music giant who defied genre restrictions, Johnny Cash got his start at Sam Phillips's legendary Sun Studios in Memphis. Though Cash aspired to sing gospel, Phillips had other plans. Sensing the effortless gravitas that the baritone singer projected, Phillips challenged Cash, pushing him toward a path that fused a rock 'n' roll attitude with elements of folk and country (while rejecting the latter's fiddles and pedal-steel guitars). "Cry, Cry, Cry" (1955) became Cash's first Sun hit, followed by his classic "I Walk the Line" (1956). Backed by the Tennessee Two (later Three), Cash embarked on an extraordinary 1,500-song career that would stretch to the 21st century.

Rocks, eggs, and tomatoes were part of the welcome Autherine Lucy received when she attempted to desegregate the University of Alabama in February 1956. Her brief attendance there was the result of a long legal battle waged by her and the NAACP against the state of Alabama. Her tenure at the school lasted only three days as Lucy was forced to leave the campus facedown in the back of a state police car on February 6, 1956. According to university officials, her suspension the next day was for her own safety. Lucy and the NAACP again fought back in the courts before conceding defeat.

Alabama State Senator and plantation owner Sam Englehart helps organize white resistance to the Montgomery bus boycott in February 1956. Racist Mississippi Senator James Eastland was to be the featured speaker. State Senator Englehart led the Alabama branch of the White Citizens' Council, a major organ of white opposition to desegregation. More "respectable" than the Ku Klux Klan, the council's membership was comprised primarily of "esteemed citizens," such as businessmen and lawyers. Although its public stance renounced violence, its overheated rhetoric often instigated violent activity. White Citizens' Councils popped up in many southern cities in the late 1950s.

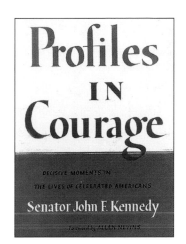

John F. Kennedy's *Profiles in Courage* was published in January 1956 to critical and popular acclaim. The book focused on the lives of eight American political leaders who had the courage to take unpopular stands. At the time, rumors circulated that Kennedy aide Ted Sorensen was actually the ghostwriter and that the idea for the book was not JFK's. Robert Dallek, Kennedy's most recent biographer, asserts that Sorensen and Georgetown professor Jules Davids drafted chapters but that the young Massachusetts senator revised and edited them. Whatever its provenance, the book boosted Kennedy's political standing as a man who was both courageous and intellectual. It also earned him (and him only) a Pulitzer Prize.

During production of Howard Hughes's *The Conqueror,* perennial cowboy John Wayne (*left*) mounted a doomed attempt to impersonate Mongol warlord Genghis Khan; Susan Hayward (*right*) tried not to laugh. But nobody laughed later when 91 of the 220 in the cast and crew contracted cancer. Forty-six died of the disease, including the Duke, Hayward, director Dick Powell, and costars Agnes Moorehead and Pedro Armendariz. The company had spent 13 weeks in Utah, downwind of A-bomb tests in Yucca Flats, Nevada. Profound levels of radiation floated across the Nevada border and over Snow Canyon, where much of *The Conqueror* was shot. The danger was compounded when Hughes innocently ordered 60 tons of radioactive dirt shipped back to Hollywood for retakes.

1956

February 18: Thomas H. Brewer, a founder of the local NAACP in Columbus, Georgia, is shot to death outside his office by a local white politician.

February 21: In Montgomery, Alabama, Martin Luther King, Jr., and 88 fellow African-Americans are indicted by a grand jury for violating a law that prohibits boycotts in the city. *See* March 22, 1956.

February 24: In a speech before the 20th Party Congress, Soviet First Secretary Nikita Khrushchev denounces the excesses of Joseph Stalin's bloody reign.

February 27: The South African parliament deliberately disenfranchises 45,000 nonwhite voters, removing them from the national electoral roll.

February 29: President Eisenhower announces that he will seek the Republican nomination for a second term in office.

March: The U.S. delegation to the United Nations asserts that its opposition to disarmament stems from a belief that nuclear weapons are a "powerful deterrent to war." • The United States accuses the Soviets of flying spy balloons over American and Allied territories. • In an effort to sidestep school integration, Virginia amends the state constitution to allow state funding for private schools. *See* September 1959. • Lawrence Ferlinghetti is arrested on obscenity charges following his publication of the Allen Ginsberg poem *Howl*.

March 2: France recognizes Morocco's independence, returning Sultan Mohammed V to the throne.

March 5: The U.S. Supreme Court affirms its ban on segregation in public schools. • The 1933 film *King Kong,* starring Fay Wray, is broadcast on television for the first time.

Beginning in 1956, Julie Andrews starred as Eliza Doolittle in the Broadway production of *My Fair Lady* (based on George Bernard Shaw's play, *Pygmalion*). Terrific acting by Rex Harrison (as Professor Henry Higgins) and a superb Lerner and Loewe score fueled the comedy's success. Such tunes as "I Could Have Danced All Night," "On the Street Where You Live," and "I've Grown Accustomed to Her Face" quickly became standards. The witty fable centered around the efforts of an upper-crust elocution teacher (Harrison) to educate a Cockney flower girl (Andrews) so that she might "pass" in aristocratic society.

The University of San Francisco dominated college basketball in the mid-1950s thanks to the heroics of 6'9" center Bill Russell. A dominant rebounder and ferocious shot-blocker, Russell led USF to NCAA championships in 1955 and '56 and a remarkable streak of 55 consecutive victories. After winning gold at the 1956 Olympics, Russell became the mainstay of the Boston Celtics, leading them to nine NBA championships in 10 years. His battles with center Wilt Chamberlain were legendary.

Martin Luther King, Jr.

BEFORE ROSA PARKS WAS arrested in Montgomery, Alabama, in December 1955, Martin Luther King, Jr., had been clear about how his life was going to proceed. After a few years of pastoring at Dexter Avenue Baptist Church, he would return to his alma mater, Morehouse College, as a philosophy professor. He even dreamed that he eventually would become the college's president.

At the time, the 26-year-old King concentrated on three things: his wife, Coretta; their daughter, Yolanda; and his duties at Dexter. The practical and pragmatic world of politics was not yet his priority. In his private moments after the bus boycott victory, King worried to his wife that people would expect too much from him and that his life had already peaked.

King's Montgomery Improvement Association slowly evolved into the Southern Christian Leadership Conference (SCLC), a loose confederation of brave black ministers and other activists. The organization was founded in 1957, with King—a brilliant orator—as its president. The Montgomery experience would plant seeds out of which the civil rights movement would emerge. Longtime movement activists—such as NAACP head Roy Wilkins and labor leader A. Philip Randolph—would make way for collective leadership coming *directly* out of the black church and committed to *direct action* against Jim Crow. The time for unswerving confrontation against white racists had arrived.

King, following the teachings of Mahatma Gandhi, believed in nonviolent protest. MLK led the Prayer Pilgrimage for Freedom on May 17, 1957, and he discussed civil rights issues with President Dwight Eisenhower on June 23, 1958. But his greatest triumphs would come in the 1960s, especially in Birmingham and Selma, Alabama, and with his "I Have a Dream" speech at the March on Washington in 1963. The power of his leadership led to the first meaningful civil rights legislation of the 20th century—the Civil Rights Act of 1964 and the Voting Rights Act of 1965.

In front of 3,000 well-wishers, Coretta Scott King embraces her husband, Martin Luther King, on the Montgomery County Courthouse steps on March 22, 1956. The young civil rights leader had just been found guilty of organizing the bus boycott in violation of Alabama's anti-boycott law. The arrest was a blunder by local authorities, as it attracted international attention and strengthened the resolve of African-Americans to continue the boycott, which was taken to a successful conclusion in December. "I knew that I was a convicted criminal," King wrote, "but I was proud of my crime . . . the crime of joining my people in a nonviolent protest against injustice."

1956

March 9: British authorities on Cyprus arrest and exile Greek Archbishop Makarios for aiding Cypriot separatist terrorists.

March 12: One hundred and one southern members of Congress sign the Southern Manifesto to reject and resist the 1954 U.S. Supreme Court ruling against segregation.

March 13: Elvis Presley's self-titled debut album is released.

March 17: Fred Allen, radio legend and regular on TV's *What's My Line?*, dies of a heart attack at age 61.

March 20: France grants independence to Tunisia. In April, Habib Bourguiba will be elected the first premier of the newly independent African nation.

March 22: Martin Luther King, Jr., is found guilty of conspiring to conduct an illegal boycott in Montgomery, Alabama. Initially sentenced to a prison term, King is instead fined $500. *See* November 13, 1956.

March 23: Pakistan becomes the Islamic Republic of Pakistan, an independent republic of the British Commonwealth. It is the first Islamic republic. • The University of San Francisco men's basketball team, led by dominant center Bill Russell, wins its second straight NCAA title.

March 27: The U.S. government seizes the *Daily Worker* newspaper, mouthpiece of the U.S. Communist Party, for tax evasion.

March 28: The Icelandic parliament votes 38 to 18 to banish U.S. troops from Iceland.

March 31: Britain opens Calder Hall, the world's first commercial nuclear electric power plant, at Sellafield. At least part of Calder Hall's function will be to secretly produce weapons-grade plutonium.

MGM PRESENTS
FORBIDDEN PLANET
AMAZING!
STARRING WALTER PIDGEON · ANNE FRANCIS · LESLIE NIELSEN
WITH WARREN STEVENS AND INTRODUCING ROBBY, THE ROBOT SCREEN PLAY BY CYRIL HUME
DIRECTED BY FRED McLEOD WILCOX · PRODUCED BY NICHOLAS NAYFACK IN CINEMASCOPE AND COLOR
A METRO-GOLDWYN-MAYER PICTURE

Take equal parts of Shakespeare's *The Tempest* and *Amazing Stories* magazine and you get MGM's *Forbidden Planet,* the splashiest and most imaginative science fiction movie of the decade. Leslie Nielsen (all business in this pre-*Airplane!* effort) is the saucer commander who reconnoiters a remote planetary settlement. There, all but a scientist and his beautiful daughter have mysteriously perished at the hands of an unseen...*something.* Before the intriguingly metaphysical climax, we meet Robby the Robot (*pictured*), one of the most endearing of all filmbots.

The son of vaudeville dancers, Sammy Davis, Jr., began touring with his father as a small boy. He sang and danced and joked, and he learned how to play the vibraphone, trumpet, and drums. In 1954 Davis lost an eye in an auto accident, and while recuperating converted to Judaism. Two years later, his career took off with his dynamic performance in the Broadway show *Mr. Wonderful* (*pictured*). In 1959 Davis became an original member of Frank Sinatra's Rat Pack. Davis's refusal to work at nightclubs that barred African-American audiences helped lead to the desegregation of Las Vegas casinos.

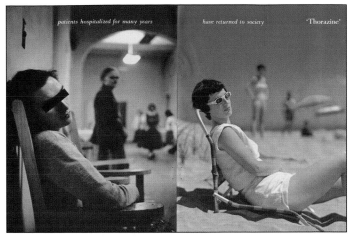

In an advertisement placed in medical journals, a woman once hospitalized for schizophrenia lolls on the beach after a few doses of the miracle drug Thorazine. In 1952 a French physician had discovered that the drug chlorpromazine had a remarkably positive effect on patients suffering from this psychological disorder. It was first marketed in the United States by Smith, Kline & French, as an anti-vomiting drug. When its effects on mental illness were discovered, the company renamed it. In spite of potentially dangerous side effects, by 1964 more than 50 million people worldwide had taken it, and the company's profits had tripled.

Hosted by Jack Bailey (*right*), television's *Queen for a Day* was a maudlin weep-fest in which audiences voted for the contestant with the most compelling sob story. Adapted from radio, the show was a huge hit among housewives, many of whom were pleased to learn that there was someone else in the world worse off than themselves. Upon winning (based on an "Applause-o-meter"), the newly chosen queen became suitably garbed in ermine and tiara, while awarded all manner of appliances and other gifts. Though those with piteous hardship stories made entertaining (if exploited) contestants, rarely was anyone with a truly woeful life chosen to compete.

"How I remember yearning for the moment when both my children would be in school for at least a few hours. All of us—I mean the women—took Dexedrine, and later Dexamil."

—JILL MORRIS, A YOUNG MOTHER WHO LIVED IN AN AFFLUENT LONG ISLAND SUBURB DURING THE 1950S

Tranquilizers

IN MAY 1956, Dr. Winfred Overholser of St. Elizabeth's Hospital in Washington, D.C., lauded the benefits of tranquilizers to *Newsweek* magazine. He contended that the sedative drugs made the patient more responsive to treatment and more interested in learning and doing things. He added that tranquilizers were also "very helpful in general practice."

Many doctors and pharmacologists shared Overholser's views, as the use of such tranquilizers as Thorazine and Meprobamate proliferated in the United States. Through the latter half of the 1950s, the drug industry flooded the market with such sedatives as Miltown, Equinal, Suavitil, and Atarax. The primary target of the drugs was the beleaguered housewife. Advertisements linked tranquilizer use with normal family life and overall happiness. Lax FDA approval standards contributed to soaring sales.

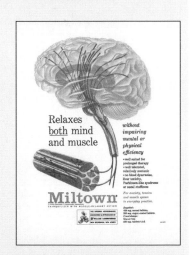

The drug industry glossed over the potential harmful effects of tranquilizers, which included addiction. Eventually, however, critics began voicing their concerns. Ronald H. Berg, the medical editor for *Look* magazine, charged that people "would be better off if they practiced self-discipline and faced up to troublesome situations; instead of running away and seeking solace in a handful of pills." By decade's end, both the House and Senate held hearings on tranquilizers, and Congress eventually passed legislation expanding the FDA's regulatory powers.

1956

April: Dr. G. D. Searle holds clinical trials of his birth control pill on women in Puerto Rico and Haiti.

April 2: In a vote of 6–3, the U.S. Supreme Court decides that individual states may not penalize anarchists who seek the overthrow of the federal government.

April 9: In *Slochower v. Board of Education of New York,* the U.S. Supreme Court rules 5–4 that New York Board of Education leaders acted improperly when they fired Professor Harry Slochower of Brooklyn College for invoking his Fifth Amendment rights before the Senate Subcommittee on Internal Security.

April 10: The de-Stalinization of Eastern Europe reaches Poland, where politician Wladyslaw Gomulka, imprisoned since 1951 for being a Polish nationalist, is freed.

April 11: While performing before a segregated, all-white audience, singer Nat "King" Cole is attacked by white concertgoers in Birmingham, Alabama.

April 14: The massive nuclear-powered aircraft carrier USS *Saratoga,* more than 1,000 feet long and capable of carrying 100 jets, enters service.

April 19: Hollywood star Grace Kelly weds Monaco's Prince Rainier II in front of more than 1,200 guests and a worldwide television audience. • In an effort to diminish the effectiveness of the NAACP, the South Carolina state legislature bans state employees from affiliating with civil rights organizations.

April 21: Leonard Ross, a 10-year-old from California, wins $100,000 on the game show *The Big Surprise.* • Elvis Presley's first major hit, "Heartbreak Hotel," reaches No. 1 on *Billboard*'s pop singles chart. It will remain there for eight weeks. • Egypt, Yemen, and Saudi Arabia sign a mutual defense agreement in Jidda, Saudi Arabia.

Prince Rainier of Monaco and actress Grace Kelly of Philadelphia exchange vows in their fairy-tale wedding on April 19, 1956. The Prince had ruled his small country of 30,000 people since 1946. Grace, the daughter of construction baron Jack Kelly, had won an Oscar in 1954 for best actress. She met the Prince while attending the Cannes Film Festival in 1955. Their whirlwind romance culminated in a three-hour televised wedding watched by some 20 million people. The Prince needed children, since without an heir, his kingdom would revert to France; Grace submitted to prenuptial tests to prove her fertility. She bore the first of their three children nine months and four days after their wedding.

Bearing the sobriquet "the hardest working man in show business," funk pioneer James Brown lived up to his billing, playing in excess of 300 dates a year on the road to stardom. Born into poverty, Brown's steely determination to succeed drove him forward, despite a four-year stint behind bars for theft. While in stir, he met Bobby Byrd, a pianist-singer who with Brown would form the core of the Famous Flames. Following success on the "chitlin' circuit," the dynamic R&B outfit recorded their first hit, "Please Please Please," in 1956. Brown's onstage pyrotechnics excited audiences and contributed to his enduring popularity.

Expectations were high when RCA brought their newest aspiring star into the studio in January 1956, just weeks after his signing. Joining Elvis Presley and his sidemen at the session were country legends Floyd Cramer and Chet Atkins, pressed into service to work on a tune inspired by a newspaper report of a suicide. Despite RCA's mortification with the result (even Presley's former producer, Sam Phillips, declared the recording "a morbid mess"), "Heartbreak Hotel" rocketed to the top of the charts in April and remained there an astonishing eight weeks. Within three months, Presley's first No. 1 became his first million-seller.

Elvis Presley

AS THE MUSICAL and social force known as rock 'n' roll entered public awareness, alarmists tying the phenomenon to juvenile delinquency had little to fear from its most successful practitioners. Singer Bill Haley was an aging, portly professional—hardly a threat to the nation's morals. Black artists could never get anywhere near a mainstream audience (at least without severely compromising their acts). None of the more salacious qualities attributed to the genre directly reached America's youth—that is, until a white, 21-year-old former truck driver from Memphis burst upon the national scene in January 1956.

Elvis Presley first found his professional footing at Sam Phillips's Memphis Recording Service. Elvis's run-through of a rural blues tune entitled "That's All Right," intended as a between-take send-up, was captured on tape, resulting in a stunning Sun Records debut in July 1954. Presley spent the following year and a half honing his act and cranking out a series of seminal rock 'n' roll releases, operating mostly through established country channels. But manager Colonel Tom Parker's gift for ballyhoo, coupled with the singer's undeniably high-voltage (and sexually charged) performances, catapulted

Elvis into the big-time via national exposure on television.

What followed is etched in rock 'n' roll legend: the record-breaking RCA contract, guest shots on Ed Sullivan's variety program (from the waist up in his final appearance), his movies, a stint in the Army, his Graceland estate. Presley's self-effacing southern charm helped disarm many of his critics. But it was his intuitive blending of country, crooner, and blues influences that he is rightly lauded for.

During the first several years of his career, Presley infused everything he touched with energy and excitement. His effortless string of million-sellers defined the decade—"Heartbreak Hotel," "Don't Be Cruel," "Hound Dog," "Love Me Tender," and "Jailhouse Rock" among them.

Eddie Constantine was an anomaly: an L.A.-born screen actor who made it big in Europe without ever achieving name recognition in the United States. Physical, glowering, and appealingly unhandsome, à la Bogart, he catapulted to popularity in 1953 when he played ferocious FBI agent Lemmy Caution in the French thriller *Les femmes s'en balancent* (*Dames Don't Care*). Constantine starred in more than 100 films during a 40-year career in France and Germany. He appeared as Lemmy Caution 13 times, most famously in Jean-Luc Godard's 1965 head trip, *Alphaville*. This Spanish poster is from a 1956 Caution thriller, *Agente Federal en Roma,* also known as *Vous pigez.*

April 23: In *South Carolina Electric and Gas Company v. Flemming*, the U.S. Supreme Court rules that segregation on public transportation is unconstitutional.

April 25: Reigning heavyweight champion Rocky Marciano hangs up his gloves with a record of 49-0. He is the first heavyweight champ to retire undefeated.

April 28: The French High Command for Indochina is dissolved with the departure of the last French soldier.

May: The Folsom Dam on the lower American River near Sacramento, California, is completed.

May 1: Secretary of Defense Charles Wilson asserts that the Soviets are ahead of the United States in the production of long-range bombers capable of delivering hydrogen bombs. • Minamata disease, a neurological disorder resulting from acute mercury poisoning, is first recognized in Japan.

May 9: Secretary of State John Foster Dulles announces that the United States, by denying arms shipments to Israel, has taken steps to avoid another U.S.-Soviet proxy war.

May 21: In the Bikini Atoll, the U.S. tests an A-bomb airburst over Namu Island.

May 26: The aircraft carrier USS *Bennington* burns off the coast of Rhode Island, killing 103 sailors.

May 27: In Tallahassee, Florida, black college students Wilhelmina Jakes and Carrie Patterson are arrested for refusing to sit at the back of a bus. The incident sparks a citywide bus boycott by black citizens, which will continue until December 1956.

June 1: Soviet Foreign Minister Vyacheslav Molotov resigns. • Alabama outlaws the NAACP throughout the state.

Although audiotape was introduced in 1948, applying the concept to visual media proved difficult, as quality reproduction required the tape to rotate at a prohibitively high speed. But in April 1956, Ampex unveiled the world's first fully operational videotaping system, the VR-1000 (*pictured*). Developed by a team that included noise reduction pioneer Ray Dolby, the system cannily employed a high-speed rotating head, keeping tape usage to an eminently manageable 15 ips (inches per second) while making precise editing possible. The invention revolutionized the industry, with CBS introducing the new technology on Douglas Edwards's evening news broadcast that November.

Youngsters down doses of the Sabin oral polio vaccine. Created by a Cincinnati doctor, Albert Sabin, in 1956, the vaccine was first tested by the World Health Organization in 1957, then administered to 80 million people outside America. The U.S. Public Health Service took four years to decide that it was as good as the Salk vaccine. It was actually superior, because it did not have to be injected and gave both bodily and intestinal immunity. At the beginning of the 21st century, polio is virtually nonexistent in the United States and rare in the rest of the world.

Poet Lawrence Ferlinghetti almost singlehandedly brought Beats to the attention of the literary world, both as publisher and principled advocate while on trial. In 1953 Ferlinghetti opened the City Lights Bookstore in San Francisco, a gathering place for poets and writers as well as fans of the Beat scene. His creation of a City Lights publishing imprint, with its Pocket Poets series, gave writers who had been rejected by mainstream publishers a place to be heard. Ferlinghetti's distribution of Allen Ginsberg's *Howl* resulted in obscenity charges in 1957, which he beat during a highly publicized trial. The resulting attention immeasurably raised the profile of Beat writers.

Director John Ford and actor John Wayne collaborated on more than 20 pictures, most of them westerns. The 1956 film *The Searchers*, a troubling tale of one man's hatred-fueled mission of revenge, is widely regarded as the high-water mark of their partnership. Wayne plays Ethan Edwards, a Confederate veteran who arrives home after the war to find his family slaughtered by Comanches and his young niece kidnapped. Many years into his pursuit, he faces a moral quandary upon discovering that the girl has become one of them. With breathtaking location photography and fine performances throughout, the film continues to win critical acclaim.

Though the work of the writers known collectively as the Beats had generated a small but devoted following, the publication of Allen Ginsberg's angry poem, *Howl*, broadened the movement considerably. First drawing notice in San Francisco in 1955, *Howl* caused a firestorm of controversy when authorities declared the work "obscene" for its brutally frank depictions of homosexuality and drug use. Written in a free-verse style reminiscent of Walt Whitman, *Howl* proved a cultural milestone.

THE POCKET POETS SERIES

HOWL
AND OTHER POEMS
ALLEN GINSBERG

Introduction by
William Carlos Williams

NUMBER FOUR

Well known for his Prairie-style home designs, Frank Lloyd Wright in 1956 saw the completion of his only skyscraper, Price Tower in Bartlesville, Oklahoma. Typical of Wright's work, Price Tower was marked by a closeness to nature. In fact, the design resembled a tree, with branchlike cantilevered floor slabs protruding from a concrete-reinforced steel "trunk." The resulting 221-foot structure had 17 stories, split between apartments and office space, sitting atop a two-story base.

"Police Affidavits!" That's the tip-in on the May 1956 cover of *Fate* magazine, which tickled the curious with allegedly true stories of the strange and paranormal. Founded in 1948 by science fiction magazine editor Raymond Palmer, *Fate* remained at the top of its esoteric field for more than five decades. The Texas saucer story in this issue was joined by tales of ghosts, religious miracles, an Antarctic threat to the earth's rotation, and even a handy primer on palm reading.

Science fiction and fantasy illustrator Richard Powers was closely linked to Ballantine Books in the 1950s and '60s, making him a key figure in the growth of paperback publishing. Surrealist and dreamlike, with an inclination to unearthly colors and disturbingly organic shapes, Powers's cover art gave Ballantine a visual identity, and helped fuel the public's growing appetite for "fantastic" literature. This 1956 cover painting for *Reach for Tomorrow,* a story collection by Arthur C. Clarke, was printed lengthwise to best showcase Powers's conception of an utterly alien landscape.

Edward D. Wood, Jr.'s delirious *Plan 9 from Outer Space* posits that extraterrestrials have arrived to create an army of conquerors comprised of the resurrected dead; actors Vampira and Tor Johnson (*pictured*) are among the none-too-alert foot soldiers. When top-billed Bela Lugosi died after Wood shot only about a minute of silent footage, the writer-director pressed on, casting his own chiropractor as Bela's "double." Although a bad movie, *Plan 9* is lively and entertaining—and a small monument to ingenuity, too, for Wood undertook principal photography with only $800 in front money. The picture was completed in 1956 but did not find a distributor until three years later.

This 1956 collage by Richard Hamilton, entitled "Just What Is It That Makes Today's Homes So Different, So Appealing?" is frequently cited as the very first example of Pop Art. By inserting familiar objects into an incongruous setting, the 34-year-old Brit offered a witty commentary on narcissism and consumer culture. In the 1960s, Hamilton became friends with Paul McCartney and produced the collage for the inside of the Beatles' "White Album."

Three black women in Montgomery, Alabama, alight from a station wagon owned by the Bell Street Baptist Church on May 31, 1956. Support from the local black community and donations from around the world allowed the Montgomery Improvement Association to purchase and operate a fleet of 15 new station wagons. Black-owned cabs also were used. In addition, more than a few whites provided transportation for their black maids to and from their homes. Some whites did so out of necessity, since their help could not get there otherwise. Others helped out because they empathized with the cause.

Whites in Montgomery, Alabama, threaten a black man during the 1955–56 bus boycott. Some of the city's white citizens did what they could to end this "crisis." Police arrested black car-pool drivers for the slightest moving violations, and pressured taxi drivers who gave rides to African-Americans. Some whites took more severe action, bombing Martin Luther King's house on January 30, 1956, and E. D. Nixon's home two days later. Nevertheless, Montgomery's black citizens would not be intimidated. The boycott continued.

"Tsk Tsk—Somebody Should Do Something About That"

In the opinion of *Washington Post* cartoonist Herblock, President Eisenhower was unassertive on civil rights issues. Historian Stephen J. Whitfield concurred, stating that Eisenhower did not "see the necessity for the enforcement or passage of laws designed to protect the civil rights of blacks in the South or elsewhere. . . . Eisenhower believed that the racial question in the United States was emotional rather than rational, that 'arbitrary laws' could not be strong enough to solve it." To his credit, Ike did send the National Guard to Little Rock, Arkansas, in 1957 to escort nine black students to school amid hostile white resistance.

1956

June 2: First Secretary Khrushchev's government announces that it will decentralize the Justice Ministry.

June 5: In response to Alabama's ban on the NAACP, Reverend Fred Shuttlesworth helps found the Alabama Christian Movement for Human Rights in Birmingham. *See* December 25–26, 1956.

June 7: The Soviets cut their standing army by 1.2 million troops, and ask the United States to match that number.

June 8: Air Force Sergeant Richard B. Fitzgibbon, Jr., becomes the first American serviceman to die in Vietnam. (His son, Richard B. Fitzgibbon III, also will die in Vietnam, in 1965.)

June 9: President Eisenhower goes under the knife at Walter Reed Army Hospital to correct an intestinal obstruction.

June 13: After a 72-year occupation, the last British troops leave the Suez Canal. The Egyptian government takes over full control of the canal. *See* July 26, 1956.

June 21: Playwright Arthur Miller appears before the House Un-American Activities Committee. He refuses to testify and is subsequently denied his passport. • According to the East German government, some 19,000 political prisoners have been released in the past seven days.

June 28–30: Communist troops crush a workers' uprising in Poznan, Poland. *See* October 24, 1956.

June 29: The Federal-Aid Highway Act, which allocates $33.5 billion for the interstate highway system, is signed into law by President Eisenhower. • Marilyn Monroe marries playwright Arthur Miller, in a civil ceremony. They will exchange vows in a Jewish ceremony two days later. Miller is Monroe's third husband.

Cars that jam U.S. Route 1 in Maryland suggest a justification of the passage of the landmark Federal-Aid Highway Act of 1956. The act massively increased funding for an interstate highway system, 90 percent of which would be financed by the federal government (and the rest by the states). The new highways, which would be free of stoplights and stop signs, would relieve much of the traffic congestion on such roads as Highway 1 and help assure more orderly evacuation of cities in case of nuclear attack. Although the system made travel easier and faster, it also caused numerous small businesses along the old routes to close, and made travel less scenic.

During a period of personal self-enrichment that saw her enroll in Lee Strasberg's Actors Studio, actress Marilyn Monroe (*right*) made the acquaintance of playwright Arthur Miller (*left*). The latter had been a colleague of admitted ex-Communist Party member Elia Kazan, and as the relationship between Miller and Monroe grew serious, members of HUAC recognized the publicity value Miller now offered. Summoned before the committee, he balked at naming names, incurring contempt-of-Congress charges. Years later, Miller revealed that his interrogator had offered to drop the charges in exchange for allowing the committee chair to be photographed with Monroe. Miller declined. The couple was married from 1956 to 1961.

> "About the capitalist states. . . . If you don't like us, don't accept our invitations, and don't invite us to come to see you. Whether you like it or not, history is on our side. We will bury you."

—NIKITA KHRUSHCHEV, SPEAKING TO WESTERN DIPLOMATS AT A MOSCOW RECEPTION, NOVEMBER 18, 1956

Comrade Khrushchev

MEMBERS ATTENDING THE 20th Communist Party Congress in February 1956 couldn't have been more shaken if a bomb had exploded in their midst. During a closed-door session, Soviet officials were subjected to a stinging indictment of former leader Joseph Stalin, delivered in passionate, angry tones by his successor as party secretary, 61-year-old Nikita Khrushchev.

Stalin, Khrushchev asserted, had "often chose[n] the path of repression and annihilation, not only against actual enemies, but also against individuals who had not committed any crimes against . . . the Soviet government." Such "treasonous" talk would have been unimaginable not much earlier. But in dramatic fashion, Khrushchev put his comrades on notice that a new era had begun, bent on dismantling the "cult of personality" that impeded true Leninism.

Khrushchev had been the dark horse among those jockeying for power after Stalin's death on March 5, 1953. Such familiar figures as Kaganovich, Malenkov, and Molotov were widely regarded as possible successors. But through cunning and circumstance, *Politburo* member Khrushchev elbowed his way past one rival after another, achieving complete power by 1958. He quickly established his reputation as a reformer by releasing millions of Stalin's political prisoners. However, Khrushchev's unpredictability and impulsive behavior were often viewed as signs of instability, even within the party.

Though he alternately charmed and repelled many in the West with his blend of colorful bluster and peasant crudity, Khrushchev could display heavy-handedness worthy of his predecessor when pressed, as he did when putting down the Hungarian revolt of 1956. Still, while his oft-quoted warning to the United States that "we will bury you" was cited as proof of Soviet designs for world domination, he insisted that he had meant it in an economic sense within peaceful coexistence. When pressed about the "threat," the premier responded, "My life would be too short to bury every one of you if this were to occur to me."

Soviet tanks scatter striking workers in Poznan, Poland, in June 1956. A number of industrial workers protested in order to gain what one observer called "bread and freedom from Soviet rule." The Soviets intervened when strikers took their protest to the streets. Some 70 Poles were killed in what became a precursor of the large Hungarian rebellion in October 1956—as well as a number of similar actions in Poland over the next three decades.

1956

June 30: Some 650,000 United Steel workers go on strike. The work stoppage will affect the national economy and force rail lines to lay off 30,000 employees. The strike will be settled when labor and management sign a three-year, no-strike contract.
• Lenin's Testament, which called for the removal of Joseph Stalin from his post as general secretary of the Communist Party, is made public in the Soviet Union.

July: The U.S. cancels free Vietnamese elections when South Vietnamese Premier Ngo Dinh Diem's refusal to participate virtually assures Ho Chi Minh's victory.

July 1: A TWA Super Constellation and a United Airlines DC-7 collide over the Grand Canyon in Arizona, killing 128 people. • The Soviets open the world's first nuclear power station, at Obinsk.

July 3: President Eisenhower agrees to reimburse the Vatican for nearly $1 million in damages resulting from the accidental World War II bombing of the summer home of Pope Pius XII.

July 9: Congress passes the Water Pollution Control Act, a forerunner to the Clean Water Act. • Dick Clark begins his long stint as host of *American Bandstand*.

July 18: President Eisenhower signs a bill that calls for the death penalty for those who sell heroin to minors.

July 23: Bell Labs' X-2 rocket plane hits 1,895 mph, a world aircraft speed record.

July 26: Egyptian President Gamal Abdel Nasser nationalizes the Suez Canal. *See* August 30, 1956. • The Italian ocean liner *Andrea Doria* sinks in 225 feet of water one day after colliding with the *Stockholm* off the coast of Nantucket, Massachusetts. Fifty-two people die, most from the initial impact.

Young women in short shorts pass time on a street corner in Salem, Illinois, in July 1956. Although the revealing style did not become widespread until the 1960s, young urban woman did experiment in the 1950s. In 1958 the rock 'n' roll song "Short Shorts" by the Royal Teens rose to No. 3 on the *Billboard* chart, suggesting that many people were interested in the idea, if not fully committed to the reality, of the provocative fashion statement.

A tanker steams through the Suez Canal. Built in the late 19th century, the canal linked the Mediterranean and Red seas through Egypt, providing a much faster trade route from Europe to the East. The canal was capable of supporting up to 14 percent of total world trade. Because it was vital to British economic interests and security, the canal was controlled by Great Britain from 1882 to 1954. When Egyptian President Gamal Abdel Nasser nationalized it in 1956, British Prime Minister Anthony Eden led a coalition that invaded Egypt to ensure that the canal remained open.

The Italian passenger liner *Andrea Doria* founders, mortally stricken, off the coast of Nantucket Island, Massachusetts, in July 1956 after colliding in heavy fog with the Swedish ship *Stockholm*. Fifty-two people lost their lives. *Andrea Doria* had been a floating work of art, decorated with paintings and sculptures that cost more than $1 million. On her 51st trip across the Atlantic, a series of ill-conceived maneuvers put her in the path of the *Stockholm,* resulting in a fatal gash. Her sinking contributed to the demise of regular transatlantic luxury liner service.

Noted Columbia University sociologist C. Wright Mills published his influential study, *The Power Elite,* in 1956. Mills argued that in spite of the alleged power of public opinion and democratic institutions, America had come to be dominated by a small group of influential, loosely connected elites from government, the corporate world, the military, the media, and higher education—often referred to as "the establishment."

Although representatives from these groups were not formally organized, they often knew each other, possessed shared interests, and tended to build consensuses, thus bypassing regular governmental channels in shaping public opinion. Mills's work profoundly influenced the anti-establishment New Left in the 1960s.

Cast as rivals during the Democratic primary season, former presidential candidate Adlai Stevenson (*left*) and Tennessee Senator Estes Kefauver (*right*) eventually comprised the 1956 Democratic ticket. It was a surprising campaign, with Stevenson chosen again as presidential candidate despite former President Harry Truman's last-minute support for New York Governor Averell Harriman. Kefauver, whose profile had been elevated by his televised Senate hearings on organized crime in 1951, was picked by the convention for the veep slot against strong competition from young Massachusetts Senator John Kennedy. Stevenson called for a "New America," advocating many of the civil rights and antipoverty programs eventually enacted by presidents Kennedy and Johnson.

A youngster feeds a bull on his family's dairy farm in the mid-1950s. The chances were high that the boy would not follow in his parents' footsteps and take over the operation. The decade witnessed a continuation of a major national trend, as the number of people owning and working on farms declined from about 18 percent of the total population in 1950 to less than 10 percent in 1960. Average farm size increased from under 200 acres to almost 300 during the decade.

1956

July 27: A U.S. B-47 bomber crashes into a weapons storage facility at the UK's Lakenheath Royal Air Force Base. Fortunately, the impact fails to ignite three nuclear bombs.

July 29: *Calypso,* oceanographer Jacques Cousteau's submersible research vessel, anchors at a record depth of 7,500 meters.

July 30: President Eisenhower signs a resolution passed by the 84th Congress making "In God We Trust" the official motto of the United States.

August: FBI Director J. Edgar Hoover establishes COINTELPRO, the FBI's anti-Communist counter-intelligence program.

August 7: The first drive-up banking window is opened at the Bridgeport, Connecticut, branch of the Mechanics and Farmers Savings Bank.

August 8: *Boxing from St. Nicholas Arena* is the final telecast of the DuMont Network.

August 11: Jackson Pollock, abstract impressionist known for his colorful, chaotic canvases, dies in a car accident while driving drunk at age 44.

August 16: Democrats holding their national convention in Chicago nominate Adlai Stevenson as their presidential candidate. Stevenson wins the nomination on the first ballot, with 905 votes.

August 17: Senator Estes Kefauver narrowly wins the Democratic vice presidential nomination over Senator John F. Kennedy.

August 22: Delegates at the Republican National Convention in San Francisco nominate President Eisenhower and Vice President Richard Nixon as their candidates for a second term in the White House.

August 25: The South African government orders 100,000-plus nonwhites to leave their Johannesburg homes.

This shocking headline came as part of a national drill held annually from 1954 through 1961. Operation Alert sought to put emergency workers through their paces as the country set aside a day to recognize the possibility of nuclear annihilation. This page was distributed to Civil Defense workers, lending an air of reality to the run-through. Though the impulse to "do something" was natural, many people—including the President—wondered about the national drill's effectiveness. In a meeting with advisers held just after the 1956 practice, Eisenhower pointed out that in a real situation, people would be "absolutely nuts."

Drive-in moviegoers sit through Cecil B. DeMille's 219-minute biblical epic, *The Ten Commandments.* A remake of his 1923 silent original, the film was producer-director DeMille's final blockbuster. The all-star cast included Charlton Heston as Moses (seen here parting the Red Sea), whose life is traced from babyhood to the Promised Land. Treated to the finest special effects of the day, audiences found the melodramatic spectacle enthralling, making *The Ten Commandments* the second-highest grossing Hollywood movie to that time.

This issue of *Vogue* offers a sampling of fall couture for well-heeled *fashionistas.* Founded in 1892, *Vogue* in the 1950s focused primarily on the fashions and the social interactions of the privileged and chic. Yet the magazine had a profound impact on fashion in general. According to *The Wall Street Journal,* from the 1950s to the 1980s, Diana Vreeland at *Vogue* and John Fairchild at *Women's Wear Daily* became "powerful arbiters of chic" during a time when "fashion trickled down slowly from elite European haute couture to the masses."

A mother and her son happily down a meal at Howard Johnson's as its parking lot fills with hungry customers. "Ho Jo's," as it was affectionately called, was a major, iconic business in the 1950s, with its welcoming colonial architecture and orange roofs. Founded in the 1920s, the chain blossomed after World War II and added a stable of motels to its restaurants beginning in 1954. Perceived as family-friendly and clean, Ho Jo's offered 28 flavors of ice cream in addition to standard restaurant fare.

Willie, Mickey, and "The Duke"

IN THE 1950s, the term "America's Game" was losing its impact. Baseball, it seemed, had become the domain of New York City. During the decade, the New York Yankees, New York Giants, and Brooklyn Dodgers made a combined 15 trips to the World Series, winning eight world championships. From spring to fall every year, pennant fever plagued New York.

Coincidentally, the greatest player on each team happened to be a center fielder: Willie Mays of the Giants, Mickey Mantle of the Yankees, and Duke Snider of the Dodgers. From Brooklyn to the Bronx, debates raged about which star was better.

Mays, the "Say Hey Kid," played with boyish exuberance. He'd crack a liner into the alley and fly out from under his cap as he slid in for a triple. One of history's greatest defensive outfielders (known for his "basket" catches), Willie also smashed 660 home runs to set a National League record. Mantle, according to Yankees manager Casey Stengel, had "more speed than any slugger and more slug than any speedster." The charismatic Oklahoman belted 536 home runs, including 52 in 1956. One of his moon shots traveled 565 feet. Snider, a graceful outfielder with a classic swing, took advantage of Brooklyn's tiny Ebbets Field. From 1950 to '53, he reached 40 homers every year, and his 336 longballs during the 1950s were more than any other major-league player.

In 1981 Terry Cashman wrote the catchy song "Talkin' Baseball (Willie, Mickey & 'The Duke')." The tune peaked at No. 28 on the adult contemporary chart—and No. 1 in the hearts of nostalgic New Yorkers.

1956

August 30: Egyptian President Gamal Abdel Nasser officially claims Egyptian sovereignty over the Suez Canal. *See* October 29, 1956.

August 30–31: The enrollment of black high school students in Mansfield, Texas, triggers rioting. Governor Allan Shivers calls in the Texas Rangers to uphold segregation, preventing integration.

September: Violence erupts in Clinton, Tennessee, over the admission of 12 black high school students. *See* October 5, 1958.

September 6: In Sturgis, Kentucky, 500 white citizens try to block the admission of eight black students to the local high school. More than 200 National Guardsmen contain the crowd.

September 9: Elvis Presley shocks America with his first appearance on the *The Ed Sullivan Show.* Presley thrusts and gyrates through "Hound Dog" and the romantic "Love Me Tender."

September 13: IBM unveils a new computer, the Model 305, which can store up to 20 megabytes of data.

September 14: IBM President Thomas J. Watson, Jr., announces the creation of the RAMAC, the first magnetic disk memory drive.

September 17: Mildred "Babe" Didrikson Zaharias, arguably the best female athlete in history, dies of cancer at age 42.

Fall: The first ultrasonic wireless TV remote control, the Zenith Space Command, goes into production.
• CBS broadcasts National Football League games for the first season of what will become a long-running partnership.

September 22: Nicaraguan dictator Anastasio Somoza is shot by assassin Rigoberto Lopez Perez. Somoza will die of his wounds on September 29.

In 1955 film director Robert Aldrich offered a bleak vision of L.A. crime and atom-age politics in *Kiss Me Deadly.* Later in the year, he released *The Big Knife,* an acidic portrait of the movie business. Aldrich's 1956 picture, *Attack!,* was a World War II drama of such cynical power that the U.S. Army refused to cooperate in its filming. Jack Palance (*pictured*) plays a lieutenant whose men are foolishly sacrificed by a disinterested lieutenant colonel (Lee Marvin) and a cowardly, politically connected captain (Eddie Albert). In a shockingly violent climax that explodes all notions of authority and command, the badly injured Palance takes justice into his own hands.

Cleo Craig (*standing, center*), chairman of the American Telephone & Telegraph Company, watches benignly as reporters in New York talk to London over the first transatlantic telephone cable. Made operational on September 25, 1956, the cables (one in each direction) were laid primarily by one ship, the USS *Monarch,* which was built for that purpose. The invention of coaxial cables with polyethylene insulation solved the main technical problems associated with the effort. This major breakthrough created much smoother and more rapid communication between the U.S. and ultimately all of Europe.

Apartheid in South Africa

DURING THE 1950s, as the United States inched toward racial integration, the all-white government of South Africa embarked on a rigorous campaign to thoroughly segregate blacks and whites. Increased industrial development during World War II had caused an influx of black residents into such large cities as Johannesburg and Cape Town, alarming white government officials. "The result [of social integration] would be a hybrid race," lamented South African Prime Minister Johannes Strijdom. "Our policy of segregation, or separate development, which we call 'apartheid,' is the means to prevent such a tragedy."

Accordingly, the government outlawed interracial marriage, restricted freedom of speech, set up separate schools for blacks and whites, and required blacks to apply for passes if they wanted to venture outside of black neighborhoods or reserves. In 1954 the ruling National Party passed the Natives Resettlement Act, which mandated the removal of nonwhites from certain cities. On August 25, 1956, the government ordered the expulsion of more than 100,000 blacks from Johannesburg.

Johannesburg, South Africa

Black activists who protested resettlement and apartheid were stifled by police oppression. In December 1956, Nelson Mandela and 156 others who criticized the government were arrested and detained on charges of treason. The repressive and highly controversial system of apartheid would continue in South Africa for another 38 years.

Businessman Frank McNamara created Diners' Club, the first credit card company, in 1950. The idea took off, with international franchises by 1952. In 1955 Western Airlines became the first airline to accept the card. In the late 1950s and 1960s, the credit card industry exploded due to the introduction of American Express cards and BankAmericard. The easy credit provided by these cards changed the spending habits of millions and helped fuel the economic boom of the 1960s.

Writer Nelson Algren spent his formative years on Chicago's impoverished south side. His familiarity with society's unnoticed and unloved was put to good use with his first novel, *Somebody in Boots*. It was not a success. After his career took off with *The Man with the Golden Arm* (1949), his publisher approached him about reissuing the earlier work. Algren agreed, if allowed to make a few changes. The result was an entirely new work, the darkly humorous *A Walk on the Wild Side*. His empathetic depiction of the peculiar wisdom found among prostitutes and derelicts was vintage Algren.

1956

September 27: USAF test pilot Mel Apt is killed when his Bell X-2 plane—the fastest, highest-flying plane in the U.S. Air Force fleet—crashes.

October: The Daughters of Bilitis launch *The Ladder,* the first regularly published national periodical for lesbians.

October 6: Dr. Albert Sabin creates an oral polio vaccine. Easier than the Salk inoculation to distribute and administer, the oral vaccine will be licensed for use in the U.S. in 1961.

October 7: Southdale Center, the first enclosed mall in the United States, opens in Edina, Minnesota.

October 8: New York Yankee Don Larsen pitches the first no-hitter in a World Series, defeating the Brooklyn Dodgers 2–0 in Game 5. Larsen actually pitches a perfect game, meaning he retires all 27 batters he faces.

October 10: The Yankees defeat Brooklyn in Game 7 of the World Series to take the title.

October 15: Eisenhower appoints William J. Brennan, Jr., to the U.S. Supreme Court. Justice Brennan will keep his seat until 1990.

October 17: The first meeting of La Leche League, an advocacy group for breast-feeding mothers, is held at the home of Mary White.

October 21: President Eisenhower responds to Soviet Premier Bulganin's calls for an end to atomic weapons tests by denouncing the overture as an attempt to interfere with U.S. policy.

October 22: The French capture the leaders of the Algerian independence movement, intercepting their plane as it heads for Tunisia.

October 23: Sparked by anti-Communist student protests in Budapest, Hungarian citizens rebel against the occupying Soviets. *See* November 1, 1956.

With the 1956 World Series tied at two games apiece, the New York Yankees needed some 1-2-3 innings from Don Larsen in the pivotal Game 5 against the Brooklyn Dodgers. He responded with nine of them, throwing the only perfect game—and, in fact, the only no-hitter—in postseason history. After Larsen struck out Dale Mitchell to end the game, catcher Yogi Berra leapt into his pitcher's arms. Afterward, a reporter asked Larsen, "Is that the best game you ever pitched?" The Yankees won the World Series in seven games.

Customers enjoy America's first enclosed shopping mall, the Southdale Regional Shopping Center near Minneapolis. Opened in the fall of 1956, in part to provide warmth for shoppers during long, cold Minnesota winters, the center's temperature was set at a constant 72 degrees. Originally, the mall contained dozens of specialty stores and was anchored by Dayton's and Donaldson's department stores. Covering some 95 acres, it was designed by noted architect Victor Gruen and became the prototype for an explosion of malls in the decades to follow.

The world's first full-scale nuclear power station (*pictured*) went on line in Windscale, England, in 1956. The plant was a realization of an international push for the peaceful use of nuclear energy. The first large-scale American nuclear power station opened in Shippingport, Pennsylvania, in 1957 and produced much of the electricity in the Pittsburgh area. While nuclear power was hailed in the 1950s and '60s as an inexpensive and efficient solution to the growing demand for power in the modern world, the 1970s and '80s saw increasing ambivalence about these plans in the wake of power plant accidents in the U.S. and the USSR.

Legendary University of Oklahoma football coach Bud Wilkinson instructs one of his players during the 1956 college season. Wilkinson, who coached the Sooners from 1947 to 1963, won 47 straight games from 1953 to 1957, an NCAA record that still stands. His Oklahoma teams won three Associated Press national championships (1950, 1955, 1956), six bowl games, and 14 league titles. Wilkinson was noted for establishing high academic standards for his players as well as conducting rigorous practices. In 1961 he became the first director of the President's Council on Physical Fitness.

Greek-American soprano Maria Callas (seen here in Bellini's *Norma*) made her triumphant New York Metropolitan Opera debut on October 28, 1956. The tempestuous diva was known as much for her stormy private life as for her riveting performances. Though Callas commanded a three-octave range, purists objected to her "flawed" voice. What they willfully overlooked was her uncanny ability to inhabit her roles, bringing an emotional truth to her singing. The charismatic star held listeners spellbound with her unpredictable but artistically valid instincts, showcased particularly well in *Norma* (her signature role), *Tosca,* and *Lucia di Lammermoor.*

1956

October 24: Thousands of Polish students take to the streets of Warsaw, protesting Soviet dominance. *See* December 17, 1956. • Egypt, Syria, and Jordan establish a joint military command in response to the growing tension in the region. • Margaret Towner's ordination makes her the first female minister in the Presbyterian Church USA.

October 29: Israel attacks Egypt on the Sinai Peninsula, stopping shy of the Suez Canal and allowing allies Britain and France to step in and occupy the canal zone. *See* November 1956. • CBS's evening news is rebroadcast using a videotape feed, a first for network television. • Chet Huntley and David Brinkley take the helm of the flagship NBC nightly newscast, which is renamed *The Huntley-Brinkley Report.*

November: The Soviets threaten to attack London, Paris, and Israel for the continued incursions against Egypt by those allied nations. Fear of Cold War escalation leads the United States to pressure the three belligerents to broker a cease-fire. *See* November 5, 1956. • North Vietnamese Communists violently suppress peasant unrest over unfair land reforms. Some 6,000 people are killed or deported. • Dr. William C. Hueper of the National Cancer Institute tells a gathering of scientists that increased rates of lung cancer coincide with an increase in air pollution levels.

November 1: Hungarian Premier Imre Nagy announces that Hungary will withdraw from the Warsaw Pact. *See* November 4, 1956.

November 3: *The Wizard of Oz* appears on broadcast television for the first time, on CBS.

November 4: An overwhelming Soviet force enters Budapest and crushes the Hungarian rebellion.

America's mid-1950s preoccupation with tropical culture peaked in 1956 with the wild success of actor-singer Harry Belafonte's *Calypso* album. The word itself, as applied to both the record and the genre, became used to describe any music of Caribbean origin. Belafonte's song "Day-o" became a smash, while the album that spawned it became the first long-playing million-seller. Before the craze finally subsided, actor Robert Mitchum and poet Maya Angelou were among those who jumped on the bandwagon with their own calypso albums.

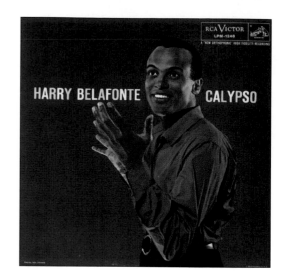

Chet Huntley (*left*) and David Brinkley (*right*) teamed up in October 1956 to host NBC's path-breaking evening news show, *The Huntley-Brinkley Report.* Their earlier coverage of the 1956 Republican Convention had grabbed the lion's share of viewers and convinced the network to replace the breezy newsreader, John Cameron Swayze, with them. Huntley and Brinkley's energy and contrasting styles, along with innovative cuts from New York to Washington, helped propel them to national celebrity.

An astoundingly prolific writer, Evan Hunter gained renown in the 1950s for his novels, including *The Blackboard Jungle* and *Strangers When We Meet,* both of which were made into successful films. But his most sustained fame came in the genre of "police procedurals" (cop novels) under the pseudonym Ed McBain. His 87th Precinct chronicles began with 1956's *Cop Hater.* Set in a fictitious stand-in for New York City ("Isola"), McBain's books seem authentic, filled with world-weary cops, lowlife criminals, and gritty situations. Continuity was maintained throughout four decades of the series, as characters developed and aged as they would in real life.

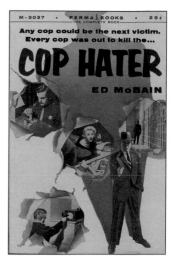

The Suez Crisis

IN 1954, TWO YEARS after the overthrow of King Farouk, Colonel Gamal Abdel Nasser rose to power in Egypt. Staunchly opposed to Western imperialism, Nasser initiated a program to industrialize and modernize Egypt. An integral part of his plan was the construction of the Aswan High Dam on the Nile River.

Funding for the dam originally came from the United States, Great Britain, and other Western nations. But once it was revealed that Egypt was receiving armaments from the Soviet Union, American and British aid ceased. In summer 1956, Nasser decided to nationalize the Suez Canal to keep the dam project afloat. The decision outraged Britain and France, who owned and operated the Canal Zone.

In late October 1956, those two countries, along with Israel, invaded Egypt. Within days, the canal was effectively under their control. The offensive, however, brought international condemnation, including harsh criticism from both the U.S. and USSR. While the Soviets threatened military intervention, President Dwight Eisenhower worked within the United Nations. The President issued a resolution calling for a cease-fire and the immediate withdrawal of British, French, and Israeli troops.

"In all the recent troubles in the Middle East, there have, indeed, been injustices suffered by all nations involved," Eisenhower maintained. "But I do not believe that another agent of injustice—war—is a remedy for these wrongs." Eisenhower's words stung Britain and France—traditional

Gamal Abdel Nasser (*in dark suit*)

American allies—who assumed that the U.S. would support or at least turn a blind eye to the invasion. But Ike was concerned about securing his reelection on November 6, and had campaigned under the banner of keeping the peace. Moreover, his administration feared that nonaction would push other Middle Eastern countries into the Soviet camp.

Shortly after Eisenhower's reproof, the invaders pulled out. The events dramatically displayed the decline of European imperialism and illuminated the new bipolar world order. Nasser went on to complete the Aswan Dam and become a champion of Arab nationalism.

British paratroopers, here securing Port Said at the northern terminus of the Suez Canal, were a major part of the invasion of Egypt in 1956. Great Britain, France, and Israel jointly attacked on October 31, 1956. The two European powers were concerned about the future of the canal, fearing that Egyptian President Nasser might impede their access. Israel, meanwhile, saw an opportunity to strike a blow against a major enemy of the Jewish state. The combined forces easily defeated the outmanned Egyptian military and captured the canal within a few days, although it was blocked by ships sunk by the Nasser regime.

The Hungarian Revolution

Hungarian rebel, age 15

ON OCTOBER 23, 1956, thousands of Hungarian students and workers marched to the Stalin monument in Budapest City Park. The crowd placed ropes around the statue's neck and tried unsuccessfully to pull it down. Then they went for its knees, melting them with blowtorches. The statue finally broke apart as the crowd chanted, "Russians go home! Russians go home!"

The Hungarian Revolution against Soviet rule had begun slowly with small protests throughout the summer of 1956. On October 23, students marched on the Budapest radio station, urging the operators to broadcast their 16-point manifesto, which included demands for free elections and withdrawal of Soviet troops. This uprising in Eastern Europe emerged in the context of changes within the Soviet Union after the death of Stalin in 1953. In the mid-1950s, with a more liberalized Soviet government under Khrushchev, more independent forms of socialism in Eastern Bloc countries seemed possible.

In response to the autumn uprising in Budapest, a Soviet armored division of 80 tanks and artillery rumbled into the city on October 24. A day later, pro-Soviet leader Erno Gero, who welcomed the Soviets, lost power to Imre Nagy, a reformer who was both pro-Moscow and pro-nationalist. Earlier in the decade, the popular leader had proposed a series of initiatives, including release of some political prisoners and a more liberal attitude toward private enterprise. During the uprising, he announced plans to create an independent Hungarian communism. For several days in late October, Hungarian citizens fought for this vision against the Soviet army in the streets of Budapest. On October 31, the Soviets withdrew troops and Nagy announced the triumph of the revolution.

In November, however, the Soviets began a brutal crackdown, sending 200,000 troops and 2,500 tanks to crush the resistance. Overall, an estimated 25,000 to 50,000 Hungarians, and 7,000 Soviet troops, died fighting. Revolutionaries executed some members of the AVH, the Hungarian secret police. Another pro-Soviet Hungarian party leader, Janos Kadar, had helped plan the second invasion, during which Nagy and others were driven from power and later executed. Soon after, more than 150,000 Hungarians fled to the West.

The Soviets portrayed the resistance as a resurgence of fascist nationalism. The Hungarian incident, despite its failure, was a clear precursor of the Czech Revolution of 1968.

Hungarians look with satisfaction at a toppled statue of deceased Soviet leader Joseph Stalin on October 24, 1956. During the previous night, demonstrators rebelling against Communist rule in their country had pulled down the statue, an act symbolizing their disgust for tyranny. Ultimately, the statue was dragged to another location, where it was smashed to bits by another crowd of angry demonstrators. Although the protesters were mainly students and workers, some dissident elements of the Hungarian army joined in.

"Hungary was Stalinism incarnate. Here in one small, tormented country was the picture, complete in every detail: the abandonment of humanism, the attachment of primary importance not to living, breathing, suffering, hoping human beings but to machines, targets, statistics, tractors, steel mills, plan fulfillment figures... and, of course, tanks."

—Author Peter Fryer, *Hungarian Tragedy*

Hungarian revolutionary forces fire at members of the Communist secret police on November 2, 1956. The next day, thousands of Soviet troops poured into Budapest to put down Hungary's attempt to carve out some autonomy within the Communist bloc. Soviet First Secretary Khrushchev, fearing that the revolution would lead to a total break with the USSR, ordered the troops in to protect what he saw as Soviet national security.

Soviet tanks maneuver in the streets of Budapest, Hungary, firing on beleaguered rebels who oppose strict Communist rule. The rebellion was doomed as soon as the massive Soviet response was triggered. Opponents of Soviet rule simply did not have the firepower to overcome tanks. Ironically, the U.S. government refused to intervene militarily even though the rhetoric of the Eisenhower Administration supported the concept of the liberation of the so-called captive nations—including Hungary—from Communist control. Eisenhower did, however, offer the moral support of the American people.

FIGHTING FOR HUNGARY

I WAS VERY, very much afraid. I can talk only about myself. Quite a few times I wanted to go home. I said, "What the heck I'm doing here? Maybe the next bullet is going to be mine." And I started to go; and when I saw the 14- and 15-year-old kids dead, I said, "I was in the service for two and a quarter years; I know how to handle a gun. And I'm going home and I'm going to leave these kids to die for our country?" The shame kept me there....

It wasn't the Soviet people or the Russian people we were against. We were against the system, the Communist system. A lot of Russian soldiers, they were sympathizing with us during the revolution.... In fact we had quite a few who died [fighting] on our side—Russian soldiers. They knew what we were fighting for, and we really didn't want anything else but a free and independent Hungary. We wanted Hungary to be for the Hungarians.

—Hungarian resistance leader Gergely Pongracz

Emotionally exhausted citizens of Budapest survey some of the damage inflicted by the Soviet military in Hungary in November 1956. The Russian juggernaut caused untold millions of dollars in property damage as well as thousands of deaths and injuries. One result of the debacle was a substantial migration of young Hungarians, who managed to sneak out of their beleaguered country. Many in this "Generation of '56" made their way to the U.S., where they remained fierce anti-Communists.

1956

November 5: French and British jets attack Egypt, dropping paratroopers just north of the Suez Canal. *See* November 6, 1956.

November 6: President Eisenhower wins a decisive victory in the federal elections, although his Republican Party loses 17 House seats and two Senate seats. • British, French, and Israeli troops halt their advance, as a cease-fire takes effect during the Suez crisis.

November 11: The earliest prototype of the American B-58, the first bomber to fly at supersonic speeds, is successfully tested.

November 13: The U.S. Supreme Court rules that segregation on intrastate buses is unconstitutional, invalidating Montgomery, Alabama's law. *See* December 20, 1956.

November 18: In a speech at a reception in Moscow, Soviet First Secretary Nikita Khrushchev issues his Cold War-defining threat to the West, saying "We will bury you."

November 22–December 8: The Summer Olympic Games open in Melbourne, Australia. Soviet athletic dominance continues, as they win 98 medals to America's 74. Several countries boycott the games, reflecting political unrest in Eastern Europe, the Middle East, and Asia. That unrest plays itself out in the pool, when the Soviet and Hungarian water polo teams engage in a bloody brawl.

November 26: Further development of the Jupiter IRBM is assigned to the U.S. Air Force when Secretary of Defense Charles Wilson rules that the Army will be unable to develop a Jupiter with a range exceeding 200 miles. • Popular big band leader Tommy Dorsey dies at age 51.

November 30: Floyd Patterson knocks out Archie Moore, becoming at age 21 the youngest heavyweight boxing champion.

Facing reelection in 1956, President Eisenhower enjoyed solid support from most Americans, even though detractors deplored his purported "laziness." Concerns over his health were less easily overlooked. His September 1955 heart attack had jolted the country, with many finding the prospect of Vice President Richard Nixon ascending to the presidency troubling. But Republicans mounted a vigorous campaign, designed to showcase their candidate's hearty recovery. Chief among issues in voters' minds were the Cold War and other foreign policy issues. When troubles arose in Hungary and at the Suez Canal on the eve of the election, the President's victory was assured. Here, the First Couples are shown celebrating their landslide victory.

The excitement of the annual model-year changeover was brought to a fever pitch by automakers in the 1950s. Many dealerships soaped their windows or covered them with newspaper just before new models arrived. Car buffs hoped for an early peek at the latest from Detroit, while others anticipated the opportunity to be the first on the block with a new Ford, Chevy, or Chrysler. All of this was the result of marketing legerdemain that convinced consumers, and the automakers themselves, that each fall's tweaks weren't just alluring but *necessary* to one's social standing and the nation's economic health. The gentleman seen here is entering a Pontiac store.

Brigitte Bardot, age 22, was launched as an international sensation in the steamy 1956 film *And God Created Woman,* directed by her husband, Roger Vadim. Though by no means a cinematic genius, Vadim did know how to properly execute an erotic tale, showcasing his wife to the greatest possible advantage. Shot mostly in St. Tropez, the film achieved maximum titillation without resorting to nudity. Iconic visuals throughout the film (particularly in the table dancing scene) forever framed Bardot's free-spirited sensuality, which mesmerized male moviegoers on both sides of the Atlantic.

Though he received third billing, no one doubted that singer Elvis Presley was the real draw of the 1956 movie *Love Me Tender,* his film debut. Cast in support of Richard Egan and Debra Paget, Presley played one-third of a love triangle in the post-Civil War South. The film was laughably anachronistic, featuring the swivel-hipped singer frantically beating on a stringless guitar between action scenes. Nevertheless, his fans came out in droves.

Split-level homes became so popular in the 1950s that Garlinghouse was able to charge for a catalog that detailed building plans. First built in the early 1930s, splits added a partial level to the traditional ranch house. These "raised ranch homes" were especially appropriate for the 1950s since they came with an additional room and a finished basement—perfect for families expanding in size due to the baby boom.

The richness and imagination evident in Samuel Beckett's *Waiting for Godot* defies easy explanation. Staged on Broadway with Bert Lahr (*left*) as Estragon and E. G. Marshall (*right*) as Vladimir, this existentialist exercise came in two acts, bereft of many of drama's traditional trappings (such as conflict and resolution). Instead, Beckett created a challenging work that defies expectations, leaving audiences either disappointed or stimulated. The Godot in question is never identified, but instead serves as a catalyst for unanswered inquiry. This haunting play epitomized the postwar trend in provoking the audience's intellect rather than providing mere entertainment.

1956

December 2: Fidel Castro and a small band of armed rebels land the *Granma* on the Cuban coast with the intention of overthrowing dictator Fulgencio Batista. It will be another two years before they succeed.

December 5: In South Africa, Nelson Mandela is arrested along with 156 others and charged with treason.

December 8: Legendary Greek-American soprano Maria Callas performs at New York's Metropolitan Opera House for the first and only time.

December 10: For the first time since adopting a code of morals, the motion picture industry revises and relaxes some aspects of the code.

December 16: New York Archbishop Cardinal Francis Spellman denounces the film *Baby Doll* sight unseen. The ensuing Catholic boycott intrigues the public, and *Baby Doll* will go on to earn a healthy $3 million at the box office.

December 17: The role of Soviet troops in Poland is limited by a Soviet-Polish agreement.

December 18: Japan is admitted into the United Nations.

December 20: With black citizens now free to sit where they please on Montgomery's city buses, the Montgomery Improvement Association calls off its 381-day boycott.

December 25: Czech radio stations suspend the occupation tradition of playing the Soviet national anthem each night before signing off. • President Eisenhower invites Robert George to serve as the official White House Santa Claus.

December 25–26: In Birmingham, Alabama, the home of Reverend Fred Shuttlesworth, a civil rights leader, is bombed, stirring unrest in the city. African-Americans defy segregation regulations on the city's buses, leading to arrests.

German expatriate Douglas Sirk directed some of the most fevered and meticulously designed soap operas in cinema history. *Written on the Wind*, an unblushing depiction of the sordid downfall of a great oil family, is one of the director's best. Passions—virtuous and (mostly) poisonous—mate with Sirk's fulsome use of color and composition to create an eye-filling tableau that vibrates with obsession and pain. Two of the story's more sympathetic characters, played by Rock Hudson and Dorothy Malone, are seen here.

Sprinter Bobby Morrow clinches a gold medal in the 200-meter race at the 1956 Summer Olympic Games in Melbourne. He also won gold in the 100 meters and the 4×400-meter relay. Overall, the U.S. came in second in medals with 74 to the Soviet Union's 98. Australia's Murray Rose won three gold medals in swimming to lead the host nation to third place. Called "the friendly games," these Olympics for the first time concluded with athletes parading together, instead of by nation. Australian teenager John Wing had inspired the idea when he wrote to organizers, "During the Games, there will be only one nation."

In 1956 New York dancer Robert Joffrey (*right*) formed a unique, six-piece company. With Gerald Arpino as choreographer, the Joffrey Ballet eschewed abridged classics in favor of dynamic original pieces. Dancers were chosen for their individual, rather than ensemble, skills. This approach should not have worked but it did, and the group soon dazzled audiences around the country. Today, the Joffrey Ballet is regarded as one of America's premier dance troupes.

It's hard to separate the word *sultry* from any description of singer-actress Julie London. Blessed with stunning looks, a fair voice, and smoldering sexuality, London applied her considerable acting ability to her recordings, turning even the most mundane material into a potential seduction. "Cry Me a River," her first and biggest hit, became her signature tune (performed by London to great effect in the 1956 film *The Girl Can't Help It*). Following the breakup of her marriage to actor-producer Jack Webb, she wed songwriter Bobby Troupe ("Route 66"), who guided her musical career through a series of jazz/pop albums.

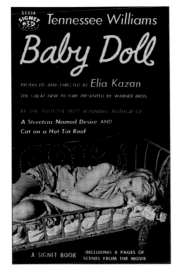

Elia Kazan's film about an oafish, middle-aged man and his thumb-sucking bride earned *Baby Doll* a "Condemned" rating from the Catholic Legion of Decency— a distinction that contributed to the picture's robust $3 million box office take. When Baby Doll (Carroll Baker, *pictured*) threatens to leave her husband (Karl Malden) on the eve of her 20th birthday (the date she had set for consummation of their marriage), her man commits a crime that encourages a slick rival to make his own play for Baby Doll. The screenplay for this provocative study was written by Tennessee Williams. Although at its core a comic piece, the film pushed the limits of what was permissible on movie screens.

After aspiring to a career in opera, Jalacy Hawkins moved on to blues and then to rock 'n' roll, changing his moniker to Screamin' Jay Hawkins. In 1956 he revisited a tender ballad that he had recorded earlier, but before rolling tape Hawkins and his band consumed a case of Muscatel. The resulting recording of "I Put a Spell on You" was an exercise in excess, punctuated with bloodcurdling screams, snorts, and assorted gurglings. Hawkins built upon this over-the-top image by emerging from a coffin in his live performances.

J. Edgar Hoover

Abetting Senator Joseph McCarthy in his relentless pursuit of the "Communist conspiracy" was a like-minded zealot, FBI Director J. Edgar Hoover. A fixture in Washington dating back to the Coolidge Administration, Hoover spent decades pursuing two goals: burnishing his bureau's image as the country's leading law-enforcement agency, and amassing a staggering collection of intelligence on all manner of perceived enemies.

Hoover's willingness to share secrets kept him in good stead with a succession of presidents. But even commanders-in-chief were leery of the powerful director: His bureau kept tabs on everyone, including the most prominent politicians; to get on the director's wrong side would be unwise.

Many have suggested that the barely concealed threat of blackmail cut both ways, for Hoover was not without vulnerabilities of his own. Though his horse-betting habit was widely known, speculation of a more personal nature kept Washington buzzing for years. The No. 2 man at the Bureau was Deputy Director Clyde Tolson, whose meteoric rise through the FBI ranks was unprecedented. Once installed as Hoover's right-hand man, the two lifelong bachelors were inseparable. Their routine of dining, entertaining, and even vacationing together inspired much whispering. Many speculated that Hoover turned a blind eye toward organized crime because the Mob possessed evidence of Hoover's homosexual relationships.

Instead of focusing on the Mob, Hoover mounted an ostentatious war against the "Red Menace." Though the agency proved adept at "educational" efforts aimed at keeping Americans on edge about national security, the FBI uncovered few bona fide subversives. All the while, the FBI's well-oiled publicity department churned out a steady stream of laudatory press releases and tomes (including Hoover's ghostwritten polemic, *Masters of Deceit*) that praised the director's abilities. In all, Hoover would serve under eight presidents. Upon his death in 1972, reams of files marked "Personal" were surreptitiously destroyed.

Don Whitehead's best-selling *The FBI Story* (1956) is a 368-page press release masquerading as a reliable chronicle of the federal crime-fighting agency. Whitehead was a two-time Pulitzer Prize winner who wrote the book under the watchful eye of the faintly paranoid FBI chief, J. Edgar Hoover. The account is effective in its sketchier outlines of Bureau history, and in its depiction of Hoover as a powerfully dominant figure. But key Bureau figures, including Clyde Tolson and Melvin Purvis (who is mentioned in the text but omitted from the index), are given short shrift. And key assertions, including one that Hoover personally arrested feared gangster Alvin "Creepy" Karpis, are simply untrue. *The FBI Story* inspired a popular 1959 film starring James Stewart.

A report to the People

THE FBI STORY

BY DON WHITEHEAD
Foreword by J. EDGAR HOOVER

"If Hoover ever calls you in, dress like a dandy, carry a notebook, and write in it furiously whenever Hoover opens his mouth. You can throw the notes away afterwards if you like."

—Charlie Winstead, a veteran FBI agent advising new agent William Sullivan

United Nations security forces take positions at Port Said, Egypt, in early December 1956. Under pressure from U.S. President Dwight Eisenhower, who threatened economic reprisals, Britain, France, and Israel agreed to a cease-fire and removal of their invading forces from Egypt. But considerable tensions still existed between the combatants. Canadian Prime Minister Lester Pearson urged the creation of a UN peacekeeping unit to defuse these tensions as the invading forces gradually departed. (Pearson would win the Nobel Peace Prize for his efforts.) The Suez Canal was soon reopened, but relations between the United States and its allies remained strained for several months.

In 1956 Grace Metalious remarked on postcard-pretty New England, her home and the setting of her novel, *Peyton Place:* "[I]f you go beneath that picture it's like turning over a rock with your foot. All kinds of things crawl out." Depressive, unskilled at relationships, and shunned by her neighbors, Metalious wrote a book that was part personal exorcism, part revenge. Major plot elements are unsavory but not improbable, and although the book is florid, it's also perceptive and powerful. Metalious wrote subsequent novels but could not duplicate the success of *Peyton Place,* one of the most widely read books of the 20th century.

A true rags to riches phenomenon, actress-singer Eartha Kitt was born in 1927 on a cotton farm in South Carolina and moved to New York when she was eight. Her apprenticeship with a dance troupe led to a tour of Europe in 1950. In Paris, Kitt developed a

cabaret act built around her sultry image and purring voice. Discovered by Orson Welles (who pronounced her "the most exciting woman alive"), she returned to New York, and Broadway stardom. By mid-decade, she had scored a number of hit records, including "*C'est Si Bon,*" holiday favorite "Santa Baby," and *That Bad Eartha*'s "I Want to Be Evil."

Because of its physical intimacy, colorful participants, and ease of broadcast, professional wrestling was much beloved by TV programmers during the 1950s. A bleached blond muscleboy who called himself Gorgeous George was an early star TV wrestler, but the quietly masculine Lou Thesz (*pictured*) had a background in the Greco-Roman style, and was a six-time world champion during four differ-

ent decades. Despite his knowledge of classical grappling, Thesz defended himself against hyperaggressive opponents with the "hooker," a devastating wristlock that could break a man's ankle or separate a shoulder.

New & Notable

Books

Howl by Allen Ginsberg
The Last Hurrah by Edwin O'Connor
The Organization Man
   by William Hollingsworth Whyte
Peyton Place by Grace Metalious
The Power Elite by C. Wright Mills
A Walk on the Wild Side
   by Nelson Algren

Movies

And God Created Woman
Forbidden Planet
Giant
The Girl Can't Help It
Invasion of the Body Snatchers
The King and I
The Man in the Gray Flannel Suit
Moby Dick
The Searchers
The Ten Commandments

Songs

"Blue Suede Shoes" by Carl Perkins
"Blueberry Hill" by Fats Domino
"Don't Be Cruel" by Elvis Presley
"Heartbreak Hotel" by Elvis Presley
"I Walk the Line" by Johnny Cash
"In the Still of the Night"
   by the Five Satins
"Memories Are Made of This"
   by Dean Martin
"Long Tall Sally" by Little Richard
"Que Sera Sera" by Doris Day
"Rock and Roll Waltz" by Kay Starr

Television

The Huntley-Brinkley Report
Playhouse 90
The Price Is Right
Queen for a Day
To Tell the Truth
Twenty-One

Theater

The Iceman Cometh
Long Day's Journey into Night
Look Back in Anger
My Fair Lady
The Quare Fellow
Waiting for Godot (Broadway debut)

Two African-Americans ride in the front of a Montgomery city bus on December 21, 1956. A day earlier, deputy U.S. marshals served notice on the city that the U.S. Supreme Court had affirmed a lower court decision declaring Alabama's state and local bus segregation laws unconstitutional. Though actually handed down on November 13, the order was not enforceable until the city exhausted its petitions. In the meantime, local authorities managed to ban the Montgomery Improvement Association's car-pool system, forcing Montgomery's black citizens to walk during the final five weeks of their campaign.

Road & Track magazine first hit the newsstands in 1947, preceding both *Hot Rod* and *Motor Trend*. It quickly appealed to former American servicemen who had become enamored of the British MG and other European sports cars. But not until 1952, when technical editor John Bond assumed full-time publishing duties, did the publication take off, ascending into the mainstream as America's premier car magazine. Filled with full-color layouts, loads of technical information, detailed reviews of new models, and Bond's erudite, often witty "Miscellaneous Ramblings," *Road & Track* set the standard for auto journalism and commentary.

information from **YOU** the taxpayer on the locations of

Implementing an angle that had worked against Al Capone, federal authorities attempted to shut down rural "moonshine" operations by pointing out that illegal profits went untaxed, thereby overburdening honest folk. Rewarding informers was often the most effective way to bring operators of illegal stills to justice, as this covert industry had become quite adept at functioning by stealth. The manufacture of bootleg liquor was a tradition as old as America, operating chiefly in rural Appalachian areas where interference was stymied by the rugged terrain. A certain heroic mythology enshrouded the distillers, epitomized by the moonshiner played by Robert Mitchum in the 1958 film *Thunder Road*.

While rock 'n' roll exploitation films were a dime-a-dozen in the mid-1950s, director Frank Tashlin's *The Girl Can't Help It* was an enormous cut above, receiving the full-color, CinemaScope treatment from 20th Century-Fox. A star vehicle for sexpot Jayne Mansfield (*pictured*), the film simultaneously sends up and celebrates the rock 'n' roll industry. The forever put-upon Tom Ewell (*seated*) stars as a washed-up agent pressed into service by a mobster (Edmond O'Brien) to make his no-talent girlfriend a singing sensation. Tashlin's earlier experience as a cartoon director is very much in evidence, and the chance to see such acts as Little Richard, Eddie Cochran, and Fats Domino in their prime is a rare treat.

For two generations of schoolchildren who faced the dreaded deadline doom of book reports, Gilberton Publications' *Classics Illustrated* comics provided fast relief. Established as *Classic Comics* in 1941 under the editorship of Albert Kanter, *CI* adapted works by Dumas, Melville, Dickens, Homer, Goethe, Shakespeare, and scores of others. Early adaptations highlighted the stories' sensational elements, but by the 1950s *CI* had become considerably more thoughtful and sedate. The cover of this 1956 version of *Huckleberry Finn* was painted by Edward Moritz.

Colo, the first lowland gorilla ever born in captivity, arrived in the world on December 22, 1956, at the Columbus Zoo in Ohio. Fearing that she would die immediately after birth, veterinarian Warren Thomas gave her mouth-to-mouth resuscitation. From the moment the public could view the baby gorilla, attendance at the zoo soared. Zookeepers dressed her for the holidays, putting her in an Easter bonnet and dresses. Five decades later, Colo was still alive and well, the mother of three, grandmother of 16, and great grandmother of two.

"Soon, [the Soviets] will be dropping bombs on us from space like kids dropping rocks onto cars from freeway overpasses."

—Senator Lyndon Johnson (D–TX), responding to the Soviet Union's successful launch of Sputnik

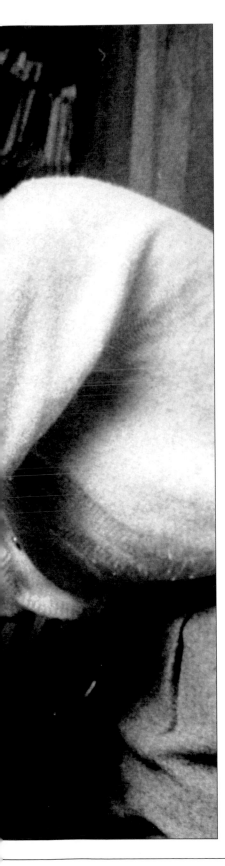

1957

The Arms Race

I N OCTOBER 1957, a teenager named John Gaddis (who would grow up to become a prominent historian of the Cold War), tracked a fast-moving glint in the night sky high over Cotulla, Texas. Like millions of people around the world, he was looking at the reflection of the Soviet rocket that had shot a 183-pound, basketball-sized aluminum sphere into Earth orbit on October 4. The little Sputnik satellite, zipping and beeping around the Earth every 98 minutes, had no particular utility, but the missile that had put it into outer space did. A rocket that could escape Earth's gravitational pull with a Sputnik on its head could fly from the Soviet Union to the United States with a nuclear warhead as its payload. The Soviets had created an intercontinental ballistic missile (ICBM).

Officially, the Soviets put a heavily inflected, Communist "gee whiz" spin on the story: "Artificial Earth satellites will pave the way to interplanetary travel, and apparently our contemporaries will witness how the freed and conscientious labor of the people of the new socialist society makes the most daring dreams of mankind a reality." Soviet First Secretary Nikita Khrushchev, soon after, stated the matter more bluntly, bragging to American publisher William Randolph Hearst: "[W]e now have all the rockets we need: long-range rockets, intermediate-range rockets. And short-range rockets . . . [which] now make it possible to hit a target in any area of the globe."

Khrushchev was blustering and bluffing, as was his style. In 1957 the Soviets had only a handful of long-range missiles, and their accuracy was poor. American government officials knew this, as top-secret aerial recon-

Ham radio operator Dick Oberholtzer and his wife listen eagerly for any signal from the Soviet-built satellite, Sputnik. A psychological victory for the Russians, the launching of Sputnik in October 1957 caught the world's attention and the American government off guard.

naissance photos made it fairly clear that the Soviet missile program was developing slowly. However, American citizens were in the dark. All they knew for certain was that a Soviet satellite spun over their heads, casting a giant shadow over American claims of military and scientific superiority.

President Dwight Eisenhower, though not willing to reveal America's classified spy photo capacity, did his best to tamp down Americans' anxieties. At a press conference a couple days after the Sputnik launch, he assured, "Now, so far as the satellite itself is concerned, that does not raise my apprehensions, not one iota."

Eisenhower was telling the truth, or at least part of the truth. In terms of security, the Russian satellite was no threat. Even the Soviets' lead in developing the ICBM did nothing to change the strategic balance; the United States had multiple capacities for delivering its nuclear weapons against the Soviet Union. But Eisenhower knew that the Cold War competition with the Soviets did not depend solely on narrow military considerations.

The day after Eisenhower had told the American people not to worry, he met with his top advisers on the National Security Council. Acting Secretary of State Christian Herter told him that international reactions to Sputnik were "pretty somber." "The United States," he told the President, "will have to do a great deal to counteract them and, particularly, to confirm the existence of our own real military and scientific strength." In the eyes of the world, the Soviets had struck a major blow for the glories of the Communist state.

About the size of a basketball and weighing a mere 183 pounds, Sputnik was the first artificial satellite. Orbiting Earth on an elliptical path every 98 minutes, Sputnik ushered in the space age as well as the U.S.-USSR space race.

The United States, Ike's men agreed, had to respond.

Public opinion at home was not in good shape, either. *Life* magazine, disregarding the President's assurances, ran a somewhat hysterical article titled "Arguing the Case for Being Panicky." Senator Lyndon Johnson (D–TX) started a Senate Preparedness Subcommittee investigation within hours of the Sputnik launch, demanding to know how the Republican Eisenhower Administration had allowed the Soviets to beat the United States to outer space.

Seeking to cool the political heat and boost American public opinion, the President announced on October 9 that the U.S. would have its own satellite in orbit before the end of the year. The news came as a surprise to the relatively underfunded team in charge of America's Vanguard satellite program. They were not ready to launch, but they vowed to give it their best shot.

On December 6, 1957, an American rocket carrying a tiny satellite no bigger than a grapefruit lifted off from Cape Canaveral in Florida. Unfortunately, after achieving a height of about four feet, the rocket toppled and exploded. Newspaper headlines assailed the "blow to American prestige." Senator Johnson, already eyeing a run for the presidency in 1960, declared the affair "most humiliating." And Soviet diplomats at the United Nations in New York sweetly asked their American counterparts if they might like to seek technical assistance from the Soviet Union's special-aid program for backward nations. It was a sad day for America.

A teacher and his students practice what to do in the event of an atomic explosion. Sputnik escalated fears of nuclear attack, with some Chicken Littles predicting that the Soviets would drop bombs on the U.S. from outer space. After Sputnik, civil defense was heightened through duck-and-cover drills as well as pamphlets issued by the federal government.

The space race was, as Eisenhower stated, not that significant in terms of security or even technology. Within two months, the United States was able to overcome its embarrassing first satellite launch, which had been dubbed "kaputnik" by the British press. The U.S. shot a rocket into outer space in January 1958 (though by that time the Soviets, preparing for a manned launch, had launched a massive satellite that held a live dog in an air-conditioned chamber). More importantly for the long-term social development of the United States, the Soviets' scientific triumph did focus attention on a very real problem: the U.S. educational system.

Critics of education in the United States suddenly made headline news as Americans struggled to understand how Communist scientists had triumphed over Yankee know-how. Admiral Hyman G. Rickover, longtime champion of government funding of scientific research, shocked many when he suggested that the United States should emulate the Soviet educational system. The Soviets drilled young children in the sciences, and those who showed promise were immediately tracked into intensive programs. Why not do the same in the United States?

Children round the bend on The H-Bomb Rocket at Rockaways Playland amusement park in Long Island, New York. "The Bomb" made its way into '50s popular culture through movies (for example, *Them!*), books (*On the Beach*), music ("Atom Bomb Baby"), and even Las Vegas showgirls (Miss Atomic Blast).

Life magazine jumped on the bandwagon with a series of articles titled "Crisis in Education." Citing overcrowded schoolrooms, underpaid teachers, and low educational standards, *Life*'s writers concluded, "Where there are young minds of great promise, there are rarely the means to advance them. The nation's stupid children get far better care than the bright. The geniuses of the next decade are even now being allowed to slip back into mediocrity." Statistics supported the lack of priority given to education. According to one study, American business and industry spent $6.5 billion on advertising while the U.S. invested only $5 billion in schools.

Politicians listened to the complaints, and in the heated atmosphere of the Cold War they came up with federal funds to do something about the "education gap." In a bipartisan effort, Congress passed the National Defense Education Act of 1958. The act stated: "The Congress finds that an educational emergency exists and requires action by the federal government. Assistance will come from Washington to help develop as rapidly as possible those skills essential to the national defense."

For the first time, the federal government funded graduate fellowships for an array of targeted fields, from the hard sciences to foreign language study. Moreover, federal money began streaming to universities all over the country to set up advanced language programs, foreign-area studies, and scientific research centers. In addition, to encourage bright high school students who might not otherwise go to college, the federal government funded national educational testing, local school-based college counselors, and the first college student-loan program. Suddenly, thanks to the Cold War and to the beep-beep-beeping of Sputnik, higher education had become a national priority.

Six times larger than its predecessor, Sputnik II was easily visible in the nighttime sky over New York City in early November 1957. The second Sputnik carried a dog, Laika, indicating that the Russians intended to put a human into space in the not-too-distant future.

Education was not the only new government priority. The Eisenhower Administration threw billions of dollars at America's space program. Before Sputnik, Congress had allowed only $500 million for space research. But by mid-1958, Congress appropriated $10.5 billion. The Cold War space race was on. To spend all that new money, Eisenhower created the National Aeronautics and Space Administration (NASA). Confounding the military, Eisenhower mandated that the space program be run by civilians.

Prior to 1958, the American armed services had been the driving force behind the rocket program, and the military had fully expected to be the major recipients of Congress's loosened purse strings. President Eisenhower, however, was becoming increasingly wary of the growing power of the military in American life. The space race, Eisenhower hoped, would not become just another aspect of the Cold War competition for new ways to blow up the planet.

Even as President Eisenhower struggled to keep the space program a primarily scientific contest with the Soviet Union, pressure was building within the United States and USSR to use rocket science breakthroughs to escalate the nuclear arms race. During Eisenhower's first term, he had embraced nuclear weapons as a cheaper method of deterring Soviet aggression. Rather than spend tens of billions on massive "low-tech" ground forces that could match the Soviets', Ike had opted to spend billions on "high-tech" nuclear weapons. Those weapons would provide first-strike capacity (primarily delivered via bomber planes) that he vowed would be used if the Russians attacked the United States or its allies.

The Soviets had not been able to match America's nuclear buildup; the Soviet Union, in fact, was falling further behind the United States in most measurable areas of economic production and technical advancement. Rockets, however, were one of the few areas in which the Soviets were having success. Khrushchev, desperate to match the American nuclear threat and to show the world that Soviet communism would bury American capitalism, publicly declared that Russia would use its advanced rocket science to create deadly long-range nuclear missiles capable of destroying the United States. The Eisenhower Administration, for strategic and political reasons, rushed into an ICBM race with the Soviets.

To the typical American, long-range, nuclear-tipped missiles did not seem any worse than nuclear bombs delivered by airplanes and submarines. But with airplane-delivered nuclear attacks, as Cold War historian John Diggins writes, "missions could be called back in case of some disastrous miscalculation. . . . With the ICBM, the time element shrank from several hours to a few minutes." Suddenly, people on both sides of the Cold War realized that with a "push of a button" the world could be unalterably, uncontrollably blown apart.

Americans' biggest concern about the launch of the Sputniks was not necessarily that the Soviets were the first into space, but the means by which they got there—the ICBM (intercontinental ballistic missile). An ICBM carrying a nuclear-tipped warhead could reach the other side of the globe within minutes.

Imagined and real horrors gripped the nation. Scientist Linus Pauling warned that the deadly effects of the nuclear era had already arrived: Open-air atomic bomb testing had introduced deadly, radioactive Strontium-90 into the atmosphere, and by 1959 it had made its way into the nation's milk supply.

A year after President Eisenhower stepped down from office in 1961, a group of college students wrote a manifesto, "The Port Huron Statement," that confronted the threat of nuclear apocalypse: "Our work is guided by the sense that we may be the last generation in the experiment with living." Even as Americans bought new homes in record numbers, marveled at their new televisions, and thought about buying a second car, they knew that at any moment their world could end. A figurative dark cloud, mushroom-shaped, loomed over America.

1957

1957: Insisting that China will not remain Communist for long, Secretary of State John Foster Dulles refuses to recognize the Asian nation. • Senator John F. Kennedy (D–MA) is appointed to the powerful Senate Foreign Relations Committee. • The Development Operations Division of the Army Ballistic Missile Agency is established, with Wernher von Braun as its chief. • Educator James Bryant Conant promotes his educational tracking theory. He suggests that public schools identify students as either gifted, average, or slow, and steer them into professions based on those designations.

1957: In a continued effort to quell rebellion, the occupying Soviet government in Hungary enacts the death penalty for strikers and those who would foment opposition. • Egyptian President Gamal Abdel Nasser rejects United Nations attempts to take a cut of Suez Canal revenues. *See* February 17, 1957. • A Jewish town named Nazerat Illit (Upper Nazareth) is built on Palestinian land. • Dr. Hilary Koprowski develops an oral polio vaccine and tests it in Africa, prompting future unsubstantiated accusations that his research provided the environment for the crossover of SIV (simian immunodeficiency virus) into HIV.

1957: A series of articles in the *New York Post* asserts that the influence of the Catholic Church has stymied contraception education and availability in New York City's public hospitals. • On the weekly program *Person to Person,* CBS airs a segment about the Cuban insurgency that includes an interview with Fidel Castro. • U.S. airports are discovering that they are too crowded. Many, including those in Detroit and Newark, New Jersey, announce multimillion-dollar expansion plans. • Norman Mailer publishes a controversial essay in *The Village Voice* called "The White Negro," about the hipster movement.

With an uncanny ability to draw disparate interests together, Senator Lyndon B. Johnson (D–TX) became majority leader in 1955. During his tenure, he became one of the most effective leaders in the history of Congress. As a civil rights advocate, Johnson potentially could have alienated his Deep South colleagues by pushing his agenda too hard. Instead, he used his position to cajole, charm, or arm-twist his fellows into voting his way on legislation. Transparently ambitious, LBJ surprised many by accepting the veep slot on John F. Kennedy's ticket in 1960.

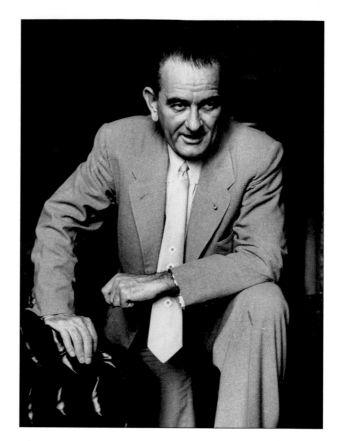

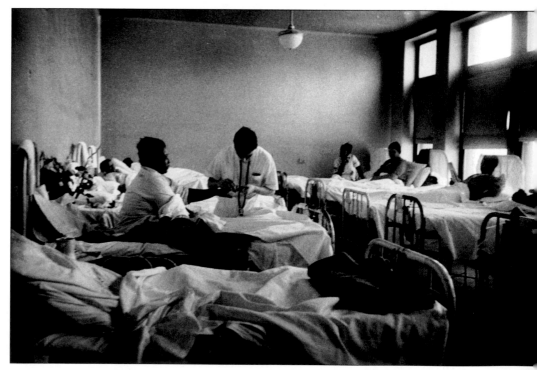

Jim Crow wore a different suit in the North, but he was still recognizable. There were few "colored" and "white" signs, and no laws on the books separated the races. However, institutions such as this Chicago hospital had clearly enforced racial policies, even if they were unofficial. This African-American ward, pictured in 1957, was in the hospital's basement. Prior to the civil rights movement, most blacks in the North accepted these policies as a trade-off for the North's increased economic opportunity and the relative safety they experienced there.

Dauntless teenage sleuths Frank and Joe Hardy (introduced in 1926) and Nancy Drew (1930) were created by writer and book packager Edward Stratemeyer, who also developed Tom Swift and the Bobbsey Twins. The mysteries were ghosted by a stable of writers and credited to the fictitious Franklin W. Dixon and Carolyn Keene, respectively. Operating from their all-American (but crime-infested) hometowns, the three amateur detectives investigated mysteries at hidden mines, swamps, caves, decrepit waterfronts, and other unsavory locales. Jacket art for the editions seen here is by Rudy Nappi.

Country-pop vocalist Patsy Cline is a show business "evergreen" who consistently sells about 100,000 CDs a year—more than 40 years after her 1963 death in a plane crash. Originally a cowgirl-type singer, she soon developed a sophisti-cated, "countrypolitan" style that showcased her smooth, gliding contralto. On January 21, 1957, Cline whipped the audience into a frenzy with "Walkin' After Mid-night" on *Arthur God-frey's Talent Scouts.* (In fact, she became the first performer ever to freeze the show's "Applause Meter.") The performance and the song estab-lished Cline as a potent musical force, and set the stage for greater triumphs.

For many, comedian Ernie Kovacs was television's first genius, an inspired innovator who used the medium in untested ways to great effect. Here he is seen in his famous "silent special" of January 1957, 30 compelling minutes bereft of dialogue. In this Kovacs sight gag, both the set and the camera are tilted, so that the poured coffee appears to defy the laws of physics. Through a series of programs and specials, Kovacs deftly blended music, simple but ingenious visual effects, and an ensemble of characters—such as the Nairobi Trio (players in overcoats and gorilla masks)—that influenced television comedy for decades.

Producer-director Roger Corman cranked out profitable B pictures at a furious pace (nine in 1957 alone), but he also had innate storytelling ability, a sense of the absurd, and an appreciation of the value of talented collaborators. Every-thing clicked in *Not of This Earth,* a smart, unnerving chiller about a blood-drinking emissary from the planet Davanna who travels to Los Angeles to round up humans for "blood pasturing." When his private nurse (hired to look after his anemia) uncovers his scheme, she fights to prevent Earth's subjugation. Top-billed Beverly Garland (a talented, assertive heroine) and thirsty Paul Birch are shown in this lobby card, which features promo art by Al Kallis.

1957

1957: Billy Barty, a prominent actor and a dwarf, founds Little People of America in Reno, Nevada. • The premiere issue of *Gentleman's Quarterly* (*GQ*) is published. • AT&T introduces the touchtone phone. • Darvon, the first non-narcotic, nonaddictive painkiller, is introduced. • Don Featherstone designs the plastic flamingo at Union Products, Inc., in Loeminster, Massachusetts. • General Foods introduces Tang breakfast drink, which will become a favorite among astronauts. • Americans are becoming increasingly medicated: Some 40 million prescriptions for tranquilizers are written this year.

1957: IBM's John Backus publishes the computer programming language FORTRAN, revolutionizing the industry. • For the first time, approximately as many women as men are registered to vote in the U.S. • The careers of comedians Mike Nichols and Elaine May take off with early appearances at New York City clubs Village Vanguard and Blue Angel. • Soldiers in the Second Army Division stationed in West Germany are told that those with German wives may leave their division or their wives, but may not bring their wives back to their home base in Fort Hood, Texas.

January: The Soviets propose a permanent division of Vietnam into a Communist North Vietnam and a separate nation of South Vietnam, but the U.S. refuses to recognize a Communist North Vietnam. • Charles Van Doren, an English professor at Columbia University, begins a winning streak on the quiz show *Twenty-One* that will net him $129,000 by the time he is finally beaten in March. *See* November 2, 1959.

Early 1957: Grove Press publishes the premiere issue of the avant-garde literary magazine *Evergreen Review,* featuring an essay by Jean-Paul Sartre and a short story by Samuel Beckett.

George Metesky, New York City's "Mad Bomber," grins from behind bars following his capture for a string of explosions that had begun in 1940. The bombs were accompanied by letters attacking Consolidated Edison (signed "F.P.," later revealed to mean "fair play"), although most of the devices failed to detonate. Metesky's bizarre campaign took a wartime hiatus before resuming, with three dozen more bombs planted in such public places as theaters and New York's public library. Stumped police finally cracked the case in January 1957 with the aid of a profiler, Dr. James Brussel, who typed the culprit down to his attire. Metesky was committed to Matteawan State Hospital.

This stunning group of models suggests the breadth of Christian Dior's 1957 collection. Bursting upon the fashion scene 10 years earlier with his New Look, Dior's stylings evolved through the famed A-Line before culminating with a softer, more limber silhouette, which encompassed tunics, chemises, and wraps. His final offerings included a waist-less, shift-style dress with a skirt that narrowed at the hem. In 1955 Dior brought young Yves Saint Laurent on board. Two years later, the gifted 21-year-old produced a new collection a mere nine weeks after the unexpected death of his mentor, setting the stage for his own fashion immortality.

Scary Crashes

On March 11, 1958, Walter Gregg was working in the garage on his farm near Florence, South Carolina, when an atomic bomb fell out of the sky and onto his house. TNT in the detonator caused an explosion that injured six people, but fortunately the bomb had not been fitted with its nuclear warhead.

The incident was just the latest in a startling number of inadvertent payload releases, collisions, and crashes during the 1950s. In 1950 alone, several accidents involving nukes shook up an already tense public. In January that year, a B-36 dropped a nuclear weapon into Puget Sound near Seattle; in April, a B-29 collided with a mountain in New Mexico; and in July, a B-50 crashed in Lebanon, Ohio, with a nuclear weapon on board.

Throughout the 1950s, with the Cold War running red hot, the U.S. military kept nuclear weapons airborne around the clock and around the globe. In this climate, mistakes were bound to happen, and they did. From 1956 to 1959, at least 12 "mishaps" or malfunctions plagued Air Force and Atomic Energy Commission officials. In 1956 a B-47

A formation of B-47s

disappeared with two weapons on board, and in 1957 a C-124 jettisoned two weapons over the Atlantic. Just a month before the South Carolina incident, a B-47 collided with an F-86 Sabre in midair, sending nuclear weapons into the drink five miles southeast of the mouth of the Savannah River in Georgia.

In a February 1958 effort to assuage public fears, the government published a statement announcing that citizens faced no threat from armed weapons. However, government agencies warned that "an accidental detonation of conventional explosives might possibly cause local scattering of nuclear materials in the form of dust." Such materials, the report added, could be "hazardous only if taken internally, as by breathing."

Government officials also described the creation of mobile "decontamination teams to protect the public from atomic dust that might result from crashes of vehicles carrying nuclear weapons," according to *The New York Times*. Despite the government's efforts to deal with the problem, the alarming number of crashes raised more questions and fears than could be easily resolved.

Famed actor Humphrey Bogart died of cancer at age 57 on January 14, 1957. In many ways, he was an unlikely leading man: He stood 5'8", had partial paralysis of the face, and spoke with a lisp. Nonetheless, his enormous talent and charisma made him a giant in his field. In the 1930s, he played convincing bad guys in a number of crime films. In the 1940s and '50s, he perfected his persona as a tough guy with a heart of gold in such classics as *Casablanca,*

The Maltese Falcon, and *The Treasure of the Sierra Madre.* Nominated for three best actor Oscars, he won the honor in 1951 for his role in *The African Queen.*

Readers encountered a haunting depiction of a nuclear apocalypse in Australian writer Nevil Shute's 1957 novel, *On the Beach.* Set in the not-too-distant future, it tells the story of a handful of survivors of a nuclear war who face certain death due to imminent radiation poisoning of the atmosphere. Rather than portray a chaotic frenzy for survival, Shute describes a resigned, calm tableau as individuals meet their fates while trying to carry on with

their business. The low-key, realistic tone makes the story all the more chilling. Success of the book and a subsequent film of the same title helped to inspire anti-nuke movements.

January 5: President Dwight Eisenhower outlines the Eisenhower Doctrine, which asserts the right of the U.S. to use force against any country trying to bring communism to the Middle East.

January 6: For Elvis Presley's third appearance on *The Ed Sullivan Show,* CBS network censors insist that the singer be shown only from the waist up.

January 9: In Atlanta, black demonstrators are arrested for picketing segregated public trolley facilities.

January 10: Harold Macmillan replaces Anthony Eden as prime minister of Great Britain. • Four black churches, as well as the homes of reverends Ralph Abernathy and Robert Graetz, are bombed in Montgomery, Alabama.

January 11: The Southern Christian Leadership Conference (SCLC) is founded to coordinate the activities of nonviolent protest groups. Martin Luther King, Jr., will be named its first president.

January 13: The Pluto Platter, the precursor to the Frisbee, is introduced by Wham-O.

January 14: Legendary screen star Humphrey Bogart dies of cancer at age 57.

January 15: The Egyptian government announces that it will nationalize all banks and insurance companies held by France and Britain.

January 16: President Eisenhower's budget proposal for the upcoming fiscal year calls for a $1.8 billion surplus.

January 18: Three B-52 Stratofortresses, led by Air Force Major General Archie J. Old, Jr., land in California upon completing the first nonstop jet circumnavigation of the world. They complete the journey in 45 hours, 19 minutes.

Finnish-born designer-architect Eero Saarinen's influence on postwar aesthetics was realized in a number of areas, notably the St. Louis Gateway Arch. With several well-known buildings to his credit (including General Motors's Technical Building), his fusion of function with form extended to some classic furniture pieces. Among the best known was his "womb" chair (*pictured*), a piece intended to look pleasing when occupied as well as when empty. These pricey but stylish innovations were expanded upon by his protégée, Florence Knoll. She achieved great success with her own Bauhaus-influenced furnishings, as well as through the marketing of Mies van der Rohe's designs.

Death personified (played by Bengt Ekerot) looms large in Swedish director Ingmar Bergman's 1957 masterpiece, *The Seventh Seal,* an allegorical exploration of man's relationship with God. Horrific, iconic images appear throughout Bergman's tale of a knight (Max von Sydow), newly returned from the Crusades, and his world-weary attempts to come to terms with God's apparent absence. Evoking the stark atmosphere of silent cinema, the film is probably the best known of Bergman's thoughtful works, which include *Wild Strawberries* (1957), *Through a Glass Darkly* (1961), and *Cries and Whispers* (1972).

Declaring "the lid is off," publisher Robert Harrison launched *Confidential* magazine in 1952. This sensational publication exposed the sordid doings of Hollywood stars with a disapproving tone, boldly going where no scandal rag had gone before. Bolstered by "gotcha!" photos and insider gossip, *Confidential*'s salacious accounts of private behavior shocked the film commu-

nity, which had been accustomed to "no publicity is bad publicity." Studios issued a flurry of lawsuits to protect their assets, but with the magazine's circulation at four million, Harrison could afford the litigation. Charges of criminal libel from the district attorney's office in 1957 eventually did compel Harrison to sell the magazine.

The Crack in the Picture Window, by social critic John Keats, is one of the 1950s' funniest and most sardonic books of nonfiction. By tracing the naive aspirations and ill-advised choices of a young couple he calls John and Mary Drone, Keats mounts a sharp attack on the new American suburbs—and the conformity, lack of adventure, and financial peril he felt awaited every resident. Greedy banks, querulous neighbors, TV

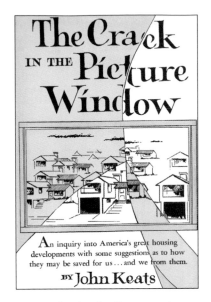

as assassin of social life . . . Keats enthusiastically warned against all of these, and more. He caused another stir in 1958 with *The Insolent Chariots,* a witty but withering critique of the auto industry and the American car culture.

After J. Fred Muggs grew a little too aggressive to suit the *Today* show's producers, another chimpanzee was drafted to fill the slot: Kokomo, Jr. (*pictured*). Introduced on the air in March 1957, the mild-mannered Kokomo provided a distinct contrast to his more mischievous forerunner. Along with the standard schtick involving many wardrobe changes, Kokomo also learned how to speak. Owner-trainer Nick Carrado spent months getting the chimp to master what speech therapists had told him was impossible; he got Kokomo to pronounce, clearly and distinctly, "Mama."

During World War II, Messerschmitt of Germany built tough, highly capable fighter planes and other aircraft. After 1945, when the blasted German economy needed to be resuscitated, and when the people needed inexpensive transportation, Messerschmitt became an automaker. The tricycle-style, single-door KR200 "bubble car" was manufactured from 1955 to 1964. The uplevel Cabin Scooter model had a heater and a defroster. An impressive top speed of 60 mph was provided by a one-cylinder, two-cycle, 10.2-horsepower engine displacing just 200 cc (12.2 cubic inches). The car had four forward gears; four reverse gears were engaged by starting the engine backward.

1957

January 21: President Eisenhower and Vice President Richard Nixon publicly take the oath of office at the east portico of the U.S. Capitol, the day after taking the same oath in a private ceremony in the White House. Marian Anderson sings the national anthem at the public service.

January 22: George P. Metesky, the "Mad Bomber" accused of planting some 30 explosive devices around Manhattan, is arrested in Waterbury, Connecticut. He will be committed to a mental hospital until 1973.

January 30: The McClellan Committee is formed to investigate the connection between organized crime and labor unions. A young Robert Kennedy serves as chief counsel to the committee's chair, Senator John McClellan.

February 1: Leo Castelli's gallery opens in New York City. It will become the home of a new art movement named Neo-Dada and characterized by the works of Jasper Johns and Robert Rauschenberg.

February 7: Moscow halts oil deliveries to Israel in retaliation for Israel's "aggressive action" against Egypt.

February 12: The members of the U.S. Communist Party hold a vote in which they decide to retain their autonomy from the Soviet Union.

February 14: The Georgia Senate outlaws interracial athletics.

February 17: In the wake of the Suez crisis, the canal reopens to traffic. *See* March 4, 1957.

February 18: *Death of a Salesman* playwright Arthur Miller is charged with contempt by a grand jury for his refusal to cooperate with HUAC.

February 26: *L'Humanité,* a Communist daily newspaper published in Paris, is shut down after publishing a report on French human rights abuses in Algeria.

Leaders of the independence movement in the former British colony of the Gold Coast celebrate the end of 55 years of Western rule. Kwame Nkrumah (*second from right*) became president following an orderly turnover of power in March 1957. The newly minted nation of Ghana was the first Central African country to decolonize in the post-war era, a period in which many empires crumbled due to the heavy costs of reconstruction and Cold War preparedness. In 1960 alone, 17 African nations would achieve independence.

Fleshed out from the 1954 teleplay, the feature film *12 Angry Men* marked Sydney Lumet's directorial debut. This tightly wound drama depicts the painstaking deliberations of an impaneled jury in a murder case, with each member bringing his own baggage to the table. The low-budget treatment actually enhanced the material, offering a touch of realism (and claustrophobia) to the proceedings. The all-star cast included E. G. Marshall (*third from left*), Henry Fonda (*fifth from left*), Jack Klugman (*foreground, right*), and Lee J. Cobb (*not pictured*). In fully drawn characterizations, each juror's prejudices, values, and strengths are revealed under gut-wrenching pressure to decide a man's fate.

Billy Graham

IN 1954 A FORCEFUL young preacher named William Franklin Graham, Jr., made the cover of *Time* magazine. The leader of the latest great American awakening had been drawing massive crowds to Christian revival meetings in Los Angeles since the beginning of the decade. From the Cold War era forward, Graham helped to define a nonsectarian brand of middle-of-the-road evangelism that struck a chord with a vast audience of Americans.

During the 1950s, Graham was an aggressive anti-Communist and an opponent of segregation. Yet he remained for the most part politically neutral despite his friendships with successive presidents, beginning with Eisenhower. His fundamentalism was orthodox, and yet he had broad appeal. His message was basic: that sinners should repent, accept Christ, and be saved.

Graham transmitted this message through his book *Peace with God* (1953), his syndicated newspaper column, and TV and radio broadcasts. But it was his giant revival meetings, like old-time tent shows, that contributed to Graham's spectacular rise. His 1957 crusade in New York City alone filled Madison Square Garden for four months running. During a three-day revival at San Francisco's Cow Palace in 1958, the preacher drew nearly 700,000 people.

Graham's mild, consensus-style evangelism was sometimes criticized by those on the right, who hoped he would take a harder and more public stand on politically controversial issues of faith. The ubiquitous preacher stayed out of the fray while tirelessly pursuing his mission to save souls.

Ten-year-old Robert Strom became the winner of one of television's biggest jackpots. Appearing on *The $64,000 Question,* he won the top prize on the strength of his knowledge of mathematics. As the popular show attempted to goose its ratings by offering even bigger prizes, Robert was given a shot at—and ended up winning—an extra $192,000. He was among the best remembered of the champions. A spin-off, *The $64,000 Challenge,* pitted past winners against each other.

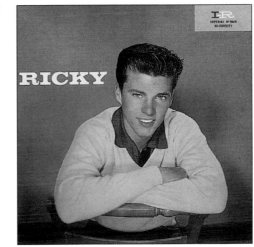

His white-bread image notwithstanding, television star Ricky Nelson was among the great rock 'n' roll singers of his era. Nelson chose songs that suited his relaxed vocal style, and surrounded himself with superb musicians, including legendary ax-man James Burton. Moreover, his discriminating tastes and command of the style led to an abundance of hits, including "Poor Little Fool," "Lonesome Town," and "Hello, Mary Lou." Nelson's weekly showcase at the conclusion of his family's sitcom, *Ozzie and Harriet,* gave his records a huge boost. It also helped soften middle America's attitude toward rock 'n' rollers.

1957

February 27: China's Chairman Mao delivers his famous speech in which he says, "Let a hundred flowers bloom, a hundred schools of thought contend." Though his words ostensibly open the door to free speech, Mao will be criticized by the masses and soon will reverse course, cracking down on those who speak out against him.

March 4: In Egypt, Israel withdraws from the Sinai after the United Nations renews its demand that Israel cease its military action in the Suez crisis. • Dr. Seuss's *The Cat in the Hat* is published.

March 6: The African nation of Ghana, comprised of British colonies Togoland and the Gold Coast, officially gains independence from Britain.

March 9: Alaska's Andreanof Islands are rocked by an earthquake that measures 8.1 on the Richter scale.

March 10: A B-47 bomber flying nuclear materials from the U.S. to Europe vanishes over the Atlantic without a trace.

March 13: Anti-Batista demonstrations turn bloody in Havana, Cuba.

March 18: The CIA begins funding of Dr. D. Ewen Cameron's Society for the Investigation of Human Ecology. Cameron, of Montreal's McGill University, will subject patients to electric shocks and megadoses of LSD in a series of mind-control experiments.

March 23: North Carolina beats Kansas (led by Wilt Chamberlain) 54–53 in triple overtime to win the NCAA men's basketball championship.

March 25: San Francisco customs officials seize 520 copies of Allen Ginsberg's poem *Howl*. Ginsberg will be brought up on obscenity charges.

In Sam Fuller's *China Gate,* set in Vietnam in 1954 at the close of the French colonial era, a Eurasian "half-caste" named Lucky Legs (Angie Dickinson, *left*) agrees to guide a perilous French military mission if the son she had by the racist squad leader (Gene Barry, *foreground*) is evacuated to America. In a provocative touch, a Communist major offers Lucky and the boy new lives in Moscow. Fuller had been a newspaperman and a WWII grunt. He had a fondness for big emotions and topical subjects, and as he saw it, Vietnam was a trap of France's own making. His sentiments cut too close to the bone to suit France, where *China Gate* was never released.

Seen here chatting with President Eisenhower during a U.S. tour in May 1957, South Vietnamese President Ngo Dinh Diem represented America's hope for stability in Southeast Asia. Appointed by Bao Dai in 1954, Diem was a devout Catholic who had been educated in the West. The U.S. believed that South Vietnam's largely Catholic populace would provide a firm base from which to unify the country. Instead, Diem systematically tightened his grip on power through suppression of enemies and would-be allies alike. Trusting no one, he installed loyal but corrupt village chiefs. With America's tacit approval, Diem canceled 1956's Geneva-mandated election, fearing a Ho Chi Minh victory. Despite misgivings about his heavy-handed rule, Eisenhower supported Diem, believing him the only viable alternative to Communist domination.

A suburban housewife hosts a makeup clinic for a group of engrossed friends in the spring of 1957. The presumed obligation to literally put on the best possible face for husbands, visitors, and even the produce clerk at the grocery store preoccupied many women during the '50s, when a "smart" appearance outside of the home was critical. In a decade in which the culture's keen attention to things visual coincided with clearly proscribed roles for women, cosmetics enjoyed a golden age. Familiar cues included declarative, arched eyebrows; false eyelashes, mascara, and eyeliner; boldly colored lips; and plenty of pancake foundation.

The Mickey Mouse Club became one of television's more enduring children's shows. Hosted by clean-cut Jimmie Dodd, the teenaged and preteen cast performed skits and musical numbers between cartoons and serial dramas. Mouse ears aside, the "Mouseketeers" provided viewers with role models (though tellingly, all were white). First among equals was Annette Funicello (*middle row, right*), the series' breakout star. Following adolescence, she segued into beach movies. Others, including Don Agrati (*My Three Sons*), Johnny Crawford (*The Rifleman*), and Paul Peterson (*The Donna Reed Show*), landed other series roles.

Jack Paar (*center*) is amused by *Tonight Show* regular Cliff Arquette as another frequent guest, French actress Genevieve, looks on. Paar took over as host of the NBC late-night show on July 29, 1957, and became an almost instant hit. Millions of viewers were charmed by his wry, self-deprecating humor and by his satirical wit (for example, he once nominated Elizabeth Taylor for the "Other Woman of the Year Award"). He welcomed an eclectic mix of guests, ranging from comedian Jonathan Winters to actor Cary Grant to politician Richard Nixon. He stepped down in 1962 after raising the show's ratings significantly.

1957

- The Rome Treaty is signed by Italy, West Germany, the Netherlands, Luxembourg, Belgium, and France. The treaty establishes the European Common Market.

March 31: The Federal Trade Commission charges the makers of three arthritis pain relief ointments with false advertising for claiming that their products "penetrate below the skin."

April 4: The British government announces dramatic cuts of up to 50 percent in both military personnel and materiel.

April 7: New York City's electric trolley system makes its final run, from Queens to Manhattan.

April 11: The Soviets put the world's largest particle accelerator into service. However, their position at the forefront of groundbreaking physics research is tenuous, as even more powerful accelerators are planned at research facilities in New York. • The U.S. Navy fires a Vanguard rocket with satellite equipment to an altitude of 126 miles.

April 13: According to the U.S. Atomic Energy Commission, the Soviets have conducted four nuclear weapons tests in the past 10 days.

April 21: The U.S. Army Air Defense Command announces that the Nike Ajax missiles with conventional warheads that are in place to defend large American cities will be replaced by Nike Hercules missiles, outfitted with atomic warheads.

April 26: The United States conducts the first test flight of the Jupiter, an intermediate range ballistic missile (IRBM).

April 29: Jordan's King Hussein accepts $10 million in direct U.S. aid to help oppose communism within his government.

In an era of strict segregation, New Orleans piano pounder Fats Domino effortlessly united audiences. Disarmingly smooth and charming, Fats was an accomplished musician whose talent transcended racial barriers. First drawing notice with his song "The Fat Man" in 1949, Domino stayed mostly beneath the mainstream radar until his 1955 release, "Ain't That a Shame," was covered by Pat Boone. A year later, Fats scored a No. 2 with "Blueberry Hill," initiating a steady chart presence that lasted for several years.

The well-meaning but frightfully nearsighted Mr. Magoo was created in 1949 by United Productions of America (UPA), and starred in nearly four dozen theatrical shorts before 1960. Amusingly conceived by director John Hubley and scripter Millard Kaufman, and given vocal life by veteran character actor Jim Backus, Magoo took home Oscars for best cartoon short in 1955 and '57. The character later made a successful transition to television. UPA utilized Magoo and a later star, Dr. Seuss's Gerald McBoing Boing, to pioneer "limited animation," whereby character movement was suggested mainly by key poses, with little or no "in between" motion. The economical approach was refined for TV use by the Hanna-Barbera studio (*Huckleberry Hound* and many others).

> "Give people a taste of Old Crow, and tell them it's Old Crow. Then give them another taste of Old Crow, but tell them it's Jack Daniel's. Ask them which they prefer. They'll think the two drinks are quite different. They are tasting images."
>
> —ADVERTISING EXECUTIVE DAVID OGILVY

The Ad Game

WHEN CROONER Frankie Laine sang about handling a hungry man with Manhandlers for Campbell's Soup commercials in the late 1950s, few Americans considered the double meaning of the lyrics. Behind the scenes, Madison Avenue advertising executives were skillfully perfecting the art and science of persuasion. Subtle suggestions of sex and other enticements, the ad execs understood, worked subliminally to sell products. From 1950 to 1960, American advertising expenditures grew from $5.7 billion a year to $12 billion as Americans were sent on a postwar spending spree.

The United States government, labor leaders, and business executives all agreed that mass consumption would play a central role in the conversion to a peacetime economy. With the rise of television, which overtook radio, newspapers, and magazines as the most important advertising medium during the 1950s, the visions of the good life dominated advertising on such programs as *Texaco Star Theater*. Television ads featured everything from Yogi Berra chugging Yoo-hoo to sexy women dressed as Old Gold cigarette packages.

As the decade progressed, so did the sophistication of advertisers and corporate marketers. General Motors, a company that had led the auto industry in earlier decades with its strategy of planned obsolescence, perfected the art of style in the 1950s. Each year, GM introduced new colors, new tailfins, and space-age designs on ever-changing car models, appealing to consumer desire, not need.

Increasingly, by the end of the decade, advertisers discovered they could segment the markets for their goods, better targeting children, women, and men at different times of the day and for specialized products. The industry also learned to pursue these carved-up markets with sophisticated demographic tools, psychological analyses, and studies of product-use patterns.

Numerous critics assailed this manipulation and conspicuous consumption. Vance Packard's *The Hidden Persuaders* (1957) was the most famous exposé of the advertising industry at the time. Packard's book warned Americans that behind the innocent appeal of ads, cunning advertising men were preying on their hidden frustrations and urges in order to sell everything "from gasoline to politicians."

Vance Packard caused a sensation with his 1957 book, *The Hidden Persuaders.* For the first time, methods by which the public was manipulated by advertisers were explored and interpreted. In somewhat overblown terms, Packard described how advertisers shaped their campaigns to best exploit a virtual checklist of human vulnerabilities. He quoted ad executives who proclaimed their power to mesmerize the unwary. While much of what Packard reported is widely known today, at the time it was revelatory and disturbing.

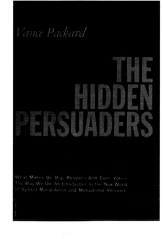

Women's undergarments were boldly marketed in Maidenform's "I dreamed . . . " campaign, which commenced in 1949. Running for the next 20 years, the seemingly endless variations on the theme presented women in countless glamorous yet assertive situations, sporting the company's bra and nothing else above the waist. Achievements seemingly made possible by wearing the product ranged from stopping traffic to barging down the Nile. While men enjoyed ogling the sexy models, the ads clicked with women for suggesting an array of fulfilling possibilities that didn't compromise femininity.

1957

May: International Brotherhood of Teamsters President David Beck pleads the Fifth Amendment more than 200 times during his testimony before the McClellan Committee, which is investigating the connection between organized crime and labor. • The medical profession takes some heat after Long Island physician Joseph Kris charges the family of seven-year-old Benny Hooper $1,500 for the doctor's role in Benny's rescue after the boy fell down a well. • Ricky Nelson of *Ozzie and Harriet* scores his first big hit with the release of his cover of the Fats Domino tune "I'm Walkin'."

May 2: Senator Joseph McCarthy dies from cirrhosis of the liver at age 48.

May 5: Eliot Ness, former federal agent and author of *The Untouchables,* dies of a heart attack at age 57.

May 10: A resolution is passed by the Supreme Soviet that asks the British Parliament and U.S. Congress to agree to talks leading to a moratorium on nuclear weapons testing.

May 11: President Eisenhower welcomes South Vietnamese Premier Ngo Dinh Diem to Washington, where the two leaders discuss the importance of stopping the spread of communism.

May 13: The U.S. denies Japan's request for the suspension of American nuclear weapons testing.

May 17: In the Prayer Pilgrimage for Freedom, 30,000 people assemble at the Lincoln Memorial in Washington, D.C., to demonstrate for voters' rights and desegregation.

May 22: A B-36 bomber accidentally drops a nuclear bomb over the New Mexico desert. The weapon is destroyed on impact and, fortunately, no nuclear detonation or radioactive contamination occurs.

May 24: Anti-American demonstrators in Taipei, Formosa, severely damage the U.S. Embassy.

The Prayer Pilgrimage, the first national event organized by the leaders of the modern civil rights movement, was designed to support the Civil Rights Bill of 1957 and to push for stronger measures. The demonstration in Washington, D.C., was held on May 17, 1957, the third anniversary of the U.S. Supreme Court's *Brown v. Board of Education* decision. It was the largest crowd that Martin Luther King (*at podium*) had ever addressed—about 30,000. "Give us the ballot," King declared, "and we will transform the salient misdeeds of bloodthirsty mobs into the abiding good deeds of orderly citizens." The crowd roared, repeating the words "give us the ballot."

A newly dispossessed child sits among the rubble caused by a tornado on May 20, 1957, outside Kansas City, Missouri. The F-5 storm cut a swath of destruction along a 71-mile path, beginning near Ottawa, Kansas. Though weather-tracking equipment recorded the storm's arrival, the means for alerting the populace proved tragically inadequate. An unforeseen consequence of the postwar construction boom had been the lack of basements in many new homes, thereby leaving residents vulnerable. That fact contributed to the 44 deaths and 500 injuries, mostly in Missouri, caused by this storm.

Imprisoned since his abortive coup attempt on Moncada Barracks in 1953, Cuban revolutionary Fidel Castro (*right photo, center*) wasted no time regrouping following parole two years later. By late 1956, he and surviving rebels had slipped back into Cuba, taking refuge in the Sierra Maestra Mountains. From there, Castro organized a guerrilla army, mounting an intense insurgency campaign throughout the island that was designed to destabilize the Batista government. Random bombings, arson, and sabotage committed by Castro's group resulted in heavy-handed punishment by Batista, who declared Castro "an agent of the Soviet Union." Meanwhile, many anti-Batista Cubans moved to South Florida. Thousands of Cuban exiles, such as the "July 26 Club" (*left photo*), raised funds and public awareness for the movement.

Well before Mayberry and Matlock, Andy Griffith gave a stunning performance as the venal Lonesome Rhodes in director Elia Kazan's *A Face in the Crowd*. Costarring Patricia Neal and Walter Matthau, the story traces the rise of a manipulative demagogue who brilliantly plays the media, parlaying his instinctive hucksterism into power and a fortune. His connection with "the people," and bypassing of the normal filtering channels, stirs powerful emotions while inspiring blind adoration. Though such cynicism did not endear the film to audiences in 1957, its knowing prescience is chilling to modern viewers.

Disneyland visitors were given a glimpse of things to come in 1957 with the new Monsanto House of the Future. This exercise in plastics development actually had been designed at MIT and featured an array of innovations. Some, such as microwave ovens, speaker phones, and electric toothbrushes, are now commonplace. Others, including atomic food preservation and ultrasonic dishwashers, await realization. The almost entirely plastic house was impervious to rot and could be dismantled and moved. When Disney decided to demolish the home of the future in 1967, the wrecking ball could not budge it. Workers had to use saws to dismantle the durable model.

1957

May 28: Baseball's National League authorizes the moves of the Brooklyn Dodgers to Los Angeles and the New York Giants to San Francisco, both in time for the 1958 season.

June: Soviet First Secretary Nikita Khrushchev turns the tables on several of his government's Stalinist ministers, successfully ousting them following their failed attempt to unseat Khrushchev with an illegal, secret vote. • Nobel Prize-winning chemist Linus Pauling, in a *Foreign Policy Bulletin* article, estimates that 10,000 Americans are suffering from leukemia caused by nuclear testing.

June 2: Soviet First Secretary Khrushchev appears on the CBS program *Face the Nation,* marking the first American television appearance by a Soviet leader since World War II. He discusses, among other things, his desire to work toward bilateral nuclear disarmament.

June 3: The U.S. Supreme Court reverses a lower court's conviction of presumed Communist and labor union official Clinton Jencks. He had been convicted of perjury for signing an affidavit that claimed he was not a Communist.

June 12: Surgeon General Leroy E. Burney asserts that there is a causal relationship between cigarette smoking and lung cancer.

June 17: The U.S. Supreme Court decrees that it is unconstitutional to criminally prosecute individuals who advocate the violent overthrow of the government. The day will hereafter be known as "Red Monday."

Summer: Enovid, a pill largely developed by Dr. Carl Djerassi back in 1951, gains FDA approval for the treatment of severe menstrual disorders.

Ford Motor Company executive William Ford admires a model of the Nucleon, an experimental automobile designed to be powered by uranium. Equipped with a scaled-down nuclear reactor inside the trunk, the vehicle was good for 5,000 miles before needing "refueling"—in this case, replacing its spent atomic matter. Widely touted at a time when atoms seemed to be the answer to everything, the Nucleon was the subject of much debate in the pages of science and technology magazines. Though the car never was produced, its design begs the question of what contingencies were in place should this warhead on wheels ever be rear-ended.

Alarmed at what he saw as an "education gap" between American and Soviet students, Harvard President James Conant in the 1950s advocated assessing the scholarly potential of pupils. Students would be typed as "gifted," "average," or "slow," and thereupon steered into the most suitable areas of study to develop their abilities. Many schools followed Conant's lead. Thus, advanced students tended to be encouraged to pursue such fields as engineering and medicine while many lesser students wound up in trade schools. Conant's theories are largely ignored today, to the detriment, some say, of the national interest.

AIP and the Teen Screen

IN HIS DEFINITIVE book about American International Pictures, film historian Mark Thomas McGee notes that in 1954 half of the nation's movie theaters were not breaking even. The major studios had been stripped of their owned-and-operated screens in a 1948 Supreme Court decision and, without guaranteed bookings, were pressing exhibitors for greater proportions of dwindling gates. Meanwhile, a generation of teenagers with disposable income was beginning to come into its own. The kids enjoyed drive-in theaters, and those theaters needed exploitable "B" product. Entertainment lawyer Samuel Z. Arkoff and a onetime exhibitor named James H. Nicholson evaluated the situation and established the American Releasing Corporation—soon renamed American International Pictures.

AIP operated on three principles: shoot 'em cheaply, put 'em out on double bills, and exploit the heck out of them. So important was marketing to AIP, in fact, that many of its pictures were written and filmed only after Nicholson had come up with a catchy title, and after the studio's imaginative staff artist, Al Kallis, created a can't-miss poster. If greeted by positive response from exhibitors, the idea was green-lighted for production.

AIP's first release was a reasonably popular road-rally melodrama called *The Fast and the Furious* (1954). In a practice that sustained the company during its earliest years, Arkoff and Nicholson barely took a breath before plowing the profits right into the next project.

HUMAN EMOTIONS STRIPPED RAW!
The terrifying story that COULD COME TRUE!

DAY THE WORLD ENDED

ATTACKED ...by a creature from hell!

SUPERSCOPE

RICHARD DENNING
LORI NELSON · ADELE JERGENS
with TOUCH CONNORS · PAUL BIRCH

AIP sci-fi, directed by Roger Corman

A typical AIP shoot lasted seven to 14 days, and was budgeted between $65,000 and $125,000. Efficient producers such as Roger Corman, Alex Gordon, Herman Cohen, and Bert I. Gordon created a low-budget "teenpic" assembly line to crank out sci-fi, hot rod, horror, western, and war pictures. On screen and behind the scenes, AIP made smart use of industry veterans and eager youngsters.

If there is a single emblematic AIP film of the '50s, it is Herman Cohen's irresistibly titled *I Was a Teenage Werewolf* (1957). It grossed nearly 20 times its $125,000 cost, and cemented AIP's status as lord of the Hollywood teenpic.

"Roger, for chrissake, hire a couple more extras and put a little more furniture on the set!"

—AIP CHIEF SAM ARKOFF TO PRODUCER-DIRECTOR ROGER CORMAN

The genius of *I Was a Teenage Werewolf* is that the title character becomes a monster not because of a curse or a freak happenstance of nature; instead, he's the hoodwinked guinea pig of a middle-aged scientist who claims he can moderate the boy's temper. The grownup turns the boy's life into a living hell, of course—and what teenager in the audience didn't share that self-pitying sensation of adolescent victimization? *Teenage Werewolf,* like its companion, *I Was a Teenage Frankenstein,* was a low-budget production that turned an impressive profit. That's Michael Landon under Philip Scheer's makeup. The timorous beauty is Dawn Richard.

1957

June 24: In the case of *Roth v. United States,* the U.S. Supreme Court rules against Samuel Roth, publisher of the quarterly publication *American Aphrodite,* claiming that gratuitous obscenity is not protected by the First Amendment.

June 25: In Tuskegee, Alabama, black citizens decide to boycott white businesses in response to a discriminatory plan by local leaders, who reconfigure the city limits so that all but a few black citizens would live outside the city. • Hurricane Audrey slams into Cameron, Louisiana, killing at least 400 people.

June 30: The American occupation headquarters in Japan, one of the last active elements of the World War II Pacific Theater, closes its doors.

July: The International Geophysical Year, a multilateral, 67-nation scientific effort to understand the Earth, gets under way. • Pugwash, Nova Scotia, hosts the first conference of the Pugwash Movement, with 22 scientists from 10 nations gathering to discuss nuclear nonproliferation.

July 2: The USS *Grayback* is launched from the Mare Island Naval Shipyard in Vallejo, California. The *Grayback* is the first submarine capable of firing guided missiles.

July 6: Tennis star Althea Gibson becomes the first African-American to win the Wimbledon women's singles championship. • John Lennon meets Paul McCartney at a church concert where Lennon is performing with his band, the Quarrymen.

July 12: In what turns out to be the first commercial use of nuclear power, the Southern California grid receives electricity from a Santa Susana test reactor.

Samuel Roth was a New York poet, bookseller, free-speech advocate, literary pirate, noisy self-promoter, and—in the eyes of the U.S. Supreme Court—a pornographer whose big mistake was sending "obscene" materials via U.S. mail. The 1957 Supreme Court decision concerned itself with Roth's hardcover quarterly, *American Aphrodite,* a pretentious and only mildly erotic magazine that ceased publication in 1955 (a 1954 issue is pictured). The court defined obscenity as material in which the "dominant theme taken as a whole appeals to the prurient interest" of the "average person, applying contemporary community standards." Precisely what constituted "community standards" was a chink in the law that civil libertarians would use to expand protections in the following decades.

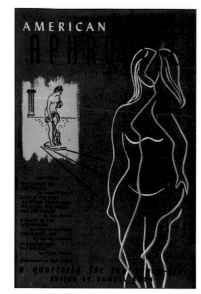

Chicago-based *Duke* was one of many men's magazines that took its cue from another Chicago publication, *Playboy.* It included sophisticated, well-written articles and stories; cartoons; a mascot (the button-eyed mannequin seen here); and, of course, undraped young models. But *Duke* was unique because it targeted middle-class black men at a time when mass media barely acknowledged the existence of African-Americans. *Duke* also was wholly black owned, the brainchild of writer and jazz musician Dan Burley. Despite good production values, the beautiful "Duchess of the Month," and contributors the likes of James Baldwin and Ray Bradbury, *Duke* survived for only about a year.

Former First Lady Eleanor Roosevelt maintained a characteristic whirlwind of activity in the years following her husband's death. In addition to championing numerous humanitarian causes, Roosevelt served as U.S. delegate to the United Nations from 1945 to 1953 (and again under President Kennedy until her death). Further, she wrote a daily newspaper column entitled "My Day" on a range of topics. It was in this capacity that she traveled to Moscow in 1957 to meet with Soviet leader Nikita Khrushchev. What resulted was less an interview than a vigorous debate, prompting Khrushchev to observe that "at least we didn't shoot each other."

The bodies of some of Hurricane Audrey's 400-plus victims lie ready for interment in the aftermath of her assault on the town of Cameron, Louisiana, on June 27, 1957. One of the most destructive tropical storms in American history, Audrey brought winds in excess of 150 mph, flattening homes and businesses to the tune of $150 million. What made the storm and its devastation particularly tragic was that despite warnings issued by the National Weather Service, many of the residents, especially older ones, failed to heed them. The locals had been unaccustomed to weather of Audrey's severity.

Written off by nearly everyone earlier in the decade, Frank Sinatra by the mid-1950s was at the top of his game. Much of his glory came through a series of "concept" albums: thematically linked releases that alternated between collections of up-tempo saloon songs and tender ballads. Working with a series of top arrangers, including Nelson Riddle, Gordon Jenkins, and Billy May, Sinatra's Capitol output formed the basis of his legend in years to come. His album *Come Fly with Me* (1957), boasting a set of escapist tunes (like the title song and "Let's Get Away from It All"), was a particular stand-out.

The Lonely Doll is a photo storybook about an unhappily solitary doll named Edith (a "Lenci" doll made in the 1920s) and her adventures with two new friends, Mr. Bear and Little Bear. In an odd turn, Mr. Bear immediately establishes himself as the haughty leader of the group, ordering Edith to do her homework before fun time, and scolding her—even spanking her—when she gets into mischief. Every picture was carefully composed and photographed by the author, Dare Wright, a former fashion model of great gifts who struggled unsuccessfully to liberate herself from her domineering mother. *The Lonely Doll* was embraced by a generation of girls, and inspired nine more books in the series.

Althea Gibson continued the pre-civil rights movement tradition of blacks achieving white acceptance through excellence in sports. The graceful athlete almost singlehandedly desegregated women's tennis. During the 1950s, she became the first African-American to compete in the U.S. Open tennis championship. In 1956 she won the French Open women's singles title. She dominated a year later, capturing the singles and doubles crowns at Wimbledon and the singles championship at the U.S. Open.

July 16: Secretary of Defense Charles Wilson orders a 100,000-man Armed Forces reduction, to be completed by the end of the year. • Marine Corps Major and future Mercury astronaut John Glenn pilots a jet from California to New York in a transcontinental record-setting time of 3:23.8.

July 19: The first nuclear-armed missile is test-fired at the Nevada Test Site.

July 20: Approximately 100,000 people pack Yankee Stadium in New York to hear Reverend Billy Graham speak.

July 26: The Soviets test-fire the first multistage intercontinental ballistic missile (ICBM).

July 27: A palace guard assassinates Carlos Castillo Armas, Guatemala's U.S.-backed president. • Fidel Castro and a force of about 200 insurgents attack a Cuban army post.

July 29: Jack Paar makes his regular hosting debut on *The Tonight Show* stage, beginning what will be a five-year run at the helm of the hit show. • The International Atomic Energy Agency is established by the United Nations to promote peaceful applications of nuclear energy.

August: Black citizens in Rock Hill, South Carolina, begin a successful boycott of the city's segregated bus system.

August 1: The U.S. and Canada agree to join forces for the creation of NORAD, the North American Air Defense Command.

August 2: Cuban dictator Fulgencio Batista suspends all constitutional guarantees, including freedom of the press, for 45 days in the wake of widespread antigovernment violence.

August 4: Racing legend Juan Manuel Fangio wins his fifth world title at the German Grand Prix in Nurburgring.

Members of the Committee for Non-violent Action demonstrate at the Camp Mercury atomic test site near Las Vegas in August 1957. Comprised largely of radical pacifists, such as Albert Bigelow, CNVA members directed most of their actions toward ending nuclear testing and the arms race. They also organized protests against the Strategic Air Command in Nebraska and a Polaris submarine facility in Connecticut. The Committee for a Sane Nuclear Policy (SANE), organized in 1957, became the largest group to oppose nuclear tests, with more than 100 local chapters.

François "Papa Doc" Duvalier (*left*) became president of Haiti in September 1957 following a tumultuous year, even by Haitian standards. A former medical doctor, Duvalier served as Labor minister before shifting political winds saw him displaced. In May 1956, Colonel Paul Magloire's rule of Haiti ended in chaos as he attempted to extend his tenure by force. Amid the turmoil, Duvalier maneuvered behind the scenes to secure the presidency, brushing aside all rivals. Papa Doc moved quickly to consolidate power; he assumed dictatorial powers while replacing the army with his own formidable guard, the fearsome Tonton Macoute.

Car Culture

O N HER WEEKLY television variety show in the mid-1950s, Dinah Shore sang a jingle for General Motors, encouraging viewers to see the USA in their Chevrolets. During the decade, increasingly affordable and curvaceous cars, such as the '56 Ford Thunderbird and the '57 Chevy, helped deepen America's love affair with the automobile.

President Dwight Eisenhower's vision of a national road system finally arrived with the Federal-Aid Highway Act of 1956, accelerating construction of an eventual 41,000 miles of limited-access highways in the United States. New roads and more reliable vehicles encouraged Americans to take Shore's advice.

On their way to national parks and family camping trips, leisure travelers could avoid the unknown thanks to an increasingly homogenous and recognizable landscape of signs and roadside iconography. Beginning in 1952, Holiday Inn began to dominate highway interchanges with its courtyard motels, which travelers felt were a lot less chancy than mom-and-pop lodgings. Meanwhile, such restaurant chains as Howard Johnson's removed the mystery of local cuisine.

For suburbanites, the car became the chief mode of daily transportation. Instead of taking the subway, streetcar, or bus to work, Dad got there faster in his new Buick. Mom needed a car (her own car if they could afford it) to drive to the new supermarket or shopping mall.

A vehicle of leisure, the car also became a pivot point of teen culture. Youths drove to the nearest hangout for a bite

A popular Hollywood, California, drive-in

to eat, a pastime that contributed to the mushrooming of fast-food burger joints across the country. Rebel teenagers also started the new ritual of "dragging the gut" (cruising through town) on Saturday nights.

The 1950s saw the rise of drive-in restaurants, movies, and even churches (in California's Orange County). Statistics proved how car-reliant America had become: From 1950 to 1960, the number of car registrations in the United States soared from 40 million to 60 million.

Tony Curtis (*far left*) and Burt Lancaster (*second from left*) portray a pair of venomous sleazeballs in director Alexander Mackendrick's *Sweet Smell of Success.* This brutal examination of New York's nightlife denizens is presented in a stark, noir-esque style and peppered with rapid-fire dialogue by Ernest Lehman. A superb Elmer Bernstein score adds to the seamy atmosphere. Curtis, in perhaps his finest performance, stars as a toadying press agent in thrall to the career-making or -breaking Hunsecker (Lancaster), an unprincipled gossip columnist. Perhaps the overall cynicism of the story put off audiences in 1957, but the film has grown in stature ever since.

August 5: *American Bandstand,* hosted by Dick Clark, premieres on ABC.

August 6: Eleven people are arrested at the Nevada Test Site during a protest against atomic weapons testing, thought to be the first of its kind.

August 7: Comedian Oliver Hardy, of Laurel and Hardy fame, dies at age 65 following a series of strokes.

August 14: The Syrian army seizes the U.S. Embassy in Damascus and deports three U.S. diplomats, claiming that the Americans were plotting to overthrow the Syrian government.

August 17: Chess player Bobby Fischer, age 14, ties for first place at the 58th U.S. Open, becoming the youngest player to earn a master rating.

August 21: President Eisenhower announces that the United States would be willing to suspend nuclear weapons tests for two years if the Soviets agree to stop producing fissionable materials and submit to weapons inspections.

August 28–29: Senator Strom Thurmond of South Carolina talks for a record 24 hours and 18 minutes during a 122-hour filibuster in opposition to the Civil Rights Act of 1957.

August 31: Malaya wins independence from Great Britain. Sir Abdul Rahman will serve as the Asian commonwealth's first leader.

September 3: President Eisenhower signs the Price-Anderson Act of 1957, which ensures that any damage compensation in the event of a nuclear reactor accident would come from any insurance carried by the owner of the reactor. • Federal District Judge Ronald N. Davies rules that Central High School in Little Rock, Arkansas, be integrated the following day. *See* September 4, 1957.

Little Rock Nine

"NIGGER, IF YOU WANT to go by me, you'll have to kill me," proclaimed a white student to a black student who hoped to integrate Central High School in Little Rock, Arkansas.

When the Supreme Court ordered in 1955 that the desegregation of the nation's public schools proceed with "all deliberate speed," school districts throughout the South balked. Nowhere was this more evident than in Little Rock. On September 2, 1957, after a federal district judge ordered that the city's schools comply with the Supreme Court's mandate, Arkansas Governor Orval Faubus called in the National Guard under the auspices of keeping the peace. But rather than desegregate Central High School, the Guard prevented nine African-American students from attending classes.

Dubbed the "Little Rock Nine," the courageous black students drew the attention of the national media, and soon a showdown between Governor Faubus and President Dwight Eisenhower ensued. The predicament came to a head on September 23 when, after widespread rioting, the Little Rock Nine again were forced out of Central High. The following day, Eisenhower federalized the Arkansas National Guard and sent in the 101st Airborne Division to uphold order and protect the black students. The guardsmen stayed at the school for the remainder of the academic year.

Though Eisenhower's actions effectively desegregated Central High, animosities continued. White students harassed the Little Rock Nine on a regular basis. Minnijean Brown, one of the nine, recalled that "not a day went by that I wasn't called something dreadful." Even worse, others were spat on and physically assaulted. The following school year, Faubus closed all four of Little Rock's high schools rather than submit to integration. When the schools reopened in 1959 after a court order, only six black students were enrolled.

Elizabeth Eckford, one of the Little Rock Nine, didn't get the message from her adviser, Daisy Bates, to meet at her house on the morning that the nine black students were set to desegregate Central High School. They were all supposed to go together by car. But it was too late; Eckford was on her own. The white mob spat on her, tore at her clothing, and called for her lynching—all in front of network news cameras and the nation's

photojournalists. And instead of protecting her, the state's National Guard turned her and the rest of the Little Rock Nine away from the school.

> "I was covered with shattered glass....I reached for the rock lying in the middle of the floor. A note was tied to it. I broke the string and unfolded a soiled piece of paper. Scrawled in the bold print were the words: 'STONE THIS TIME. DYNAMITE NEXT.'"
>
> —DAISY BATES, ADVISER FOR THE LITTLE ROCK NINE, RECALLING AN INCIDENT AT HER HOME

Daisy Bates, copublisher of the *Arkansas State Press* (a black newspaper), also was Arkansas president of the NAACP. In 1957 she served as adviser and mentor to the Little Rock Nine. As such, she was the target of attacks and murder threats by white segregationists, who launched a rock through her window and twice burned a cross on her front lawn. Yet Bates remained steadfast, determined to force Arkansas to desegregate its schools. However, Arkansas Governor Orval Faubus (pictured on the TV screen), a segregationist, also would not budge. It would take the clout of the President and the might of the U.S. military to decide this local battle.

THEY'RE IN THE SCHOOL!

WHILE I WAS DICTATING, someone yelled, "Look! They're going into the school!"

At that instant, the eight Negroes—the three boys and five girls—were crossing the schoolyard toward a side door at the south end of the school. The girls were in bobby sox and the boys were dressed in shirts open at the neck. All were carrying books.

They were not running, not even walking fast. They simply strolled toward the steps, went up and were inside before all but a few of the 200 people at that end of the street knew it.

"They've gone in," a man roared. "Oh, God, the niggers are in the school."

A woman screamed, "Did they get in? Did you see them go in?"

"They're in now," some other men yelled.

"Oh, my God," the woman screamed. She burst into tears and tore at her hair. Hysteria swept the crowd. Other women began weeping and screaming.

—ASSOCIATED PRESS REPORTER RELMAN MORIN, SEPTEMBER 23, 1957

Members of the 101st Division of the Airborne Command escort 15-year-old Minnijean Brown (*pictured*) and eight other black students to Central High School on September 25, 1957, nearly four weeks after their first attempt to desegregate the school. Arkansas Governor Orval Faubus had ordered the state National Guard to prevent the Little Rock Nine from entering the school. The paratroopers' escort, as approved by President Dwight Eisenhower, was the last word in a weeks-long standoff between Faubus and racist white mobs on one side, and a federal court order and the U.S. Constitution on the other.

1957

See September 20, 1957.

September 4: Under orders from Governor Orval Faubus, the Arkansas National Guard prevents nine black students from entering Little Rock's Central High School on the second day of classes. *See* September 20, 1957. • The *Wolfenden Report,* published in Great Britain, calls for an end to the criminalization of homosexuality. • The Ford Motor Company introduces the 1958 Edsel, which will prove to be a marketing failure.

September 5: With U.S. assistance and air support, Cuban dictator Fulgencio Batista suppresses an uprising by the Cuban navy at Cienfuegos. • The U.S. State Department announces that it plans to expedite arms shipments to Iraq, Turkey, Jordan, and Lebanon.

September 8: Female tennis star Althea Gibson becomes the first African-American to win the U.S. Open.

September 9: President Eisenhower signs the Civil Rights Act of 1957. The act establishes a civil rights division within the Justice Department and calls for the creation of the U.S. Commission on Civil Rights. The act also allows the federal government to bring suit against anyone interfering with another person's right to vote. • A bomb explodes at Hattie Cotton Elementary School in Nashville during a week in which white citizens protest the admission of a black student.

September 13: Cuban dictator Fulgencio Batista announces, in an NBC interview broadcast in the U.S., that he will not seek reelection in Cuba's next round of national elections, scheduled for June 1958.

September 19: For the first time, the U.S. conducts an underground nuclear test. The test is held in an isolated part of the Great Basin Desert, some 100 miles outside of Las Vegas.

Dorothy Counts, age 15, and Dr. Edwin Thompkins, a family friend, brave a white mob as Counts desegregates Harding High School in Charlotte, North Carolina, in September 1957. With both *Brown* decisions and the Civil Rights Act of 1957 backing them up, attempts to desegregate schools continued sporadically in communities across the South. While federal legislators may have liked to take the credit, it was brave black teenagers like Counts, who were willing to face socially sanctioned harassment, that made school desegregation a reality below the Mason-Dixon line.

Television's Paladin (Richard Boone) of *Have Gun, Will Travel* was a western adventurer noted for his cerebral approach to gun-fighting. Paladin viewed life as a chess game, as he aimed to stay several moves ahead of his opponents. Cultured and erudite, he typically strategized his way out of a problem rather than simply pull the trigger. This departure from the standard western formula suggested the producers' aim to attract a more sophisticated audience.

Of Jim Thompson's 29 novels, all but three were first published as paperback originals. Although ignored by the literati of the 1950s, Thompson's hard-edged, gravely bleak stories attracted a core of dedicated fans. As Thompson saw things, nothing is as good as it seems, everybody's a chiseler, and they're probably going to do it to you before you can do it to them. In *Wild Town,* a violent and none-too-bright ex-con is handed a job as a hotel detective. And then he meets the

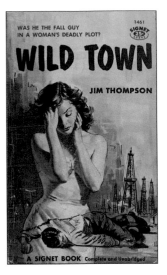

trampy wife of the hotel's old, rich owner. Look out, danger ahead. Cover art on this 1957 original is by prolific paperback illustrator Robert Maguire.

Little known outside of labor circles, Teamsters President Jimmy Hoffa became a national figure during McClellan Committee congressional investigations of union corruption in 1957. Hoffa became president that year following the jailing of his predecessor, Dave Beck, on grand larceny charges. The Teamsters had drawn scrutiny for an assortment of racketeering and ethical violations, eventu-

ally leading to their expulsion from the AFL-CIO in 1957. Hoffa's reputation as a shrewd strategist was matched only by his renown as an abrasive, inflexible man for whom "guts" was paramount. Personal enmity with McClellan Committee counsel Robert Kennedy resulted in a virtual blood feud.

Growing up poor in segregated Mobile, Alabama, Hank Aaron was rail-thin, as square meals were hard to come by. He later experienced racism while playing in the Negro Leagues, minor leagues, and majors. Yet he overcame all obstacles to win the National League MVP Award in 1957 on the strength of a .322 batting average and 44 home runs. That fall, "Hammerin' Hank" led the Milwaukee Braves to their first National League championship and a seven-game World Series triumph over the New York Yankees. Seventeen years later, Aaron would break Babe Ruth's career home run record.

Actor Raymond Burr enjoyed a journeyman film career playing heavies (notably Lars Thorwald in Hitchcock's *Rear Window*), but not until television's *Perry Mason* did he achieve stardom. Mason was a cool, patient defense attorney who typically won acquittals for the apparently guilty at the last minute in highly dramatic fashion—usually involving a courtroom confession by a witness. *Perry Mason,* which captured viewers with Fred Steiner's memorable opening theme, made for addicting, if formulaic, viewing. Actress Barbara Hale costarred as Mason's able assistant, Della Street.

1957

September 20: Federal District Judge Ronald N. Davies orders Arkansas Governor Orval Faubus to remove the Arkansas National Guard from Central High School. Faubus announces he soon will comply with the order but asks black students to stay away from the school in the meantime. *See* September 23, 1957. • The Thor intermediate range ballistic missile (IRBM) is successfully test-flown 1,250 miles.

Fall: Twenty-seven Africanized queen bees are inadvertently released in Brazil. These "killer bees" will colonize and migrate steadily northward, killing some 1,000 people throughout the century.

September 23: The "Little Rock Nine" are admitted to Central High School, but they soon are sent home when the police fear they won't be able to maintain control of the mob waiting outside the school. *See* September 24, 1957.

September 24: On national television, President Dwight Eisenhower announces he is sending U.S. Army troops from the 101st Airborne Division to Little Rock to enforce the court-ordered desegregation of Central High School. He also federalizes the Arkansas National Guard. *See* September 25, 1957.

September 25: Federal troops escort the Little Rock Nine to their classes at Central High School. • The Soviets disclose that they have carried out training exercises with their army and navy involving the use of atomic and hydrogen weapons.

September 26: *West Side Story,* a Leonard Bernstein-Stephen Sondheim musical, premieres at Broadway's Garden Theatre.

September 29: An explosion of radioactive waste at the Mayak plant near the Russian city of Kyshtym contaminates a 17-square-kilometer area.

This prototypical 1950s diner stands as a prime example of "Googie" architecture. So-called after a Los Angeles coffee shop (designed by John Lautner), the style was characterized by a "futuristic" motif that favored extensive use of glass, upswept roofs, "boomerang" or "amoeba" shapes, and exposed steel I-beams. Reaching its heyday by the mid-1950s, Googie was largely, but not entirely, a West Coast phenomenon. Though derided by serious architecture critics as a transient, frivolous design, Googie left its mark in the form of Seattle's Space Needle.

The 1957 film *Jailhouse Rock* tapped into Elvis Presley's raw, animalistic energy to great effect. Thrown into prison on a manslaughter charge, the angry, antisocial Vince (Presley) discovers he can sing. Mentored by a fellow con (Mickey Shaughnessy, *left*), he finds success as a rock 'n' roll singer upon his release, capitalizing on his notoriety with a striking musical number built around the title song. From there, he reverts to form—despite guidance from a comely industry insider, *Howdy Doody*'s Judy Tyler (tragically killed after filming finished). Presley's cinematic promise would be squandered in subsequent films.

Composed by Leonard Bernstein and Stephen Sondheim, *West Side Story* was a widely celebrated updating of Shakespeare's *Romeo and Juliet*. Transplanted from Verona to contemporary New York City, the show recast the feuding families as rival street gangs. Originally conceived as *East Side Story* (featuring a doomed romance between a Jewish-Catholic couple), a six-year genesis saw its creators retool the concept, resulting in a Broadway hit that featured such timeless tunes as "Somewhere," "America," and "I Feel Pretty." Here, actresses Chita Rivera (*right*) and Liane Plane suggest some of Jerome Robbins's high-energy choreography. The show earned seven Tony Award nominations.

In a decade in which gay life was freely condemned and conducted surreptitiously, author Ann Bannon forged new paths with a series of empathetic, well-written lesbian-themed novels. The title of her first book, *Odd Girl Out,* refers to Laura, a college student whose romance with her sorority sister, Beth, shatters when Beth elects to go back to her male sweetheart and live the straight life. Alone, Laura sets out for New York City and new experiences. Despite its then-outré theme, *Odd Girl Out* was the second-best selling paperback original of 1957. The autographed copy seen here is a 1960 edition.

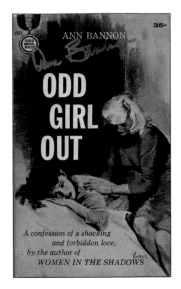

Because Barney Rosset's Grove Press prided itself on publishing avant-garde books other publishers were afraid to touch, Rosset's 1957 launch of *Evergreen Review,* an iconoclastic literary quarterly, seemed natural. The first issue (*pictured*) included an essay by Jean-Paul Sartre, short fiction by Samuel Beckett, and a portfolio by cover photographer Harold Feinstein. In the second issue, Rosset and *Evergreen* editor Don Allen focused on Beat writers, confirming *Evergreen Review* as a one-stop source for work by innovative European and American authors.

With the premiere of *Leave It to Beaver* in 1957, the Cleavers of Mayfield became one of television's most popular families. Centering on the doings of the "Beaver" (or Theodore, played by Jerry Mathers, *front*) and big brother Wally (Tony Dow, *top right*), the sitcom's childhood perspective had a low-key charm. Heading the household were June (Barbara Billingsley, *left*) and Ward (Hugh Beaumont, *right*), whose occasional fallibility helped humanize what might otherwise have been stereotypical TV parents. The show's informed sentimentality gave it a certain sweetness, essential to its appeal on two networks and through countless reruns.

1957

October: The Viet Minh launch a nationwide bombing and assassination campaign across South Vietnam. They will murder more than 400 South Vietnamese officials by year's end. • An epidemic of Asian Flu, which was first identified in February in the Far East, reaches its peak in the United States.

October 1: U.S. Air Force B-52 bombers begin a program of remaining on patrol full-time, in anticipation of an attack by the Soviets. • Thalidomide is introduced in West Germany. Developed by Chemie Gruenethal, it is widely prescribed to treat morning sickness in pregnant women, but it causes severe birth defects.

October 3: The people of West Berlin, Germany, elect Willy Brandt as their new mayor.

October 4: The U.S.-Soviet "space race" begins when the Soviets stun the Americans by launching Sputnik, the Earth's first artificial satellite. Sputnik will remain in orbit until January 4, 1958. • *Leave It to Beaver* premieres on CBS for the first of its six seasons.

October 7: Two hundred square miles of British countryside north of Liverpool are contaminated when a fire in a graphite-cooled nuclear reactor leads to a major radiation leak.

October 10: President Eisenhower personally apologizes to Ghana's finance minister, Komla Agbeli Gbdemah, after Gbdemah reveals that he was refused service in a Dover, Delaware, restaurant. • The Milwaukee Braves, led by slugger Hank Aaron, beat the New York Yankees in the Game 7 finale of the World Series.

October 11: A B-47 carrying nuclear materials crashes in Florida, setting off two minor detonations.

Cosmopolitan magazine, established in 1886, soon became a vehicle for politically oriented articles and fiction; contributors included Theodore Dreiser, Upton Sinclair, H. G. Wells, and George Bernard Shaw. Monthly circulation reached a new high of two million during World War II, when *Cosmopolitan* was dominated by fiction, but by 1955 readers were more interested in lifestyle and celebrity articles. Circulation diminished to about one million, and *Cosmo* pitched itself to women with more fervor than before. It was not until 1965, when Helen Gurley Brown was installed as editor, that *Cosmopolitan* once again became a publishing powerhouse. The cover portrait of film star Kim Novak on this 1957 issue is by illustrator Jon Whitcomb.

Actress Joanne Woodward (pictured on the jacket of the British edition of the 1957 source book) gave a bravura performance in a complex study of multiple personalities, *The Three Faces of Eve* (1957). Based on a true-life case study by Corbett Thigpen and Hervey Cleckley, the film depicts three distinct personas—an unassuming housewife, a wild party girl, and a sober, intelligent woman—inhabiting the same body. Though the film's tone varies from documentary-style narrative to light farce, it is an engrossing study of a little-understood malady. Actor Lee J. Cobb provides able support as Eve's psychiatrist. Woodward's imaginative, often touching portrayal rightly earned her an Academy Award for best actress.

James Garner played gambler-rogue Brett Maverick, the title character of this subversive television western. Though originating in 1957 as a standard-issue western horse opera, the series soon found its footing by utilizing Garner's natural comic gifts, as he steered the show toward black comedy. *Maverick* was the brainchild of producer Roy Huggins, who called it "a conventional western, turned inside out." The program quickly became a hit, beating out a plethora of competition to win an Emmy for best western. Garner left the series after three seasons to make films, but returned to the small screen in the 1970s for *The Rockford Files*.

Raid at Apalachin

IN NOVEMBER 1957, U.S. narcotics agent Joseph Amato spoke before a Senate hearing on the Mafia and organized crime. "We believe there does exist in the United States a society loosely organized for the specific purpose of smuggling narcotics and committing other crimes," he testified. Amato's words were not only controversial, but to many they were the ramblings of a delusional witness. Indeed, J. Edgar Hoover, the longstanding chief of the FBI, had claimed that the Mafia was a myth.

Then, just days after Amato's testimony, New York state troopers surrounded and raided the estate of Joe Barbara in the small hamlet of Apalachin, New York. What they discovered was a national meeting of *La Cosa Nostra*—the American Mafia. The crime bosses tried to make a break for it, climbing through windows and running through the woods, but dozens were arrested.

Months before the raid, such leading mafiosi as Vito Genovese, Carlo Gambino, Paul Castellano, and Stefano Magaddino had decided that they should convene to discuss the growing narcotics trade and the recent murder of crime boss Albert Anastasia. The gathering was not atypical; ever since the bloody Castellammarese War of 1931, *La Cosa Nostra* had held meetings to check interfamily violence and settle disputes.

The planners of the 1957 meeting chose Apalachin for its proximity to New York City and its isolated location, which they wrongly thought would deter the police. "It was horrendous," recalled crime boss Joseph "Bananas" Bonanno, "all those men caught in the same place, a ton of publicity, a public-relations coup for law enforcement, a field day for journalists."

Though the state troopers had little with which to charge the 63 gangsters they apprehended, they finally settled the question of the Mafia's existence. As one law enforcement official noted, "One thing you can be sure of—those characters weren't meeting to start a Red Cross chapter."

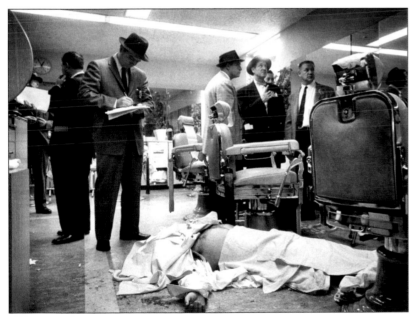

Mobster Albert Anastasia (of Murder, Inc., notoriety) lies dead in New York's Park Sheraton barbershop. With a well-deserved reputation for brutality throughout his criminal career, Anastasia had incurred the wrath of fellow gangsters Vito Genovese and Carlo Gambino, both members of the "New York Commission"—an organization with links to underworld operations stretching from coast to coast. Anastasia's hit on Arnold Schuster, an "outsider," had alarmed his associates, who recognized that public tolerance of their activities was contingent upon their confining killings to their own. Once the necessary alliances were assembled, Anastasia's October 1957 execution became a *fait accompli*.

Plainfield, Wisconsin, farmer Ed Gein was a quiet man who baby-sat local children. He also was a murderer and grave robber who turned his ramshackle farmhouse into a chamber of horrors decorated with the bones, organs, and skin of the two women he killed and the many whose bodies he had secretly exhumed. He cooked and ate human organs, and wore a woman's tanned torso. When deputies raided Gein's property, they found the headless body of his last victim, hung by the heels and field-dressed like a deer. A Milwaukee writer named Robert Bloch absorbed the news accounts and wrote a novel entitled *Psycho*. Gein died in a mental hospital in 1984.

October 16: Speaking at a press conference, Secretary of State John Foster Dulles warns the Soviets that the U.S. will retaliate for an attack against Turkey with an attack against the Soviet Union.

October 17: England's Queen Elizabeth II arrives for a state visit in Washington following visits to Ottawa, Canada, and Williamsburg, Virginia.

October 18: The Soviet Union's Rudolf Ivanovich Abel is convicted in the United States of espionage.

October 22: François Duvalier is elected president of Haiti with the backing of the army, beginning a brutal 14-year dictatorship.

October 24: French fashion pioneer Christian Dior dies in Italy at age 52. His assistant, Yves Saint Laurent, will take over leadership of the Dior fashion house.

October 25: Murder, Inc., crime boss Albert Anastasia is gunned down in a Manhattan barbershop. Though suspicion focuses on several perpetrators, nobody will be arrested for Anastasia's murder.

November: Britain's Vivian Fuchs and New Zealand's Edmund Hillary lead the first trans-Antarctic expedition to establish a base at the South Pole. • Project Orion begins when a team of scientists at General Atomics proposes a spaceship powered by nuclear pulse propulsion. Ultimately, the project will be abandoned when nuclear test ban treaties prohibit explosions in space.

November 1: The longest suspension bridge in the world opens over Michigan's Mackinac Straits.

November 2: The citizens of Pleasanton, Texas, vote overwhelmingly in favor of integrating the local public schools. The process is carried out peacefully.

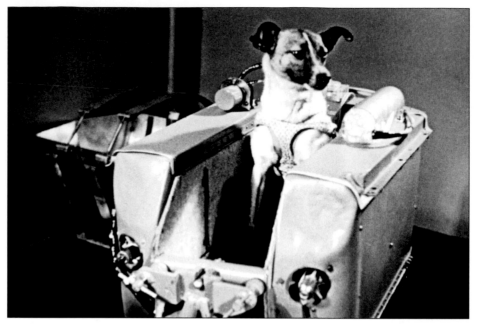

Less than a month after stunning the world with Sputnik, the Soviets' launch of Sputnik II upped the ante by putting a live passenger into orbit. Laika, a three-year-old female dog, became the unwitting recipient of that distinction, for her departure came with no contingency for a safe return to Earth. Laika's mission was meant to demonstrate that the stress of a launch and weightlessness was eminently survivable. Alas, Laika perished from overheating several days into the sojourn, something that Soviet scientists subsequently expressed their regrets over. Her lifeless body completed 2,370 orbits before incinerating during reentry.

While most Americans found the launch of the Sputniks unnerving, others sought to make light of the Soviets' achievements. This woman samples the "Sputnikburger," created by an Atlanta eatery. Sporting a Spanish olive "satellite" affixed with three toothpick "antennae," the burger was fittingly doused with Russian dressing. Laika, Sputnik II's hapless passenger, was memorialized with a cocktail wiener.

In 1957 television's *Zorro* became a successful incarnation of Johnston McCulley's literary creation. The story, set in Spanish California, concerned the swashbuckling exploits of nobleman Don Diego, who righted injustices through exceptional swordplay while in the guise of the title avenger. Guy Williams followed in the footsteps of movie Zorros Douglas Fairbanks and Tyrone Power as the handsome, mysterious hero. Though the character embodied sophistication, the plotlines in the Disney-produced series were mild and therefore accessible to children, who were pitched a vast array of merchandise.

Pop crooner Johnny Mathis occupied a unique niche in the recording market, appealing to adults as much as youth. His lush, well-produced sound proved extremely popular, beginning with the single "Wonderful, Wonderful" (though curiously, not included on the album of the same name). Mathis had begun his career after turning down a slot on the 1956 U.S. Olympic track team. Once the ball was rolling, a succession of hits followed, including "Chances Are" and "Twelfth of Never." His steady stream of releases led to the very first greatest-hits compilation. Mathis also recorded one of pop's more enduring holiday tune collections.

The Cat in the Hat

ON THE STRENGTH of whimsical illustrations and a knack for rhyme and rhythm, Theodor Geisel introduced American children to a new world of creative wordplay with *The Cat in the Hat* (1957).

Thirty years before his cat arrived on young readers' welcome mats, Geisel began his career as a cartoonist for national magazines. During World War II, he worked for Frank Capra's Signal Corps, lending his illustrations to war-related films. After the service, Dr. Seuss—a moniker that combined his mother's maiden name and his never-completed doctorate from Oxford—began writing popular children's books under his new name. Titles included *Bartholomew and the Oobleck* (1949) and *If I Ran the Zoo* (1950).

Geisel's talent coincided serendipitously with a perceived literacy problem during the 1950s. Various studies and an influential *Life* magazine article blamed low literacy rates among American children on boring reading primers, such as the "Dick and Jane" series. But *The Cat in the Hat* was anything but dull, as readers discover on page seven, when a confident feline flings open the door toting an umbrella and spouting sly rhymes.

Dr. Seuss followed *The Cat in the Hat* with a succession of classics, including *Green Eggs and Ham* and *One Fish Two Fish Red Fish Blue Fish*, both published in 1960. Overall, more than 500 million Dr. Seuss books have been sold worldwide.

1957

November 3: The Soviets launch Sputnik II, occupied by a dog named Laika, who will survive for several days. Sputnik II will leave orbit on April 13, 1958.

November 7: The Ford Foundation's Gaither Report is presented to President Eisenhower. The report fuels fears of a U.S.-Soviet "missile gap," and recommends increased military buildup.

November 8: Great Britain conducts its first successful test of a hydrogen bomb.

November 13: In a nationally broadcast address, President Eisenhower announces the need to dramatically increase future defense spending in order to keep pace with the technologically advanced Soviets.

November 14: New York state police raid the Apalachin estate of crime boss Joseph Barbara, arresting about 60 of Barbara's associates. Mafia bosses had gathered to discuss the illegal drug trade in New York. The raid provides the first proof of the Mafia's far-reaching criminal empire.

November 15: To prove his assertion of Soviet missile supremacy, First Secretary Nikita Khrushchev challenges the U.S. to a rocket-shooting competition. • SANE, the National Committee for a Sane Nuclear Policy, is founded by Norman Cousins, editor of the *Saturday Review.*

November 16: Ed Gein, ghoulish grave robber and inspiration for the film *The Texas Chainsaw Massacre,* butchers his final victim before he is caught by authorities.

November 25: His health in continued decline, President Eisenhower suffers a mild stroke. • The longest-ever college football winning streak, 47 games, comes to an end when Notre Dame shuts out Oklahoma.

Rivaling Elvis Presley, Jerry Lee Lewis became a rock 'n' roll sensation in 1957 with a string of hits, including "Whole Lotta Shakin'," "Great Balls of Fire," and "Breathless." However, the unpredictable piano-pounder fought inner demons that put his career in conflict with his fire-and-brimstone fundamentalist upbringing (as embodied by his evangelist cousin, Jimmy Swaggart). Further, his December 1957 marriage to his 13-year-old cousin, Myra Gale Brown (*right*)—while still married to his second wife (he had married his first wife at age 16)—erupted into a national scandal. Lewis suffered a public backlash from which he never fully recovered. Because of his marriage to Myra, Lewis was actually booed off the stage in England.

Based on Humphrey Cobb's stirring antiwar novel, the film *Paths of Glory* (1957) was a stunning look at war's folly and the cost exacted by pride and vanity. Stung by the failure of his men to execute a foolish, ill-conceived order, General Broulard (played by Adolphe Menjou) and his underling, General Mireau (George MacReady), set about to arbitrarily punish selected troops for their "cowardice." Colonel Dax (Kirk Douglas, *pictured*) is given the thankless task of defending the doomed men against a judicial *fait accompli*. This powerful depiction of military injustice was artfully directed by Stanley Kubrick, then in ascendancy as one of cinema's giants.

Meredith Willson's brassy show, *The Music Man,* opened on Broadway in December 1957. With actor Robert Preston in the title role, the energetic comedy-romance featured dynamic dancing, country corn, and 76 bombastic trombones. The musical was an immediate hit, spawning a soundtrack album that held down the No. 1 slot for 12 weeks while winning a Grammy Award. Preston, who would reprise the Harold Hill role on film in 1962, shone as an unsavory musical-instrument salesman who attempts to put one over on the town of River City before love intervenes.

In director Hall Bartlett's *Zero Hour!* (1957), pilots become incapacitated midflight, triggering panic on the airplane. Eventually, crew members enjoin a battle-scarred passenger to bring the plane to safety. This film would be parodied almost in its entirety as *Airplane!* in 1980. However, *Zero Hour!* is a white-knuckle potboiler with a first-rate cast, including fill-in pilot Dana Andrews (*pictured*). The script was written by Arthur Hailey, who later would write the best-selling novel *Airport.*

Russian-born Ayn Rand arrived in America in 1925, determined to make it as a successful screenwriter. That she accomplished, but it is for her novels, including 1943's *The Fountainhead* and 1957's *Atlas Shrugged,* that she is best known. Though she demurely claimed nothing loftier than literary ambitions, Rand's books served as vehicles for her didactic philosophizing. Having lived under Leninist Russia, she espoused a worldview that celebrated individualism and exalted the creative above all. *Atlas Shrugged* depicts this in stark detail while cast as science fiction.

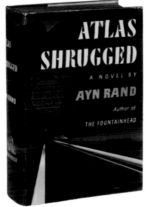

In the 1950s and '60s, puppeteer Shari Lewis was one of television's most successful ventriloquists. Discovered on *Arthur Godfrey's Talent Scouts,* she began her career on local television in New York, armed with little more than a sassy sock puppet named Lamb Chop. Along with Charlie Horse and Hush Puppy, Lewis and Lamb Chop became dominant figures in children's programming. Lewis won an array of honors and awards for her efforts to nurture imagination.

1957

November 27: Jacqueline Bouvier Kennedy, wife of Senator John F. Kennedy, gives birth to a daughter, Caroline.

November 30: Six children die and 100 are injured in a grenade attack on a Jakarta school. Indonesian President Sukarno, the intended target, is unhurt.

December 2: The first privately run nuclear power plant in the U.S. opens its gates in Shippingport, Pennsylvania.

December 5: New York City passes a Fair Housing Practices Law, designed to prevent racial and religious discrimination in housing.

December 6: The first U.S. attempt to send a satellite into orbit ends with a Cape Canaveral launchpad explosion. • In response to racketeering charges against Jimmy Hoffa and other members of the International Brotherhood of Teamsters leadership, the AFL-CIO votes to expel the Teamsters.

December 17: The American-made Atlas ICBM (intercontinental ballistic missile) is successfully test-fired for the first time. *See* November 28, 1958. • Minnijean Brown, one of the nine black students at Little Rock's Central High School, dumps a bowl of chili on the head of a white boy who had been taunting her. She is given a six-day suspension.

December 19: NATO member nations reach an agreement allowing for the installation of U.S. intermediate range ballistic missiles in Europe.

December 20: Elvis Presley receives a notice from the Selective Service that requires him to appear for induction into the U.S. Army. *See* March 24, 1958.

December 28: The FBI announces that the number of major crimes in the U.S. has risen by an estimated 7.5 percent in 1957.

Dr. Wernher von Braun coupled a genius for rocket engineering with a flair for public relations, becoming the unlikely face of America's space program prior to the advent of the Mercury astronauts. As the former architect of the Nazis' V-2 rocket program, which killed thousands of Brits and Belgians during the war, von Braun was viewed by many—including President Eisenhower—with distaste, to say the least. But the government found his expertise indispensable for maintaining parity with the Soviets, whose launch of Sputnik blindsided the world in October 1957. Von Braun and his team created the Redstone rocket, America's first viable entry in the space race.

Though possessing the technological edge, Americans hadn't launched a rocket into space before Sputnik. The buzz created by that event put the U.S. under pressure to better their Soviet counterparts. Amid much hoopla, the Vanguard rocket (chosen over Wernher von Braun's Redstone rocket) was intended to launch the first American satellite. But on December 6, this dream went up in smoke with a spectacular launchpad explosion (*pictured*). A mere three successes out of the following 10 attempts underscored American humiliation in the face of the Soviets' achievements.

On December 17, 1957, 54 years to the day after the Wright Brothers first flew at Kitty Hawk, America's first ICBM, the Atlas, was successfully launched from Cape Canaveral in Florida. At last on equal footing with the Soviets, the U.S. rapidly accelerated its arms buildup. The Atlas was a liquid-fueled rocket designed to carry low-orbit payloads—or nuclear weapons. Six Atlas F launch facilities were built around the country, ready to fly when necessary. A less apocalyptic purpose was served in the early 1960s when all but two of the Mercury spacecraft were launched by these rockets. The Atlas was decommissioned in 1965.

A real-life occurrence at an Allied POW camp in Burma formed the basis of Pierre Boulle's novel *The Bridge on the River Kwai,* and the subsequent screen adaptation. Director David Lean (*Lawrence of Arabia, Dr. Zhivago*) presented a lavish widescreen tour de force that went on to win seven Academy Awards and become the top-grossing picture of 1957. The story was built around the clash of wills between British Colonel Nicholson (Alec Guinness, *right*) and the camp's commander, Colonel Saito (Sessue Hayakawa, *left*). Scripted in part by Boulle (*Planet of the Apes*), the film's depiction of war's brutality underscored the heroism of the men involved.

Blind from birth, composer-pianist George Shearing led one of jazz's most popular quintets in the 1940s and '50s. Utilizing what became known as the "locked hands" style of playing, his sound was built upon his harmonized block chordings locked in with the vibraphone and guitar. This underscoring of the melody provided a catchiness that made his music accessible to non-jazz listeners. Shearing first caught the public's ear with his take on "September in the Rain," and he later composed the standard "Lullaby of Birdland." The 1950s saw him move in an increasingly lush direction, typified by this 1957 Capitol release.

1957

New & Notable

Books

Atlas Shrugged by Ayn Rand
Doctor Zhivago by Boris Pasternak
The Hidden Persuaders
    by Vance Packard
Kids Say the Darndest Things
    by Art Linkletter
No Down Payment by John McPartland
On the Beach by Nevil Shute
On the Road by Jack Kerouac
The Wapshot Chronicle by John Cheever

Movies

The Bridge on the River Kwai
Funny Face
Invasion of the Saucer Men
Old Yeller
Paths of Glory
12 Angry Men
Will Success Spoil Rock Hunter?
Witness for the Prosecution

Songs

"April Love" by Pat Boone
"Diana" by Paul Anka
"Jailhouse Rock" by Elvis Presley
"Little Darlin'" by the Diamonds
"Rock and Roll Music"
    by Chuck Berry
"That'll Be the Day" by Buddy Holly
"Wake Up Little Susie"
    by the Everly Brothers
"Whole Lotta Shakin' Goin On"
    by Jerry Lee Lewis

Television

American Bandstand
Have Gun, Will Travel
Leave It to Beaver
Maverick
Perry Mason
The Ruff and Reddy Show
Sea Hunt
Wagon Train

Theater

The Dark at the Top of the Stairs
The Entertainer
A Long Day's Journey into Night
Look Back in Anger
The Music Man
West Side Story

When blondeness was buffed to a seductive gloss by Marilyn Monroe in the early 1950s, imitators popped up like peroxide dandelions. Some, such as Kim Novak and Jayne Mansfield, had significant careers. Pictured here are "Britain's answer to Marilyn Monroe," the pneumatic Diana Dors (*left*), and Universal's "platinum powerhouse," Mamie Van Doren (*right*). Despite a big buildup, Dors never succeeded in Hollywood; she returned to Britain and steady employment as a respected character actress. Van Doren was cannier, and seemed content to be a B-movie bombshell. One of her 1957 vehicles, *Untamed Youth,* is a small masterpiece of drive-in cinema.

A stylish living room in the late 1950s usually featured contemporary and perhaps even abstract furnishings. Kidney-shaped conjoined tables, wrought-iron wall hangings, oddly shaped lamps, and simple, functional furniture—often in neutral colors—marked a clear rebellion against the sort of cluttered, ornate furnishings of an earlier period. Many rooms in middle- and upper middle-class homes were dominated by large windows, which gave an open, airy feeling.

American chess prodigy Bobby Fischer, age 14, intently battles Philippine champion Rodolfo Tan Cardoso in New York in 1957. A year later, Fischer earned the designation "international grandmaster," becoming the youngest player ever to achieve that honor. The previous year, he had won the U.S. championship, setting an age record in that event as well. Fischer had started playing at age six when his sister bought him a chess set to keep him amused. Bobby's passion ultimately led to a world championship against supposedly unbeatable Russian Boris Spassky in 1972.

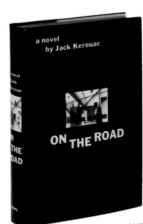

Jack Kerouac's genre-defining novel, *On the Road* (1957), chronicled a drug-fueled, cross-country odyssey undertaken by a group of free spirits. According to legend, Kerouac wrote the manuscript during a three-week creative burst, with little thought of editing, on a single scroll of paper. In reality, he typed on 12-foot-long rolls of onion skin and later taped them together to form a scroll 119 feet long. He also was a more disciplined writer than most suspected. The hedonistic experience described in his Beat masterpiece was carefully culled from Kerouac's scrupulous notes. The result was a work comparable to a master jazzman's improvisations.

A Cub Scout and a Brownie give patriotic salutes in this image of wholesome Americana. The number of scouts grew phenomenally in the 1950s, as the first members of the baby boom grew up. Cub Scout membership in the U.S. soared by more than 200,000 a year in the mid-1950s, while from 1949 to 1957 the number of Girl Scouts doubled to more than three million. According to historian Jay Mechling, scouting's popularity was enhanced by patriotic and religious sentiment induced by the Cold War. It "effectively conflate[d] duty to God and country as a single duty," Mechling stated, and was seen by many as a bastion against communism.

Welsh playwright John Osborne burst onto the theatrical scene in 1956 with his critically acclaimed play, *Look Back in Anger,* about a bright, working-class protagonist who becomes bitter because he cannot find meaningful work in postwar Britain. By 1958 Osborne and such novelists as John Braine and Alan Sillitoe were identified by the media as "the angry young men." According to the *Columbia Encyclopedia,* they might be described more accurately as "disgruntled," as they "expressed discontent with the staid, hypocritical institutions of English society."

"I detested the United Broadcasting Corporation . . . and the only reason I'm willing to spend my life in such a ridiculous enterprise is that I want to buy a more expensive house and a better brand of gin."

—A CHARACTER IN THE SLOAN WILSON NOVEL *THE MAN IN THE GRAY FLANNEL SUIT*

1958

The Organization Man

"ONE DARK MORNING this winter," began a 1958 *Look* magazine article on the plight of the American male, "Gary Gray awakened and realized he had forgotten how to say the word 'I.' ... He had lost his individuality. In the free and democratic United States of America, he had been subtly rooked of a heritage that Communist countries deny by force."

In the pages of *Look, The New York Times, Playboy,* and *Ladies' Home Journal,* writers in the late 1950s confronted the specter of conformism in America. They wrote of a people stripped of individual initiative, and of men emasculated in postwar society.

This vision of conformity had been most compellingly articulated in a 1956 book by *Fortune* magazine editor William Hollingsworth Whyte. Whyte—called Holly by his friends—was an old-stock WASP, the son of a railroad executive from West Chester, Pennsylvania. Following a familiar path for young men of his background and generation, he went to Princeton, graduated in 1939, and enlisted in the Marine Corps close on the heels of the Japanese bombing of Pearl Harbor. After the war, he landed in Henry Luce's publishing empire, where he developed a terse, colloquial prose style typical of the Time, Inc., publications. In his articles, Whyte wrote powerful critiques of American society and business culture. He also wrote a book that became a surprise bestseller and provided, in its title, a shorthand label for male conformity: *The Organization Man.*

Dressed virtually alike, commuters arrive home in Park Forest, Illinois, after another day at the office. In the 1950s, men spent a large portion of their incomes on suits, hats, overcoats, and briefcases in order to meet corporate expectations. In fact, it was not uncommon to spend a week's salary on one new suit.

Like never before, advertisers in the 1950s encouraged men, women, and children to buy, buy, buy. But fathers, typically their families' sole breadwinners, often felt buried by work, bills, and debt. The situation was exacerbated during the recession of 1958.

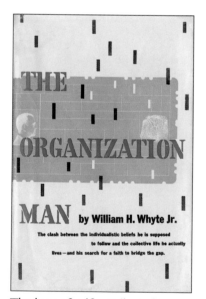

The loss of self, attributed to 1950s corporate conformity, was the major theme of William Whyte's *The Organization Man.* Whyte described men who identified their own well-being with that of their companies.

Whyte found, in the large corporations that dominated American business in the 1950s, a shift away from the values of individual initiative and the so-called Protestant ethic, which he defined as "the pursuit of individual salvation through hard work, thrift and competitive struggle." Instead, modern Americans adhered to a "social ethic." They looked to the group as a source of creativity, to "belonging" as a higher good.

Whyte chronicled the "modest aspirations of organization men who lower their sights to achieve a good job with adequate pay and proper pension and a nice house in a pleasant community populated with people as nearly like themselves as possible." Though Whyte bent over backward to downplay the judgmental—"Unless one believes poverty ennobling, it is difficult to see the three-button suit as more of a straitjacket than overalls," he wrote—his disdain for corporate conformity was clear. The book's appendix, in fact, offered advice on how to cheat on the increasingly used corporate personality tests that, to him, represented the ultimate extension of organizational control over the individual.

The Organization Man was just one of many books critical of American society—some of them dry academic treatises—that became bestsellers in the 1950s. They included David Riesman's 1953 book, *The Lonely Crowd: A Study of the Changing American Character* ("The other-directed person wants to be loved rather than esteemed"); Vance Packard's 1957 book, *The Hidden Persuaders* ("many of us are being influenced and manipulated, far more than we realize, in the patterns of our everyday lives"); and Sloan Wilson's 1955 novel, *The Man in the Gray Flannel Suit* (whose title rivaled Whyte's as shorthand for what had, presumably, been lost). Although these books were quite different from one another, all captured and confirmed a powerful feeling that something had gone wrong in American society.

It's hard to say whether or not Americans became less individualistic and more conformist during the 1950s. Later generations have tended to take this criticism at face value, reading it as objective description of social trends rather than as evidence that Americans were confronting profound changes in their society and had ambivalent feelings about them. From the era of the Great Depression forward, Americans increasingly found their lives shaped by large and powerful institutions: the federal government, the military, large corporations. In many ways, these were positive experiences. The Allies won the war, and by the 1950s a greater proportion of Americans than ever before could expect a basic level of economic security and material comfort.

The changes, however, produced tensions. Even as Americans immoderately celebrated "the American way of life" and turned blind eyes to the problems that continued to plague the nation, they were as profoundly self-critical as any generation in the 20th century. The critical impulse was strongest among members of an older, urban elite who saw cultural decline in the rise of suburban tract housing and a national "mass culture." These critics disproportionately shaped public discussions as the nation moved into its powerful postwar role and attempted to define "the American character."

Many '50s commentators felt that masculinity had become endangered due to the rise of office work and the shared roles of men and women at home. Separate identities were renewed through certain upscale men's magazines, such as *Playboy* and *Esquire*.

Though the critique of conformity focused mostly on the impact of large organizations and on the workplace, some of the most vocal—and angriest—critiques targeted the private sphere. In 1956 *Woman's Home Companion* presented a vision of the "captive male" burning leaves in his suburban yard on a Sunday afternoon. "It is a comfortable, relaxed scene," the author wrote, "even if the women do look like keepers of a prosperous zoo and the men like so many domesticated animals inside of it." Even the "quietest Sunday gardener," the author insisted, "may have his indestructible dream of greatness and adventure" stolen away in such female-dominated domestication. Robbed

365

of his "chance at heroism... seeing this gap between his dream and his daily life," he wonders: "is he even a man."

The picture of men as domesticated animals, caged by women in a suburban zoo, is simply a colorful version of a story often told in the popular culture of the 1950s. While women's discontent simmered at the end of the decade (when *Redbook* asked its readers to explain "Why Young Mothers Feel Trapped," it got 24,000 replies), the "crisis of masculinity" was a perpetual topic. Arthur Schlesinger, Jr., in a 1958 article for *Esquire* magazine, wrote: "[T]oday men are more conscious of maleness not as a fact but as a problem. The way by which American men affirm their masculinity [is] uncertain and obscure."

From the mid-1950s through the early 1960s, writers in popular magazines railed against the cult of "togetherness." They predicted that the loss of masculine virtues of aggressiveness and competitiveness in a feminized, corporatized world would lead to the downfall of American civilization, and they sought protected spaces where masculinity could flourish. Hugh Hefner, by the late 1950s, claimed that *Playboy*'s mission was to solve the problem of male identity, and to foster separate identities for men and women.

Even though the concept of buying on credit existed in earlier eras, its popularity soared in the 1950s. Throughout the decade, consumer debt increased as loans were extended for the purchase of houses, automobiles, appliances, and furniture.

This story of loss and frustration is an odd story, for in many ways white men in America never had it so good. The 1950s were a time of great opportunity. White men faced almost no competition from women, or from men of color. Blue-collar union jobs paid better than ever, and from 1947 to 1957 the proportion of middle-class salaried workers jumped 61 percent. Home ownership rates skyrocketed. The number of registered cars more than doubled from 1945 to 1955, from 25 million to 51 million, and by 1960 almost one-fifth of suburban families had two cars. Moreover, consumer goods were widely available, as the number of shopping centers in the United States jumped from a mere eight at the end of World War II to 3,840 in 1960. People who had grown up in the Great Depression lived much more comfortable, affluent lives than had seemed possible just two decades before.

But with these new ways of life came new pressures. Consumer debt grew dramatically during the 1950s. Today, in a society inured to debt—one in which many people finance their lives by juggling credit card balances—'50s debt appears modest and sensible. Most of it was mortgage debt, an investment that would pay off handsomely for a great many of that generation. The only available credit card through most of the 1950s was Diners Club, although it wasn't widely accepted.

The great extravagance was automobiles, which grew more and more lavish as the decade progressed. Cars became bigger and sleeker, with tailfins and excessive chrome. Cars came to signal success, and rapid style changes pushed consumers to want new, up-to-date models. "We design a car to make a man unhappy with his 1957 Ford 'long about the end of 1958," said Ford designer George Walker. In addition, many suburban families found it necessary to have two cars—one for the husband to commute to work, one for the wife to do the necessary chores. A second car meant a second set of car payments.

Each debt, whether for a house, car, or television, was a new pressure. Those who had lived through economic hard times were keenly aware that debt could be dangerous, that strong economies could crash. And men, as the bread-winners, bore the burden of providing for their families. They had to guarantee financial stability and make possible the comforts that their families were beginning to take for granted. Writers at the time pointed to a rise in alcoholism as evidence of the new stresses in American life.

While some members of America's growing white middle and upper-middle class regretted the trade-offs they had made in embracing stability and comfort, many Americans had no such luxury. In an age of affluence, more than one in five Americans were poor. A quarter of that number was the elderly, the majority of whom had no health insurance and whose average Social Security payment, for those covered in the system, was about $70 per month. Almost half of the nation's African-American citizens were poor, as were more than half of Native Americans. As suburban communities expanded, and as increased farm productivity forced sharecroppers and poor farmers from the land, poverty became increasingly concentrated in blighted inner cities. The problem was largely invisible to the middle class and largely ignored in the debates about America's failings.

While most white Americans prospered in the 1950s, the same could not be said for African-Americans. In fact, nearly half of all black citizens lived in poverty. Many still toiled as field-workers for pitiful wages in the South, while hundreds of thousands of others lived in the slums of northern cities.

The decade of the 1950s, contrary to the popular stereotype, was not simply a time of contentment. It also was a time of social and self-criticism, and—for many millions—continued impoverishment.

1958

1958: The American Association of Retired Persons (AARP) is founded by retired schoolteacher Dr. Ethel Percy Andrus. • McDonnell-Douglas unveils its F-4 Phantom, which will become the U.S. Air Force workhorse bomber through the Vietnam War era and beyond. • The U.S. Treasury produces the last "wheat ear" penny. The pennies featuring the wheat design have been in production since 1909.

1958: Vancomycin, an antibiotic found effective against staphylococcal and streptococcal infections, is fast-tracked by the FDA. • A contraception controversy erupts when New York City's Kings County Hospital prevents Dr. Louis Hellman from providing birth control to a diabetic mother of three, citing Catholic mores of the day. Hellman leaks his story to *The New York Times,* and within two months the hospital rescinds its policy. • *High School Confidential!,* starring Mamie Van Doren and Russ Tamblyn, is released. It is the first mass-market movie to deal with the issue of teenagers and drugs. • Self-described investigative satirist Paul Krassner launches his anti-establishment magazine, *The Realist.*

1958: Viking Press publishes *The Dharma Bums* by Jack Kerouac, the follow-up to his popular beat novel, *On the Road.* • Clifton Hillegass founds Cliffs Notes in his basement with $4,000 seed money. • William Higinbotham, of Brookhaven National Lab, creates the world's first video game, a tennis game, as part of a display for visitors to the lab's Instrumentation Division. • Eugene Gilbert's syndicated column, "What Young People Are Thinking," based on his extensive polling of teenagers, gives manufacturers a new way to market to that key demographic. • RCA unveils the first LPs recorded in stereo. Although it is initially very expensive to produce, stereo vinyl will soon become the recording industry's dominant format.

Members of the John Birch Society open a meeting by pledging allegiance to the American flag. This ultraconservative organization was founded by candy manufacturer Robert Welch in 1958. It was named after an American pilot and missionary killed by the Chinese Communists in 1945. The society preached a fierce anticommunism, and it strongly supported efforts to root out internal Communist subversion. It even declared that presidents Roosevelt, Truman, and Eisenhower were sympathetic to communism. The society's members tended to come from the more conservative elements of the business world.

Editor John Gates holds one of the last issues of his newspaper, *The Worker* (titled *Daily Worker* until 1958). This organ of the Communist Party USA was founded in 1924, and for more than 30 years it propounded the official party line. The paper folded, mainly because of diminishing circulation due to hostility toward communism. Gates resigned from the CPUSA because, in his words, the party "had ceased to be an effective force for democracy, peace, and socialism in the United States."

New York's Seagram Building (*left*) and Lever House (*right*) were two notable office towers designed by Ludwig Mies van der Rohe and Gordon Bunshaft, respectively. The 24-story Lever House was one of the first examples of the International style of architecture, with its steel frame, glass curtain wall, and open plaza. The Seagram Building followed this example and enlarged upon it, boasting 38 stories and a larger expanse of public area in front. Its golden hue (meant to simulate the color of gin) contrasted nicely with Lever House's green tones, transforming the character of Park Avenue.

This collection of essays from *Dissent* magazine was published in 1958. First appearing in 1954, this quarterly journal became a voice for left-wing intellectuals, including founders Irving Howe and Lewis Coser, who bitterly opposed Stalinism. Its contributors and readers wanted to carve out a space between hard-line communism and what they saw as the mindless anticommunism of Senator Joseph McCarthy and his followers. In early articles, including Howe's "The Problem of U.S. Power" in 1954, the magazine called for left-wing, non-Communist socialism.

The Kingston Trio (*left to right:* Dave Guard, Bob Shane, and Nick Reynolds) enjoyed widespread popularity in 1958 on the strength of their first single, a grim little number about a hanging entitled "Tom Dooley." Unlike other folk artists of the era, the members of the Kingston Trio (named after Kingston, Jamaica, in a nod to the Calypso craze) were largely apolitical. Recognizing their own musical limitations, the trio developed a comic onstage banter, which contrasted with the rather earnest demeanor of other folk acts. The group's success spawned similar outfits, including the Limelighters, the Highwaymen, and the Chad Mitchell Trio.

1958

1958: Both Toyota and Datsun enter the U.S. market, but weak sales force both manufacturers to pull back and reevaluate the wants and needs of the American consumer. • Wham-O toy developers Richard Knerr and Arthur Melin unveil the hula hoop. At less than two dollars each, more than 100 million hula hoops are sold in their first year of production. • The Ford Motor Company creates a concept car powered by a portable nuclear reactor. Designers claim that the Ford Nucleon could drive 5,000 miles before refueling.

1958: New products for the U.S. consumer include Cocoa Krispies, Cocoa Puffs, Sweet 'n' Low, and Tater Tots. Also, the Jolly Green Giant pushes his vegetables on television for the first time. • Ludwig Mies van der Rohe's steel and glass Seagram Building is completed on New York City's Park Avenue. • McDonald's sells its 100th million hamburger, just three years after the company was incorporated and its first franchise opened. • American Express and BankAmericard credit cards are introduced. • Brothers Frank and Dan Carney borrow $600 from their mother and open the first Pizza Hut restaurant on a busy intersection near their Wichita, Kansas, home.

January: Painter Jasper Johns has his first show, at New York's Castelli Gallery. The Museum of Modern Art buys three of his pieces. • Work begins on a massive fallout shelter under the Greenbrier Resort in White Sulphur Springs, West Virginia. Authorized by President Dwight Eisenhower, the shelter was designed to house members of Congress and key staff in the event of a nuclear strike on Washington, D.C.

January 1: The European Economic Community, also known as the European Common Market, is implemented.

On January 31, 1958, the United States successfully launched its first orbiting space satellite, Explorer I, almost four months after the Soviets' successful Sputnik, and more than a month after America's Vanguard rocket exploded on the launchpad. Lifted by a massive Jupiter rocket, Explorer carried a device to measure the flow of cosmic radiation. Project leader Dr. James Pickering recalls being stunned when he went to a press conference at 2:00 A.M. after the launch and found that a huge hall "was completely filled" with media. Americans were clearly relieved by this successful effort to match the earlier Soviet accomplishment.

A determined high school student in New York City conducts a science experiment in the late 1950s. Millions of American high school, college, and graduate students benefited from the National Defense Education Act, passed in 1958, mainly as a response to the Sputnik space satellite launched by the Soviet Union. Designed primarily to spur American scientific and technological education, as well as the study of foreign languages, the act provided for significant federal aid in those areas. Money was allocated for science education in high schools, low-interest loans for college students, and graduate fellowships.

The Starkweather Murders

FOR EIGHT DAYS in January 1958, teenagers Charles Starkweather and Caril Ann Fugate embarked on a murder spree that took them from Lincoln, Nebraska, to Douglas, Wyoming. By the time the police finally caught up, the couple had claimed 11 victims, including three members of Caril's family.

The killings began when Starkweather held up a gas station in Lincoln, killing the attendant, Robert Colvert. His next victims were Caril's mother, stepfather, and three-year-old half-sister. The two holed up in Fugate's home for a few days before making their getaway in Starkweather's 1949 Ford. Killing people along the way, they headed toward Wyoming's Badlands.

Exactly what set off Starkweather is hard to determine. As a schoolboy, his poor eyesight, bad hearing, speech impediment, and short stature made him the butt of jokes among his classmates. After dropping out of school at age 16, Starkweather drifted around Lincoln, unable to hold down a steady job. "Everything just built up inside Charlie until he went berserk," explained his father.

On June 25, 1959, Starkweather was executed. Fugate was imprisoned until paroled 18 years later.

Fugate and Starkweather

In 1958 Japanese automakers began to export their wares to America, the biggest market of all. But lacking a clear strategy, knowledge of the market, and a suitable product, their efforts went for naught. This Toyopet Crown typified the problem. The automobile was apparently modeled after American cars from much earlier in the decade, and the name suggested frivolity. Only 919 of Toyota's initial offerings were sold in the U.S. that year, while Datsun didn't fare much better. At a time when "Made in Japan" was still the kiss of death, few Americans were interested in these cars. A decade later, however, Japanese automakers would begin to find success in the States.

FBI Director J. Edgar Hoover, with the help of ghostwriters, published his exposé of Communist tactics and infiltration of American institutions in 1958. It was part of Hoover's master plan to promote the image of the FBI as a tough and patriotic crime- and subversion-fighting organization. Approximately 2.5 million copies of the book were sold, and, along with the "10 Most Wanted List" and junior G-men clubs for kids, became part of pop culture iconography. Most historians believe that Hoover grossly exaggerated the internal Communist menace in this work.

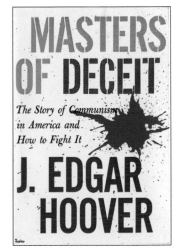

MASTERS OF DECEIT

The Story of Communism in America and How to Fight It

J. EDGAR HOOVER

1958

January 2: Composer Leonard Bernstein is appointed the musical director of the New York Philharmonic.

January 3: The British West Indies Federation is created, and Lord Hailes is named governor general. Member states include Trinidad, Tobago, Jamaica, Barbados, and the Windward and Leeward Islands.

January 6: Continuing a trend begun the previous year, the Soviets announce that they have trimmed their armed forces by some 300,000 men.

January 10: Chess phenom Bobby Fischer wins the U.S. championship at age 14, making him the youngest chess champion in history.

January 13: President Eisenhower writes Nikolai Bulganin, chairman of the Council of Ministers of the USSR, proposing that the U.S. and the Soviets agree to use outer space for peaceful purposes. • John Gates, editor of the U.S. Communist Party newspaper *Daily Worker,* quits the party and resigns his post at the paper. • In a major gay rights victory, the U.S. Supreme Court rules that the homophile magazine *One* is protected speech and may be sent through the mail.

January 15: An annual Gallup poll of the most admired women in the U.S. gives top honors to former First Lady Eleanor Roosevelt. • Linus and Eva Pauling present a petition urging a multilateral agreement to halt nuclear weapons testing to UN Secretary-General Dag Hammarskjöld. More than 9,000 scientists have signed the petition.

January 23: Venezuelan military dictator General Marcos Perez Jimenez flees the country after being ousted in a military coup.

January 27: U.S.-Soviet cultural exchanges are formally established.

Egyptian President Gamal Abdel Nasser (*left*) meets with President Shukri el Kuwatly of Syria during a March 1958 visit. That year, the two countries merged into a single unit, called the United Arab Republic. Nasser was named president, and Egyptian and Syrian citizenship was abolished. The new entity was clearly an attempt to shore up and ultimately expand pan-Arabism, and served as a message to Israel to restrain itself in the post-Suez invasion years. But the UAR mainly served to heighten tensions in the area. The union lasted only until 1961, when Syria withdrew after a military coup.

Elvis Presley is sworn into the U.S. Army on March 24, 1958. Although fans complained that such a "national treasure" as Elvis should not be drafted, he was. His manager, Tom Parker, made sure he served in a regular military unit rather than special services, so as to highlight his patriotism. Elvis, a former truck driver, was assigned to drive a jeep in a tank unit. Although some assumed that his career would be severely damaged, previously unreleased songs continued to appear. In fact, according to VH1's *Artists A–Z,* "When he re-entered civilian life in 1960, his popularity, remarkably, was at just as high a level as when he left."

The toy industry most commonly fell back on cowboy six-shooters to reflect the American preoccupation with new frontiers and firearms, but six-shooters had a rival: ray guns. Sometimes inspired by comic strips or TV shows, other times not, the typical ray gun was a gaudily colored tin toy that whirred, burped, or sparked when the trigger was pulled. The vintage *rakétapisztoly* pictured here was manufactured in Hungary, confirming that the spirits of adventure—and commerce—were not restricted to the United States.

One year after arriving in America, Mexican-born composer-conductor Juan Garcia Esquivel brought his audio imagination to the masses with *Other Worlds, Other Sounds,* a collection of tunes fraught with exotic instrumentation and unusual effects. Esquivel (or Esquivel!, as he usually was credited) was one of the best-known purveyors of space-age pop, a bold exploration of stereophonic sound (typified by much speaker-to-speaker panning). Whether they were covers of standards or his own bizarre compositions, Esquivel's sonic experiments were uniformly adventurous, even if they were an acquired taste.

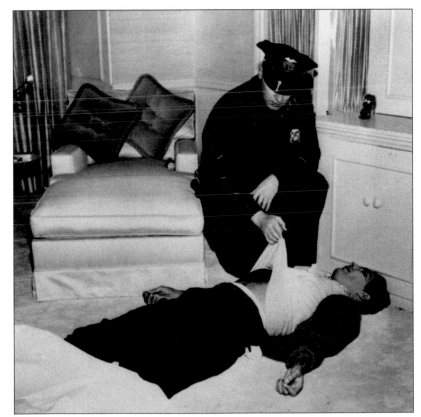

Cheryl Crane (*right photo*), age 14, awaits justice after being charged with stabbing mobster Johnny Stompanato to death (*above*). The daughter of famed Hollywood actress Lana Turner, Crane told authorities that she had rushed to her mother's defense after hearing Turner's paramour threaten to "cut" her. What happened next was examined in court: Crane said she grabbed an eight-inch knife and rushed into the room, whereupon Stompanato ran into the blade, severing his aorta. The lurid case became a media sensation, with Turner testifying in her daughter's defense. A verdict of "justifiable homicide" was rendered, with Crane remanded to her grandmother until she turned 18.

1958

January 28: The Thor intermediate range ballistic missile is successfully tested at Cape Canaveral, Florida. • Dodgers great Roy Campanella is paralyzed after his car skids on ice and crashes into a telephone pole.

January 29: Film stars Paul Newman and Joanne Woodward marry at the El Rancho Hotel and Casino in Las Vegas. • Charles Starkweather and his accomplice girlfriend, Caril Ann Fugate, are arrested in Wyoming after a multistate killing spree. *See* November 21, 1958.

January 30: Christian Dior's fashion design protégé, Yves Saint Laurent, has his first solo showing.

February: Explorer I, the first U.S. satellite to reach orbit, is launched from Cape Canaveral aboard a Jupiter rocket. • The global Asian Flu pandemic, which was first identified in the Far East the previous year, winds down in the United States.

February 1: Egyptian President Gamal Abdel Nasser, who envisioned a united Arab world, successfully negotiates the merger of Egypt and Syria within the United Arab Republic.

February 3: Belgium, the Netherlands, and Luxembourg sign a free-trade agreement that will come to be known as the Benelux union.

February 4: Banana industry giant United Fruit Company settles an antitrust suit by agreeing to create a competitor in its Latin American market.

February 5: A B-47 flying over Georgia accidentally drops a nuclear bomb at the mouth of the Savannah River. The unarmed bomb does not detonate and is never found.

February 8: French jets strike Tunisia, bombing the village of Sakiet-Sidi-Youssef, killing 68 people and injuring nearly 100.

In the 1940s, Pennsylvania golf pro Deacon Palmer taught his son a slashing, hard-hitting style of play. By 1958 Arnold Palmer's go-for-broke golf game, down-to-earth charm, and winning smile earned him a legion of admirers known as "Arnie's Army." In that year's Masters, Palmer carded an eagle on Augusta National's 13th hole on Sunday. He needed it, as he won his first major championship that day by a single stroke. Palmer ultimately would count four Masters wins among his 62 PGA Tour victories.

Out-of-work citizens pack an unemployment office in Illinois in April 1958. From August 1957 to February 1958, industrial production in the United States declined by 10 percent and the number of unemployed workers rose to its highest level since the end of World War II. In addition, many striking automobile workers were out of work. When the terms of their 1958 contract with major companies revealed that work conditions were not addressed, more than 70 percent went on wildcat strikes—a clear repudiation of their leader, Walter Reuther, who had negotiated and signed the contract.

Fans pack the Los Angeles Coliseum to watch the L.A. Dodgers baseball team. For years, the Dodgers had been the pride of Brooklyn, but in 1958 owner Walter O'Malley moved them to L.A. The major reason was financial. New York had refused to help O'Malley build a new ballpark, while Los Angeles promised one designed specifically for baseball, Dodger Stadium. Moreover, massive postwar population growth in California suggested a potentially huge fan base, while advances in air travel made cross-country trips feasible for visiting Major League teams. The New York Giants moved to San Francisco in 1958, depriving the Big Apple of a National League franchise and causing much fan bitterness there.

At a time when American prestige suffered due to Soviet achievements in space, a measure of pride was recouped through the success of 23-year-old classical pianist Van Cliburn. The Louisiana-born prodigy had begun playing as a toddler, and eventually furthered his gifts at the prestigious Julliard School in New York City. Displaying an extraordinary command of the keyboard and considerable star power, Cliburn won numerous competitions. These victories set the stage for his triumph in Moscow at the Tchaikovsky Competition on April 13, 1958. His virtuosity proved just the tonic that disheartened Americans needed. Upon his return to the U.S., he was honored with a ticker-tape parade in New York.

Brilliant painter and graphic artist Ben Shahn was a social realist who had keen concerns about critical issues, particularly institutionalized oppression and the misapplications of power. He also had been a New Deal/Farm Security Administration photographer. Besides creating the cover illustration and lettering on this 1958 book, Shahn contributed one or more pen-and-ink illustrations to each page. *Ounce Dice Trice,* written by Scottish poet Alastair Reid, is an antic rumination on the meaning and sound of peculiar words, both real (*flurr, bugbear*) and fanciful (*mumbudget, poose*).

Actress Joan Collins models the "sack" dress. Introduced to the fashion world in 1957, the design's origins went back considerably further, to a time when folks were resourceful in meeting basic needs. Original sack dresses were literally sacks, once filled with grain or seeds. The 1950s sack dresses started the trend toward straighter, waist-less shift dresses, which lasted into the 1960s. Many men claimed to hate the style.

1958

February 9: Airman Donald G. Farrell begins a simulated seven-day trip to the moon in a flight simulator at Randolph Air Force Base in San Antonio, Texas.

February 12: The SCLC begins its Crusade for Citizenship with meetings in 22 southern cities. Its goal is to double the number of black voters by 1960.

February 13: Great Britain warns the Soviets that any attack on the West, conventional or otherwise, will be met with a nuclear response.

February 14: Iraq's King Faisal and Jordan's King Hussein unite to form the Arab Federation.

February 22: The United States and Great Britain sign an agreement outlining the terms under which the U.S. would deploy Thor missiles in Britain. It is agreed that the missiles and sites will remain under British control, while the Americans will continue to own the nuclear warheads within the missiles.

February 25: Former Cuban President Carlos Prio Socarras is arrested along with eight accomplices for planning an invasion of the United States. • Social philosopher and peace activist Bertrand Russell founds his Campaign for Nuclear Disarmament, a loosely structured campaign characterized by peaceful, mass protest marches.

March 5: The U.S. satellite Explorer II fails to achieve orbit. Explorer missions III through V will follow before the end of the year, with Explorer III and Explorer IV building on Explorer I's discovery of the Van Allen Radiation Belt. Explorer V also will fail to reach orbit.

March 10: A report reveals that Americans own some 47 million television sets, about two-thirds of the world's total.

In 1958 writer-director-actor Orson Welles (*center*) unveiled his final Hollywood masterpiece, *Touch of Evil,* a noir-esque thriller that starred Janet Leigh (*left*) and Charlton Heston (not shown). Unfortunately, the film was butchered by the studio without Welles's consent, almost certainly contributing to its commercial failure in 1958. But hindsight reveals its strengths and visual richness, beginning with an arresting three-minute continuous-take opening shot. Several stars make cameo appearances, including Marlene Dietrich, Welles alumnus Joseph Cotten, and radio actress Mercedes McCambridge. The film's frank depictions of drugs, racism, corrupt cops, and sexual ambiguity challenged '50s sensibilities.

Vice President Richard Nixon yells back at heckling students in Lima, Peru, during his 1958 visit to Latin America. Nixon had embarked in May on a goodwill tour of eight nations in the region. He was booed by angry demonstrators everywhere he went, mainly because of U.S. support for unpopular dictators in the area. In Caracas, Venezuela, he actually was set upon by a mob, who stoned his car. Although he generally responded to the attacks with aplomb, Nixon cut his visit short. Columnist Walter Lippmann referred to the trip as a "diplomatic Pearl Harbor."

American commercial radio was built on block programming, by which designated periods (blocks) of a station's broadcast day were given over to big band, soap opera, chat, and other distinct formats. Something quite different, Top 40, arose around 1953 as a reaction against the growing popularity of television. Variously credited to radio visionaries Todd Storz, Bill Stewart, and Gordon McLendon, Top 40 ceaselessly flogged a predetermined group of rock 'n' roll hits, augmenting the tunes with lively deejays, stunts, breathless newscasts, and hard-to-forget jingles. Top 40 stations (or "35," as with L.A.'s KDAY 1580, *pictured*) distributed weekly hit lists. "Witch Doctor," by David Seville, topped the chart that accompanied this promo art on April 18, 1958.

The Nipco transistor radio, first manufactured in 1958, was one of many produced in Japan in the 1950s. Sony, which set the pace in 1955 with the first transistor radio, was followed by a herd of imitators, including Candle, Crown, Koyo, and others. Interestingly, this Nipco model had exactly the same jet wing decoration used on an earlier Motorola model. Transistor radios revolutionized the way people listened to music by making favorite sounds portable.

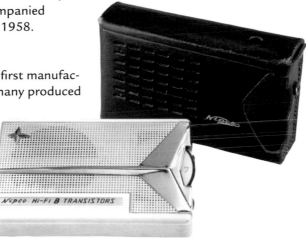

Russ Meyer was a combat cameraman who couldn't crack the Hollywood cinematographers' union after World War II. So, he set himself up as a still photographer, taking cheesecake shots of his fulsome wife, Eve, and numberless other models and starlets. In 1959 Meyer capped the decade's sexual revolution when he directed and shot *The Immoral Mr. Teas,* a 63-minute Eastman-color farce about a timid deliveryman who develops X-ray eyes whenever attractive young women wiggle into his field of vision. Meyer made increasingly ambitious films for another 20 years, and eventually became a potent box office force and a darling of critics. This 1958 publication celebrates Meyer's still-photo technique.

American film director Martin Scorsese has recalled that when he and his young moviegoing pals saw the Hammer Films logo, "we knew it was going to be a very special picture . . . a surprising experience, usually—and shocking. . . ." So-called "period" horror, with its castles, fog, and vampires, was displaced by science fiction during the 1950s. Hammer, a small British production company that had made B pictures of all sorts since the 1930s, gambled in 1958 with *Dracula (Horror of Dracula* in the States), bringing crimson color, lush sets, heaving bosoms, and a fresh snarl to period chills. Christopher Lee (*pictured*) and Peter Cushing (playing Van Helsing) became stars, and Hammer became synonymous with "horror."

1958

March 11: An economic recession in the United States sends the unemployment rate soaring to 7.7 percent. • A nuclear bomb is accidentally released from a B-47 bomber over Mars Bluff, South Carolina. The trigger detonates, leaving a 75-foot diameter crater, but the nuclear warhead remains dormant.

March 12: Fulgencio Batista's cabinet resigns after the dictator suspends constitutional rights in Cuba.

March 14: Former President Harry Truman publicly explains that he dropped the atomic bombs on Hiroshima and Nagasaki to bring the war to a quick end and save American and Japanese lives. • Perry Como's *Catch a Falling Star* is awarded the Recording Industry Association of America's first gold record.

March 15: The U.S. State Department calls a recent Soviet proposal "wholly unacceptable." The Soviets had asked the United Nations to ban military uses of space and to oversee the liquidation of military bases, including U.S. military bases in Europe, the Middle East, and North Africa.

March 17: Vanguard I becomes the second U.S. satellite to be successfully launched into orbit. It will transmit data back to Earth for the next three years.

March 24: Elvis Presley reports for duty with the U.S. Army.

March 25: West Germany grants the U.S. permission to deploy nuclear missiles in its country. • Middleweight boxer Sugar Ray Robinson earns his fifth championship with his victory over Carmine Basilio.

March 27: Nikita Khrushchev is named premier of the Soviet Union. • President Eisenhower approves a Department of Defense plan to fund two military missions to the moon.

The rich and elegant partake in a bit of leisurely shopping at an upscale department store in Los Angeles. In response to the growing wealth of many American families in the mid- to late 1950s, such high-end specialty shops grew apace. Older department stores, such as Macy's and Marshall Field's, added designer lines to appeal to the affluent. In boomtown Dallas, Neiman-Marcus expanded its commitment to such fashion mavens as Coco Chanel and catered to such upscale shoppers as Grace Kelly.

THE FIRST LERNER-LOEWE MUSICAL SINCE "MY FAIR LADY"

GiGi

M-G-M Presents
AN ARTHUR FREED PRODUCTION

LESLIE CARON
MAURICE CHEVALIER · LOUIS JOURDAN
HERMIONE GINGOLD · EVA GABOR · JACQUES BERGERAC · ISABEL JEANS
Screen Play and Lyrics by ALAN JAY LERNER · Music by FREDERICK LOEWE · Based on the Novel by COLETTE
Costumes, Scenery and Production Design by CECIL BEATON · In CinemaScope and METROCOLOR · Directed by VINCENTE MINNELLI

If anyone seeing director Vincente Minnelli's 1958 musical, *Gigi,* got a sense of déjà vu, it might only be expected. The film was scored by Alan Jay Lerner and Frederick Loewe, who also composed the music for the Broadway show *My Fair Lady,* which had a similar plot. (Indeed, a rejected tune from the latter was dusted off and inserted into *Gigi.*) Quibbling aside, the film was a smash, with Leslie Caron in the title role and Maurice Chevalier performing his deathless song, "Thank Heaven for Little Girls." *Gigi* went on to win nine Academy Awards.

Master of Suspense

ONE OF FILMDOM'S best-loved figures, director Alfred Hitchcock was a singularly gifted talent, known as much for his macabre-humor persona as for his signature filmmaking style.

Beginning in the silent era, the British-born "Hitch" created a body of cinematic work that, while eluding Academy recognition (for himself, anyway), proved to be as popular among audiences as it was influential among his peers. In the 1940s and '50s, he hit his artistic stride with a string of Hollywood classics that solidified his reputation as a master of the psychological thriller. "Hitchcockian" entered the language as shorthand for menace and intrigue.

Such films as *Strangers on a Train* (1951), *Dial M for Murder* (1954), and *Rear Window* (1954) demonstrated his command of building tension. Hitchcock's dry wit was evident in such works as *To Catch a Thief* (1955) and *The Trouble with Harry* (also 1955). Notorious as an on-set taskmaster, he

nonetheless assembled a virtual stock company of players (including stars Cary Grant, Jimmy Stewart, and Grace Kelly), drawing forth some of their finest performances.

Certain thematic elements were recurrent throughout his work, such as mistaken identity, voyeurism (a powerful part of *Vertigo,* 1958), and disquiet beneath sedate surfaces. Hitchcock's genius was to assemble the elements in a way that played upon audience's fears while providing satisfying entertainment. For example, *North by Northwest* (1959) is a thriller that is alternately terrifying and amusing. It also is Hitchcock's splashiest interpretation of a favorite theme: the innocent man wrongly accused.

In 1955 television gave him the opportunity to bring his brand of suspense into American homes each week with *Alfred Hitchcock Presents.* By the end of the decade, the ubiquitous Mr. Hitchcock had primed audiences for perhaps his most disturbing feature of all, 1960's *Psycho.*

When Alfred Hitchcock's *Vertigo* was released in 1958, audiences and critics greeted it coolly. Certainly, its pitiless examination of a man who pines for a dead lover, and who attempts to re-create her by molding another woman in her image, is unsettling and peculiar. But the film's artfulness is readily apparent. Precisely because of smart underplaying by James Stewart and (in a dual role) Kim Novak (*pictured*), *Vertigo* is a highly charged, emotionally devastating depiction of male romantic obsession. That it's also a murder mystery adds a violent twist to its unusual allure. In a psychological sense, *Vertigo* may be the most daring big-studio movie of the decade.

1958

March 30: Alvin Ailey's American Dance Theater, a groundbreaking African-American dance troupe, is born with a performance at Manhattan's 92nd Street Young Men's Hebrew Association. • Tensions simmer between Israel and Syria as periodic skirmishes and episodes of shelling keep border communities on alert.

April 1: President Eisenhower signs the $1.8 billion Emergency Housing Bill in the hopes of giving the economy a shot in the arm.

April 2: San Francisco columnist Herb Caen coins the term "beatnik." • The UN Economic Commission for Europe releases a report predicting that the Soviet Bloc will soon face severe labor shortages unless it dramatically cuts troop levels. • The U.S. government halts arms shipments to Batista's Cuban government.

April 3: Fidel Castro and his band of guerrillas launch attacks on Havana, Cuba.

April 4: New York Mafia figure Johnny Stompanato is stabbed to death by the daughter of his girlfriend, actress Lana Turner. Turner and Stompanato had been arguing when Turner's 14-year-old daughter, Cheryl Crane, appeared with a knife. • Bertrand Russell's Campaign for Nuclear Disarmament stages its first protest march, from London's Hyde Park to Aldermaston, Berkshire. Some 5,000 protesters gather in Trafalgar Square in London to speak out against nuclear proliferation.

April 6: Arnold Palmer wins his first Masters tournament at the Augusta National Golf Club, with a total score of 284, 4 under par.

April 13: Top honors at Moscow's Tchaikovsky International Competition go to American pianist Van Cliburn.

Seen on its maiden flight on May 27, 1958, the McDonnell F4H-1 jet fighter plane, aka the Phantom, represented a bold leap forward in technology. Powered by twin engines, this Navy aircraft was built for speed (Mach 2), with all-weather, long-range capabilities. Versatility was key to its success. Designed as an interceptor armed with air-to-air missiles, the Phantom also could launch nuclear weapons, if need be. As an active workhorse for some 38 years, the Phantom served all branches of the American military. It also was adopted by nearly a dozen other nations.

Algis Budrys's 1958 Cold War novel, *Who?*, concerns itself with Martino, a missing American scientist who is inexplicably returned by the Soviets. But when Martino strides across the checkpoint border in Berlin, onlookers see that he has acquired a grotesque metal head and a mechanical hand. Has Martino given his weapons secrets to the Soviets? Or is he a brainwashed cat's-paw programmed to do ill once back in Allied hands? Indeed, is the man Martino at all? Tense and explicitly political, *Who?* is also a chilling exploration of what it means to be oneself—or not.

A captivating teen model demonstrates the latest in fashion for young women on the cover of this 1958 issue of *Seventeen*. Teen-oriented magazines flourished in the late 1950s, as the first of the Baby Boomers reached adolescence. Competing with the fairly upscale *Seventeen* (which had premiered in 1944) were such flashy upstarts as *Teen Screen, Teen Star Album,* and *Teen Magazine.* These magazines focused on movies, music, fashion, and romance. *Seventeen* also ran stories for soon-to-be brides, since so many young women of the era got married as teenagers.

The Affluent Society

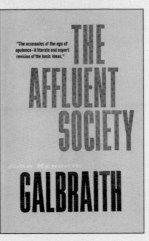

"The economics of the age of opulence—A literate and expert revision of the basic ideas."

THE AFFLUENT SOCIETY

John Kenneth

GALBRAITH

ONE OF JOHN KENNETH Galbraith's provisional titles for *The Affluent Society* (1958) was *Why People Are Poor*. That rejected title perhaps better captured his attempt to explain the persistence of poverty and the excess of consumerism in the 1950s.

A Harvard economist and a veteran of the New Deal, Galbraith was able to connect with a popular readership at a time of questioning and unease. *The Affluent Society* appeared soon after the Soviets' launch of Sputnik and as Americans began to wonder what their productivity and consumer culture were achieving. What broader social goals—such as the exploration of space—were being sacrificed as Americans preoccupied themselves with items of luxury? Galbraith, along with sociologist C. Wright Mills and other intellectuals, were troubled by an America that indulged in shiny consumer goods but invested little in public parks, schools, and social infrastructure.

Galbraith asked, "Might there not one day be discontent with a society in which there is a single-minded concentration on the goal of economic success?" *The Affluent Society* suggested a path toward more federal management of the economy and away from economic growth based on consumerism. Economists and politicians began to support Galbraith's ideas, which would comprise the heart of President Kennedy's New Frontier and President Johnson's Great Society.

In this advertisement, a happy suburban husband rides his spiffy new Springfield riding mower. Having a neat lawn became an obsession with many middle-class suburban families who had escaped from the concrete of large cities during the 1950s. Advances in power mowers enabled men and women to join in the ritual of creating and maintaining neat green spaces. The joy of lawn care was perhaps a bow to America's rural past as well as evidence of a powerful pride of ownership.

Youngsters partake in the biggest fad of the 1950s: twirling hula hoops around assorted body parts. In 1957 Richard Knerr and Arthur Melin of America's Wham-O company picked up on the popularity of wooden hoops in Australia and invented colorful plastic ones. First marketed in the United States in 1958, they became almost instant successes, with 25 million sold in just two months. People all over America gyrated their hips to see who could keep the hoops whirling the longest. The fad died out in the 1960s.

April 14: Poland Premier Wladyslaw Gomulka declares workers' strikes illegal and decrees that unions must submit to Communist Party authority.

April 16: The interstate highway system is born when President Eisenhower signs the Federal-Aid Highway Act.

April 18: After 13 years of incarceration, poet Ezra Pound is discharged from Washington, D.C.'s St. Elizabeth's Hospital. Pound was declared legally insane and committed for his support of Mussolini's fascist Italian government. • The former Brooklyn Dodgers play their first game in Los Angeles. They face off against the San Francisco Giants, who recently moved from New York.

April 27: Evangelist Billy Graham kicks off his three-day revival at San Francisco's Cow Palace. The event will draw close to 700,000 people.

April 28: CIA chief Allen Dulles claims that the Soviet economy is growing twice as fast as the U.S. economy.

April 29: Egypt agrees to pay $81 million to British and French stockholders in exchange for ownership of the Suez Canal.

May: Chairman Mao launches China's "Great Leap Forward," a disastrous social experiment in which China tries to modernize its economy by focusing on industrial production quotas to the detriment of the nation's agricultural output. A massive famine will result, and within a few years millions of Chinese will die of starvation.

May 1: Egyptian President Nasser, visiting the Soviet Union, promises his support for the USSR in exchange for Soviet support of African and Asian independence.

May 8: U.S. Representative Adam Clayton Powell (D–NY) is brought before a grand jury on charges of tax evasion.

Hungarian political leader Imre Nagy speaks to his nation during the abortive 1956 revolution against Soviet domination. Nagy had become prime minister during the rebellion, which he supported. After the Soviets crushed the rebels, Nagy took refuge in the Yugoslav Embassy and was guaranteed free passage out of the country by the Soviets. They subsequently reneged, arrested the rebel leader, and executed him in Budapest on June 16, 1958, after a secret trial. Nagy had become too powerful a symbol for the USSR to tolerate.

Texas-born Alvin Ailey gained fame in the 1950s as one of the biggest proponents of modern dance. Educated at Lester Horton's dance school (where he became director upon Horton's death in 1953), Ailey absorbed an array of influences—ballet, jazz, African—and coalesced them into a singular vision. The results were enacted through the company he founded, the Alvin Ailey American Dance Theater in New York City. The group quickly became noted for its bold explorations of black culture while eschewing traditional choreographic values.

> "In socialism, all is well, even if there is nothing to eat."
>
> —A PEASANT IN YANSHI, CHINA

China's Great Leap Forward

IN EARLY 1958, Chairman Mao Zedong and other leaders of the Communist Party of China were unsatisfied with the economic progress in the rural regions of their country. To remedy the problem, they abandoned Soviet-style socialism and embarked on a rigorous new course that would thoroughly communize the country as quickly as possible. Accordingly, Mao called for "a great leap" from agrarian backwardness to modern industrialization.

Central to the Great Leap Forward was the advent of the commune, which in theory would boost productivity. By the end of the decade, about 500 million peasants were

A poster to promote the development of agriculture in China

organized into roughly 24,000 communes, where they toiled for up to 18 hours a day, seven days a week producing steel. "Three years of hard labor for one thousand years of happiness," Mao reminded them.

Happiness, however, did not come to those subjected to the commune system. Labor platoons replaced the traditional family unit, as husbands were separated from wives while children were placed in communal nurseries. Even worse, the emphasis on industrialization caused labor shortages in agriculture. The resulting drop in crop output, coupled with droughts and flooding, led to widespread famine. By 1962 some 20 million peasants had starved to death.

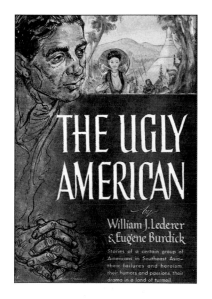

The Ugly American (1958), by journalists William J. Lederer and Eugene Burdick, was a "fictional" account of American officials and their actions in the Southeast Asian nation of "Sarkhan" (read: South Vietnam) in the early 1950s. It featured Americans who were incompetent and arrogant toward native leaders whom the U.S. was supposedly helping in their fight against communism. The book's title became an evocative phrase, referring to ignorant and rude American representatives in foreign countries, especially in the developing world. In 1963 the book was made into a successful movie starring Marlon Brando.

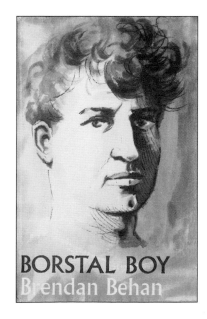

Irish writer Brendan Behan's Borstal Boy was published in 1958. Behan had been sent to an English reform school (a "borstal") in 1940 for IRA terrorist activities. This autobiographical account of his time at the school is filled with details of the horrors of the experience as well as anecdotes about his love of musical theater and gardening. Behan became a symbol of vigorous resistance to the British. He was also a prodigious drinker and partier who died in 1964 at age 41, partly as a result of alcohol abuse. The jacket illustration seen here is by B. S. Biro.

May 13: Protesters angry with U.S. policies in Latin America throw stones at Vice President Richard Nixon when he stops in Caracas, Venezuela, on his goodwill tour of South America. • French troops seize control of the Algerian capital of Algiers after French mobs storm the streets protesting what they see as the French government bowing to pressure from Algerian nationalists.

May 15: The Soviets launch Sputnik III, the world's first space laboratory.

May 18: Lockheed-Martin's F-104 Starfighter, designed by C. L. "Kelly" Johnson, sets a world speed record of 1,404.19 mph.

May 19: NORAD, the North American Air Defense Command, is officially established by the United States and Canada for their mutual protection.

May 23: Ten die when eight Nike missiles explode in an accident at a Nike base in Middletown, New Jersey.

May 24: The United Press and the International News Service merge to form United Press International.

May 27: Ernest Green, the only senior among the Little Rock Nine, graduates from Central High School.

May 29: Twenty-nine U.S. oil companies are indicted by a federal grand jury in Alexandria, Virginia, for oil and gas price fixing in the wake of the Suez crisis.

May 30: Unidentified casualties of World War II and the Korean War are laid to rest at the Tomb of the Unknown Soldier at Arlington National Cemetery.

June: In preparation for Ho Chi Minh's "People's War" to unite all of Vietnam under the Communist banner, the Communists organize 37 companies of troops in a coordinated command structure in the Mekong Delta.

Ford Motor Company's 1950s effort to fill the market niche between the Ford and Lincoln brands is universally regarded as the biggest misstep in automotive history. The Edsel, named after Henry Ford's son, was the result of extensive research and test-marketing. (Poet Marianne Moore was commissioned to contrive a name for the product, with laughable results; for example, the "Utopian Turtletop.") Despite featuring many innovations that one day would become commonplace (such as an inside trunk release), the Edsel was doomed by poor timing (arriving during the 1958 recession), overhype, indifferent workmanship, and a distinctive grille design that launched a thousand jokes.

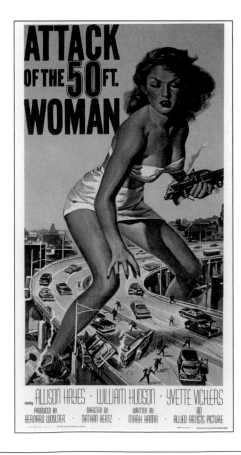

Size preoccupied science fiction moviemakers throughout the atomic-age 1950s. The decade brought a shrinking man, an amazing colossal man, an astonishing array of gargantuan insects, and even puppet people. New heights of unintentional hilarity were reached in 1958 when an unhappily married heiress launched the *Attack of the 50 Ft. Woman*—not to dominate Earth (though her condition had been caused by contact with a giant extraterrestrial)—but to get even with her philandering husband. Statuesque Allison Hayes, in the title role, and blonde Yvette Vickers, as the local tramp, were hot stuff indeed. The now-famous poster illustration is by Reynold Brown.

The New Highways

IN CITIES AND RURAL AREAS during the 1950s, Americans made way for highways. New legislation in the 1950s, including the Federal-Aid Highway Act of 1956, made these changes possible. From 1956 to 1969, the federal government appropriated $25 billion to construct more than 41,000 miles of highways.

Military and political leaders encouraged this massive spending for reasons of national defense. The new roads could provide the efficient movement of troops and materiel; they could even serve as airplane landing strips if the need arose.

City planners, flush with federal money, trumpeted the coming of the modernized metropolitan landscape, as the old city could efficiently accommodate traffic moving between the suburbs and downtown. In New York City, construction crews built concrete ramps and expressways right through the center of neighborhoods, where poor people (largely minorities) lived.

Highways made it possible for drivers to commute quickly from the suburbs to downtown businesses. Thus, many families (mostly white) moved to the appealing, new houses on the outskirts of town. They also took their ample tax dollars with them, leaving little money for the big cities' schools, public transportation, and other services. Moreover, cars on the jammed freeways spewed noxious fumes. In the 1960s and beyond, many large cities would become impoverished, run down, and hazardous to residents' health.

Highways also affected small towns and the rural landscape. Farms near cities were subdivided for housing, manufacturing, and shopping malls. From 1950 to 1980, more than 40 million acres of farmland were lost to developers. Moreover, older business districts on two-lane highways became veritable ghost towns as drivers traversed the new expressways instead.

The new roadways allowed middle-class Americans to travel at high speeds throughout the United States—to explore the coasts, the Grand Canyon, Yellowstone, and so much more. Highways were a boon to the tourism industry, and also contributed to the growth of such chains as Holiday Inn and Howard Johnson's. For better and worse, the new highways dramatically changed American society.

The Mackinac Bridge, joining Michigan's lower and upper peninsulas, was completed in 1958. At 8,614 feet in length, it is the longest suspension bridge in the world. Although plans for a connection had been unveiled as early as 1921, bonding authority for the project was not approved by the Michigan legislature until 1952. With its length, height (552 feet above water), and weight of the cables (11,849 tons), it is indeed a magnificent feat of engineering.

1958

June: William Levitt, developer of Levittown, tells the media that he will not sell any homes to African-Americans at his latest development in Burlington County, New Jersey.

June 4: French Prime Minister Charles de Gaulle sends mixed messages on the future of French Algeria, declaring in a speech before a mostly French crowd, "I have understood you!" while seeking to mend fences with Algeria's FLN separatist movement.

June 16: The U.S. Supreme Court rules that the State Department does not have the right to deny a passport based on a person's Communist Party affiliation. • Former Hungarian Prime Minister Imre Nagy, popular leader of the 1956 anti-Soviet uprising, is executed by the occupying Soviet authorities.

June 23: President Eisenhower discusses civil rights issues at the White House with Martin Luther King, Jr., and other civil rights leaders.

June 25: Michigan's Mackinac Bridge, the world's largest suspension bridge, is dedicated.

June 28: French authorities release 30 Algerian political prisoners in an effort to win Muslim support for French policies in the region.

June 29: In Birmingham, a bomb explodes at the church of Reverend Fred Shuttlesworth—one of numerous bombings throughout the South during the year. • Brazil wins soccer's World Cup over Sweden by a score of 5–2. Brazil's 17-year-old sensation, Pelé, scores two of his team's goals.

June 30: In *NAACP v. Alabama,* the U.S. Supreme Court validates the right of the NAACP to conceal its lists of members. • The Pennsylvania Supreme Court denies an appeal by the Board of Directors of City Trusts of Philadelphia, allowing Girard College to continue as a segregated school under a private board of trustees.

As sexual mores loosened in the 1950s, many teenagers felt pressured to meet the new "standards." That feeling of conflict opened the door for such drive-in fare as American International's *High School Hellcats,* a tawdry but lively tale of delinquent girls who corrupt an innocent newcomer. Yvonne Lime (who dated Elvis at about this time) is earnest as the good girl. But she seems merely a satellite to the sexy bad seed, played by starlet Jana Lund with a sly, humorless smile calculated to cow other girls and make boys do as she wishes. Director Edward Bernds had graduated to features after working on Three Stooges shorts. The arresting poster art is by Al Kallis.

Some 4,000 demonstrators descend upon London in June 1958 to protest the existence of nuclear weapons. These activists were members of the British Campaign for Nuclear Disarmament (CND), which was founded in 1958 and launched a series of such protests in the late 1950s and early 1960s. Its most prominent leader was philosopher Bertrand Russell. Similar organizations sprouted in the United States, including the Committee for Non-violent Action (CNVA), which steered a boat into a nuclear test area in 1958.

The baby boom, combined with the growing affluence of millions of middle-class Americans, helped spur the sale of portable motion picture cameras so that families could chronicle their lives. The development of 8mm film made smaller, relatively inexpensive cameras feasible. According to the Kodak Company Web page, "by the 1950s, 8mm home movie cameras were a common sight at family parties, special events and on vacations."

Brazilian soccer sensation Pelé dribbles past a helpless defender. In 1958 the 17-year-old phenom (born Edson Arantes do Nascimento) led his nation's team to a World Cup championship. He netted six goals in the final round, including two in the last game against Sweden. Pelé would go on to become the greatest player in soccer history, scoring an astounding 1,280 goals in 1,360 career games. Pelé was so revered that, in 1970, factions involved in a civil war in Nigeria agreed to a 48-hour cease-fire so that they could watch Pelé play an exhibition game.

A Michigan man listens to a radio report about the landing of American Marines, including his son, in Lebanon in July 1958. President Eisenhower was concerned about the influence in Lebanon of Egyptian President Gamal Abdel Nasser, who pushed the twin agendas of Arab nationalism and socialism throughout the Middle East. Fearing that the Egyptian leader would take advantage of unrest in Lebanon, Eisenhower dispatched the troops at the request of Lebanese President Camille Chamoun. The troops limited their action to capturing Beirut and its airport. Within four months, the civil unrest in Lebanon died out, Nasser was unable to establish a foothold, and the last Marines left.

Two French holiday-goers show off their bikini bathing suits in 1958. The bikini became popular in the late 1950s, in large measure because French actress Brigitte Bardot wore an especially skimpy one in her steamy 1956 film, *And God Created Woman*. Unveiled by French designer Louis Reard in 1946 (and named after the South Pacific islands), the bikini initially was considered far too risqué for "nice" girls to wear. In fact, most beauty contests, including the Miss America Pageant, banned it. After Bardot's performance, the bikini became all the rage in Europe, although it did not make much of a dent in the U.S. market until the 1960s.

1958

July 7: President Eisenhower signs legislation making Alaska the 49th state.

July 13: The last Studebaker-based Packard is built.

July 14: The pro-American Lebanese government is overthrown by leftist rebels. The following day, President Eisenhower will order 5,000 U.S. Marines into the country to maintain order. • The pro-Soviet army of Iraq assassinates King Faisal and takes control of the country.

July 18: Thousands gather at the U.S. Embassy in Moscow to protest the presence of American troops in Lebanon.

July 19: Using a "sit-in" technique, members of the NAACP Youth Council begin the successful desegregation of dozens of lunch counters in Wichita and Oklahoma City.

July 26: Britain's Prince Charles is made Prince of Wales, a title that can be held only by the eldest son of the monarch. Charles is the first Prince of Wales since Edward II was given the title in 1936.

July 28: In Haiti, an attempted coup and takeover of François Duvalier's presidential palace is put down.

August 2: The United States recognizes the new Iraqi government.

August 3: A Jehovah's Witness rally at Yankee Stadium in New York City attracts 250,000 faithful. • Chairman Mao Zedong receives Soviet Premier Khrushchev in Peking to discuss a Communist alliance. •The atomic submarine USS *Nautilus* crosses the North Pole under the Arctic ice cap.

August 4: *Billboard* magazine inaugurates its Hot 100 list, based on both airplay and sales data. The first No. 1 record on the new list is Ricky Nelson's "Poor Little Fool."

Iraqi troops guard the presidential palace in Baghdad after participating in a successful coup against King Faisal. In 1958 the king, the crown prince, and the prime minister were all assassinated. The leader of the coup, General Abdul Karim Qassim, opposed the monarchy's pro-Western policies and membership in the Baghdad Pact, an alliance led by the United States. Qassim became prime minister and tried to steer a neutral path between the virulent pan-Arabism of President Nasser of Egypt and acquiescence to U.S. demands. The coup did cause tensions to rise in the Middle East.

An X-15 rocket plane streaks across the skies near Edwards Air Force Base. Designed by North American Aviation in 1955, the X-15 was part of the Air Force's assumption that the "the key to dominating the skies was to fly faster than the opponent," according to the U.S. Centennial of Flight Commission. The experimental plane set records for both speed (4,534 mph) and altitude (354,000 feet) for aircraft. The X-15s never saw air combat, and were grounded for good in 1968.

It took great courage to participate in a sit-in. African-Americans and their supporters could be badly abused—cursed at, spat at, beaten—in public, without protection from anyone. In Oklahoma City in August 1958, a group that sat in at Brown's Basement Luncheonette had their table taken away and were harassed by whites. When sit-ins mushroomed throughout the South in 1960—and began to work as a way to nonviolently strike a blow against Jim Crow—the abuse increased, as did the personal risk.

The Royal Crown Cola Co. coupon seen here highlights RC's 1958 line of soft drinks, including brand-new Diet Rite Cola, which brought fresh fizz to this highly competitive industry. Diet Rite was the first cola with no calories, sodium, or caffeine, and in just a few years it would be the No. 4 cola in America. Innovation was part and parcel of RC: In 1954 the company was the first to put soft drinks in cans, and, in another bold 1958 move, the first with a 16-ounce bottle.

Nationalist Chinese troops on Quemoy Island protect themselves against shelling from Communist Chinese forces. In August 1958, China began artillery and aerial attacks directed at the offshore islands of Quemoy and Matsu, occupied and claimed by Taiwan. The Communists said they feared that the islands might be used to launch an invasion of the mainland. President Eisenhower affirmed America's commitment to help defend the islands, and ordered the U.S. Seventh Fleet to escort Taiwanese convoys resupplying the islands. (He refused to sanction the possible use of tactical nuclear weapons against Chinese airfields, however.) The Communists stopped their shelling after Taiwanese leader Chiang Kai-shek agreed to renounce the use of force to reunite the two Chinas.

1958

August 23: China fires on the islands of Quemoy and Matsu, sinking a Taiwanese supply ship and reigniting the Taiwan Straits crisis between the U.S. and China. • In a speech in Brazzaville, Congo, French Prime Minister Charles de Gaulle makes it clear that he intends to oversee the decolonization of the French African empire. • President Eisenhower signs into law legislation establishing the Federal Aviation Administration.

August 27: Operation Argus, a series of three high-altitude nuclear tests, begins. This operation proves a theory that asserts that high-altitude explosions would create a radiation belt in the earth's atmosphere.

August 29: The Soviets keep the pressure on the Americans in the space race, claiming to have successfully sent two dogs to an altitude of 280 miles and safely returned them to Earth.

September: The Atomic Energy Commission reports that Soviet nuclear testing in the Arctic has resumed.

September 2: President Eisenhower signs the National Defense Education Act, intended to make the U.S. more globally competitive by strengthening students' background in math, the sciences, and language.

September 6: Joint Chiefs of Staff Chairman General Nathan F. Twining asks President Eisenhower to grant the commander of the Seventh Fleet authority to order nuclear strikes against China, but the request is denied.

September 7: The Soviet Union tells President Eisenhower that any American attack on China would be answered by both the Chinese and the Soviets. The Soviets will restate their threat 12 days later.

At a time when typical horror films utilized creatures from outer space to terrify audiences, director Kurt Neumann offered considerable shock value with a common housefly. *The Fly* (1958) stars Al Hedison and Vincent Price in the story of a scientist whose careless experimentation in

matter transfer results in horrific disfigurement. Despite the obvious gaps in logic (the fly's head retains the scientist's intellect), Neumann skillfully builds suspense and empathy, culminating with the tiny fly/human's piteous cry of "Help me!" at the film's climax. The scene is a jolter that has achieved cinematic immortality.

The greatest rock 'n' roll partnership of all time was formed in 1957, when 16-year-old John Lennon (*right*) invited fellow Liverpudlian Paul McCartney (*left*) into his band, known as the Quarrymen. Along with lead guitarist George Harrison, drummer Colin Hanton, and piano player John Duff Lowe, the youths recorded their first songs in 1958—a cover of Buddy Holly's "That'll Be the Day" and a McCartney/Harrison original entitled "In Spite of All the Danger." The Quarrymen drifted apart in early 1959, but John, Paul, and George would become the core of a promising new band, called the Beatles, in 1960.

TV Westerns

IN THE EARLY 1950s, fictional western heroes galloped into America's homes and dominated the television viewing schedule. When the genre made the transition from radio and movies to the suburban living room, it first moved in next to Howdy Doody and Kukla, Fran, and Ollie—in other words, as children's programming.

Gene Autry, the Cisco Kid, Roy Rogers, and Hopalong Cassidy were among the many kid-friendly western heroes. Lucrative merchandising only cemented the new craze. Children couldn't wait to buy the coonskin caps popularized on the Davy Crockett program, or the white hat, black mask, and revolvers of the Lone Ranger.

Chuck Connors as *The Rifleman*

Have Gun, Will Travel and The Rifleman, reiterated the heroic iconography of the stand-alone gunslinger. *Maverick*, starring James Garner, even parodied the popular genre. But by far the most popular western of the late 1950s was *Gunsmoke*. The trials and tribulations of Miss Kitty and Marshall Dillon and their hometown, Dodge City, epitomized the new western, which focused on family and community. Another huge favorite, *Bonanza*, centered around the hardships and togetherness of the Cartwright clan.

The craze reached a high point in 1957, when *Life* published "TV Goes Wild over Westerns." The magazine remarked that at least one-third of nighttime television hours were dom-

Then, westerns grew up. During the second half of the 1950s, adult westerns ran in prime time every day. Some of the new programs reflected the bipolar Cold War climate with their black and white themes. Other shows, such as inated by the genre. "[T]he 1957 fall season opened with 28 new Westerns," the article stated. Of the 50 shows canceled for the 1956–57 season, according to *Life*, none were westerns.

Director Irwin S. Yeaworth, Jr.'s *The Blob* was conceived as little more than drive-in fodder, but its imaginative story line and the performance by lead actor Steve McQueen won the film attention beyond its typical audience. The title entity is a hungry, jellylike mass that arrives from space via meteorite. A curious elderly gentleman (played by Olin Howlin, *pictured*) inadvertently releases the protoplasmic creature, which proceeds to wreak havoc upon everything and everyone in its path. Despite its low budget and limited production values, *The Blob* has the extra allure of color, and is an effective piece of genre filmmaking.

1958

September 12: In *Cooper v. Aaron*, the U.S. Supreme Court overturns a U.S. district court's decision to suspend further integration of Little Rock schools for two and a half years. It also rules that public money cannot be used to fund private schools that sidestep federal desegregation orders. *See* September 27, 1958. • Texas Instruments unveils the integrated circuit, or silicon chip. The brainchild of two of its scientists, Jack Kilby and Robert Noyce, the silicon chip will revolutionize technology. Noyce will go on to found the Intel Corporation.

September 17: Fidel Castro, ensconced in the Sierra Maestra, launches a major offensive against Fulgencio Batista's Cuban army.

September 20: In a Harlem department store, Martin Luther King, Jr., is stabbed by Izola Curry, a black woman.

September 22: Presidential assistant and former New Hampshire Governor Sherman Adams resigns in the wake of a scandal. Adams had accepted gifts in exchange for helping a Boston industrialist obtain special treatment with the Federal Trade Commission and the Securities and Exchange Commission.

September 27: The citizens of Little Rock vote against the integration of their city's public schools, 19,470 to 7,561. *See* September 30, 1958. • Typhoon Vera smashes into the Japanese island of Honshu, leaving 5,000 dead.

September 28: French voters approve the new constitution, which establishes the Fifth Republic and enhances Charles de Gaulle's power at the expense of Parliament. De Gaulle will be elected president of the Fifth Republic on December 21. • The U.S. Air Force chooses the Thor over the Jupiter as a mass-production intermediate range ballistic missile.

Martin Luther King, Jr., exchanges a loving gaze with his wife, Coretta Scott King, in Harlem Hospital on September 30, 1958. Ten days earlier in New York, a deranged African-American woman named Izola Curry stabbed King in the chest with a letter opener as he signed copies of his new book, *Stride Toward Freedom*. According to Dr. Aubre Maynard, the head of the interracial surgical team, King would have died if he had sneezed because the tip of the opener had reached his aorta. Two ribs and a portion of King's breastbone had to be removed to free the blade.

Desperate for a means to monitor Soviet activity, the CIA commissioned Lockheed Aircraft Corporation to develop a state-of-the-art spy plane. The result was the U-2, an unarmed, single-seat aircraft that was capable of staying airborne for nine hours while flying high enough to elude attack. U-2 pilots began reconnaissance flights in 1956, gathering valuable intelligence all over the world. Though the U-2 could be detected on radar, it was not until 1960 that the Soviets successfully brought one down, precipitating a major diplomatic crisis.

Created by Don Featherstone for Union Products in 1957, pink flamingo lawn ornaments were made out of polyethylene. The eye-catching birds became immensely popular as millions of Americans moved to the suburbs and were convinced they needed cutesy lawn creatures to decorate their green spaces. Many found the color, hot pink (aka flamingo pink), irresistible.

Years of playing "the good girl" in movies paid off well for Donna Reed in 1958. *The Donna Reed Show,* which premiered that September, was typical of the sitcom genre of the day. The parents (Donna and Alex Stone, played by Reed and Carl Betz) lived in domestic bliss with their children, Jeff (Paul Petersen) and Mary (Shelley Fabares). The family confronted and resolved a nonproblem in 30 minutes, including commercials. The sitcom was one of many in the 1950s and early 1960 that portrayed an ideal American family.

Producer-director Stanley Kramer, long known for his "message" pictures, presented a contrived but engaging examination of racial tensions in the 1958 film *The Defiant Ones.* The movie stars Tony Curtis (*left*) as "Joker" Jackson and Sidney Poitier (*right*) as Noah Cullen, a pair of escaped, handcuffed convicts who must overcome personal animosity and racial prejudice in order to survive. Fleeing a southern chain gang, the two are literally bound to each other, compelling them to work together to avoid recapture. The film reveals the common humanity the two men share beneath their hardened facades.

Beginning with the Hopalong Cassidy model in 1951, young Baby Boomers hopped on the school bus every morning toting metal lunch boxes that featured their favorite fictional characters. In the 1950s and '60s, more than 120 million metal lunch boxes were sold in the United States.

Kids' favorites included the characters they saw on TV: Davy Crockett, Superman, the Lone Ranger, Howdy Doody, Mickey Mouse, and others. This Roy Rogers and Dale Evans "chow wagon" model was introduced in 1958.

1958

September 30: Arkansas Governor Orval Faubus rules that public high schools in Little Rock will be closed for the rest of the school year. *See* June 18, 1959.

Late September: Alabama Governor James Folsom commutes the death sentence of Jimmy Wilson, a black man, to life imprisonment. Wilson was convicted of stealing $1.95 from an elderly white woman.

October: Patrice Lumumba founds the National Congolese Movement.

October 1: The National Advisory Committee on Aeronautics (NACA) disbands, as NASA is founded to lead the U.S. through the space race.

October 2: The West African nation of Guinea proclaims its independence from French rule.

October 4: For the first time, a passenger jet flies from London to New York. The jet is a De Havilland Comet owned by BOAC, the predecessor to British Airways.

October 5: In Clinton, Tennessee, a bomb destroys 16 classrooms at the recently desegregated local high school. • Joe Perry of the San Francisco 49ers breaks the career NFL rushing record of 5,860 yards set by Steve Van Buren. • Jimmy Lyons and Ralph Gleason stage the first Monterey Jazz Festival, featuring performances by legendary artists Dizzy Gillespie, Billie Holiday, Duke Ellington, and Louis Armstrong.

October 9: Pope Pius XII dies at age 82. *See* October 28, 1958. • The New York Yankees take the World Series over the Milwaukee Braves, four games to three.

October 12: The Temple, a reform synagogue in Atlanta, is heavily damaged by a bomb. Five members of the National States Rights Party are arrested, but not charged with the crime.

Jazz aficionados listen in rapt attention at the first Monterey Jazz Festival on October 5, 1958, a milestone event that became the West Coast answer to the Newport Jazz Festival. Organized by disc jockey Jimmy Lyons and San Francisco music critic Ralph J. Gleason (who later would help found *Rolling Stone* magazine), the gathering was intended to showcase lesser-

known performers alongside the genre's biggest stars. Among the stellar acts that first year were Louis Armstrong, Max Roach, Billie Holiday, and Dizzy Gillespie (who performed the national anthem). Local favorite Dave Brubeck became a mainstay of the fest, which also included art and educational programs.

The remains of Clinton (Tennessee) High School, dynamited on October 5, 1958, made clear that school desegregation would be a hard-won fight. In Georgia that year, the state legislature suspended the compulsory school-attendance law. Meanwhile, the U.S. Supreme Court rejected a lower-court order that had suspended integration of public schools in Little Rock, Arkansas; the high court called on local officials to make "a prompt and reasonable start" on desegregation. Arkansas Governor Orval Faubus responded by closing all high schools in Little Rock to "prevent disorder."

The Mattachine Society, founded in Los Angeles in 1950, was a pioneer gay rights organization that included among its members such luminaries as fashion designer Rudi Gernreich. The society was named after a character in Italian theater who would tell his king the truth when others feared to. Its major goals were to challenge antihomosexual legislation and actions and to build a strong culture. *Mattachine Review* wanted people to see homosexuals not as "swishes"—a pejorative descriptor like "queer"—but as equals with a different sexual orientation.

American Bandstand

TEENS ACROSS AMERICA finally were given a show of their own with the national arrival of *American Bandstand* in August 1957. Originating in Philadelphia five years earlier, the program found a nationwide audience once the producers recognized that kids were interested in checking out *other kids*—their opinions, their fashions, and, mostly, their dances. Original host Bob Horn was a balding former disc jockey with a good grasp of which new music was important and which wasn't. But following Horn's dismissal (for drunk driving), the new host parlayed a winning formula into a national institution.

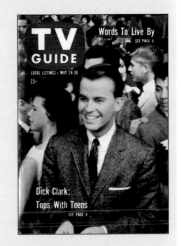

Youthful and telegenic, deejay Dick Clark possessed an innate rapport with teens that his predecessor lacked. Unfortunately, he proved less than discriminating with his choice of records. The result: Legions of well-scrubbed, made-to-order "singers" (often named Bobby) found overnight stardom, while authentic but less attractive rockers fell by the wayside.

Ultimately, *Bandstand*'s showcase for the transient dances of the day—such as the bop, the stroll, and the jive—proved irresistible to audiences, keeping viewers from coast to coast apprised of what their peers were up to. While spawning imitators for demographically precise variants (such as *Soul Train*), *American Bandstand* remained TV's preeminent rock 'n' roll show for more than 30 years.

Minnesota native Eddie Cochran began his career as one half of a country-western duo, but the example of Elvis led him, like so many others, to a different path. In partnership with Jerry Capehart, Cochran penned a series of classic rock 'n' roll tunes that rivaled Chuck Berry's in capturing the teen experience with humor and panache. His immortal "Summertime Blues" (1958) is a particularly popular example; others include "Twenty-Flight Rock" (performed by Cochran in *The Girl Can't Help It*) and "Somethin' Else." At age 21 in 1960, Cochran was killed in a London car crash that injured fellow rock 'n' roller Gene Vincent.

October 13: Fidel Castro pronounces on Cuban radio that candidates appearing on the November 3 election ballot will be executed for treason.

October 14: The District of Columbia Bar Association votes to accept black lawyers as members. • *Look* magazine publishes an article, "I Am a Student," that reveals that 72 percent of college students believe that a well-rounded personality should be the ultimate aim of their college degree.

October 15: The X-15 rocket plane, capable of flying 500 mph at an altitude of 45,000 feet, is unveiled by its Los Angeles-based manufacturer, North American Aviation, Inc.

October 20: Reverend Fred Shuttlesworth heads the organization of a bus boycott in Birmingham. Fourteen months later, a federal court ruling will mandate that the city's buses be desegregated.

October 25: About 10,000 students participate in the Youth March for Integrated Schools in Washington, D.C. They're led by A. Philip Randolph, Harry Belafonte, and Jackie Robinson. *See* April 18, 1959.

October 26: Fidel Castro warns the U.S. against meddling in Cuba's affairs.

October 28: Cardinal Angelo Roncalli is elected pope. He takes the name John XXIII.

October 29: Under pressure from Soviet authorities, *Dr. Zhivago* author Boris Pasternak refuses the Nobel Prize for literature. Pasternak's masterpiece is considered out of line with Russia's Communist Party and has been banned in the USSR.

October 31: President Eisenhower suspends U.S. nuclear testing, and the Soviets reciprocate, asking other nations to join as well. The moratorium will hold for nearly three years.

British children pray for Pope Pius XII at a Catholic school in London after the Pope suffered a stroke on October 8, 1958. He died the next day. Born Eugenio Pacelli, he began his papacy in March 1939 and served during some of the most challenging days in the history of the Catholic Church. His most controversial act was signing an ambiguous concordat with Adolf Hitler in 1933. Critics claim it helped the German dictator consolidate power, while supporters argue that it was a pragmatic response that helped save the Catholic Church in Germany. During the war, the Vatican remained neutral, although Pius was critical of Nazi Germany and privately encouraged Catholic clergy to help Jews.

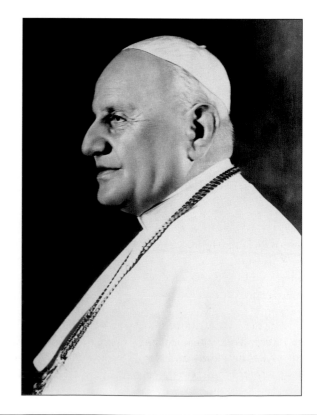

Cardinal Angelo Roncalli became Pope John XXIII in October 1958 after the death of Pius XII. During World War II, Roncalli had been praised for helping to save thousands of Jewish refugees. As pope, he surprised the world with his good humor and informality. Early in his papacy, it became clear that he had a liberal bent, as he met formally with the Archbishop of Canterbury—something that a pope had not done in 400 years. In the early 1960s, he convened Vatican II, a meeting of Catholic Church leaders that created a new liturgy and emphasized increased cooperation with non-Catholic groups.

Perhaps the best-known proponent of "found objects" as art, Louise Nevelson achieved success in the 1950s after years spent seeking a suitable outlet for her creative drives. Ignoring the prevailing trend of using permanent, unyielding materials for her sculptures, Nevelson worked with such malleable matter as plastic, wood, and even Plexiglas. Intending her work to be fluid, she sometimes deconstructed and rearranged pieces, finding endless possibilities.

Rockabilly queen Wanda Jackson was a protégée of country star Hank Thompson. She signed with Decca in 1954 while still a teenager, but her girlish innocence didn't click with record buyers. Jackson began to hit her stride at Capitol with a 1958 release, "Riot in Cell Block #9," in which she alternately purrs and growls in what would become her trademark vocal style. The same year brought the sensational "Fujiyama Mama," a memorable shouter in which Jackson likens herself to the A-bombs that took out Hiroshima and Nagasaki. She is almost certainly the greatest white female vocalist of the early rock era.

Unlike earlier recitations, fables, and Bible stories that taught children to read, primers that aimed to provide a "controlled vocabulary" were introduced in the 1930s and carried on for decades. Featuring a cast of characters that spoke in an artificial, repetitious manner, this format was believed to be vital to the development of basic reading skills. "Dick and Jane" arrived first, followed by similar series from other publishers. The "Alice and Jerry" books (*pictured*) covered parallel ground, as did "Jack and Janet," "Tom and Susan," and many other pairings. Though eventually supplanted by phonics, these teaching tools are fondly recalled by several generations of students.

Dubbed "Little Miss Dynamite," singer Brenda Lee became one of rock 'n' roll's first crossover artists, encompassing country, pop, and rockabilly. Lee had sung on radio and television until her recording career commenced in 1956. Three years later, at age 14, she scored her first Top 10 hit, "Sweet Nothings." This was followed months later by her first million-seller (and signature tune), "I'm Sorry." Her rich, plaintive voice frequently fooled people into believing that she was older than she was. Lee (seen here departing London for Milan) enjoyed stardom around the world during her hit-making years.

1958

November: Whipple "Whip" Jones opens the Aspen Highlands Ski Area with a rope tow and two chairlifts. • *Good Housekeeping* magazine runs a full-page editorial urging construction of family fallout shelters. • The Second Berlin Crisis is precipitated when Soviet Premier Khrushchev issues an ultimatum demanding that the U.S. and its Western allies leave West Berlin within six months.

November 4: The Republican Party suffers substantial losses in the midterm elections, giving up 13 seats in the Senate and 48 in the House of Representatives. • Republican Nelson Rockefeller is elected governor of New York over Democrat Averell Harriman. • A B-47 bomber crashes near the Dyess Air Force Base in Texas. The nuclear bomb on board does not detonate, but a TNT detonation leaves a 35-foot-wide crater.

November 10: New York Jeweler Harry Winston donates the Hope Diamond to the Smithsonian Institution. It will become one of the most popular and enduring exhibits at the National Museum of Natural History in Washington, D.C.

November 20: The Country Music Association holds its first meeting at WSM Radio in Nashville.

November 21: Caril Ann Fugate, accomplice and girlfriend of Charles Starkweather, is sentenced to life in prison for her role in the pair's January 1958 killing spree.

November 28: The Atlas ICBM completes its first successful full-range flight test, traveling approximately 6,300 miles from Cape Canaveral across the Atlantic Ocean. *See* July 28, 1959. • Louisiana's athletic segregation law is ruled unconstitutional by a federal court in New Orleans.

Raised by his great grandmother in segregated Georgia, Jim Brown first attended school in a two-room shack. From there, he rose to become arguably the greatest running back of all time. After averaging 14.9 yards per carry as a high school senior, and a legendary career at Syracuse, Brown was named NFL Rookie of the Year in 1957. The following season, he earned league MVP honors after romping for 1,527 yards and 18 touchdowns. A classic combination of power and speed, Brown led the NFL in rushing eight times in his nine seasons. His average of 5.2 yards per carry remains an NFL record.

In 1958 Soviet writer Boris Pasternak was awarded the Nobel Prize for Literature for his efforts in both lyric poetry and fiction, particularly his 1957 novel, *Dr. Zhivago.* Pressure from the Soviet government forced him to decline the award. The novel had been banned in the USSR, and Pasternak kicked out of the Union of Soviet Writers, in part because of his objections to the official Soviet literary emphasis on socialist realism. Largely as a response to unrest in Eastern Europe, Soviet censorship hardened in the late 1950s, with Pasternak one of the victims.

Cocktail Culture

O**F THE MANY CULTURAL** changes that took place in postwar America, the casual consumption of alcoholic beverages ranks as one of the most distinctive and far-reaching. A variety of broad socioeconomic factors gave rise to the "cocktail culture," including an overall increase in standard of living and the advent of the white-collar "organization man." A simpler explanation is that after decades of prohibition, economic depression, and war, Americans were ready to let loose.

Though people of all economic brackets enjoyed social drinking during the 1950s, the evening gin and tonic, or scotch and soda, was a feature of the white middle class. The standardized "cocktail hour," which took place around 6 P.M., was a way for both men and women to unwind.

"You need a drink" became a socially acceptable solution for daily stress and anxiety—which affected many men in the 1950s due to a more competitive working environment and pressure to keep up with the Joneses. Many women, perhaps stressed from a houseful of kids or feeling unfulfilled in their often-thankless role as homemaker, also felt the need to escape through alcohol.

The cocktail party was a related phenomenon of the decade. On Saturday nights, couples in formal attire mingled with neighbors and office buddies at the hosts' plush suburban home. Guests enjoyed cocktails and *hors d'oeuvres* throughout the evening.

Though the vast majority of adults consumed alcohol, only *moderate* drinking was considered acceptable. Excessive or compulsive drinking was frowned upon. Nevertheless, the numbers don't lie. From 1950 to 1960, America's gin production soared from six million gallons per year to 19 million gallons.

SNEAKING DRINKS

I **WAS HAPPY AS A CLAM** when we first moved to Winnetka. I loved my little house, loved decorating it, choosing the drapes and slipcovers. We were the first on our block to have kitchen appliances that weren't white, and that *matched*; we had an avocado-colored General Electric refrigerator and range. Very nifty.

But once the house was finished I found myself very lonely. There really wasn't much to do and the women on my block were all preoccupied with their children. I was trying very hard to get pregnant. It was around that time that I started drinking a little. Well, I'd always liked to drink, but I had cut back when Jimmy and I got engaged. Anyway, I decided to teach myself to cook and would spend hours poring over cookbooks, making these elaborate dishes like *coq au vin* and *boeuf bourguignon*—and sipping away on the cooking wine, of course. I did make it a point never to have a mixed drink during the day. But I'd meet Jimmy in the driveway when he got home at six with a martini in my hand. And he used to wake up in the middle of the night and find me kneeling next to my bureau drinking scotch out of a bottle I kept there. I did finally go to a psychiatrist and he told me, "Your only problem is that you don't have children," and that if I had a baby my drinking would stop. Which, of course, was what I thought, too.

—EILEEN HANLEY, DISCUSSING HER LIFE IN A WEALTHY CHICAGO SUBURB IN THE 1950S

In 1958 Jules Feiffer published his first book, a collection of his *Feiffer* strips done for the *Village Voice*. His elegant, free-flowing drawing style was unusually sophisticated, and his subject matter was even more unconventional. Prefiguring such later strips as *Doonesbury,* his panels skewered the high and mighty in both the political and pop culture worlds. Feiffer became a self-styled "rebel," taking on such topics as the Cold War and The Bomb.

1958

December 1: Representatives from the U.S., USSR, Argentina, Australia, Belgium, Britain, Chile, France, Japan, New Zealand, Norway, and South Africa sign a treaty agreeing to maintain Antarctica as a wildlife preserve.
• Ninety-two students and three nuns perish in a fire at Chicago's Our Lady of the Angels elementary school. •
The Department of Health, Education, and Welfare reports that nearly a million student days were lost in 1958 due to the closing of schools to avoid integration.

December 9: Robert Welch and 11 of his colleagues gather in Indianapolis to organize the anti-Communist John Birch Society.

December 10: The first domestic passenger jet service, a National Airlines Boeing 707, delivers 111 passengers from New York to Miami.

December 15: Arthur L. Schawlow and Charles H. Townes of Bell Labs publish *Infrared and Optical Lasers* in American Physical Society's journal, *Physical Review*. The report discusses their invention of the laser, an acronym for light amplification by stimulated emission of radiation. The laser will revolutionize industries ranging from medicine to communications.

December 19: A memo circulates in the Eisenhower White House outlining the administration's "pre-delegation authority," which authorizes senior military commanders to respond to a nuclear attack on the U.S. if the President is incapacitated.

December 28: The Baltimore Colts defeat the New York Giants 23–17 in overtime (the first in NFL history) in the NFL Championship Game.

December 30: Fulgencio Batista's sons arrive in New York with their grandfather, fleeing in advance of a Castro victory.

In 1958 Fidel Castro's years of struggle against Cuban dictator Fulgencio Batista's regime came to a head. Castro's forces were bolstered by news that America was cutting off military aid to Batista. Their cause was furthered by the desertion of thousands of regular army troops. In May, the outnumbered rebels scored a smashing victory against Batista during Operation Verano. But the decisive blow may have come from Castro's right-hand man, Argentine-born Ernesto "Che" Guevara (*reclining on right*). The former physician's December 1958 attack on an army train in Santa Clara finally prompted Batista to cut his losses and flee.

Mourners attend a mass funeral for children killed in a devastating fire at Chicago's Our Lady of the Angels school. On December 1, 1958, flames swept through a building ill-prepared for such a disaster. There were no sprinklers, no automatic fire alarms, and only one fire escape. Before firefighters arrived, the blaze was out of control. In the end, 92 children and three nuns were killed. Although a 10-year-old student initially confessed to setting the fire, he later recanted. Officially, the cause of the tragedy remains unknown.

"The Greatest Game"

FOR MOST OF THE 1950s, the NFL wasn't even in the same league (figuratively speaking) as Major League Baseball. But that all changed on December 28, 1958, when quarterback Johnny Unitas led the Baltimore Colts to a dramatic victory over the New York Giants in the NFL Championship Game. It has been dubbed "The Greatest Game Ever Played."

For several reasons, interest in televised football was on the upswing by 1958. The quality of the broadcasts improved, as did the marketing of the game, and more and more people owned television sets. For the 1958 title game at Yankee Stadium, an estimated 50 million people tuned in.

By the third quarter, the Colts seemed to have the game in hand, as they led 14–3 and were knocking on the door again. But the Giants reversed the momentum, stopping Baltimore on the 1-yard line and moving ahead 17–14. Then, after the Colts got the ball with 1:56 left in the game, Unitas marched his troops downfield. After Baltimore's Steve Myhra kicked a 20-yard field goal at 0:07, the game entered the first sudden-death overtime in NFL history.

In overtime, Unitas led a masterful, 13-play drive. When running back Alan Ameche plunged in from the 1, the Colts

Colts fullback Alan Ameche scoring the winning touchdown

prevailed 23–17. NFL Commissioner Bert Bell led the cheers, proclaiming, "This is the greatest day in the history of professional football!"

Bell apparently could see into the future. A dazzled nation couldn't wait for the start of the next season—nor could television executives. In upcoming years, the NFL would expand, sign increasingly fatter TV contracts, and, in 1967, launch what would become the greatest spectacle in sports: the Super Bowl.

The NFL's Pittsburgh Steelers drafted quarterback Johnny Unitas in 1955, but cut him after concluding that he wasn't smart enough to run a pro offense. In 1956 Unitas signed with the Baltimore Colts, with whom he became the league's greatest field general. He led the Colts to NFL championships in 1958 and '59 and won the NFL MVP Award three times.

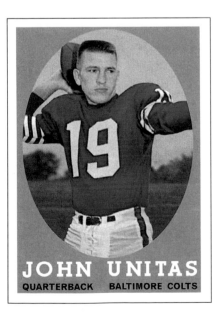

Off the field, he was seen as a clean-cut, straight arrow with a neatly trimmed flattop—the quintessential '50s role model.

Prolific suspense writer John D. MacDonald was a Harvard MBA and onetime OSS agent who made the leap from pulp magazines to such "slicks" as *Esquire*. He also was a key player in the paperback-original phenomenon of the '50s, becoming a "franchise" author whose name alone was sufficient to sell books. One of his 1958 novels, *Clemmie,* charts a suburban husband's descent into alcoholism and joblessness during his masochistic romance with a sexy, controlling sociopath. Like all of

MacDonald's work, *Clemmie* is marked by intense characterizations, gnawing anxiety, and a powerful feeling for *place*—in this case, American suburbia turned into a landscape of debauchery. Cover art is by paperback mainstay Barye Phillips.

1958

New & Notable

Books

The Affluent Society
   by John Kenneth Galbraith
Anatomy of a Murder by Robert Traver
Breakfast at Tiffany's by Truman Capote
Inside Russia Today by John Gunther
No More War! by Linus Pauling
Stride Toward Freedom
   by Martin Luther King, Jr.
The Ugly American by William J. Lederer
   and Eugene Burdick

Movies

Ashes and Diamonds
The Blob
Cat on a Hot Tin Roof
Gigi
High School Confidential!
Party Girl
Thunder Road
Vertigo

Songs

"Book of Love" by the Monotones
"Fever" by Peggy Lee
"Get a Job" by the Silhouettes
"It's Only Make Believe"
   by Conway Twitty
"Johnny B. Goode" by Chuck Berry
"My True Love" by Jack Scott
"Poor Little Fool" by Ricky Nelson
"Summertime Blues"
   by Eddie Cochran
"Who's Sorry Now"
   by Connie Francis
"Witch Doctor" by David Seville

Television

Bat Masterson
Desilu Playhouse
The Donna Reed Show
The Huckleberry Hound Show
Peter Gunn
The Rifleman
77 Sunset Strip

Theater

The Birthday Party
Flower Drum Song
Suddenly, Last Summer
Sunrise at Campobello
Two for the Seesaw

Political cartoonist Reg Manning portrays Soviet Premier Nikita Khrushchev as a Jekyll and Hyde figure who both puzzles and threatens the world. The specific context for this cartoon was the Soviet leader's ultimatum that the Western powers vacate their zones in Berlin, leaving the city entirely in Communist hands. (Khrushchev angrily referred to Western occupation as a "thorn," a "cancer," and "a bone in my throat.") This was the same leader who only two years before had condemned the excesses of Stalinism and seemed willing to support a thaw in relations with the West.

French President Charles de Gaulle makes an emphatic point in a 1958 speech. De Gaulle had led Free French forces during World War II and had headed two provisional governments after the war, but he resigned in a huff in 1946 because of disputes with some parties in his coalition. In 1958 French President René Coty called on him to return to power as prime minister because a crisis in Algeria (a French colony rebelling against France) threatened to lead to Algerian civil war. Although some feared his arrogance and dictatorial streak, de Gaulle was elected president of France in December 1958, and given broad powers. Ultimately, he oversaw transition from colonial rule to Algerian independence in 1962.

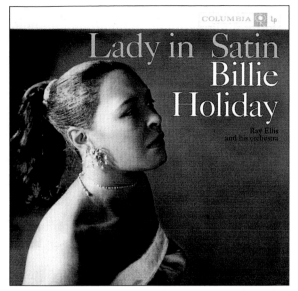

Legendary vocalist Billie Holiday was reaching the end of a long, downward spiral in 1958. After a superlative singing career going back to the 1930s (which saw her record with such giants as Benny Goodman, Count Basie, and Lester Young), her health was in decline. The uniquely gifted vocalist struggled with heroin addiction, and nowhere was her battle better documented than on the powerful and moving *Lady in Satin* collection. There, the effects of her illness were obvious in her croaky, ragged voice. She instinctively chose songs of anguish and heartache, well suited to her condition. Holiday died in 1959 at age 44.

The melodramatic saga of convicted murderer Barbara Graham was depicted to Oscar-winning effect by actress Susan Hayward in director Robert Wise's *I Want to Live!* Graham, a troubled young mother with a record of prostitution, got caught up with small-time criminals in 1953, and was implicated in the robbery and murder of an elderly California widow. Whether or not Graham herself directly caused the death was in dispute; what wasn't were her jailhouse efforts to bribe others into providing an alibi. Her credibility destroyed, Graham endured considerable legal wrangling before finally meeting death in San Quentin's gas chamber in 1955.

Songwriter and part-time actor Ross Bagdasarian scored big in 1951 with his novelty composition "Come On-a My House," recorded by singer Rosemary Clooney. In 1958 he parlayed speeded-up vocals into another No. 1 with "Witch Doctor," released

under the name David Seville. Anticipating the possibilities of three voices singing in harmony, Bagdasarian created the Chipmunks characters. Their debut, "The Chipmunk Song," was a 1958 holiday smash that introduced the public to Simon, Theodore, and the incorrigible Alvin. In subsequent years, Seville's comic trio enjoyed a string of successes on record and television.

Speedy, Alka-Seltzer's mascot, first appeared in women's magazines in 1952, but he grew in fame when he was featured on television commercials in the late 1950s. The little guy could fashion more than 30 facial expressions through a secret process that actually prompted the company to lock tapes of the

commercials in a vault. During the 1950s, Speedy was joined by other highly effective animated pitchmen, including Mr. Clean and Charlie Tuna.

"It's the beat generation, it be-at, it's the beat to keep, it's the beat of the heart, it's being beat and down in the world and like oldtime lowdown and like in ancient civilizations the slave boatmen rowing galleys to a beat and servants spinning pottery to a beat...." —JACK KEROUAC, IN HIS BOOK *DHARMA BUMS*

1959
The Beat Generation

ON SEPTEMBER 9, 1959, CBS introduced the sitcom *The Many Loves of Dobie Gillis*. As the show's theme song proclaimed, Dobie was a clean-cut teenager who just wanted a pretty girlfriend. But alongside Dobie's mainstream teen silliness lay something off-center. The show was told from his teenage perspective, a television first, and this particular teenager regularly expressed some doubts about the American dream. Specifically, he did not want to end up like his work-obsessed, humorless father, a grocer. In the Dobie Gillis show, father did not know best. The people at CBS had decided that its television audience might like some gentle cultural rebellion.

Cheering on Dobie's teen revolt was his unlikely best friend, Maynard G. Krebs. If Dobie had doubts about traditional American verities such as "hard work pays off" and "play by the rules," Maynard was practically allergic to them. In a ripped sweatshirt and sporting a sketchy goatee, Krebs played the bongos and listened to Dizzy Gillespie and Thelonious Monk. He absolutely hated the idea of a 9 to 5 job. Krebs was a "Beatnik." Though he was television's very first, he was by the fall of 1959 a familiar type to Americans.

"Beatniks" were a commercialized, parodic version of the Beat generation. Novelist Jack Kerouac had come up with the phrase "Beat generation" late in 1948. In his usual elliptical manner, Kerouac explained: "It's sort of furtiveness…with an inner knowledge there's no use flaunting on that level, the level of the public, a kind of beatness…a weariness with all the forms,

In the late 1950s, the Beat movement became a cultural phenomenon. Swearing off the 9 to 5 workday and the conformity of the era, the Beats found solace in such alternative pastimes as jazz and poetry. Pictured (*left to right*) are Verta Kali Smart, Herb Kohl, Jonathan Kozol, Ginette, and Pug (a folk singer).

all the conventions. . . . You know . . . I guess you might say we're a beat generation." Over the next decade, the phrase seeped its way into the nation's consciousness.

Then, in 1958, San Francisco newspaper columnist Herb Caen coined the term "Beatnik." Caen intended to mock the hipsters and not-so-hip people who were flocking to such Bay Area clubs as the Cellar, where poet Kenneth Rexroth booked his genuinely "Beat" friends to shout out their new work in time to live jazz performances. The columnist had borrowed the "nik" from "Sputnik," the recently launched, orbiting satellite shot into space by the Soviet Union. Beatniks, in others words, were foolish young people who were way out there, circling the planet in a spacey, "pinko" trajectory that, in Caen's opinion, led to nowhere good. Magazines such as *Time* and *Life* embraced Caen's mocking neologism in their stories about the growing number of artistic nonconformists who hung out in coffeehouses and jazz clubs throughout America's urban bohemias.

Real or not, the most visible of all Beatniks was Dobie Gillis's friend, Maynard G. Krebs, a television character played by Bob Denver. Krebs dug jazz, played the bongos, and shuddered whenever the word *work* was mentioned. *The Many Loves of Dobie Gillis* ran on CBS from 1959 to 1963.

Most Americans found the "beatnik" craze either ridiculous or vaguely unsettling. But during the late 1950s, tens of thousands of young people began to tune in to the serious challenge Beat writers such as Jack Kerouac, Allen Ginsberg, William Burroughs, and Gary Snyder were giving to the American cultural establishment. The Beats rejected materialism, traditional politics, and mainstream religion. They promoted Eastern spirituality, illegal drugs, brazen sexual expression, and, in general, partaking in new experiences.

In October 1955, Ginsberg issued one of the first and most powerful announcements of the Beats' cultural presence in a legendary reading of his long poem *Howl* at a San Francisco art gallery. The opening lines were unforgettable, as Ginsberg laments that the most intelligent people of his generation were being destroyed by madness, and that they wandered through black neighborhoods at dawn looking for "an angry fix." In the poem's penultimate section, Ginsberg condemns the United States as a monstrous "Moloch" whose blood runs money and whose fingers are 10 armies. The poem inspired a new generation of young rebels.

Howl was printed in 1956 by poet Lawrence Ferlinghetti, who ran a small publishing business out of his City Lights bookstore in San Francisco. The San Francisco police attempted to stop the poem's distribution by claiming that it was obscene—among other things, the poem celebrated homosexual sodomy—but in 1957, in a pathbreaking decision, a California state judge ruled that the poem was art and, thus, could not be censored. The trial only served to publicize both the poem and Ginsberg, one of the relatively few Americans in the 1950s who was openly and proudly gay.

Ginsberg's close friend, Jack Kerouac, spread the Beat message even further with his 1957 novel, *On the Road,* an autobiographical account of his frenetic runs across the United States. The novel became an instant hit, and the book's protagonists—including Ginsberg, Neal Cassady, and William Burroughs (though given pseudonyms)—became countercultural heroes. In his ode to the freedom of the road, written to resemble a roaring stream of consciousness, Kerouac declares: "The only people for me are the mad ones . . . the ones who never yawn or say a commonplace thing, but burn, burn, burn like fabulous yellow roman candles, exploding like spiders across the stars. . . ."

The next year, Kerouac published *The Dharma Bums.* It was a more meditative but still mostly autobiographical novel. During mountain hikes and wine parties, character Japhy Ryder gives Ray Smith (the Kerouac character) and the book's readers a full-bore, wild-man introduction to Zen Buddhism, exotic sex practices, and a host of other Eastern esoterica. *The Dharma Bums,* as the book's publicist later said, was the "book that turned on the psychedelic generation." By 1959 Kerouac had become one of the best-known novelists in the United States.

Another Beat novelist, William Burroughs, was a longtime friend of Ginsberg and Kerouac. Older by about a decade than the other two, he had been deeply involved in the New York City subculture of the early post-World War II years. Furtively homosexual and an on-again, off-again heroin addict, Burroughs poured his obsessions about drugs and sex into a hallucinatory, fragmented set of writings that added up to some thousand pages. In Tangiers, Ginsberg helped Burroughs edit the work into the 1959 book *Naked Lunch.*

In this highly unconventional novel, fearsome sexual predators, pig-headed racists, grisly con men, and worn-down hopheads retch and cower and murder and debauch. In the 1950s, no commercial publisher in the United States was ready to take on the legal headaches that the publication of *Naked Lunch* undoubtedly would produce. The book first came out in Paris, and it was an immediate sensation. But for the next half dozen years, *Naked Lunch* would be in the courts, serving as the last great test case of literary censorship in the United States.

Beat writers were not operating in a cultural or political vacuum. Though the political establishment's fierce and broadly applied anticommunism made direct challenges to the American status quo a risky proposition, social critics,

Author Jack Kerouac was the most prolific writer to emerge from the Beat movement. Kerouac had spent the early 1950s struggling for literary success, but he earned national acclaim when *On the Road* was released in 1957.

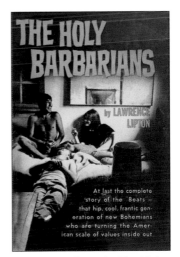

Lawrence Lipton's *The Holy Barbarians* (1959) was one of the first books to document the experiences of the Beat generation. Lipton described who the Beats were and what they believed in. He also described life in Venice Beach during the Beat heyday of the late 1950s.

cultural rebels, and political radicals were popping up all over the American scene by the end of the 1950s. Right in the mass media mainstream, a new 1959 television series, Rod Serling's *The Twilight Zone,* took a hard look at American culture. Though the series was avowedly only a science fiction/fantasy drama, many of the episodes offered thinly veiled critiques of American social problems. Racism was exposed, militarism pilloried, and mindless conformity attacked. *The Twilight Zone* was a studiously subversive look at everyday life in the United States.

Those within America's burgeoning academic community also were becoming more vocal. In *The Sociological Imagination* (1959), Columbia University professor C. Wright Mills argued that social scientists had a duty to explain how private problems, such as individual economic failure or personal alienation, were linked to deliberate public policies and societal decisions. He insisted that scholars had to be social critics, not apologists for the government or Big Business.

New York's literary scene also began to take on a harder edge at the cusp of the 1960s. In 1959 well-known novelist Norman Mailer published a collection of his essays, *Advertisements for Myself.* Among the pieces was "The White Negro: Superficial Reflections on the Hipsters." Seeking to provoke, Mailer argued that whites who were looking for a more authentic existence, freed from the artificial constraints of an uptight society, should look to the experience of black Americans, who knew firsthand that society's moral claims were often nothing more than a merciless front for brutal oppression. Mailer insisted that

Allen Ginsberg, author of the widely acclaimed and controversial *Howl and Other Poems* (1956), was the Beat movement's most eloquent and tireless spokesman. He remained active in counterculture activities in the 1960s and beyond. In fact, he coined the term "Flower Power" as an alternative to military aggression.

whites needed to liberate themselves psychologically from the unquestioning conformity typical, he believed, of the 1950s era. Though Mailer was not associated with the Beats, his cultural critique resonated with theirs.

A far more radical political challenge to American conventional wisdom came from just outside the United States. At the very beginning of 1959, a 32-year-old revolutionary named Fidel Castro overthrew the government of Fulgencio Batista, the American-supported dictator of Cuba. Teenager Todd Gitlin, who would go on to become a prominent '60s radical, recalled: "We saw the black and white footage of bearded Cubans wearing fatigues, smoking big cigars, grinning big grins to the cheers of throngs deliriously happy at the news that Batista had fled; and we cheered, too.... [It was] a revolt of young people, underdogs who might just cleanse one scrap of the earth of the bloodletting and misery we had heard about all our lives." When Castro visited the United States in April 1959, thousands of young people cheered him

About a decade older than Jack Kerouac and Allen Ginsberg, William S. Burroughs was the unofficial godfather of the Beats. A heroin addict and a worldly cynic, Burroughs made his mark on the Beat literary scene with the 1959 publication of *Naked Lunch*.

as he toured the East Coast. That Castro was an admitted leftist did not seem to dim the ardor of his American supporters; just the opposite. A crack in the American anti-Communist consensus had begun to form.

Seeking to widen that crack was a varied group of political dissidents. Since the mid-1950s, anti-Soviet, democratic socialist Irving Howe had been using the pages of his small, independent monthly, *Dissent,* to call for new, progressive politics in the United States. I. F. Stone, likewise, had started his own iconoclastic political broadsheet, the *Weekly,* to challenge the dictates of McCarthyism and the secrecy that surrounded Cold War decision-making.

In 1957 activists opposed to nuclear weapons formed the National Committee for a Sane Nuclear Policy. That same year, Martin Luther King and other civil rights supporters formed the Southern Christian Leadership Conference. In 1958 a religious pacifist, A. J. Muste, organized the Committee for Nonviolent Action. And in 1959, the young members of the Student League for Industrial Democracy, which had been formed during the great left-wing political resurgence of the 1930s, began rethinking their mission and the name of their group. In early 1960, they would rename themselves the Students for a Democratic Society.

The 1950s era *was* characterized by political repression, Cold War anxieties, suburban conformity, and cultural rigidity. But by the end of 1959, some Americans—Beat poets, angry writers, discontented students, leftist agitators, civil rights activists, and even a few television executives—were more than ready to overthrow the old verities of the Eisenhower years and break out into a new era of unforeseen possibilities.

Norman Mailer's *Advertisements for Myself* (1959) contained a reprint of a controversial essay entitled "The White Negro." The piece defined white hipsters as those who philosophically assimilated elements of African-American society into their own, thus becoming "white Negroes."

1959

1959: A half century of ethnic slaughter begins in Rwanda when the Hutu majority overthrows the government of the ruling Tutsis. As many as 20,000 Tutsis are killed—a small fraction of the death toll that will mount over the next several decades. • In Buffalo, New York, Russian immigrant Sam Marcy founds the Workers World Party—a Communist party independent of the Soviet power base.

1959: In Cairo, Egypt, oil-producing nations hold their first conference. They aim to set up a cartel to control the supply and therefore the price of oil. • The Bracero Program, a federal government initiative designed to admit legal Mexican workers into the U.S. under controlled circumstances, peaks this year with 450,000 admissions. • Future President Ronald Reagan spends much of the year stumping as a "Democrat for Nixon."

1959: "Therapeutic Abortion: A Problem in Law and Medicine" is published in the *Stanford Law Review,* shedding light on the issue of both legal and underground abortions in the U.S. • The American Medical Association officially sanctions birth control. • Eleanor Flexner publishes *Century of Struggle,* a highly acclaimed history of women's suffrage in the United States.

1959: California becomes the first state to impose emissions standards for cars. • Swedish auto manufacturer Volvo makes Nils Bohlin's invention, the three-point seat belt, standard equipment on all its new cars. • One of every 10 cars sold in the United States this year is an import. • The Super Cub becomes the first Honda motorcycle sold in the U.S.

1959: The New York Police Department assigns 1,400 officers to fight juvenile crime. • Allen Gant, of the Glen Raven Mills textile company in North Carolina, invents panty hose.

Castro's Coup

ON NEW YEAR'S DAY, 1959, Fidel Castro and his band of ragtag soldiers triumphantly made their way to Havana, where they seized control of Cuba's government. Castro's coup shocked the world. To most observers, it seemed impossible that a small guerrilla army could topple military dictator Fulgencio Batista and his 10,000 American-armed troops.

"No one—including Batista and the American government—believed that our strength could develop to the point that we could defeat the army. They thought they had time, but they did not," Castro recalled years later. What swung the balance to the rebel leader was his enormous popularity throughout the Cuban countryside, as well as widespread discontent with Batista's notoriously corrupt and repressive regime.

Once in power, Castro initiated a series of radical reforms. He reduced urban rents and utility rates while raising workers' wages. Even more significant, his land-reform program led to the confiscation of vast tracts of territory from wealthy landowners. None of this went over well with Cuba's upper class or with American investors, who controlled most of the country's cattle, sugar, mining, and railroad industries—as well as its hotels, nightclubs, and casinos. The Eisenhower Administration was equally appalled. Government officials not only disliked Castro's leftist reforms and overt nationalism, but they also worried that he would influence other Latin American countries to follow Cuba's lead. Consequently, the United States cut off all economic aid to the country.

Though he had never openly identified with the Communist Party, Castro turned to the Soviet Union for support after the American rebuke. The United States, in turn, severed all diplomatic ties with Cuba, imposed an economic boycott of the island, and enlisted the CIA to devise a plan to overthrow Castro's revolutionary government. Such an attempt failed in 1961 in what came to be known as the Bay of Pigs fiasco.

"I am Fidel Castro, and we have come to liberate Cuba."   —CASTRO

Followers of Fidel Castro jubilantly await his arrival in Havana on January 1, 1959. Castro's rebellion garnered most of its support from rural peasants, the urban working class, and some intellectuals, especially those who were sympathetic to communism. Former members of ex-president Batista's official government rightly feared Castro's revenge, as did most upper-middle-class and upper-class businessmen and large landowners. Outsiders with financial interests in Cuba, including organized crime figures and such American companies as United Fruit, feared a regime that would move increasingly toward socialism.

A Castro supporter makes a symbolic statement in Havana during the Cuban Revolution. Batista had resigned from office and hurriedly left the country at 2:00 A.M. on January 1, just ahead of the rebel march into Havana. Thus, resistance to Castro's forces in the capital city was minimal. The rebellion's success actually had been sealed earlier when some 1,000 to 2,000 rebel guerrillas under Castro and his second in command, Che Guevara, captured the major cities of Santiago and Santa Clara. Since Castro had wanted Batista arrested and tried, the American-supported dictator sneaked away during the night. He lived in Portugal and Spain until his death in 1973.

TERROR IN HAVANA

[T]HE REBEL UNDERGROUND stepped up its sabotage and terroristic activities throughout the country, including Havana. Homemade bombs would explode intermittently at different points in the Capital and people would be driven from motion picture theaters and other places of amusement. Fire bombs were also employed, and show windows of stores suffered from the impact of the explosions. Rebel bands harassed army outposts and even ventured into towns to capture arms.... [B]uses, both in cities and on highways, trucks carrying freight and merchandise, passenger and freight trains, railroad and highway bridges, public buildings and homes and businesses of "Batistianos" were blown up or burned as part of the agitation and terror designed to maintain a constant state of alarm.

—ANONYMOUS EYEWITNESS, AS QUOTED IN *FIDEL CASTRO—REBEL, LIBERATOR OR DICTATOR?* BY JULES DUBOIS

• Just six years after its premiere issue, *Playboy* reaches a monthly circulation of one million. • According to federal government data, nearly half of the new brides in America are under age 19. • According to a nationwide poll of American teenagers, 59 percent of them are "going steady."

1959: The U.S. mint begins to print the Lincoln Memorial on the penny in honor of the 16th president's 150th birthday. • The microchip is simultaneously patented by Jack Kilby of Texas Instruments and Robert Noyce of the Fairchild Semiconductor Corporation. • The De Beers Corporation announces that it has created a flawless synthetic diamond. • Häagen-Dazs ice cream and Hawaiian Punch fruit drink are the latest additions to American supermarket shelves.

1959: Jerrie Cobb becomes the first female astronaut candidate. Although she tests better than many of the original Mercury 7 astronauts, NASA will adopt a rule that all candidates must have military test pilot experience, which automatically eliminates females from consideration. • Jet-powered airline travel reaches the Hawaiian Islands.

January 1: Fidel Castro arrives in Havana shortly after President Fulgencio Batista flees the country. Castro will lead the Cuban military and appoint Manuel Urrutia as provisional president.

January 2: The Soviets launch Luna, the first man-made satellite intended to orbit the sun.

January 3: Alaska is admitted as the 49th state in the Union.

January 7: The United States recognizes Castro's new Cuban government on the same day that Castro declares a new constitution.

January 8: Charles de Gaulle, newly elected president of France's Fifth Republic, takes office.

New Jersey-born Connie Francis became one of the top female performers of the rock 'n' roll era (although few of her recordings genuinely qualify as "rock"). An accordion prodigy as a child, Francis got her start on a local talent show. At 16, she signed a recording deal with MGM, which bore fruit with a 1920s tune suggested by her father (and recorded over her objections), "Who's Sorry Now?" No less an authority than Dick Clark pronounced it a No. 1, which it soon became. A string of smashes followed, making Francis a familiar visitor to the Top 10 for several years.

The American art movement that came to be called Magic Realism began in the early 1940s and was perpetuated throughout the 1950s. One of the leading interpreters was George Tooker, whose 1959 egg tempera painting, "The Waiting Room," is seen here. Typical of Magic Realism, the work is marked by semirealistic figures and objects in a surreal setting. Tooker was fascinated by walls, fences, cubicles, stairwells, concrete enclosures, and other physical boundaries that inhibited freedom. Emotionally, "The Waiting Room" suggests apathy, despair, and paranoia.

Aloha, Alaska

Not since New Mexico and Arizona became states in 1912 had an American possession been admitted to the union. But after 1945, Congress began debating the ins and outs of statehood for the territories of Alaska and Hawaii.

The drive to include the two territories was primarily a result of World War II and the subsequent Cold War. Both Alaska and Hawaii were strategically located and thus were important military outposts. During the recent world war, they had experienced substantial population gains, as burgeoning defense spending drew civilians and soldiers alike to the far-off territories. Their continued importance during the Cold War—Hawaii as a chief naval outpost and Alaska as a bridge to Soviet Russia—were further incentives to admit the territories into the union.

But not everyone supported the statehood cause. In Alaska, the owners of large salmon canneries feared that statehood would mean higher taxes and greater restrictions on fishing. They also worried about the effects of increased oil exploration. As for Hawaii, many Southerners in both the House and Senate did not like the racial composition of the islands. Caucasians comprised a minority of the islands' population, while most Hawaiians were of Asian and Pacific Islander ancestry. Despite such opposition, both territories achieved statehood in 1959, Alaska on January 3 and Hawaii—as the 50th state—on August 21.

U.S. Representatives Ralph J. Rivers of Alaska (*left*) and John A. Burns of Hawaii.

Joyful Alaskans toss a youngster into the air after Alaska became America's 49th state on January 3, 1959. A new American flag (*pictured*) was designed, with seven rows of seven stars each. (A short-lived creation, the flag was replaced eight months later when Hawaii achieved statehood.) Congress passed the Alaskan statehood bill in part because discovery of oil on the Kenai Peninsula had led some members to believe that the resource would be developed more rapidly and efficiently if Alaska were a state. President Eisenhower gave his support after the bill reserved huge areas of Alaska for federal military purposes.

1959

January 21: Cecil B. DeMille, legendary filmmaker and director of *The Ten Commandments*, dies at age 77.

January 25: With the Boeing 707, American Airlines begins the first regularly scheduled jet service between New York and Los Angeles.

February 3: Rock legend Buddy Holly, along with fellow rockers Ritchie Valens and J. P. "Big Bopper" Richardson, is killed in a plane crash near Clear Lake, Iowa. • Martin Luther King, Jr., arrives in India. While there, he will study Gandhi's methods of social change through nonviolent resistance.

February 6: The U.S. successfully test-fires the behemoth Titan ICBM from Cape Canaveral, Florida.

February 7: The Soviets sign a pact with China to promote industrial expansion in that country.

February 16: Fidel Castro takes the oath of office and is sworn in as premier of Cuba.

February 17: The 9.8-kilogram Vanguard II, the first American weather station in space, is successfully launched.

February 19: Britain, Turkey, and Greece sign an agreement that grants independence to Cyprus.

February 20: The Federal Communications Commission establishes a rule that mandates equal television broadcast time for political candidates.

February 22: One of stock car racing's signature events, the Daytona 500, is run for the first time. Driver Lee Petty prevails.

February 28: The Corona Project, a top-secret U.S. photo-reconnaissance satellite mission, gets under way with the first of 145 launches.

March: Ho Chi Minh declares his People's War in his ongoing effort to unite all of Vietnam under his rule.

In an era in which the TV western was commonplace, CBS's *Rawhide* was notable for two things: its catchy theme song, composed by Dimitri Tiomkin and sung by Frankie Laine, and as a career-making launching pad for actor-director Clint Eastwood (*left*). As ramrod Rowdy Yates, Eastwood was second lead to Eric Fleming (*right*), who played trail boss Gil Favor. Weekly, the series depicted their adventures along the cattle drive from Texas to Kansas. Fellow cast members included singer Sheb Wooley as Pete Nolan and Paul Brinegar as Wishbone, the camp cook.

With a development period of seven years, a $6 million budget, and a 70mm widescreen treatment, Walt Disney's *Sleeping Beauty* proved to be among the studio's most ambitious works. Alas, it was not a hit at the time, winning audience adoration only through subsequent reissues. Like many Disney films, it pitted good (as embodied by Princess Aurora, *left*) against evil (the witch Maleficent, *right*). Featuring a score built upon Tchaikovsky's ballet of the same name, *Sleeping Beauty* would be Disney's last entirely hand-drawn animated feature.

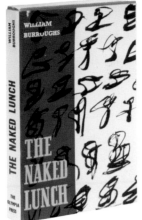

In *The Naked Lunch,* novelist and drug addict William Burroughs gives us a series of loosely connected autobiographical stories. The main character wanders through life buying drugs, taking drugs, having sex on drugs, being caught on drugs, and being subjected to the wiles of medical science in an effort to control drug addiction. The subject matter and nonlinear, episodic style made the book a cult classic. Burroughs was the grandson of the inventor of the adding machine, but he rejected his wealth and status for a life of drugs and writing—for a while as a part of the Beat generation.

Producer-director William Castle fashioned himself into the king of the gimmick horror thriller. A journeyman filmmaker with the instincts of a Barnum, he came up with such stunts as Emergo, an illuminated skeleton swept over the heads of the audience (*House on Haunted Hill,* 1958, *pictured,* with Carol Ohmart about to take a dip in an acid bath); an insurance policy for death against fright (*Macabre,* 1958); and Percepto, theater seats wired to give unwary patrons a startling buzzing sensation (*The Tingler,* 1959). Later innovations included the Coward's Corner, the Punishment Poll, and the Fright Break. *House on Haunted Hill* is a deft combination of dark humor and genuine scares, and is the most fondly remembered of Castle's pictures.

Just as Elvis provided a road map for aspiring rock 'n' roll singers, Buddy Holly (*center*) and the Crickets laid the blueprint for rock bands. Holly's initial lineup included drummer Jerry Allison (*top*), bassist Bill Mauldin (*bottom*), and rhythm guitarist Niki Sullivan. Their backup work along with Holly's hiccuping vocal style and self-penned lyrics led the way for countless bands in their wake, most notably the Beatles. Though scoring only one chart-topper, "That'll Be the Day," countless Holly tunes permeate rock's tapestry, including "Peggy Sue" and "Everyday." Holly's career was cut short on February 3, 1959, when, at 22, he perished in a plane crash along with rock prodigy Ritchie Valens and J. P. "Big Bopper" Richardson.

Look magazine, founded in 1937, was often mentioned in the same breath as *Life* magazine in the 1950s, but they were, in fact, quite different. The editors of *Life* considered their publication a weekly news magazine, while the biweekly *Look* focused on feature articles. *Look* was noted for tackling controversial subjects, such as civil rights for African- 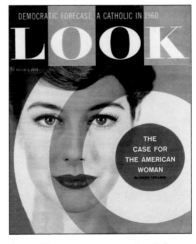 Americans and, as trumpeted on this cover, women's rights. The magazine also featured articles by noted writers, including Ernest Hemingway and Norman Mailer.

1959

March: *Consumer Reports* publishes the article "The milk all of us drink and the fallout," asserting that levels of strontium-90, a radioactive isotope, are rising in dairy milk.

March 2: Modal jazz pioneer Miles Davis records *Kind of Blue* with the rest of the Miles Davis group: Cannonball Adderley, John Coltrane, Philly Joe Jones, Paul Chambers, and Bill Evans.

March 3: The first U.S. satellite intended to orbit the sun, Pioneer IV, is launched. It will fall into solar orbit after passing within 37,000 miles of the sun. • Lou Costello, comedic film partner of Bud Abbott, dies at age 52.

March 9: Mattel's Barbie doll makes its debut at the American Toy Fair.

March 10: The people of Lhasa, Tibet, stage an uprising against the occupying Chinese. The Chinese crackdown will result in the exile of the Dalai Lama to India.

March 11: President Dwight Eisenhower asserts that the United States will not fight a war in Europe over the Berlin crisis, but does not rule out the use of tactical nuclear weapons.

March 19: The U.S. government announces that it conducted a nuclear test at an altitude of 300 miles in September 1958.

March 20: MIT scientists announce that radar contact was made with Venus on February 10, 1958.

Spring: A new fad spreads across college campuses, as students stuff themselves into phone booths.

March 23: In response to the continuing conflict on the Korean Peninsula, President Eisenhower extends the peacetime draft through July 1, 1963.

March 24: Iraq withdraws from the Baghdad Pact on the heels of an announcement by the U.S. that it will continue to provide military aid to Iran, Turkey, and Pakistan.

Comedian Lou Costello, who died on March 3, 1959, and partner Bud Abbott (*standing*) first appeared together in 1936 and became one of America's best-loved comedy teams. With Abbott as the more or less dignified straight man and Costello as the fast-talking simpleton, they began a string of successful movies in 1939, making 34 in all. *The Abbott and Costello Show* allowed the team to perform their standard routines on television, including the classic "Who's on First?" skit. The two dissolved their partnership in 1957, two years before Costello's death.

Dr. William Pickering, director of the Jet Propulsion Laboratory (JPL), explains how the Juno II rocket was launched. On March 3, 1959, the Juno II carried the Pioneer IV satellite toward the moon. Intended to crash on the lunar surface, it instead went into orbit around the sun. Pickering headed the JPL from 1954 to 1976. Among his accomplishments were overseeing the launches of the U.S. satellite Explorer I (1958) and Mariner IV (1964), which was the first U.S. space probe launched toward Mars. He twice was featured on the cover of *Time* magazine and was dubbed an original "rocket man."

Trouble in Tibet

IN 1950 COMMUNIST CHINA invaded Tibet with the stated intention of "liberating" the Buddhist country from Western imperialist influences. The Dalai Lama, Tibet's political and spiritual head, tried negotiating with China, but ultimately failed. The Chinese military ravaged the country, destroying monasteries and killing or imprisoning anyone who resisted.

In March 1959, the Chinese Red Army surrounded Tibet's capital city, Lhasa. As mortar shells crashed into the Dalai Lama's palace, the Tibetan National Assembly decided that their leader should immediately leave the country for India. Disguised as a Chinese soldier and aided by a blinding sandstorm, the Dalai Lama slipped out of Lhasa and headed to the Himalayan Mountains. "For the first time in my life I was truly afraid—not so much for myself but for the millions of people who put their faith in me," he later recalled.

The Dalai Lama's escape party meandered its way through the Himalayas, with the Chinese hot on its heels. After a two-week ordeal during which they endured blizzards and dysentery, the Tibetans crossed into India. According to one observer, it was "one of the most remarkable escapes in history." From India, the Dalai Lama agitated for Tibetan freedom and independence—a goal that has yet to be realized.

Tibetan refugees

The Dalai Lama escapes from Tibet over a tortuous route in March 1959 after sneaking past Chinese troops who had surrounded the capital city. Earlier that year, Tibetans had rebelled against Chinese rule in their territory. The rebellion was put down ruthlessly, with China later admitting to the deaths of 87,000 Tibetans. (Tibetan exiles have claimed that more than 430,000 died at the hands of the Chinese from 1959 to 1984.) In 1959 and 1960, the International Commission of Jurists concluded that China had committed genocide. For the remainder of the century and beyond, the Dalai Lama lived in northern India.

1959

March 26: Raymond Chandler, author of the Philip Marlowe detective novels, dies at age 71.

April: African-American Hazel Payne nearly dies in Little Rock, Arkansas, because state law prohibits the transfusion of "white blood" into black people.

April 4: Delivering an address at Gettysburg College in Pennsylvania, President Eisenhower underscores the need for an aggressive program of foreign aid to derail the global spread of communism.

April 5: According to tests conducted by the U.S. Naval Research Laboratory, atmospheric radiation in the eastern U.S. increased 300 percent following a series of Soviet nuclear tests in the fall of 1958.

April 7: The Atomic Energy Commission announces that a nuclear reactor has converted energy directly into electricity. • After 51 years, prohibition comes to an end in Oklahoma.

April 9: NASA announces that it has winnowed its list of Mercury astronaut candidates to seven: Alan Shepard, John Glenn, Virgil "Gus" Grissom, Donald "Deke" Slayton, Wally Schirra, Scott Carpenter, and Gordon Cooper. • The Boston Celtics, led by coach Red Auerbach and center Bill Russell, win their first of eight consecutive NBA titles. • American architect Frank Lloyd Wright dies at age 92.

April 10: Crown Prince Akihito marries a commoner, Michiko Shoda, becoming the first heir to Japan's Chrysanthemum throne to do so.

April 12: The Soviet Bolshoi Ballet begins an eight-week tour of North America.

April 15: Diagnosed with terminal cancer, Secretary of State John Foster Dulles resigns his post. President Eisenhower will name Christian Herter as Dulles's successor on April 18.

Boston Celtics point guard Bob Cousy flicks a no-look pass against the Cincinnati Royals. The 6'1" floor general led Boston to six NBA championships, including his second in 1959. Nicknamed the "Houdini of the Hardwood," Cousy dazzled fans with such ball tricks as the behind-the-back dribble and twice-around pass. Until physical giants such as Bill Russell and Wilt Chamberlain emerged in the late '50s, Cousy was widely hailed as the greatest player in the history of basketball.

The trip to Mahatma Gandhi's homeland made a great impression on Martin Luther King (pictured with his wife, Coretta Scott King, *center*). India's leaders were honored to show off their relatively new democracy to a "Negro Gandhian." King's goal was to immerse himself in Gandhi's philosophy and find a way to apply it to the civil rights movement. He found the answer in the sacrificial quality of Gandhi's followers. They were determined to live and die without owning anything but their convictions. King raised the Indian press's hackles, however, when he called for India to take nonviolence to its logical end and disarm itself, even in the shadow of its enemy, Pakistan.

One of the decade's most sensitive interpreters of the Great American Songbook was Nebraska-born Jeri Southern, a classically trained pianist who gravitated to jazz in the mid-1940s. At the urging of her manager, she became a singer-

pianist, and was initially active in the Chicago club scene. Southern judged a song by its lyrics, which she conveyed with uncommon warmth and intelligence. Her vocals were subtle and completely unmannered—so much so that, despite commercial success with "You Better Go Now," "When I Fall in Love," and other singles, Southern was best appreciated by the jazz *cognoscenti*. The LP seen here was released in 1959.

Milan, Italy's Pirelli Tower was designed by Gio Ponti, a painter, poet, publisher, industrial designer, and architect. The diamond was a motif he used freely as a personal trademark, and given the shape of the 32-story building, one can see what he meant when he called it "a graphic slogan." The tower opened in 1956 as the world's tallest reinforced-concrete structure, and it soon was recognized as a symbol of modern Italy. Its slender profile eventually proved hazardous, as it was struck by a small plane in 2002.

In 1959 Walt Disney Studios began shifting its focus to live-action properties, beginning with *The Shaggy Dog*. The movie starred Fred MacMurray (*center*), in the first of many such roles, along with former Mouseketeers Tommy Kirk (not shown) and Annette Funicello (*top right*). The film itself, a juvenile Cold War spoof concerning a boy (Kirk) who turns into a sheepdog, was a major hit. Disney followed with similar movies, including *The Absent-Minded Professor* (1961), *The Love Bug* (1968), and *The Shaggy DA* (1976).

In 1955 the Sperry Corporation merged with Remington Rand, and four years later Sperry Rand marketed this Remington men's shaver. Made of urea plastic and acrylic, the heavy shaver body was dominated by the Remington crest, which evoked the upscale "V"-crest motif of Cadillac and the recently departed Packard. The shaver epitomized functional, everyday industrial design at its most persuasive, utilizing shapes and colors to suggest dependability and prestige.

1959

April 15: Fidel Castro begins a goodwill tour of the United States in Washington, D.C.

April 18: More than 25,000 students partake in the second Youth March for Integrated Schools in Washington, D.C. Thousands sign a petition for school integration. • The Montreal Canadiens defeat the Toronto Maple Leafs in the Stanley Cup Finals for their fourth straight NHL title.

April 20: British ballerina Margot Fonteyn is arrested in Panama on suspicion of planning an antigovernment revolt.

April 25: A lynch mob storms a Poplarville, Mississippi, jail and murders African-American Mack Parker, who had been accused of raping a white woman.

April 26: According to the Panamanian government, Cuban guerrillas attempted to invade Panama but were turned back. Within the week, more than 80 guerrillas will surrender to Panamanian forces.

April 28: Clare Boothe Luce is confirmed as ambassador to Brazil by the U.S. Senate. However, she will resign three days later at the request of her husband amid accusations of incompetence from Senator Wayne Morse, who has staged a one-man campaign against her appointment.

April 29: The Congress of Racial Equality (CORE) organizes nonviolent sit-ins at segregated establishments in Miami.

May: Josef Mengele, who personally selected 400,000 prisoners to die at the Nazis' Auschwitz death camp, flees from Argentina to Paraguay. • Ho Chi Minh's war begins in earnest with the construction of the Ho Chi Minh Trail and the establishment of the Central Office of South Vietnam to oversee the war theater in the South.

On March 11, 1959, Lorraine Hansberry became the first black female playwright to have work produced on Broadway. Hansberry's *A Raisin in the Sun* starred Sidney Poitier (*left*) and Ruby Dee as Walter Lee Younger and his wife, Ruth. After Walter Lee's father dies, the family agonizes over what to do with a $10,000 insurance check. Should they buy a house in a white neighborhood, invest in a liquor store with Walter Lee's friends, or help Walter Lee's sister, Beneatha, go to medical school? Conflicts and crises abound, including the visit of a representative of a white neighborhood, who offers the Youngers money to abandon the idea of moving there.

Pat Boone, seen opening sacks of fan mail, was second only to Elvis as the biggest teen idol of the era. The Florida native first drew notice with his white-bread covers of R&B songs, including Fats Domino's "Ain't That a Shame" and Little Richard's "Tutti Frutti." Though laughably soulless to modern ears, his recordings helped ease acceptance of the original artists. Boone eventually adopted a more fitting crooner style, scoring with such tunes as "April Love" and "Love Letters in the Sand." Despite his popularity, Boone's squeaky-clean image precluded his acceptance by rock purists, who viewed him as the anti-Elvis.

Widely regarded as Hollywood's greatest comedy, *Some Like It Hot* follows the misadventures of a pair of Chicago jazz players (Tony Curtis, *left,* and Jack Lemmon, *center*) who go on the lam disguised as "girl musicians" after witnessing the St. Valentine's Day Massacre. They dodge gangsters and a lecherous old tycoon who has designs on Lemmon, and meet singer Sugar Kane Kowalczyk (Marilyn Monroe, in one of her best performances). The hit film was a high-water mark for all three stars, as well as for coscripter-director Billy Wilder and his writing partner, I.A.L. Diamond, not least because its subversive wit bent gender rules and allowed for screamingly funny double entendres.

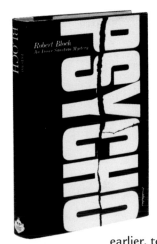

Robert Bloch's 1959 novel, *Psycho,* derives much of its power from the central assumption that the "ordinary" person next door could be a homicidal maniac. Bloch based this premise on a true crime involving a Wisconsin man, Ed Gein, who engaged in grave robbing, murder, and cannibalism. In the novel, a female guest in Norman Bates's motel is murdered while she showers. We eventually discover that Bates, who had killed his domineering mother 10 years earlier, took on her personality and was the murderer. Director Alfred Hitchcock used the novel as the basis for his classic 1960 film of the same name. The famed "PSYCHO" logo was designed by Tony Palladino.

Yukio Mishima's *The Temple of the Golden Pavilion* first appeared in English in 1959. The most commercially successful of the famed Japanese author's works, it tells the story of a Buddhist monk who burns down a beautiful ancient temple because he can not see the same level of beauty in himself. In his own strange life, Mishima became obsessed with martial arts and with the quest for the perfect body. He also was fiercely nationalistic and fascinated by Japan's samurai past. In 1970, shortly after he and a band of followers occupied a military headquarters in an attempt to inspire a return to pre-World War II patriotism, he committed ritual suicide.

One of many Bozo the Clowns offers up a trainload of Bazooka bubble gum. The original Bozo—a clown named Pinto Colvig—was hired by Capitol Records in 1946 for "sing-along" records aimed at the children's market. He became so popular that in the 1950s promoter Larry Harmon, who had purchased Bozo's rights from Capitol, hired actors to play the role on television in major U.S. (and eventually foreign) markets. By the mid-1960s, more than $150 million of Bozo merchandise was being sold per year.

1959

May 2: Fidel Castro asks the United States to spend $30 billion over the next decade to promote the democratization of Latin America.

May 10: In Rome, Italian archaeologists discover the ruins of Emperor Nero's gardens.

May 11: Representatives of the Big Four—the U.S., Britain, France, and the Soviet Union—meet in Geneva to discuss the reunification of East and West Germany.

May 12: Singer Eddie Fisher, recently divorced from Hollywood actress Debbie Reynolds, becomes Elizabeth Taylor's fourth husband.

May 15: Scientists studying whaling industry records warn that the blue whale is heading toward extinction.

May 18: Fidel Castro's Cuban government passes a law that calls for the confiscation of all sugar plantations owned by American companies.

May 19: The Atlanta Public Library allows African-American patrons for the first time.

May 20: U.S. passports are returned to Japanese-Americans who were stripped of their citizenship during World War II.

May 24: Former Secretary of State John Foster Dulles dies of cancer at age 71.

May 26: Pittsburgh Pirates pitcher Harvey Haddix throws 12 perfect innings in a game against the Milwaukee Braves, but then loses the game in the 13th.

May 28: Two monkeys, Able and Baker, become the first animals to survive a space mission after NASA sends them rocketing 300 miles into space on a Jupiter missile.

June 2: Musing on a subject close to his heart, San Francisco Beat poet Allen Ginsburg pens "Lysergic Acid."

Compulsion, a critically acclaimed 1959 film from director Richard Fleischer, is based on the infamous Leopold-Loeb case. In 1924 two wealthy, genius-level Chicago teenagers, Nathan Leopold and Richard Loeb, pleaded guilty to murdering an acquaintance, Bobby Franks. Their hearing was highlighted by defense lawyer Clarence Darrow's successful 12-hour plea against the death penalty. The film adaptation of Meyer Levin's novel uses different names, but the plot is essentially the same as the true story. Although the film does deal with the two youths' intimate relationship, it portrays homosexuality as sinister and dangerous.

In 1951 Dr. Carl Djerassi (*pictured*) created progesterone, a synthetic hormone, marking the first major step in the development of oral contraceptives. But neither he nor the company he worked for were interested in testing it. Later in the decade, Harvard scientist Dr. John Rock, along with Dr. Gregory Pincus, used progesterone to create the first birth control pill, Enovid, in cooperation with Searle Drugs. The Federal Drug Administration approved the sale of Enovid as a birth control pill in 1960, which—argue many historians—set the stage for the sexual revolution.

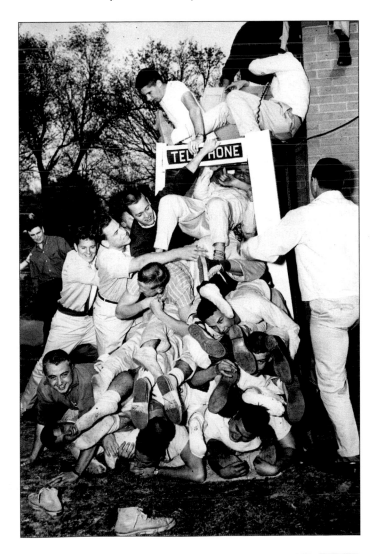

Reexamining historical characterizations of America's foreign policy, academic William Appleman Williams's *The Tragedy of American Diplomacy* postulated a counter-theory to prevailing views. Rather than accept at face value the mythic goals of spreading "freedom" and "democracy" around the world, Williams offered an analysis that pointed to economics as the engine of U.S. policy. He argued that what seemed like altruism was merely a by-product of efforts to establish market footholds for American business interests. Such foreign policy, the author noted, stirred resentment overseas. Naturally, Williams's radical notions spurred much spirited debate.

Cuban leader Fidel Castro lays a wreath at the Lincoln Memorial during his visit to the United States in April 1959. If Castro had hoped for American approval of his revolution, he was greatly disappointed. Based on intelligence reports from the CIA, President Eisenhower had concluded that the Cuban leader had aligned himself too closely with Communists in Cuba to warrant U.S. support. Indeed, Eisenhower concluded that the only hope for Cuba "lay with some kind of nondictatorial third force" that rejected the authoritarianism of both Castro and former dictator Fulgencio Batista. Some historians have argued that Ike missed a real chance to move Castro away from the Communist camp.

Thirty-five students at Southeast Missouri State College set a world record for telephone booth stuffing in April 1959. This strange fad actually began in South Africa earlier that year, when 25 college students crammed themselves into a booth. The fad moved to London, where a phone call needed to be made for the "stuff" to count, then to MIT in the United States, where students used calculus to maximize numbers. It finally spread to the American heartland, where the record was set.

Barbie Arrives

IN EARLY 1959, Barbie enjoyed her coming-out party, delighting girls across America. Introduced by Mattel, Inc., Barbie was modeled after the mildly erotic German doll Bild Lili, which was geared toward adult males. The original Barbie retained some of Lili's features, including the sidelong glance, thick eyeliner, and undersized waistline.

What made Barbie such a hit was that she was not a baby doll—she was not intended to be nurtured, cuddled, or fed. Rather, Barbie was an independent teenager that young girls could emulate, and guide through imaginary situations. The world of Barbie was one of fashion, leisure, and play; it did not include parents, children, school, or marriage. In addition, Mattel launched an entire line of clothes for Barbie. Outfits such as "Roman Holiday," "Easter Parade," and "Enchanted Evening" fascinated young consumers and stoked their interest in the doll.

Over time, Barbie acquired a boyfriend, Ken (in 1961), and such friends as Midge, Francie, and Skipper. The Barbie business skyrocketed in subsequent years as Mattel introduced an array of other accessories, including cars, houses, and even dune buggies. By the 21st century, Mattel had sold more than one billion Barbies (and friends) worldwide.

Crooner Eddie Fisher eyes actress Elizabeth Taylor while his wife, actress Debbie Reynolds, appears oblivious to what is going on. The three formed the most notorious celebrity scandal of the late 1950s, when Fisher left his wife (and two small children) to marry Taylor. Eddie and Debbie, who had married in 1955, were Hollywood's premier "cute couple," and Fisher's affair with the voluptuous Taylor led many fans to scorn him. His May 12, 1959, marriage to Taylor ended in divorce in 1965, and two years later Fisher married singer Connie Stevens.

In 1954 Nash Motors's popular Rambler compact was joined by an even smaller companion model, the 42-horsepower (later 52-horse) Nash Metropolitan, a British-made two-seater with American, distinctly Nash-like styling. The Met sold well during a big-car era in which every U.S. trend, poll, and self-appointed expert predicted that such a vehicle would fail spectacularly. The up-level, "Luxury in Miniature" 1500 model that bowed in 1956 (a '59 is shown here) topped out at 80 mph—but required 22 seconds just to get from 0 to 60! The recession of 1958 was good for the Met, which achieved all-time high sales of 22,000 units for the 1959 model year.

McCall's, first published in 1876, became one of America's most popular magazines in the 1950s, reaching 4.75 million readers. Its slogan became "Togetherness," as it preached that women would find happiness in a harmonious family life. Specifically, McCall's focused on sewing patterns, fashion, and stories of joy in romance and marriage. It joined Cosmopolitan and Good Housekeeping in emphasizing to women the virtues of the domestic arts and sciences, such as knowing the right party sandwiches to serve.

Hiroshima, Mon Amour, Alain Resnais's powerful, emotional film, stirred audiences with its nonsequential story line and seeming abandonment of linear plot. But the story, of a French actress (Emmanuelle Riva) and Japanese architect (Eiji Okada) who seek healing from their traumatic wartime experiences, marked the high-water mark of French "New Wave" cinema. Although its complex, innovative flashback structure and repetition made for sometimes jarring viewing, critics hailed the film as a lyrical depiction of the subconscious mind's efforts to grasp the elusive. The film's poetic stylings and fractured sense of time were widely imitated.

Soviet ballerina Galina Ulanova danced her way into the hearts of thousands of Americans during the Bolshoi Ballet's triumphant U.S. tour in spring 1959. Critics and audiences were especially taken with the company's rendition of Romeo and Juliet. In their comments about the tour, Soviets tended to emphasize the positive side of cultural exchanges, while U.S. observers fretted that the Russian enemy might be scoring propaganda points. Ballet fans just enjoyed the beauty of the art.

1959

June 3: Singapore is granted a government largely independent of Britain, although Britain will retain control of Singapore's foreign relations and defense.

June 9: The USS *George Washington*, the first American submarine equipped with ballistic missiles, is launched in Groton, Connecticut.

June 11: The postmaster general bans D. H. Lawrence's recently released book, *Lady Chatterly's Lover*. Seven years will pass before a court rules that the book is not obscene.

June 18: A federal court rules that Arkansas's law to close its public schools is unconstitutional. The school board will not appeal the ruling and will reopen Little Rock's schools in the fall.

June 23: After nine years in a British prison, convicted atom spy Klaus Fuchs is released.

June 25: The Cuban government takes advantage of its new agrarian reform initiative, seizing 2.35 million acres of privately held land. • Charles Starkweather is executed in the electric chair at the Nebraska State Penitentiary for his multistate killing spree the previous year.

June 26: The Canadian-American St. Lawrence Seaway opens, creating access between the Atlantic Ocean and Great Lakes ports. • Ingemar Johansson defeats Floyd Patterson to capture the heavyweight boxing crown.

July: Ho Chi Minh sends 4,000 Viet Minh guerrillas to infiltrate South Vietnam. • Singer-songwriter Joan Baez launches her career at the first-ever Newport Folk Festival.

July 1: Israel's Knesset approves the sale of arms to West Germany.

July 4: For the first time, a 49-star flag is raised over the U.S. Capitol. The 49th star represents Alaska.

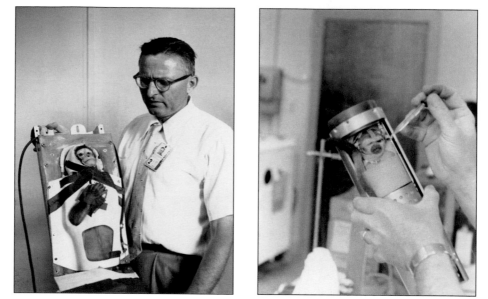

A NASA scientist examines a rhesus monkey named Able (*left photo*) while another scientist feeds Able's colleague, a squirrel monkey dubbed Baker. On May 28, 1959, the two simians were hurled into space in the nose cone of a Jupiter rocket. Scientists used them to test the impact of high acceleration and weightlessness, a necessary precursor to sending humans into space. Both monkeys survived the undoubtedly harrowing 16-minute flight, although Able died four days later while undergoing surgery to remove a medical electrode. Baker lived at the Alabama Space Center until 1984.

The USS *Mason,* an American heavy cruiser, steams through the Eisenhower Lock of the St. Lawrence Seaway. Officially opened on June 26, 1959, by Queen Elizabeth II of Great Britain and President Eisenhower, this miracle of engineering skill could support ocean-going vessels. The seaway had seven locks and extended from Montreal to Lake Erie. The commercial advantages for Great Lakes states and provinces were enormous. Since 1959 more than three billion tons of cargo have moved through the seaway, with almost half traveling to and from overseas ports.

NASA Takes Off

On October 4, 1957, the USSR successfully launched Sputnik, the first artificial satellite to orbit the earth. As the Soviets celebrated their achievement, Americans were left wondering about the state of their own space program.

The National Advisory Committee for Aeronautics (NACA) had a staff of thousands and was run by some of the brightest minds in the country, but it had failed to beat the USSR into space. Matters became aggravated after the success of Sputnik II and the launchpad explosion of Vanguard I—the first U.S. satellite attempt. U.S. government officials agreed that something had to be done.

Congress immediately held hearings on the matter. Their solution was the creation of the National Aeronautics and Space Administration (NASA) in July 1958. Unlike NACA, which was run by the military, the new agency was civilian operated. Along with this change came a reorientation in what the U.S. hoped to achieve in outer space. Previously, the space program was geared toward reconnaissance and was essentially an outgrowth of the U-2 spy-plane program. The creation of NASA marked a shift away from the militaristic approach toward a more scientific one.

Allotted a $145 million budget in 1959 (and $401 million in 1960), NASA sent into orbit a series of satellites that reported on the earth's weather patterns, its atmosphere,

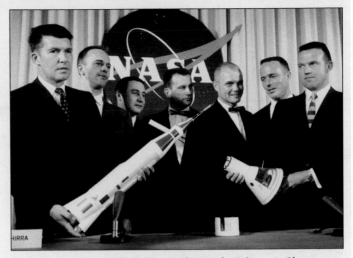

Astronauts (*from left*) Schirra, Shepard, Grissom, Slayton, Glenn, Carpenter, and Cooper

and the planet's magnetic field. Such endeavors were followed by interplanetary probes to the moon and Venus. On April 9, 1959, NASA announced the selection of the first astronauts who would be sent into space as part of the Mercury program. Alan Shepard, Gus Grissom, John Glenn, Deke Slayton, Scott Carpenter, Wally Schirra, and Gordon Cooper went on to become national heroes as they blazed the trail for successive generations of space travelers.

World War II and Korea brought out the adventuresome spirit in men who had fought, and self-conscious longing in many who had not. Whatever the case, civilian life could be dull, so many working-class men welcomed the "sweat" magazines—*Man to Man, Stag, Male,* and countless others—which gloried in tales of hyper-masculine heroes who rescue half-clad beauties from the

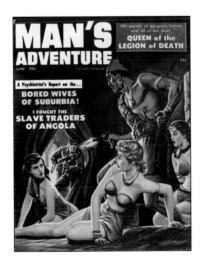

predations of slave traders, Nazis, cannibals, gorillas, army ants—you name it. (The genre's most beloved cover blurb is "Weasels Ripped My Flesh!") Interior text was unabashed pulp, but some of it was churned out by Mario Puzo, Bruce Jay Friedman, and others who went on to notable careers. This 1959 *Man's Adventure* cover painting is by Clarence Doore.

Blind from the age of six, musician Ray Charles became one of popular music's best-loved entertainers, creating a sound that encompassed gospel, jazz, and even country. Possessing a gritty, soulful voice, superb piano chops, and an ear

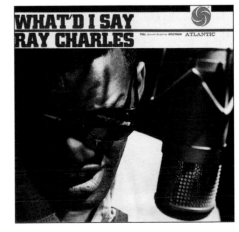

for exciting arrangements, Charles enjoyed a solid, if unspectacular, career until his 1959 hit, "What'd I Say." Featuring dynamic call and response vocals and his signature keyboard riffing, the song established him in mainstream consciousness. From then on, Charles's prodigious output guaranteed a steady chart presence. Such hits as "Georgia on My Mind" and "Hit the Road, Jack" helped ensure his musical immortality.

1959

July 8: Major Dale Buis and Sergeant Chester Ovnand, U.S. military advisers, are killed in Bien Hoa, Vietnam, by hostile fire. They are considered the first U.S. fatalities in what Americans will come to know as the Vietnam War.

July 12: Castro denounces the United States for offering asylum to the former head of the Cuban air force.

July 13–17: ABC airs *The Hate That Hate Produced*, a five-part documentary about Malcolm X and the Nation of Islam.

July 17: Jazz singer Billie Holiday dies at age 44. • Anthropologist Louis Leakey finds a 1.75 million-year-old hominid skull—the oldest to date—in Olduvai Gorge, Tanzania.

July 21: The U.S. launches the USS *Savannah,* the first nuclear-powered merchant ship.

July 24: Vice President Richard Nixon engages Soviet Premier Nikita Khrushchev in the "Kitchen Debate" at the U.S. Trade and Cultural Fair in Moscow.

July 28: After three previous test-fires exploded in midflight, an Atlas ICBM test rocket is launched successfully from Cape Canaveral, Florida. This final Atlas prototype is declared operational and will be deployed within the year.

August 7: The U.S. Navy announces that it has developed a radar system that can monitor, from U.S. bases, Soviet nuclear tests and missile launches. • Explorer 6, also known as the "Paddlewheel Satellite," is launched. It is capable of sending images to Earth from 17,000 miles up.

August 15: The Soviets deny Vice President Richard Nixon's request to tour one of their munitions plants.

August 17: A half million New Yorkers are left in the dark when a massive power failure strikes the city.

Jimmy Stewart (*left*) stars as a lawyer defending a jealous husband accused of murder in Otto Preminger's *Anatomy of a Murder* (1959). The film presents a frank, nuanced look at the blurring of conventional morals, where nothing is clear-cut. Preminger's shrewd casting included George C. Scott (*right, back turned*) as an aggressive prosecutor; Ben Gazzara (*not shown*) as the accused; newcomer Lee Remick (*second from right*) as his wife; and real-life lawyer Joseph "Army v. McCarthy" Welch (*center*) as the judge. The incomparable Duke Ellington added an undercurrent of gritty disquiet to the film with his incisive jazz score.

Singer Bobby Darin may have been rock's first Renaissance man. Following his initial success with "Splish Splash" and "Queen of the Hop"—conventional pop/rock fare—he confounded expectations by dusting off an old Weill-Brecht chestnut and recording it in a style reminiscent of Sinatra. "Mack the Knife" topped the charts for nine weeks, selling two million copies and broadening Darin's audience. Eventually, Darin would successfully tap the country and folk markets, spurred by an obsession to achieve greatness by an early age. This desire was fueled by knowledge of heart trouble, which finally claimed him at age 37 in 1973.

The Kitchen Debate

IN JULY 1959, Vice President Richard Nixon flew to Moscow to open the U.S. Trade and Cultural Fair in Sokolniki Park. The event was intended to be a goodwill gesture, but the American organizers also hoped to show off American technology.

Nixon walked through the exhibit with Soviet Premier Nikita Khrushchev, pointing out the merits of the various items on display. As they made their way into the "American household" section of the fair, Nixon showed the Russian leader a washing machine and emphasized that it made women's work easier. Unimpressed, Khrushchev said, "Don't you have a machine that puts food into the mouth and pushes it down?...These are merely gadgets."

Soon the two were embroiled in a heated debate about communism and capitalism. "We hope to show our diversity and our right to choose," exclaimed Nixon. "We do not wish to have decisions made at the top by government officials...." But Khrushchev had his own take on the matter: "In America, if you don't have a dollar, you have the right to [sleep] on the pavement." The debate continued as the American and Russian argued over which country was more advanced.

Two months later, Khrushchev began an extended tour of the United States. Galvanized by the events in Moscow,

Khrushchev (*light suit, pointing*) and Nixon

American crowds and even some local officials—such as the mayor of Los Angeles—greeted the leader coolly. The volatile Khrushchev responded by deriding the Hollywood filming of *Can-Can,* calling the near-nude dancing "immoral." Despite such episodes, the trip went relatively well. Khrushchev capped off his visit by meeting with President Dwight Eisenhower at Camp David. The two leaders did not hammer out any concrete initiatives, but they did agree that their differences should be resolved peacefully.

ROCKETS AND COLOR TV

KHRUSHCHEV: We have existed not quite 42 years, and in another seven years we will be on the same level as America. When we catch you up, in passing you by, we will wave to you....

Nixon: There are some instances where you may be ahead of us, for example in the development of the thrust of your rockets for the investigation of outer space; there may be some instances in which we are ahead of you—in color television, for instance.

Khrushchev: No, we are up with you on this, too. We have bested you in one technique and also in the other.

Nixon: You see, you never concede anything.

Khrushchev: I do not give up.

Nixon: Wait till you see the picture.

—EXCHANGE BETWEEN KHRUSHCHEV AND NIXON AT THE AMERICAN NATIONAL EXHIBIT IN MOSCOW, JULY 24, 1959

"Don't you have a machine that puts food into the mouth and pushes it down? Many things you've shown us are interesting but they are not needed in life. They have no useful purpose. These are merely gadgets."

—KHRUSHCHEV TO NIXON AT THE AMERICAN NATIONAL EXHIBIT IN MOSCOW, JULY 24, 1959

1959

August 20: More than 2,300 people die when Typhoon Iris hits China.

August 21: Hawaii joins the Union as the 50th state.

August 22: The New York Philharmonic, led by Leonard Bernstein, receives a standing ovation in Moscow.

August 23: According to the federal government, some 400 U.S. schools will offer Russian language courses during the 1959–60 school year.

August 26: President Eisenhower sends money to Laos to help fight the Communist insurgents who are pouring over the border from North Vietnam.

August–September: Making a goodwill tour of Europe, President Eisenhower is received as a hero by both the French and German people.

September: The USS *Observation Island* launches the first successful test of a Polaris missile from sea, about seven miles off Cape Canaveral. • In Prince Edward County, Virginia, public schools are closed to avoid integration. White students are placed in private schools, and black students are left with no schools at all.

September 4: In an effort to end racketeering, Congress passes the Labor Reform Act, which seeks to reduce the power of labor unions. • Following a series of stabbings, Bobby Darin's hit song "Mack the Knife" is pulled from New York City radio station WCBS.

September 7: Citing widespread black disenfranchisement, the U.S. Civil Rights Commission asks President Eisenhower to provide electoral oversight in certain districts.

September 9: In an address to the United Nations, the Dalai Lama requests intervention in Tibet against the occupying Chinese.

Director Alfred Hitchcock ended a decade of brilliant work with a rollicking cross-country chase in *North by Northwest*. The alternately lighthearted and terrifying spy thriller stars Cary Grant (*center*) as Roger Thornhill, a man mistaken for a government agent who is pursued through a series of memorable locales, including the UN building (*pictured*) and Mount Rushmore. Actress Eva Marie Saint costars as the mysterious femme fatale who seduces Thornhill with coolly ribald dialogue. The film contains one of Hitchcock's most unforgettable sequences, in which Grant is buzzed by a crop-dusting plane.

Steelworkers picket outside a U.S. Steel plant during a strike against that corporation and most other steel companies, which lasted 116 days. The action shut down 90 percent of U.S. steel production. On October 19, President Eisenhower invoked the Taft-Hartley Act, ordering the strikers back to work while negotiations went on, a move upheld by the Supreme Court. The strike was settled in January 1960, with major wage concessions made by the companies. One long-term result was an increase in steel imports to the U.S. The strike was part of a wave of labor unrest in 1959, which included a major walkout by autoworkers.

The Beat Generation, a transparent (and late) attempt to cash in on the beatnik craze, was the baby of producer Albert Zugsmith, whose résumé encompassed superior films (*Written on the Wind, Touch of Evil*) as well as cheese (*High School Confidential!, Girls Town*). Promotional material for *The Beat Generation* promised "the wild, weird world of the Beatniks . . . beyond belief!" In truth, the movie is a crime thriller about a serial rapist and the woman-hating cop who tracks him down. Mamie Van Doren and a lot of awful poetry are bonuses. The film is unintentionally funny, and suggests that the Beat/beatnik scene had run its course in the popular imagination.

Comedian Lenny Bruce did not tell jokes. Instead, he railed against society's institutions and injustices, challenging and redrawing the boundaries of what was acceptable as entertainment and public discourse. Sex, politics, commercialism, religion, and hypocrisy were favorite subjects. His act was frequently vitriolic or childish, but mostly it was truthful and darkly funny. His on-stage demeanor was fearless, and he had a little boy's sense of bravado—useful attributes because Bruce was almost continually in trouble with the law; his monologues cut too deeply, and encouraged prosecutions for obscenity. In the live routines on this 1959 album, he sends up doctors, Hitler, evangelism, and even mass murder.

The Missing Link

ON JULY 17, 1959, anthropologist Mary Leakey went out to one of the archaeological sites in Tanzania's Olduvai Gorge that she and her husband, Louis, had been excavating. Accompanied by her two dalmatians, Mary was inspecting the surface of a rocky incline when she noticed a piece of bone that resembled part of a human skull. When she brushed away the loose dirt, she exposed a jawbone and teeth. What Mary Leakey uncovered turned out to be the skull of *Zinjanthropus boisei,* or "Nutcracker Man," an early ancestor of humankind.

The discovery sent shock waves through the scientific community. Until then, the oldest remains of a tool-using hominid were those of "Peking Man," which had been found in China and dated back some 500,000 years. The Leakeys' find was dated at 1.75 million years, revealing that Africa, not Asia, was the birthplace of human evolution.

Louis declared that the Nutcracker Man was the "missing link between the near-men or ape men of South Africa and true man as we know him from primitive Java or

Louis and Mary Leakey with the jaw of the Nutcracker Man

Peking." The discovery of Nutcracker Man rearranged the field of anthropology and inspired a new generation of archaeologists to build on the Leakeys' work.

1959

September 11: Congress passes a bill that will provide food stamps for low-income Americans.

September 12: The Soviets launch Luna 2, which will become the first man-made object to hit the moon.

September 14: President Eisenhower signs the Landrum-Griffin Act in an effort to curb union corruption.

September 15: Black Army veteran Clyde Kennard is arrested on false charges of possession of liquor and theft of chicken feed, shortly after being turned away during his third attempt to register at Mississippi Southern College. He will be convicted, and—despite the best efforts of attorney Thurgood Marshall—will serve much of a seven-year sentence before dying in prison.

September 17: The X-15 rocket plane makes its first flight from a B-52 bomber. It attains a speed of 1,400 mph, about twice the speed of sound.
• Typhoon Sara slams into the Japanese islands and the Korean Peninsula, claiming more than 2,000 lives.

September 19: The SETI movement—the Search for Extra-Terrestrial Intelligence—is born when scientists Giuseppe Cocconi and Philip Morrison publish a paper in *Nature* claiming that terrestrial radio telescopes are now able to detect radio signals from other stars.
• Soviet Premier Khrushchev, on a state visit to the U.S., loses his temper when he is told that security concerns will prevent him from visiting Disneyland. *See* September 25, 1959.

Fall: Xerox releases its model 914 copier, complete with a built-in fire extinguisher (the "scorch eliminator").

September 22: Communist China is once again thwarted in its decade-long campaign to gain admittance to the UN. • The transatlantic telephone cable between the United States and Europe is completed.

The Comics Code Authority was built on the graves of dozens of comic book publishers that went under during the anti-comics crusade of 1954–55. For the remainder of the decade (and beyond), every page of every American comic was pre-inspected by Code staffers. DC Comics had always been squeaky clean, and benefited from the erasure of pesky competition. Although the company wanted the Authority's seal of approval, it elevated inoffensiveness to a new plateau when it depicted the Man of Steel as a frustrated house-husband on the gimmicky cover of this 1959 issue. The handsome art is by Curt Swan and Stan Kaye.

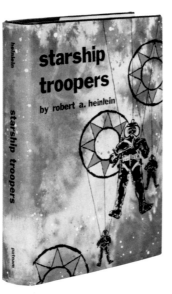

Prolific science fiction writer Robert Heinlein published the controversial novel *Starship Troopers* in 1959. On one level, it is a classic human-versus-alien story, as the hero, a young soldier named Juan Rico, learns the skills needed to battle an invading race of man-sized spiders. On another level, it is a vehicle for Heinlein's moral conservatism, marked by a strict hierarchy of authority under which orders of the true "leader" must be carried out unquestioningly. In this "ideal" world, public floggings are legal and only military veterans can vote—characteristics that led some to see this as a proto-fascist vision.

Astro Boy was created in 1951 by Japan's most popular writer-illustrator of comic books, Osamu Tezuka. Known in Japan as *Tetsuwan Atom* (Mighty Atom), the noble little robot has the mind and personality of a young boy who died in an auto accident; he was given a mechanical body by his grieving father, a scientist. Immensely powerful but gentle at heart, Astro Boy becomes Earth's champion against a vivid array of high-tech aggressors. The tale is, in effect, about second chances and the use of force for defensive purposes only. Not surprisingly, Astro Boy struck a chord in a postwar Japan eager to regain its dignity and find an appropriate role in the world.

Louisiana Governor Earl Long (*right photo*) campaigns for election as lieutenant governor in 1959. (He could not succeed himself as governor.) One of the most colorful politicians of the decade, Long was best known for his eccentric behavior, especially his well-publicized affair with burlesque dancer Blaze Starr (*above*), who appeared in "revues" at clubs across the country. In June 1959, Long's wife had him committed to a mental institution, from which he ran the state government by telephone. He was released after a short stay to continue his election bid, which he lost. Long was elected to Congress in 1960, but died before taking office.

This *Saturday Evening Post* cover (by Constantin Alajálov) shows a young couple dreaming the American dream of unlimited material possessions. Although many Americans in the 1950s achieved affluence, there were nonetheless substantial pockets of poverty in the United States, especially among racial minorities. The National Poverty Center notes that "in the late 1950s, the poverty rate for the total U.S. population was 22.4 percent, or approximately 39.5 million individuals." Moreover, the recession of 1958–59 put a damper on the aspirations of middle-class Americans, as well.

The Three Stooges made nearly 200 short comedies for Columbia over a span of more than 20 years, but the two-reel format faded badly after World War II. The Stooges' contract was not renewed in 1957, and it looked like the act was finished. Although none of the Stooges received a dime from Columbia's subsequent sale of the shorts to television, the exposure won the boys a new generation of fans. Suddenly, they were hot properties. Their comeback began with an outer-space comedy, *Have Rocket, Will Travel,* in which (*from left*) Moe Howard, Larry Fine, and Curly Joe DeRita meet their android duplicates—not to mention a space unicorn and a fire-breathing giant spider.

A Hawaiian girl celebrates the announcement of statehood for her island chain. After President Eisenhower signed a statehood bill on March 18, 1959, Hawaiians voted on Proposition 1, which asked, "Shall Hawaii immediately be admitted to the Union as a state?" Ninety-four percent of voters said yes. On August 18, 1959, Hawaii was admitted to the Union. Massive celebrations erupted on the island, with bonfires burning, horns honking, and thousands dancing in the streets.

Classically trained bandleader Martin Denny became the foremost purveyor of what was known as "exotica" music, a blend of faux Poly-nesian sounds melded with animal noises. Despite the considerable musicianship and arranging skill involved, critics

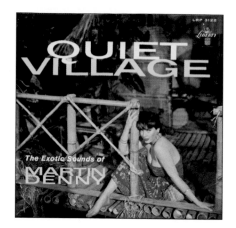

viewed the genre as little more than a cheap novelty. But Denny was quite popular with the public, scoring a Top 10 smash with "Quiet Village" in 1959. With his use of unusual instrumentation, Denny helped nurture the public's taste for what became known as "world music." Model Sandy Warner (*pictured*) appeared on most of Denny's LP sleeves.

In an era of simpler entertainment, when audiences had relatively modest expectations, drive-in theaters and "hardtop" movie houses sometimes turned to "spook acts" to boost box office receipts. A show might feature a gruesome magic act, a fake seance, or monsters that snarled and grabbed at young patrons. Some spook shows were mounted by

professionals; others were simply the labors of costumed ushers and other theater employees. This 1959 ad placard issued by a Kentucky drive-in promises that "some will faint!" Another common ploy was the rhetorical challenge to male pride: "Guys, are you man enough to bring your girl?"

Actor Errol Flynn looks faintly out of it as he holds hands with his 17-year-old companion, Beverly Aadland. The former swashbuckling Hollywood heartthrob died after years of substance abuse at age 50 in October 1959, a few weeks after this photograph was taken. During his peak years, 1935 to '42, he made several adventure movies, including *The Adventures of Robin Hood*, that put him at the top of the Hollywood heap. In his last film, *Cuban Rebel Girls*, he played a reporter-adventurer on the scene of Fidel Castro's Cuban Revolution, with Aad-land as his costar. It was a perfectly awful 68-minute pseudo-documentary, called by one reviewer a "miserable screen epitaph" for an actor who had been a movie hero.

Trumpeter Miles Davis was that rare musician whose command of his art placed him at the forefront of every stylistic development within his field, keeping jazz alive at a time when other idioms threatened to marginalize it. At age 18, during the war years, Davis had traveled to New York to absorb direct inspiration from Charlie Parker and Dizzy Gillespie. Stylistically, he soon forged his own path, pushing the music beyond its established boundaries. The culmination of his explorations came with *Kind of Blue* (1959), on which he teamed with saxophonists John Coltrane and Cannonball Adderley. Davis's use of modal scales profoundly influenced music for years.

Bandleader-singer Louis Prima and his wife, accomplished jazz vocalist Keely Smith, were among the kings and queens of Las Vegas in the 1950s. Backed by "jump jazz" ensemble Sam Butera and the Witnesses, Louis cavorted around the stage and let loose with his hoarse, blues-styled vocals while Keely stood almost stock-still as she sang, deadpan, trying her best to ignore the antics of her husband. Audiences loved it. Louis and Keely dominated Vegas lounges—the entertainment/bar areas off the casino floors—and enjoyed modest success in movies. Their recording of "That Old Black Magic" was a major hit.

Soviet Premier Nikita Khrushchev and his wife, Nina Petrovna, flank actress Shirley MacLaine on a Hollywood set. The Soviet leader visited the United States from September 15 to 27, 1959, meeting MacLaine during the filming of *Can-Can* and touring an American supermarket. He also met with President Eisenhower at Camp David. Even though the two leaders did agree to set up a summit meeting later, with Charles de Gaulle of France and Harold Macmillan of the United Kingdom, Ike was disappointed that he didn't seem to charm the Russian. "I can't get anywhere with this guy," he complained to an adviser.

Bonanza, which premiered on NBC on September 12, 1959, initially struggled against *Perry Mason,* but soon built an enormous following. The NBC western centered around Ben Cartwright (played by Lorne Greene, *far right*) and his three hearty sons (*from left*), Little Joe (Michael Landon), Hoss (Dan Blocker), and Adam (Pernell Roberts). Like their widowed father, each son was loyal, hardworking, and resourceful as they tended to the family's thousand-square-mile ranch (The Ponderosa). *Bonanza* ran for more than 13 years and was the top-rated show on television from 1964 to '67.

1959

September 25: President Eisenhower welcomes Soviet Premier Khrushchev to Camp David, in rural Maryland, to discuss arms control. *See* September 27, 1959. • S.W.R.D. Bandaranaike, prime minister of Ceylon, is assassinated by a Buddhist monk.

September 27: Soviet Premier Khrushchev leaves the United States after withdrawing his earlier ultimatum—that the U.S. and its Western allies quit Berlin. Khrushchev also made headlines for visiting the set of the film *Can-Can* and touring an American supermarket.

October 2: CBS introduces Rod Serling's *The Twilight Zone,* a sci-fi television series with strong social commentary.

October 4: The Soviets launch the Luna III satellite, which will photograph 70 percent of the far side of the moon while in orbit.

October 7: Opera sensation Mario Lanza dies of a heart attack in Italy at age 38.

October 8: The Los Angeles Dodgers win the World Series, defeating the Chicago White Sox in six games.

October 10: Pan American Airlines becomes the first airline to offer around-the-world itineraries.

October 11: Pope John XXIII announces that Mother Elizabeth Ann Seton will be beatified by the Roman Catholic Church, making her the first American to receive the honor.

October 14: Actor Errol Flynn dies at age 50.

October 15: An Air Force B-52 bomber collides with a refueling plane over Kentucky. Two unarmed nuclear weapons are recovered from the debris.

October 16: General George C. Marshall, architect of the reconstruction plan that rebuilt postwar Europe, dies at age 78.

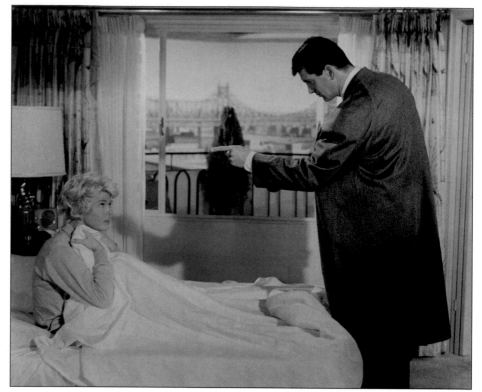

Actress-singer Doris Day (*left*) made her most enduring and best-loved movies when cast opposite Rock Hudson (*right*), beginning with 1959's *Pillow Talk.* Their onscreen chemistry was undeniable. In this risqué sex farce, which costars Tony Randall, the two leads are locked in a combative telephone party-line battle. Simultaneously, Day falls for a handsome out-of-towner (Hudson) without realizing that he's the annoying guy on the phone. The witty script and smart performances made the film a hit, leading to two other movies with the same three stars, *Lover Come Back* (1961) and *Send Me No Flowers* (1964).

In 1959 singer Fabian Forte (known simply as Fabian) was cast in an Elvis-like movie vehicle to capitalize on his chart success. *Hound Dog Man,* though unconnected with Presley's hit song, shrewdly tied the two entertainers together. Along with Frankie Avalon and Bobby Rydell, Fabian epitomized the Philadelphia sound, an artificial phenomenon that saw good-looking, clean-cut young males molded into inoffensive rock 'n' roll personalities for mass consumption. Exposure via Dick Clark's Philadelphia-based *American Bandstand* proved key to Fabian's massive but transient popularity.

The Twilight Zone

ON FRIDAY EVENINGS beginning in October 1959, an eerie, tension-producing guitar line crept into America's living rooms, beckoning viewers to enter...*The Twilight Zone*. Rod Serling, a successful television writer for CBS's popular *Playhouse 90*, created a "middle ground between light and shadow" in the new sci-fi/fantasy program.

The Twilight Zone, according to *The New York Times*, featured stories that "lie somewhere between down-to-earth reality and outer space." The popular weekly anthology garnered two Emmy Awards and much critical acclaim during its run on CBS. Serling, who held a cigarette while standing against a starry background, introduced each week's program. Moreover, he wrote more than 90 of the 156 episodes that aired from 1959 to 1964.

The half-hour teleplays sometimes suggested other-worldly themes, but the stories usually offered strong moral

Rod Serling

messages and transparent allegories of contemporary political and social issues, including race relations, capital punishment, and the threat of nuclear annihilation. In the pilot for the program, entitled "Where Is Everybody?," an airman in a jumpsuit wanders an empty town. He wonders where everybody is and begins to break down mentally. It turns out that he is the guinea pig in a top-secret operation by the Air Force, which wants to simulate solitude in preparation for journeys to the moon.

Prior to *The Twilight Zone*, network executives had tried to soften Serling scripts that directly engaged contemporary issues, such as the race-based murder of African-American Emmett Till. But the benign-seeming fantasy genre allowed Serling to tell socially conscious stories that may not otherwise have made it to TV. "You know, you can put these words into the mouth of a Martian and get away with it," he said.

Oscar-winning animators William Hanna and Joseph Barbera first found success on the big screen, creating MGM's *Tom and Jerry* series during the 1940s. But following the liquidation of the studio's animation department, Hanna and Barbera turned their talents to develop-

ing original material for television. One year after their initial offering, *The Ruff and Ready Show,* premiered in 1957, their *Huckleberry Hound Show* hit the air. Featuring the laconic, top-hatted title character, the show served as a springboard for the burgeoning Hanna-Barbera troupe, launching supporting "players" Yogi Bear, Quick Draw McGraw, and Augie Doggie. Schtick-driven plots coupled with "limited animation" became the Hanna-Barbera trademark.

Ferdinand "Fred" Demara became notorious in the 1950s as "The Great Imposter." Beginning in 1942, he assumed the identities of other people and passed himself off as a member of various professions, including psychologist, civil engineer, and prison warden (which he learned during a stint in jail). His most famous

impersonation came during the Korean War, when he posed as a Canadian doctor and performed successful surgeries! He finally got a degree from a Bible school, and when he died, he was a legitimate hospital clergyman. He was played by Tony Curtis in a biographical 1960 movie.

1959

October 20: The U.S. begins its economic embargo against Cuba, which will continue into the 21st century.

October 21: Soldiers loyal to ousted Cuban President Fulgencio Batista set off bombs in Havana. • Architect Frank Lloyd Wright's New York masterpiece, the Guggenheim Museum, opens its doors.

October 23: Fidel Castro accuses the United States of a secret aerial assault on Havana. • Juanita Kidd Stout is appointed judge of the Common Pleas Court in Philadelphia, becoming the first black female judge in the United States. • Troop skirmishes at the Chinese-Indian border leave 17 dead. • Antiwhite mobs riot against police and troops in Stanleyville, Belgian Congo.

October 31: The U.S. Defense Department deploys the Atlas D, its first fully functional intercontinental ballistic missile.

November: The Nashville Christian Leadership Conference stages sit-ins in downtown department stores. • After a year with the Harlem Globetrotters, Wilt Chamberlain begins his legendary NBA career with the Philadelphia Warriors.

November 1: Congolese nationalist leader Patrice Lumumba is arrested for allegedly inciting riots. • The Federal Trade Commission cracks down on misleading ads in the wake of the year's quiz show scandals. • Jacques Plante of the Montreal Canadiens pioneers regular use of a goalie mask in the NHL.

November 2: Charles Van Doren testifies that the producers of the hit quiz show *Twenty-One* fed him the correct answers.

Anne Bancroft (*left*) plays Annie Sullivan and Patty Duke portrays Helen Keller in the critically acclaimed William Gibson play, *The Miracle Worker*. First shown on television's *Playhouse 90* in 1957, the piece was lengthened for Broadway, where it premiered in October 1959. (Keller read the script ahead of time, in braille.) It dramatized the powerful true story of how Sullivan overcame Helen's stubbornness to teach the deaf and dumb child to read and speak. Powerful performances by the lead actors held audiences in thrall. *The Miracle Worker* won six Tony Awards, including best play and best actress in a drama (Bancroft). It is still being performed today.

A government soldier brings a Communist prisoner in for questioning in northern Laos during October 1959. The situation there was almost indecipherably complicated. Three factions—the Communist-led Pathet Lao under Kong-Le, the neutralists surrounding Prince Souvanna Phouma, and anti-Communist forces led by Prince Boun Oum and General Phoumi Nosavan—competed for power. The Eisenhower Administration supported Oum and Nosavan, fearing that the neutralists would be too weak to prevent Communist takeover. Although many feared another Korea, the conflict was ultimately settled peaceably in 1962, when the Declaration on the Neutrality of Laos was signed by multiple nations in Geneva. However, Pathet Lao rebels continued to be active.

Quiz Show Scandals

HOW MUCH OF TELEVISION was phony? In the wake of the 1950s scandals that exposed the rigging of TV quiz shows, Congress and the general public demanded an answer to that difficult question. For the first time, Americans began to turn a critical eye toward the programming that they welcomed into their living rooms every evening.

The most explosive moment of the 1950s quiz show scandals occurred when a smart but untelegenic man named Herb Stempel blew the whistle on a Geritol-sponsored game show called *Twenty-One*. A successful contestant on the rigged program, Stempel was asked to take a fall, thus allowing WASPy, Columbia University English professor Charles Van Doren to win the mounting cash prize. Stempel's admission revealed a conspiracy that cut across the genre. On *Twenty-One* in particular, producers and ratings-hungry corporate sponsors had manufactured drama by manipulating the outcome of seemingly fair competitions. Stempel and Van Doren, like contestants on other shows, were fed answers and given acting cues to amp up the tension.

The quiz show scandals unnerved Americans, who had regarded TV as a trusted institution. Overnight, revelations of deception placed the medium's innocent conventions—

Charles Van Doren, Jack Barry, and Herb Stempel

including corporate sponsorship, "canned applause," and the TelePrompTer—under the microscope. What was real and what was theater, after all? The uproar and dismay reached a fever pitch in 1959 when Congress investigated the matter. The events led to a healthy skepticism about media and offered a hint of the cynicism that would grow during the 1960s.

Classroom educational films were dominated by a few production companies: Encyclopaedia Britannica, Centron, Coronet, and Sid Davis Productions. Common topics included grooming, study habits, dating etiquette, good sportsmanship, and other innocuous issues. Many of these short movies, though, explored dark themes, such as homosexual predation, teen pregnancy, violent traffic deaths, child kidnapping, and drug abuse. The typical "warning" film—with plenty of overacting by earnest semiprofessionals—was a blunt tale of common sense or morality gone by the wayside. This scene is from Centron's 11-minute VD film, *The Innocent Party* (1959), in which good-girl Betty discovers that boyfriend Don has infected her with syphilis.

1959

November 3: Anti-U.S. riots erupt throughout the Panama Canal Zone over U.S. control of the canal. • President Eisenhower presides over a cornerstone-laying ceremony at the site of the new CIA headquarters in Langley, Virginia. • French leader Charles de Gaulle announces that France will withdraw from the North Atlantic Treaty Organization (NATO).

November 7: A court order enforcing the Taft-Hartley Act upholds the illegality of the latest steel strike (the sixth since World War II). The order forces a half million U.S. steelworkers back to work after a 116-day walkout.

November 10: The U.S. Navy commissions the USS *Triton,* the largest nuclear submarine to date.

November 15: The Clutter family of Holcomb, Kansas, is brutally murdered by Richard Hickock and Perry Smith. Truman Capote will base his 1965 novel, *In Cold Blood,* on the case.

November 17: The 10th Circuit Court of Appeals sides with the Navajo Tribal Council, which objected to the Native American Church's use of peyote on Navajo tribal lands. The court determines that the Navajo nation is a dependent nation not bound by the U.S. Constitution.

November 19: The last Edsel rolls off the Ford Motor Company's assembly line. Ford lost more than $350 million on the ill-fated car.

November 20: The National Shrine of the Immaculate Conception is dedicated in Washington, D.C.

November 21: *The Jack Benny Show* features a show-stopping duet by Richard Nixon on piano and host Benny on violin.

November 24: The United States and the Soviet Union sign a pact in which they agree to collaborate on advancements in science, sports, and culture.

A lone U.S. soldier holds back demonstrators during an anti-American riot in Panama in November 1959. Fired up by a nationalistic media, several hundred protesters crossed into the U.S.-controlled Canal Zone to try to raise a Panamanian flag. They subsequently were repulsed by U.S. troops. The mob managed to break the windows of the U.S. Information Agency Library and to stomp on an American flag that had flown at the U.S. ambassador's home. Order was restored, but tensions remained high for years afterward.

The Herb Clutter farm in Holcomb, Kansas, was the scene of one of the decade's most horrific crimes. Lured by a former farmhand's claims of abundant cash on the premises, jailbirds Dick Hickock and Perry Smith left prison in 1959 and set out for the "perfect score." What they found instead on November 15 was a bewildered Clutter and his frightened family: invalid wife Bonnie; daughter Nancy, 16; and son Kenyon, 15. Frustrated by their failure, the pair summarily executed the home's occupants and fled with $43. Their subsequent capture and execution became the subject of Truman Capote's best-selling "nonfiction novel," *In Cold Blood* (1965).

The Richard Condon novel *The Manchurian Candidate* (1959) was a popular and critical success. It tells a complex tale in which Communist Chinese brainwash Raymond Shaw, a captured American soldier, during the Korean War. He is programmed as an assassin, whose  code is triggered during the 1960 presidential race. Filled with twists and turns and a surprise ending, it is also, in the words of one reviewer, "an incredible cynical work full of ugly Americans," as well as "an enjoyably disturbing read." The book's jacket art is by former EC Comics artist Bernie Krigstein.

Former film critic Jean-Luc Godard's *Breathless* is frequently cited as the archetypical French "New Wave" film. Stylistically, this is so, with its reliance on handheld cameras and jump shots—revolutionary at the time. But beyond that, it's a paean to cinema, with nearly everything in the film being a reference to another movie or moviemaker. Jean-Paul Belmondo (*left*) plays the film's attractive yet despicable antihero. His love interest is played by doomed American actress Jean Seberg (*right*). Her leftist causes would subject her to intense FBI scrutiny and harassment, contributing (along with depression and the death of her baby) to her suicide in 1979.

Coloratura soprano Joan Sutherland appears in her breakthrough performance as the title character in a 1959 production of Donizetti's *Lucia di Lammermoor.* Born in Australia in 1926, Sutherland studied at the Royal College of Music in London. In the 1950s and early 1960s, she became the best-known exponent of the brightly sung bel canto repertoire, serving as a popular successor to the great Maria Callas, whose powers were waning. Sutherland's 1960 album, *The Art of the Prima Donna,* is an enduring classic.

Illustrator Gil Elvgren produced appealing oil paintings for Coca-Cola, General Electric, *Good Housekeeping* magazine, and many other clients during his 45-year career. He achieved his greatest popularity, though, with his matchless calendar art. A long association with the Brown & Bigelow illustration studio resulted in hundreds of pin-up paintings that deftly combined expressive innocence and glamour. B&B sold rights to pieces by Elvgren and other artists to companies large and small for promotional use, usually as calendars that hung in garages, union halls, and home workshops. Neely Enterprises was just one company that picked up Elvgren's "Smoke Screen" (*pictured*).

1959

November 27: Protesters take to the streets of Tokyo to object to the recently signed U.S.-Japan mutual defense treaty.

November 29: The National Academy of Recording Arts and Sciences holds the first Grammy Awards ceremony in New York City, honoring music recorded in 1958.

December 1: The first arms control agreement of the Cold War, the Antarctic Treaty, is signed by 12 nations. The treaty will establish Antarctica as a nuclear-free area.

December 2: The Malpasset Dam on the French Riviera's Reyran River collapses, flooding the town of Frejus and killing some 420 people.

December 4: An American research monkey named Sam survives the trip to space and back again.

December 7: The Federal Communications Commission opens hearings on television standards and televised depictions of crime and violence.

December 14: Berry Gordy founds Motown Records in Detroit.

December 18: Twenty alleged Mafia bosses are convicted of obstruction of justice in New York.

December 22: President Eisenhower and King Mohammed agree that U.S. forces will withdraw from Morocco within four years.

December 23: President Eisenhower wraps up an 11-nation, three-continent holiday goodwill tour.

Late 1959: The first Denny's restaurant opens. • The number of soldiers in the U.S. Army has dropped to 862,000, from a 1953 high of approximately 1.4 million. Some in government worry that the shrinking army will be less capable of responding to an international crisis.

The United States Housing Act of 1949 provided federal funding for urban redevelopment in inner city areas. The Pruitt-Igoe project (*pictured*) in St. Louis was ambitious but came to exemplify the failure of public housing policy. Designed in 1951 and opened in 1956, the 33 11-story buildings encompassed 2,870 apartments. These high-rise "streets in the air" were intended to be safe and clean, but their "warehouse" feel encouraged anger and vandalism. They also were disastrously inappropriate for the infirm and families with children: In a maladroit effort to avoid congestion, elevators stopped only at the first, fourth, seventh, and 10th floors. Even the buildings' 11'×85' communal galleries were shunned by most residents because of graffiti and criminal activity. Demolition of Pruitt-Igoe began in 1972.

Moviegoers' taste for spectacle reached its zenith with the success of *Ben-Hur*, winner of a record-setting 11 Academy Awards. Perhaps the finest "sword and sandal" picture ever made, the sprawling 212-minute epic was larger than life in every way, made at a cost of $15 million. Director William Wyler spared no expense to re-create the Roman Empire at the time of Christ. His script (which featured uncredited input from novelist Gore Vidal) called for a cast of thousands, expensive sets, and challenging stunts, climaxing with the film's famous chariot race. Charlton Heston (*center*), in the title role, spearheaded the cast.

Composer Henry Mancini was not only prolific but versatile. From the sinister rumble of the "Peter Gunn Theme" to the sublime majesty of "Moon River," Mancini displayed an effortless ability to create unique and memorable pieces throughout four decades of film and television scoring. Schooled on a variety of instruments, Mancini received his first break at the twilight of the Big Band era, arranging for Glenn Miller's Orchestra. From there, he moved into film work, straddling jazz and pop with a style that enhanced plenty of cinematic drama—as exemplified by his *Touch of Evil* score.

In his 1957 bestseller, *The Untouchables,* Eliot Ness (writing with sportswriter-biographer Oscar Fraley) recounted his years fighting organized crime (including mobster Al Capone) in Depression-era Chicago. Ness did not live long enough to collect royalty checks or to see the premiere of the TV adaptation of his book. *The Untouchables,* which ran on ABC from 1959 to 1963, starred Robert Stack (*right*) as Ness; Keenan Wynn (*left*) appeared only in the unofficial *Desilu Playhouse* "pilot." Narrated by broadcasting legend Walter Winchell, the successful drama upped the violence quotient of 1950s television, and brought feature film technique to the small screen.

Wilt Chamberlain, a 7'1", 275-pound center for the Philadelphia Warriors, scores on a finger-roll in 1959–60, his rookie season in the NBA. Not only was "Wilt the Stilt" the biggest, strongest player the league had ever seen, but he ranked among its greatest athletes. As a rookie, he smashed NBA records for scoring average (37.6 points per game) and rebounding (27.0 per outing), earning league MVP honors. In 1961–62, he would average 50.4 points per game, thanks in part to a 100-point night against the New York Knicks.

Pat Frank's 1959 post-apocalyptic novel, *Alas, Babylon,* resonates with Cold War fears, relating the awful impact of nuclear war on Fort Repose, a peaceful Florida town. Although its citizens escape the immediate consequences, the secondary effects caused by the destruction of

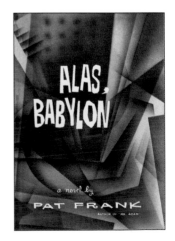

the national infrastructure force them to cope in ways that reveal human strengths and weaknesses. Praised by critics for its sophistication, the book is still popular among reading groups.

The Friendly Skies

IN THE MID-1950s, millions of Americans regularly traveled by air—yet the experience could be nerve-racking. Businessmen and vacationers, flying mostly on loud, slow propeller planes, often found the flights grueling, despite the relatively recent conveniences of heated interiors and pressurized cabins. In 1958 traveling became much more pleasurable when Boeing introduced the 707 jet.

Faster jets and multiplying domestic carriers helped expand the scope of business and leisure travel. In the U.S. West, where commercial aviation industries had blossomed after the war, rapidly growing cities such as Albuquerque converted air bases into hub airports to serve a growing region. In the Midwest, Chicago's O'Hare International Airport was opened to commercial passenger flights in 1955.

The advent of jet travel cut the time needed to journey from New York to London from 12 hours to six. Vacationers on the eastern seaboard quickly exchanged the Poconos and the Berkshires for Miami when National Airlines inaugurated service between New York and that city on December 10, 1958. Increasingly, vacationers traveled farther faster.

On the way to the jet age, the decade saw more than its share of airplane crashes. In July 1956, 128 people died when a pair of four-engine propeller planes—a TWA Constellation and a United Airlines DC-7—collided over the Grand Canyon. The crash raised the issue of how to prevent such disasters in the future.

When it came out that both pilots in the crash had been flying in uncontrolled airspace under visual flight rules, Americans became alarmed. In the wake of the tragedy, the industry began to invest in safety systems. In 1958 Congress established the Federal Aviation Agency (FAA) to ensure air-traffic safety.

In the mid-1950s, Warner Bros. became a powerhouse of television production with a slate of slick, formulaic westerns and crime shows. *Maverick* and *Cheyenne* were among the former; included among the latter was *Hawaiian Eye,* which had an appealing cast, an "exotic locale" (the Warner lot in Burbank!), and plenty of action. Warner worked its young TV contract players hard, paid them little, and capitalized on their popularity with record albums and other cross-merchandising. This LP features (*from left*) Anthony Eisley, Robert Conrad, Connie Stevens, and *Hawaiian Eye*'s purported comic relief, Poncie Ponce.

Trans World Airlines promotes its overseas jet service to London in this double-page 1959 magazine advertisement. Actually, TWA entered the international jet market a year after its major competitors, preferring to concentrate on its domestic flights. Because travelers responded so positively to the incredible convenience of the speedy jets, airline companies worldwide rapidly replaced their propeller-driven aircraft to meet the growing demand. Interestingly, the first regularly scheduled jet service appeared in the USSR in 1956, two years before National Airlines made its first U.S. commercial flight.

Brother Theodore was perhaps the darkest of the American comedians who practiced the art of black humor in the late 1950s. Born Theodore Gottlieb to wealthy German-Jewish parents in 1906, he was the only family member to survive the Dachau concentration camp. After fleeing to America, he developed a bizarre one-man comedy show, played bohemian clubs, and earned a small but ardent cult following. According to historian Ronald Smith, Theodore "rage[d] a losing battle against existentialism." His signature line: "The best thing is not to be born."

A Summer Place (1959) was a soapy potboiler (with a great theme song) that served to launch its young stars into the big time. Sandra Dee (*right*) was a former model who specialized in sweet, girl-next-door roles, epitomized by the *Gidget* series. (Her widely perceived wholesomeness was parodied in *Grease* with "Look at Me—I'm Sandra Dee.") The self-described "junior Doris Day" enjoyed further high-profile stardom with her marriage to singer Bobby Darin. Troy Donahue (*left*) was the latest in a series of "pretty" male youths pitched to teen audiences, wherein any actual acting ability was beside the point.

Warren Miller's bleak novel, *The Cool World* (1959), portrays the lives of young African-Americans in Harlem in the 1950s. Remarkable for its realistic detail, the novel was nominated for a National Book Award. Miller himself was white and lived on 96th Street near East Harlem, but his grasp of the material was so firm that even famed African-American novelist and essayist James Baldwin did not realize that Miller wasn't black. The book jacket, by noted graphic artist Edward Sorel, helps establish the mood of desperation that permeates the novel.

Mary Martin as Maria leads the talented von Trapp children in song in the smash Broadway musical *The Sound of Music*. Based on the true story of an Austrian family who escaped from Nazi rule, it opened in November 1959. Although it changed some of the details of the source story, the play retained the spirit of this musical family's incredible tale. It won five Tony Awards, including best musical and best actress in a musical (Martin). Its enduring hit songs include "Edelweiss," "My Favorite Things," and "Do-Re-Mi," as well as the title song.

1959

New & Notable

Books

Advertisements for Myself
  by Norman Mailer
The Elements of Style by William Strunk,
  Jr., and E. B. White
Goodbye, Columbus by Philip Roth
The Haunting of Hill House
  by Shirley Jackson
Henderson the Rain King by Saul Bellow
The Manchurian Candidate
  by Richard Condon
Naked Lunch by William Burroughs
The Tin Drum by Günter Grass

Movies

Anatomy of a Murder
Ben-Hur
Black Orpheus
Breathless
The 400 Blows
Hiroshima, Mon Amour
North by Northwest
Room at the Top
The Shaggy Dog
Sleeping Beauty
Some Like It Hot

Songs

"Charlie Brown" by the Coasters
"Donna" by Ritchie Valens
"Kansas City" by Wilbert Harrison
"Love Potion No. 9" by the Clovers
"Mack the Knife" by Bobby Darin
"16 Candles" by the Crests
"Sweet Nothin's" by Brenda Lee
"What'd I Say" by Ray Charles

Television

Bonanza
Dennis the Menace
The Many Loves of Dobie Gillis
Rawhide
The Twilight Zone
The Untouchables

Theater

Becket
Gypsy
The Miracle Worker
A Raisin in the Sun
The Sound of Music
Sweet Bird of Youth

The stunning Guggenheim Museum in New York City, completed in 1959, featured unique spiral galleries and sculptural massing. Famed architect Frank Lloyd Wright designed this repository for modern art. According to Wright, it provided "the best possible atmosphere in which to show fine paintings," in part because the building suggested a sense of "the quiet unbroken wave." This was the great man's last work. He died at his winter retreat in Phoenix on April 9, 1958.

Artist Franz Kline was an American Abstract Expressionist famous for his minimalistic use of color and canvas. His *Orange and Black Wall* (*pictured*) typified his deceptively simple approach. Kline sometimes took months to complete a work, painstakingly plotting out his use of pigment to best depict the movement and emotion he wished to convey. His background included studies in London, with early works being mostly urban scenes. After meeting Willem de Kooning, Kline quickly abandoned traditional aesthetic values while discovering his own artistic vision. By the mid-1950s, Kline's work was world-renowned.

Though former lifeguard Gordon Scott had taken over the role of Tarzan from Lex Barker in 1955, not until four years later did he truly make his mark on Edgar Rice Burroughs's immortal character. A change in studios (from MGM to Paramount) and producers brought new life to the franchise, as the creators aimed to recapture the novels' original flavor. Tarzan was revamped as a literate, albeit savage, jungle lord. Gone were the low production values and cookie-cutter plots. Instead, for *Tarzan's Greatest Adventure* (1959, *pictured*), care was taken with character development and plausibility.

Pianist Glenn Gould burst upon the classical scene in the mid-1950s with his recording of a piece that he would forever be linked with, Bach's *Goldberg Variations*. His unparalleled artistry and singular technique were well suited to producing revelatory performances of pieces originally scored for the harpsichord. Distantly related to composer Edvard Grieg, Gould was a child prodigy, labeled a genius by age 12. But such brilliance came with a persona deemed "eccentric." He frequently bundled up in warm weather and had the curious habit of humming while he performed. Gould eventually reduced his social interactions to telephone calls and letters.

"A modern masterpiece of automotive sculpture"—that's how General Motors described the 1959 Cadillac, one of the iconic symbols of the 1950s. Towering tailfins and twin-pod taillamps are obvious highlights of what was the last full creative expression of GM design chief Harley Earl, who retired in 1958 (by which time the '59 Caddy had already been finalized). Earl's love of aircraft-inspired styling cues and feminized bodyside shapes reached an apex with this year's Cadillacs. The 4,855-pound Eldorado Seville (*pictured*) was a comfortable cruiser that wallowed softly over dips, and felt loose in cornering. In those shortcomings, it was little different from other cars of its time. As a tangible expression of the optimism that characterized the American '50s, it may be without peer.

"We were young, self-righteous, reckless, hypocritical, brave, silly, headstrong, and scared half to death." —1960s ACTIVIST ABBIE HOFFMAN

Epilogue
Birthing the '60s

AMERICANS' PRACTICE of turning decades into eras—such as the 1950s into "the Fifties"—leaves those eras spilling out of their chronological boundaries. The Sixties, some argue, were put to rest only with Watergate in 1973. The 1950s, obviously, ended on December 31, 1959. But when did "the Fifties" end? What symbolic moment or event closed off this complex decade?

Conventional narratives of postwar America tend to find the end of the Fifties (or perhaps more accurately, the beginning of the Sixties) in the presidency of John F. Kennedy. Those who, in simplest terms, see the Sixties as an awakening from the quiescence and conformity and repression of the Fifties tend to point to the young JFK, hatless in the winter cold of his inauguration day in January 1961, proclaiming to one and all that the torch had been passed to a new generation. And those who see the Sixties as a violent and turbulent decade tend to find the end of the Fifties in an assassin's bullets, in little John-John's salute, in what seemed, in those dark hours, a nation's loss of innocence.

The 1950s, of course, were neither quiescent nor innocent. And despite the temptation to see the young JFK as the harbinger of the 1960s and Eisenhower, his predecessor, as the old, gray embodiment of the 1950s, it was never so clear. In fact, Kennedy's inaugural speech was steeped in the Cold War assumptions of the 1950s, framed around the division between "two great and powerful groups of nations."

The 1950s were a decade of great hopes and powerful fears, and both extremes would give rise to the difficult and divided decade of the 1960s.

Much of what was dubbed revolutionary in the 1960s had its roots in the '50s, when youngsters developed a sense of cultural identity that evolved into a unique sort of social awareness. Washington also evolved after the '50s, embracing extreme measures to protect policies that no longer enchanted the public. In this encounter of May 19, 1969, students at the University of California–Berkeley stroll to class in the shadows of National Guard bayonets.

Cold War fears led to America's intervention in the ongoing war in Vietnam, which tore the nation apart and cost the lives of tens of thousands of Americans and many more Vietnamese. And 1950s hopes—for prosperity and security, for a society of opportunity for all, for a more democratic and inclusive nation—led not only to 1960s government programs to combat poverty and to major gains in civil rights for many of the nation's citizens, but also to widespread protest and social division. Whether as an outgrowth of postwar culture or in reaction to it, much of the extravagant grandeur—and horror—of the 1960s has roots in the more modest decade of the 1950s.

President Kennedy's inaugural pledge, that America would "pay any price, bear any burden" in the ongoing global struggle shows the Cold War roots of 1960s foreign policy. The world reached the brink of nuclear apocalypse during the Cuban missile crisis of 1962, as the two superpowers squared off over reconnaissance photos that showed Soviet missiles positioned in Cuba, within firing range of the southeastern United States. In the aftermath of the crisis, President Kennedy and Soviet Premier Nikita Khrushchev took steps to improve relations between the U.S. and USSR, installing a "hot-line" between the nations' leaders, deescalating Cold War tensions in Europe, and signing a limited nuclear test ban.

Although President Kennedy was young and seemed philosophically innovative, he was very much a Cold Warrior molded in the late 1940s and '50s. Like Truman and Ike, he was determined to take aggressive positions relative to the expansionist policies of the Soviet Union. Here, JFK and his counterpart, Soviet Premier Nikita Khrushchev, meet in Vienna in June 1961.

However, the Cold War continued in other ways and in other places. The U.S. and USSR engaged in a massive arms race, and they competed for influence over Third World nations. They offered these developing countries foreign aid and cultural and educational programs, and they engaged in covert actions and proxy wars. The war in Vietnam had been in progress for decades as a nationalist struggle against a colonial power (France) and then as civil war between north and south. But it became—in the Cold War calculus of influence—defined as a critical part of the global struggle between (as the U.S. saw it) communism and democracy, with Vietnam the domino whose fall would destabilize the whole region.

It is clear that the United States was not willing to "pay any price" for victory in Vietnam. Even Kennedy, as he sent military "advisers" there in the early 1960s, hoped to combat insurgency in Vietnam through "nation building" and not force of arms. But Cold War logic led American leaders to invest more and more of the nation's men and resources in the war. They feared that withdrawal or defeat would signal to America's Cold War enemies that American power was limited, and would indicate to America's allies that they could not put their faith in U.S. guarantees. As American troop levels in Vietnam reached a half million in 1968, CBS-TV anchorman Walter Cronkite—the "most trusted man in America"—declared the war a quagmire. War protests increasingly divided the nation, interrupting a Cold War consensus that had held for two decades.

As Cold War tensions contributed to America's war in Vietnam, post-WWII hopes helped to transform American society, culture, and politics. The major 1960s social programs of President Lyndon Johnson's "Great Society" owed much to the postwar culture of optimism and increasing prosperity. The economic boom of the post-WWII years moved large numbers of Americans into the economic middle class, spreading relative prosperity much more broadly than before. With the assistance of the federal government, most notably in the form of the GI Bill, more Americans gained a college education or vocational training, and more Americans obtained inexpensive mortgages and became homeowners.

Not all shared in the prosperity, but in 1962, when Michael Harrington published his influential *The Other America* (an account of the widespread poverty that continued in the midst of American plenty), the inequity seemed obviously wrong and the solutions possible. The range of liberal social programs enacted by President Johnson and the Democratic Congress of the mid-1960s varied in effectiveness, but they alleviated the effects of poverty, especially on the elderly, whose poverty rate fell from 40 percent in 1960 to 16 percent in 1974.

The most lasting legacy of the 1960s would be a revolution in the reach and meaning of civil rights in American society, and it, too, has roots in the 1950s. It was in the aftermath of World War II that black citizens launched what became a mass movement for civil rights, and some of the most courageous and dramatic moments of that struggle came in the "quiescent" '50s. The Montgomery bus boycott not only propelled the young Martin Luther King, Jr., to national leadership, but it also demonstrated the power of grassroots commitment and nonviolent protest.

It was in the 1950s, also, that the federal government began to reckon with the role it would play in enforcing national civil rights laws. The NAACP had worked hard to get school segregation cases before the Supreme Court, and in 1954 the High Court rejected the doctrine of "separate but equal." The "Little Rock Nine," who integrated Little Rock's Central High, showed remarkable courage. But it was President Eisenhower's decision to directly confront

The sophisticated and well-equipped French army had been driven from Vietnam by Communist forces in 1954. The lesson was clear enough to comprehend at that time, but American involvement began, slowly, during the Eisenhower Administration. By the summer of 1968, when President Johnson listened to a tape recording made at the front by his son-in-law, Marine Captain Charles Robb, he knew the war was hopeless.

Black civil rights activists who came of age in the '60s were frustrated by the slow slog to respect and equality. By 1969, when this photo was snapped at Cornell University, they had endured the murders of Martin Luther King and other heroes. The determined spirit of the 1950s had hardened and now wore a new face.

Women, the "minority" that outnumbered men in America, internalized many of their frustrations in the 1950s and early '60s. A few years later, women who were tired of lives restricted to housework or the "pink ghetto" of dead-end jobs raised their voices—and their placards, as at this rally in New York City in 1968.

the conflict between federal authority and states' rights proponents by deploying the federalized Arkansas National Guard to preserve order and protect the Little Rock Nine that set a major precedent. The federal government, when local custom or state authority came into conflict with national law and guarantees of civil rights for all, would use its power.

Of course, some of the most significant struggles of the 1960s were in reaction against the 1950s, not a development from them. Many young black Americans, frustrated with the slow pace of change and angered by continuing discrimination and oppression, rejected the universalist, color-blind vision that King's followers had embraced in the 1950s, along with their nonviolent tactics. Calling for "Black Power," they proclaimed a version of black nationalism that rejected the culture and politics of white America. The Black Power movement would play a key role in shaping other race- and ethnicity-based movements.

Women also reacted against the conventions of '50s culture. The rumblings of discontent had been present throughout the decade that celebrated the American housewife and mother; women's magazines were full of advice for unfulfilled and unhappy housewives. When Betty Friedan described women's discontent as "the problem with no name" in her 1963 book, *The Feminine Mystique,* she broke new ground by blaming society for stifling women, not women for poor adjustment to society's expectations. In the 1960s, women challenged the model of the 1950s' perfect woman in ways that ranged from conventional politics—lobbying for equal opportunities in employment—to radical protest. American women did not necessarily agree on goals or tactics, but many forcefully rejected the dominant model of the '50s woman.

Finally, the roots of 1960s culture also can be found in the 1950s. Beat culture is an obvious forerunner to the cultural dissent that characterized the 1960s, but we can find roots in mainstream culture, as well. The young adults of the 1960s had a different upbringing than any previous generation. In the years following WWII, high school became mandatory for all American youth to the age of 16. That meant that these young people were the product of a much longer-lasting and intensive peer culture than any previous generation. From childhood, they were targeted by marketers of toys and soft drinks and clothes and music. They were studied and monitored and discussed, and American leaders and educators worried about how to help them become the sorts of citizens who could face the challenges of democracy in a difficult Cold War world.

Many of these young people took the notion of responsibility seriously. Confronted with the terrible flaws in American society—racial discrimination, poverty, the war in Vietnam—that so contradicted the idealized public portrayals of Cold War American culture, many sought change. Untroubled by memories of economic hardship, others rejected the careful practices of their parents, immersing themselves in a peer culture that worried little about notions of respectability and other middle-class virtues. The youth of the late 1960s bore little resemblance to the youth of a decade before, those that critics had worried were too careful, too conformist, too old before their time. But the youth culture of the 1960s—exuberant, idealistic, and hedonistic in its various manifestations—was at least in part the product of the youth-oriented culture of the 1950s.

Standing at the end of the 1960s, looking back a decade, one would be hard-pressed to see the continuities. The U.S. was mired in an unwinnable and increasingly unpopular war. Violence erupted in the streets of Chicago when protesters challenged the legitimacy of state power and the Democratic National Convention's "democratic" process. Ghettos had burned during the long, hot summers. Black youth proclaimed "Black Power," while white youth seemed to have embraced "sex and drugs and rock 'n' roll." The nation was divided along the fault lines of race, age, region, politics, and culture. Little of the landscape was recognizable, and Americans either gloried in the distance from what seemed, in retrospect, the stability and order of the 1950s or mourned its passing. But the transformations of American society that took place in the 1950s were as fundamental in their own way as those that roiled the waters of the 1960s, and they prepared the way for a half century of complex social change to come.

When citizens assembled outside the 1968 Democratic National Convention in Chicago to protest U.S. war policy, many—including bystanders—were beaten and arrested. Demonstrators had forced a confrontation for the nation and the world to see. Their decision was a climax to the first stirrings of dissent, expressed in the '50s when a brave few had agitated against racism, nuclear hazards, covert actions abroad, and other government lapses.

Index

465

Acknowledgments

The editors wish to thank the following people for their contributions to this book: Cheryl Bensenjack and the Permissions Group; Colonel Walter Boyne, USAF (Ret.); William H. Dodge; Michael W. Evans; Ian Hogan; Diana Honts; Mark McGee; Ted Okuda; Keith L. Smith.

Permissions

Page 18. Sylvia Porter excerpt from Mary Beth Norton, et al., *A People and a Nation*, seventh edition, Houghton Mifflin, 2004, p. 801.

Page 21. David Mace, "Is Chastity Outmoded?" *Woman's Home Companion*, September 1949, p. 101.

Pages 36 and 297. "Tsk, Tsk—Somebody Should Do Something About That," from *Herblock: A Cartoonist's Life* (Times Books, 1998) and "We Now Have New and Important Evidence," copyright 1950 by Herblock in *The Washington Post*.

Page 39. "Crusader Rabbit" ©1957 Twentieth Century Fox Television. All rights reserved.

Page 40. Joan John Cobbs account from "The History of Jim Crow," http://www.jim-crowhistory.org, Teacher Resources, Naratives. Reprinted with permission.

Page 47. William Levitt quote from "Dream Town" by Penn Kimball, December 14, 1952, *The New York Times*.

Page 53. Helen Gahagan Douglas quote from Greg Mitchell, *Tricky Dick and the Pink Lady*, Random House, 1998.

Page 57. "One" by Jackson Pollock, 1950. ©The Pollock-Krasner Foundation/Artists Rights Society (ARS), New York. Reprinted with permission.

Page 67. "Massacre in Korea" by Pablo Picasso, 1951. ©2005 Estate of Pablo Picasso/Artists Rights Society (ARS), New York. Reprinted with permission.

Pages 82, 118, 166, and 402. "Does it bother you," "The Korean Story," "McCarthy!" and "It's getting harder" editorial cartoons by Reg Manning reprinted with permission from David Manning.

Page 87. Haywood Baugh account from "Interview with Haywood Baugh" by Samantha Wilhelm and Samara Saylor, March 21, 1992. Virginia Commonwealth University, Special Collections and Archives-Cabell Library, Virginia Black History Archives.

Page 121. "Woman I" by Willem de Kooning. ©2005 The Willem de Kooning Foundation/Artists Rights Society (ARS), New York. Reprinted with permission.

Page 209. Lester P. Monts account from University of Michigan Library, Brown v. Board of Education Archive, Oral Histories. ©2004 The Regents of the University of Michigan. Reprinted with permission.

Pages 234, 289, and 338. All included material by Dr. Martin Luther King, Jr., reprinted by arrangement with the Estate of Martin Luther King, Jr., c/o Writers House as agent for the proprietor, New York, New York. Delivered on 5 December 1955. Copyright 1969 Martin Luther King Jr., copyright renewed 1997 Coretta Scott King.

Page 239. "Untitled" by Mark Rothko, 1955. ©1998 Kate Rothko Prizel & Christopher Rothko Artists Rights Society (ARS), New York. Reprinted with permission.

Page 261. J. W. Milam quote from *Look* magazine, January 24, 1956, issue. Reprinted with permission from Hobby-Catto Properties, LLC.

Page 263. Yolande Betbeze quote from *Miss America. American Experience*, produced by WGBH, 2002.

Page 271. Raymond Parks quote from Virginia Durr, *Memoir, Vol. II*, Nov. 24, 1976.

Page 296. "Just What Is It That Makes Today's Homes So Different, So Appealing?" by Richard Hamilton. ©2005 Artists Rights Society (ARS), New York/DACS, London. Reprinted with permission.

Page 299. Khrushchev, Nikita S. *Khrushchev in America: Full Texts of Speeches Made by N.S. Khrushchev on His Tour of the United States, September 15–27, 1959*. New York: Crosscurrents Press, 1960.

Page 305. Johannes Strijdom quote from *US News and World Report*, Sept. 14, 1956, p. 47.

Page 314. John Wing quote from 1956 Summer Olympics ©2005 Wikipedia. Permission is granted to copy, distribute, and/or modify this document under the terms of the GNU Free Documentation License, Version 1.2 or any later version published by the Free Software Foundation; with no Invariant Sections, no Front-Cover Texts, and no Back-Cover Texts. A copy of the license is included in the section entitled "GNU Free Documentation License."

Page 336. MR. MAGOO and associated character names, images, and other indicia are trademarks of and copyrighted by UPA Productions of America. All rights reserved.

Page 347. "LOOK! THEY'RE GOING INTO THE SCHOOL!" excerpt by Relman Morin from the AP report, Sept. 23, 1957. Reprinted with Permission. Used with permission of The Associated Press Copyright ©2005. All rights reserved.

Pages 365–366. Louis Lyndon, "Uncertain Hero," *Woman's Home Companion*, November 1956, pp. 41–107.

Page 424. Letty Nunez quote from "Barbie Doll Revolutionized Toy Industry," By Belem Ramos, Borderlands: An El Paso Community College, El Paso, Texas, Local History Project.

Page 435. Nikita Khrushchev's "secret speech" from Complete text of Khrushchev's "Secret Speech": February 25-26, 1956. ©Paul Halsall, August, 1997. "Internet Modern History Sourcebook," Fordham University, Bronx, New York.

Page 446. "Orange and Black Wall" by Franz Kline. ©2005 The Franz Kline Estate/Artists Rights Society (ARS), New York. Reprinted with permission.

Photo Credits

Front cover (top row): **AP Wide World Photos; Getty Images/Time Life Pictures; The Image Works; Getty Images/Time Life Pictures; AP Wide World Photos;** (center row): **National Archives; AP Wide World Photos; Getty Images/Time Life Pictures;** (bottom row): **Getty Images; Photofest/Universal Pictures; Getty Images/Time Life Pictures.**

Back cover: **Getty Images.**

AP Wide World Photos: 12, 13, 15, 26 (bottom), 31 (bottom left), 37 (top), 38 (top & bottom right), 41 (bottom), 43 (top right & bottom right), 51 (bottom), 53 (top left & bottom), 54 (top & bottom), 59 (bottom), 68, 70 (top), 75 (bottom), 76 (bottom), 78 (bottom), 79 (bottom left), 81 (bottom), 87, 88, 89 (bottom left & bottom right), 90 (bottom), 94 (top), 95 (top), 104 (top), 106, 108 (bottom), 110, 112 (bottom), 115 (bottom left), 116 (bottom), 121 (bottom left), 122 (top), 130 (top left & bottom right), 135 (bottom right), 141 (top left & bottom left), 142, 143 (top), 157 (top right & right center), 162 (bottom), 163 (bottom left), 165 (top & bottom left), 167 (left center), 170 (bottom), 171 (left center), 173 (top & bottom left), 178 (top), 182 (top left), 194 (top), 195 (top), 199 (top left), 202 (bottom), 205 (top), 211 (top left), 212 (bottom right), 213 (top left & bottom), 214 (top), 221 (top left), 228 (top), 234 (bottom), 237, 243 (center), 246 (bottom), 251 (bottom left), 252 (top), 258 (top), 270 (bottom), 282 (top), 283 (right), 286 (bottom), 288 (bottom), 289, 297 (top), 299 (bottom), 301 (top right), 304 (bottom), 306 (top), 310 (bottom), 311 (top left), 312 (top), 313 (bottom right), 318 (top), 319 (top left), 323 (top), 328 (top), 334 (bottom), 339 (top left & top right), 345 (top), 348 (top), 349 (bottom left), 354 (bottom), 356 (top), 373 (bottom left), 380 (top), 382 (top), 388 (bottom), 392 (top), 393 (right center), 397 (bottom right), 398, 401 (top), 411 (right), 413 (bottom left), 418 (bottom), 423 (top left & bottom right), 433 (top right), 434 (top left), 440 (top), 443 (left center), 448-449, 450, 451, 452, 453; **Art Resource:** 213 (top right); © 2005 Estate of Pablo Picasso/Artists Rights Society (ARS), New York, 67 (top);

© 2005 The Franz Kline Estate/Artists Rights Society (ARS), New York, 446 (bottom); © 2005 The Pollock-Krasner Foundation/Artists Rights Society (ARS), New York, 57 (bottom); © 1998 Kate Rothko Prizel & Christopher Rothko/Artists Rights Society (ARS), New York, 239 (top right); Smithsonian American Art Museum, Washington, DC, 412 (bottom); © 2005 The Willem de Kooning Foundation/Artists Rights Society (ARS), New York, 121 (bottom right); **© 2005 Artist Rights Society (ARS), New York/DACS, London:** 296; **Between the Covers Rare Books, Inc.:** 91 (bottom right), 123 (bottom left), 141 (top right), 154 (center), 161 (top left), 165 (bottom right), 177 (bottom right), 179 (top right), 211 (bottom right), 243 (top left), 263 (top right), 357 (bottom left), 361 (top right); **Courtesy of the Boston Public Library, Print Department:** 25 (bottom left); **British Film Institute:** 272 (bottom left); **Brown Brothers:** (top right & bottom right), 27 (bottom), 46 (bottom), 78 (top), 82 (bottom), 86 (bottom), 115 (bottom), 117 (bottom), 124 (top left), 148 (top), 152 (top), 154 (top), 157 (left center), 179 (bottom right), 183 (bottom left), 195 (bottom), 206 (top), 258 (bottom left), 263 (bottom), 280, 292 (top), 299 (top), 311 (bottom), 313 (top left), 315 (top right), 369 (bottom), 370 (top), 391 (top), 396 (bottom), 412 (top), 426, 437 (bottom right), 446 (top); 20th Century Fox, 436 (bottom); Paramount Pictures, 219 (top); **As published in the Chicago Sun-Times, Inc. copyright 2005. Chicago Sun-Times, Inc. Reprinted with permission.:** Carmen Reporto, 174 (top); **Courtesy of The Conelrad Collection:** 196 (bottom right); **© 2005 Coolstock.com Collection:** 350 (top); **William H. Dodge:** 424 (top); **Farnsworth House:** Jon Miller, Hedrich Blessing, 55 (bottom); **Getty Images:** 17 (center), 21, 22 (top), 27 (top right), 31 (top left), 32 (bottom), 34 (bottom), 49 (bottom left), 51 (top right), 55 (top left), 67 (bottom left & bottom right), 77 (bottom right), 92 (bottom right), 93 (top), 95 (bottom left), 96, 98 (bottom), 100 (bottom), 109 (top right), 111 (top right & bottom left), 112 (top), 115 (top left), 116 (top), 118 (bottom), 120 (bottom), 123 (top right), 124 (bottom left), 126, 127, 128 (top), 136 (top), 139 (top & bottom left), 140 (top), 144 (bottom), 146-147, 150, 153 (bottom